booksonline

Read SAP PRESS online also

With booksonline we offer you online access to leading SAP experts' knowledge. Whether you use it as a beneficial supplement or as an alternative to the printed book – with booksonline you can:

- Access any book at any time
- Quickly look up and find what you need
- Compile your own SAP library

Your advantage as the reader of this book

Register your book on our website and obtain an exclusive and free test access to its online version. You're convinced you like the online book? Then you can purchase it at a preferential price!

And here's how to make use of your advantage

1. Visit www.sap-press.com
2. Click on the link for SAP PRESS booksonline
3. Enter your free trial license key
4. Test-drive your online book with full access for a limited time!

Your personal **license key** for your test access including the preferential offer

h63d-x8vf-pbum-42tj

Enhancing Supplier Relationship Management Using SAP® SRM

 PRESS

SAP PRESS is a joint initiative of SAP and Galileo Press. The know-how offered by SAP specialists combined with the expertise of the Galileo Press publishing house offers the reader expert books in the field. SAP PRESS features first-hand information and expert advice, and provides useful skills for professional decision-making.

SAP PRESS offers a variety of books on technical and business related topics for the SAP user. For further information, please visit our website: *www.sap-press.com*.

PadmaPrasad Munirathinam and Ramakrishna Potluri
Consultant's Guide to SAP SRM
2008, 512 pp.
978-1-59229-154-0

D. Rajen Iyer
Effective SAP SD
2007, 365 pp.
978-1-59229-101-4

Martin Murray
Understanding the SAP Logistics Information System
2007, 328 pp.
978-1-59229-108-3

Martin Murray
SAP MM – Functionality and Technical Configuration
2008, 588 pp.
978-1-59229-134-2

Sachin Sethi

Enhancing Supplier Relationship Management Using SAP® SRM

Galileo Press

Bonn • Boston

Galileo Press is named after the Italian physicist, mathematician and philosopher Galileo Galilei (1564–1642). He is known as one of the founders of modern science and an advocate of our contemporary, heliocentric worldview. His words *Eppur se muove* (And yet it moves) have become legendary. The Galileo Press logo depicts Jupiter orbited by the four Galilean moons, which were discovered by Galileo in 1610.

Editor Meg Dunkerley
Copyeditor Lori Newhouse
Cover Design Jill Winitzer
Photo Credit Image Copyright Oria. Used under license from Shutterstock.com.
Layout Design Vera Brauner
Production Editor Kelly O'Callaghan
Assistant Production Editor Graham Geary
Typesetting Publishers' Design and Production Services, Inc.
Printed and bound in Canada

ISBN 978-1-59229-312-4

© 2010 by Galileo Press Inc., Boston (MA)
2nd Edition, updated

Library of Congress Cataloging-in-Publication Data
Sethi, Sachin.
  Enhancing supplier relationship management using SAP SRM / Sachin Sethi. — 2nd ed.
      p. cm.
  Includes bibliographical references and index.
  ISBN-13: 978-1-59229-312-4 (alk. paper)
  ISBN-10: 1-59229-312-3 (alk. paper)
  1. SAP SRM.   2. Business logistics — Computer programs.   3. Integrated software.   I. Title.
  HD38.5.S478 2010
  658.7'2 — dc22

                                                                2009042520

To my late mother, who was most proud of my first edition and would have loved to see the second edition.

To my parents, whose incessant sacrifices to "do the right thing" no matter how tough the path always inspires me to make the right choices.

To my wife Ekta for her unconditional support, boundless understanding, and infectious energy. Her endless efforts helped me bring this book concept to life.

Contents at a Glance

Contents

PART III SAP SRM Implementation, Integration, and Upgrades

6 Catalog and Content Management — Crafting Your Catalog Strategy 239

7 Choosing Implementation Scenarios 271

13 Architecture and Technology of SAP SRM 481

14 Upgrade — A How-To Approach 499

15 Performance Reporting via SAP NetWeaver BW 529

16 SAP NetWeaver Portal and SAP SRM 561

Contents

PART IV   Industry Solutions

20   Procurement for Public Sector 613

PART V   Selected Configuration in SAP SRM

21   Selected Configuration in SAP SRM 623

Appendices

*"We're at the beginning of one of the most important revolutions in busi-
ness. The Internet will forever change the way business is done. It will
change every relationship, between our businesses, between our customers,
between our suppliers. Distribution channels will change. Buying practices
will change. Everything will be tipped upside down. The slow become fast,
the old become young. It's clear we've only just begun this transformation."*
— *Jack Welch, Chairman GE; Fortune Magazine*

Preface

In the spirit of the axiom that change is the only real constant, procurement has
undergone its full share of renewal. Paradigms shifted, rules changed, and boundaries disappeared. In the 1990s, with the advent of the Internet, e-procurement burst
on the scene, ushering in a new era. Simply stated, e-procurement is the business-to-
business exchange of goods and services over the Internet that provides means for
organizations to automate their internal purchasing processes. e-Procurement forced
organizations to redefine their processes in preparation for a new, highly competitive, boundary-less economy.

As procurement processes in organizations matured and software solutions offered
by vendors improved, the need to enhance e-procurement followed. This book
addresses that need and aims to provide an in-depth understanding of the SAP Supplier Relationship Management (SAP SRM) solution offering. According to SAP, the
SAP SRM application tightly and cost-effectively integrates strategic practices for
supplier qualification, negotiation, and contract management with other enterprise
functions and their suppliers' processes through a single analytical framework and
support for multi-channel supplier enablement.

The contents of this book are inspired by my consulting engagements with some
of the leading companies on the landscape today. This book extends beyond configuration. It strives to fill the need for a comprehensive guidebook on strategies in
the areas of content management, workflow, integration to financials and human
resources, security management, business intelligence, enterprise portals, e-Sourcing, and so on.

Since SAP introduced its first e-procurement solution in 1999, it has enjoyed explosive growth and evolved into what we know as SAP SRM. Today, SAP SRM is the market leader in its field. SRM enjoys the incongruent distinction of being both an industry term and the name of a host of software solutions.

This book clarifies both aspects and attempts to empower the reader with the information and tools needed to understand and implement SAP SRM. After reading this book, readers will possess an overview of the industry term SRM, an understanding of what is the SAP SRM solution, and have a comprehensive guidebook to use for developing strategies in implementing the SAP SRM solution.

Who This Book Is For

This book targets SRM project managers, consultants, cross-functional leads, technical teams, and support leaders who want to deploy SAP SRM successfully in the real world.

It is organized into five logical parts, enabling readers to delve directly into the part most relevant to them. However, readers new to SRM will find it more valuable to start with Part I, which provides an overview of SAP SRM.

Experienced consultants familiar with SAP SRM and its core functionality might be drawn to Part III, which deals with implementation, integration, and upgrades.

The content and capabilities in this book are based on SAP SRM 5.0 and SAP SRM 7.0 releases. The first edition of this book introduced a lot of essential concepts within SRM and detail about the capabilities of SAP SRM 4.0. In the last couple of years, SAP SRM has gone through a considerable shift in both technology changes and in capability. With SAP SRM 7.0 providing an entirely new user-interface, large technology change, and a new workflow engine, it became imperative for me to author this second edition. In this edition, I build upon the concepts discussed in the first edition and introduce the new capabilities that have emerged in SAP SRM 5.0 and SRM 7.0.

In addition, the SAP E-Sourcing solution has gained a lot of traction in the marketplace and a number of organizations are looking at E-Sourcing as a real driver for strategic sourcing. I have included a new chapter dedicated on explaining the concepts of E-Sourcing and its integration with SAP ERP.

Based on reader feedback, I have also included a new chapter on sharing real customer case studies with implementing SAP SRM, E-Sourcing, and SAP ERP. These case studies will allow organizations implementing SAP SRM to view what others may have done and possibly gain additional insight on their strategic roadmap.

I am extremely grateful for the support that customers, consulting organizations, and independent consultants have given me in making the first edition of this book a huge success. I have received excellent feedback on the value readers have gained from reading this book and I hope to continually provide that experience to new readers of this second edition.

I recommend that this book be used in conjunction with SAP SRM training, release notes, other SAP PRESS books, and the help guide available in the Service Marketplace. This book does not aim to replace any of the other content provided by SAP.

About This Book

Let's take a quick look at what the various part of this book contain, so you can get an idea of how to best use it for your needs. Some of you might read it from beginning to end. Or you might use it as a modular resource, dipping into specific chapters as needed. Let's get an idea of what is included in this resource.

Part I: How SRM Fits Within an Organization

This part gives an overview on Supplier Relationship Management (SRM). It answers the question: "What is SRM?"

Part II: What Is SAP SRM?

This begins with an introduction to SAP's Supplier Relationship Management application, SAP SRM. It then provides a detailed understanding of the three supply processes within SRM: operational procurement, strategic sourcing, and supplier enablement. "What is SAP SRM?" and "Where does it fit in the overall SAP solution landscape?" It then guides you through the detailed functionality and capability of SAP SRM.

Part III: Implementation, Integration, and Upgrades

This part outlines valuable and relevant tools for implementation, integration, and upgrade processes. It guides you through finer the points that cannot be learned from SAP training alone. Most of these insights are based on my real-life implementations and experiences.

This part also offers knowledge that would distinguish configuration consultants from process consultants and answers to key project questions such as the following:

▶ "We are considering SRM/EBP for global e-Procurement along with a global SAP ERP project. What are the decision criteria for selecting a scenario? How do scenario decisions affect the communication to the supply chain?"

▶ "There seem to be a lot of different options for catalogs. Should we merely implement punch-out catalogs? What is the SAP solution for catalog management?"

▶ "How does SRM integrate with the SAP ERP Financials? We're using the Funds Management functionality in SAP; what integration touch points should we be aware of?"

▶ "We are looking at upgrading from EBP 3.0, which currently fronts SAP 4.6c MM. I am looking for some summary documentation setting about the functional and technical pros and cons for upgrading to EBP 3.5.5.0."

▶ "We are implementing SRM with BW and SAP R/3. Is there a guide to assist us with the security knowledge?"

Part IV: Industry Solutions

This part highlights the new Procurement for Public Sector solution (SAP PPS) offering from — based on SAP SRM. Originally branded as Government Procurement (GP), this solution focuses on the unique requirements for government and other public sector companies.

Part V: Selected Configuration in SAP SRM

This part arms the reader with selected solution configuration information. While not a step-by-step cookbook for configuration, it discusses key setup and configuration areas in SAP SRM.

Appendices

The appendices contain valuable extras that readers will find extremely helpful in their projects: SRM functionality matrix, job scheduling, Business Add-Ins (BAdIs), customer fields, a quiz to test your SRM knowledge, and more.

Summary

In this preface, I tried to give you a general idea and overview of the book. I hope that the contents of this book, along with the examples I have chosen to illustrate important concepts and processes, furthers your understanding of how you can use SAP SRM to enhance procurement in your company.

Let's now move on to Chapter 1, where I will give you a general understanding of supplier relationship management and its important concepts.

Special Thanks

When I embarked on the journey to write this book, I had no idea how, when and where I would find the time between running TSE (The SRM Experts), working on client engagements, completing my EMBA and trying to be a good husband and father. It is during times like these that we are amazed by what true support from friends and family can do. I have been fortunate to be blessed with incredible relationships whose support made this book possible.

I am indebted to my friend, Abhijit Umbarkar, for his unstinted and unparalleled efforts in helping me author the first edition. He spent countless hours reviewing every chapter and providing his expert advice. As an SAP PRESS author himself, I am extremely thankful to him for his contributions in the integration to financials chapter.

I thank my extraordinary colleagues and friends who spent numerous hours combing through the chapters of the book and provided invaluable reviews. I wish them the very best in every endeavor.

I am continually thankful for the support and direction of my two brothers Randhir and Rahul. Their unparalleled advice always keeps me focused towards the goal and helped me find the time in authoring this second edition.

I also want to thank all my customers that have given me the opportunity to gain the experience and knowledge by working with them and implementing SAP SRM and E-Sourcing solutions globally.

To SAP PRESS for giving me this wonderful opportunity and a special thanks to my editor, Meg Dunkerley for her relentless patience, belief, and dedication in making this second edition a reality.

Last but not the least, I express gratitude towards all the readers of the first edition, their wonderful comments, feedback and support to make the first edition a best seller and giving me the inspiration to author the second edition of this book.

PART I
How SRM Fits Within an Organization

Supplier relationship management (SRM) is rapidly developing as a key business priority for companies as they look for tangible savings and enhanced collaboration, communication, and visibility in the procurement life cycle.

1 Introduction to Supplier Relationship Management

The ever-changing economy, globalization, reduced product margins, and offshoring of manufacturing and services have all promoted and elevated the need for a tighter and more robust integration of business partners throughout the value chain. The new customer–supplier relationship involves not just the procurement and supply of goods and services but a relationship that demands true partnership.

Today, organizations are learning that the way to gain the most value from their business partners is by enhancing their collaboration throughout their supplier base. Internet connectivity has defined new ways to identify, negotiate, and engage with suppliers and partners worldwide, while other data-aggregation and enrichment tools provide greater insight into procurement trends and best practices.

This is where SAP Supplier Relationship Management (SRM) provides value for organizations. SAP SRM streamlines all the processes and communication channels between an organization and its supplier base.

Example

An organization used to take 10 to 15 days to requisition and process a purchase order (PO). They can now process a PO in one to two days using SAP SRM processes and applications. Supplier organizations have greater visibility in customer processes. Suppliers can, for example, view their invoice statuses and payment information by logging in to supplier portals provided by customer organizations implementing SAP SRM.

Let's begin the next part of this chapter by talking about the evolution of procurement and about how SAP SRM has matured over the last five years.

1.1 e-Procurement and SRM

Some form of communication and collaboration between the buyer and the supplier has always existed, so procurement in its basic form has been around for a long time. According to procurement services provider ICG Commerce, the term *procurement* refers to the process of managing activities associated with a company's need to procure the goods and services required to either manufacture a product (direct) or to operate the organization (indirect). Breakthrough inventions in communication and collaboration technologies such as the telephone, fax, and Internet have had significant impacts on the procurement process over the years. Figure 1.1 illustrates the evolution of procurement in a simple way.

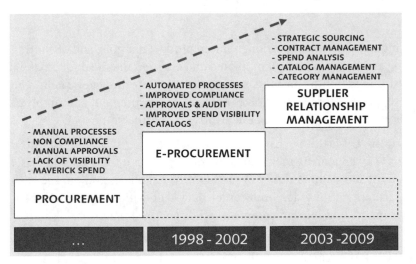

Figure 1.1 Evolution of Procurement

Until the late 1990s, most organizations still had manual, costly, and inefficient procurement processes. Limited standardization in the requisition-to-order process, no approvals or manual approval processes, none or minimal visibility into spending, along with no strategic sourcing capabilities, all created a highly inefficient procurement environment.

This is why the advent of the Internet and e-commerce gave birth to *e-procurement* (electronic procurement), which became the buzzword for buying and selling of products and services using the Internet. e-Procurement was adopted by organizations to automate their manual procurement processes, and reduce costs by directing spending on primarily indirect goods to negotiated supplier catalogs.

Ariba, i2, SAS, and Commerce One pioneered the e-procurement marketplace. And their entire solution offering was branded as e-procurement. Interestingly, most of these software providers were niche players and none were major enterprise resource planning (ERP) software providers. Companies like Ariba were too far ahead for any ERP software providers to provide a competing product for e-procurement.

A number of Fortune 500 companies implemented Ariba and Commerce One applications, touting these as best of breed. Over the past four to five years, the big ERP software providers have finally caught up and developed a compelling application for customers. Not only have they built "best-of-breed" solutions, but they also possess a front door into all the large customers that for years have implemented the ERP applications in their organizations. Furthermore, ERP application providers offer integrated solutions, a great benefit.

Another key development over the past few years has been that customers have demanded more than automation of processes. Organizations realized that e-procurement tools were not enough to provide the cost reductions and savings that were projected by the market. Other drivers, such as sourcing, contract management, reporting, and analytics, were all equally important in gaining the true benefits promised for e-procurement. This is where the industry shift has given birth to SAP SRM, which is broader in scope than e-procurement and represents the next step in the evolution of procurement.

SAP SRM applications take a comprehensive approach toward managing an enterprise's interactions with the organizations that supply the goods and services it uses. SAP SRM manages the flow of information between suppliers and purchasing organizations and ensures the integration of supplier information in the procurement process. The goal of SAP SRM is to make all the interactions between the enterprise and its suppliers streamlined and effective. Some of its key objectives are to optimize the processes designed for acquisition of products and services, to replace inefficient paper trails, and to maximize on savings by using companywide supplier contracts.

A simple Google search on *supplier relationship management software* provides more 2.43 million results. Interestingly, a search on *e-procurement software* provides around 3.03 million results. The question arises whether the shift from e-procurement to SRM has really happened. The answer is yes, because SAP SRM is not just a re-branding of e-procurement but rather an umbrella term for a suite of tools, one of which is procurement or e-procurement. Catalog Mgmt., Sourcing, Contract Mgmt., Spend Analysis, and Supplier Enablement are all tools within the SAP SRM umbrella (as illustrated in Figure 1.2).

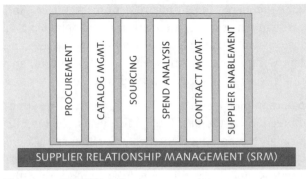

Figure 1.2 SAP SRM Suite

As illustrated in Figure 1.3, procurement is a core part of the SAP SRM suite, accounting for 52% of the suite. Market studies show that procurement solutions are still the leader in revenue share in the overall SAP SRM market segment. There is no mystery behind this growth, because at its core, e-procurement is the automation of the requisition-to-order process. Every organization that ventures down the path of SRM has to overcome its first challenge of automation.

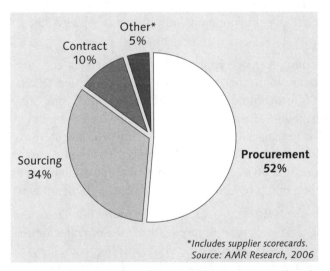

Figure 1.3 Procurement and Sourcing License Revenue Share by Application Segment, 2006

SRM is more than just about cost savings; it is also about value generation. Leading organizations understand that their business partners can be a key element in their overall success. Together, they can improve business processes, share information to reduce wasted time and resources, and improve overall margins.

The value proposition for SRM allows companies not only to reduce costs but gain considerable competitive advantage. Figure 1.4 illustrates some of the benefits that buying organizations and suppliers gain by implementing SRM solutions and processes.

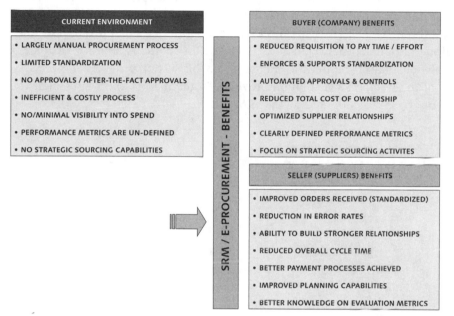

Figure 1.4 SRM Value Generation

SRM reaches beyond just the automation of business processes and the reduction in operating costs gained by this automation. This was best expressed by Bill Knittle, global procurement director for downstream procurement at BP International: "SRM is about much more than cost reduction...it's about ensuring continuity of supply and obtaining collaborative value from a select group of strategic suppliers. The key is to focus on the right suppliers in the first place, and then to work with them in a structured and disciplined manner. We have implemented a formal process of segmenting our supply base to choose the appropriate engagement approach for each supplier, and we're continuing to put structure and discipline around relationship and performance management."

Section 1.1 discussed the evolution of procurement to SRM. In the next two sections, 1.2 and 1.3, we will briefly discuss the SRM vendor landscape and introduce why SAP with the SAP SRM application is the market leader for SRM applications.

1.2   The SRM Vendor Landscape

In 2002, Frost & Sullivan identified SRM as a promising growth area, forecasting a compound annual growth rate (CAGR) of 18% over the 2001 to 2006 period. This growth was more than sustained, and in 2006, a leading supply-chain research organization, AMR Research, projected that the SRM market segment will experience an 8% CAGR through 2010. This provides a market opportunity for software providers to continue to build efficient and cost-effective SRM solutions, and for customers to have a wide array of solutions to choose from. This section provides an overview of some of the leading SRM solution providers in the market and shares industry research on the leaders dominating the SRM market.

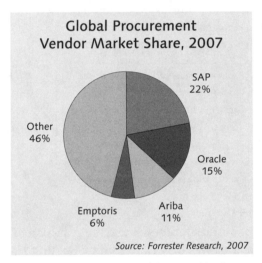

Figure 1.5   Procurement and Sourcing Vendors

According to leading research firm Forrester Research, the market for global procurement software providers is led by SAP with 22% of the overall procurement and sourcing market, with Ariba and Oracle at a close second and third place with 15% and 11% respectively. Figure 1.5 illustrates the top procurement and sourcing vendors by 2007 vendor market share.

1.3   Why SAP SRM?

In a market with so many best-of-breed solution providers, organizations may ask why they should implement SAP SRM, the supplier relationship management solution from SAP.

SAP introduced its initial e-procurement solution in 1999, called *Business-to-Business procurement* (B2B). This happened at a time when market leaders such as Ariba were years ahead of the SAP solution. It was also an era when e-commerce was the leading buzzword, and ERP vendors had missed the boat on *"e"* or web-based commerce. Many organizations that had existing implementations of the SAP ERP solution, SAP R/3, opted to implement *best-of-breed* e-procurement solutions such as Ariba.

This has since changed considerably. Over the last ten years, SAP has drastically improved its SAP SRM application and become a leading application provider. The current application is SAP SRM, and everything from the user interface to its functionality for operational procurement, strategic sourcing, and supplier enablement provides a highly competitive offering for customers. SAP SRM was the fastest growing SAP application in two of the three years prior to 2006, and SAP has added significant investments in the overall SAP application.

> **Note**
>
> According to sources in SAP, there are over 3,500 implementations of SAP SRM across the globe. These include customers with productive and nonproductive environments across the entire suite of SAP SRM application.

Figure 1.6 provides results from a 2005 SAP Annual Report for investors in which the SRM application gained 20% in revenue. Notice that, compared to the other applications including SAP ERP, SAP SRM had the largest percentage change compared to any SAP single application offering.

In addition to being a competitive solution as compared to Ariba and others in the market, SAP SRM has a big advantage in its tight integration to the core SAP ERP software. A recent survey conducted by Accenture (with findings illustrated in Figure 1.7) concluded that the most important deciding factor for organizations that are evaluating SRM software solutions is the functionality available in the software. The second most important factor is the ease of integration with existing ERP systems.

The Accenture survey results are further strengthened with the testimony of customers that have implemented the SAP SRM solution illustrated in Figure 1.8. SAP conducted research across many SAP SRM customers and published an SAP SRM customer reference book.

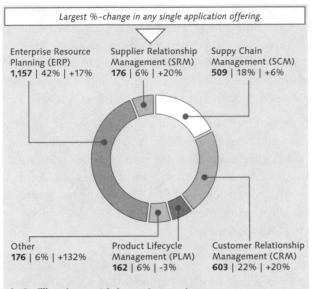

Figure 1.6   SAP SRM Software Product Revenue Breakdown

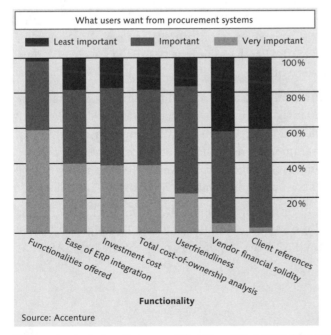

Figure 1.7   Accenture Survey on What Users Want From Procurement Systems

The companies listed in Figure 1.8 are just a few of the many listed in the survey reference book. It is important to notice that four out of the six companies listed cited leveraging their existing investment and integration as their key deciding factor for choosing to implement SAP SRM.

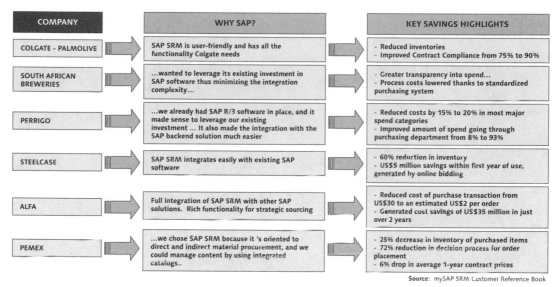

COMPANY	WHY SAP?	KEY SAVINGS HIGHLIGHTS
COLGATE - PALMOLIVE	SAP SRM is user-friendly and has all the functionality Colgate needs	- Reduced inventories - Improved Contract Compliance from 75% to 90%
SOUTH AFRICAN BREWERIES	...wanted to leverage its existing investment in SAP software thus minimizing the integration complexity...	- Greater transparency into spend... - Process costs lowered thanks to standardized purchasing system
PERRIGO	...we already had SAP R/3 software in place, and it made sense to leverage our existing investment ... It also made the integration with the SAP backend solution much easier	- Reduced costs by 15% to 20% in most major spend categories - Improved amount of spend going through purchasing department from 8% to 93%
STEELCASE	SAP SRM integrates easily with existing SAP software	- 60% reduction in inventory - US$5 million savings within first year of use, generated by online bidding
ALFA	Full integration of SAP SRM with other SAP solutions. Rich functionality for strategic sourcing	- Reduced cost of purchase transaction from US$30 to an estimated US$2 per order - Generated cost savings of US$35 million in just over 2 years
PEMEX	...we chose SAP SRM because it 's oriented to direct and indirect material procurement, and we could manage content by using integrated catalogs..	- 25% decrease in inventory of purchased items - 72% reduction in decision process for order placement - 6% drop in average 1-year contract prices

Source: mySAP SRM Customer Reference Book

Figure 1.8 Why Organizations Chose SAP SRM

As illustrated in Figure 1.8, companies like Steelcase have chosen SAP's SRM application for its ease of integration with their existing SAP software. They have attained results of more than 60% reduction in inventory along with a $5 million savings by using the SAP SRM bidding solution.

1.4   Summary

In this chapter, we introduced the term supplier relationship management (SRM). We talked about the evolution of procurement into e-procurement and then into today's SRM. We also briefly discussed the current SRM vendor landscape and how SAP is today's market leader in SRM with 22% of the overall procurement and sourcing market.

Chapter 2 will introduce SAP's supplier relationship management application, SAP SRM. The goal of the next chapter is to help readers answer the question: What is SAP SRM, and where does it fit into the overall SAP application landscape?

PART II
What Is SAP SRM?

"With the SAP Supplier Relationship Management (SAP SRM) solution, we want to enable our customers to unleash the value potential of a holistic and strategic approach to purchasing and supply management by offering a purchasing platform for continuous savings and value generation."
— *Peter Kirschbauer, General Manager, SAP AG, SAP Applications*

2 SAP SRM — An Introduction

2.1 Evolution of SAP SRM

SAP introduced its e-procurement solution in 1999. Since then, the application offering and its acceptance have seen tremendous growth. The solution has seen over eight releases over the last nine years, with a latest Business Suite release of SAP SRM 7.0 in Q2 2009. Customers that were early adopters of this solution remember the solution branding as Business to Business Procurement (BBP) or Enterprise Buyer (EB). Over the years, the solution has grown from a Web-based catalog requisitioning solution aimed at operational excellence to the solution today that offers complete supply management. Figure 2.1 provides a chart that shows the progression of this application from B2B to SAP SRM.

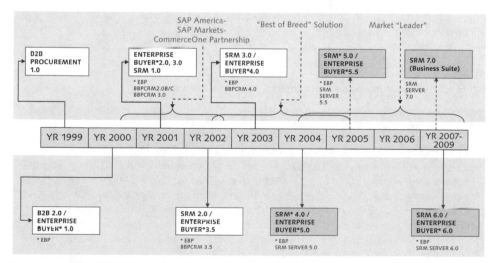

Figure 2.1 SAP SRM Solution Growth — From B2B–EBP to SAP SRM

In 1999, SAP introduced the B2B Procurement 1.0 application and has since re-branded the offering from BBP to EBP to the application available today as SAP SRM. The application release generally available to customers today is SAP SRM 7.0. The SAP SRM 6.0 release, which was rebranded as SAP SRM 2007 was short lived because it was stopped by SAP for general release to customers. Only a select group of customers received the SAP SRM 6.0 application in a controlled-release fashion. The SAP SRM 7.0 application is built on top of the SAP SRM 6.0 foundation. Most of the technology around use of the Portal, WebDynpro, and Process-Controlled workflow was introduced in SAP SRM 6.0. We will discuss these technologies with the later chapters in this book.

2.2 SAP SRM and SAP Enterprise Applications

The SAP SRM application integrates seamlessly with SAP ERP, SAP Product Life-cycle Management (PLM), and SAP Supply Chain Management (SCM) applications to ensure an effective implementation of cross-application business processes (see Figure 2.2).

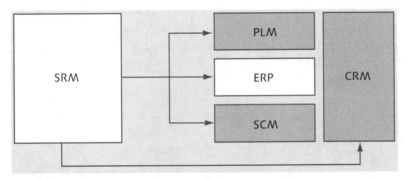

Figure 2.2 SAP SRM Integrates Cross-Enterprise Business Processes

> **Note**
>
> SAP SRM is a separate solution, independent of SAP ERP. It is common for people to forget that SAP SRM is installed and implemented within its own three-tiered architectural land-scape, independent from the SAP ERP landscape. However, it is still an SAP system; the graphical user interface (GUI) for SAP SRM is the same as for native SAP ERP, with an IMG for core-configuration. The difference lies in the actual end user interface for SAP SRM. End users only require a web browser to access all the transactions. Figure 2.3 provides an ex-ample of the user interface in SAP SRM. End users use the SAP portal-based user interface for creating shopping carts and performing approvals, etc. And configurators use the SAP GUI application to configure and setup the SAP SRM system.

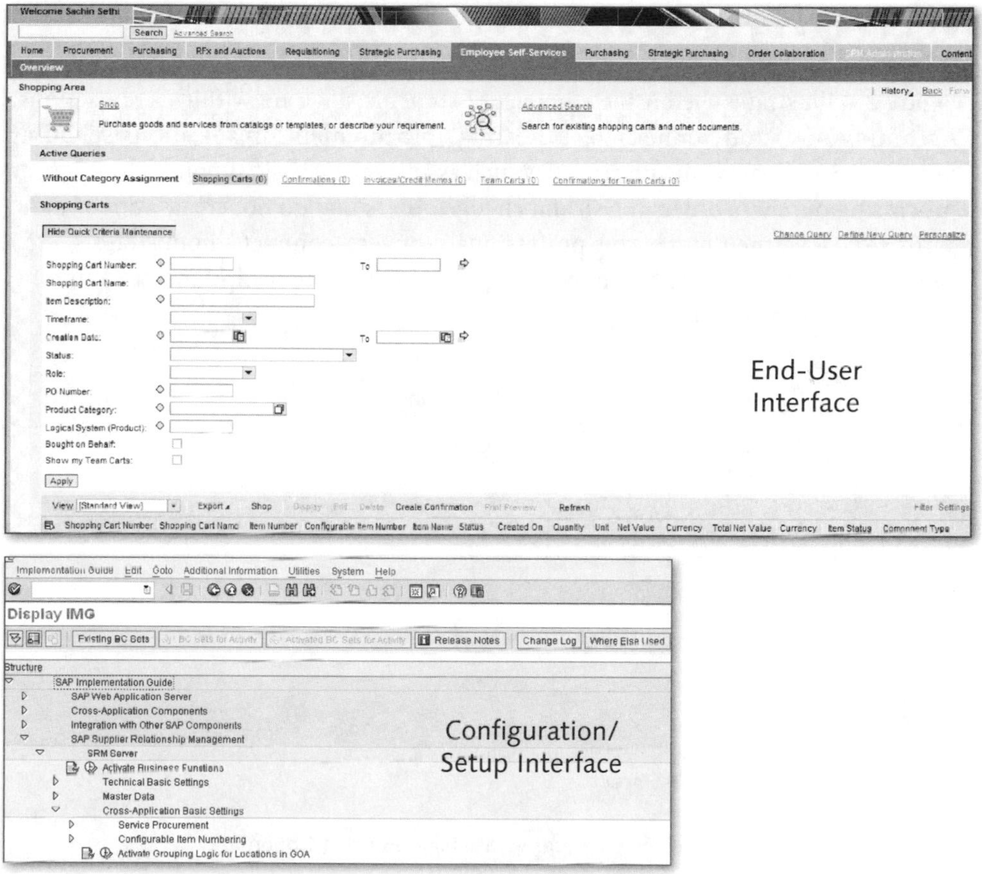

Figure 2.3 SAP SRM User Interface — End User and Configurator

> **Note**
>
> Until SAP SRM 5.0, the user interface for SAP SRM was based on an ITS and BSP technology. Beginning with SAP SRM 2007 (or SAP SRM 6.0), and now SAP SRM 7.0 the ITS and BSP user interface has been replaced by a portal user interface for SAP SRM based on WebDynpro technology.

2.3 Benefits of SAP SRM

Often, it's not easy to clearly understand the business benefits within a solution offering or a new business process unless at some level we're able to understand the underlying business challenges within the organization. Once we as users realize and understand the challenges faced, we then can be open to hearing about the solutions. We frequently question why we need to change our current system or business processes.

It is advisable for organizations to review the challenges faced by their internal business systems and processes and then review the business benefits offered by SAP SRM.

Figure 2.4 illustrates the business impact of strategic sourcing within organizations. According to a study done by A.T. Kearney, procurement organizations spend as much as 85% of their time on activities such as answering basic supplier inquiries, or processing purchase orders (POs), and change orders that do not create added value. With SAP SRM, their purchasing professionals (buyers, contract administrators, etc.) can focus their efforts on building strategic supplier relationships and streamlining the procure-to-pay process.

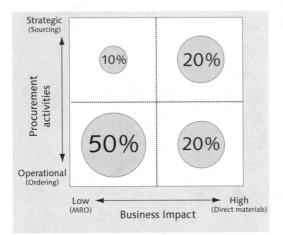

Figure 2.4 Operational Procurement Focus vs. Strategic Sourcing Opportunity

Example

Organizations using SAP SRM empower end users to keep track of their orders using real-time status checking. Requisitioners do not have to call the purchasing department to find out the status of their shopping cart request; they can use the Check Status application in SAP SRM to monitor the status of their orders. Using the Biller Direct application, your organization can enable suppliers to view the status of their invoices and view in real time what payments have been disbursed. This reduces drastically the time spent by the purchasing and accounts payable departments in handling end user and supplier calls.

2.3.1 Opportunities and Business Benefits Within SAP SRM

Solutions driven solely by technological enhancements only provide a siloed response to the competitive and strategic needs of organizations today. World-class business solutions need to use advancements in technology as a strategic advantage to provide solutions that cater to the unique business processes that exist in organizations.

Organizations that are leaders in their markets and industries are better at using IT to enable business strategy. The SAP SRM solution provides benefits that exist in three realms, which are listed as follows and illustrated in Figure 2.5:

▶ Process benefits

▶ Technology benefits

▶ People benefits

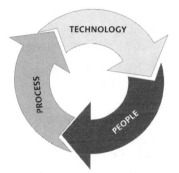

Figure 2.5 The Three Realms — Process, Technology, and People

2.3.2 Process Benefits

SAP SRM is based on SAP best practices that stem from proven business and industry expertise. In addition, with the SAP SRM solution, SAP provides a wide range of preconfigured business scenarios that organizations can quickly deploy and benefit from with improved efficiency in their business processes. Let's examine some process benefits now:

▶ Overall reduction in requisitioning, order processing, and supply-management cycle time are a direct result of the streamlined procure-to-pay processes within SAP SRM.

▶ Efficiencies in business processes eliminate costly process-related errors and increase productivity by implementing adequate internal controls.

▶ SAP SRM replaces manual procurement processes with a streamlined requisitioning and approval process. Delays caused by lengthy manual approvals are replaced by faster electronic workflows and online status displays.

▶ Web-based catalogs provide a quick and easy mechanism for finding negotiated goods and services, comparative prices, and required attributes. Additionally, catalog-based selection ensures compliance with approved vendors.

▶ An Internet-based request for proposal (RFP) and bidding process reduces the source evaluation cycle time.

▶ Greater visibility of the historical spending data reduces the source determination time. Purchasing professionals can optimize sourcing decisions based on such criteria as past supplier performance data to determine the best source for goods and services. This helps to continuously enhance the sourcing knowledge within the organization.

▶ Synchronization of back-office functions by integrating with corporate finance and ERP systems. SAP SRM integrates with one or many SAP and non-SAP backend systems.

▶ Improved contract compliance and governance are achieved by driving spending toward selected suppliers with negotiated products and prices. Spending analysis within SAP NetWeaver® Business Warehouse (BW) matches contracts with purchase transactions to monitor off-contract spending.

2.3.3 Technology Benefits

SAP SRM provides real-time integration with SAP ERP as the backbone, ensuring real-time data validation across SAP applications, such as SAP ERP Financials Financial Accounting and SAP ERP HCM. Let's take a look at some technology benefits:

▶ Web-based requisitioning, bidding, and supplier interaction provide ease of use and increased collaboration across the supply chain.

▶ Out-of-box, ready-to-use workflow business sets promote reduced implementation efforts.

▶ SAP SRM replaces paper approvals with online approvals, reducing the processing time drastically. It also provides greater visibility and awareness with an electronic audit trail.

▶ Email integration with standard mail clients such as Microsoft Outlook or Lotus Notes provides greater productivity and user acceptance.

▶ Pre-delivered business packages within SAP NetWeaver Portal provide end users with a single interface for all purchasing needs.

▶ Better on-demand reporting and improved compliance.

▶ Flexible and scalable architecture and implementation scenarios provide organizations the opportunity to configure for their specific business requirements.

▶ Integration technologies such as XML and Supplier Networks promote opportunities to standardize supplier adoption.

▶ Users only require a web browser to access the functionality in SAP SRM. This in turn reduces end user maintenance costs with a lower total cost of ownership (TCO).

2.3.4 People Benefits

Benefits for the organization's users are listed here:

▶ Streamlined Wizard and Professional Form requisition navigation in SAP SRM provide a solution for both casual and power users.

▶ Personal Object Work lists (POWL) provide users with an ability to create real-time queries and quick visibility on the status of their orders and reduces time-consuming follow-up.

▶ Professionals within the purchasing organization can focus on strategic supplier relationships and contract negotiations instead of requisition processing.

▶ Online supplier catalogs in SAP SRM ensure that users can quickly search for goods and services. This greatly reduces the need for intervention by purchasing professionals for negotiated goods and services ordered from these catalogs.

▶ An intuitive Web-based Portal interface provides single logon to multiple SAP and Non-SAP applications increasing user efficiency and stronger adoption.

▶ The end-user requisitioning experience is similar to online applications such as Office Depot, Staples, and Dell, easing organizational change management and training needs.

▶ A single interface to all the procurement functions allows users to focus on their tasks and activities improving productivity. Additionally, business packages for SAP SRM direct information to different user groups on an individual basis, which increases productivity and enhances user acceptance.

In SAP's published *SAP SRM Statement of Direction 2005*, SAP outlines the business benefits of SAP SRM and describes how SAP SRM addresses the business challenges faced by organizations today. Table 2.1 is an excerpt from the document.

Capability	Business Need	Business Benefit
Sourcing	Gain visibility into and actively control more spending categories and manage demand; ensure compliance across business units and supply base	Better sourcing decisions that optimize overall value contribution from suppliers
Procurement	Simplify, standardize, automate, and integrate the procure-to-pay process	Streamlined procure-to-pay process with less administration and more efficiency, resulting in elimination of errors, increased productivity, reduced cycle times, and lower processing costs
Supplier Enablement	Enable the supply base to collaborate and work more effectively	Increased adoption of e-procurement practices through scalable supplier-connectivity capability

Table 2.1 Some Business Benefits of SAP SRM

Organizations interested in reading the statement of direction can download a copy from SAP's website at *www.sap.com/solutions/business-suite/srm/brochures*.

Now that you are familiar with the key benefits of SAP SRM, let's use the next section to further dissect the SAP SRM solution. In Section 2.4, we'll introduce three key concepts:

▶ Core supply processes
▶ Business scenarios
▶ Technology components

2.4 Dissecting SAP SRM

There are a few terms and concepts that we need to define o properly understand SAP SRM. SAP constantly changes the SAP SRM framework and often introduces new concepts for arranging SAP SRM. Fundamentally, there are three key concepts to understand: core supply processes, business scenarios within each core process, and underlying technology components that enable the business processes.

For the implementation of each business scenario, one or more SAP components or third-party applications might be required. For example, the Supplier Enablement business scenario is powered by a number of underlying technology components, such as, supplier self-services, SAP Biller Direct, SAP NetWeaver Portal, Supply Network Planning (SNP), to name a few.

2.4.1 Core Supply Processes

SAP defines three core supply processes that collectively make up the SAP SRM solution:

▶ Operational procurement
▶ Strategic sourcing
▶ Supplier enablement

Chapters 3, 4, and 5 are dedicated to each of these core supply processes.

2.4.2 Operational Procurement

Each core supply process has multiple business scenarios:

▶ **Self Service Procurement**
   Indirect procurement enables your employees to create and manage their own requirement requests. This relieves your purchasing department of a huge administrative burden while making the procurement process both faster and more responsive.

▶ **Plan-driven Procurement (direct procurement)**
This automates and streamlines ordering processes for regularly needed core materials. Because SAP SRM is integrated with planning, design, and order-processing systems, you can link your procurement processes to a plan-driven strategy that gets you the materials you need for core business processes exactly when you need them. Plan-Driven Procurement integrates seamlessly with backend systems such as enterprise planning and production. The scenario allows you to integrate operational procurement with your existing supply-chain management solution.

▶ **Service Procurement**
e-Procurement has produced great opportunities for saving costs in the purchasing process. However, companies generally fail to extend cost saving measures to services, even though services amount to more than 50% of annual purchasing volumes. The Service Procurement business scenario within SAP SRM covers a wide range of services such as temporary labor, consulting, maintenance, and facility management.

2.4.3 Strategic Sourcing

It is estimated that sourcing accounts for up to 75% of the total opportunity for procurement savings within an enterprise. The following business scenarios enable the strategic sourcing capabilities within SAP SRM to fulfill supply needs, negotiate supplier contracts, and evaluate supplier performance:

▶ **Catalog Content Management**
This scenario provides a solution for creating, maintaining, and managing catalog content within your e-procurement application. This concept will be discussed in detail in Chapter 6.

▶ **Strategic Sourcing and Contract Management**
This application in SAP Enterprise Buyer (EB) provides professional purchasers with a wide range of actions and information to help them source their requirements. As a purchaser, you can use the interface to process the requirements and determine the best source of supply. Once you have done this, you can create a PO or contract directly from the sourcing application or SAP Bidding Engine. Save it either locally or in the backend system, depending on the technical scenario you are using (Classic, Extended Classic, or Standalone).

▶ **Spend Analysis**
This is a decision-support application that enables you as a purchaser to analyze your total spending across system and organizational boundaries. You can perform the analyses per supplier, per product, or per product category.

2.4.4 Supplier Enablement

Supplier Enablement provides a quick and easy process for suppliers and customers to collaborate along the supplier relationship life cycle. Supplier organizations can connect to a customer-hosted portal to communicate across a number of supplier-related activities.

▶ **Supplier Self-Registration**
With this application, organizations can provide a simple Web-based self-registration process for potential suppliers. The main aim for this process is to allow strategic purchasers to identify new suppliers for doing business; accepted suppliers can then participate in strategic sourcing events such as bidding and auction events.

▶ **Design Collaboration**
This scenario allows organizations to involve suppliers beginning with the product design stage, which enables collaboration on design objects like specifications and bills of materials. Organizations using the SAP PLM application can use C-folders to invite suppliers to participate in the design aspect of acquiring specialty products and services.

▶ **Order Collaboration**
Organizations can use the supplier self-services component to exchange business documents with their suppliers. POs, PO acknowledgements, and invoices are examples of some of the business documents that can be exchanged with suppliers using a Web-based application hosted by the customer. Suppliers only require a web browser to log in to the application and receive POs and can collaborate on all procurement-related activities.

▶ **Collaborative Replenishment**
Collaborative replenishment optimizes the supply-chain performance by enabling suppliers to access customer inventory data and making them responsible for maintaining the inventory levels required by customers through exception-based replenishment.

2.5 SAP Components

SAP components are the underlying technologies that enable the SAP business scenarios. The key SAP components are listed below and described in detail following:

▶ SAP Enterprise Buyer (SAP EB)
▶ SAP Bidding Engine
▶ Supplier self-services

► SAP Catalog Content Management (SAP CCM) or SRM-MDM Catalog

► SAP NetWeaver BW

► SAP NetWeaver Process Integration (PI)

► SAP NetWeaver Portal

2.5.1 SAP Enterprise Buyer (SAP EB)

SAP EB promotes *self service* procurement. It is a Web-based solution that provides the complete procurement process for the procurement of both direct and indirect goods and services. The process begins with the creation of a *shopping cart* and ends with the entry of an *invoice*. SAP EB is the execution hub for the majority of processes within SAP SRM, as shown in Figure 2.6.

Most organizations initiate their supplier-relationship management journeys with implementing the EB component in SAP SRM. Once implemented, SAP EB acts as a catalyst for all the other components. For example, the SAP CCM component is not used by itself; instead, users creating shopping carts or purchasing professionals creating POs in EB use catalogs to quickly search for and order products and services.

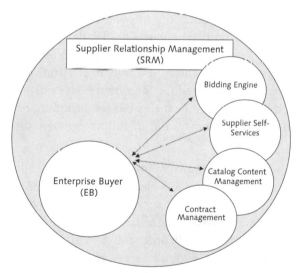

Figure 2.6 SAP EB — Execution Engine in SAP SRM

2.5.2 SAP Bidding Engine

The Bidding Engine is an Internet solution that provides organizations the ability to strategically source and obtain optimal prices for goods and services. Tools such as

RFx, Auctions, Reverse Auctions, and Bid Evaluation enable organizations to create and process bid invitations and auctions to source products and services. Suppliers access the bid invitations using a web browser where they can submit bids and access all the details of the bid.

An example of how an organization might use the Bidding Engine capabilities is as follows. Let's say your company wants to replace all the existing computers because they're getting outdated and wants to purchase state-of the-art laptops for all 5,000 users in the organization.

This type of a purchase could cost an organization between $75,000 to $100,000 just in equipment purchase, apart from the services and maintenance cost. Organizations could use the SAP Bidding Engine to invite a select group of suppliers such as Dell Corporation, IBM Corporation, or Hewlett-Packard (HP) to a Bidding Event where they would get competitive bids electronically. Your company can then evaluate the bids received in an electronic manner based on a number of different criteria and select the most suitable supplier to contract the purchase.

2.5.3 Supplier Self-Services

Supplier self-services is a hosted Internet application that provides an integrated application for organizations to collaborate with their business partners. A web browser such as Internet Explorer is all that is required for accessing supplier self-services. This offers smaller and mid-sized suppliers the opportunity to electronically integrate the procurement processes without the need for their own sales systems. Supplier self-services provides hosted order management capabilities, including PO processing, goods-receipt confirmation, invoice entry, and the ability to view the payment status.

Organizations can invite strategic suppliers that are smaller in size and those that do not have the capability to exchange business documents electronically using XML or EDI. By enabling smaller suppliers with supplier self-services capabilities, your organization can ensure that documents are delivered to the supplier electronically via a hosted solution. Supplier organizations can assist in order collaboration and can acknowledge the PO receipt and delivery of the goods and services electronically, alleviating the manual efforts required by your purchasing department.

Also, suppliers can enter invoices electronically using supplier self-services, and these can then be sent to the appropriate individuals in your organization for proper approvals using workflow prior to payment. This can reduce the manual efforts for your accounts payable department to enter invoices.

2.5.4   SAP Catalog Content Management (SRM-MDM Catalog)

Beginning with SRM 7.0, the go-to catalog option is the SRM-MDM catalog. Although, SAP will continue to support its previous solution (SAP CCM), it is recommended that upgrade customers move to the SRM-MDM catalog, because for new SRM 7.0 implementations only the SRM-MDM catalog application will be supported.

The SRM-MDM catalog solution enables organizations to manage enterprise and supplier content. Users can search for products and services using a robust search tool with added flexibility to search cross-catalogs, comparisons, and get detailed information on products or services. SRM-MDM catalog is a competitive offering to the previously used catalogs of SAP CCM and BugsEye products offered by Requisite. SAP support for Requisite products expired in 2005.

SAP initially announced the strategic shift in content-management strategy in May 2006 to move toward the SRM-MDM Catalog. Chapter 6 will discuss the SRM-MDM catalog solution in detail.

2.5.5   SAP NetWeaver BW

SAP NetWeaver BW is a packaged, comprehensive business-intelligence (BI) product centered around a data warehouse that is optimized for (but not limited to) the ERP environment from SAP. SAP NetWeaver BW is an integral component of the SAP suite of applications with an added advantage of being a software package that can be used in both SAP and non-SAP environments.

All analytics in SAP SRM are powered by the business warehouse. This is one reason why SAP's NetWeaver BW application is integrated as a component within the SAP SRM application; organizations need to implement analytics in SRM. The positive aspect for organizations is that they can quickly use more than 100 reports and queries that are provided via the standard content in SAP NetWeaver BW for SAP SRM. SAP predelivers these reports for SAP SRM that can be used out of the box.

2.5.6   SAP NetWeaver Process Integration

SAP NetWeaver Process Integration (previously SAP NetWeaver Exchange Infrastructure [SAP XI]), provides open integration technologies that support process-centric collaboration among SAP and non-SAP applications, both within and beyond enterprise boundaries. SAP NetWeaver PI is a middleware solution that organizations can use to exchange data between SAP SRM and business partner systems or electronic marketplaces, over the Internet. SAP NetWeaver PI is used in SAP SRM, to integrate processes between SAP EB, supplier self-services, and SRM-MDM.

Organizations that want to exchange business documents such as POs, acknowledgments, and invoices electronically via XML or EDI with their suppliers need to implement the SAP NetWeaver PI component.

2.5.7 SAP NetWeaver Portal

SAP NetWeaver Portal unifies key information and applications to give users a single view that spans IT siloes and organizational boundaries. With the SAP NetWeaver Portal, you can quickly and effectively integrate SAP solutions, third-party applications, legacy systems, databases, unstructured documents, internal and external Web content, and collaboration tools.

With SAP SRM 7.0, the SAP NetWeaver Portal is a mandatory component, because it offers the entire user interface for SAP SRM solution, based on a WebDynpro technology. Unlike previous release such as SAP SRM 5.0, where an SAP NetWeaver Portal was nice to have, in SAP SRM 7.0, all user interaction is enabled using the portal interface.

2.6 Summary

Thus far, we have talked about supplier relationship management in general and have briefly defined the SAP SRM application. In this book, we will try to describe in detail the functionality available in SAP SRM. Chapters 3, 4, and 5 focus on SAP supply core processes: operational procurement, strategic sourcing, and supplier enablement, respectively.

In Chapter 3, we discuss in detail operational procurement, which is primarily enabled using the SAP EB component. We will introduce the concept of the shopping cart in SAP SRM, which is similar to a requisition in SAP ERP. In addition, we discuss in detail the business scenarios: Self Service Procurement, Plan-Driven Procurement, and Services Procurement.

The aim of operational procurement is to effectively manage the procurement activities in organizations from purchase to payment.

3 Operational Procurement

Let's begin this chapter by defining procurement and then operational procurement. We defined procurement in Chapter 1 as the process of managing activities associated with a company's need to procure the goods and services required to either manufacture a product or to operate the organization. The process of procurement typically differs from one company to another.

> **Note**
>
> Procurement processes within a government institution may have unique regulatory requirements, which might be different compared to a nongovernmental company such as Intel. However, the need to purchase is the same across all the organizations: to efficiently support the company business.

Procurement activities are often divided into two distinct categories:

- Direct: Production-related goods
- Indirect: Nonproduction-related goods and services

When we talk about direct procurement, we are referring to raw materials or production goods that directly affect the production process within an organization. An example of raw material is coal. Coal primarily generates electricity. Therefore, most energy companies purchase coal as a raw material to produce energy in some form.

In contrast, indirect procurement deals with the purchase of goods and services to support maintenance, repair, and operating (MRO) activities within the organization. Indirect procurement also encompasses procurement of capital goods and services for the organization as well. Some examples of indirect procurement are the purchase of spare parts for a shop-floor machine, office supplies such as paper and pencils, and an MRI machine for a hospital.

Operational procurement is the effective management of all procurement activities within an organization, both direct and indirect. However, most organizations that have implemented SRM solutions or are evaluating these solutions have initially targeted management of their indirect spending.

Most organizations that have already implemented SAP SRM or are planning to implement it in the future begin with the process of automating their core procurement processes. It is amazing to see many large organizations that are leaders in their industries having largely inefficient internal procurement processes within their organizations. It seems as though they have been so busy trying to gain a competitive edge over their competition that they've worked on everything but controlling their internal spending and laggard processes.

In Figure 3.1, you can see an example of what the core procurement process still looks like at many organizations today (or used to for companies that have already moved ahead with SAP SRM).

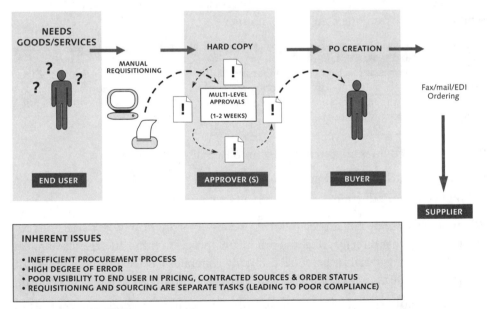

Figure 3.1 Traditional Procurement Process

In the process illustrated in Figure 3.1, the requisition-to-delivery time amounts to days and sometimes weeks, making the overall procurement process inefficient. Because of the manual processes involved, the visibility to the end user and the buyer is poor. In most organizations, delays happen because movement of paper-based requisitions require multiple levels of authorization and budgets and commitments have to be checked manually. In nonpublic organizations, there may be no budget checks at all.

An organization implementing an operational procurement solution expects the following key benefits:

▶ Elimination of inefficient processes; standardized and automated procure-to-pay processes

▶ Reduction in overall procurement costs; control over maverick buying

▶ Reduction in the overall requisition-to-pay cycle time

▶ High user adoption via a simple, easy-to-use procurement application

▶ Reduced dual entry and error rates

▶ Increased user and regulatory compliance

According to a study done by the Warwick Business School, some organizations spend $84 in requesting and processing a purchase order (PO). The same study found that this number could be reduced to approximately $31 if an efficient e-procurement system and its processes were implemented. Figure 3.2 illustrates this finding.

Function	Traditional Process	E-procurement
Requisition Generation	66.76	29.2
Requisition Distribution	7.36	0.0
Order Generation	8.87	1.5
Order Distribution	1.87	0.0
Expediting	0.91	0.3
Goods Receipt	3.83	1.5
Invoice Processing	10.40	0.7
TOTAL	100.0	33.2

The above table, taken from a report by Warwick Business School, highlights the administrative costs of a traditional procurement system compared with the costs of e-procurement (using the manual system costs as the base index (= 100).

Figure 3.2 Administrative Costs of Traditional Procurement Systems vs. e-Procurement

The procurement capability of SAP SRM automates purchasing transactions for goods and services. It helps companies reduce costs by automating and streamlining the purchasing process, connecting buyers and vendors, and controlling corporate spending. Figure 3.3 illustrates at a high level the procurement capability of SAP SRM.

Within operational procurement, there are three main business scenarios, illustrated in Figure 3.4. When we talk about operational procurement in SAP SRM, we are primarily referring to the Enterprise Buyer (SAP EB) component. SAP EB was introduced in Chapter 2.

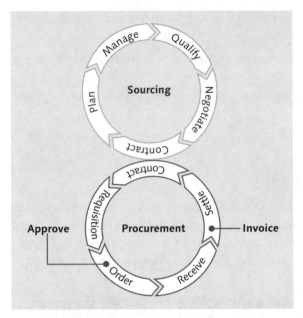

Figure 3.3 SAP SRM Closes the Loop Between Procurement and Sourcing (Source: SAP America)

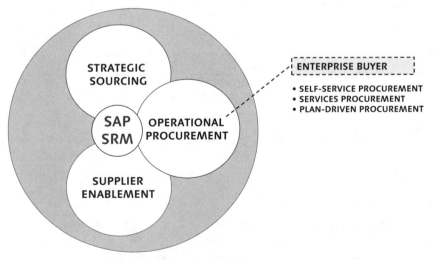

Figure 3.4 Operational Procurement in SAP SRM

In the remainder of this chapter, we will discuss in detail the functionality available within each of the three business scenarios illustrated in Figure 3.4: self-service procurement, services procurement, and plan-driven procurement.

3.1 Self-Service Procurement

The *self-service procurement* business scenario empowers users in the organization to be self-sufficient in ordering day-to-day goods and services without buyer intervention. It provides end users with the appropriate tools to find the items they need via easily searchable product catalogs that have been prenegotiated by procurement professionals.

Self-service procurement enables your employees to create and manage their own requirement requests. This relieves your purchasing department of a huge administrative burden while making the procurement process both faster and more responsive. It ensures compliance and reduces process costs by decentralizing the procurement process while maintaining central control, allowing purchasing professionals to focus on managing relationships instead of transactions. The main objectives for self-service procurement are as follows:

▶ To increase the speed of procurement and reduce overall costs
▶ To provide an integrated purchasing environment
▶ To foster and maintain compliance

Simply put, the self-service procurement process can be described by the five steps illustrated in Figure 3.5. We will discuss each of these process steps in detail.

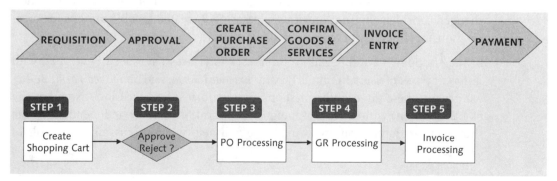

Figure 3.5 Self-Service Procurement Process

3.1.1 Step 1: Create Shopping Cart

Many organizations still use manual, paper-based forms for their requisition processes. Even those that use electronic media still separate their requisition applications from their PO creation applications. This prevents users from accessing any prenegotiated contracts or supply sources in ways that could reduce unnecessary administrative work by the procurement departments. SAP SRM streamlines this procurement process. Let's start by reviewing the requisitioning process in SAP SRM, as illustrated in Figure 3.6.

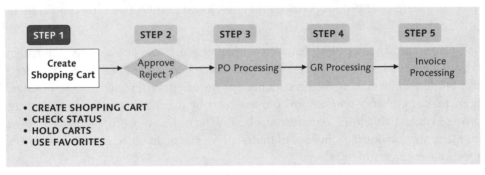

Figure 3.6 Requisition Process — Creating Shopping Carts

There are many definitions of a purchase requisition, but in its simplest form, a requisition is *a written, printed, or electronic request for something that is needed*. In SAP SRM, a requisition is created using a shopping cart. The shopping cart application is split into a number of different areas.

As of release SAP SRM 3.0, the user interface for the Shopping Cart application changed considerably from previous releases. SAP created flexible options for organizations to choose from to create a shopping cart.

In the Shopping Cart application, three user interfaces have been developed with different types of users in mind: *Wizard*, *Extended Form*, and *Simplified Form*. Before we explain these three different shopping cart forms, let's talk about some of the global functions within the shopping cart application that are independent of the shopping cart form. Understanding these will help when discussing the details of the shopping cart.

User Settings (my Settings)

The *User Settings* function allows users to review and set their personal settings such as email address, address information, and assignment of attribute defaults. These settings act as default values that are automatically entered in each new shopping cart created by the user. In the shopping cart, the user still has the ability to override these defaults if needed. Figure 3.7 illustrates the settings application.

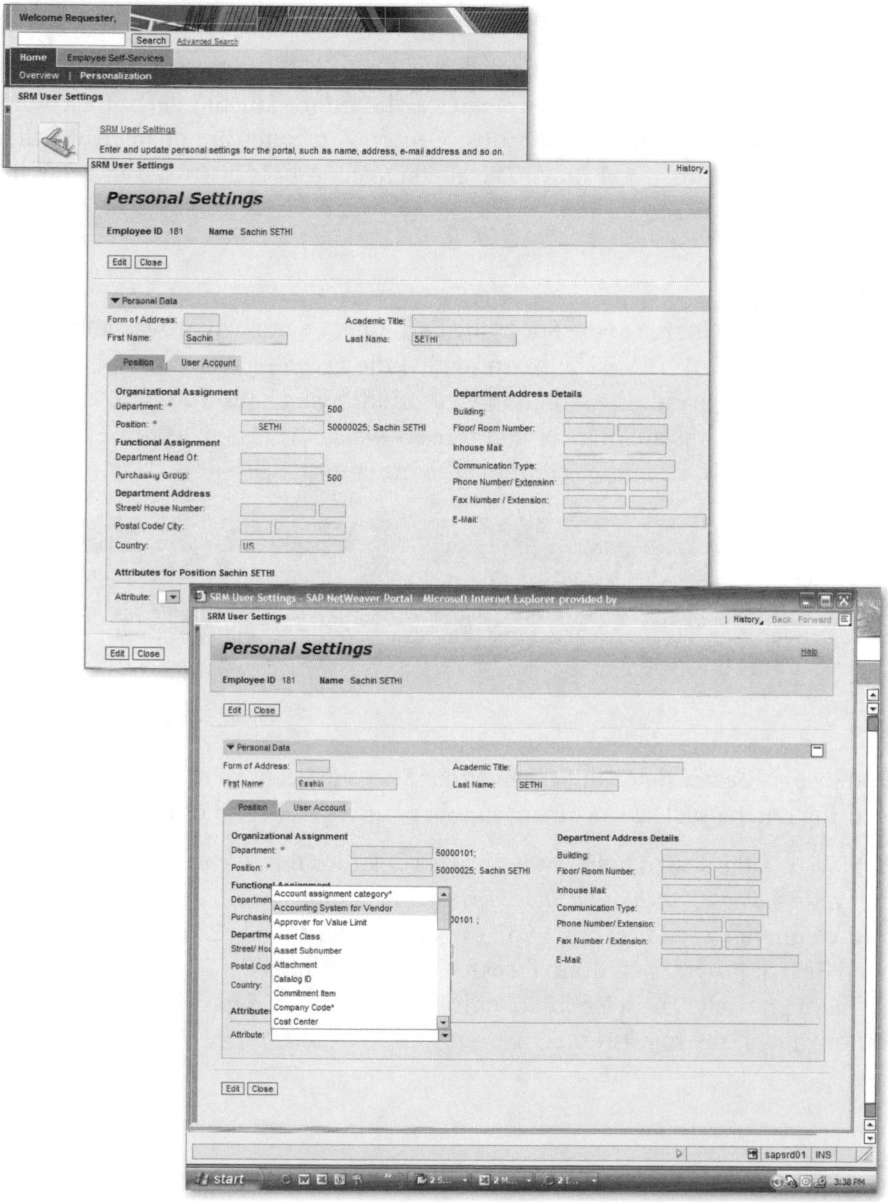

Figure 3.7 User Settings

The *Mandatory Data* tab allows users to review and set information such as First Name, Last Name, and E-Mail Address. The Address Data tab allows users to set a default Building, Room Number, and Floor, which can then be used as a default in the shopping cart. The Attributes tab allows users to set a default value for attributes that are available in the Attribute drop down.

For example, in Figure 3.7, the user has selected Cost Center as the default Account assignment category. When this user creates a shopping cart, the default account assignment category will always be a Cost Center. Attributes are enabled via the Organizational Structure in SAP SRM. The attribute concept is discussed in detail in Chapter 8.

Extended Details

As part of the overall design of the Shopping Cart, Check Status, Approval, and other applications within SAP SRM, SAP has provided the *Extended Details* option in SAP SRM 5.0. The user expands the screen to view additional details for that section. In standard use, the details are hidden, and if users want, they can click on Extended Details to expand this section for additional information.

> **Note**
>
> In SAP SRM 7.0, the Extended Details is replaced by the "Advanced Search" option. In addition, the Quick Search query provides many criteria to search. Users can open or hide the Quick Search function. Figure 3.8 illustrates the Advanced Search and Quick Search.

Search

Users can use the *Search* function in the various SRM applications to search for documents, using criteria such as document number, description, and others.

In SAP SRM 5.0, the search function is always constructed in the same way and can be displayed as *Simple Search* or *Extended Search*. The Simple Search generally contains the most commonly used fields that you can use to specify your search criteria. The Extended Search provides additional search criteria to target the information you require more precisely. The selection of entry fields available depends on the chosen application and on the role assigned to you.

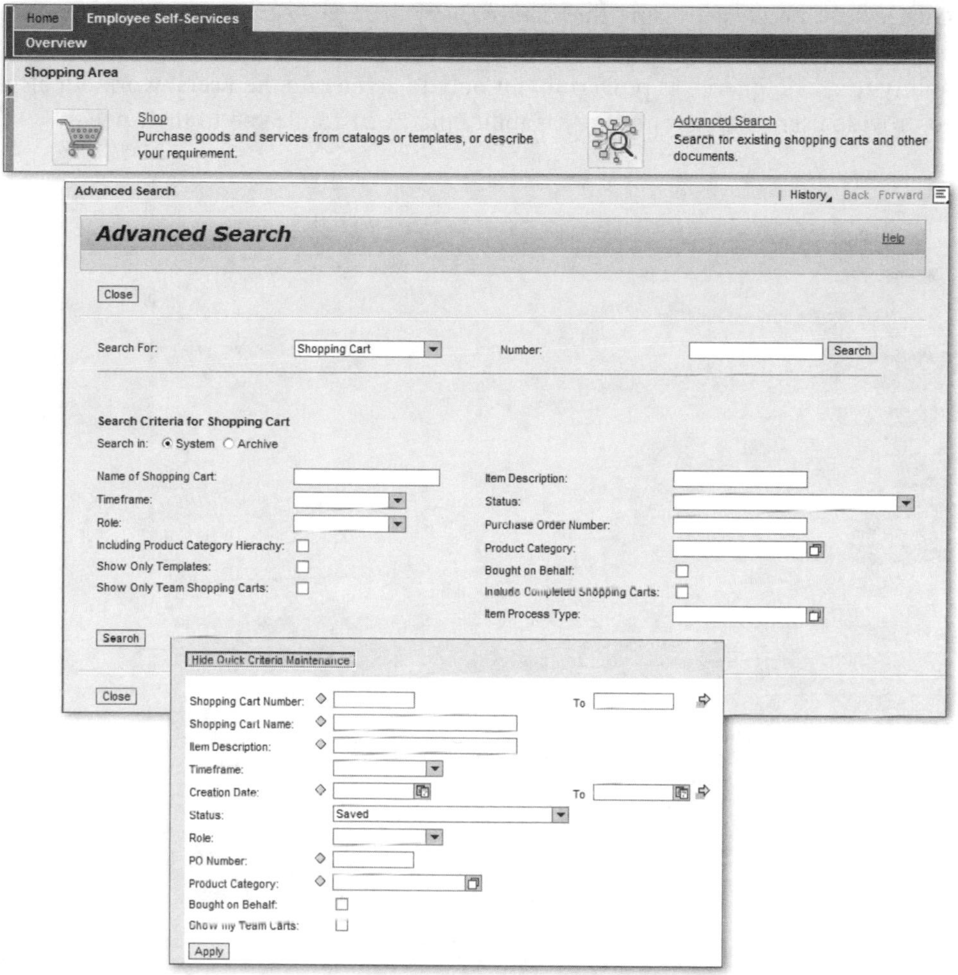

Figure 3.8 Extended Details in the Shopping Cart

Note

In SAP SRM 7.0, the search feature is provided using the Personal Object worklists (POWL) queries and the Quick Criteria Maintenance, as illustrated in Figure 3.9.

The *Active Queries* can be defined by end users so they don't have to maintain search criteria each time they want to search for documents. For example, if they normally search for shopping carts created in the last 30 days, then they can create an Active Query for that. The next time the user accesses the Shopping Cart application, the query will be readily available with updated information.

Queries can be created using the *Change Query* or *Define New Query* functions that are hidden in the far right in the portal screen layout (illustrated in Figure 3.9). The ability to create queries is powerful, not only to accelerate the users' work but also to provide users with a reporting capability that is customizable to their needs.

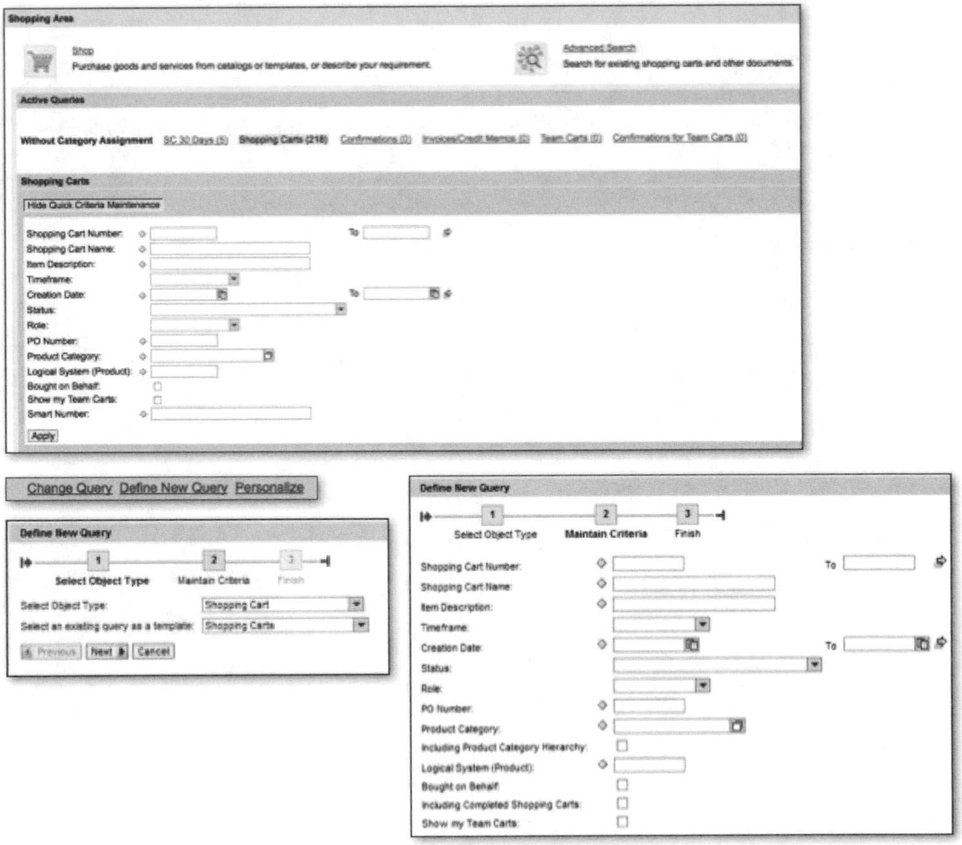

Figure 3.9 Search Function

Approval Preview

As a part of the overall design of the Shopping Cart, Confirmation Entry, PO, Invoice Entry, and other applications, SAP provided the *Approval Preview* function. This allows users to preview who needs to approve their shopping carts (or other documents), and users can additionally add reviewers or approvers to influence the approval process.

The ability to view all those in the approval chain promotes a self-service approach and allows the end user to be more knowledgeable. The user can also add additional approvers or reviewers using the Add Approver and Add Reviewer buttons.

> **Note**
>
> In SAP SRM 5.0 and previous releases, the approval preview could be displayed as a graphic or in a tabular view. As of release 2007 (SAP SRM 6.0), the graphical view is no longer available; only the table view is provided as illustrated in Figure 3.10.

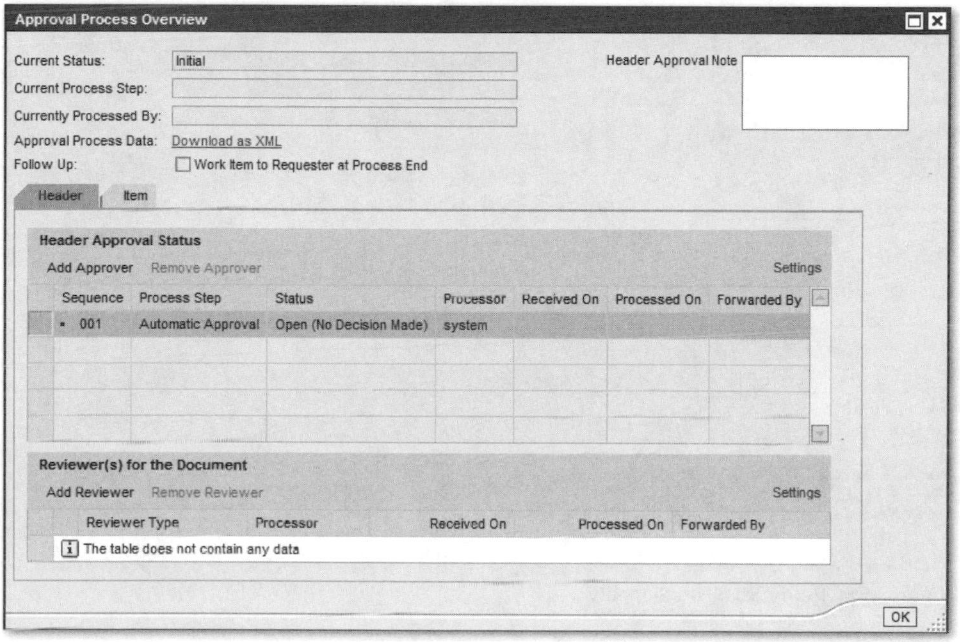

Figure 3.10 Approval Preview

Hold or Save Functionality

The *Hold* or *Save* functionality allows users to temporarily save a document for processing at a later time or date. This is helpful if a user is creating documents such as a shopping cart and adding multiple items. If the user has not completed a shopping cart, he can put it on Hold so that it can be accessed at a later date and time.

An example is when a user is awaiting response from the vendor on a quote for items within the shopping cart. Figure 3.11 illustrates this functionality. The held/saved shopping carts can be accessed using the Shopping Cart Quick Criteria Maintenance application.

> **Note**
>
> In SAP SRM 7.0, the Hold functionality has been renamed Save. The capability stays the same as previous SAP SRM releases.

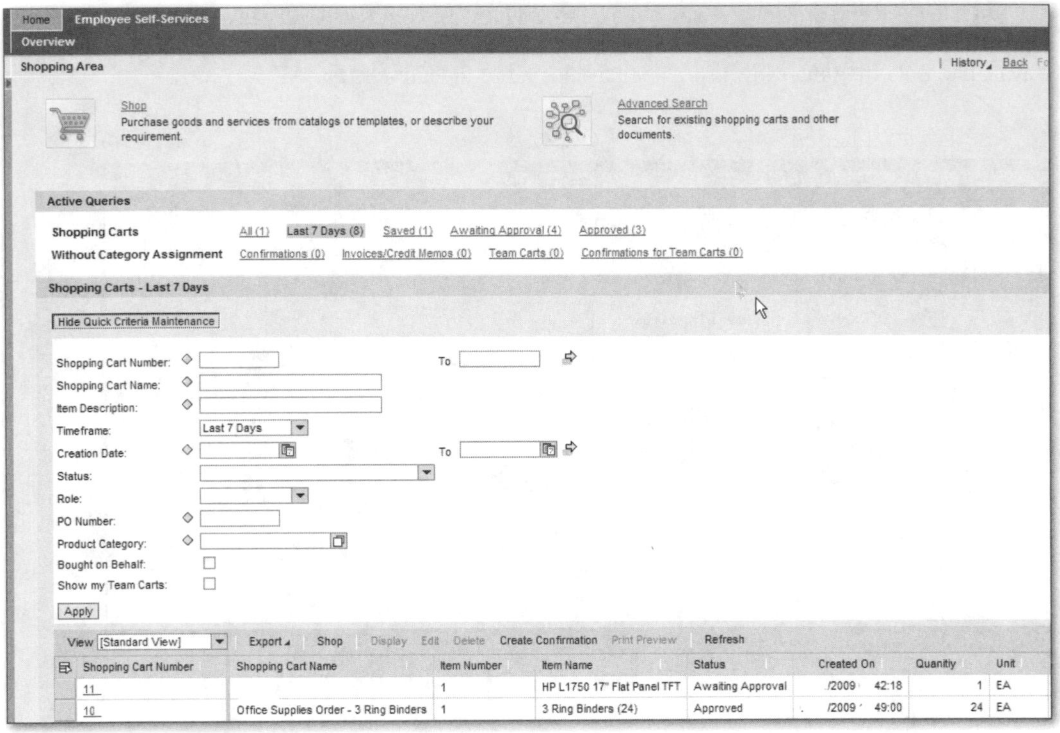

Figure 3.11 Hold / Save Functionality

Check Functionality

The *Check* functionality was introduced in the SAP SRM 3.0 release, and checks the documents for errors. These checks could be standard system checks provided by SAP, or organizations can use their own business rules to include checks for documents.

One example of the standard system check is for *Cost Assignment*. A shopping cart cannot be completely saved if the user has not specified a valid Cost Assignment. Therefore, if the SAP General Ledger account or cost center is invalid, the system will issue an error message. An example of a check that an organization might want to include is whether shopping carts with zero dollar values are allowed. In the standard design, a shopping cart of zero value can be created.

The check's results are displayed either in the bottom of the screen or on the top of the screen, depending on the type of document. In the shopping cart, the checks are typically provided on the top of the screen; however, in the PO, they are in the bottom of the screen. A message with a red icon indicates an error, a message with a yellow icon indicates a warning, and a message with a green icon is an informational message.

Figure 3.12 illustrates checks within the shopping cart. In the shopping cart, the end user can click on the Check button to determine whether the shopping cart is completed free of any errors. In Figure 3.12, a system message is issued with a red icon No SAP General Ledger account was entered. Enter an SAP General Ledger account. This indicates that the user has not provided an SAP General Ledger account in one of the line items in the shopping cart.

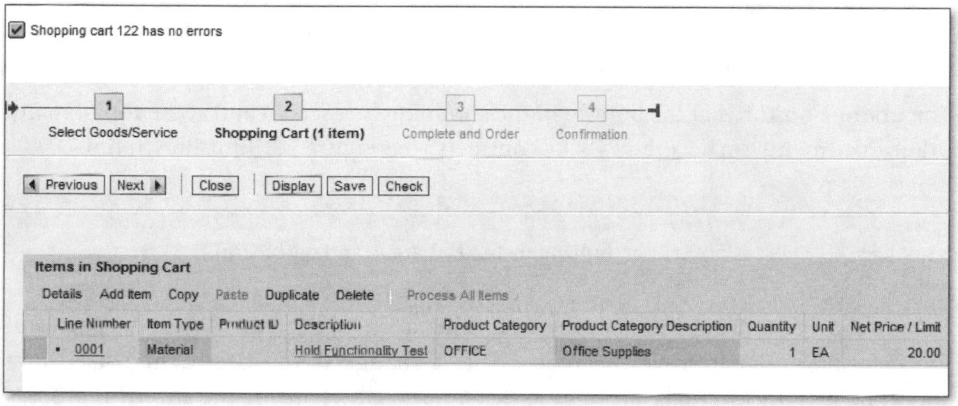

Figure 3.12 Check Functionality

Save or Order Functionality

In all documents created in the SAP SRM system, once the document entry is complete, the end user needs to either select the option to *Save* or *Order*. The Save and Order buttons perform the same function. For example, in the shopping cart, a user clicks the Order button once they have completed their shopping carts and are ready to order. However, during approval of a shopping cart, an approver clicks the Save button to approve or reject.

Change or Edit Functionality

The *Change* functionality allows users to change the documents, such as shopping carts or POs that had already been created. This gives you the flexibility to make changes to these documents while they are in approval. However, document changes can only happen until a particular point.

Note

In SAP SRM 7.0, the Edit functionality replaces "change." The capability stays the same, but SAP has changed the terminology.

For example, the shopping cart can be changed (edited) while it is in approval, but once all approval steps have been created, the shopping cart no longer can accommodate any changes. Many organizations expect the shopping cart to be changed even after a PO has been created, but this is not possible. Once a PO has been created, any further changes are only allowed in the Purchase Order application; the shopping cart can no longer be changed.

For example, if the requisitioner finds out from the vendor that they can only deliver half the quantity within the specified delivery date, assuming that the PO has been created, at this point, the end user cannot make any changes to the shopping cart, only users who have authorization to change POs can make further changes.

The **Change** button is at the bottom of the shopping cart screen and at the top of many other documents such as the POs or contracts (see Figure 3.13 for illustration).

Note

In SRM 7.0, there is no Change button; instead, there is an Edit button.

Based on user authorization, approvers can make changes to the documents as well. For example, if an approver needs to make a change to the Cost Center used in a shopping cart, he can make changes to the shopping cart during the approval process as long as he has the appropriate authorizations.

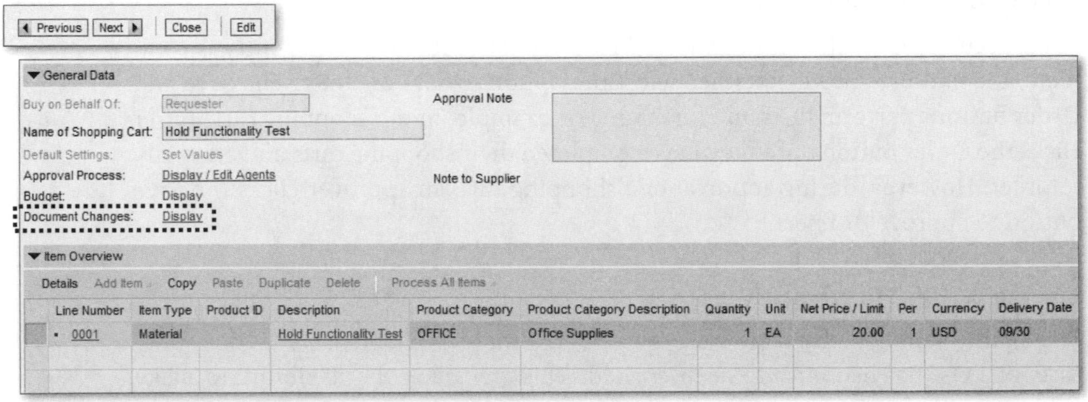

Figure 3.13 Changes to Documents

Once changes are made to the document, a change history is created in the shopping cart, which is useful from an audit perspective. Figure 3.14 illustrates this capability.

Header/Item Attribute	Old Value	New Value	Changed By	Changed On	Changed At	Version
▼ Header						
▼ Basic Data						
• Total Value of Shopping Cart / Target ...	20.00 USD	200.00 USD	Requester	09/30/2009	15:14:16	
▼ Status						
• Held Indicator: Status Is Inactive		X	Requester	09/30/2009	15:03:59	
• Awaiting Approval Newly Added			Requester	09/30/2009	15:03:59	
• Shopping cart ordered Newly Added			Requester	09/30/2009	15:03:59	
▼ Item Number 1 – Hold Functionality Test						
▼ Basic Data						
• Net Total Value	20.00	80.00	Requester	09/30/2009	15:14:16	
• Net Value	20.00 USD	80.00 USD	Requester	09/30/2009	15:14:16	
• Quantity in Order Unit	1.000 EA	2.000 EA	Requester	09/30/2009	15:14:16	
• Net Price	20.00 USD	40.00 USD	Requester	09/30/2009	15:14:16	
• Gross Price	20.00 USD	40.00 USD	Requester	09/30/2009	15:14:16	
▼ Item Number 2 – Hold Functionality Test						
▼ Basic Data						
• Newly Added			Requester	09/30/2009	15:14:16	
▶ Partner						
▼ Account assignment						
• Newly Added			Requester	09/30/2009	15:14:16	

Figure 3.14 Display Changes to Documents

Now that you have an understanding of some of the global functions within a shopping cart, let's discuss the different shopping cart forms that are available in SAP SRM. We will start by briefly reviewing the three different shopping cart interfaces and then discuss in detail the various areas available within the shopping cart application, such as Default Settings for Items, Add Items, and Item Details.

Shopping Cart: Wizard

The *Wizard* is the default user interface for employees. It helps employees find, select, and add goods or services to their shopping carts quickly and easily. This wizard interface is ideal for casual shopping cart users who request goods or services occasionally. This interface provides a user with three steps to complete the request for ordering goods and services. This allows the user to view graphically the particular stage of the purchasing process he has reached, as illustrated in Figure 3.15.

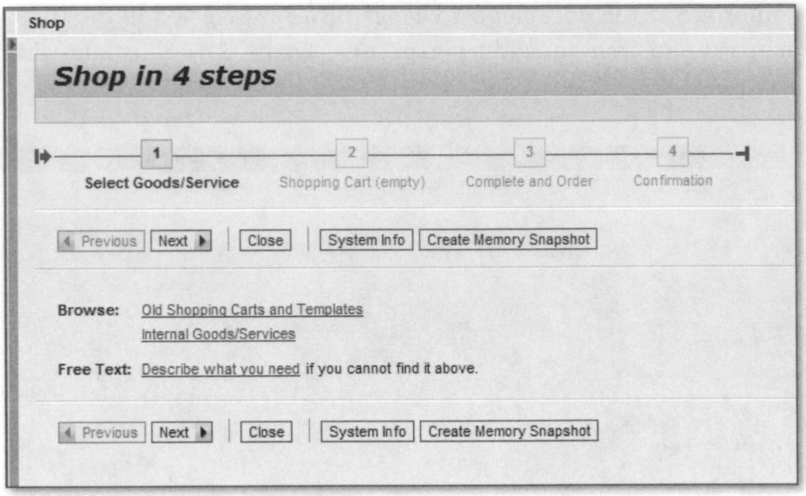

Figure 3.15   Wizard-Based Shopping Cart

Each of the steps in the Wizard-based shopping cart is explained in the following bullet points. In Step 1, you can search for goods or services and then add them to your shopping cart. In Step 2, you can display your shopping cart and check it. In Step 3, you can order your shopping cart. Step 4 confirms the shopping cart number that is generated from Step 3.

1. **Select goods or services**

    This step allows users to select goods or services and add them as items in the shopping cart. Users can add one or more items within their shopping carts from a variety of sources such as electronic catalogs, old POs and templates, and internal goods or services. If users are unable to find required goods or services, then they can simply describe their needs using the Describe Requirement option. This is sometimes referred to as free-text or free-form text shopping cart where a user simply describes his requirement, as illustrated in Figure 3.16. In the figure, we show that the end user can click on the Describe Requirement link, which opens a new section allowing the user to provide a Description, Quantity, Price, and Required on date for the requirement.

2. **Shopping cart**

    In this step, a user can review his overall shopping cart and make any changes, such as update quantities in the Quantity field. Additionally in Step 2, a user can review the details of each line item and provide additional details such as account assignment information, attachments, or notes to buyer or suppliers, as illustrated in Figure 3.17.

The end user can make additional changes in the Item Details section within the Basic Data, Cost Assignment, and other areas as illustrated in Figure 3.17.

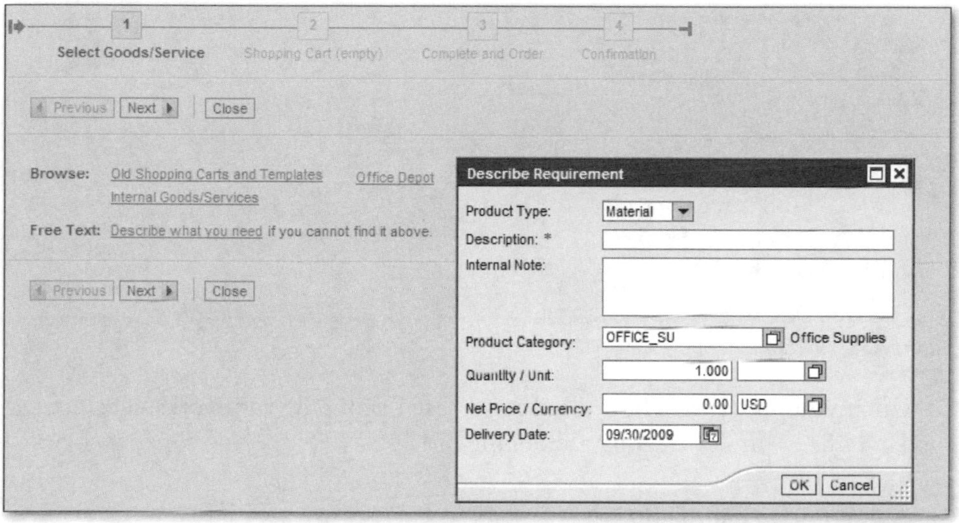

Figure 3.16 Wizard Shopping Cart — Free-Text Item

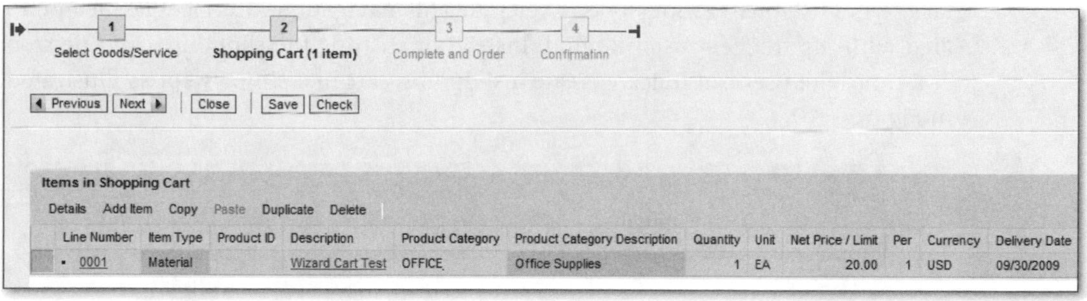

Figure 3.17 Wizard Shopping Cart

3. **Complete and order**

The user has completed his shopping cart and is now ready to place the order, as shown in Figure 3.18. At this point, he has the option to check if any approval is needed for this order by clicking on Approval Preview. Also, the user can enter any notes for the approver in the Notes for Approval section.

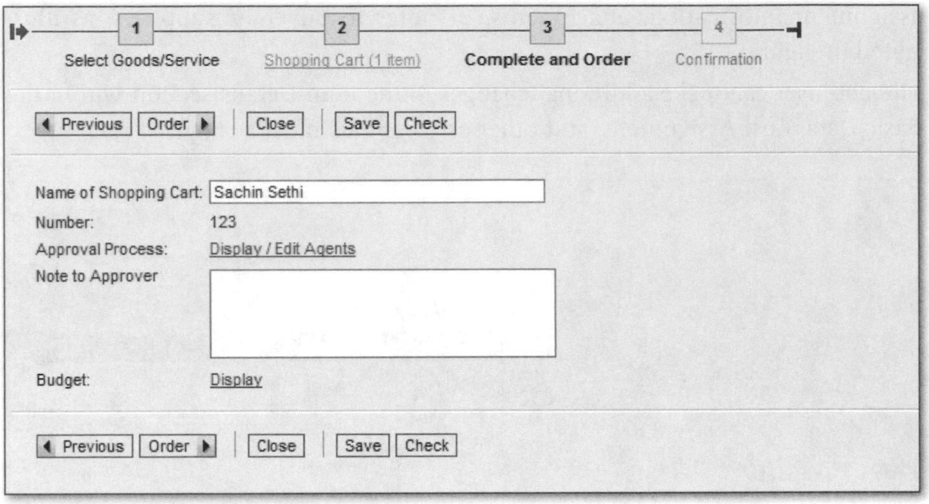

Figure 3.18 Wizard Shopping Cart

Now that you understand how the Wizard-based shopping cart works, let's discuss the Simplified Form of creating a shopping cart.

Shopping Cart: Simplified Form

The *Simplified Form* allows a user to create a shopping cart in one-single form interface, where the navigation style is vertical. This navigation interface has been created with the frequent user in mind. Instead of creating the shopping cart one step at a time, the user can quickly create a shopping cart in a single step, as illustrated in Figure 3.19.

> **Note**
>
> As of SAP SRM 7.0, the Simplified form is no longer utilized. Only the Wizard and Professional forms are available.

The end user is able to view the Default Settings for Items section, which was not available in the Wizard form. He can use the Add Items section to Search in Individual Catalogs. As he adds items to the cart, a user can view the line items in the Items in Shopping Cart section. He can look at the Approval Preview or add notes for the approver in the Additional Specifications area of the form.

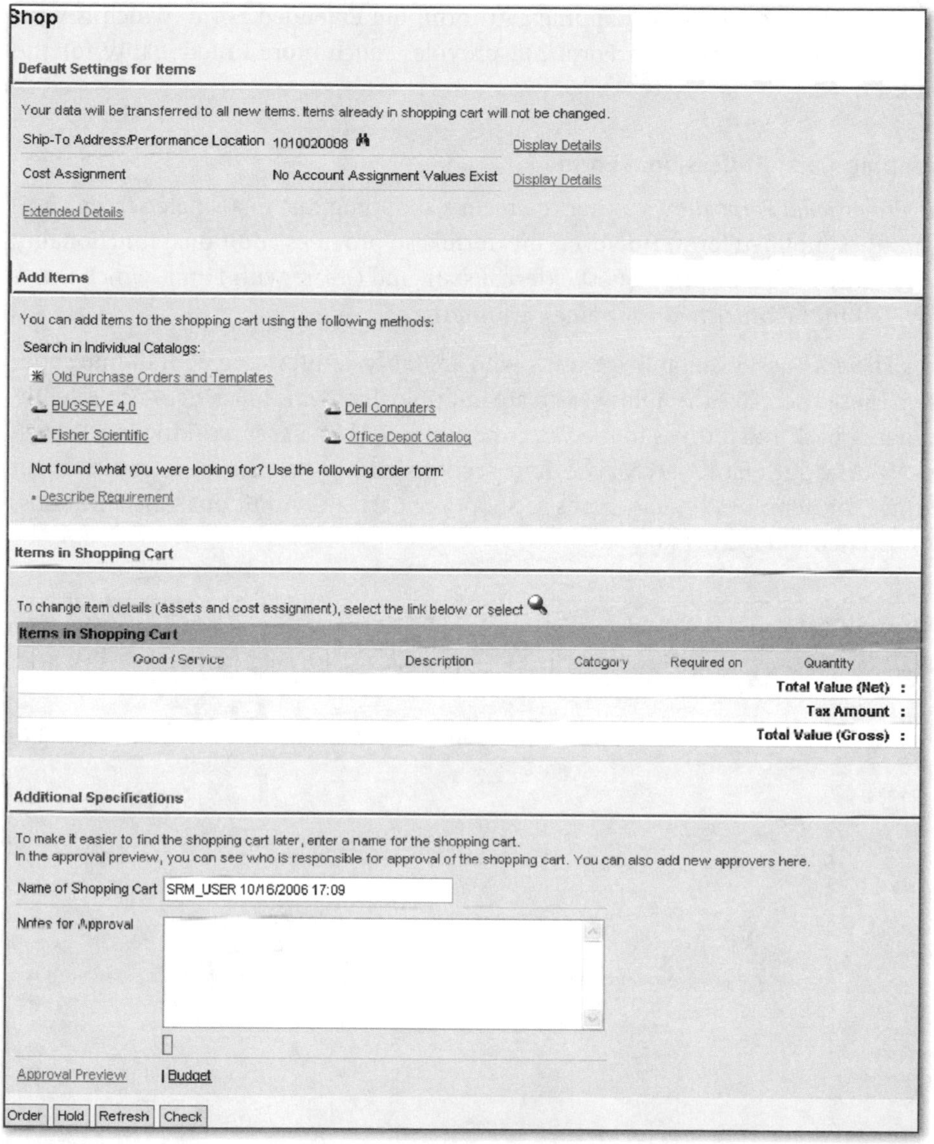

Figure 3.19 Simplified Form — Shopping Cart (SAP SRM 5.0 Screenshot)

However, this navigation style does not provide users the functionality to create shopping carts for ordering services using Create with Limit (discussed later). Additionally, the Simplified Form interface does not allow users to create shopping carts using products (material master) on the overview screen. Another disadvantage of the Simplified Form is that it does not allow users to use the Buy-on-behalf of functionality, also called Shop for.

Let's now discuss the third shopping cart form, the Extended Form, which is visually similar to the Simplified Form but provides much more functionality for the end user.

Shopping Cart: Professional Form

The *Professional Form* allows a user to create a shopping cart in a single screen similar to the simplified form. However, this form also provides additional functionality such as Buy-on-behalf of, Request external staff, and Create with Limit, which is not provided in the other two shopping cart interfaces.

The *Extended Form* is suitable for users who are fairly comfortable with online shopping. These users like the ability to create multiple line items in a single screen without going back and forth as in the Wizard interface. Also, a user working in a Professional form can quickly access the four sections within the shopping cart: Default Settings for Items, Add Items, Items in Shopping Cart, and Additional Specifications, as illustrated in Figure 3.20.

Create Shopping Cart

Number 34   Document Name C-SSETHI 09/16/2009 22:15   Status In Process   Created On 09/16/2009 22:16:00   Created By Sachin SETHI

Order | Close | Save | Check

▼ General Data

Buy on Behalf Of: Sachin SETHI
Name of Shopping Cart: C-SSETHI 09/16/2009 22:15
Default Settings: Set Values
Approval Process: Display / Edit Agents
Document Changes: Display

Approval Note

Note to Supplier

▼ Item Overview

Details | Add Item ▲ | Copy | Paste | Duplicate | Delete

Line Number	Item Type	Product ID	Description	Product Category	Product Category Description	Quantity	Unit	Net Price / Limit	Per	Currency	Delivery Date
•	Undefined Item Type			SOFT_R/P	Software Rent/Purch	1.000		0.00	1	USD	09/16/2009
•	Undefined Item Type			SOFT_R/P	Software Rent/Purch	1.000		0.00	1	USD	09/16/2009
•	Undefined Item Type			SOFT_R/P	Software Rent/Purch	1.000		0.00	1	USD	09/16/2009
•	Undefined Item Type			SOFT_R/P	Software Rent/Purch	1.000		0.00	1	USD	09/16/2009
•	Undefined Item Type			SOFT_R/P	Software Rent/Purch	1.000		0.00	1	USD	09/16/2009
•	Undefined Item Type			SOFT_R/P	Software Rent/Purch	1.000		0.00	1	USD	09/16/2009
•	Undefined Item Type			SOFT_R/P	Software Rent/Purch	1.000		0.00	1	USD	09/16/2009
•	Undefined Item Type			SOFT_R/P	Software Rent/Purch	1.000		0.00	1	USD	09/16/2009
•	Undefined Item Type			SOFT_R/P	Software Rent/Purch	1.000		0.00	1	USD	09/16/2009
•	Undefined Item Type			SOFT_R/P	Software Rent/Purch	1.000		0.00	1	USD	09/16/2009

Figure 3.20 Professional Form — Shopping Cart

The shopping cart is displayed as a table-style list that includes an easy entry form that is particularly useful for items that a user might enter regularly. Figure 3.21

illustrates the additional capabilities available to an end user when creating a shopping cart using the Extended Form. He can use the Requests and Order functionality within the Add Items section to request external staff or other services. He can use Create Limit Items to create a shopping cart line item with a fixed maximum amount for a product or service. Also, the user can quickly enter a material or product number in the Good/Service field to create a line item using the product master (material master) in SAP SRM.

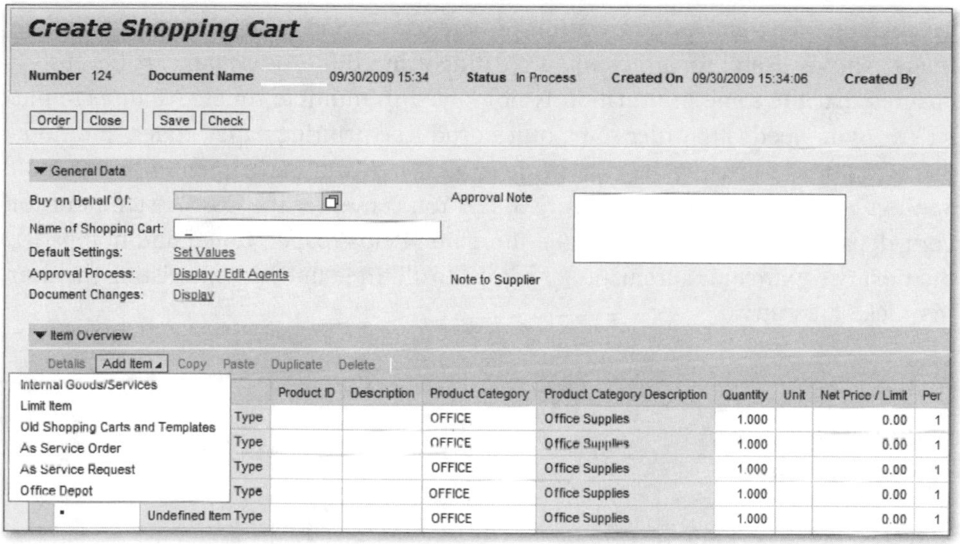

Figure 3.21 Professional Form Shopping Cart

SAP SRM allows organizations to enable all three user interfaces within a single production environment. Each of the interfaces has its own transaction in SAP SRM: BBPSC01, BBPSC02, and BBPSC03. Based on roles and authorizations, the business can decide which users get access to the Wizard, Simplified Form, or the Extended Form. Although this is technically feasible, most companies do not enable all three shopping cart forms. There are multiple reasons for this; training and on-going support are the most frequent.

These different shopping carts user interfaces are assigned to users via roles in SAP SRM (e.g., employee user, secretary, professional purchaser).

Depending on the role assigned to a user, that user can access the appropriate forms. Review Chapter 11 on security to understand how roles and authorizations impact a user's access within SAP SRM. Additionally, review Appendix D on custom development and BAdIs to see what other options organizations have to override the standard user-interface settings provided by SAP.

So far, you have learned that the Shopping Cart application has three different forms: Wizard, Simplified Form, and Extended Form. Now we will detail the Shopping Cart application by discussing the different areas within the shopping cart. The Shopping Cart application is divided into four distinct sections: Default Settings for Items, Add Items, Items in Shopping Cart, and Additional Specifications.

Default Settings for Items

The Default Settings for Items of the shopping cart provides users assistance with quick data entry; entries that you make here are copied to the shopping cart line items. This is useful for users when creating a multiline shopping cart because it ensures that the same information is not keyed in multiple times. As an example, let's say you needed to order some office products: printing paper, toner, and notepads. You need to charge the costs of these goods to your department in the Default Settings for Items section (see Figure 3.22). You can enter the Cost Assignment for your department. When you add the three line items (paper, toner, and notepads), the Cost Assignment is automatically copied to all three line items, assisting the user in quick data entry.

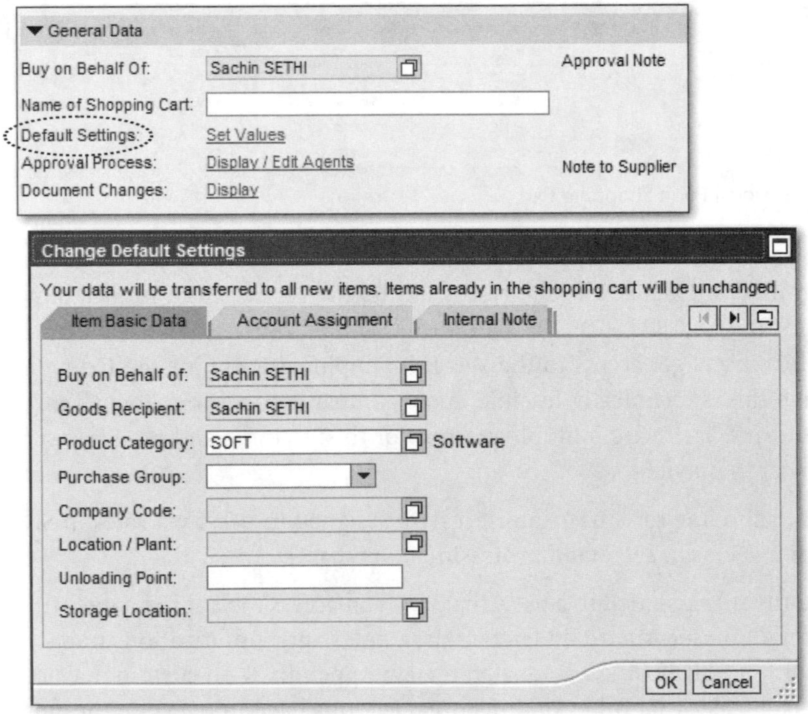

Figure 3.22 Default Settings for Items

> **Note**
>
> Once you have started to create line items within the shopping cart, any changes to the default settings do not affect the shopping cart. Only settings made prior to adding items in the shopping cart are copied to all line items.

The default setting also provides the functionality to order products on behalf of other users. In previous SAP SRM releases, a separate transaction was available for this function, called *Buy-on-behalf of*. The functionality offered is still the same but is accessed via the Default Settings for Items section instead of an entirely separate transaction.

The Buy-on-behalf of functionality is also called Shop for. This functionality allows authorized users the ability to purchase goods or services on behalf of their colleagues or managers. The approval process invoked in the system is based on the Shop for user; therefore, compliance is still achieved. Additionally, the user for whom the order is placed can still continue to create the confirmation and the invoice for the products bought on his behalf. Figure 3.23 illustrates the Shop for functionality.

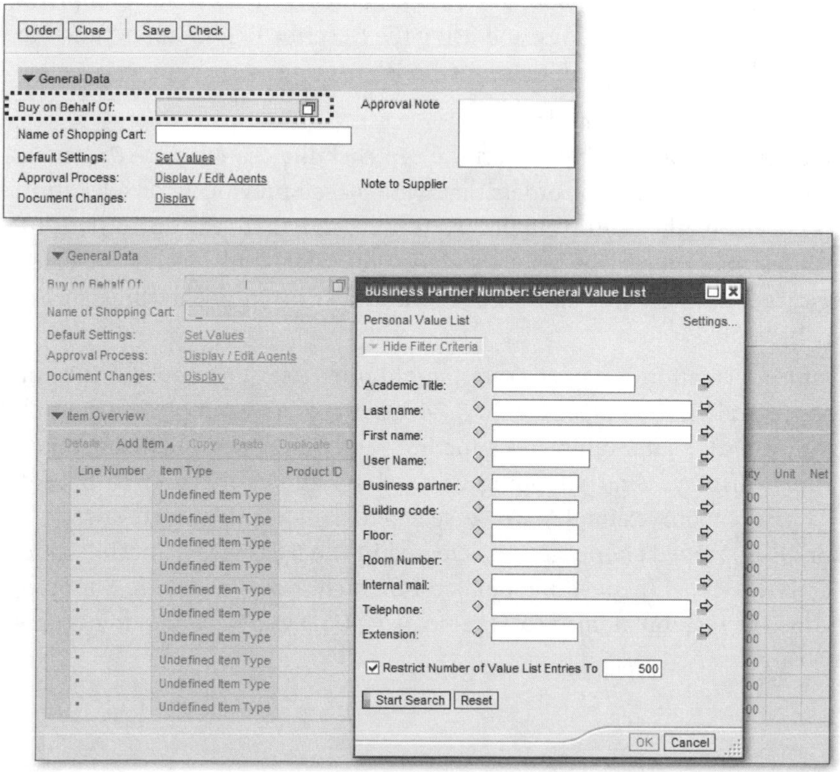

Figure 3.23 Shop For or Buy-on-Behalf Of

> **Note**
>
> The users for whom individuals can shop must be specified as values in the attribute RE-QUESTER in the Organizational Structure. This is further explained in Chapter 8.

As a standard, the Default Settings for Items section is only available within the Extended Form shopping cart. However, organizations using the other forms, Wizard or Simplified Form, can activate the Default Settings for Items section via the Change Display in Shopping Cart BAdI (BBP_SC_MODIFY_UI).

Project teams interested in this functionality should work with their development teams to activate and code this BAdI. Also review Section D.2.1, BAdI: Change Display in Shopping Cart (BBP_SC_MODIFY_UI), in Appendix D to get more information about this BAdI. Let's now discuss the Add Items section of the shopping cart.

Add Items

In the *Add Items* section of the shopping cart, the requisitioner can select goods and services using a few different methods such as Old Purchase Orders and Templates, Search Internal and External Catalogs, and using the Describe Requirement function. The following bullet points explain these methods in further detail:

▶ **Old Purchase Orders and Templates**

Once the user is within a shopping cart, he can click the *Old Purchase Orders and Templates* function to search for orders that were placed previously or select from templates created by the central purchasing team. Using these existing orders, the user can select individual line items or complete orders and quickly recreate a shopping cart. This allows the user to save time and effort in re-entering data that can easily be copied.

All relevant information is copied from the old purchases or templates into the new shopping cart line item(s). Figure 3.24 illustrates an example of using the Old Purchase Order and Templates function. Once the user clicks on this, a search screen displays Find Shopping Cart, which allows the user to provide search criteria. In our example, we've selected the default search criteria to search for all Approved shopping carts created in the Last 7 Days. In the Search Results area, we select the test line item and then click on the Add to Shopping Cart button. The test line item at total value of 10 USD will be added to our new shopping cart.

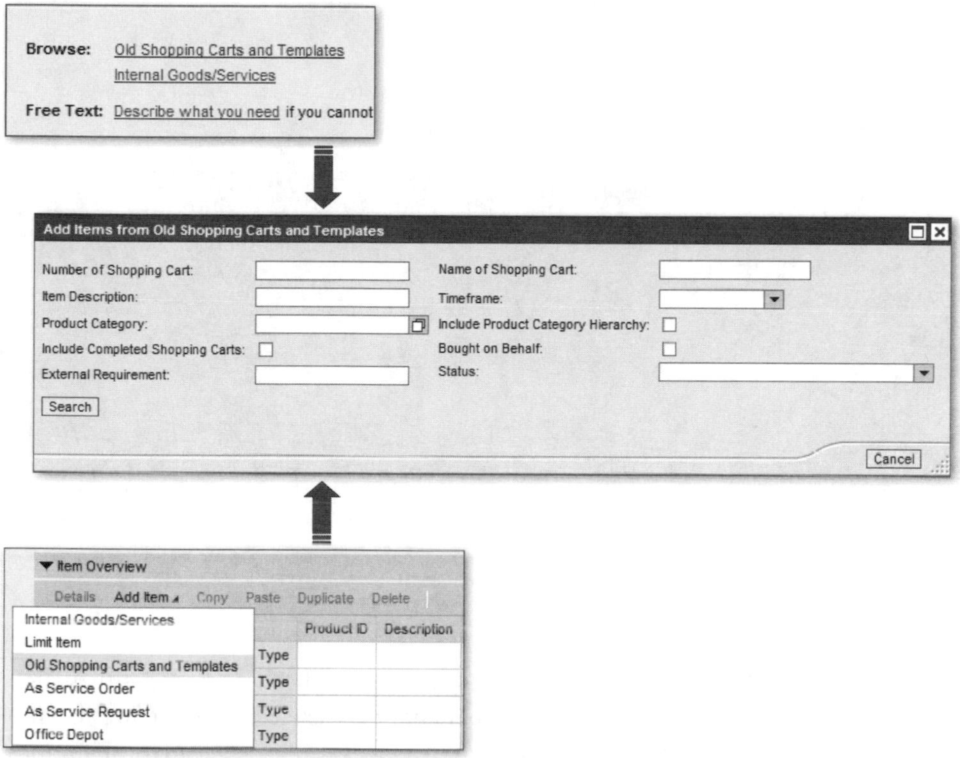

Figure 3.24 Old Purchase Orders and Templates

A template can be used as a reference when creating and processing shopping carts. Individual items or entire shopping carts can be transferred from old POs and templates to a new template or shopping cart. These are usually useful when processing recurring procurement transactions.

For example, suppose a department administrator orders a set of products from an office-supply vendor on a monthly basis. In such a case, purchasing professionals can define templates that can be used by employees as references when creating and processing their shopping carts. In the standard design, users need the Purchasing Assistant or Purchaser role assigned to create templates.

The template creation process is similar to creating a shopping cart with a few differences. For instance, there is no cost assignment functionality when creating a template because it's supposed to be generic for use across all departments that have access, as illustrated in Figure 3.25.

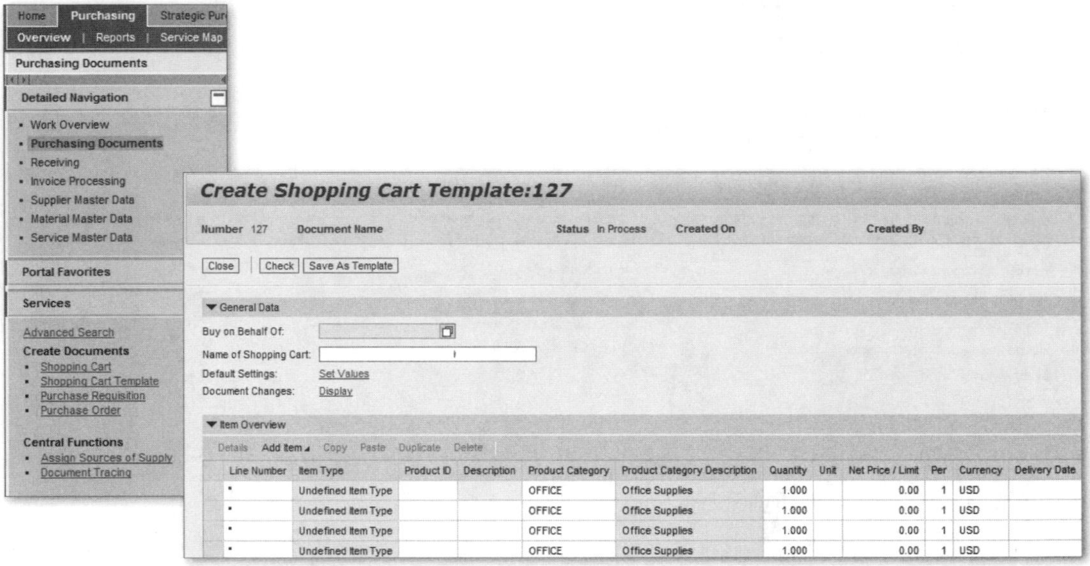

Figure 3.25 Creating Templates

▶ **Search External and Internal Catalogs**

Users can search both *external* and *internal catalogs* to quickly and efficiently search for negotiated goods and services. The benefit of these electronic catalogs is multifold. Users can quickly find products and services using rich search capabilities provided by the catalogs, and once they find what they need, all the information about the product or service is seamlessly transferred back to the shopping cart line item(s). The user does not have to retype information.

  ▶ **External Catalogs**

  External catalogs are typically maintained by your suppliers and hosted on their systems; users can access these catalogs via the Internet. An example of an external catalog is Office Depot. Users can seamlessly log on to the Office Depot catalog directly from within the shopping cart, search for goods, and then bring all the information for the product back to their shopping carts as line items. Figure 3.26 illustrates how a user can click on a Fisher Scientific link to launch the external catalog and search for products.

  ▶ **Internal catalogs**

  Internal catalogs are catalogs that are created and maintained by your organization. These could be items that are a part of your existing material master or products that your suppliers have provided you for listing in your catalog.

Chapter 6 will introduce readers to the concept of catalog and content management and explain in detail how organizations can use catalogs to drive efficiency in their overall procurement process. Both internal and external catalogs are explained in detail in Chapter 6.

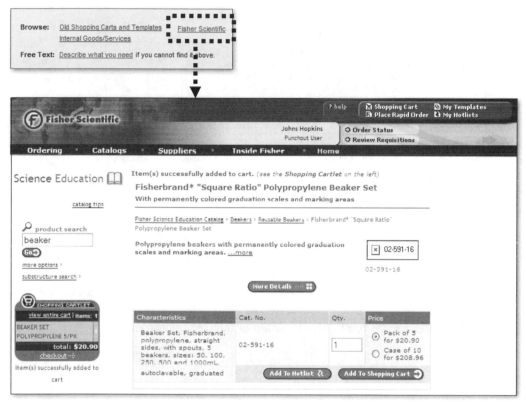

Figure 3.26 External Catalogs

▶ **Internal goods or services**

Internal goods or services are products that are housed within the SAP SRM system (product master). The product master represents either a material or a service master. If you have a material or service master in another system, it can be replicated to the SAP SRM system as well.

For example, if you use a materials management in SAP ERP that contains material masters, you can replicate the material master items from SAP ERP into SAP SRM as products. Users can search for these products using a selected set of criteria including the Product ID, Product Description, Category, and others as illustrated in Figure 3.27.

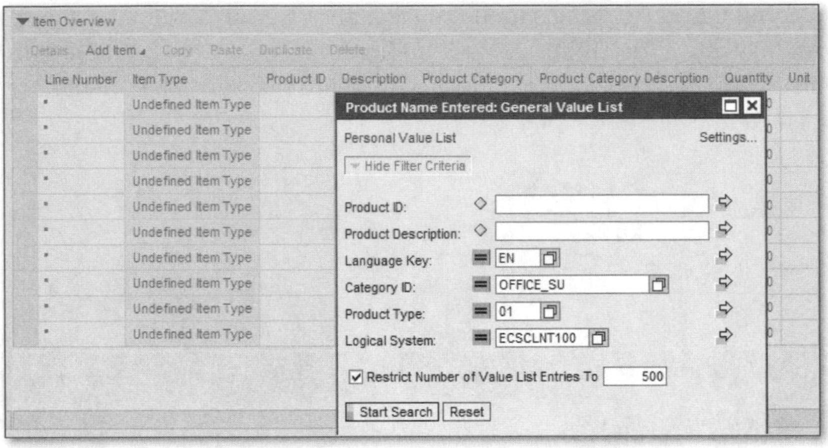

Figure 3.27 Internal Goods and Services

▶ **Describe requirement**

If the requisitioner is unable to find the goods or services he wishes to procure in any of the catalogs, a text description can be entered in the shopping cart. Users can click on Describe Requirement in the Add Items area to enter a free-form text description of what they need. The user needs to provide enough information to the purchasing team so they can find the appropriate vendor and price. Figure 3.28 illustrates the Describe Requirement function. Often, the requisitioner might actually know the price and vendor who can supply the goods or services and therefore can provide this information in the free-text order.

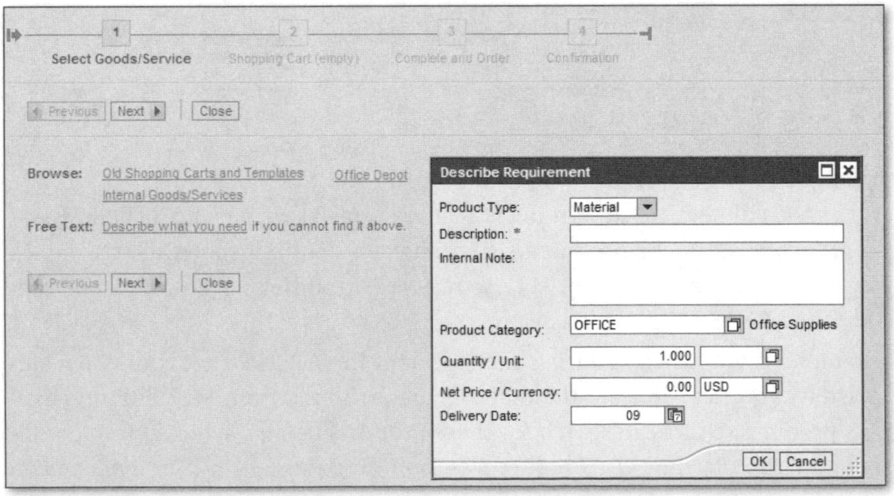

Figure 3.28 Describe Requirement — Free-Form Text Requisition

Items in Shopping Cart

This section of the shopping cart provides users with a running list of items they have added from the Add Items functions such as catalogs or old purchase orders and templates. For example, if the requisitioner launched the Fisher Scientific catalog as illustrated in Figure 3.26, selected three items from Fisher's catalog, and added those to his shopping cart, then all three items will be available in the section Items in Shopping Cart.

In the Extended Form version of the shopping cart, the requisitioner also has the flexibility to directly create line items in the Items in Shopping Cart section. As a default, three blank lines are available for entry in this area and the requisitioner can use them to quickly enter the appropriate product number or item description in the available fields.

Let's use Figure 3.29 to illustrate the Items in Shopping Cart section. The first line item was created by the requisitioner by just entering some information of the required product in the Description field. In addition, the user can select an appropriate product Category, OFFICE SUPP & EQUIP in our example. Additional information can be entered in the Required on, Quantity, and Price fields.

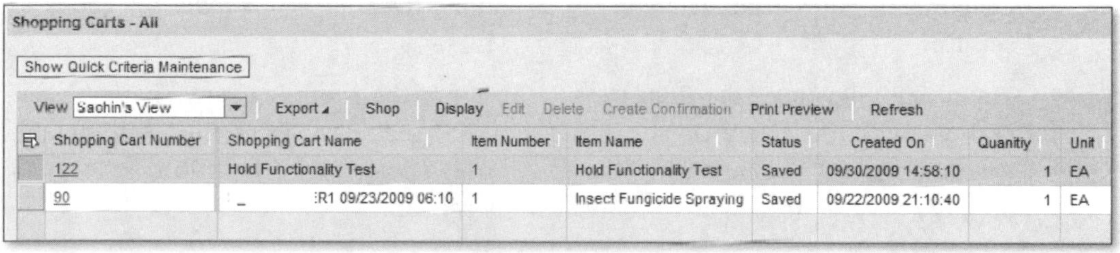

Figure 3.29 Items in Shopping Cart

The second line item in Figure 3.29 was created by simply entering a product ID 3425 in the Good/Service field. This allows the user to enter multiple product numbers in the open line items and quickly create a multiline shopping cart.

This is useful when the requisitioner knows the product IDs in the SAP SRM system. Alternately, he can click on the Binocular icon to search for products or services available within the SAP SRM system.

The requisitioner can also simply copy a line item by clicking on the Copy icon in the Action column. This is especially useful when the user might want to create multiple line items with the same basic information but with small changes such as Quantity and Required on date.

In situations when a user needs to provide additional information for the shopping cart line items, such as entering the vendor part number, adding a vendor note, or changing the account assignment details, they can go to the line item details by clicking on the Magnifying Glass icon in the Action column. The Item Details section is discussed in greater detail in the next section.

Additional Specifications

Once the user adds all items to the shopping cart, he can provide some additional information within the Additional Specifications section. The Additional Specifications section was illustrated in Figure 3.20. To make it easier to find the shopping cart later, the user can enter a unique name in the Name of Shopping Cart field. The user also can view whether an approver is needed for the cart. The Approval Preview functionality was discussed and illustrated in Figure 3.10.

Item Details

Once users have added one of more items to their shopping carts, they can choose to continue and place the order, or they can provide additional item details related to their individual line items. These could be details on specifying the location, cost assignment, notes or attachments, or specifying the source of supply for goods or service.

Figure 3.30 illustrates the Item Details section of the shopping cart. There are five sections within the Item Details of the shopping cart: Basic Data, Cost Assignment, Documents and Attachments, Ship-To Address/Performance Location, Sources of Supply / Service Agents, and the Availability section.

- ▶ **Basic data**
  This section allows the end user to review and provide additional information pertaining to the shopping cart line item. Figure 3.31 illustrates the fields available on the Basic data section of the cart. The users are unable to select the purchasing organization in the shopping cart; this is similar to a purchasing requisition in SAP ERP. If there are multiple purchasing organizations, only the buyer has the ability to select the purchasing organization in the Process Purchase Order application.

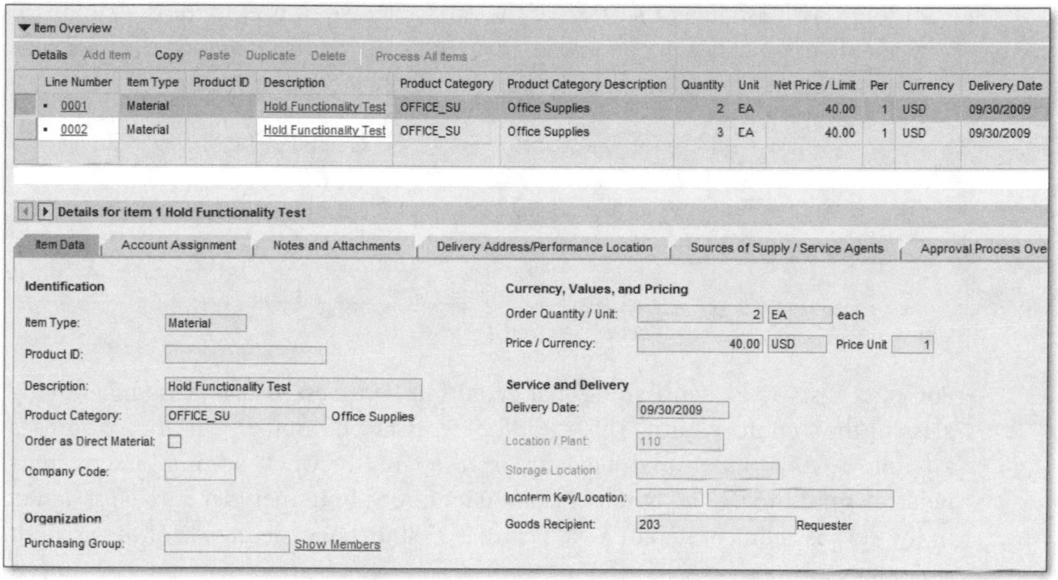

Figure 3.30 Shopping Cart Line Item Details

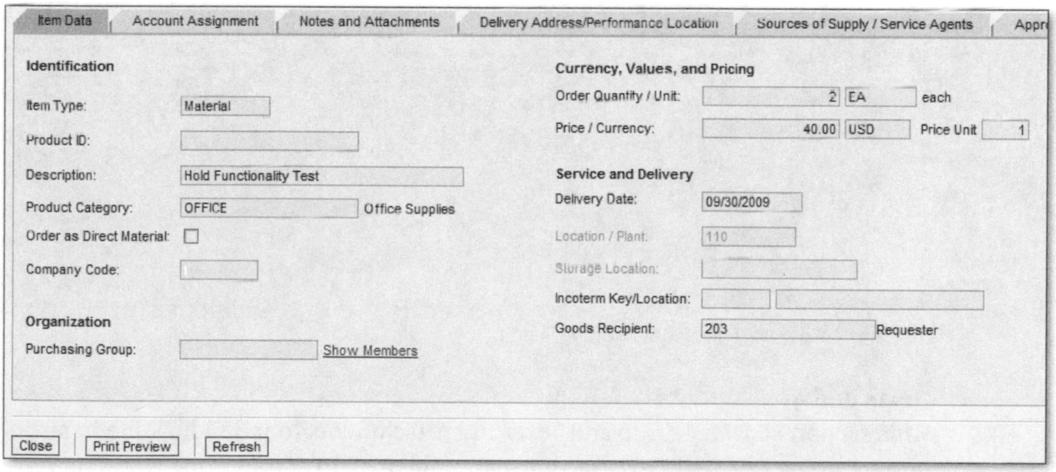

Figure 3.31 Basic Data Section in the Shopping Cart

▶ **Cost assignment**

The Cost Assignment section allows users to provide information on where the goods or services being purchased are going to be charged. Users can allocate costs toward a variety of cost assignments available in SAP ERP Financials Financial Accounting. This functionality is defined in detail within Chapter 9, where we discuss integration to SAP ERP Financials. Figure 3.32 illustrates the fields available on the Cost Assignment section of the cart. For ease of use, there is a clipboard available to quickly copy and paste the cost assignments. Also, costs can be split across multiple cost allocations by Percentage, By Qty, or By Value.

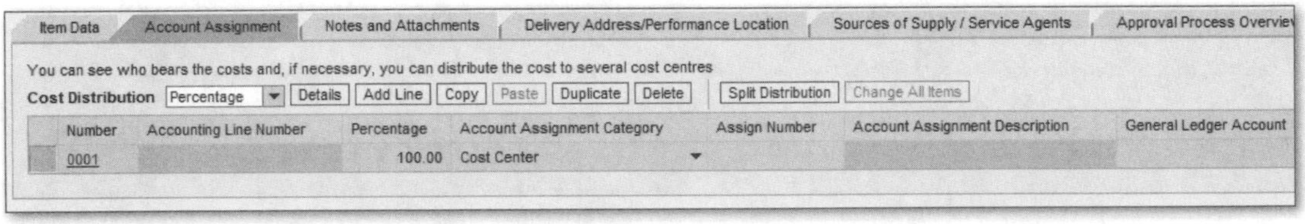

Figure 3.32 Cost Assignment Section — Overview

For each cost assignment, additional detail can be accessed using the magnifying glass in the Action column. This could be necessary if your organization also uses a public sector solution and needs to use the Fund or Grant account assignments fields. Also, if the cost assignment is an Asset, the Subnumber can only be assigned in the cost assignment details area. Figure 3.33 illustrates the details of the account assignment.

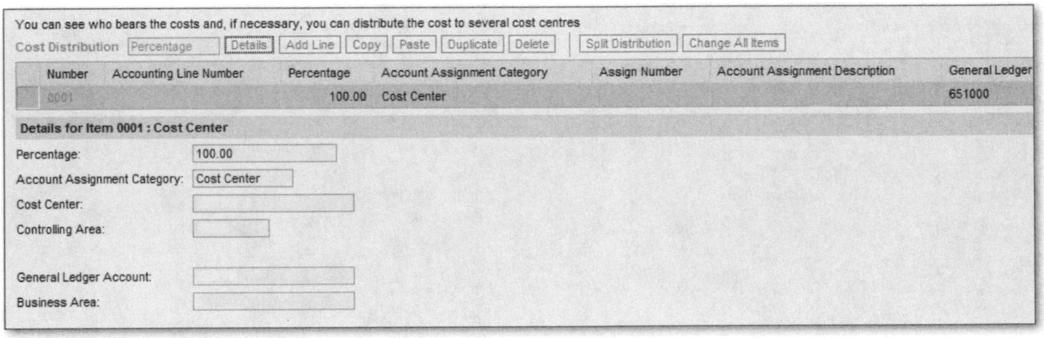

Figure 3.33 Cost Assignment Section — Detail

▶ **Texts and attachments**
This section allows users to add Texts and Attachments to individual line items in the shopping cart. The Texts section allows the user to add Internal Notes or Vendor Text.

The Internal Notes provide additional information to the buyers and approvers within the organization. These are not printed on the corresponding PO. However, the Vendor Text is intended for the use of the vendor or supplier and by default is printed on the PO sent to the vendor or supplier.

Figure 3.34 illustrates the Texts and Attachments section of the shopping cart. The Attachments area allows the user to attach documents such as Microsoft® Word®, Microsoft Excel®, or Adobe® Acrobat® PDF. Attachments can be internal or external, and can be identified using the Internal check box. The internal attachments are for the approvers and buyers internal to the organization and all other attachments are sent to the suppliers as information that needs to accompany the PO, such as a copy of the estimate or quote.

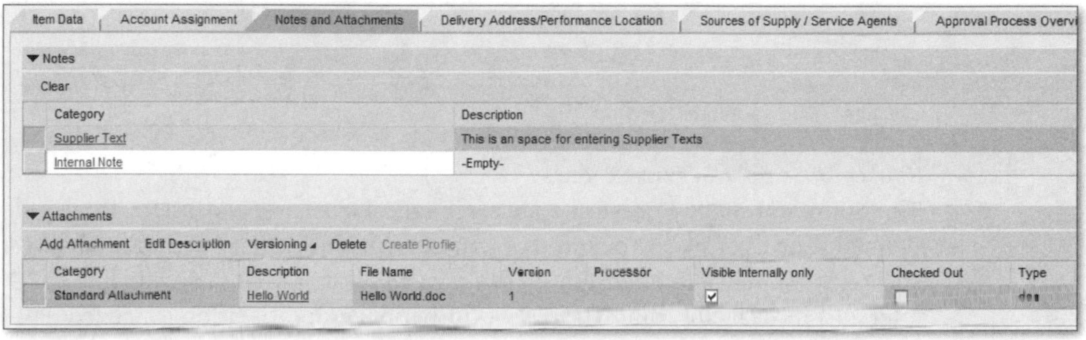

Figure 3.34 Texts and Attachments

> **Note**
>
> Attachments do not output automatically when the PO is sent via a print, fax, or XML. Only if email is the output medium are the attachments sent automatically. Organizations that want to output attachments when the PO is printed need to work with the developer to use BAdIs.

▶ **Ship-to address/performance location**
The Ship-to address/performance location section allows a user to provide a shipping point where the goods/services are to be delivered. Typically, a default ship-to address is populated in the shopping cart. This is based on the Organizational Structure or whether a delivery-address attribute was maintained in the Settings application illustrated in Figure 3.7. The user can change this ship-to address in certain cases. A list of existing delivery addresses is available to the user based on his organization, or the user can enter a one-time ship-to address. Figure 3.35 illustrates the ship-to address section.

This delivery address can be set up on each line of the shopping cart; therefore, users can create multiple line item shopping carts where each is delivered to a separate location. The plant or location identified in the Basic Data section can also provide a default address.

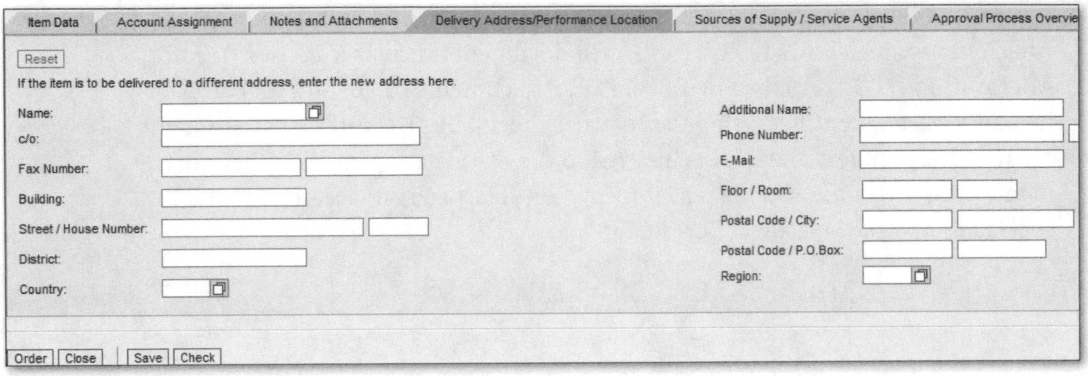

Figure 3.35 Ship-to Address Section

▶ **Source of Supply/Service Agents**

The Source of Supply/Service Agents section allows users to select from pre-defined sources of supply or specify a source to purchase from. Use of predefined sources of supply allows the shopping carts to automatically convert into a PO after all approvals are complete and no further buyer intervention is needed. Purchasing organizations utilize this process to alleviate buyers from the nonvalue processes of creating POs.

If there are contracts or agreements that the organization has set up with vendors for specific products or product categories, those contracts and vendor lists can be available for end users to use seamlessly. This promotes compliance, process improvement, and cost reduction. The following sources of supply are considered fixed in the SAP SRM system. This typically means that buyer intervention is not required if the goods and services are provided using these following sources of supply:

▶ Catalogs

▶ Contracts

▶ Vendor lists

Figure 3.36 illustrates the Contract and Vendor List as fixed sources of supply. If no pre-defined source of supply is found, users can search the vendor database in SAP SRM and suggest a vendor from which to purchase the goods or services being ordered, as shown in Figure 3.36. In this scenario, the system creates an incomplete PO (locally) or purchase requisition (in the backend).

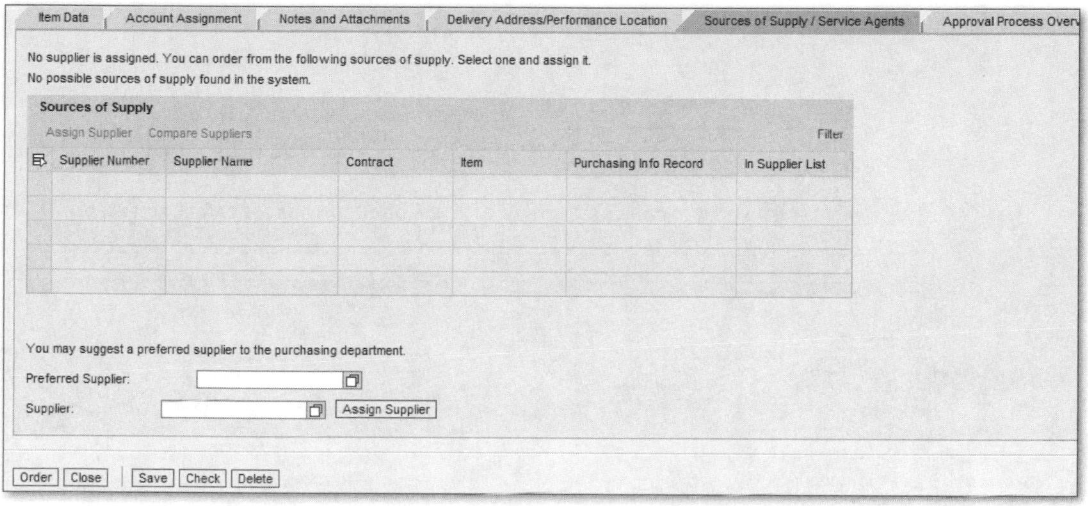

| Item Data | Account Assignment | Notes and Attachments | Delivery Address/Performance Location | Sources of Supply / Service Agents | Approval Process Overv |

No supplier is assigned. You can order from the following sources of supply. Select one and assign it.
No possible sources of supply found in the system.

Sources of Supply

Assign Supplier   Compare Suppliers   Filter

	Supplier Number	Supplier Name	Contract	Item	Purchasing Info Record	In Supplier List

You may suggest a preferred supplier to the purchasing department.

Preferred Supplier:
Supplier: Assign Supplier

Order   Close   Save   Check   Delete

Figure 3.36 Source of Supply — Assign Manually

The SAP SRM system provides all valid possible sources of supply (local sources available in SAP SRM or the SAP backend) for the product or free-text items. If a unique source of supply is found for a product or service, it is automatically assigned; otherwise, the user can select from a list of other predefined sources. If you do not want to use the source assigned, you can replace it with a preferred vendor. However, these purchases are then sent to professional buyers to review and complete.

Depending on the Customizing settings, the system displays either all vendors or just those in a vendor list. When a user changes a product category, company code, or plant field in the shopping cart, sourcing is redetermined.

▶ **Availability**

Availability allows a user to review the availability of products; he can check whether the quantity required is available by the requested delivery date. However, this functionality is only valid for product-based purchases (e.g., material master items).

The SAP SRM system checks the availability of products across multiple plants. A list is returned from the check, showing the quantity available and date. For example, 100 pieces are available now, and in four days, 250 pieces will be available. You can select the plant that can provide the required product quantity.

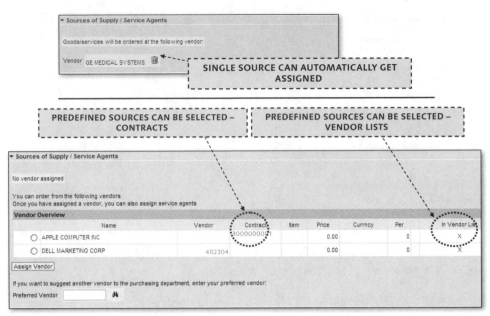

Figure 3.37 Source of Supply — Predefined (SAP SRM 5.0 Screenshot)

Now that you understand the Item Details section of the shopping cart in detail, let's learn about how users keep track of the shopping carts they create, using the Check Status application.

Check Status

One of the key capabilities of SAP SRM self-service scenario is the real-time access users have to the status of their orders and what stage the orders have reached in the business process. In the *Check Status* application users, can review the follow-on documents that have been created for the shopping cart, such as requisitions, POs, confirmations, invoices, or payment status. Users can use a variety of search criteria available to find their shopping carts, such as the Shopping cart name, number, or status, as illustrated in Figure 3.38.

> **Note**
>
> In SAP SRM 7.0, there is no function specifically named Check Status. However, the same functionality is provided using Active POWL queries and Quick Criteria maintenance. Users can search for the same criteria as in SAP SRM 5.0 and more.

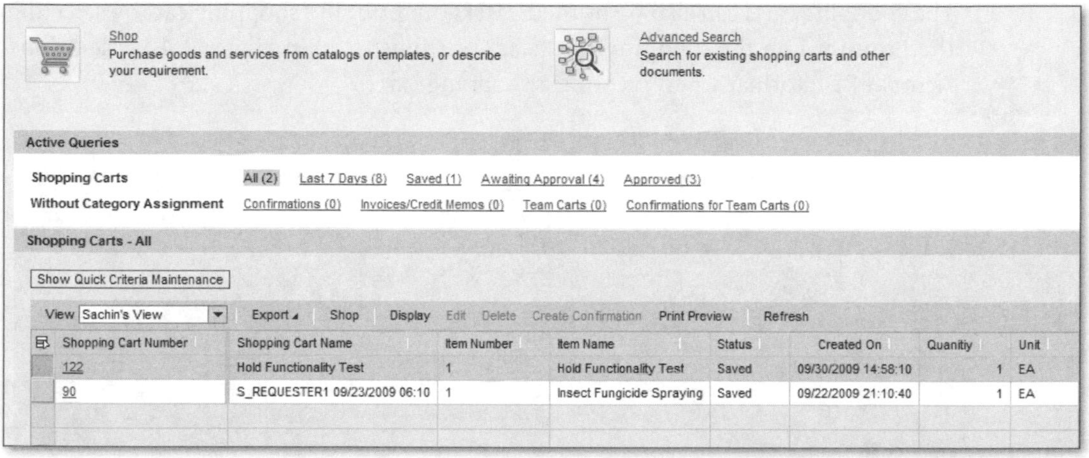

Figure 3.38 Check Status

A user can also check his document status based on Buy-on behalf of functionality or his role as an approver, as shown in Figure 3.39.

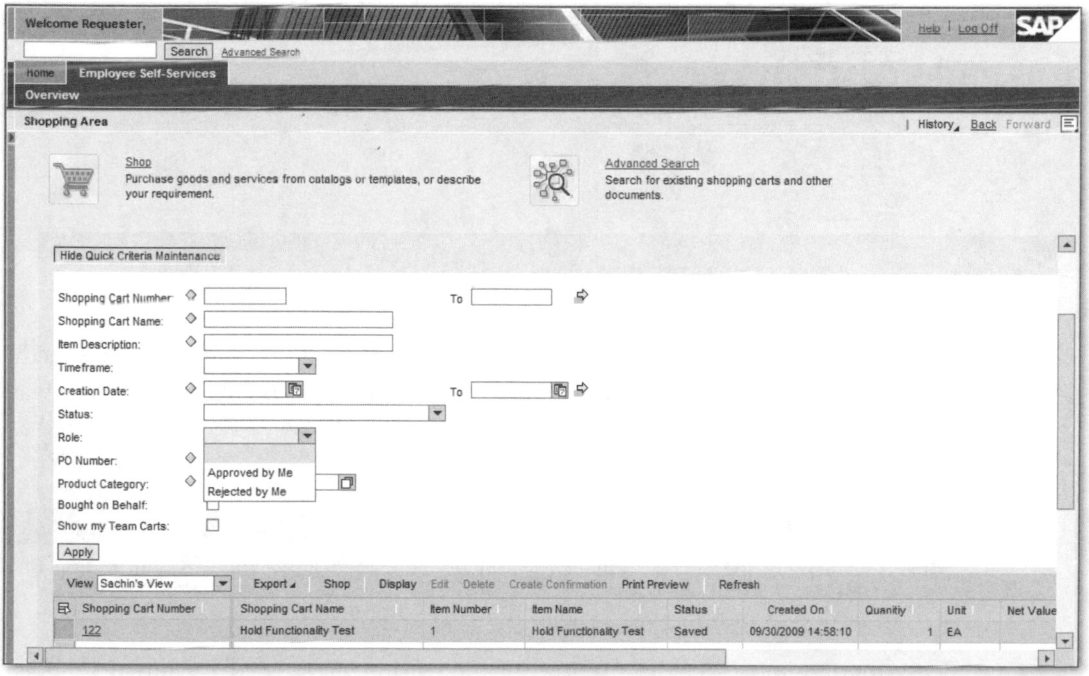

Figure 3.39 Approvers Search for Approved or Rejected Carts

The shopping carts can also be printed. Users can print the shopping cart by selecting the Print icon on the shopping cart header, as illustrated in Figure 3.40. Use Adobe Acrobat PDF format when printing a shopping cart.

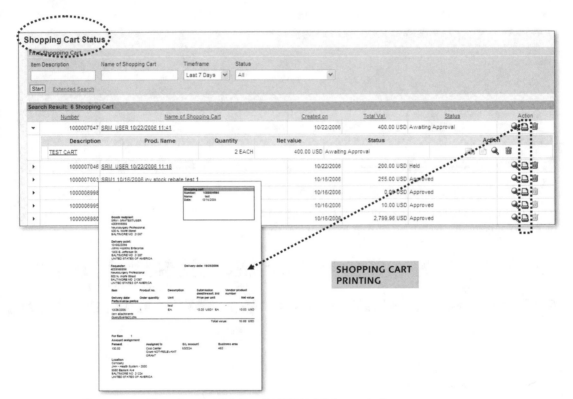

Figure 3.40 Shopping Cart Printing (SAP SRM 5.0 Screenshot)

In addition to the status, users can also execute confirmations and invoices directly from the Check Status transaction (illustrated in Figure 3.41). This functionality was added in the SAP SRM application beginning in SAP SRM 4.0. These are referred as *Express Confirmation* or *Express Invoice*.

> **Note**
>
> In SAP SRM 7.0, there is no longer the functionality for using Express Confirmation or Express Invoice.

The shopping cart order history is available within the Related Documents tab, as illustrated in Figure 3.42.

Figure 3.41 Express Confirmation and Invoice Entry (SAP SRM 5.0 Screenshot)

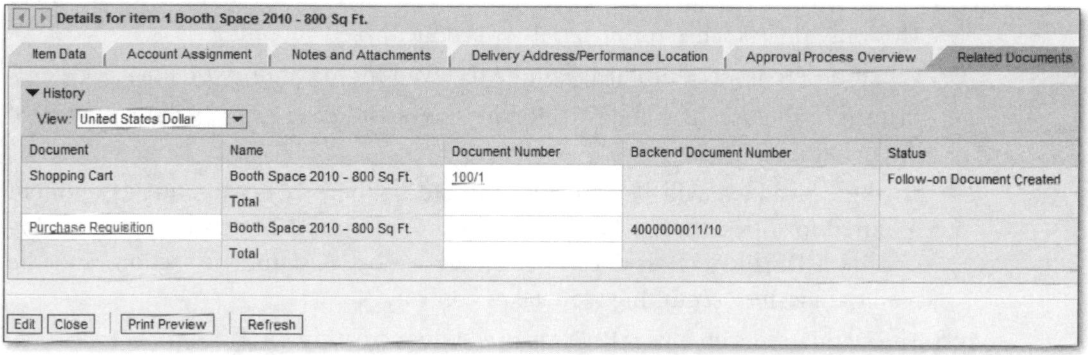

Figure 3.42 Related Documents (Follow-on Documents) Within a Shopping Cart

As a standard in SAP SRM, the following PO types are created as follow-on documents to shopping carts:

▶ **ECPO PO**
This is for all Expense item purchases.

▶ **ECDP PO**
This is for all POs with stock items that need to be received into inventory in SAP ERP (also called *direct procurement*).

▶ **Requisitions**
These can be created for all shopping carts of ECPO document type (given that the Classic implementation scenario is configured and a requisition instead of a PO is desired).

▶ **Reservations**
This is for all shopping cart line items that contain materials or products subject to inventory management, regardless of whether stock is available in SAP ERP.

An organization can determine what type of document is created in SAP SRM or the SAP backend based on the Customizing settings in the IMG. Review Chapter 7 to understand the impact of the implementation scenario on the follow-on document creation.

Next, you'll learn how to create shopping carts for ordering direct materials.

Ordering Direct Materials in the Shopping Cart

When we talk about the self-service procurement, we typically associate that with ordering indirect materials. In SAP SRM, we can also create spot direct procurement orders in the shopping cart. The overall direct procurement and plan-driven procurement scenario is discussed in detail in the following section. The key attributes of ordering direct materials are:

- This only makes sense for material- or product-based shopping carts.
- When ordered, those products will be received into inventory or stock.
- Instead of the user as a goods recipient, the plant becomes the valid recipient of the materials.
- As these products will be received into stock, there is no account assignment required for direct material orders in the shopping cart. Therefore, the shopping cart Item Details section does not contain a Cost Assignment section, and the material master Accounting view takes control.
- The standard document of ECDP is used when creating the PO.
- These orders are created in the backend materials management system, but any further changes are only possible in SAP SRM.

A user decides when to order a product as Direct by selecting the Order as Direct Material check box in the shopping cart line item. This is available within the details of the individual line item. Once this option is selected, it cannot be reversed. Figure 3.43 illustrates the Order as Direct Material functionality.

If a valid and definite source of supply exists (for example, a contract, or vendor list) and the predefined approval criterion has been met, a PO will be automatically generated in SAP SRM. Otherwise, the buyer will need to source this shopping cart to create a PO manually.

In the next section, we'll discuss Step 2 of the self-service procurement scenario, Approve Reject?, as illustrated in Figure 3.5.

Details for item 1 LCD Monitor

| Item Data | Account Assignment | Notes and Attachments | Delivery Address/Performance Location | Sources of Supply / Service Agents | Table Extensions | Availab |

Identification

Item Type: Material

Product ID: 500000138

Description: LCD Monitor

Product Category: 508   Comp Hardware & S/W

Order as Direct Material: ☐

Company Code: 3300   ABC LP

Organization

Purchasing Group: Maintenance Grp ▼ Show Members

Currency, Values, and Pricing

Order Quantity / Unit: 1   EA   Each

Price / Currency: 129.99   USD   Price Unit   1

Service and Delivery

Delivery Date: 08/17/2009

Location / Plant: 254   Suwanee Plant

Storage Location: 5201   Suwanee Garden

Incoterm Key/Location:

Goods Recipient: 82   Britto Manoj SMART02

Order Close   Save Check System Info Create Memory Snapshot

Figure 3.43 Ordering Direct Materials

3.1.2   Step 2: Approve Reject?

Automated and standardized *approvals* are the cornerstone of any e-procurement and SAP SRM solution. Timely approvals and notifications help speed procurement execution and provide a documented audit trail. In SAP SRM, organizations can trigger one or more approval steps to gain approvals at different steps within the requisition-to-pay process.

Approval procedures are available upon creation, change, or deletion of a number of purchasing documents including shopping carts, POs, goods receipts, and invoices. Figure 3.44 illustrates Step 2 of the self-service procurement scenario within operational procurement. You should have already created a shopping cart (Step 1) before this stage.

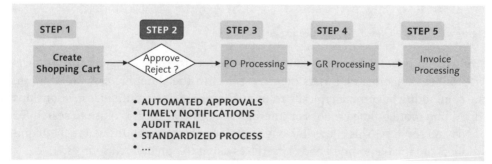

Figure 3.44 Approvals — Automating the Overall Procurement Process

Workflow and approvals provide key functionality within SAP SRM. Workflow is the SAP technology that allows organizations to develop approval procedures that align with their business needs. SAP SRM provides predefined workflow templates for organizations to use out of the box. In SAP SRM, all applications, such as the Shopping Cart, PO, Confirmation, Contract, Bid Invitation, and others use workflow extensively.

A workflow needs to be triggered within the SAP SRM system to create a successful shopping cart, and a no-approval workflow can be triggered if approvals are not required. Workflow plays an important part in the functioning of the SRM system. Chapter 10 introduces and explains role of workflow in SAP SRM. Readers can either directly jump to Chapter 10 now or continue to read the other sections in this chapter and then read Chapter 10 at a later time.

3.1.3   Step 3: PO Processing

In the self-service procurement scenario, purchasing professionals empower the end users so they can request for goods and services easily and at the same time access and select from prenegotiated sources of supply that users can select from. In doing so, they bypass the need for intervention by purchasing professionals. Some of the concepts woven into this section are listed as bullets in Figure 3.45.

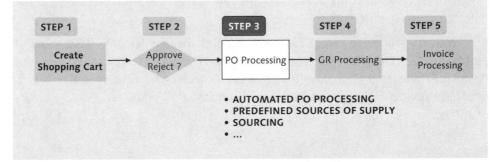

Figure 3.45   PO Processing — Completing and Ordering

Professional buyers can create contracts or vendor lists in the system for products or product categories that users then can select in the shopping cart. In addition, the commodity buyers are typically responsible for enhancing supplier relationships for adding more online catalogs or internal catalogs that users can use to search for goods and services. This allows the buyers to focus on transactions where the requisitioners are unable to find goods or services using the predefined sources.

Sourcing and professional procurement involves the core purchasing process of analyzing, qualifying, selecting suppliers, and processing orders. In this section, we're going to concentrate on PO processing. The other processes will be discussed in Chapter 4.

These concepts are based on the idea that the purchasing professionals in your organization (also called buyers) are going to be processing the POs within the SAP SRM system instead of the backend SAP ERP system. If your organization plans to implement the Classic Scenario, then PO processing will be handled in either the SAP ERP back-end.

Purchase Order Processing and Order Management

The PO processing functionality in SAP SRM allows professional purchasers to create and maintain POs. Organizations that want to use this functionality need to implement the Extended Classic or Standalone scenario. This functionality is not relevant for the Classic scenario implementations, because in that scenario the professional purchasers process POs in the materials management in SAP ERP software.

There is usually confusion about what type of a shopping cart or PO is necessary for the business need of the organization. There are many different shopping carts such as Request, Shop, Shop with Limit, or Purchase order. Table 3.1 provides some clarity.

The Process Purchase Order application provides professional purchasers with a worklist containing incomplete POs that need further processing. An incomplete PO is one that requires attention from the buyer. It could be the result of a shopping cart created by the requisitioner needing a price and a source of supply.

The PO is either created automatically by the system or manually by the purchaser. Professional purchasers can select documents from their Worklists and either display them using the Magnifying Glass icon or change them using the Pencils icon.

Business Need	Shopping Cart Type	PO Type	Self-Service, Service, or Plan-Driven Procurement
Departments request for items for consumption and expense	Shop	ECPO	Self-service
Purchasing agreement between organization and vendor that goods or services be delivered over a specified period of time for a specified dollar value	Limit	ECPO	Service procurement

Table 3.1 Shopping Cart and PO Type

Business Need	Shopping Cart Type	PO Type	Self-Service, Service, or Plan-Driven Procurement
Storeroom users that manage an inventory in SAP	Shop	ECDP	Self-service and plan-driven procurement
Departments within organization request items stocked within a central warehouse or storeroom within the enterprise	Shop	Reservation document created in ERP	Self-service

Table 3.1 Shopping Cart and PO Type (Cont.)

This application also provides a Find function, which allows buyers to search from a variety of different criteria. Figure 3.46 illustrates the Process Purchase Order application. The purchaser can also create a new PO by first selecting the type of PO in the Purchase Order with Transaction Type dropdown menu and then clicking on the Create button.

> **Note**
>
> In SAP SRM 7.0, the Purchase Order application has been changed to look similar to the overall floor plan similar to Shopping Cart and Confirmation. Figure 3.46 also shows the new Purchase Order transaction in SAP SRM 7.0
>
> Also, the Find function is now replaced with the Personal Object Worklist (POWL) search queries.

Similar to other documents in SAP SRM, the Process Purchase Order application is split into two tabs: Header Data and Item Data.

▶ **Header Data**

On the PO header, there are a number of sections available that apply for the entire PO (all line items). These include Purchasing Organization, Purchasing Group, Vendor, and others. If the PO was created from a corresponding shopping cart, the purchaser can change the purchasing organization assignment on the PO if there are multiple purchasing organizations. The purchasing organization is not available for users to change in the shopping cart or for buyers in the Sourcing application. Figure 3.47 illustrates the Basic Data section of the PO header.

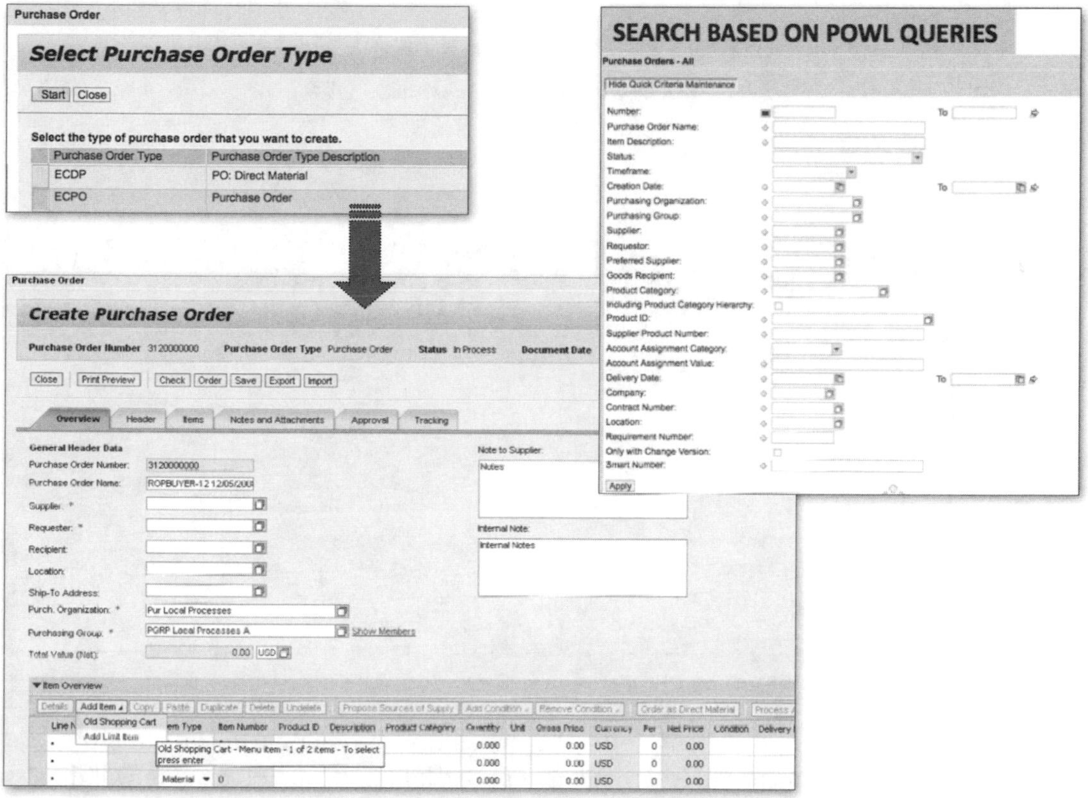

Figure 3.46 Process Purchase Orders

Note

In SAP SRM 7.0, the following terms have been changed:

▶ Basic Data is now General Data.

▶ Follow-on documents section is replaced with a Tracking Tab.

▶ Instead of a separate area for Payment, that information is included on the General Data section.

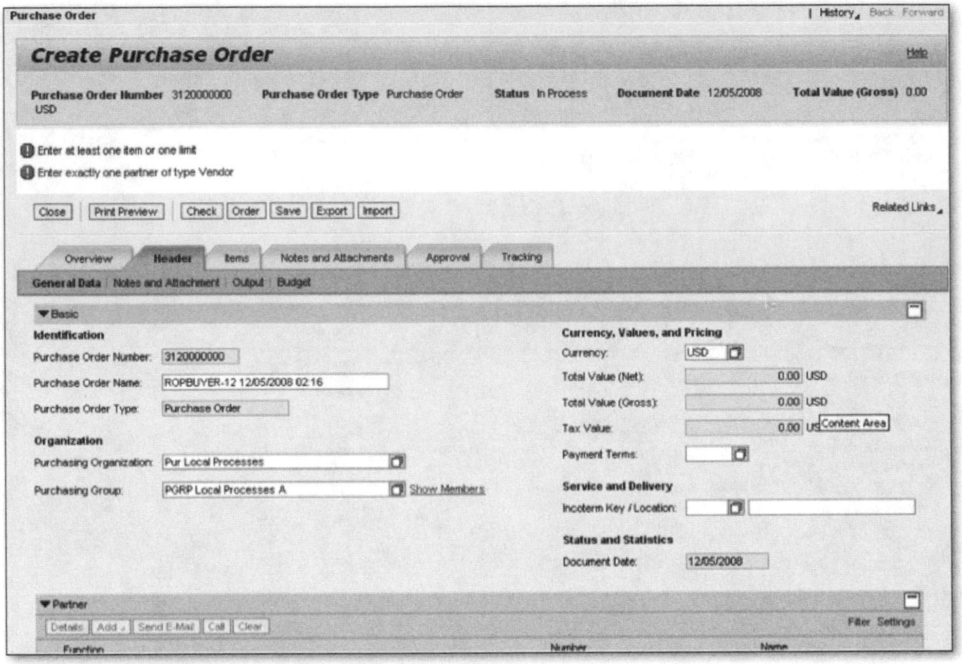

Figure 3.47 Purchase Order Header — Basic Data

A number of the sections on the PO are similar to other documents in SAP SRM, such as Document and Attachments, Approval, Budget, and others. We will discuss the Payment, Output, Follow-on documents, and Version sections of the Header Data tab in the following bullets:

▶ **Payment**
In the *Payment* section, buyers can select and change the terms of payment that might be set up with a particular vendor for the PO. Typically, these terms are defaulted based on the definitions in the vendor master; however, these can be changed on a spot basis (illustrated in Figure 3.48). In SAP SRM 7.0, the Payment information such as "payment terms" are on the GENERAL DATA • BASIC SECTION, as illustrated in Figure 3.47.

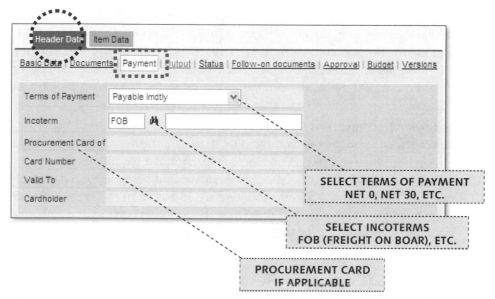

Figure 3.48 Payment Area (SAP SRM 5.0 Screenshot)

▶ **Output**

Once the PO is free of all errors, it can be ordered and sent to the vendor. Typically, the minimum of *output* is based on the definition in the vendor master record, however. Occasionally, buyers might need to output the PO in a different medium or re-output an existing PO again (as shown in Figure 3.49). An output preview is available that displays the PO in an Adobe Acrobat PDF format; this can be viewed prior to the transmission of the manual POs. Organizations can define their own forms for POs in Customizing.

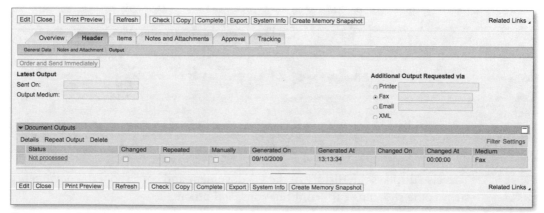

Figure 3.49 Output Area

It is important for organizations to ensure that if the Extended Classic scenario is implemented, then the POs are created in SAP SRM and a copy of the PO is sent to SAP ERP backend. The output of the PO can only be triggered from the SAP SRM system; no output is triggered from the SAP backend system for these POs. In SAP SRM, the configuration setting needs to be completed in Customizing to enable document output.

▶ **Follow-on Documents or Tracking**

The *Follow-on Documents* section provides details on the documents that might be required after the PO creation. For example, if it is a requirement to receive a PO response from the PO vendor, then this would be selected. Again, typically this information is automatically defaulted based on the vendor master definition but can be altered by the purchaser in this section. Figure 3.50 illustrates the Follow-on Documents section of the PO.

> **Note**
>
> In SAP SRM 7.0, the Follow-on Documents section has been renamed as "Tracking," and is now available within a separate tab by itself. The functionality is the same as in SAP SRM 5.0, but the structure has been changed, as illustrated in Figure 3.50.

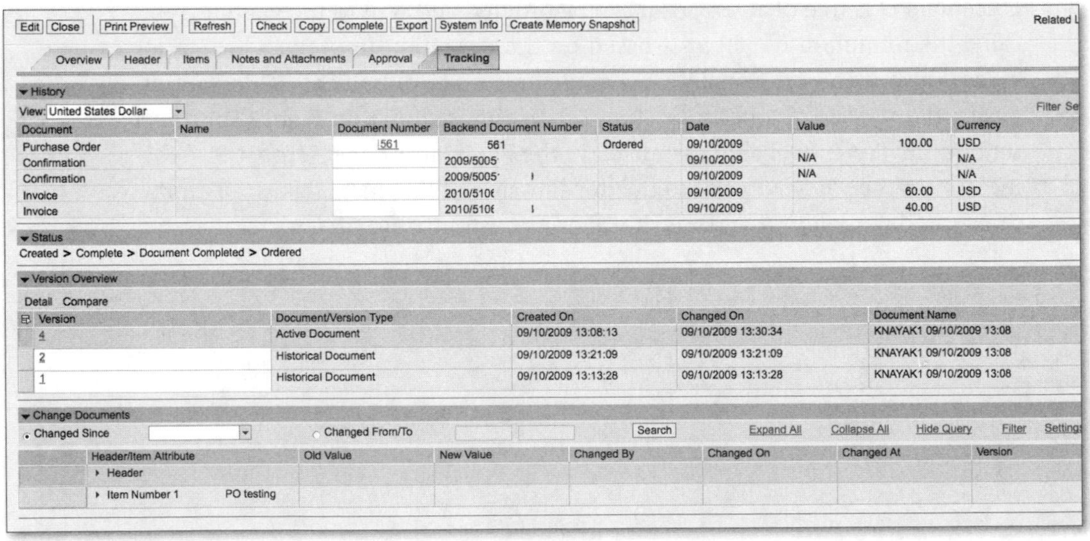

Figure 3.50 Follow-On Documents (SAP SRM 5.0) or Tracking (SAP SRM 7.0) Area

This also displays the History of the PO document and corresponding documents such as the shopping cart, confirmations, and others.

► **Versions**

PO changes are made in SAP SRM using the Transaction Process Purchase Orders. Changes made directly to the PO result in the creation of a new version for the original PO. Buyers can then compare the different PO versions. Changes that are initiated by the vendor can be captured using the PO Response (POR) application.

Versioning is an important functionality available in many purchasing documents, including the PO. This captures the needed trail of changes made to the PO and allows for quick comparison for changes.

Figure 3.51 illustrates the Compare function within the Versions section. Both the active and historical version of the PO has been selected for comparison. The changes are displayed at a Header Data and Item Data level. In our example, Version 2 of the purchase order contains a Quantity of 10, which is the change that was made compared to Version C1.

> **Note**
>
> In SAP SRM 7.0, the versioning functionality is similar to SAP SRM 5.0, but the versions are now available in the "Tracking" tab, as illustrated in Figure 3.50.

Now that readers are familiar with the sections within the Header Data tab, let's discuss the Item Data tab and the sections that exist within it.

► **Item Data**

The Item Data tab on the PO can contain one or more line items. All the line items can only be for the same purchasing organization, purchasing group, and vendor. The Item Data section is similar to the shopping cart document in SAP SRM because it offers the functionality to create line items using multiple options such as catalogs, internal goods, and services, or simply describe the product or service.

Figure 3.52 illustrates the Item Data tab within the PO. The line items within the PO Item Data tab contain many fields and typically are not visible in the browser window; you will find yourself scrolling to the right. Therefore, the line items are divided so that they are visible on one screen in Figure 3.52.

In the Item Data tab, a purchaser can create line items in the same way he does when creating a shopping cart, by entering a product ID in the Product field or entering text within the Description field. Also, the purchaser can add items using internal and external catalogs. This can be done by selecting a catalog in the Find in Catalog dropdown menu and then clicking to launch the catalog.

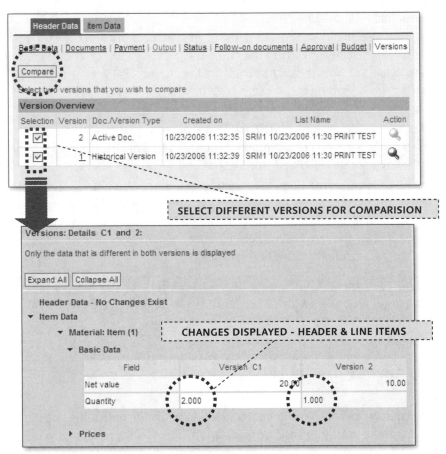

Figure 3.51 Comparing Versions for Documents (SAP SRM 5.0 Screenshot)

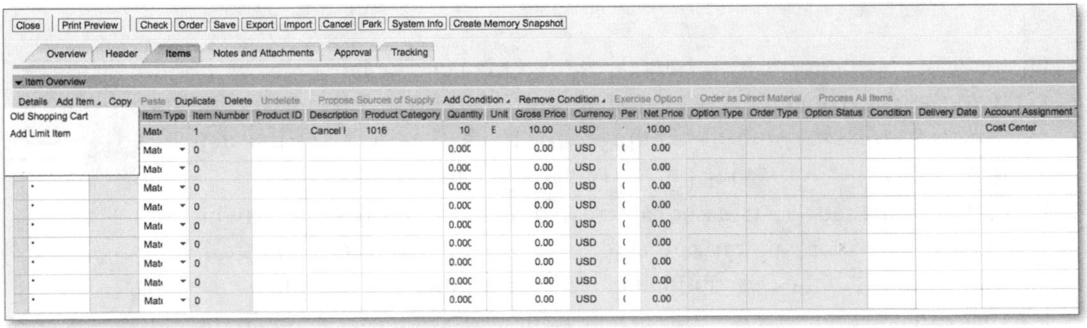

Figure 3.52 Purchase Order Item Data Section

Once the purchaser is done with entering the line items in the PO, he can click on the magnifying glass to review the details of the PO line item. The sections within the item details are discussed next:

▶ **Basic Data**
The *Basic Data* section provides a detailed view of the line item. It contains additional fields such as Incoterm, Vendor Product Number, and Under/Over-delivery Tolerance, to name a few. Figure 3.53 displays the Basic Data section.

▶ **Partner**
The *Partner* section provides information about the requisitioner (Requester), Goods Recipient, Location, and Ship-to Address. Typically, this information is entered in the Partner Overview section of the Header Data tab, but the purchaser can override that information at a line-item level. This section is seldom used.

Figures 3.53 and 3.54 illustrate the various areas within the Item Data tab on the PO.

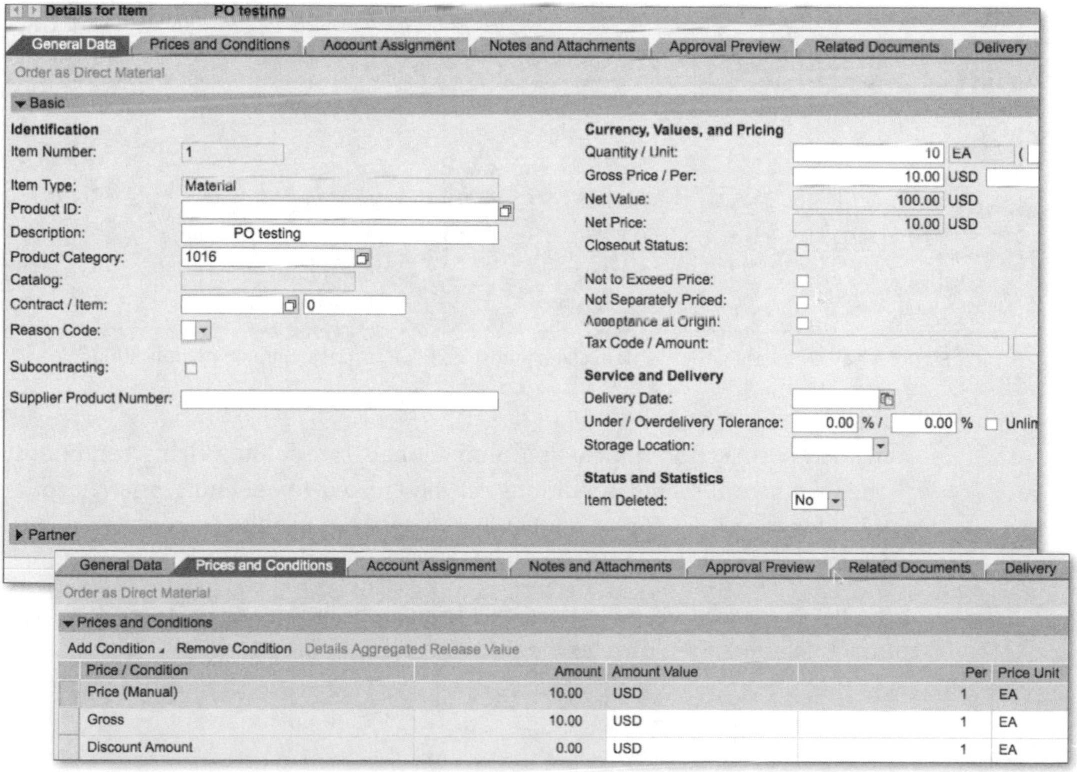

Figure 3.53 Purchase Order — Item Data: Basic Data, Prices

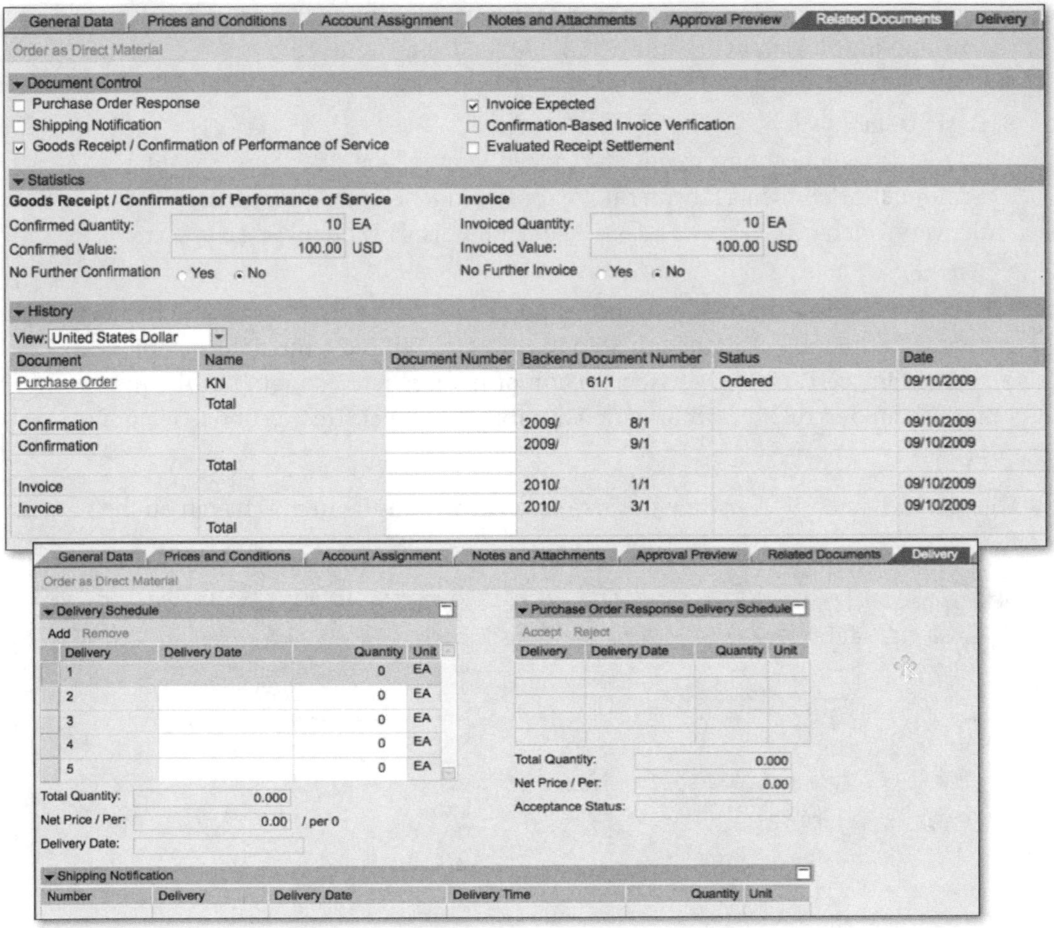

Figure 3.54 Purchase Order — Item Data: Statistics, PO Response, Shipping Notification

▶ **Prices**

In the *Prices* section, purchasing professionals can define pricing conditions. This is where discount conditions can be created for defining price negotiations for each line item of the PO. Purchasers can use the Discount (Percent), Discount (Absolute), or Header Discount (%) conditions in the Prices section.

If the PO is sourced via a contract, the pricing conditions are adopted from the contract. Figure 3.53 illustrates the Prices section.

▶ **Documents**

The *Documents* section allows purchasers to add Notes and Attachments at a line-item level. This functionality is similar to the Documents and Attachments functionality discussed in the Shopping Cart application.

▶ **Account Assignment**

Similar to the shopping cart, the PO items can also contain multiple cost assignments with split distributions. The *Account Assignment* section provides the same functionality as discussed in the Account Assignment section of the Shopping Cart application.

▶ **History**

The *History* section provides a graphical and table view of all the documents that have been created relevant to the PO line item.

▶ **Statistics**

The *Statistics* section in the Item Data provides information on the confirmed and invoiced quantity for the particular line item. Purchasing professionals can select the No further confirmations expected checkbox to indicate that no further deliveries are expected from the vendor, essentially closing the PO line item. Also, they can select the No further invoices expected checkbox to indicate that no further invoices are expected from the vendor. This allows you to close the PO. The Statistics section is illustrated in Figure 3.54.

▶ **Purchase Order Response**

The *Purchase Order Response* (also called POR) functionality was introduced in the SAP SRM 4.0 release. This allows suppliers or purchasing professionals to enter a response from the vendor regarding the PO sent. When a PO is sent to a supplier for goods or services, the supplier typically acknowledges the receipt of the PO. The supplier may respond for one or more goods or services to acknowledge its receipt, confirm the acceptance of the order with an agreement on delivery dates, quantities and prices, or to propose changes to the PO. Figure 3.55 illustrates the process flow for PO response.

> **Note**
>
> In previous releases, this functionality was termed Order Response/Acknowledgement. Just as with a shopping cart, the PO response is a separate application in SAP SRM with a Business Object BUS2209.

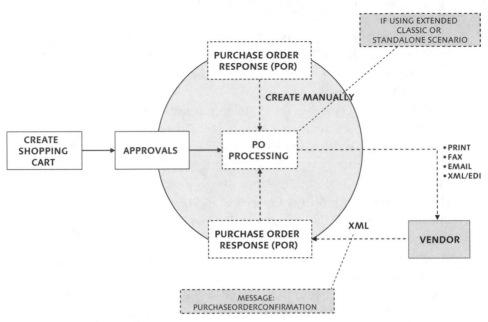

Figure 3.55 Purchase Order Response

Purchasers can create a POR manually to attach the changes indicated by the supplier such as delivery dates, prices, and others. This PO response gets attached to a specific PO that was transmitted to the supplier. From then on, creation of an auditable document can be tracked and followed up independently of the PO that was sent by the organization. Figure 3.56 illustrates the POR application. In the PO response application, the professional purchasers can search across multiple Status categories such as Party Confirmed by Vendor, Rejected by Vendor, Variance in Purchase Order Response, and others shown in Figure 3.56.

When processing a PO response, a professional purchaser can create a POR manually, approve or reject, or compare the PO to the POR.

If the purchaser selects the Accept all or Reject all icon in the Action column, a POR is automatically created with the status of Accepted or Rejected for all the line items in the PO. When comparing the POR against the PO that was sent to the vendor, a version log is available for tracking and comparison, as illustrated in Figure 3.57.

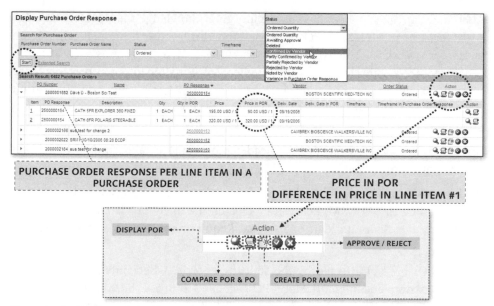

Figure 3.56 Purchase Order Response Application (SAP SRM 5.0 Screenshot)

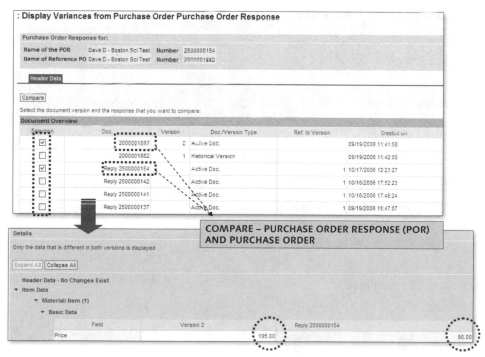

Figure 3.57 Comparing a POR and a PO (SAP SRM 5.0 Screenshot)

Alternately, if the suppliers have the ability to acknowledge the PO electronically, SAP SRM can receive XML PO responses and display them automatically in the purchaser's worklist. This worklist also shows the document status such as Party-confirmed if there are changes by the supplier. This functionality is also available for suppliers to process in the supplier self-services (SUS) application. This application is a component within the SAP SRM application and will be discussed in detail in Chapter 5.

Up to this point, we've explained the Header and Item Data tabs within the Purchase Order application in detail.

We'll conclude this section by addressing the splitting criteria used during the creation of a PO. In SAP SRM, POs can be created manually or via an existing document such as a Shopping Cart or External Requirement (e.g., Materials Resource Planning).

Manual POs are not affected by the splitting criteria, when only a PO is created using an existing document. If a local PO is generated in SAP SRM from an existing shopping cart, it could result in one or more POs based on the line item detail of the shopping cart. This results from the split criteria of the POs. The following criteria are used for splitting a PO in SAP SRM 4.0:

- Purchasing organization
- Purchasing group
- Company code
- Procurement card company
- Procurement card number
- External quotation
- Logical financial system
- Logical system that is the source of an external requirement
- External requirement item number
- Subtype (extended, local scenario)
- Vendor
- Desired vendor
- Ship-to address fields
- Document type or process type

In the next section, we'll discuss Step 4 of the self-service procurement scenario, GR Processing, illustrated in Figure 3.5.

3.1.4 Step 4: GR Processing

Many organizations are lax about the process of goods receipt (*GR Processing*). A three-way match between a PO, goods receipt, and invoice is not mandated. However, companies implementing SAP SRM are realizing the value of implementing this process across their organizations. This process provides a check and audit for the goods orders received and payments processed.

In this section, we'll discuss the goods receipt (known as *confirmation*) functionality in SAP SRM. Some of the key areas covered in this section are Confirmation Entry, Express Confirmation, and Returns as illustrated in Figure 3.58.

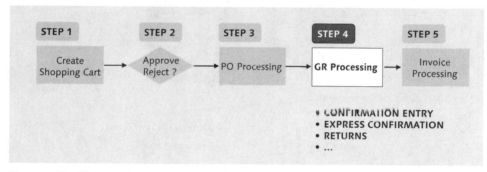

Figure 3.58 GR Processing — Entering Confirmations

In SAP SRM, a confirmation is synonymous with a goods receipt. A user can create a confirmation in SAP SRM, and if a backend SAP ERP system is connected, a corresponding goods receipt is created. Depending on your implementation scenario, the organization can choose to create a confirmation in SAP SRM or a goods receipt in the backend SAP ERP system. Figure 3.59 illustrates the possible scenarios for creating confirmations in SAP SRM.

Goods receipts and service entry (confirming service related purchases) are performed using the Confirm Goods/Services application in SAP SRM. Role-based authorizations control who can receive goods and services, as illustrated in Figure 3.60. The SC Creator in Figure 3.60 is the shopping cart creator.

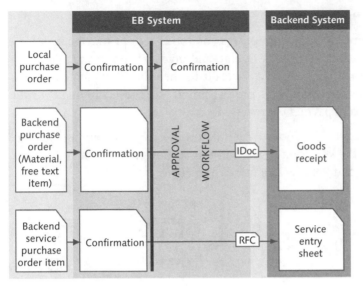

Figure 3.59 Creating Confirmations

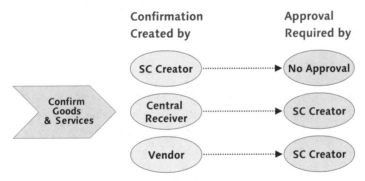

Figure 3.60 Who Can Confirm Goods and Services

Let's discuss the confirmation of goods and services by the shopping cart creator, central receiver, and vendor in further detail.

Confirmation for Goods and Services by Shopping Cart Creator

The *shopping cart creator* can confirm goods and services that they requested themselves or that others requested for them, where they are the goods recipient (for example, in the Shop for application). In the shopping cart or PO transactions, the user creating the document defaults as the Goods Recipient automatically. However, others can be assigned as recipients instead, as illustrated in Figure 3.61.

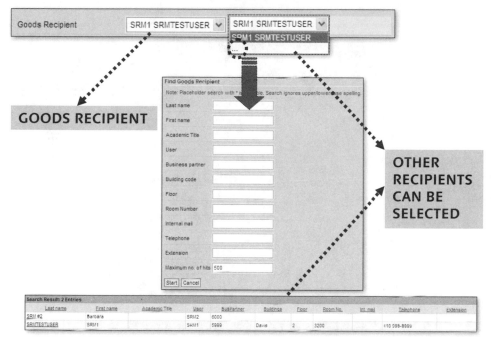

Figure 3.61 Goods Recipient

Users can either choose the Confirm Goods/Services application in SAP SRM, or they can choose the Express Confirmation icon in the Check Status application.

> **Note**
>
> Unlike previous SAP SRM releases, in SAP SRM 7.0, there is no "Express Confirmation" transaction.

The Confirm Goods/Services application provides end users more flexibility in creating goods receipts. They can create receipts for multiple POs, multiple lines, receive partial quantities, and also perform cancellations and returns. The Express Confirmation functionality does not provide any of these capabilities. Also, the Express Confirmation icon only allows confirmation of a single item at a time. Figure 3.62 illustrates the Confirm Goods/Services application.

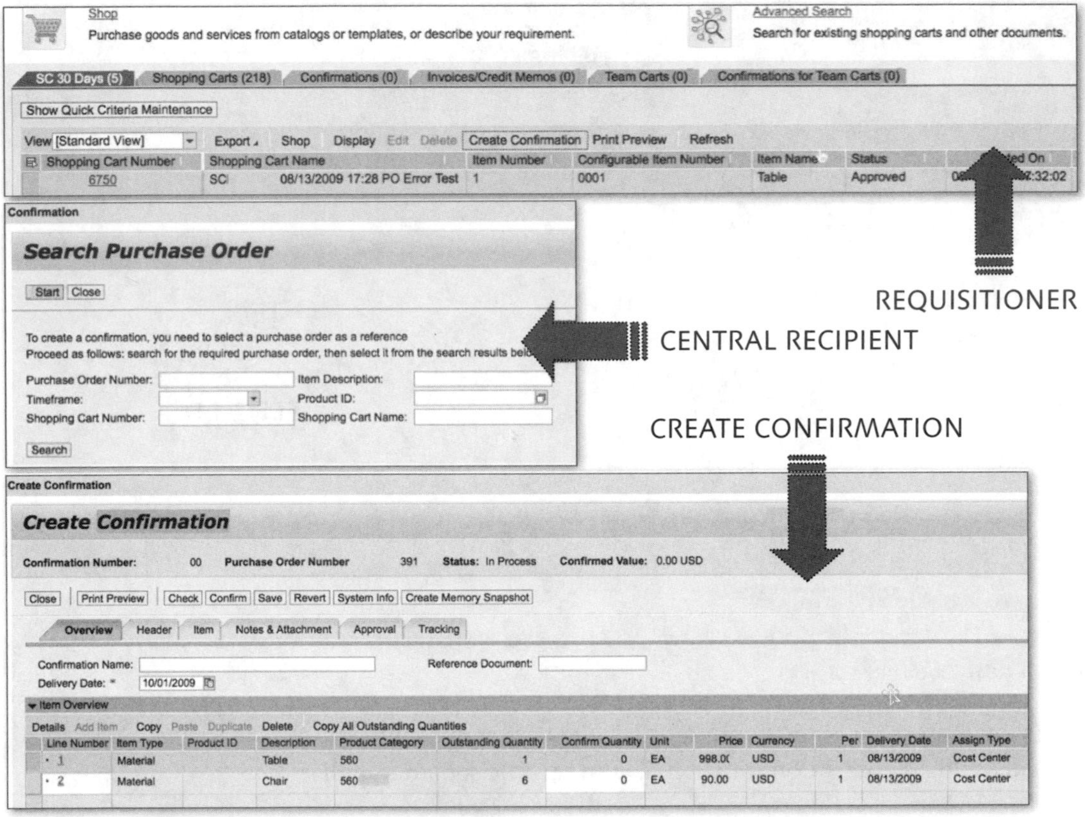

Figure 3.62 Confirm Goods or Services

In SAP SRM, a confirmation can be created multiple ways as discussed in Figure 3.60. Figure 3.62 illustrates the Employee vs Central receiver confirmation. When an employee does a confirmation, he can directly trigger the confirmation creation based on an existing shopping cart, select it, and click on Create Confirmation.

If a Central recipient does the confirmation, he can search for the purchase order for which a confirmation needs to be entered. Figure 3.62 illustrates some of the search options available.

We will now explain the key areas within the confirmation application:

▶ **Item Data Tab**
When the Create Confirmation application is selected, the process for creating a confirmation is started. As a default, the Overview tab is opened for the PO that

needs to be confirmed, showing all the line items to confirm. The Overview and the Item Data tab show the same information in this transaction.

Here, the user can receive one or multiple line items at once and also can receive complete or partial quantities for each of the PO lines being received. Figure 3.63 shows an example where Line item #1 is received completely and Item #2 is received partially.

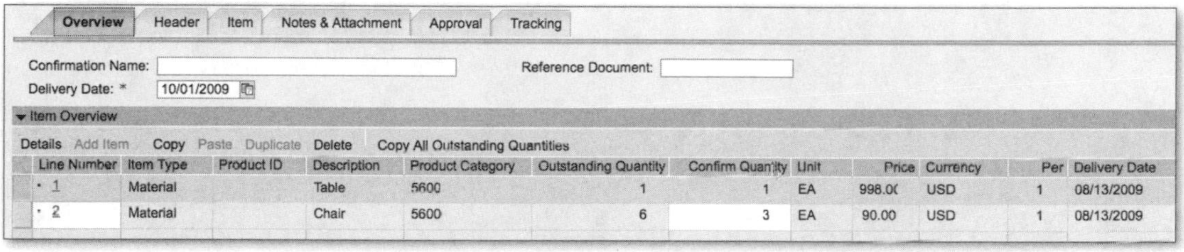

Figure 3.63 Items to Confirm

Users can also set the Last Delivery indicator in the Item Data tab as well. This indicator is useful when no additional deliveries are expected from the vendor. This is shown in Figure 3.64. In a three-way match scenario where the PO, Goods Receipt, and Invoice are expected, make sure deliveries are completed. Otherwise, a discrepancy will be found during invoice processing.

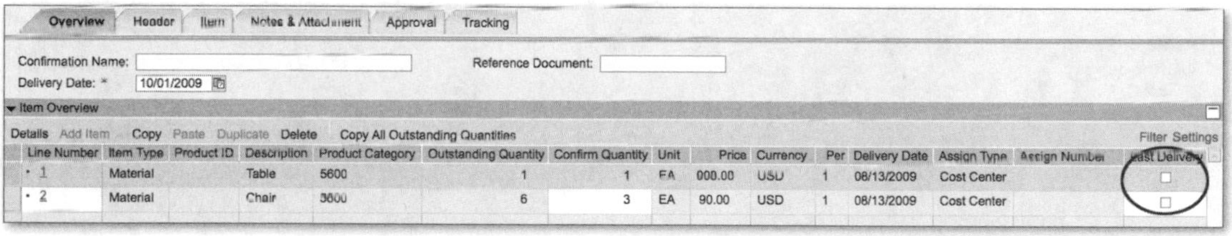

Figure 3.64 Delivery Complete Indicator

▶ **Header Data Tab**

The Header Data tab allows users to enter additional information about the confirmation entry including the vendor's Bill of Lading, the Goods Receipt Slip. Additionally the Header Data tab allows the user to create notes and attachments in the Documents section. Figure 3.65 illustrates the Basic Data, Partner, and Documents section of the Header Data tab.

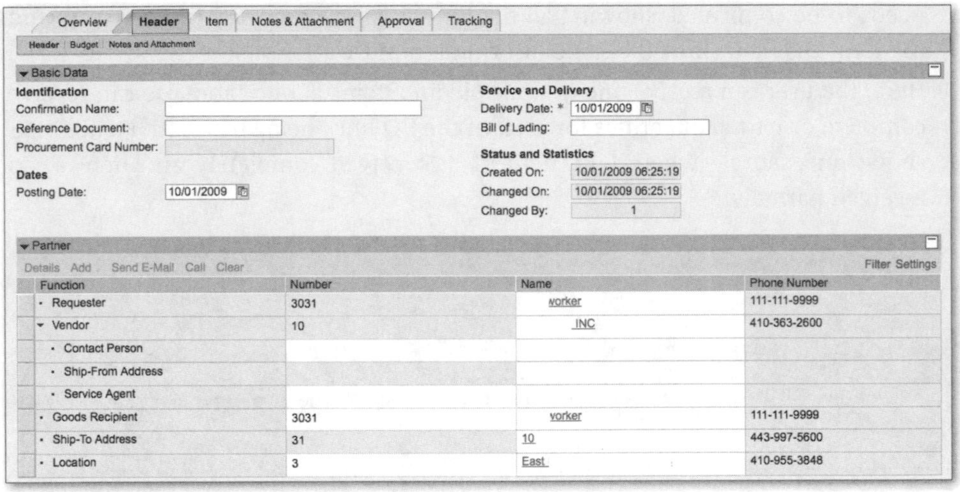

Figure 3.65 Header Data Tab

Figure 3.66 illustrates the History and the Status sections of the Header Data tab. In SAP SRM 7.0, as we mentioned earlier, the History and Status sections have been replaced by the "Tracking" tab, as illustrated in Figure 3.66.

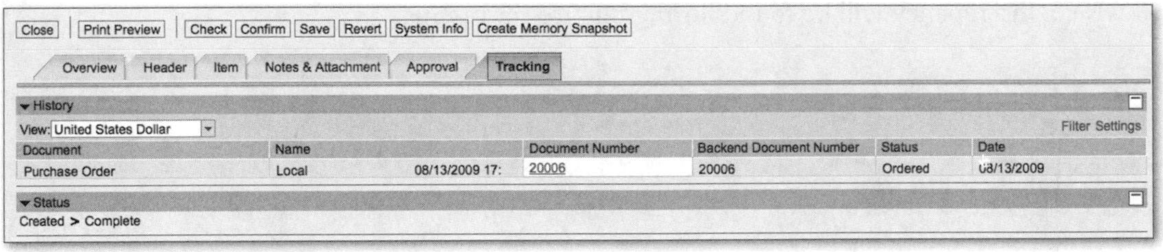

Figure 3.66 Header Data tab

▶ **Approval Preview Tab**
  Depending on whether the organization wants to use approvals for confirmation entry, the Approval Preview tab shows the preview of the approval process if required. Approvers can be added as well. The approval functionality in SAP SRM is discussed in detail in Chapter 10. Figure 3.67 illustrates the Approval Preview tab in the Confirmation application. In this example, the system made an automatic decision for no approval based on the configured business rules.

| Overview | Header | Item | Notes & Attachment | **Approval** | Tracking |

Current Status: Initial

Header Approval Note

Current Process Step:

Currently Processed By:

Approval Process Data: Download as XML

Follow Up: ☐ Work Item to Requester at Process End

| Header | Item |

Header Approval Status

Add Approver Remove Approver   Settings

	Sequence	Process Step	Level Status	Status	Processor Determination	Processor	Received On	Processed On	Forwarded By
•	001	Automatic Approval	Valid (Can be Started)	Open (No Decision Made)	SYSTEM	system			

Reviewer(s) for the Document

Add Reviewer Remove Reviewer   Settings

	Reviewer Type	Processor	Work Item Created At	Received On	Processed On	Forwarded By
⊡ The table does not contain any data						

Figure 3.67 Approval Preview Tab

Confirmation for Goods and Services by Central Receiver

A Central Goods Recipient can perform confirmations for all POs. These POs could originate in SAP SRM or the backend system.

Organizations need to be careful when assigning users' access to Confirm Goods/Services centrally, because there is no ability to restrict the POs that can be received. All POs across all departments and plants can be received by the individual having access to the central role. This role is typically given to users such as administrative assistants who typically order for multiple people and who also serve as a central point for the delivery of goods and services.

> **Note**
>
> If it is necessary to provide this transaction to many users, organizations can use BAdIs to restrict the POs that are available for the central receiver to confirm. BAdIs are development objects that need to be developed based on customer-specific logic.

Cancellation or Returns

A user also has the ability to cancel his confirmation or return goods using the Confirm Goods/Services transaction.

Once a determination is made that an item needs to be returned, the receiver or requisitioner contacts the vendor to obtain a return authorization number. A Return

Goods Authorization (RGA) form is completed, indicating the return authorization number, reason for return, and any additional information required by the vendor.

When a return delivery is posted in SAP SRM, a movement type of 122 is posted in the backend SAP system (if the Standalone scenario is being used, then a local return is posted). This return only posts a transaction in SAP SRM and has no correspondence to the Return Material Authorization (RMA) that needs to be obtained from the vendor. Typically, the person who posts the return should call the vendor to get the RMA number for the return prior to posting it in SAP SRM. Figure 3.68 illustrates a sample process flow for returns.

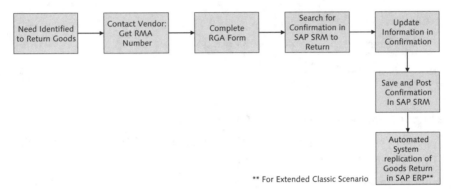

Figure 3.68   Return Goods Process Flow

A user can begin the process for return delivery or cancellation using the Display/Process Confirmation option in the Confirm Goods/Services application.

Figure 3.69 shows that the Return delivery button can be used to return the previously confirmed product Office Depot® Wood 2, Pencils, Medium 5. Alternately, the Delete button can delete or cancel confirmation number 6000000222. Figure 3.70 illustrates the return delivery and cancellation confirmation.

> **Note**
> Only confirmations that have not yet been invoiced can be cancelled or changed.

Once the return of goods process is completed in SAP SRM, the user can return the goods to the vendor or ask the receiving dock personnel to return the goods on the behalf of the requisitioner.

Display and Process Confirmations

Make a Selection: Display/Process Confirmation

To display or edit confirmations, first find a confirmation.

Find Confirmation

Item Description	Confirmation Number	Timeframe	Purchase Order Number
		Last 7 Days	

Start   Extended Search

To display or edit confirmations, choose the number below or 🔍

Search Result: 1 Confirmation

Number	Specific.	Name	Ref. Document	Created by	Status	Action
6000000222		SACHIN TEST	AB-0123	SRM2 SRMTESTUSER	Approved	🔍

RETURNS AND CANCELLATIONS ARE AVAILABLE VIA THE DISPLAY AND PROCESS SELECTION OPTION

Display and Process Confirmations

Confirm Hold Check Refresh Recreate Change Display Delete Return delivery Evaluate   Back to Initial Screen

In order to process the confirmation, choose an active pushbutton

Confirmation Number   6000000222
Confirmation Name   SACHIN TEST   Purchase Order Number 2000001703
Delivery/Performance Date * 10/22/2006   Reference Document AB-0123

PROCESS RETURN DELIVERY

Header data   Item Data   Approval Preview

Item Overview

	Item	Description	Product	Quantity*	Unit	Net Price	Assigned to	Description	Purchase Order / Item	Product Category	Last Delivery	Actions
☑	1	Office Depot(R) Wood 2 Pencils, Medium S		12	PAC	0.92 USD Per 1 PAC	Cost Center 4800000000	JHH UNALLOC INST	2000001703 / 1	OFFICE SUPP & EQUIP	☐	🔍 📋 🗑

* Required Entry

DELETE / CANCEL CONFIRMATION

Figure 3.69 Cancellations and Return Delivery (SAP SRM 5.0 Screenshot)

Display and Process Return Deliveries

Confirm Hold Check Refresh Recreate Change Display Delete Return delivery Evaluate   Back to Initial Screen

Save your return delivery, you can process this action again later.

Returns Number 6000000223

Name of Returns SACHIN TEST   Purchase Order Number 2000001703
Returned on * 10/22/2006   Reference Document AB-0123

RETURN DELIVERY PROCESSING

Header data   Item Data   Approval Preview

1. If necessary, change the quantity (for partial return deliveries, for example), and other details.
2. Choose "Confirm" above

Item Overview

	Item	Description	Product	Quantity*	Unit	Net Price	Assigned to	Description	Purchase Order / Item	Product Category	Last Delivery	Actions
☑	1	Office Depot(R) Wood 2 Pencils, Medium S		12	PAC	0.92 USD Per 1 PAC	Cost Center 4800000000	JHH UNALLOC INST	2000001703 / 1	OFFICE SUPP & EQUIP	☐	🔍 📋 🗑

* Required Entry

Display and Process Confirmations

Confirm Hold Check Refresh Recreate Change Display Delete Return delivery Evaluate   Back to Initial Screen

In order to process the confirmation, choose an active pushbutton

CANCELLING A CONFIRMATION

Confirmation Number   6000000222
Confirmation Name   SACHIN TEST   Purchase Order Number 2000001703
Delivery/Performance Date * 10/22/2006   Reference Document AB-0123

Header data   Item Data   Approval Preview

Item Overview

	Item	Description	Product	Quantity*	Unit			Description	Purchase Order / Item	Product Category	Last Delivery	Actions
☑	1	Office Depot(R) Wood 2 Pencils, Medium S		12	PAC			LOC INST	2000001703 / 1	OFFICE SUPP & EQUIP	☐	🔍 📋 🗑

Windows Internet Explorer ☒

⚠ Confirmation 6000000222 canceled

OK

* Required Entry

Figure 3.70 Cancel Confirmations and Return Delivery (SAP SRM 5.0 Screenshot)

Express Confirmation

This functionality provides end users with the ability to quickly create a goods receipt (confirmation). This is especially useful for users who are casual requisitioners and do not want to create the regular goods confirmations. This function supports the self-service scenario in that it provides the end users with the ability to complete the entire purchase process from shopping cart to invoice-entry seamlessly.

> **Note**
>
> In SAP SRM 7.0, there is no longer an Express Confirmation function. A user can create a confirmation document by selecting an existing shopping cart that has been converted into a purchase order.

The express confirmation can be accessed from the Check Status application, illustrated in Figure 3.71. From a process perspective, a goods receipt or confirmation is only available for entry after the PO is complete and transferred to the vendor. All shopping carts that have a corresponding PO are available for confirmation.

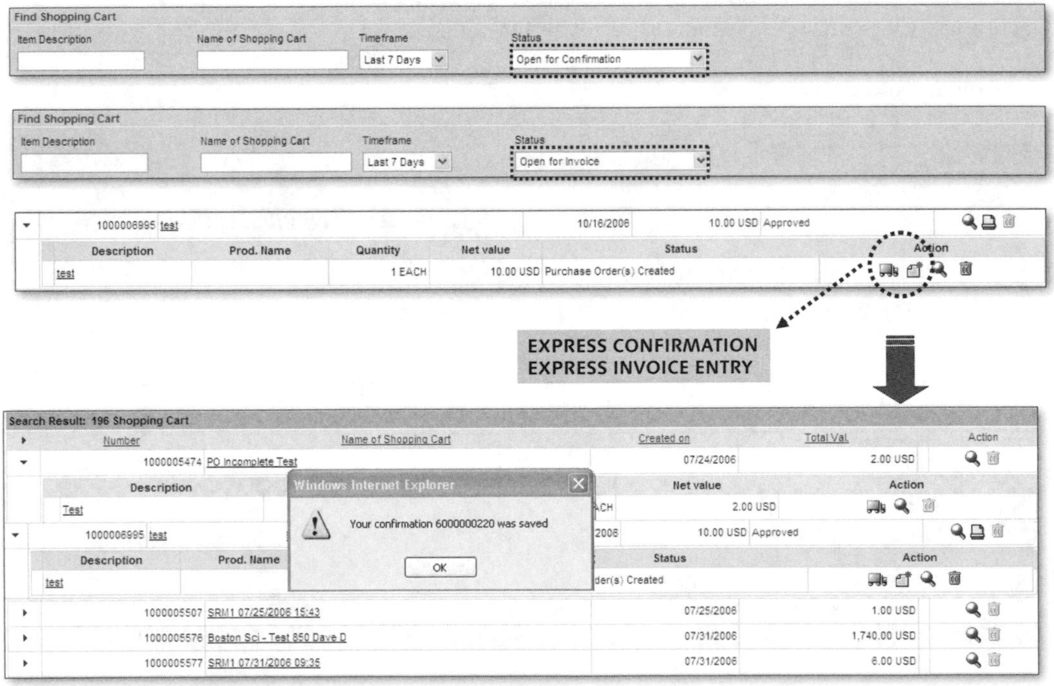

Figure 3.71 Express Confirmation (SAP SRM 5.0 Screenshot)

When the user selects the Express Confirmation Truck icon, a goods receipt is automatically processed in the background. A message box is provided to the end user once the confirmation is created successfully. In this function, there is no capability to enter any information such as bill of lading and others. Therefore, a user can only process the confirmation completely. Partial confirmations are not supported, for example, if the PO was for a quantity of 10, and the express confirmation only needs to be created for a quantity of 6.

> **Note**
>
> You cannot create Express Confirmations or Express Invoices for unplanned items or for shopping cart items split between several POs.

Confirmation for Goods and Services by Suppliers

Suppliers can use the confirmation function as well to create, edit, and send confirmations using SUS. The core advantage of this functionality is that small and mid-sized suppliers can be enabled by your organization to electronically respond to POs.

Using SUS, suppliers can create confirmations and invoices that are then sent to responsible users within your organization for approval. Not only does this reduce data-entry efforts for the customer, it allows for an electronic mechanism to collaborate on the entire procurement process. This functionality is discussed in detail in Chapter 5.

The next section discusses the last step in the self-service procurement scenario, illustrated in Figure 3.5.

3.1.5   Step 5: Invoice Processing

An *invoice* is usually created after the goods receipt or service performance has been confirmed. It includes general invoice information, such as total amount, total tax, freight costs, vendor and invoice recipient, and detailed information (header information, item information, and approval preview). Some of the key areas in this section are Invoice Entry, Credit Memo Entry, Partial Invoices, and Invoice with and without PO as illustrated in Figure 3.72.

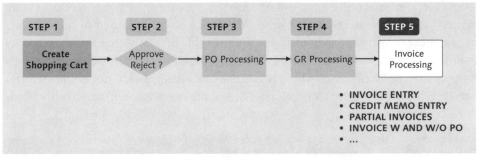

Figure 3.72 Invoice Processing — Entering Invoices and Credit Memos

In SAP SRM, a single entry transaction is available for processing invoices and credit memos. Invoices and credit memos are created using the *Enter Invoice/Credit Memo* transaction in SAP SRM, as illustrated in Figure 3.73.

Enter Invoices

Select: Invoice ⌄ Create with PO Reference ⌄

To enter an invoice for a purchase order, first find a purchase order.

Search for Purchase Order

Item Description	Name of Shopping Cart	Timeframe	Purchase Order Number
		Last Year ⌄	
Product	Product Category	Vendor	Role
	⌄		Goods/Services Requested by me ⌄
Account Assignment Category	Account Assignment Value	Delivery Date From	Delivery Date To
⌄			
Company Code			

Start   Simple Search

EXTENSIVE FUNCTIONALITY ➡

✓ Partial returns and credit memos
✓ Invoice exception processing
✓ Invoice entry without PO reference
✓ Tolerances
✓ Settings to process erroneous and incomplete documents
✓ Delivery complete indicator
✓ Invoice sampling
✓ Evaluated Receipt Settlement (ERS)

✓ Catalog integration
✓ Tax calculation
✓ Texts and attachments
✓ Collective invoices
✓ Central/desktop receiving and invoice verification
✓ Approval for inbound documents
✓ Express confirmation and invoice

Figure 3.73 Invoices and Credit Memos (SAP SRM 5.0 Screenshot)

Role-based authorizations control who is allowed to access this transaction, as illustrated in Figure 3.74.

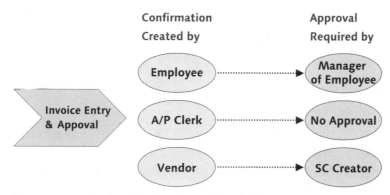

Figure 3.74 Who Can Enter Invoices and Credit Memos

In SAP SRM, a user can create an invoice or credit memo in and if a backend SAP ERP system is connected. Depending on your implementation scenario, the organization can create invoices in SAP SRM or directly enter invoices in the backend SAP ERP system. Figure 3.75 illustrates the possible scenarios for creating invoices in SAP SRM.

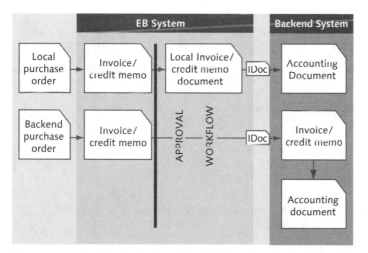

Figure 3.75 Creating Invoices and Credit Memos

When the invoice or credit memo is posted in the SAP SRM system, the payment information is transferred to the corresponding SAP backend financial system. Once the invoice is transferred to the backend system, all accounting documents are updated and commitments are reduced. Additionally, an invoice or credit memo document is created in materials management in SAP ERP and becomes visible in the PO history. Invoices in SAP SRM can be created using one of the following options:

- ▶ Entering invoices with PO reference
- ▶ Entering invoices without PO reference
- ▶ XML invoice receipt
- ▶ Using Express creation

Entering Invoices with PO Reference

As in SAP ERP, SAP SRM allows users to create invoices with reference to a PO or without reference. When creating invoices, one of the most important things an invoice processor needs is the ability to search using multiple criteria such as PO Number, Vendor, and Product, as illustrated in Figure 3.76.

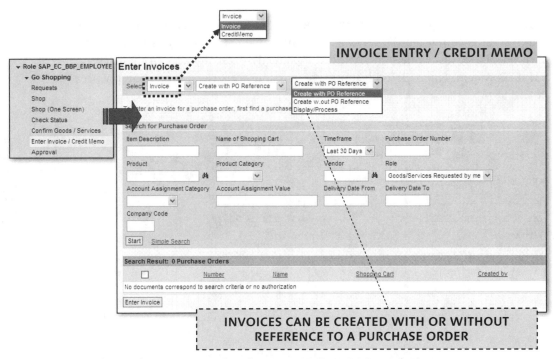

Figure 3.76 Enter Invoices with Reference to PO (SRM 5.0 Screenshot)

As the PO is being referenced, all information in the invoice is pulled in from the corresponding PO. If all the criteria of total invoice value and PO value match, then the invoice can be posted. If there are discrepancies, the invoice processor can either put the invoice on Hold or send it for further approvals. The approval functionality available in SAP SRM is discussed in detail in Chapter 10.

When invoices are created with reference to a PO, the system automatically proposes the data from the system in which the PO was originally entered (local PO or backend PO). All the line items from the PO are automatically shown in the invoice for easy entry.

Invoices in SAP SRM can be entered for more than one PO at a time. This is called collective invoice processing. However, the PO needs to maintain the same:

- Vendor
- Company code
- Currency
- Backend financial system

Entering Invoices Without a PO Reference

Similar to SAP ERP, SAP SRM allows users to create invoices with reference to a PO or without reference. When there is no PO, the invoice creation process begins with the selection of a vendor. Naturally, in this process, the invoice processor has to enter most of the information manually because there is no reference document.

XML Invoice Receipt

Organizations implementing SAP SRM have also embarked on the electronic document exchange via XML. Vendors such as Office Depot, Fisher Scientific, and Dell are all examples of organizations that encourage customers to engage in document exchange using Internet technologies such as XML to streamline operations and reduce costs.

Invoices in SAP SRM can be processed using inbound XML invoices from suppliers. Since SAP SRM release 4.0, SAP has included functionality that allows organizations to process XML invoices even if no goods receipts documents are processed.

Instead, the incoming invoice is created with a status of waiting and awaits the creation of a goods receipt. The status on the SRM invoice is Waiting for Preceding Document as seen in Figure 3.77. A new program has been created (BBP_IV_AUTO_COMPLETE) that can be scheduled so that invoices are automatically posted once the corresponding goods receipts documents are posted.

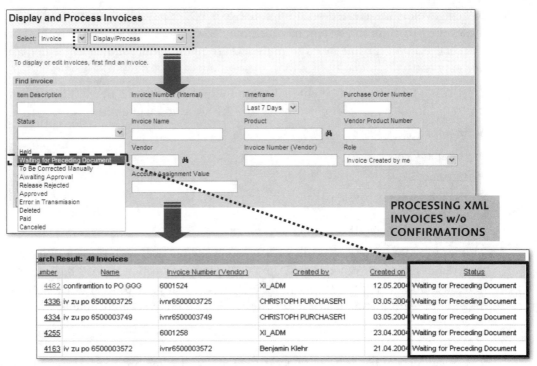

Figure 3.77 Processing XML Invoices Without Goods Receipts (SAP SRM 5.0 Screenshot)

When incoming invoices are received with errors, a status of To Be Corrected Manually is assigned to the invoice document, as illustrated in Figure 3.78. A background workflow notifies the responsible users, and they can manually correct the errors or send the invoice back to the vendor. To keep the original invoice intact, version-management functionality is available.

Express Invoices

The *Express Invoice* functionality gives end users the ability to quickly create an invoice. This supports the self-service scenario, in that end users can complete the entire purchase process from shopping cart to invoice entry seamlessly.

The express invoice can be accessed from the *Check Status* application, illustrated in Figure 3.79. From a process perspective, an invoice is only available for entry after the PO is complete and transferred to the vendor. All shopping carts that have a corresponding PO are available for invoice entry. If the PO requires a goods receipt as well, then the Confirmation/Goods Receipt step is mandatory prior to entry of invoices.

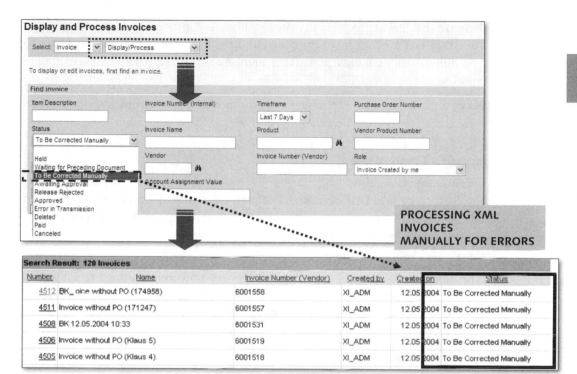

Figure 3.78 Processing XML Invoices to Correct Errors Manually (SAP SRM 5.0 Screenshot)

Note

In SAP SRM 7.0, there is no longer an Express Invoice functionality.

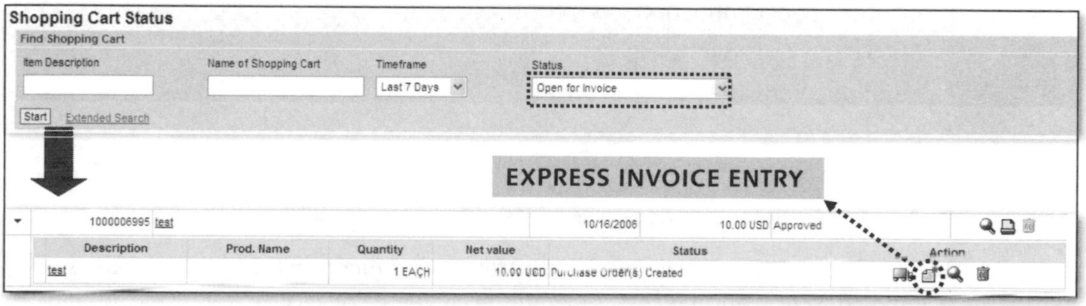

Figure 3.79 Express Invoice Creation (SAP SRM 5.0 Screenshot)

When the user selects Express Invoice, an invoice is processed in the background automatically. A message box is provided to the end user once the invoice is created successfully. A user can only process the invoice completely; partial invoices are not supported.

It is not possible to create express invoices for unplanned items or for shopping carts that are split across multiple POs.

Processing Credit Memos

A credit memo is required when the goods or services that were provided by a supplier need to be returned because of defective product or other discrepancies. A credit memo allows the organization to reduce its liability for the goods or services received within its financial system. The credit memo transaction is the same as the invoice-processing transaction in SAP SRM.

In the next section, we will introduce the services procurement process within the operational procurement business scenario. You will learn about the capabilities of SAP SRM for the procurement of services.

3.2 Services Procurement

In many organizations, spending on services consumes up to 50% of the overall procurement expenditure. Considering this huge number, it is imperative for organizations to focus on the services procurement process and reduce costs for greater profitability. Some of the most important services that organizations procure are:

- Consulting
- Business and administrative services
- Marketing and advertising
- Building and maintenance services
- Legal services
- Technology services
- Air travel and transportation services

Services demand the same process controls as product procurement — such as budget and contract compliance — but add the challenge of service items that are mostly undefined at the time of requisition. Unplanned items are a significant cost within services procurement and can overrun budgets for projects unless they're allocated upfront.

Until recently, most SAP SRM applications did not provide much support for procurement of services. Now that many organizations have realized the benefits of the nonservice categories, they have started to focus on the opportunities to reduce costs within the procurement of services. SAP SRM supports services procurement via the following three options:

▶ Creation of shopping carts with value limits

▶ Request and ordering of external staff

▶ Creation of shopping carts with service products within the materials management in SAP ERP software

3.2.1 Create with Limit

In the Shop transaction, a user with appropriate authorization can create a shopping cart with a value limit or validity period using the Create with Limit application. These could be used for creating orders for a limited period of service or dollar value. Some organizations refer to such purchases as a Blanket order. Confirmations for goods receipts or services, as well as invoices can be entered up to this limit.

This application gives the user flexibility to determine, when creating a limit shopping cart, whether only an invoice will be required as a follow-on document or both the confirmation and invoice will be required. This provides flexibility for simple service transactions such as snow removal, general landscaping, or cutting grass, where the service is performed on a regular basis and there is no one person responsible for the confirmation. Figure 3.80 illustrates the Create with Limit application.

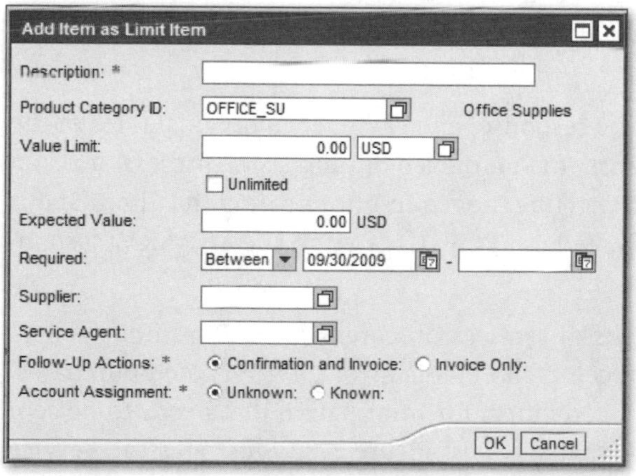

Figure 3.80 Create with Limit

In the Extended Classic implementation scenario, when creating shopping carts with more than one limit, separate POs will be created for each item when ordering, regardless of the data (vendor, document type, purchasing group, company, location, performance period, etc.) in each item. For example, if a shopping cart with two limit positions is ordered, two POs always will be created but not one PO for two items.

3.2.2 Request for External Staff

In this section, we're specifically discussing the procurement of *external staff*, which was referred as *temporary labor* in earlier releases. The Requests application initiates a request for information/request for proposal (RFI/RFP) process to send a request for a service to a vendor before creating the actual PO. This allows an organization to find a better match of a service agent to their core requirement.

In SAP SRM, the services procurement process can be initiated by an employee or purchasing assistant in the shopping cart or by the purchasing buyer in the SAP Bidding Engine component.

This scenario supports the process for both the request for information from a vendor and the actual purchase of the service. Depending on the service request, an organization might need to get detailed information from the vendor(s), prior to ordering the services. These could be a request for contracting or consulting service, for example.

Using the Requests application, a user can initiate the process of detailing the services required, including adding detailed information on the skill sets needed for the service agents. Once the request is complete, it is then sent to the vendor via an email link for response. Vendors can use the Bidding Engine component in SAP SRM to respond to the service requests.

The vendor can specify agents in the response, and can reject individual lines of the request. Upon receiving the response, the employee or purchasing professional can review and decide on accepting or rejecting the request from within the Check Status application. If the response is accepted, a PO is triggered in the SAP SRM system. This process is illustrated in Figure 3.81.

Because of the unique requirements of services procurement, SAP introduced specific transactions for the request, receipt, and invoicing of service-related purchases. These transactions contain specific containers for information that needs to be captured on a typical request for external services. Figure 3.82 illustrates the Service Request application in SRM.

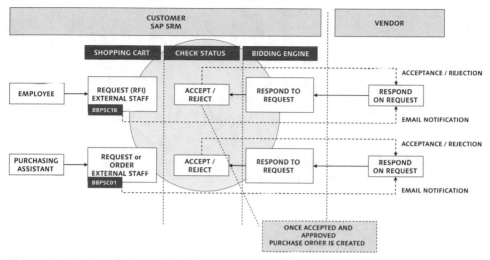

Figure 3.81 Request for External Staff — Process Overview

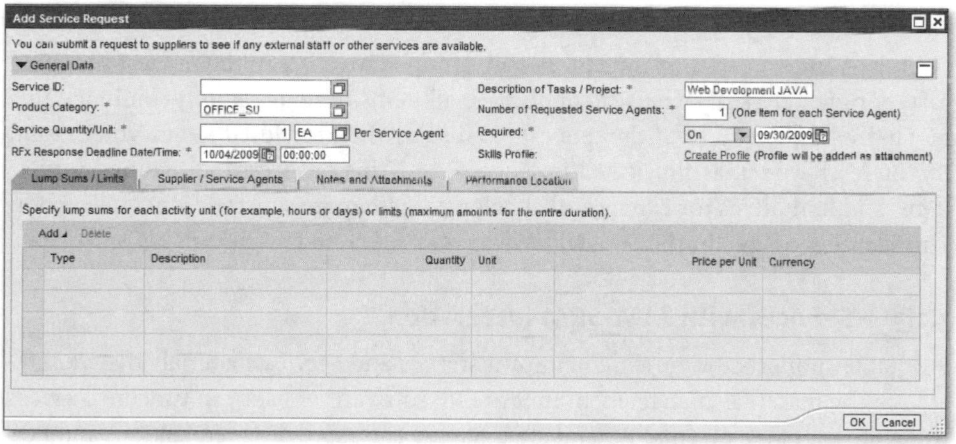

Figure 3.82 Request for External Staff

The service request can be entered directly as free-form text or can be added from the service master if there are services defined in the product master. A performance period can be defined to identify when the service is to be performed.

Besides the usual additional information that you can include in the request using texts and attachments, organizations can also create a skills profile as an Adobe Acrobat PDF form in the request. In this Adobe Acrobat PDF form, you enter the prerequisites that a service agent must fulfill, and specific skill sets can be defined that are required for the service project. You can use a BAdI to modify the list of skills available for selection in the PDF form.

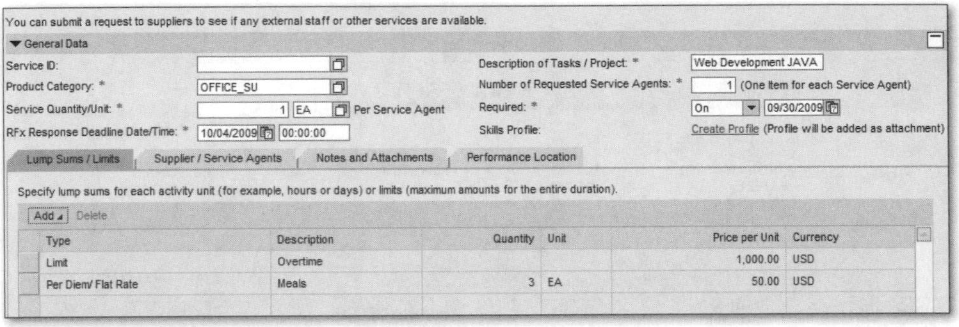

Figure 3.83 Request for External Staff — Adding Lump Sums and Limits

The Lump Sum and Limit capability in the application enable organizations to allocate unplanned buckets (e.g., expenses or overtime) for the service request and assign specific not to exceed limits. These costs typically cannot be allocated explicitly, so a maximum limit is defined that can be charged during the entire duration of the service project. Both the Lump Sum and Limit categories provide free-text description fields that offer flexibility for a variety of uses.

Both the planned and unplanned items are grouped together in the request shopping cart. For greater clarity, the system displays all items of your request combined in a hierarchy before you send the request. To display the individual items, you expand the hierarchy item, as illustrated in Figure 3.83. This ensures that planned service items and limit items for expenses that belong together are sourced from one vendor. This is only possible in the Standalone and the Extended Classic scenarios.

3.2.3 Services with MM-SRM Integration

SAP SRM supports the procurement of materials and service materials that are created in the materials management in SAP ERP software. A user can procure services using the shopping cart and PO and integrate the corresponding requisitions and POs within the SAP backend (ERP) system. This is the scenario where services are created within materials management in SAP ERP and replicated to SAP SRM.

The process starts with the creation of a shopping cart in SAP SRM with a Product Type of Services as seen in Figure 3.84. In Figure 3.85, line item 1 is for ENGINEERING SERVICE — ELEVATOR 1002, which is a service material 102948. The Product Type for this item is Services, which allows the user to enter a Timeframe for the delivery date.

The Required field in the item details provides the ability to define a timeframe for the service performance using a Between or Begin on date. When the product type is Goods, the Required on field only allows a user to enter a specific date for delivery.

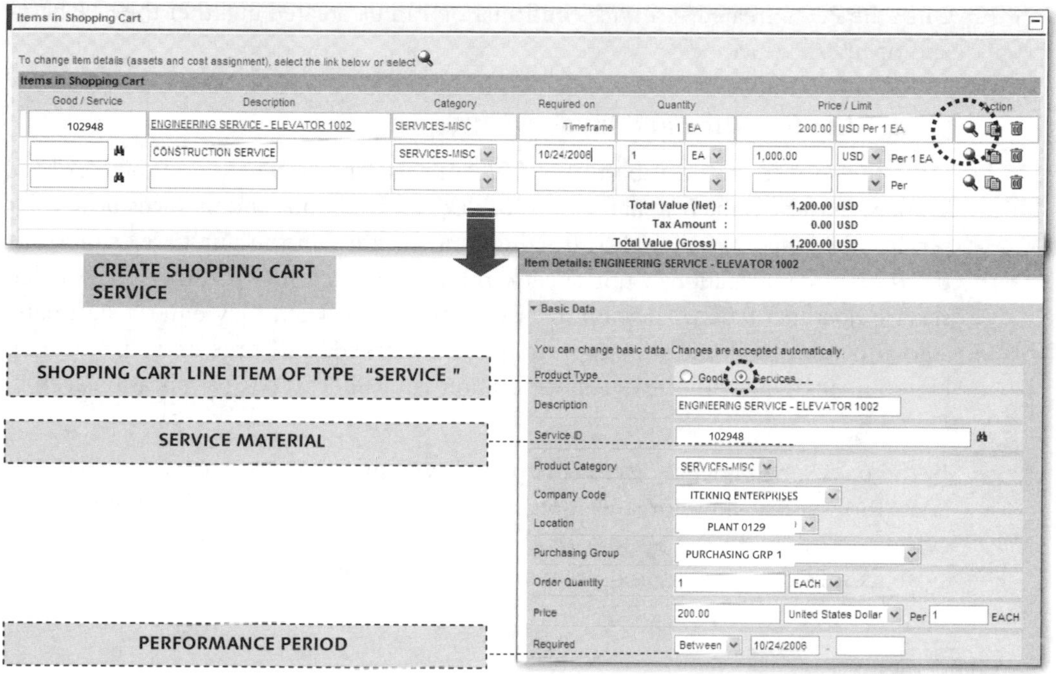

Figure 3.84 Shopping Cart of Type Service (SAP SRM 5.0 Screenshot)

Once the shopping cart is complete and ordered, based on system configuration, either a purchase requisition or PO of type Item Category D is created in SAP ERP, as illustrated in Figure 3.85.

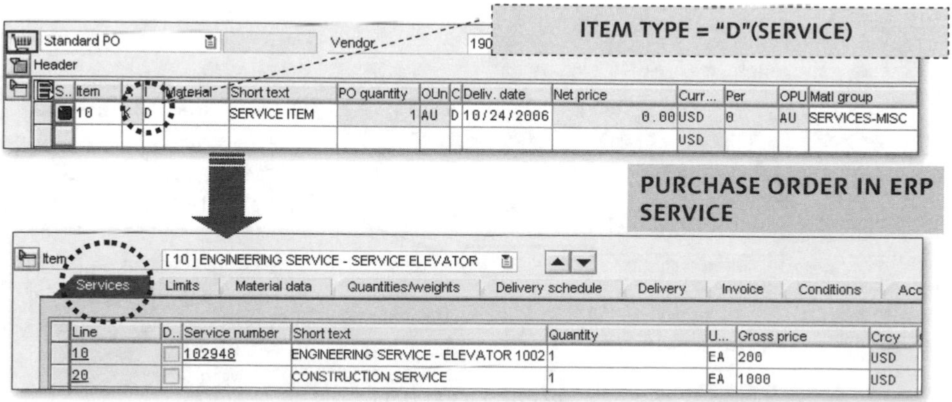

Figure 3.85 Service Purchase Order in SAP Backend

Once the PO is created, a service confirmation can be created in either the SAP back-end or in SAP SRM.

3.2.4 Confirmation and Invoice Entry

Once the service has been performed, a confirmation can be entered to record the services. Based on the original request or PO, confirmations and invoices posted for services can only be entered to the duration specified in the purchase request. At the time of confirmation, a timesheet can be maintained for capturing the detailed service documentation. The timesheet supports users when they enter a start date, start time, and end times for capturing hours worked. This time entry is not integrated in any way with the Cross Application Time Sheet (CATS) application seen in Figure 3.86.

In the next section, we'll discuss the plan-driven procurement business scenario in SAP SRM, which allows organizations to integrate demand from other supply chain systems such as Project System (PS), Plant Maintenance (PM), or demand-driven systems such as Materials Requirement Planning (MRP).

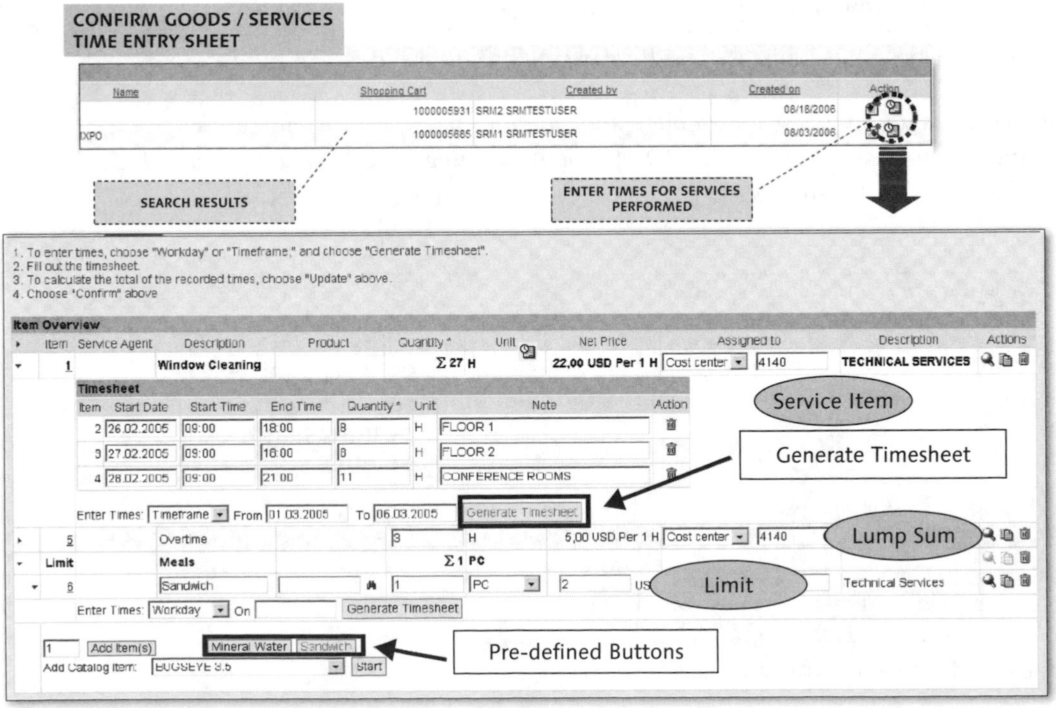

Figure 3.86 Confimation of Goods and Services — Time Entry Sheet (Figure Credit: SAP)

3.3 Plan-Driven Procurement

The plan-driven procurement business scenario integrates operational procurement with the existing SAP (SCM), plant maintenance, and SAP Project System applications. This is also sometimes referred to as *direct material procurement*. In this scenario, requirements from external systems (both SAP and non-SAP) are transferred into the SAP SRM system for sourcing and PO processing. Figure 3.87 illustrates plan-driven procurement.

Organizations have the option in customizing to define whether the requirements that are transferred from external systems are processed in the Sourcing or the Process Purchase Order application. The sourcing application provides greater value, because the transferred requirements can then either be grouped into a single PO or initiate a bid invitation when no sources of supply are suitable.

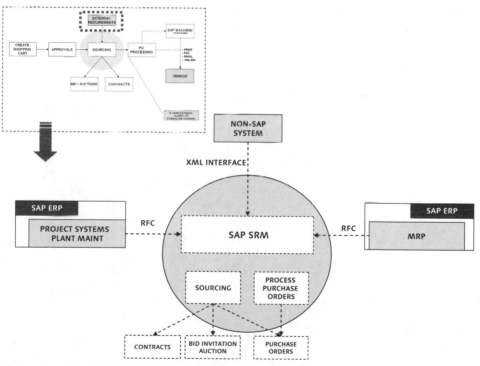

Figure 3.87 Plan-Driven Procurement — Overview

Two of the key objectives of plan-driven procurement are:

▶ Improve supplier selection and efficiency compliance
▶ Centralize purchasing and integrate with external planning systems

The standard plan-driven procurement process is illustrated in Figure 3.88. Let's walk through each of the steps illustrated in Figure 3.88 to understand the plan-driven procurement business scenario:

❶ Create a purchase requisition in the SAP ERP system from the MRP, Project System, or Plant Maintenance applications.

❷ Based on pre-defined conditions (product categories, etc.), a requisition is transferred from the SAP backend to SAP SRM.

❸ Based on configuration in SAP EB, the transferred requisition is converted into a shopping cart and is called an external requirement. The external requirements are transferred into SAP SRM as shopping carts that are preapproved. No additional approvals are possible.

❹ Based on Customizing rules within SAP SRM, the requirement is either processed in the Process Purchase Order application or in the Sourcing application. If unique sources of supply (contracts, vendor lists, etc.) exist, a PO is created automatically. Otherwise, the purchaser has to intervene and manually complete the requirement, as illustrated in Figure 3.89.

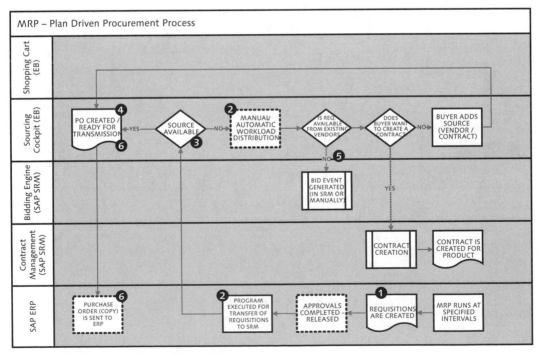

Figure 3.88 Plan-Driven Procurement

❺ The purchaser processes the requirement in SAP SRM, provided that a Source of Supply exists, or begins creating a Bid Invitation to request vendor quotes (RFQ).

❻ Once the appropriate source is assigned to the requirement, a complete PO is created in SAP SRM, an output is generated for the vendor, and a copy of the PO is transferred back to the original backend system (SAP ERP).

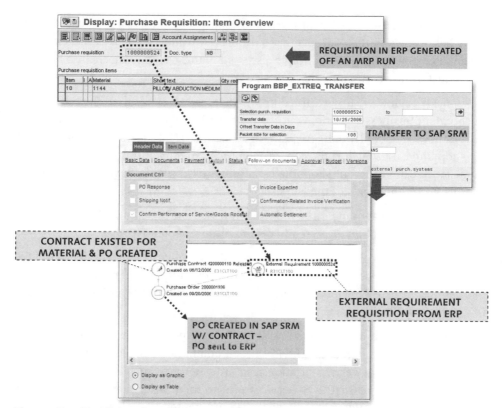

Figure 3.89 Plan-Driven Procurement — MRP requisition, PO in SAP SRM

> **Note**
>
> The PO transferred to the backend SAP system is a read-only PO; further changes to the PO are only allowed in the SAP SRM system.

After Step 6 shown in Figure 3.88, the goods receipt can be created in either SAP SRM or the SAP backend system. Once this is done, the inventory levels are automatically updated in SAP In-Store Merchandise and Inventory Management.

We have described the three business scenarios that exist within the operational-procurement business process: self-service procurement, services procurement, and plan-driven procurement. In the next section, we'll briefly discuss the new enhancements in the operational-procurement business process since SAP SRM release 5.0.

3.4 Summary

This concludes the operational procurement chapter, which was a long chapter due to the importance of the concepts that have been introduced, such as the shopping cart and PO applications. The concepts discussed in this chapter will create a baseline for the rest of the discussion within this book.

Let's quickly review what we learned in this chapter. We introduced the self-service procurement business scenario, which is the most widely used business scenario in organizations that implement SAP SRM. In Section 3.1.1, we introduced the concept of a shopping cart, which is the core of the procurement solution within SAP SRM. We discussed the different shopping cart forms that provide flexibility of deployment based on the needs of the end user.

In addition to the shopping cart, we briefly touched on the approvals functionality in SAP SRM. This will be discussed in detail within Chapter 10.

We also introduced you to the confirmation and invoice-entry functionalities in SAP SRM. We noted that user organizations have the flexibility to enter confirmations or invoices either in SAP SRM or continue to create goods receipts and invoices in the backend SAP ERP system.

In Section 3.2, we discussed the create with limit, requests, and order external services applications that target the services procurement needed within organizations. We discussed how answer organizations can order services such as temporary labor using SAP SRM and learned how services procurement integrates seamlessly with the SUS functionality, which will be discussed in Chapter 5.

In Section 3.3, we explained how organizations can integrate demand from external supply chain systems with SAP SRM. The plan-driven procurement business scenario provides the capability to integrate demand from MRP, project systems, and plant maintenance systems into the SRM system.

In Chapter 4, we will introduce the Strategic Sourcing and Contract Management capabilities of SAP SRM. You will learn about the Sourcing application, Bidding Engine, Live Auction, and the Contract applications within SAP SRM.

SAP SRM automates processes between sourcing and procurement, within the enterprise and across the supply base. It increases supply-chain visibility and gives you closed-loop insight into global spend.

4 Strategic Sourcing and Contract Management

Sourcing is the process of identifying, conducting negotiations with, and forming supply agreements with vendors of goods and services. In SAP SRM, sourcing is the core purchasing process of analyzing, qualifying, and selecting suppliers. It is also the process that enables compliance of purchasing strategies by creating contracts for goods and services that can be leveraged across the enterprise.

Sourcing has become the new buzzword now that e-procurement and SRM have become familiar terms within corporate procurement networks. However, the concept of sourcing is anything but new. Organizations that have already reaped the benefits of the process improvements of operational procurement are now getting ready to reduce costs further by focusing on their strategic sourcing processes and capabilities.

In simple terms, *strategic sourcing* is the process of identifying and qualifying suppliers who can provide the goods and services needed by the organization. It also includes the process of negotiating with suppliers using auction and bidding techniques to negotiate the best possible terms and conditions without sacrificing quality and dependability.

Contract management is the process of creating, maintaining, and monitoring contractual agreements between the buyer and supplier organizations. In SAP SRM, organizations can integrate data from request for proposals (RFP), request for quotations (RFQ), and auctions to create and update contract terms, conditions, and prices. These contracts can then be used as sources of supply to purchase goods and services.

> **Note**
>
> Each SAP SRM application provider in the marketplace focuses on highlighting their strategic sourcing and contract management capabilities.
>
> SAP provides two separate strategic sourcing applications: one in the core SAP SRM and another via the Hosted & OnPremise offering of SAP E-Sourcing. This chapter discusses the Strategic Sourcing capabilities in the Core SRM product. Chapter 18 provides a brief understanding about the SAP E-Sourcing solution.

In this chapter, we'll discuss the capabilities of SAP SRM in the areas of strategic sourcing and contract management. We've combined the sourcing and contract management capabilities of SAP SRM into a single chapter. When we talk about strategic sourcing, we should cover all aspects of the selection and negotiation processes with suppliers.

Once negotiations are complete with the supplier for the procurement of goods or services, the buying organization either enters into a contract with the supplier or just creates a one-time purchase order (PO). This chapter discusses the contract management capabilities in SAP SRM whereby contracts can be used as a valid source of supply by professional purchasers when making sourcing decisions.

4.1 Strategic Sourcing

In SAP SRM, Strategic Sourcing deals with the following aspects of supplier selection:

- Supplier screening and selection
- Source of supply determination (Sourcing)
- Request for qualification, bidding, and live auctions

4.1.1 Supplier Screening and Selection

Supplier screening and selection is simply the process of choosing the right supplier for a certain product, service, or product category. This process allows organizations to prescreen suppliers using detailed and customized screening questionnaires, allowing professional purchasers to determine whether those suppliers should be considered potential business partners.

The process of supplier screening begins when the organization invites potential suppliers to visit its external website and register as potential suppliers. A link on the organization's website can present potential suppliers with the registration process within SAP SRM. Once the supplier completes the required information and submits its information to the organization, it is sent to the designated purchasing professional for review and screening. The supplier registration process is discussed in further detail in Chapter 5.

During the screening process, the purchasing professionals can accept or deny a particular supplier. The suppliers that are accepted can then be available in the organization's supplier directory within SAP SRM. Suppliers contained in the supplier directory are not automatically available as sources within the SAP SRM applications (shopping cart, PO, etc.). These suppliers need to be transferred into the SAP SRM system using the *Transfer supplier* action if you want them available in applications such as Bid Invitation.

> **Note**
>
> The supplier directory is contained within the SAP SRM system and is not the same as the vendor master in the SAP ERP system.

The supplier-screening process is triggered by using the transaction *Pre-select Vendors*. In this transaction, professional purchasers in the organization can accept or reject suppliers that have registered. Suppliers that are accepted can be transferred to the SAP SRM system as business partners. Rejected suppliers cannot be transferred. Once the suppliers are accepted, they are added to the supplier directory, and can be accessed via one of the following applications:

- Sourcing
- Bid Invitations
- Vendor Lists
- Manage Business Partner

Figure 4.1 illustrates the supplier registration and screening process. This process is discussed in further detail in Chapter 5.

4.1.2 Source of Supply Determination (Sourcing)

In SAP SRM, the *Sourcing* application provides the professional buyers with sourcing-relevant information that enables them to select the most appropriate source of supply for an open user requirement. If multiple sources of supply are available, the buyers can compare them and select the best source.

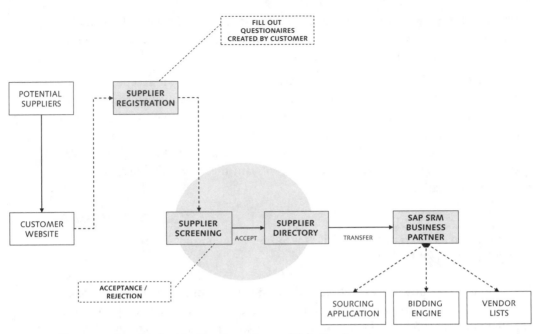

Figure 4.1 Supplier Registration, Screening, and Selection Process

According to SAP, *sourcing* is a central concept in SRM where open requirements from local or back-end systems are assigned sources of supply either in the Sourcing application or via the SAP Bidding Engine component. The resulting document (PO or contract) resides either in the local or backend system, depending on the scenario being used.

Contracts, vendor lists, and catalogs are considered approved sources of supply within the SAP SRM system. When end users have requirements to purchase goods or services, they can select from these approved sources of supply without needing intervention from the purchasing department. However, organizations can have business rules that require intervention of the purchasing department for PO creation, and these rules can be defined in Customizing.

Therefore, the source determination is sometimes done automatically by the system when an exact match is found. Alternatively, professional purchasers can use the available sourcing options to determine the best source of supply for the requirement. Figure 4.2 illustrates the sourcing relationship in operational procurement and strategic sourcing.

Organizations can choose when implementing SAP SRM whether they want their professional purchasers to use the Sourcing application or work directly in the Process Purchase Orders application.

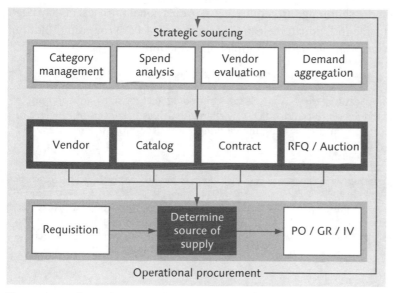

Figure 4.2 Relationship Between Sourcing and Operational Procurement when Determining Source

Reasons for Using the Sourcing Application

Because purchasing professionals can simply process shopping carts directly in the Process Purchase Order application, readers might wonder how they would benefit by adding a middle layer with the Sourcing application. Some of the key benefits of using the Sourcing application are as follows:

▶ Central repository for processing requirements from internal (e.g., shopping carts) and external systems (e.g., requirements generated via materials resource planning)

▶ Ability to access various sources of supply (e.g., the suggest sources of supply function)

▶ In SAP SRM 7.0, the operational purchaser can also use the "Replace with Catalog Item" function to convert a free-text based shopping cart line item with a corresponding item from a catalog.

▶ Capability to aggregate multiple requirements to create POs using grouping functionality (e.g., combine multiple shopping carts into a single PO)

▶ Ability to launch bid invitations and auctions directly

▶ Ability to create contracts from existing requirements

However, the sourcing application provides the capability to initiate the follow-on documents (PO, bid invitation, and contract). Once the follow-on document has been created from the shopping cart requirement, professional purchasers may need to work further in the individual SAP SRM applications of PO Processing, Bidding Engine, and Contract Management to complete the document.

Example 1

In the Sourcing application, the buyer selects a shopping cart, assigns an appropriate source, and takes the action to create a PO. Any changes such as the Terms of Payment or Purchasing Organization on the PO can only be done within the Process Purchase Order application.

Example 2

This example creates a contract from a shopping cart, when further detailed processing such as total release quantity or value on the contract can only be maintained within the Contract application. Figure 4.3 illustrates a simple flow for Sourcing and Process Purchase Order.

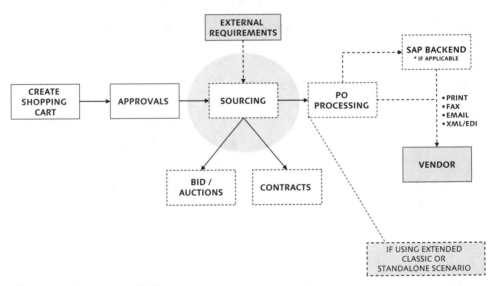

Figure 4.3 Sourcing Application

In essence, there are three key sources of supply that act as fixed sources. When a fixed source is selected in a shopping cart, the document is considered complete by the system and no buyer intervention is required for any subsequent PO processing. This is dependent on the business rules defined in Customizing (IMG). The following bullet points list the sources of supply that are considered as fixed in SAP SRM:

▶ Catalogs

▶ Contracts

▶ Vendor lists

In the SRM shopping cart, line items that require additional processing can be routed to the professional purchaser in the Sourcing application. All other line items that are complete with a fixed source or supply and price can generate a PO automatically. Alternatively, reservations can also be generated in SAP ERP for items that are subject to SAP In-Store Merchandise Inventory Management (if using the Classic or decoupled scenario). This can be controlled within Customizing.

When working in the Sourcing application, professional purchasers are provided with a *worklist* of requirements that need to be processed on a daily basis. The purchaser in SAP SRM 7.0 can choose to create predefine the worklist search criteria or search for the open requirements each time he executes the Carry Out Sourcing application.

The main goal at this point is to process the requirements available within the worklist and create one of the follow-on documents of PO, contract, bid invitation, or auction. In Figure 4.4, the Carry Out Sourcing application illustrates the options for the purchaser's worklist and the open requirements that exist for processing. In SAP SRM 7.0, a guided procedure provides the purchaser with a four-step process to Assign Sources of Supply to open requirements (shopping carts from SAP SRM or external systems like MRP).

Each shopping cart line item is individually listed in the Requisition/Item column. Therefore, a shopping cart with multiple line items could be distributed to multiple purchaser worklists and eventually result in multiple POs. The Remove button can be used by the purchaser if the requirement is no longer required. Once this is selected, the requirement is removed from the Sourcing application and can no longer be processed.

Once the purchaser wants to process one or more items in the worklist, he can simply select the requirements and click on the Create Draft button for further processing, as illustrated in Figure 4.5. The purchaser needs to make a decision to either create an RFx, Contract, Purchaser Order, or an Auction when creating a draft. If "Purchase Order" is selected, the purchaser can now enter a supplier number in the Supplier field or select the Search icon to search for a vendor in the Vendor database in SAP SRM. Once the vendor and price information has been entered and no further changes are required, the purchaser can review the draft and confirm the creation of the PO or another document such as RFx, Auction, or Contract.

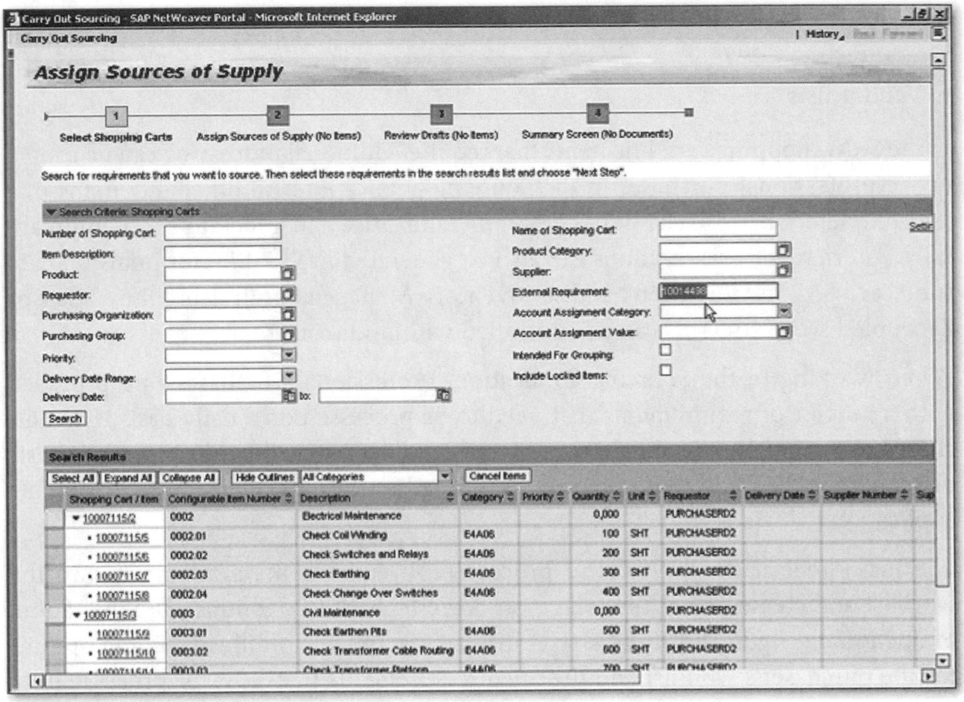

Figure 4.4 Sourcing Worklist (Figure Credit: SAP)

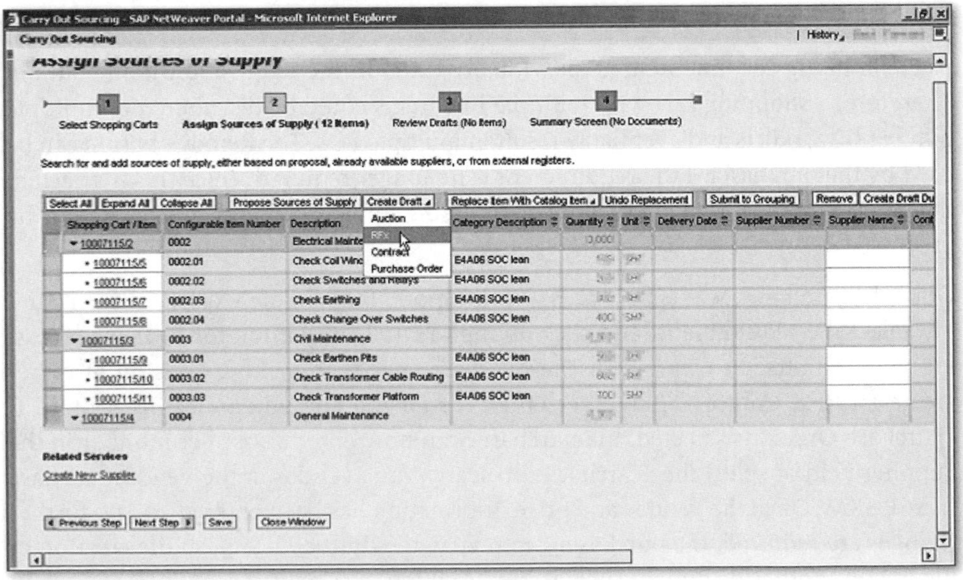

Figure 4.5 Assign Sources of Supply in the Sourcing Application (Figure Credit: SAP)

In the work area, the professional purchasers can select one of the many actions to process the requirement further. The following bullets explain each of the Action buttons:

▶ **Propose Sources of Supply**

Purchasers can search for negotiated sources of supply using the Propose Source of Supply button in the Sourcing application. The SAP SRM system will propose any existing sources of supply and the buyer can assign a source to an open item. These sources will be from one of the following: contract items, vendor lists, or manual selection of a vendor at the buyer's discretion. If multiple sources of supply are available, the purchaser can compare them and select the best source. This can be seen in Figure 4.6.

▶ **Create Purchase Order**

Once the buyer has assigned an appropriate source of supply or price to the open requirement item, a PO can be created. The purchaser can create an incomplete PO by leaving either the Vendor or Gross Price field blank and then clicking the Create Purchase Order button. This is required when the purchaser knows that additional information needs to be changed in the PO, such as terms of payment or maybe the purchasing organization. These fields are not available in the shopping cart and can only be changed in the PO.

▶ **Submit to Grouping**

The Submit to Grouping button allows multiple shopping carts or line items to be grouped into a single PO. Organizations that use the plan-driven procurement scenario to integrate the MRP requirements from SAP ERP into SAP SRM can also use the grouping functionality to automatically combine the multiple requisitions created from MRP.

▶ **Create Bid Invitation**

When an appropriate source of supply is not available for requirement(s), professional purchasers can create a bid invitation for the selected requirements directly from within the Sourcing application by clicking on the Create Bid Invitation button. Once the bid invitation is created, it can be further processed in the Bidding Engine application to enhance or send to selected suppliers.

▶ **Create Contract**

A buyer has the ability to create a contract instead of a PO via the Sourcing application and do so by clicking the Create Contract button.

▶ **Create Auction**

When an appropriate source of supply is not available for requirements, a professional purchaser can create a bid invitation for the selected requirements or Alternatively can create an auction event by clicking on the Create Auction button (see Figure 4.8).

► **Hold**

This button allows the buyer to Hold the requirement in the work area to process later. Requirements that are held will also appear in the worklist of the other members of the same purchasing group.

► **Remove**

This button allows the purchaser to remove the requirement from his work area so other buyers can process if required or work on the requirement at a later time. For example, let's say that while processing a requirement, the purchaser needed to discuss the delivery information with the requisitioner. If the requisitioner is unavailable, the purchaser can remove the requirement from the work area to process at a later time.

In the Sourcing application, based on authorizations, professional purchasers can change the product, quantity, desired delivery date, goods recipient, or account assignment information on the shopping cart line item. This can be done by clicking on the document number in the Requirement column. For example, the purchaser can make changes to the any of the shopping cart line items listed in Figure 4.5 prior to creating a draft document. All changes are noted in the Change History field of the shopping cart. No approval workflows are started for changes made to requirements in the Sourcing application.

Finding Requirements to Process

In the Sourcing application, professional purchasers can also process requirements for which they are not typically responsible. This could be a scenario when another buyer is not available or is on leave. The *Find* tab in the Sourcing application allows buyers to search for requirements using a variety of criteria, as illustrated in Figure 4.6. For example, the purchaser could search by the Number of Shopping Cart and search for external requirements from a planning system by entering the requirement number in the Ext. requirement field.

All the requirements available in the Sourcing application are already approved, as illustrated in Figure 4.7. No further approval processes are triggered within Sourcing. Once the follow-on document (e.g., a PO) is created, additional approval workflows may apply.

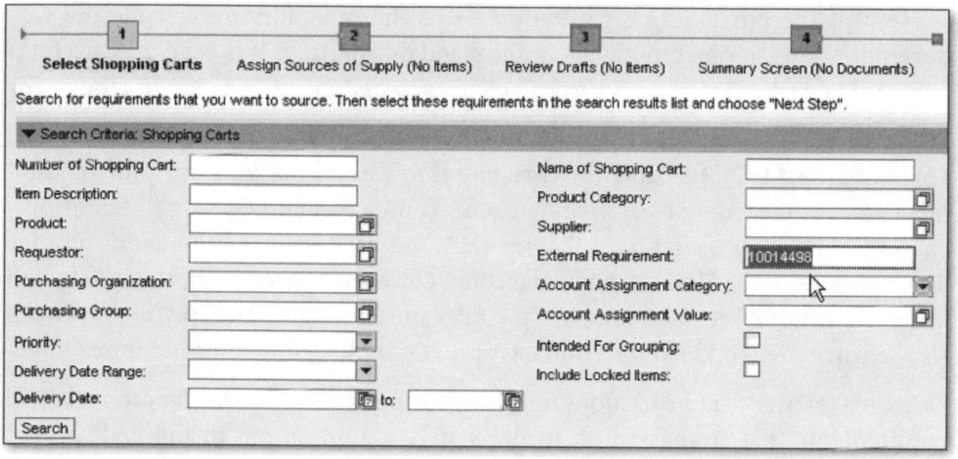

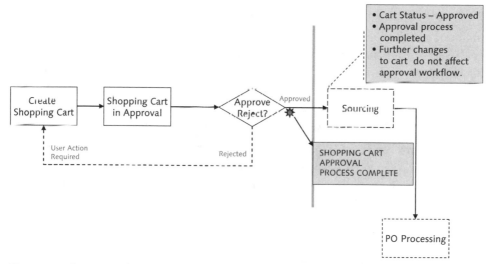

Figure 4.6 Searching for Requirements in Sourcing Application

- Cart Status – Approved
- Approval process completed
- Further changes to cart do not affect approval workflow.

Create Shopping Cart → Shopping Cart in Approval → Approve Reject? — Approved → Sourcing

User Action Required

Rejected

SHOPPING CART APPROVAL PROCESS COMPLETE

PO Processing

Figure 4.7 Preapproved Requirements in Sourcing Application

The Sourcing application supports all of the implementation scenarios for SAP SRM (Classic, Extended Classic, or Standalone).

Workload Distribution (Reassignment of Workload)

From the SAP SRM 4.0 release, a new functionality has been introduced to assist with the reassignment of purchaser workload. This process allows purchasing managers to distribute the workload of documents among purchasers. This functionality is useful if the purchasing organization needs the capability to override the way documents are allocated to buyers in the standard solution. It is especially useful if a buyer is overburdened or is unavailable to process documents due to absence or other circumstances.

This functionality is available for changing the responsible purchaser for requirements (shopping carts or external demand), contracts, and POs to a different purchasing group. For example, in Figure 4.11, we have selected the check box for Requirements in the Find Documents section. Once we click on Start, the system will provide a list of all requirements for the relevant Purchasing Group. The buyer can also redistribute workload for Contracts and POs by selecting the check box.

Based on roles and authorizations in SAP SRM, purchasing managers can access all requirements that are passed on to the Sourcing application. In the Redistribute Workload application, purchasing managers have the ability to distribute requirements to the other buyers. This lets them control and allocate requirements based on the workload or the availability of buyers in their organizations.

In the standard solution, shopping cart requirements are sent to the responsible buyers based on the product commodities that the purchasing groups are responsible for. In other words, if there are five buyers and each is responsible for a particular product category (such as office supplies, lab suppliers, or construction), then in Customizing, organizations can assign these product categories to responsible buyers and those requirements are displayed in their buyers' worklists.

If the standard product category based solution does not work and organizations want to build their own business rules to distribute the work effort for processing requirements, they can use the Redistribute Workload application. Documents can be distributed via the following methods:

- **Manual Assignment**
  Purchasing managers can manually reassign the documents by accessing the Redistribute Workload application.

- **Automatic Assignment**
  Based on business rules defined by the organization, documents can be automatically assigned to another purchasing group. This can be done using BAdI: BBP_PGRP_ASSIGN_BADI.

In the Redistribute Workload application, the purchasing manager can select from a variety of criteria and then select one or more documents that need to be redistributed from one purchasing group assignment to another. The results list displays any document that might already be undergoing processing by the responsible buyers.

Once the manager selects one or more documents to reassign, he can choose the new purchasing group from a drop down selection and click the Start Manual Assignment function to reassign the documents (as illustrated in Figure 4.8).

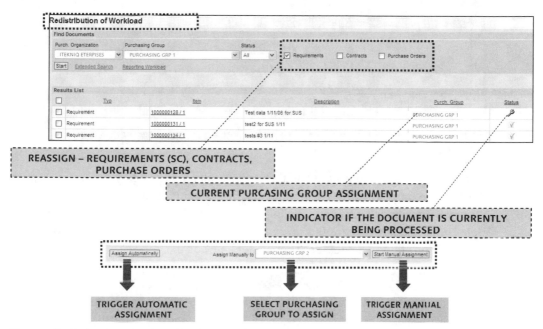

Figure 4.8 Redistribution of Workload (Screenshot from SAP SRM 5.0)

In Figure 4.8, there are three shopping carts in the Results List of the Redistribution of Workload application. The Purchasing Group column shows the current purchasing group assigned to these shopping carts, which is PURCHASING GRP 1. To reassign these shopping carts to another buyer, follow these steps:

1. Select one or more requirements in the results list.

2. Select a new purchasing group in the Assign Manually to dropdown menu. In our example, this is PURCHASING GRP 2.

3. Click on the Start Manual Assignment button to manually assign the new purchasing group or click the Assign Automatically button to trigger automatic assignment based on predefined business rules.

Once this is done, the system provides a confirmation screen indicating whether the reassignment was successful. These documents are then automatically available for processing in the worklist of the new buyer.

In the standard solution, an organization can determine in Customizing when Sourcing is triggered for a shopping cart line item. Figure 4.9 illustrates these options.

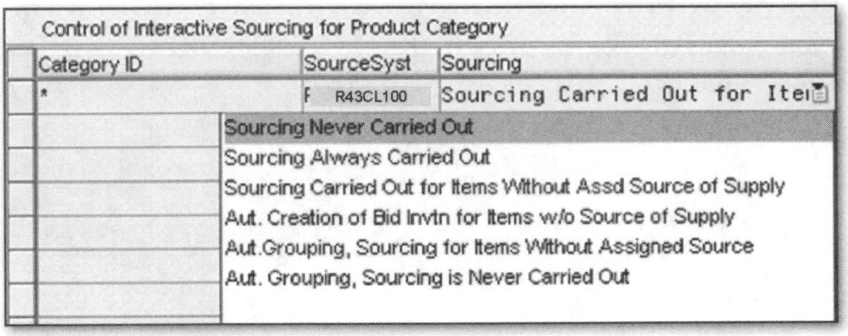

Figure 4.9 Control of Interactive Sourcing

However, this selection is based on the product category (Category ID, seen in Figure 4.12) of the shopping cart, which might not be a suitable criterion for determination. Organizations find themselves needing to determine business rules that can apply to determine whether a shopping cart is routed to the Sourcing application for buyer intervention. Table 4.1 provides some guidelines for this process.

Shopping Cart line item	Buyer Intervention in Sourcing
No fixed vendor in shopping cart	Yes
No price in shopping cart	Yes
Shopping cart for material reservations	No
High-dollar-value shopping carts	Yes (for reviewing source and any sole-source justifications)
Capital goods and leases	Yes
Replenishment of stock materials	No (if contract or vendor list exists)

Table 4.1 Guidelines for Developing Business Rules for Buyer Intervention (Sourcing)

Now that you understand the need for using the Sourcing application and are familiar with the different functions in Sourcing, we'll discuss the request for qualification (RFQ) and bidding capabilities within SAP SRM.

4.1.3 RFQ and Bidding

The SAP Bidding Engine sits at the heart of the strategic-sourcing solution within SAP SRM and facilitates the RFQ and bidding processes between the organization and the vendor. Purchasing professionals use the SAP Bidding Engine to create and process RFQs and bids for products and services. Contact persons (bidders) at the vendor organization in turn use the SAP Bidding Engine to submit bids in response to these bid invitations.

The RFQ and bidding functionality in SAP SRM helps the purchasing professional negotiate the best possible prices, terms, and conditions with vendors.

To understand the bidding process, it is important to distinguish between the following two key terms:

▶ **Bid Invitation**
RFQ is typically the request that a customer sends out to one or many vendors, inviting them to provide a quotation for a set of goods or services. The difference between the RFQ and request for information (RFI) is that the RFQ requires a price, while the RFI does not require any prices on the response from the vendors.

▶ **Bid**
Also known as a quote, this is typically the response from the vendor based on the requirements outlined in the RFQ. Vendors who receive bid invitations can log on to the SAP SRM system and enter their bids against the product and service requirements outlined in the bid invitations.

In SAP SRM, professional purchasers initiate Bid Invitations from multiple different SAP SRM applications: Sourcing, Contract Management, and Bidding Engine, as illustrated in Figure 4.10.

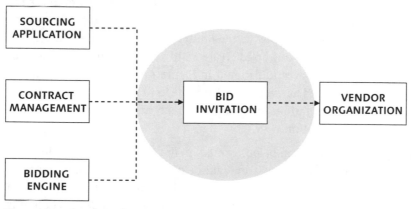

Figure 4.10 Creating a Bid Invitation

Figure 4.11 illustrates the same concept as Figure 4.13 but provides additional information regarding the processes that lead up to the creation of a bid invitation. For example, in the Sourcing application, a bid invitation can be created to source shopping carts that have gone thru the approval process. However, in the Bidding Engine application, a bid invitation can be created manually or using predefined templates. Let's discuss each of these three options in further detail.

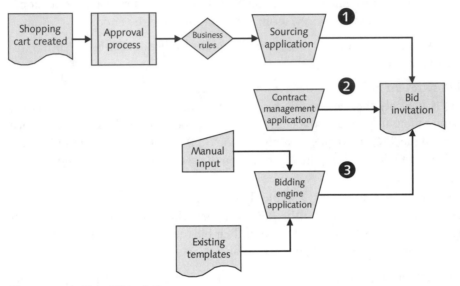

Figure 4.11 Initiate Bid Invitation

Via the Sourcing Application

Using SAP Bidding Engine, buyers can create a bid invitation directly from the *Sourcing application*. This will be especially useful if there is an open requirement and the buyers need to find a source of supply. In the Sourcing application, the buyer will click on the Create Bid Invitation button to create a Bid Event for any item that is in the Sourcing application work area (illustrated in Figure 4.12). All data relevant to the bid invitation will be copied automatically from the item in the Sourcing application to the item in the bid invitation. Any additional texts and attachments will also be transferred to the bid invitation.

At this point, no further activity can be performed on the shopping cart line items in the Sourcing application. Further processing will be handled in the Bidding Engine. Buyers will not be able to add any items to the bid invitation that have not been carried over automatically from the Sourcing application. Before a Bid Invitation is published, additional information, such as a submission deadline and chosen suppliers, have to be added in the Bidding Engine.

Any follow-on functions to either create a PO or contract will be performed from within the Bidding Engine application.

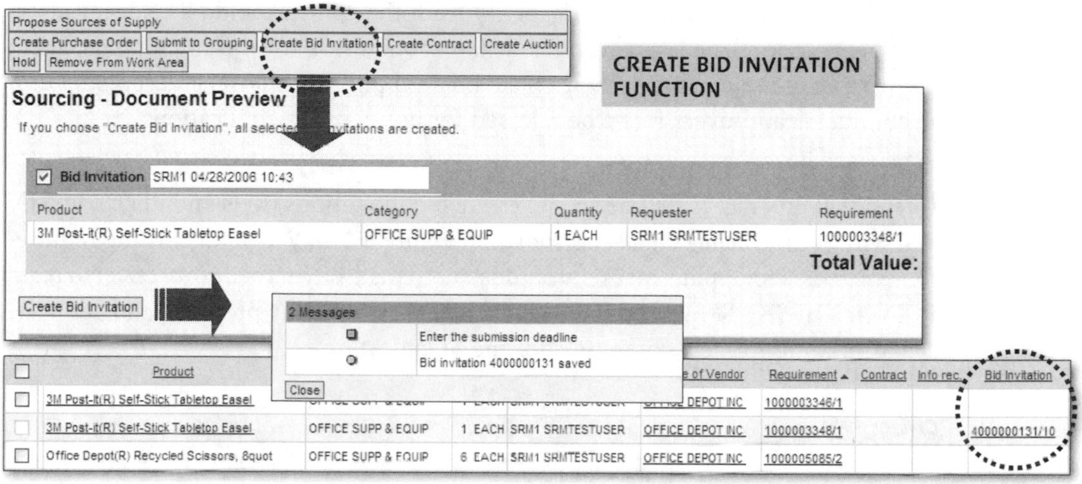

Figure 4.12 Create Bid Invitation via the Sourcing Application (Figure Credit: SAP)

Via the Contract Management Application

Buyers can monitor contracts that are about to expire and can subsequently create a bidding event directly from the contract management application to renegotiate expiring contracts (illustrated in Figure 4.13). In releases prior to SAP SRM 4.0, this was termed the *Create Bid Invitation*; it is now called *Negotiate*.

Figure 4.13 Negotiate Contracts (Screenshot from SAP SRM 5.0)

The bid invitation is created automatically from the contract and all relevant information is autopopulated in it. Vendors will respond using the Bidding Engine, and a new version of the contract will be created if a supplier's proposal is accepted. Once the contract is approved, it can be released for use in other applications.

Via the Bidding Engine

Professional purchasers will be able to create bid invitations (RFIs and RFQs) directly from within the *Bidding Engine* (as shown in Figure 4.14). When an existing requirement such as a shopping cart request does not exist, buyers will proactively create Bid Events in SAP SRM to initiate strategic negotiations for products and services, such as bidding for new computers for the organization.

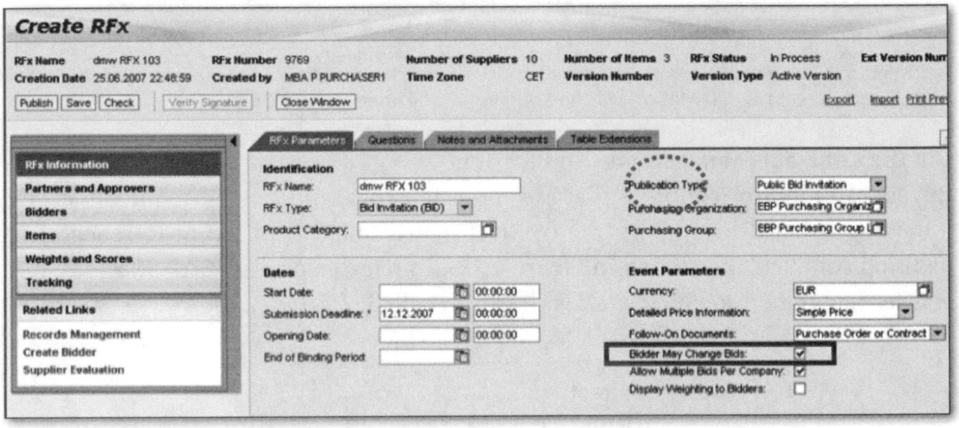

Figure 4.14 Create Bid Invitations Directly (Figure Credit: SAP)

In the Bidding Engine application, a bid invitation can be created in the following two ways:

▶ **Using Templates**
This will help professional purchasers process recurring transactions more quickly and efficiently. In the Create Bid Invitation section, the purchaser can use the Create Template button to create a bid invitation template.

▶ **Manually**
Professional purchasers can initiate the RFQ process by creating a bid invitation manually in the Bidding Engine. As illustrated in Figure 4.17, the purchaser can select the type of bid from the dropdown menu and then click the Create button to create a new Bid Invitation, invite appropriate bidders, add products or services and free form requirements. Purchasers also can add attachments and notes relevant for the bid response.

4.1.4 The Bidding Engine — Bid Invitation in Detail

So far, you have learned that a bid invitation can be initiated from multiple different applications in SAP SRM. In this section, we will discuss the Bidding Engine application in detail.

The bidding process in SAP SRM is initiated with the creation of a complete bid invitation. Using the Bidding Engine, suppliers are invited to submit their proposals as *bids*. Once their proposals have been submitted, buyers can compare and evaluate the proposals and accept the best bid or bids, which eventually result in a follow-on document such as a *contract* or a *PO*. Figure 4.15 illustrates the bidding process and the bullets after the figure explain each step in the process in greater detail.

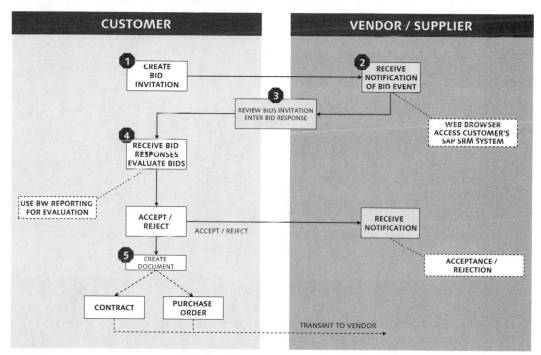

Figure 4.15 Bid Invitation and Bid Process (Figure Credit: SAP)

▶ In Step 1, we begin by creating a bid invitation. In the bid invitation, the buyer enters relevant information about the bid and selects the suppliers that need to be invited for the bid. Additionally, they select the type of bid to be created. In SAP SRM, the following two types of Bid Invitations are supported:

▶ **Restricted Bid Invitations**
Restricted Bid Invitations are qualified, predetermined suppliers that are active in the SAP Vendor Master and should have been replicated in SAP SRM.

▶ **Public Bid Invitations**
Public Bid Invitations are potential bidders that are not in the SAP Vendor Master and are invited to bid on requirements at the discretion of the professional purchasers creating the bid invitation. The bid invitation is published on SAP marketplace bulletin boards.

▶ In Step 2 in Figure 4.15, the supplier(s) RECEIVE NOTIFICATION OF the BID INVITATION via email which includes a link to the bid invitation in SAP SRM (note: the Vendor Master in SAP SRM needs to contain supplier information including email addresses). An organization may have to customize the information in this email because the standard email content might not be sufficient. Figure 4.16 shows a restricted or private bidding option.

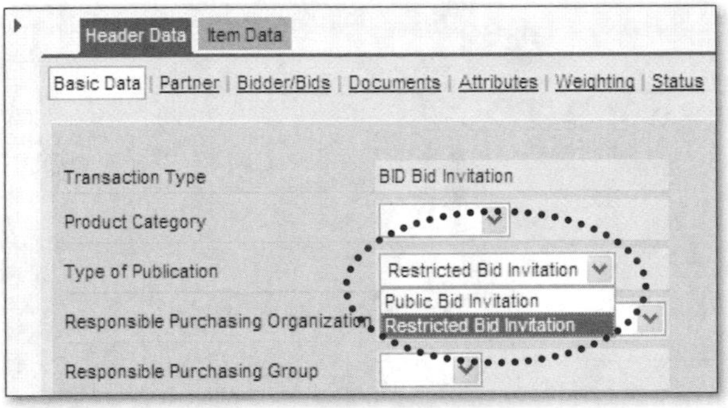

Figure 4.16 Restricted or Private Bidding (Screenshot from SAP SRM 5.0)

> **Note**
> In SAP SRM 7.0, a new functionality has been added around the confirmation of the Bidder's participation in an RFx. When the bidders receive a notification of a new bid event, they can indicate their intent to participate (select one of three actions: Participate, Do Not Participate, or Tentative). The purchasing organization has a better view of which bidders are going to participate and decide whether they want to include new participants or make changes to the bid event overall.

▶ In Step 3, the bidder or a contact person at the vendor organization logs on to the Bidding Engine application in SAP SRM to review the bid invitation (as shown in Figure 4.17). He is able to enter some of the following information on the bid response:

- Details on price and conditions, such as price scales
- Changes to quantity
- Vendor text and comments. The bidder can attach documents at Header Data and Item Data levels of the bid.
- Information on any customized attributes in the bid invitation; for example, if the bid invitation contains an attribute of color. The vendor can provide information that is relevant to the attribute.
- Create additional line items, if this option has been allowed in the bid invitation.

> **Note**
>
> In SAP SRM 7.0, a new functionality has been added for bidders to a propose response modification (expressive bidding) for items presented in the bid. This functionality provides a greater degree of flexibility to the bidders. Purchasing organizations can choose to allow the bidders to propose modifications to specific line items in the bid. Options include:
>
> - Bidder can propose an alternate item
> - Substitute an item if bidder cannot provide original item
> - Supplement item, if a bidder wants to propose an additional item
>
> Also, a new functionality is where bidding suppliers can Withdraw from a bid that they might have submitted. In this event, the purchaser can obviously not award a bid that may have been withdrawn by the supplier. This is useful especially when the purchasing company makes changes to the bid event in the middle of the process, and the supplier can no longer provide the goods/service in accordance with the new changes. Figure 4.17 also illustrates the new capabilities of Participation and Withdraw.

- In Step 4 in Figure 4.15, the strategic purchasers in SAP SRM receive all the bid responses from the vendors with relevant information. By using evaluation tools in the Bidding Engine or the SAP NetWeaver Business Warehouse (SAP NetWeaver BW) component, purchasers can compare all the bids before deciding on the best supplier. Figure 4.18 illustrates the comparison of a bid submitted by two vendors. VENDOR1 has submitted his bid at a price of 20.00, and VENDOR2 has submitted the price of 23.00. The system evaluates each criterion in the bid and automatically suggests the winning Valuation Score in green and others in red. Figure 4.18 shows an example of a simple bid comparison using VENDOR1 and VENDOR2 and the more complex bid comparison on the right between C.E.B Berlin and BIDDERCOMP1. We'll discuss the bid evaluation capabilities in SAP SRM in detail in the next section.

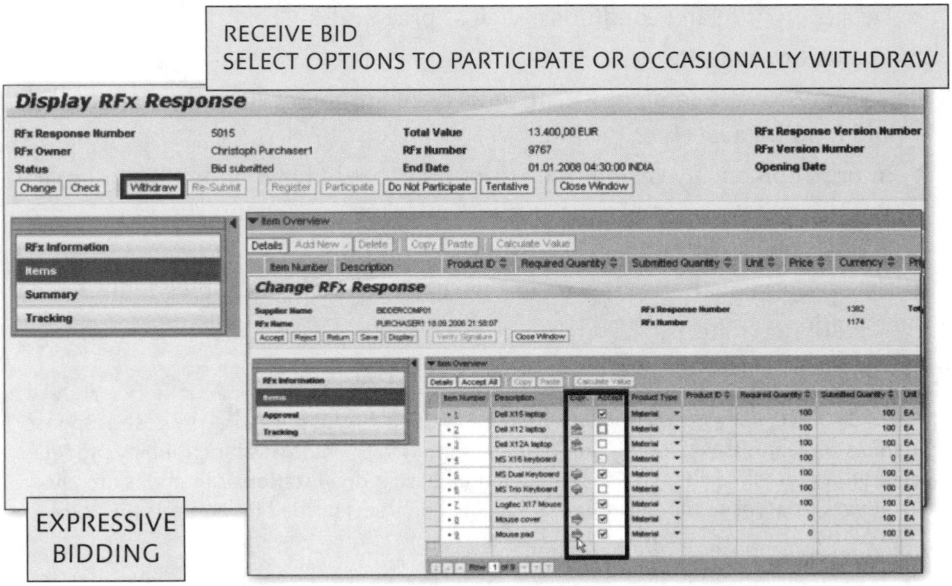

Figure 4.17 Bid Invitation Accessed by Supplier Contact (Figure Credit: SAP)

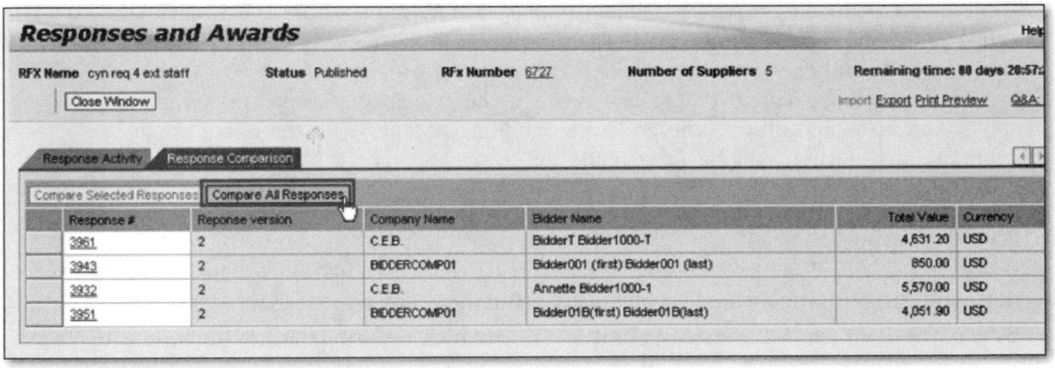

Figure 4.18 Bid Evaluation (Figure Credit: SAP)

▶ In Step 5, once the bid evaluation is complete and a bid is awarded to a supplier(s), the strategic purchaser can create a CONTRACT or PURCHASE ORDER document and transmit to the vendor.

4.1.5 Bid Evaluation in Detail

In the Bidding Engine, strategic purchasers can use the tools described in the following subsections to evaluate bids submitted by vendors.

Weighting and Ranking

In the Bidding Engine, organizations can use the *Weighting and Ranking* functions to evaluate and compare different bids that are submitted in response to a bid invitation. They can perform these evaluations at Attribute and Field, Item, Outline, and Bid levels, a fact that provides flexibility in prioritizing the items and attributes in the bid invitation.

At the time of creating a bid invitation, the buyers decide whether to use the Weighting and Ranking function. It cannot be used subsequently to analyze the bids in terms of their scores. By using the Weighting and Ranking function, buyers will be able to weigh attributes or standard fields according to how important they are for the requirements, using a weighing factor. Figure 4.19 illustrates the process steps in creating attributes. Weighting is assigned and then used when evaluating bids.

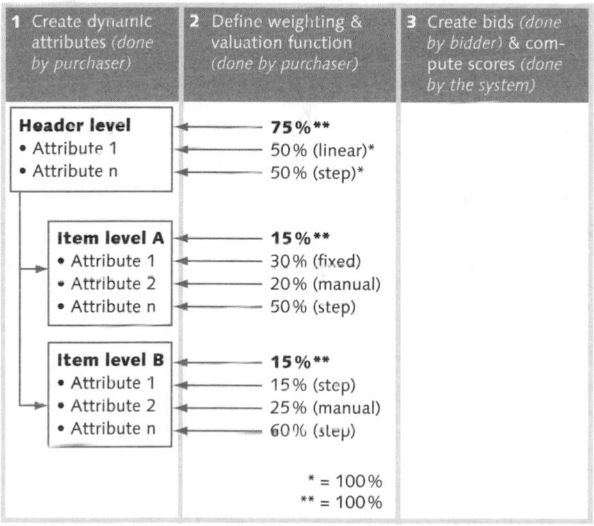

1 Create dynamic attributes *(done by purchaser)*	2 Define weighting & valuation function *(done by purchaser)*	3 Create bids *(done by bidder)* & compute scores *(done by the system)*
Header level • Attribute 1 • Attribute n	**75%**** 50% (linear)* 50% (step)*	
Item level A • Attribute 1 • Attribute 2 • Attribute n	**15%**** 30% (fixed) 20% (manual) 50% (step)	
Item level B • Attribute 1 • Attribute 2 • Attribute n	**15%**** 15% (step) 25% (manual) 60% (step)	
	* = 100% ** = 100%	

Figure 4.19 Dynamic Attributes — Concept

For example, weighting and ranking is useful if the delivery time is more important than the actual price of the item. In our example, we describe the weighting on standard fields of delivery date and price. However, dynamic attributes can be defined in the bid invitation and then analyzed based on the weighting and ranking. Dynamic attributes are specific characteristics of products and services that can be incorporated into the bidding process in the Bidding Engine. They customize bid invitations and appear as additional fields requesting specific information. These attributes can be created and used for a specific bid invitation or made available to all bid invitations.

In addition to the Weighting and Ranking function, the following four functions can be used to calculate valuation factors (illustrated in Figure 4.20):

▶ **Linear**

The Linear function is especially suitable for amount fields. The parameters of this function are minimum and maximum attribute values together with minimum and maximum function values. If a bidder enters a value that is outside of the defined range, the minimum or maximum value is taken as the score value.

▶ **Step**

The Step function is especially suitable for information items such as delivery dates. When you are entering the intervals, you must ensure that the new interval begins where the previous one ends, for example, 1 to 9 and 10 to 19.

▶ **Fixed**

The Fixed function is especially suitable for attributes with determined fixed values. If fixed values are defined for an attribute, the score values can be assigned to particular fixed values, such as the color of a product.

▶ **Manual**

The Manual function is especially suitable for text fields with no fixed values. In this case, the purchaser will manually evaluate the contents of the fields in the bid document once received from the bidder.

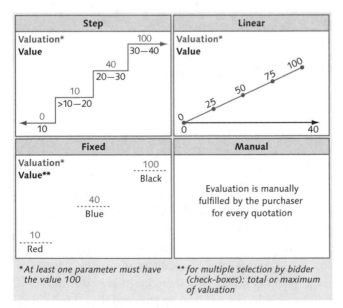

Figure 4.20 Bid Evaluation Factors

Downloading Bids to Excel

Purchasers can use the Download button to download bids to their desktops for comparison and evaluation using Microsoft® Excel®.

Using Reports in SAP NetWeaver BW

SAP NetWeaver BW is the reporting tool in SAP. The following reports are examples of analytics available in SAP NetWeaver BW that enhance a purchaser's ability to evaluate the bids received and determine a winner.

▶ Bidder history

▶ Vendor evaluation

▶ Price comparison list

▶ Detailed bid comparisons with attributes

Chapter 15 explains in detail the capabilities of SAP NetWeaver BW as it relates to SAP SRM.

4.1.6   Live Auction

The *Live Auction* functionality in SAP SRM is an integral part of the SAP Bidding engine and replaces the previous functionality of reverse auction. It is implemented as a part of the SAP SRM strategic sourcing business scenario. In a typical auction, the buying organization creates an auction event for one or more products and services that it wants to purchase. Multiple suppliers bid for the products and services, and depending on the nature of the auction (English, Dutch, or other), the winner is determined.

Most organizations use multiple criteria, not just cost alone, to select suppliers. The criteria could include quality of delivery, financial stability, supplier capabilities, and of course, total cost. Auctions foster competition among suppliers, as opposed to simply aggregating demand and then selecting the appropriate supplier.

Organizations have been able to gain huge savings by executing auctions. For example, in a success story published by SAP, SEA Containers Ltd., a logistics service provider, leveraged the auction capabilities in SAP SRM to generate savings of €1.4 million.

It is common for readers to question the core difference between the bid- invitation process of RFI and RFQs (discussed in Section 4.1.3, RFQ and Bidding) and the auction process, which also uses bid invitations. Figure 4.21 illustrates at a high level the difference between bid invitations and live auctions.

BID INVITATION	LIVE AUCTION
RFI & RFQ INVITATIONS INCLUDING PRICE AND NON-PRICE VARIABLES	BIDDING IS BASED ON PRICE ONLY EVALUATION CAN BE W/ OTHER VARIABLES
LONGER RESPONSE TIME FOR BIDDING VENDORS – DAYS TO WEEKS	TYPICALLY A SHORTER TIME-FRAME FOR BIDDING – HOURS TO DAYS
BIDDER'S ARE NOT ABLE TO SEE ANY INFORMATION ON COMPETITOR BIDS	RANK, BEST BID, AND NEXT BID CAN IS AVAILABLE IN REAL-TIME FOR BIDDERS
WELL SUITED FOR A LARGE VARIETY OF GOODS AND SERVICES, INCLUDING RAW MATERIALS, SERVICES, AND PROJECTS	WELL SUITED FOR COMMODITIES, OR GOODS AND SERVICES WITH STANDARDIZED ATTRIBUTES THAT VARY ONLY SLIGHTLY FROM ONE SUPPLIER TO ANOTHER SUPPLIER
TYPICALLY SOURCING IS BASED ON VALUE PROPOSITIONS (E.G. HIGH QUALITY, DELIVERY TIME) INSTEAD OF JUST PRICE	MARKET DYNAMICS OF AUCTION WORKS BEST WHEN THE BUYER / SUPPLIER RELATIONSHIP IS LOOSELY-COUPLED

Source: SAP America

Figure 4.21 High-level Difference Between Bid Invitation and Live Auction

Strategic purchasers can use the Bidding Engine to create live auctions for products and services. Alternatively, auctions can also be initiated from either of the following sources (as illustrated in Figure 4.22):

▶ **Via the Sourcing Application**
Shopping carts and external demand in the Sourcing application can be directly converted into an auction event. It is important to note that auctions created from the Sourcing application do not allow adding additional items.

▶ **Convert a Bid Invitation**
If a bid invitation has already been created or submitted, it can be converted into an auction as well for further processing.

▶ **Manually in the Bidding Engine**
Manually in the Bidding Engine can be done when there is no existing requirement and the strategic purchaser wants to initiate a strategic bid event. In this scenario, the resulting PO from the auction can only be saved locally.

SAP SRM delivers standard predefined auction profiles for organizations to use. These profiles use auction best practices and are listed as follows:

▶ **English Auction**
There is one simple rule: The lowest bidder wins the auction.

▶ **Rank-only Auction**

A bidder can only bid lower than his last bid. The lowest bid from all suppliers ranks on top.

▶ **Blind-bidding Auction**

Same as rank-only auction, but a bidder's rank is only displayed when that bidder is ranked first.

▶ **Company Best-bid Auction**

Bids are validated against the best bid submitted so far by bidders from the same company.

> **Note**
>
> In SAP SRM 7.0, SAP has provided a new auction type called Dutch auction. In a Dutch auction, the price for the item on auction starts low and then goes up every "X" -time increment. If no one accepts the item within initial price, then the price increases and continues to increase every "X" time defined. The first bidder to raise his hand wins the auction. A purchasing organization can define a ceiling price as an option as well so there is a limit to the increase in the price of the auction.

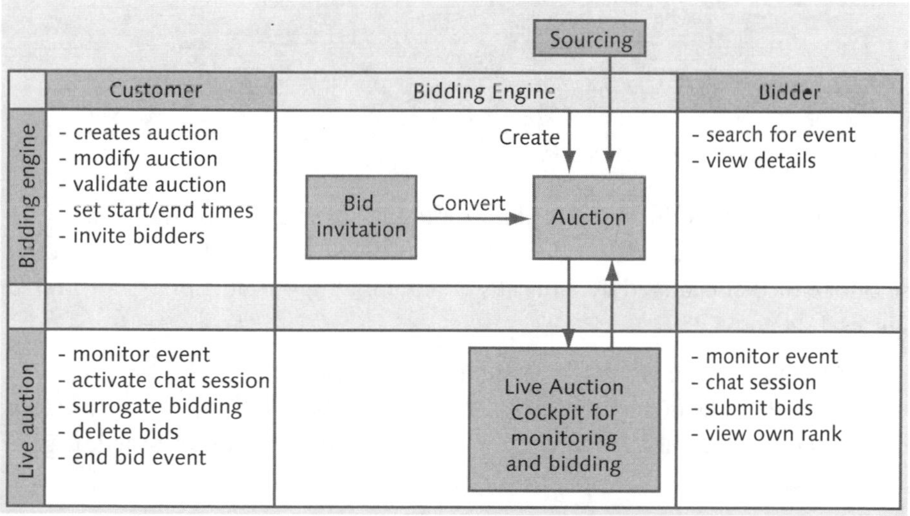

Figure 4.22 Creating an Auction

An organization can select an auction profile based on the type of auction being conducted, along with the supplier community being invited. For example, an English auction is the opposite of the bidding event experienced on sites such as eBay®, where the highest bidder wins. In the English auction, the lowest bidder wins, because the aim of the organization is to find the cheapest source for the product or service. Figure 4.23 illustrates the difference between these auction profiles.

Profile type	Definition	Bidder sees (selection)	Bidder can't see (selection)
English	Basic reverse auction, bids validated against overal best bid, that is, the lowest bid ranks first	Rank Best bid Next bid Bid price No. of bidders	Bidder name Company best bid Company name First place
Rank-only	Bidder can submit a bid as long as it is lower than his own last bid, but it will not be ranked as first unless it is lower than all other bids.	Rank No. of bidders	Best bid First place Next bid Bid price
Blind bidding	Same as rank-only auction, excepted that a bidder's rank is only displayed when that bidder is ranked first.	First place	Best bid Rank Next bid Bid price
Company best bid	Bids are validated against the best bid submitted so far by bidders from the same company	Rank Rank in company Best bid Company best bid Bid price	First place Company name

Predefined profile types are delivered with SAP SRM.

Figure 4.23 Predefined Auction Profiles

An organization can modify the auction profile in Customizing to change the validation rules and the information displayed to vendors during the auction process. These can be further changed dynamically when initiating the auction, as illustrated in Figures 4.24 and 4.25.

The interface for auction creation is similar to the Bidding Engine. Figure 4.25 illustrates the Basic Data section within the Header Data tab of the auction. An organization can select the type of auction to be created using the Transaction Type dropdown menu.

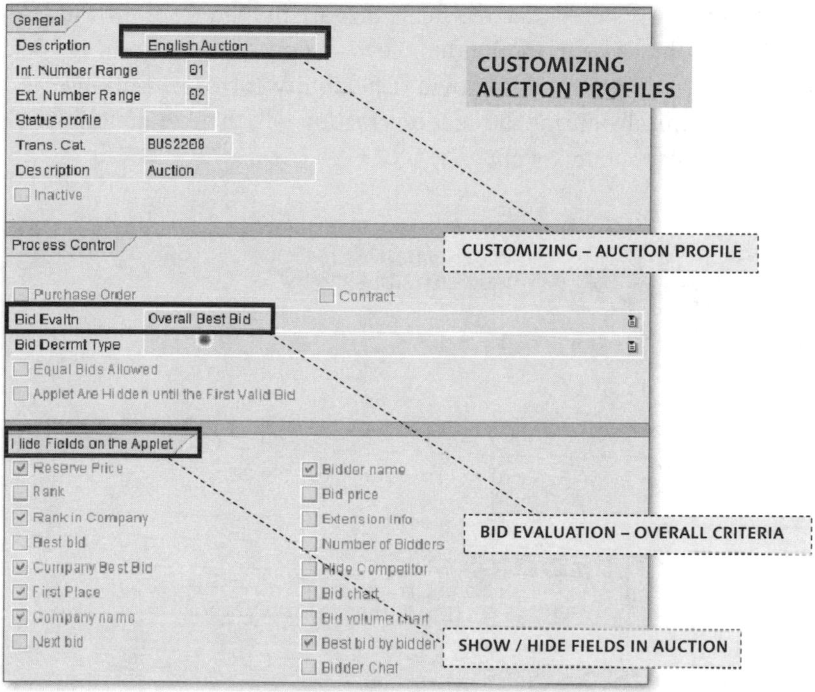

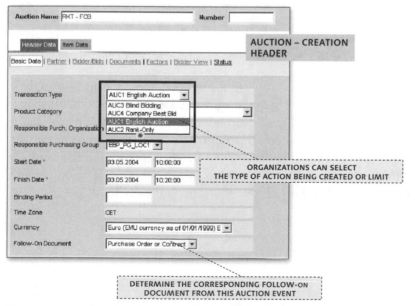

Figure 4.24 Customizing Auction Profiles

Figure 4.25 Auction Creation — Header (Screenshot from SAP SRM 5.0)

The strategic purchaser can also redefine the fields that are hidden from the bidders in the auction. This can be done in the Bidder View section of the auction header (shown in Figures 4.26 and 4.27). This provides flexibility for organizations that want to determine dynamically during the auction creation whether certain information is valid for a particular auction event.

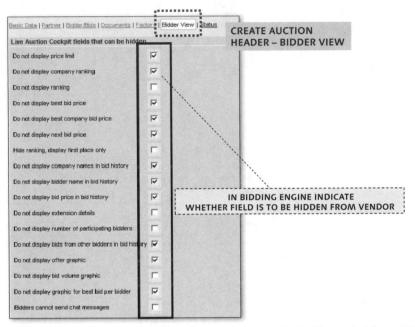

Figure 4.26 Bidder-View — Hide and Un-Hide Auction Fields (Screenshot from SAP SRM 5.0)

Similar to the dynamic attributes available in the bid invitation, the auction application contains *factored-cost* bidding. These allow for considering factors other than just the lowest price, such as the quality of the product or service or past performance of the supplier or vendor. In addition, organizations can assign bidding advantage or disadvantage to specific bidders while defining factors. The definition of factors is available at both the Header and Line-item levels of the bid event (auction). Figure 4.28 illustrates the factored-cost concept provided by SAP within SAP SRM.

1. INFORMATION SUCH AS *BEST BID* AND *NEXT BID* IS HIDDEN.

Name:	RKT - Blind Bidding			Requester:	Jaden Moore
Number:	0000002220	Currency: EUR		Start Date:	05/03/2004 3:20:00 PM CEST
Rule Profile:	Reverse auction with broken lot, full quantity, anonymous bidding			End Date:	05/03/2004 4:00:00 PM CEST
Description:				Time Remaining: 00:12:33 (Active)	

Item	Description	Quantity	Unit	Price Unit	Start Price	Decrement	Rank	My Bid	Bid Price
	Champagne	100 piece(s)	EN	1	50.00	0.00	-	45.00	

2. RANK IS ONLY SHOWN IF BIDDER IS IN 1ST PLACE.

Total Bid Price: | Submit

	Company	Bidder	Bid Price	Bid Date
Details	BIDDERCOMP01	bidder001(first) bidder001(last)	45.00	05/03/2004 3:45:20 PM CEST
	BIDDERCOMP01	bidder001(first) bidder001(last)	49.00	05/03/2004 3:44:58 PM CEST
	BIDDERCOMP01	bidder001(first) bidder001(last)	50.00	05/03/2004 3:41:21 PM CEST

3. BIDDER CAN ONLY SEE HIS OWN BIDS IN THE BID HISTORY. NO PRICE INFORMATION IS AVAILABLE FROM OTHER BIDDERS.

Figure 4.27 Bidder's View in the Auction

1 Select/invite potential bidders (by purchaser)	**2** Assign an advantage or disadvantage (by purchaser)	**3** Create (by bidder) & Compute Bids* (by the system)
Auction 123		
• Bidder A ←	±0% (none)	
• Bidder B ←	+10% (disadvantage)*	
• Bidder C ←	+20% (disadvantage)	
• Bidder D ←	-10% (advantage)	
• Bidder E ←	+7€ (disadvantage)**	
• Bidder F ←	+8% (disadvantage)	
• Bidder n ←	-5.5€ (advantage)	
Assign bidders	* = Multiplier ** = Adder	* Price transformation for: • Start price • Reserve price • Next valid bid price

Figure 4.28 Factored-Cost Concept

Live auctions are started, ended, and extended automatically according to the parameters set during the creation of the auction. However, once the auction is started, the strategic purchaser has the capability to pause, extend, or end the auction at any point. Both purchasers and bidders can monitor the auction and bidding activity in real time. The purchaser's view of the auction is illustrated in Figure 4.29. The purchaser can view the best bid for each item in the auction. The purchaser can also initiate a chat session with any of the bidders to ask questions and provide additional information. The purchaser can also see the overall savings in the Total Savings field.

The bidder's view of the auction is illustrated in Figure 4.30. The bidder can view his overall rank in the Company Rank column. Additionally, he can also view the best bid and how it compares to his own bid. The Bid Price column allows the bidder to enter the next bid price.

Typically, in the auction process, the strategic purchaser(s) only monitors the auction to review the progress and status of the auction. However, there are times when the purchaser might have to intervene during the auction process, in one of the following ways:

▶ **Ban specific vendors**
Ban specific vendors is required when you don't want a particular vendor to be a part of the auction process anymore.

▶ **Bidding on behalf**
Bidding on behalf, or surrogate, bidding may be required if the vendor is unable to bid. Although, the application provides this capability, there might be legal ramifications to this action.

▶ **Delete bids**
Sometimes, a vendor might request that the purchasing organization delete a particular bid entered during the auction process. Although the application provides this capability, there might be legal ramifications.

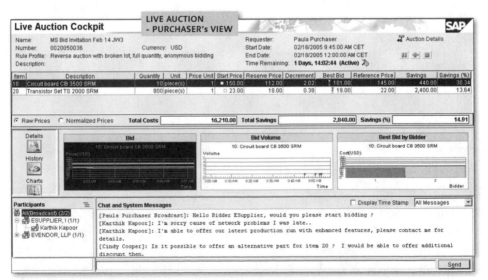

Figure 4.29 Live Auction Cockpit — Purchaser's View

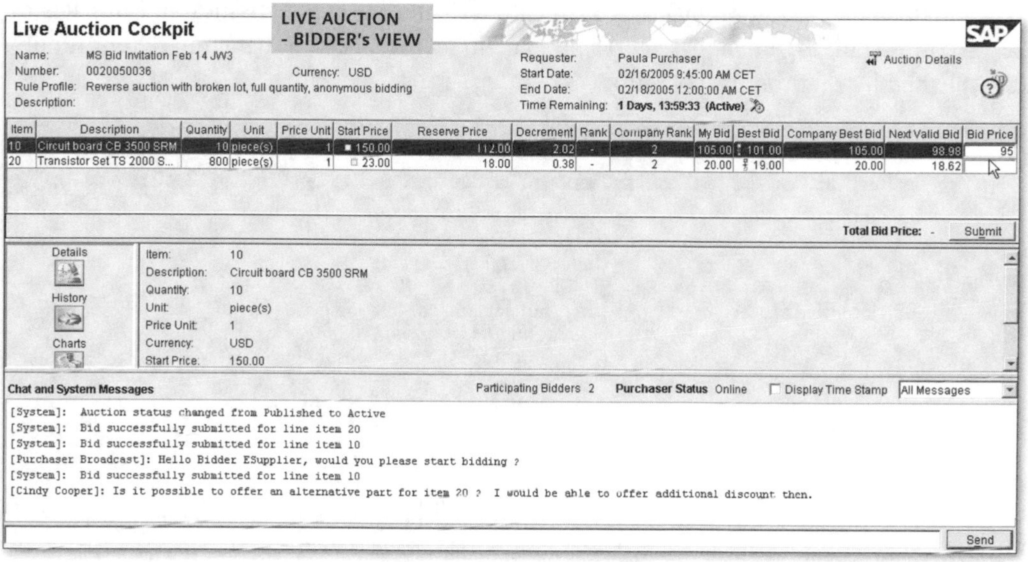

Figure 4.30 Live Auction Cockpit — Bidder's View

In this section, we discussed the strategic-sourcing capabilities in SAP SRM such as the Sourcing application, the Bidding Engine, and the Live Auction cockpit.

In the next section, we'll cover the contract management capabilities in SAP SRM.

4.2   Contract Management

Based on the current industry trends, *contract management* is one of the most talked-about processes within supplier relationship management. In 2005, Forrester Research concluded that:

> *Contract lifecycle management (CLM) applications will experience rapid growth of 40% in demand in 2005, driven by the growing desire of enterprises to manage contract creation, negotiation, and compliance on an enterprisewide basis, to help ensure compliance with Sarbanes-Oxley, and to capture savings buried in contracts with suppliers and sales or licensing revenues in contracts with customers or licensees of intellectual property.*

That is underscored by recent research by the Aberdeen Group, which found that "…an astounding 80% of enterprises are using manual or only partially automated processes to carry out contract-management activities."

It is difficult for organizations to realize continuous cost benefits and achieve organization compliance in procurement unless a robust contract management process and accompanying application is used within the overall supplier relationship management system. Figure 4.31 illustrates some of the key issues and impacts of contract management based on a 2006 contract management benchmark report published by the Aberdeen Group.

Issue	Impact on Procurement
Fragmented procedures	• Increased maverick buying • Increased supply and financial risk • Under-leveraged spending
Labor-intensive process	• Long sourcing and contracting cycles • Less spend under contract / management • Non-competitive negotiations
Poor visibility into contracts and terms	• Poor compliance • Inconsistent and risky terms • Limited visibility into spending
Ineffective compliance monitoring and management	• Increased maverick buying • High purchase price variance, missed rebates, and discounts • Overpayments and performance risks
Inadequate performance analysis	• No view into category performance • Policy and regulatory violations • Under-leveraged spending and high risk

Figure 4.31 Impact of Poor Contract Management

Note
This chapter discusses the operational contract management capabilities available within SAP SRM core. Operational Contracts contain characteristics such as payment terms, price, part information, supplier, and others that enable purchasers to source open requirements against these contracts. In addition to these capabilities, the SAP Contract Lifecycle Management (SAP CLM) application available within the SAP E-Sourcing application provides full contract lifecycle management capabilities for the management of the lifecycle of a contract, including contract clauses, authoring, and legal contract generation. Chapter 18 discusses SAP E-Sourcing solution in detail.

In SAP SRM, the contract management process deals with the development, negotiation, execution, and monitoring of contracts. Organizations can use these contracts to enhance their operational procurement processes, improve compliance, and achieve significant cost savings across the enterprise.

Contract management functionality in SAP SRM allows for a central repository of all the purchase contracts and pricing agreements of a purchasing organization. Purchase contracts represent long-term buying strategic agreements between the purchasing organization and suppliers to purchase certain goods or services over a specified period. These contracts will provide the necessary flexibility for storing local exceptions, future prices, location-dependant prices, and minimum and maximum constraints as requirements demand.

Within SAP SRM, contracts are a source of supply in shopping carts and POs. Requisitioners can order goods and services using prenegotiated suppliers that have been selected as strategic for the product or commodity being purchased. Therefore, purchasing professionals don't need to intervene for purchases initiated with products and services that have active contracts in the system. In the contract management functionality in SAP SRM, the following processes are supported, as shown in Figure 4.32:

- Contract development (create)
- Contract negotiation
- Contract execution (release and use)
- Contract monitoring

Figure 4.32 Contract Management Process

Sometimes, organizations misunderstand the difference between contracts and catalogs. Although, they are both considered valid sources of supply in SAP SRM, they differ in ways that are described in the following bullet points:

- **Contracts**
  Contracts are legal agreements between two parties, with detailed terms and conditions, clauses about penalty, warranty, and a determined validity period. A contract can contain products or product categories with specific discounts and other terms and conditions. In SAP SRM, the contract is a document in the system, not the same as a PO and therefore users cannot receive or invoice against a contract. However, they can release POs against a contract.

- **Catalogs**
  Catalogs contain products and list prices for users for easy searching and comparison. A catalog is often supported by a contract to integrate the binding details existing in the contract. However, contracts are not required in the system to support catalogs. In the SAP Catalog Content Management application (SRM-MDM), organizations can transfer contracts from SAP SRM into the catalog.

Purchasing professionals and users with appropriate authority have the ability to create contracts in SAP SRM with the appropriate terms and conditions. In addition, they can assign to a contract an appropriate status: *Held, Approved or Released, Locked, Completed*. Requisitioners then have the ability to use the contracts that are in a Released status when creating their shopping carts as approved sources of supply to request for goods or services.

Contracts are used against purchases, and purchasing professionals can analyze and monitor the use of these contracts. This will assist in tracking vendor performance and overseeing internal contract compliance. Alert notifications via email allow professional purchasers to be aware of upcoming contract expiration dates.

Figure 4.33 illustrates the contract management process in SAP SRM. We will discuss each of these process steps in Sections 4.2.1 through 4.2.5.

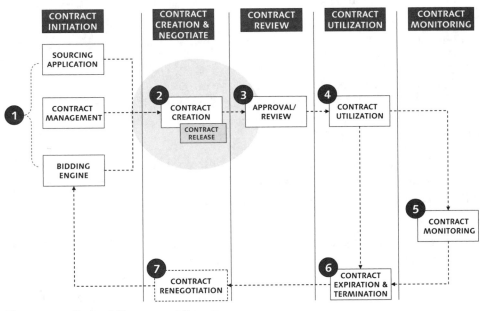

Figure 4.33 Contract Management Process

4.2.1 Contract Initiation

In Step 1 of Figure 4.33, we illustrate that in SAP SRM professional purchasers can initiate contracts from any one of the following applications:

▶ From within the Sourcing application
▶ From directly in Contract Management
▶ From within the Bidding Engine

In Figure 4.34, we show the creation of a contract from Sourcing, Process Contract, and Display Quotation applications in SAP SRM.

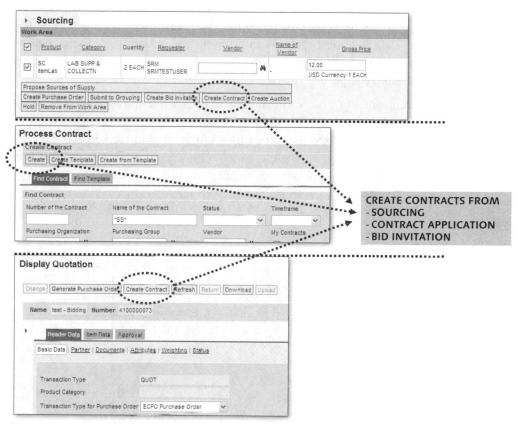

Figure 4.34 Contract Initiation from Sourcing, Process Contracts, and Bid Invitations (Screenshot SAP SRM 5.0)

4.2.2 Contract Creation and Negotiation

In Step 2 of Figure 4.33, we show that once the contract is initiated, the contract-creation process begins. In SAP SRM, organizations can create contracts or global outline agreements (GOA). A GOA is a purchasing document within SAP SRM created as a negotiated agreement with a vendor for the entire enterprise. It is typically created when multiple backend systems are integrated within the landscape.

> **Note**
>
> In SAP SRM 7.0, SAP has introduced the Central Contract Management capability. This new functionality is explained in Section 4.3.1.

The Contract application is similar in structure to the Process Purchase Order application discussed in Chapter 3. The application is divided between the Header Data tab and the Item Data tab.

Figure 4.35 illustrates the Basic Data section within the Header Data tab of a contract. In the Header Data tab, the contract administrator needs to complete the mandatory field marked with an asterisk next to the field. For example, Vendor is a required piece of data when completing the Header Data tab of the contract.

Additionally, the administrator can maintain a Target Value for the contract indicating the overall value that can be used on this contract. Once the contract is released, the Rel. Value field is updated to indicate how much value in the contract has been used and what is remaining. Also, a tolerance can be defined in the Under/Overdelivery Tolerance field or the check box can be selected to indicate that the items within this contract can be received with Unlimited over-delivery.

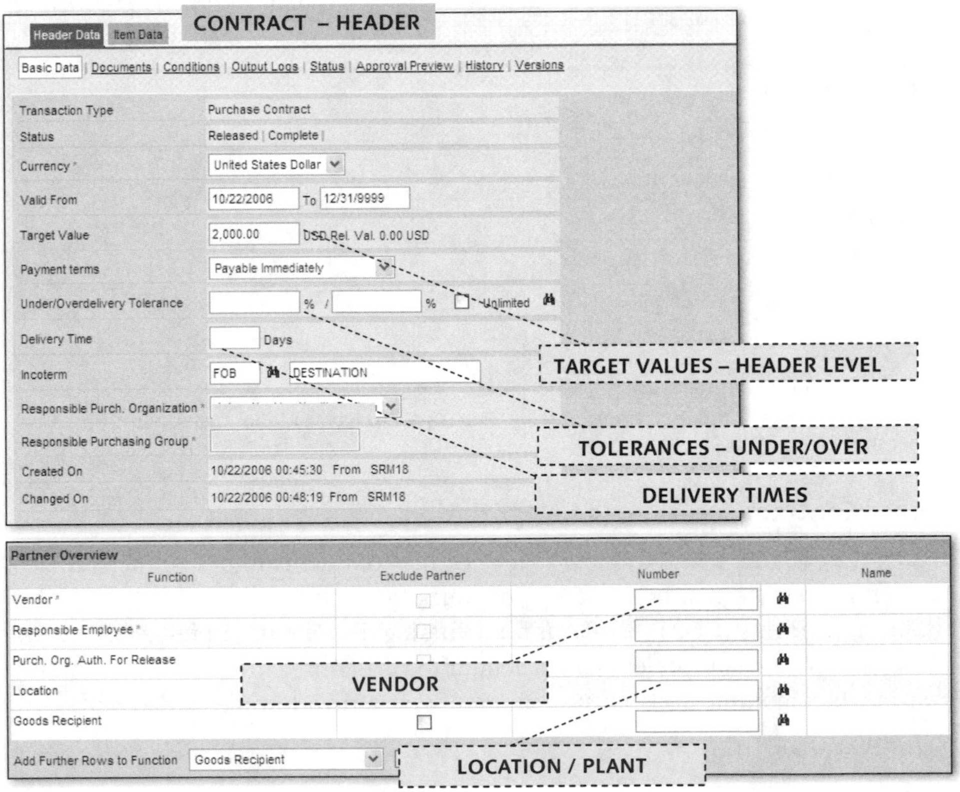

Figure 4.35 Contract Creation — Header Data Level (Screenshot SAP SRM 5.0)

Figure 4.36 illustrates the Basic Data section within the Item Data tab of a contract. The contract administrator can create a contract item that is a Product (material master based) or Description based. In our example in Figure 4.36, the item is description based, called *TEST*.

It is important that when a description is used, the administrator also enters the Vendor Product Number in the contract line item; this allows for sourcing the contract correctly. Now, when a shopping cart or PO is created, the end user needs to ensure that the same vendor product number is used in the shopping cart line item so that this contract will be available as a source of supply.

An Under/Overdelivery Tolerance can also be set at the item level, as we saw in the Header Data tab. This allows more flexibility to set tolerances for individual items instead of the overall contract. The contract administrator can also set a Minimum Order Qty or a Minimum Order Value for each item within the contract.

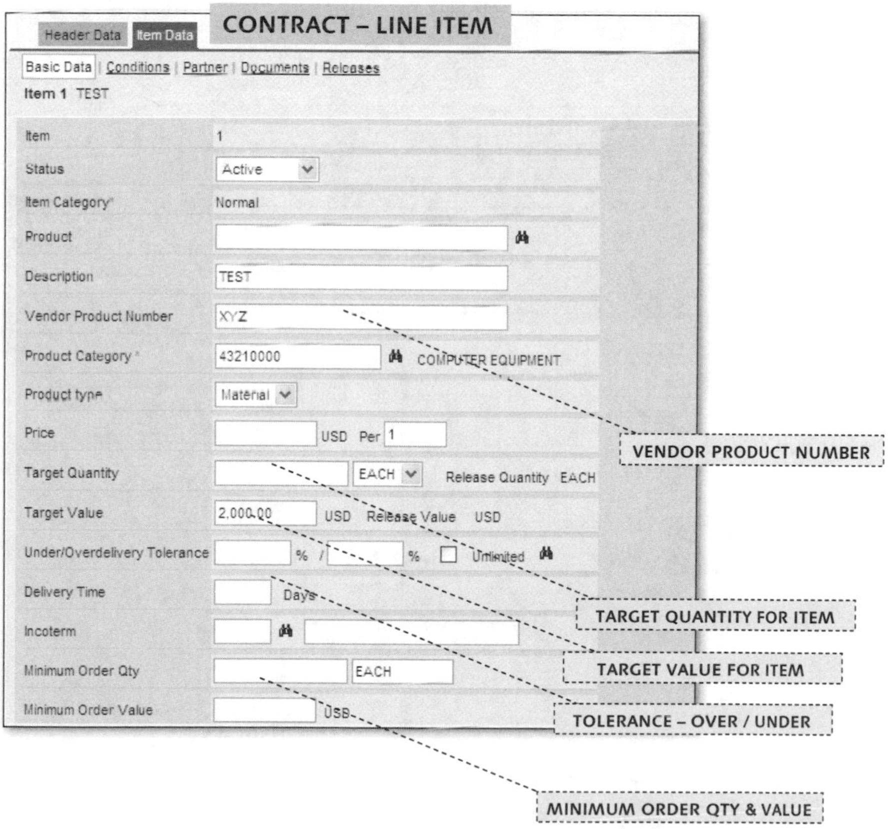

Figure 4.36 Contract Creation — Line-Item Level (Screenshot SAP SRM 5.0)

During the creation and maintenance of contracts in SAP SRM, the contract administrator can use the functions described in the following subsections.

Release Contracts

Using the Release button in the contract, the contract administrator can release complete (error-free) contracts. This contract can then be used as a source of supply for releases against POs. Until a contract has the status of Released, it cannot be used in shopping carts or POs.

Lock

Using the *Lock* function, the contract administrator can lock an active document for releases. No POs can be made with reference to this document. For example, purchasers can set this status to temporarily remove a contract from Sourcing. If only a single item needs to be locked in a contract, it can be made Inactive in the Basic Data section on the line item. Figure 4.37 illustrates this function.

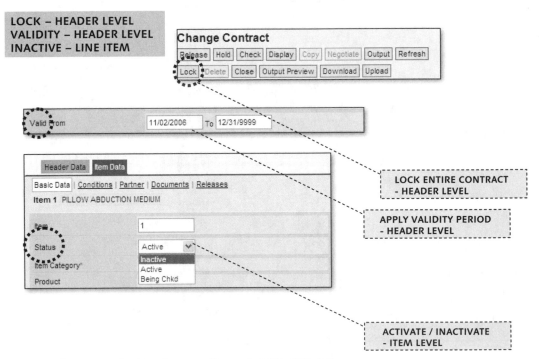

Figure 4.37 Locking Contracts (Screenshot SAP SRM 5.0)

Download and Upload

Using the *Download and Upload* function, professional purchasers can download the contract documents to their PCs as files, process them locally, and then upload the changed document data to the SAP SRM application. From SAP SRM, a tabular file structure (in CSV format) is delivered. This provides additional flexibility for organizations to create and process contracts with a large number of items and also to make bulk changes.

> **Note**
>
> The download data file of the contract is not pretty to look at. The example illustrated in Figure 4.38 has been reformatted to make it more legible. SAP provides BAdIs so organizations can apply additional business rules to augment or enhance the standard solution for upload and download (BBP_PD_DOWNLOAD).
>
> In addition, SAP also provides a consulting solution, where customers can purchase a prede-livered application that enhances the layout of the download and makes it easier to use the upload of contracts and line items. Review the OSS notes later in this chapter for details.

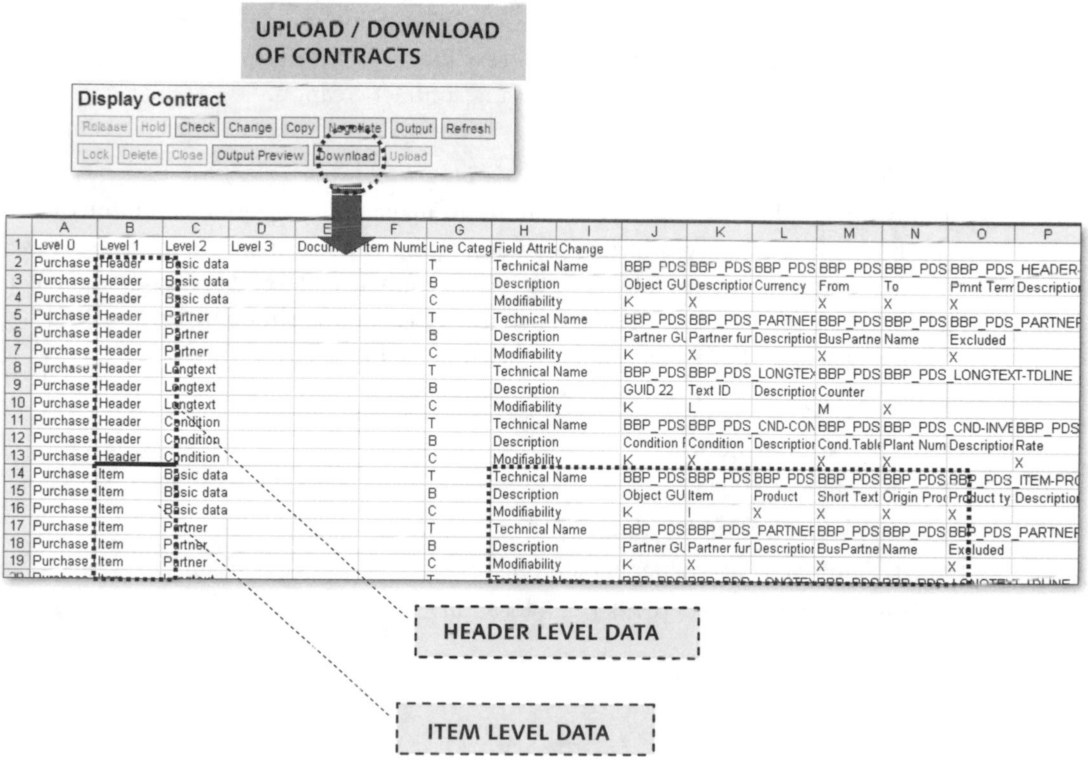

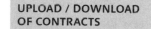

Figure 4.38 Download of Contract and GOA with Excel

Negotiate

Using the *Negotiate* function, the contract administrator can create a bid invitation for an expiring contract to determine new vendors and possibly to negotiate improved conditions. Using SAP Bidding Engine, the contract administrator can then either create a new contract or update an existing one. This is discussed further in Section 4.2.6, Contract Renegotiation.

Attachments

Using the *Attachments* function, the contract administrator can attach terms and condition documents along with any electronic document used in the contract negotiation process. This allows for a central repository for all pertinent documentation for a contract document.

Copy Contracts

The ability to *copy contracts* simplifies the process of renewing existing contracts or creating new ones. In addition, contract templates are available that can be used to quickly and efficiently create new contracts based on a standard format. Templates are linked to the standard approval process for the contract document. Figure 4.39 shows the various options available during contract creation.

Pricing

The contract administrator has the ability to manage item *pricing* conditions with conditions functionality, which is used in creating and maintaining contracts. These master conditions are used by the pricing functionality in SAP SRM to determine a net price for products and services that are bought in the shopping cart or PO. The following standard SAP conditions are used in a contract:

- Fixed price
- Percentage discount
- Absolute discount
- Price dependent on location
- Discount (percentage) dependent on location
- Discount (absolute) dependent on location

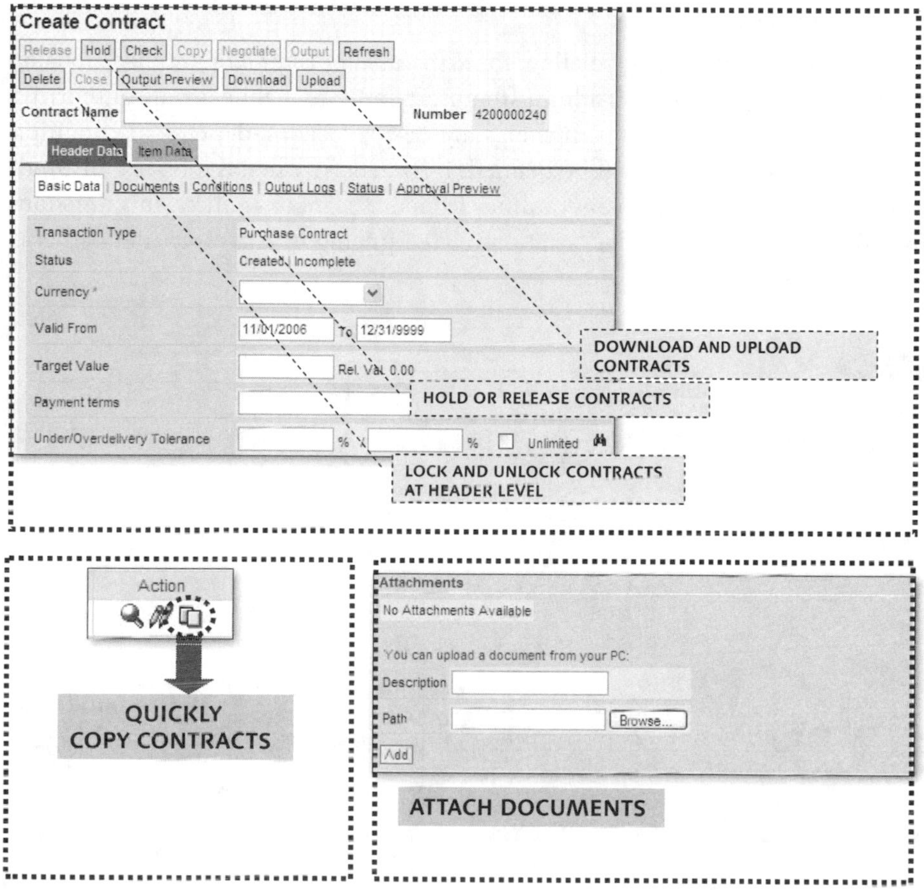

Figure 4.39 Contract Creation (Screenshot SAP SRM 5.0)

For gross-price determination order, SAP provides the standard prioritization of condition types (according to the delivered calculation schema) as follows:

► Manual price-buyer override

► Contract price

► Catalog price

► Price from product

The pricing application guarantees that a manual price has priority over a contract price, which has priority over a catalog price, which in turn has priority over a price from product. This order illustrates how a price is derived when a source of supply is needed.

Restriction for Location

Organizations have the ability to allow for *Restriction for Location* reference globally. For contract items, the contract administrator can indicate that he is only authorized for release for specific locations. If this is the case, a location-dependent condition exclusive to these locations will be defined. In situations when the prices for products that are delivered from a vendor differ from one plant to another, this functionality makes it possible to define location-related pricing in a contract item. This is illustrated in Figure 4.40.

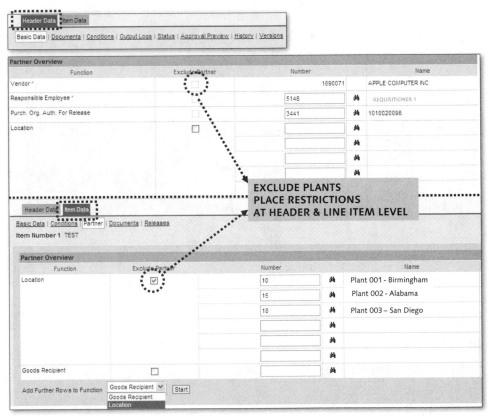

Figure 4.40   Restriction for Locations and Recipients (Screenshot SAP SRM 5.0)

Quantity or Value Scales

The condition types used, *Quantity* or *Value Scales*, in contracts will provide for a scaling facility. In a separate subscreen for scales, professional purchasers will be able to define scales based on prices or quantities. Figure 4.41 shows how scales can be used in the contract application.

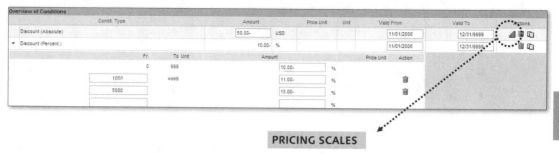

Figure 4.41 Pricing Scales (Screenshot SAP SRM 5.0)

Status Management

Using the *Status Management* functionality in SAP SRM, purchasing professionals have access to the following document status categories, some of which they can manually assign and some of which are assigned automatically by the system. Figure 4.42 shows this functionality at work. Contract administrators can manage the following status categories in a contract:

- ▶ Held/Hold
- ▶ Released
- ▶ Locked
- ▶ Closed

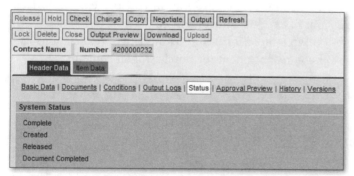

Figure 4.42 Status Management (Screenshot SAP SRM 5.0)

In turn, the SAP SRM system then manages the following status categories:

- ▶ Created
- ▶ Document Completed
- ▶ In Negotiation

- In Renewal
- Deleted
- Archived
- Incomplete
- Complete

Version Management

When documents are modified, it is important that change history is maintained. In the Contract Management application in SAP SRM, version management provides the capability to keep track of changes made to contracts. In contrast to the change documents that retain a change history, a version displays the status of a document at a specific point in time. An example is a situation in which you wish to display a PO in the form in which you transferred it to the vendor on a particular day. A version provides clarity in contract negotiations.

Once a contract is in *released* status, there are changes. These changes are saved in a change version of the original documents. They are subject to an approval process (based on business rules for your organization) before the changes are transferred to the active document. The change workflow is started once the changed version is released.

Once the changed version gets the status approved, a historical version is saved as a copy of the active document. It cannot be changed but only displayed. Authorized users can then compare versions of a contract document and list the differences both at a Header and Line Item level in tabular form. In Customizing, organizations can choose whether to enable version management for purchasing documents.

> **Note**
>
> SAP provides BAdIs for organizations to apply additional business rules to augment or enhance the standard solution for controlling the circumstances under which the system creates a version for contracts (BBP_VERSION_CONTROL).

In SAP SRM 7.0, with Central Contracts, a new tab has been introduced for "Tracking" the changes to the contract at a Header and Line Item level.

Distribute Contracts to the SAP Catalog

Once contracts are created and released for use, they can be distributed to the SAP Catalog for easier search and selection. This is enabled using a standard process that integrates the contract application with the SAP Catalog (SRM-MDM Catalog) using the SAP NetWeaver Process Integration (PI) solution.

Once the Customizing requirements are completed, all contracts that have a status of Released and have also been selected for transfer to the catalog (Header level) are available for transfer to the SAP Catalog Content Management application.

> **Note**
>
> With SAP SRM 7.0, new capability has been introduced to allow the distribution of contract items to the catalog. Therefore, an organization can define on an item which items should be distributed to the SRM-MDM catalog. In previous releases, the distribution of contract data was only possible on the header level of the contract. The following fields are transferred to the contract in the standard (or else a BAdI can be used to transfer customer specific fields):
>
> ▶ Supplier/Vendor, Vendor ID, Vendor Part number
>
> ▶ Product, Product ID, Product Category
>
> ▶ Price, Price unit, Percentage
>
> ▶ Payment terms, if also on item level

4.2.3   Contract Review

Step 4 in Figure 4.33 showed that once a contract is created and released it may require approvals or review by others within your organization. For example, business rules in your organization may dictate that all contracts created in excess of $50,000 require the approval of the purchasing director. In this example, the contract will not be available for use as a valid source of supply until it has been approved by the purchasing director. Once all the required approvals are complete, the status in the contract changes to released.

In SAP SRM, a number of workflow templates are predelivered that organizations can use out-of-the-box without any development. As part of the system setup and configuration, project teams decide which workflows to activate and also define business rules within the workflow condition editor. Workflow in SAP SRM and its use in the different documents such as contracts are explained in detail in Chapter 10.

4.2.4   Contract Utilization

Step 5 in Figure 4.33 illustrated that once contracts are created and released, they are available for use and utilized within the system to create POs. Additionally, professional purchasers can use these contracts within the Sourcing application to assign contracted vendors as sources of supply when completing open shopping cart requirements. As a contract gets used within the shopping cart or PO, the contract release gets updated subsequently and can be reviewed in the contract application. In this way, contract administrators can be aware of the use of the quantity or total value of the contract and make appropriate decisions. For example, let's assume that there is a contract created in the system for the purchase of computers with the Dell Corporation. The contract administrator can review the Header Data section of the Dell contract to check the Release Value of the contract.

4.2.5 Contract Monitoring

Contract monitoring is a continuous process of reviewing purchasing activity against the contract and contract budget. When monitored periodically, this activity ensures adequate performance and contract compliance. Industry research shows that although most organizations create and use contracts in some form with their vendors, they lack visibility into the way these contracts are used or complied with.

Step 6 of Figure 4.33 illustrates that released contracts are available for use in business documents such as shopping carts and POs, and once they are used, the contract administrator can being the monitoring process. Using the contract monitoring functionality, contract administrators can monitor contract usage, contract renewal, volume of a contract, and overview of ordered products and categories. One of the key methods to ensure procurement compliance is for organizations to monitor purchasing activity periodically.

Progress should be matched with baseline metrics defined for the organization. When contracts are created, a validity period can be assigned to indicate the start and end dates of the negotiated terms and conditions in the contract. Once the contract end-date is reached, a contract attains status of Expired. Contracts with the expired status are not available as sources of supply for selection by end users or professional purchasers. In Step 7 in Figure 4.33, we showed that once a contract is expired the contract administrator needs to take action to either renegotiate the contract or terminate the contract. We will discuss the renegotiation of contracts in the next section.

In SAP SRM, contract monitoring can be further enhanced by using the SAP SRM alert-management functionality and reports in SAP NetWeaver BW. In the previous paragraph, we explained that organizations can monitor individual contracts to review the contract use and expiration. To attain true contract monitoring, however, the SAP NetWeaver BW application provides access to predefined monitoring reports and alerts that can be triggered when contracts are about to expire.

From a process perspective, when specific events occur in SAP SRM, alerts are generated and can be reported via the Contract Management content in SAP NetWeaver BW. This does not have to occur when a contract is nearing expiration; an alert could be configured for contract changes as well. The reporting capabilities of SAP NetWeaver BW as it relates to SAP SRM are described in detail in Chapter 15.

4.2.6 Contract Renegotiation

Contract administrators have the capability in SRM to renegotiate existing contracts directly with the vendor using the Bidding Engine. This is illustrated as Step 7 — Contract Renegotiation — as you saw in Figure 4.36.

Renegotiation is typically done to renew the terms and conditions of an existing contract. To initiate the negotiation, a bid invitation is generated directly from within the contract application, which can then be enhanced within the Bidding Engine before it is sent out as an email request to preferred vendors. The vendor(s) can then submit new contract terms and conditions, such as target value or price conditions. If the professional purchaser or contract administrator accepts the vendor's bid, the data is transferred to the existing contract and it is renewed.

> **Note**
>
> In releases prior to SAP SRM 4.0, this function was called Create Bid Invitation in the Contract Management application and is now called Negotiate.

Contracts that are about to expire can be renegotiated via the SAP Bidding Engine, as illustrated in Figure 4.43. In this figure a GOA with the number 4200001316 is shown in display mode. The Negotiate button is used to begin the process of renegotiation. Once this is clicked a pop-up window is displayed indicating that a bid invitation is created and held. In our example, the message is Bid invitation 0000003316 Held. The contract administrator can review the status of this contract at any time by clicking on the History link in the contract Header Data screen.

Figure 4.43 Negotiate Function in the Contract Application

Once the negotiation process is started, the system assigns different statuses based on the stage of the negotiation. This allows for flexible search capability. The In Negotiation status indicates that negotiations for a particular contract have started with the vendor. The In Renewal status indicates that a released contract has undergone negotiation and the bid invitation is currently in a Held status. This status tells the professional purchasers that additional work may need to be performed on the bid invitation before it can be published and sent to the vendor.

Once the generated bid invitations are enhanced and completed, a bid notification is sent to the supplier, who can then choose to change the bid by adding new items or change information on the target quantities or values for an item, the conditions, or delivery times. The bid invitation and bid process are the same as described in the bidding section earlier in this chapter.

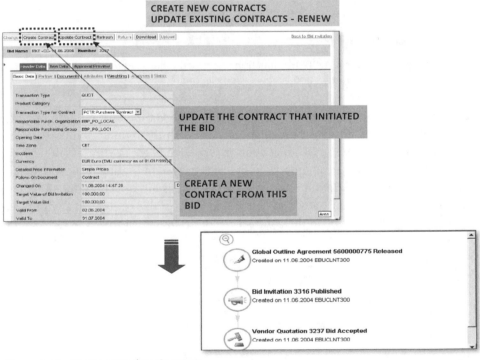

Figure 4.44   Create or Update Contracts

Once the bid is received by the customer, and accepted, the contract administrator has two choices: Create a new contract, or update the existing contract. Figure 4.44 illustrates that the Update Contract button can update the contract that initiated the bid (a new version of the original contract is generated in SAP SRM). The Create Contract button can create a new contract from the bid award. Based on defined business rules, an approval for the contract update or creation might be required.

4.2.7 Contract Distribution

With SAP SRM, organizations can create contracts or GOAs. A GOA is a purchasing document within SAP SRM created as a negotiated agreement with a vendor for the entire enterprise. It is typically created when multiple backend systems are integrated within the landscape. Once these GOAs are created, organizations can choose to distribute these documents to backend SAP systems if needed. The backend purchasing organizations can be notified about these new contracts via email, and at that point the purchasing organizations can register for these contracts and begin to use them for creating POs in the SAP backends (as illustrated in Figure 4.45).

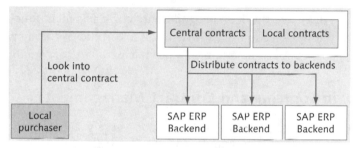

Figure 4.45 Distributing Contracts to Backend Systems

> **Note**
>
> As of SAP SRM release 4.0, both the contract and scheduling agreement can be distributed compared to just the contracts in previous releases. Organizations cannot create local contracts within SAP SRM and also distribute that same contract to an SAP backend. Only one of the options is allowed in release 4.0. Figure 4.45 illustrates Central contracts separately from Local contracts.
>
> Organizations implementing SAP SRM 7.0 should review the Central contract functionality that replaces GOA in SAP SRM 5.0 and earlier. This is explained in Section 4.3.1, Central Contract Management concept.

When distributing the contracts or scheduling agreements, a separate document is created based on the purchasing organization and location (plant) defined within the contract document. The actual distribution is enabled using a standard IDoc: BLAREL — BLAORD03, COND_A02 — BLAREL02.

> **Note**
>
> SAP provides BAdIs for organizations to apply additional business rules to augment or enhance the standard solution for the contract distribution (BBP_CTR_BE_CREATE in SRM; BBP_CTR in SAP R/3).

Organizations that want to distribute the contracts or scheduling agreements to the SAP backend need to be aware of the following restrictions (SAP SRM 4.0 release):

▶ Only releases SAP ERP 4.0B or higher are supported.

▶ No distribution of central contracts to SAP EB are allowed.

▶ No automatic split of target quantity and target value is allowed.

▶ Service items are not allowed for distribution from a GOA in SAP SRM to a scheduling agreement in the SAP backend.

▶ Contract hierarchies are not supported.

▶ Attachments are not transferred to the SAP backend.

In Sections 4.1 and 4.2, we discussed the Sourcing and Contract Management functionality in SAP SRM. In the next section, we'll briefly discuss some of the new enhancements in sourcing and contract management since release of SAP SRM 5.0.

4.3   What's New in Sourcing and Contract Management?

SAP has been continuously enhancing the SAP SRM solution every year with new releases that have produced a variety of rich and useful functionality. This section highlights some of the new functionality introduced in Sourcing and Contract Management applications since SAP SRM 5.0.

4.3.1   Central Contract Management concept

Prior to SAP SRM 7.0, there were two types of Contract objects in SAP SRM: a local contract and a GOA contract, as illustrated in Figure 4.46.

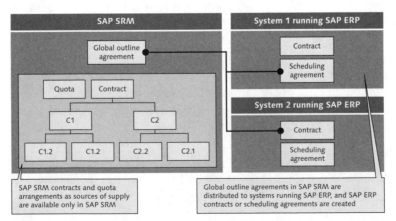

Figure 4.46 Contract Management in SAP SRM in SRM 5.0 and Previous Releases (Figure Credit: SAP)

▶ The Local contract was used as a source of supply for the Standalone and Extended Classic Scenarios, and

The GOA created contracts in SAP SRM and then distributed to one or more back-end SAP ERP systems as an umbrella outline agreement.

However, GOA could not be used as a source of supply in SAP SRM. Limiting the use of the Contract Management capabilities in SAP SRM – Release Management, Hierarchies, Line Item–based payment terms, and others.

In SAP SRM 7.0, local SAP SRM and GOA objects have been harmonized into a single business object as a Central contract that is essentially created in SAP SRM and can still be distributed to one of more SAP backend systems. A central repository for all contracts is available across SAP SRM and SAP ERP systems. Therefore, organizations can now handle releases centrally in the contract in SAP SRM for purchase orders created either via SAP SRM or SAP ERP (use as a source of supply in SAP SRM and also in SAP ERP). Figure 4.47 illustrates the Central contract concept with SAP SRM 7.0.

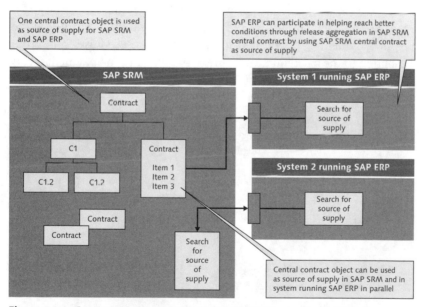

Figure 4.47 Contract Management in SAP SRM 7.0 (Figure Credit: SAP)

> **Note**
>
> In SAP ERP, either a specific type of Contract or a scheduling agreement is created from the SAP SRM Contract.

The restriction for the central contract object is having a backend ERP release of ECC 6.0 EhP04. Prior to EhP04, the GOA functionality distributed contracts to the backend. The data, which is relevant for a source of supply determination, is sent to SAP ERP through Enterprise Services Repository (for SAP ERP release 6.0 EhP4) or through intermediate documents (for earlier SAP ERP releases).

In SAP SRM 7.0, the following new enhancements have been extended to the Contracts application.

▶ **Extended information in Source of Supply area**

The source of supply section in the shopping cart has been enhanced to show extended information about the contract. Each contract now shows the Line Item description, Supplier part number, and Priority in supplier list if it exists, illustrated in Figure 4.48.

▶ **Payment terms on Line Item level**

Prior to SAP SRM 7.0, payment terms were on the Header level of the contract. Now payment terms are available at a Line Item level, providing enhanced capabilities to manage contracts. Because SAP ERP supports payment terms only at the Header level, the payment terms of the central contract are used as a split criterion for distribution to the backend ERP. Figure 4.49 illustrates the payment terms on the item level of the contract.

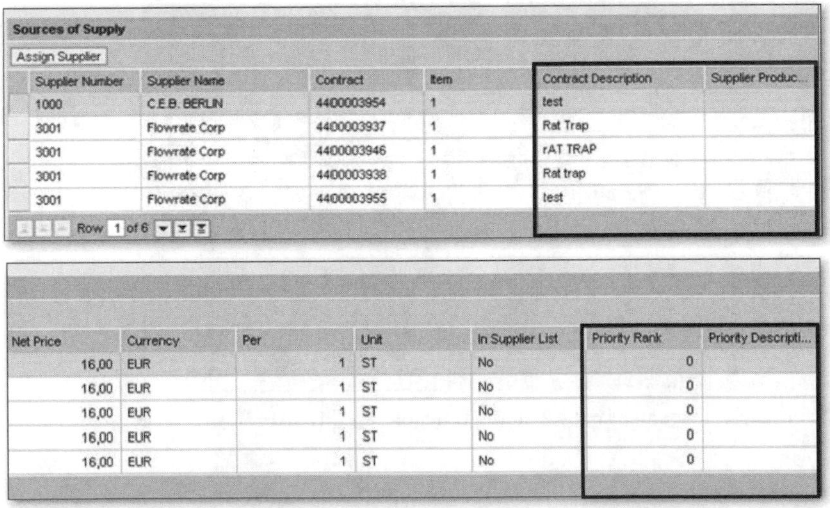

Sources of Supply

Assign Supplier

Supplier Number	Supplier Name	Contract	Item	Contract Description	Supplier Produc...
1000	C.E.B. BERLIN	4400003954	1	test	
3001	Flowrate Corp	4400003937	1	Rat Trap	
3001	Flowrate Corp	4400003946	1	rAT TRAP	
3001	Flowrate Corp	4400003938	1	Rat trap	
3001	Flowrate Corp	4400003955	1	test	

Row 1 of 6

Net Price	Currency	Per	Unit	In Supplier List	Priority Rank	Priority Descripti...
16,00	EUR		1 ST	No	0	
16,00	EUR		1 ST	No	0	
16,00	EUR		1 ST	No	0	
16,00	EUR		1 ST	No	0	
16,00	EUR		1 ST	No	0	

Figure 4.48 Source of Supply Section in Shopping Cart (Figure Credit: SAP)

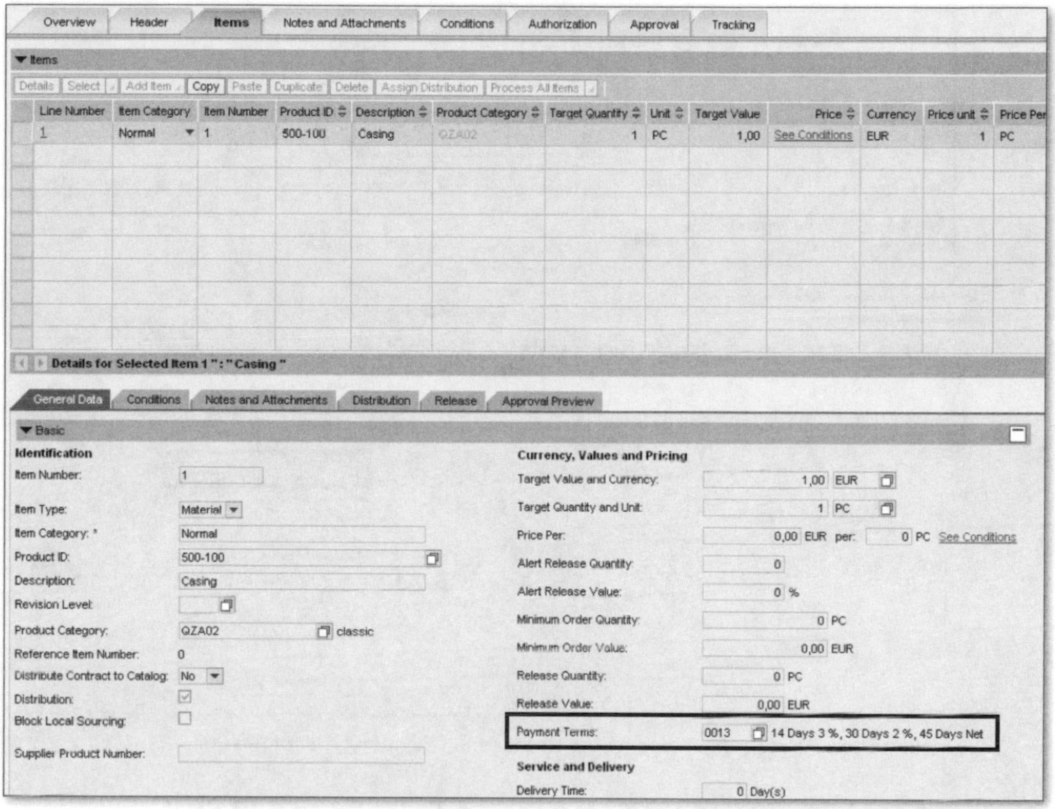

Figure 4.49 Item Level Payment Terms on Contract (Figure Credit: SAP)

▶ **Configurable Alerts for Contract Monitoring**

Prior to SAP SRM 7.0, there has always been an ability to provide alerts to the purchaser on the contract expiration. However, it was based on a report (BBP_CONTRACT_CHECK). With SAP SRM 7.0, organizations can either configure alerts for contracts in the IMG as a customizing function or define them for individual contracts in the Header and Line Item of the contract. Figure 4.50 illustrates the alert configuration on the Header and Line Item level of the contract.

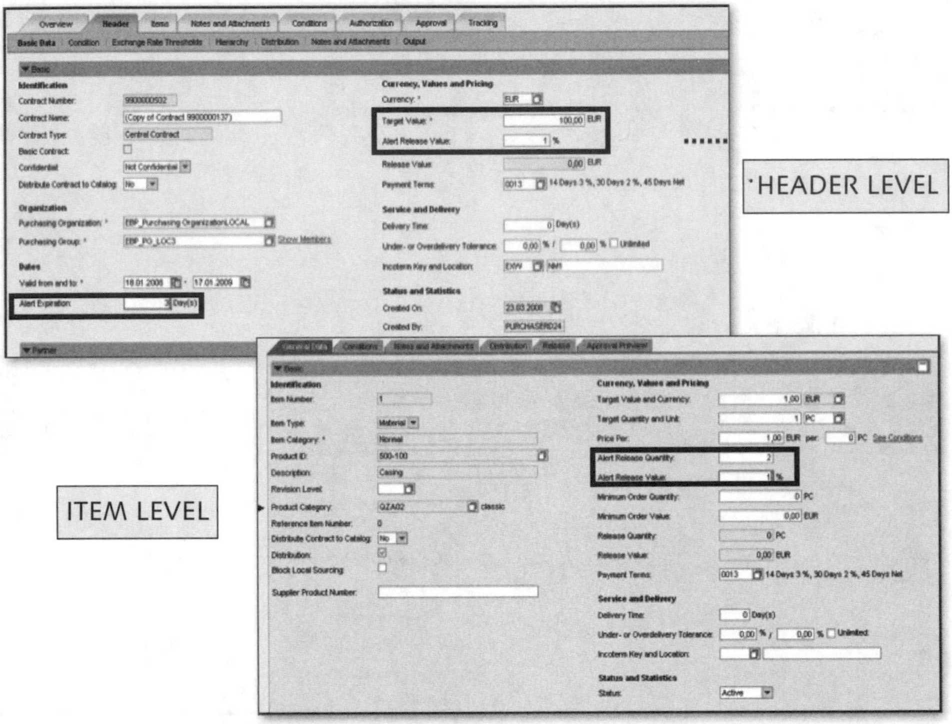

Figure 4.50 Alert Configuration on the Header and Line Item Level of the Contract

4.3.2 Initial Upload of Contract from SAP ERP to SAP SRM

A number of organizations that have been using the SAP ERP solution use the materials management in SAP ERP for purchasing. As these organizations are moving toward the SAP SRM application, they need to replicate the existing master data within these systems into the SAP SRM system.

For example, the Contract Management functionality is now only being developed within SAP SRM. Therefore, it is beneficial for organizations to use SAP SRM to create and manage all contracts within SAP SRM and then distribute those of other systems within the organization if required.

A new report — BBP_CTR_INIT_UPLOAD — has been created as a standard tool to upload contracts and scheduling agreements from the backend SAP ERP system into SAP SRM.

4.3.3 New Strategic Sourcing Offering — On-Demand Sourcing

On-demand solutions that assist in the overall delivery of supplier relationship management are one of the key trends emerging in the marketplace. These applications allow companies more flexibility and the ability to maximize their current technology investments. These solutions work with virtually any existing procurement or ERP system, including SAP, Oracle, PeopleSoft, and others. Some of the reasons on-demand is becoming a huge market lie in the following benefits driven by these solutions:

▶ Operational implementation is completed in a short amount of time compared to typical in-house solution installation and operation (typically within weeks).

▶ Implementation and start small and grow over time.

▶ Full payback and return on investment (ROI) occur within months because the costs of installation, setup, and ongoing maintenance are reduced dramatically.

▶ Start-up fees are dramatically lower than those for traditional software.

SAP acquired Frictionless Commerce, a leading on-demand supplier of e-sourcing solutions, in 2006. With this acquisition, SAP now offers a strategic sourcing on-demand solution. Frictionless Commerce's On-Demand edition offers e-sourcing capabilities available through a web browser. Within days, organizations can run sourcing events and begin managing suppliers. The On-Demand edition offers shorter time-to-benefit, as well as measurable cost savings with a minimal investment in time, resources, and training.

The SAP E-sourcing on-demand functionality provides the following capabilities, referenced from the frictionless website:

▶ **Project management and reporting**
Manage activities, tasks, milestones, and alerts. Capture supporting documents and files into one repository. Track a portfolio of savings opportunities.

▶ **RFx (RFI, RFQ, and RFP) creation, management, and analysis**
Source simple-to-complex negotiation events in direct, indirect, and services categories. Conduct multiround sourcing events without re-entering data.

▶ **Wide variety of reverse auction capabilities and settings**
Manage advanced bidding rules such as bid visibility, automatic extensions, ranked-bidding format, weighted-bidding format, staggered line-item start and end times, and reserved prices.

The Frictionless offering was already NetWeaver compliant prior to the acquisition by SAP. Therefore, SAP advises that the migration path to SAP SRM for customers is fairly seamless.

> **Note**
>
> As of Q4 2009, SAP offers primarily two solutions for e-sourcing: Hosted and On Premise. The latter is installed within your firewall. Currently, the Hosted solution offers integration of master data, executing RFx/Auctions and the creation of POs or contracts in SAP ERP. The E-Sourcing solution has no integration with SAP SRM in the standard. However, some customers have enabled integration of Contracts from E-Sourcing with SAP SRM using custom development within SAP NetWeaver PI. SAP plans to offer a product later in 2010 that will integrate the solution offering for integration with both SAP SRM and SAP ERP. The integration between E-Sourcing and SAP ERP is enabled using SAP NetWeaver PI.

4.4   Summary

In this chapter, you were introduced to the two key capabilities within SAP SRM: sourcing and contract management. We discussed how organizations can use the bidding and auction capabilities in SAP SRM to enhance their entire sourcing process to better identify quality suppliers as well as to negotiate the best possible terms and conditions without sacrificing quality.

We also discussed in detail the contract management functionality in SAP SRM. You should remember that contracts can be created from multiple different applications in SAP SRM. Contract management allows organizations to prepare, create, update, and monitor contractual agreements electronically within the system.

> **Note**
>
> In Q2 of 2007, SAP announced a new application for contract management, branded as CLM. The current CLM 2.0 release is based on the legal contract authoring capability that controls the creation of contracts in Microsoft® Word®, along with legal clauses and terms. Contract management within SAP SRM still remains, but CLM will be a valuable tool for organizations that want the capability of authoring contracts using Microsoft Word and enabling the complete contract lifecycle management. The CLM solution is part of the SAP E-Sourcing offering. Chapter 18 provides an overview of the E-Sourcing solution and its capabilities.

In Chapter 5, we'll look at the Supplier Enablement concept in SAP SRM. We'll discuss in detail how buying organizations can integrate with suppliers for order collaboration and inventory replenishment. Chapter 5 will also introduce the SUS functionality of SAP SRM.

The age of proprietary information systems is coming to an end, and the age of shared services is dawning. The traditional corporate boundaries are falling down, giving way to cross-company sharing of business processes.

5 Supplier Enablement

According to Webster's dictionary, *enablement* is "The act of enabling, or the state of being enabled; ability." When we generally talk about supplier enablement, we are referring to enabling the interaction, visibility, and collaboration between buying organizations and their suppliers.

While it's true that some companies have done a great job streamlining their internal processes, their shared processes — those that involve interactions with other companies — are largely a mess. Think about your own procurement process. It's the mirror image of your supplier's order fulfillment process, with many of the same tasks and information requirements.

When your purchasing agent fills out a requisition form, for instance, he's performing essentially the same task that the supplier's order entry clerk performs when he takes the order. Yet there is probably little or no coordination between the two processes. Even if you and your supplier exchange transactional data electronically, the actual work is still being performed in isolation, separated by a large intercompany divide.

Because cross-company processes are not coordinated, many activities end up being duplicated. The same information is entered repeatedly into different systems, the same forms are filled out and passed around multiple times, and the same checks are done over and over. When the activities and data make the jump between companies, inconsistencies, errors, and misunderstandings routinely arise, leading to even more wasted work. Often, many employees have to be assigned to manage the cumbersome interactions between the companies. Although all of these inefficiencies may be hidden from your accounting systems, which track only what happens within your own walls, the costs are real, and they are large. Today, efficiency ends at the edges of the company.

To better understand supplier enablement, let's take an example from the 2006 benchmark report published by the research company, Aberdeen Group. This benchmark examined the supplier enablement processes, activities, benefits, shortcomings, and technology use of 120 enterprises. Figure 5.1 provides analysis of the data gathered from a question posed to customer organizations: How much data do you share with your supplier community?

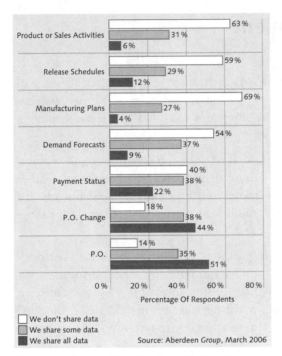

Figure 5.1 Buyer's Data-Sharing with Suppliers

The data in Figure 5.1 illustrates that most companies that responded to the survey exchange Purchase Order (PO) and Purchase Order Change data with the supplier electronically. Of the respondents, 51% exchange all PO data electronically, 44% of the respondents exchange PO Change data, 38% of the companies share some payment status data, and 22% share all data related to payment status. Notice, however, that there is a big disparity for buying companies to provide visibility to suppliers about their demand forecasts and release schedules, with only 9% to 12% of companies sharing all data in these areas.

Organizations are increasingly looking at technology for exchanging information with their suppliers. Based on the Aberdeen report, half of the respondent companies already use some form of Web-based supplier portal and Internet-based electronic data interchange (EDI), and about six of every seven enterprises will have programs in place within 12 months. Another interesting fact reported by Aberdeen was that in their 2004 benchmark report, the average e-procurement deployment had only 17% of suppliers enabled. Today, that number has jumped to 29%. This data is evidence that organizations are increasingly integrating their businesses processes with those in their supplier communities.

Streamlining cross-company processes is the next great frontier to reducing costs, enhancing quality, and speeding operations. The leaders will be companies that are able to take a new approach to business, and who will work closely with partners to design and manage processes that extend beyond the traditional corporate boundaries.

This chapter focuses on how companies can use SAP SRM to closely integrate processes in order management, inventory and demand planning, and design collaboration. In the next section, we will provide a brief overview of all of the integrated processes that exist within the SAP Supplier Collaboration solution.

5.1 Supplier Enablement Using SAP SRM

The SAP SRM application provides organizations with the ability to integrate with suppliers of all sizes. SAP provides this functionality to organizations using the core SAP SRM solution along with the SAP Supply Chain Management (SCM) application. Organizations can integrate their suppliers using a Web-based solution that is scalable and provides suppliers with immediate access to supply side transactions and other relevant information. It provides a single point of entry where, among several other capabilities, purchasing organizations and suppliers can:

▶ Collaborate on exchanging orders and acknowledgments
▶ Share inventory and supply-demand plans
▶ Access uploaded supplier catalog data
▶ Check payment status
▶ Collaborate on new and existing product design plans

Over the last few years, SAP has enhanced their supplier collaboration applications. Today, there are multiple components that integrate together to provide a holistic solution for supplier enablement. The main components are as follows:

▶ Supplier self-services (SUS, a component of SAP SRM)
▶ Supply network planning (SNP, part of SAP SCM)

▶ SAP NetWeaver® Portal (a component of SAP NetWeaver)

▶ SAP Product Lifecycle Management (SAP PLM)

▶ Supplier network (an integrated offering of SAP SRM)

Figure 5.2 illustrates how these components enable collaborative processes along the entire supplier relationship lifecycle.

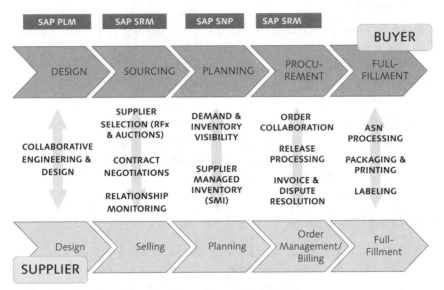

Figure 5.2 Integrated Processes Within Supplier Collaboration

This chapter focuses on the processes that are powered by the SAP SRM components (SUS and supplier network), and, where appropriate, provides an overview of the functionalities available for supplier enablement using the other SAP software (SNP, SCM, PLM, etc.).

As mentioned earlier, suppliers only need a Web browser to access the SUS application.

5.1.1 Direct Access of SUS Application via BSP URL

> **Note**
>
> In SAP SRM 7.0, the SUS application screens have not changed from what they were in SAP SRM 5.0. Therefore, this portion of SAP SRM looks the same as before.

Figure 5.3 illustrates an example of accessing the SUS application.

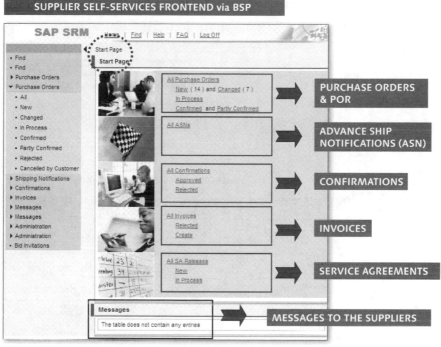

Figure 5.3 SUS Main page

5.1.2 Business Package or iView in the SAP NetWeaver Portal

The *Business Package* is suitable for organizations implementing the SAP NetWeaver Portal solution. The *supplier collaboration* business package can be used in the SAP NetWeaver Portal to readily access portal roles iViews and applications. The core benefit of using the SAP NetWeaver Portal is that the supplier is provided with a unified solution that could contain content from multiple SAP components with information from SUS, SAP SRM, SAP NetWeaver Business Warehouse, and SAP ERP.

For instance, your organization wants to share several reports (from SAP NetWeaver BW) with a supplier for performance evaluation. You can easily add these reports into the portal environment and then the supplier can access the SUS component processes and the SAP NetWeaver BW reports using a single login to the SAP NetWeaver Portal.

Additionally, if you invite the same supplier to a Bidding event, the portal can again be used as a seamless interface to the supplier. Further, the Bidding Engine component can be integrated with the SUS application in such a way that the supplier view is unified. Figure 5.4 shows an example of the SUS application after accessing it via the SAP NetWeaver Portal.

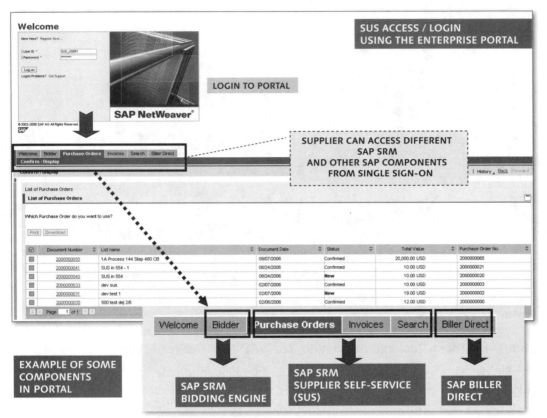

Figure 5.4 Accessing SUS via the SAP NetWeaver Portal

According to SAP America, the vision for supplier collaboration is: "Unified access to collaborative applications and information gateway, providing suppliers with a single point of access. This enables collaborative processes along the entire supplier relationship lifecycle."

5.2 Supplier Registration

For an organization to reduce administrative overhead with the help of supplier enablement, SAP SRM provides multiple options to register prospective suppliers that are going to engage in collaborative processes with the organization. The *Supplier*

Registration process is integrated with the overall Supplier Selection and Use process in SAP SRM. This process is discussed below and also described briefly in Chapter 6. Suppliers can be registered in SAP SRM in the following ways:

- The buyer organization registers the supplier manually
- The supplier self-registers on the buyer's website

The process of self-registration in SAP SRM is enabled using the Supplier Registration concept, which utilizes SAP SRM, Supplier Registration, and SUS to complete the entire process. The process for manually creating the suppliers does not utilize the Supplier Registration application available in the SAP SRM system.

5.2.1 Buyer Organization Registers the Supplier

If your organization already has the necessary detail about a supplier's company, you can *register* the supplier manually. You can register the supplier either as a business partner in SAP SRM, or you can create a vendor master record for this supplier in the SAP ERP backend. Once you've created the vendor or business partner (or replicated the organization from SAP ERP), a user ID and password is created for the supplier in the SUS application. This ID is automatically sent to the vendor or business partner via the email specified. This process is illustrated in Figure 5.5.

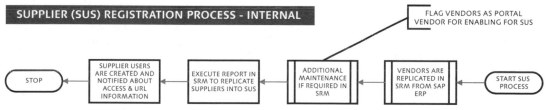

Figure 5.5 Buying Organization Registers Suppliers Manually

You need to create the appropriate supplier users (contact persons) in SAP SRM, in the SUS application. Additionally, the roles you assign to these users are SUS roles, which are different from roles in SAP EB or SAP ERP. Often, organizations forget that these are different applications and therefore the security is independent in each of these applications. The security teams responsible for creating users need to know that the users need to be created with the User management application in SUS, and cannot be created using the Create User (SU01) transaction in the system. This is illustrated in Figure 5.6.

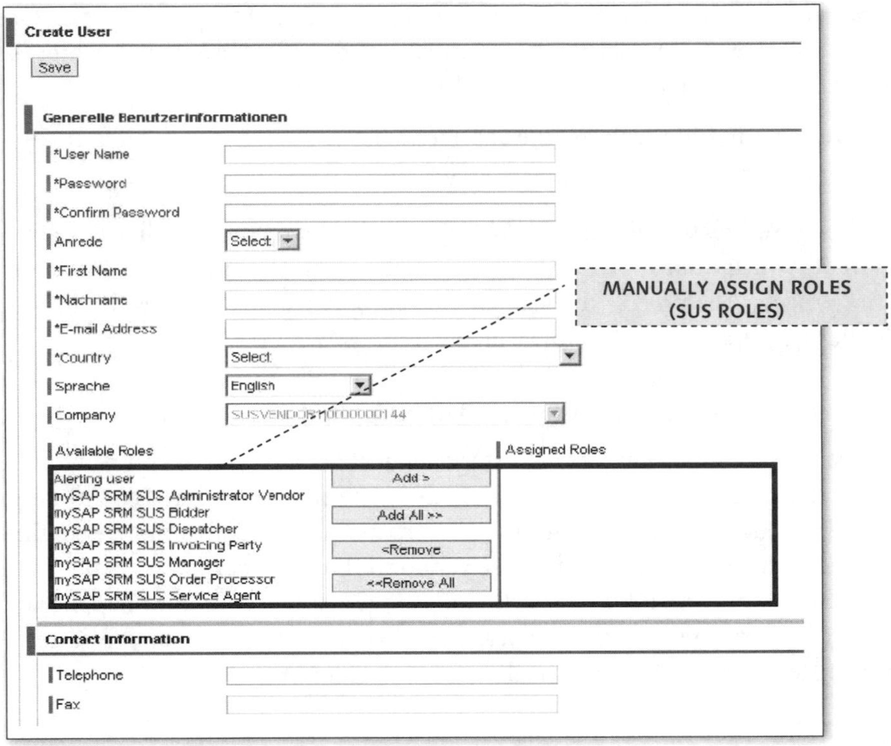

Figure 5.6 Creating Users in SUS User Management

5.2.2 Supplier Self-Registration

An organization can invite selected suppliers to self-register on the organization's website. Suppliers can register using an anonymous user account (no logon required) on the website to fill out a basic application form. In addition to requesting standard information about the supplier, an organization can send category-dependent or -independent questionnaires to suppliers for gathering detailed information regarding the supplier's capabilities for providing goods and services for those categories.

The data in the registration application and the relevant questionnaires is used by purchasers to prescreen suppliers. The supplier information and questionnaires are evaluated by the appropriate purchasing professional who decides to approve or reject a supplier. If approved, you can create a business partner for the supplier in SAP EB and later replicate the business partner as a vendor in supplier self-services.

This process is illustrated via a process flow in Figure 5.7. Each of these processes is further discussed in this section.

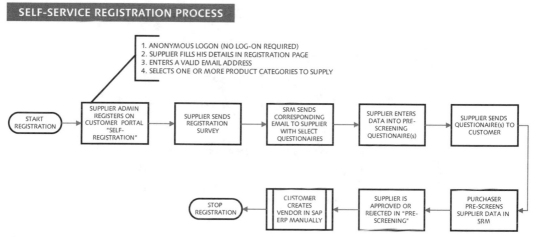

Figure 5.7 Supplier Registers via Self-Service

- **Self-Registration Application**

  To self-register, a supplier can fill out a simple application form to enter its company information. This form requests information that in the past was received from prospective suppliers via fax or mail and was then entered into an SAP system manually. Instead, an organization can now leverage the Self-Registration functionality to electronically receive supplier information. Figure 5.8 shows that the Supplier Registration form contains three main areas to capture supplier details: Company Information, Address Data, and supplier commodity details.

- **Questionnaires**

  An organization can also design specific questionnaires for a specific product category that can then be used for the supplier prescreening process. Figure 5.9 illustrates the customization area for Supplier Registration. You can use the Create/ Change Questionnaire functionality to configure how the questionnaire should be created. Figure 5.9 shows the standard questionnaire available in SAP SRM, which contains three sections: General questions, Certification, and Revenue. This questionnaire is very generic and most organizations will find the need to use BAdIs available in SAP SRM to modify the questionnaire and/or create a new questionnaire.

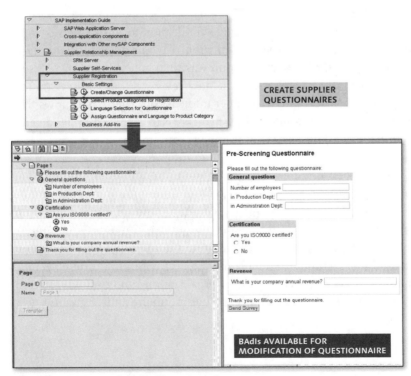

Figure 5.8 Supplier Registration Form

Figure 5.9 Creating Supplier Questionnaires

▶ **Supplier Prescreening**

Once prospective suppliers have submitted their registration applications and relevant questionnaires, the purchasing professionals in the buying organization can prescreen the suppliers, and review their submitted details and questionnaires. Based on the evaluation, they can approve or reject a prospective supplier by clicking on the Accept or Reject buttons.

▶ **Transferring Screened Suppliers to SAP EB**

Once prospective suppliers have been screened and approved as accepted partners, purchasers can individually transfer these suppliers into the SAP EB application as business partners. The supplier can be selected from the list of approved Business Partners and then transferred to SAP EB using the Transfer button. At this time, you can add information to this business partner record, if required. These business partners are then available to purchasers in SAP EB for selection in the Sourcing, Vendor Lists, and other applications.

> **Note**
>
> The Supplier record is at this point only created in the SAP EB system as a business partner. An organization using SAP ERP as an enterprise backend might need to also create the supplier record in the Vendor Master in the SAP system for follow-up functions (PO, Invoice, etc.). The Vendor Master record needs to be created manually, because there is no process to create these automatically. In the EB-SUS scenario, the supplier business partner is created in the SAP EB system. In the MM-SUS scenario, a supplier needs to be created in the SAP backend manually.

▶ **Transferring Business Partners from SAP EB to SUS**

Suppliers created in SAP EB are transferred to the SUS application using the SAP NetWeaver Process Integration (SAP NetWeaver PI). Once this is done, a sales organization is created in SUS and the supplier administrator (registered user) is sent an email containing a registration ID and password that they can use to create an administrator UserID for their company in SUS. The sales organization is then created in the Organizational Structure in SUS.

Once suppliers (business partners) are available in SAP SRM, these suppliers can be replicated to the Organizational Structure in SUS. This replication is carried out using standard programs in SAP SRM.

> **Tip**
>
> If an organization does not want to use the automated process of sending the registration ID via an email, it can deactivate the standard workflow for this process.

Once users are created in the SUS application, the buying organization and the supplier organizations can begin to collaborate on exchange of orders, inventories, invoices, payment status, and others.

5.3 Supplier Collaboration: Order Collaboration

The *supplier collaboration* process in SAP SRM utilizes the SUS component as its core application. The SUS application is, in simple terms, a hosted system that suppliers can easily access using a web browser. SUS provides collaboration capabilities for goods and service orders and integrates suppliers into the procurement processes of large buying organizations. Such suppliers do not require their own sales systems for receipt and processing of orders; external suppliers can then access designated purchasing documents that have been sent from the buying organization for order management or collaboration.

> **Note**
>
> The objective of order collaboration and settlement is to provide an extended number of suppliers, specifically those without sophisticated technical capabilities, with self-service access to orders.

Figure 5.10 illustrates a simple scenario for order collaboration using the SUS application. Here, the process begins with the creation of a purchase order in SAP SRM. If the vendor is a SUS supplier, the purchase order is sent to the SUS application for processing by the supplier. Orders can then be viewed and changed by the supplier to begin the process of order collaboration.

In this section, we'll discuss the detailed functionality available to organizations in SAP SRM for collaboration of purchasing documents with their suppliers. Most organizations today exchange purchase documents with their suppliers using a variety of communication methods, including fax, EDI, XML, and others.

The SUS application is not a one-size fits all solution; organizations cannot expect all of their suppliers to forgo their existing electronic integrations and move to the SUS environment. Typically, this functionality is more relevant for suppliers that are smaller in size and can benefit from electronic order collaboration. Additionally, using this platform makes sense when organizations and suppliers can strategically integrate their inventory and design processes using real-time collaboration in a Web-based environment. Typically, organizations provide SUS access to only a select group of vendors.

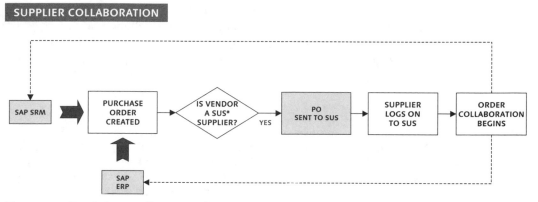

Figure 5.10 Simple Process Illustration of Order Collaboration

In Chapter 3, we discussed service procurement and plan-driven procurement business scenarios. An overview of the two processes is illustrated in Figure 5.11.

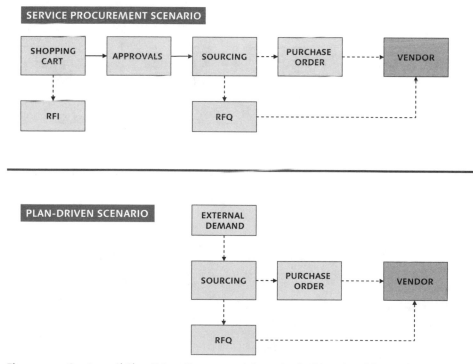

Figure 5.11 Service and Plan-Driven Procurement Scenarios in Operational Procurement

SUS provides capabilities for organizations to utilize the same business processes with select suppliers in a hosted environment (SUS) to collaborate on orders, RFIs, RFQs, and others (illustrated in Figure 5.12). In Figure 5.12, instead of communicating the PURCHASE ORDER directly with the VENDOR, you send the PO to SUS. The supplier can then log in to SUS and access its orders.

> **Note**
>
> The Suppliers/Vendors are enabled in SUS by replicating them from the SAP SRM system. In the SAP SRM transaction, Manage business partners, an email address, standard communication protocol Exchange Infrastructure, and Portal vendor flag must be maintained. After saving these changes, the vendor will be replicated to SUS system automatically. A manual replication can be executed with Transaction BBP_SP_SUPP_INI.
>
> In the SUS-MM scenario, a vendor can be replicated using Transaction BD14 from the SAP ERP system to SUS. The vendor is then visible in SUS in Transaction PPOMV_BBP. Also, an email notification is sent to the supplier notifying them of the creation of their business partner.

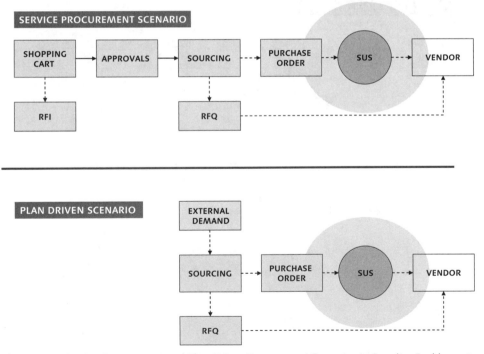

Figure 5.12 Service Procurement and Plan-Driven Procurement Scenarios in Supplier Enablement

In SUS, the following two order management scenarios are supported:

▸ Service procurement with Supplier Integration (also called *EB-SUS*)
▸ Plan-Driven procurement scenario (Integration with SAP Materials Management, also called *MM-SUS*)

These order management scenarios are discussed in detail in the next two sections.

5.3.1 Service Procurement with Supplier Integration (EB-SUS)

Service procurement covers a wide range of services, such as temporary labor, consulting, maintenance, marketing, legal, printing, and facility management. It represents a significant opportunity for procurement cost savings. For services, processes are more complex and less standardized. SAP SRM incorporates the necessary flexibility, collaboration, and constraints for widespread services adoption. We discussed the service procurement process in detail within Chapter 3, Operational Procurement.

This section discusses how the service procurement scenario is integrated with the SUS application, enabling suppliers to collaborate electronically without investing in infrastructure or technology. The buying organization hosts the order management solution and suppliers simply use a web browser for accessing and collaborating in the overall procurement process (as illustrated in Figure 5.13).

Figure 5.13 Supplier Collaboration in the Overall Procurement Process

The processes described in Figure 5.12 are the same as those described in the self-service procurement scenario in Chapter 3. The main difference is that in the self-service procurement with supplier integration scenario, which we'll call the EB-SUS scenario, the supplier logs in to a hosted environment of the buying organization to collaborate on processes such as responding to a service request, receiving orders, confirming goods or services, and entering invoices.

> **Note**
>
> All of these processes are illustrated in Figure 5.14. The difference between what you're learning in this chapter and what you learned in Chapter 3 is that here we discuss the capabilities suppliers have to perform collaborative functions in the context of a hosted SUS solution.

An organization that is implementing the Extended Classic Scenario needs to under-stand that the EB-SUS scenario is not completely supported when Extended Classic is activated in SAP SRM. The scenario works for collaboration of POs, PO response, and change orders but not for confirmation and invoice entry. If the Extended Classic scenario is activated in SAP EB and you send a purchase order from SAP EB to SUS, you cannot send the confirmation and invoice with reference to this purchase order back from SUS to SAP EB. However, some organizations have enabled this function-ality using customizations and BAdIs.

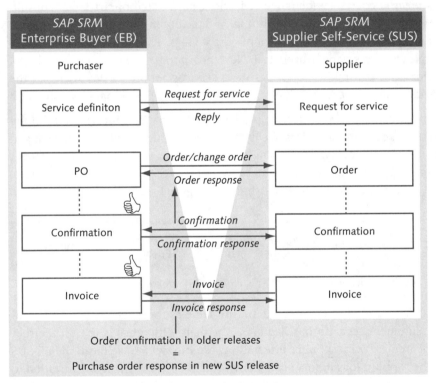

Figure 5.14 Service Procurement with Supplier Integration (EB-SUS)

This chapter focuses specifically on the functionality available to a supplier for per-forming these functions. The functionality available to the purchaser is discussed in Chapter 3. Figure 5.15 shows that the Order, Confirmation, Service entry, and Invoice documents can be created in SAP EB or in the SUS application for select sup-pliers. As mentioned earlier in this chapter, the SUS application makes more sense for a select group of smaller suppliers but not for all suppliers. Smaller suppliers can use SUS to communicate electronically with (larger) buying organizations.

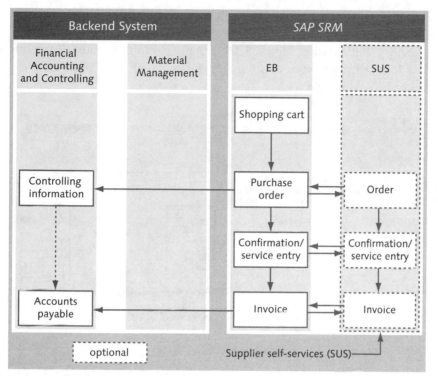

Figure 5.15 SUS Integration with SAP EB

The self-service procurement business scenario only supports the procurement of services and indirect materials; it does not support the procurement of direct materials or planned orders.

<table>
<tr><td>Note</td></tr>
<tr><td>The EB-SUS scenario utilizes the SAP NetWeaver PI component for the communication of all purchasing documents between the SAP EB and SUS application. SAP NetWeaver PI contains standard business content scenarios that enable organizations to distribute orders, order confirmations, and invoices out of the box; however, the SAP NetWeaver PI component needs to be installed and configured.</td></tr>
</table>

SAP EB Purchase Orders

SAP EB Purchase Orders are converted into sales orders in the SUS application. This is because, technically, the hosted SUS application acts as a sales application for the supplier organization. Therefore, in SUS, each PO that is sent from SAP EB has a corresponding sales order number (generically termed as a document number). This is illustrated in Figure 5.16.

Once a PO is created in SAP EB for a SUS vendor, it is automatically sent to the SUS application via SAP NetWeaver PI. In SUS, the PO is available as a New order in the list of POs section (illustrated in Figure 5.16). Suppliers can use a number of different criteria to search for new or existing POs that require further processing for confirmation or invoice entry.

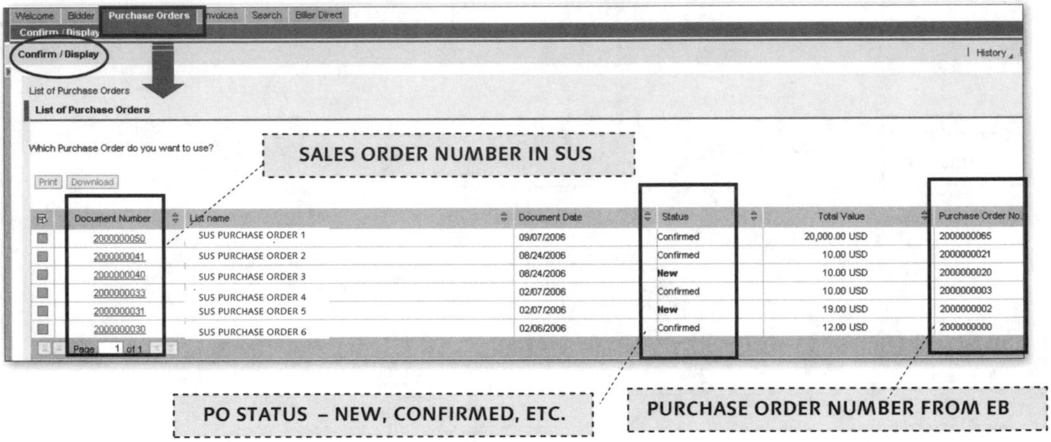

Figure 5.16 List of POs in SUS

To create a confirmation, suppliers can select any new orders that have been sent to them from the buying organization. Once they select an order to process, they can display the different sections of the order, as shown in Figures 5.17 and 5.18. In Figure 5.17, the different areas that exist within the Process Purchase Order application in SUS have been collapsed.

Figure 5.18 illustrates the different areas within a PO in SUS. The Basic Data section shows the sales order number (2000000050) in the Document Number field in SUS and the PO number (2000000065) sent from SAP EB in the Order Number field. A PO sent by a customer becomes a sales order for the supplier. The Items section shows all of the items that are in the PO.

The Messages section enables the supplier to review any messages sent by the purchaser in the Message from Purchaser box or enter new messages in the Message to Purchaser box. The Terms of Payment and Delivery section displays the payment terms for the PO and the information on how any delivery charges will be handled. In the Attachments section, suppliers can review attachments sent by the purchaser, or they can attach any documents that should be reviewed by the buying organization.

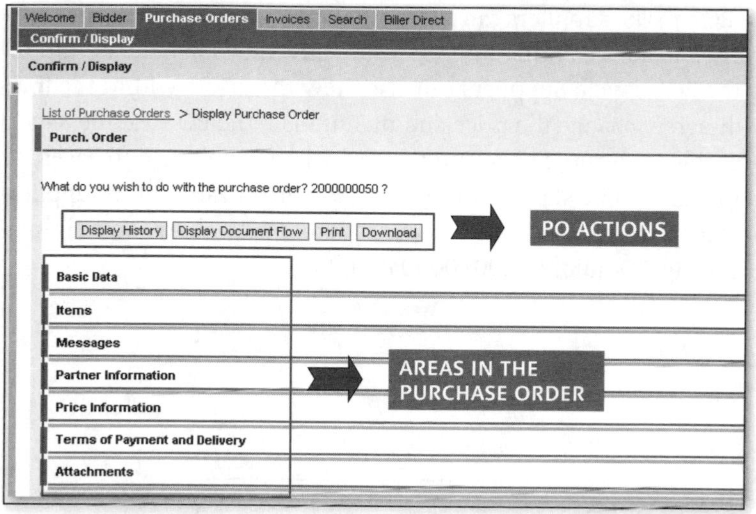

Figure 5.17 PO Sections

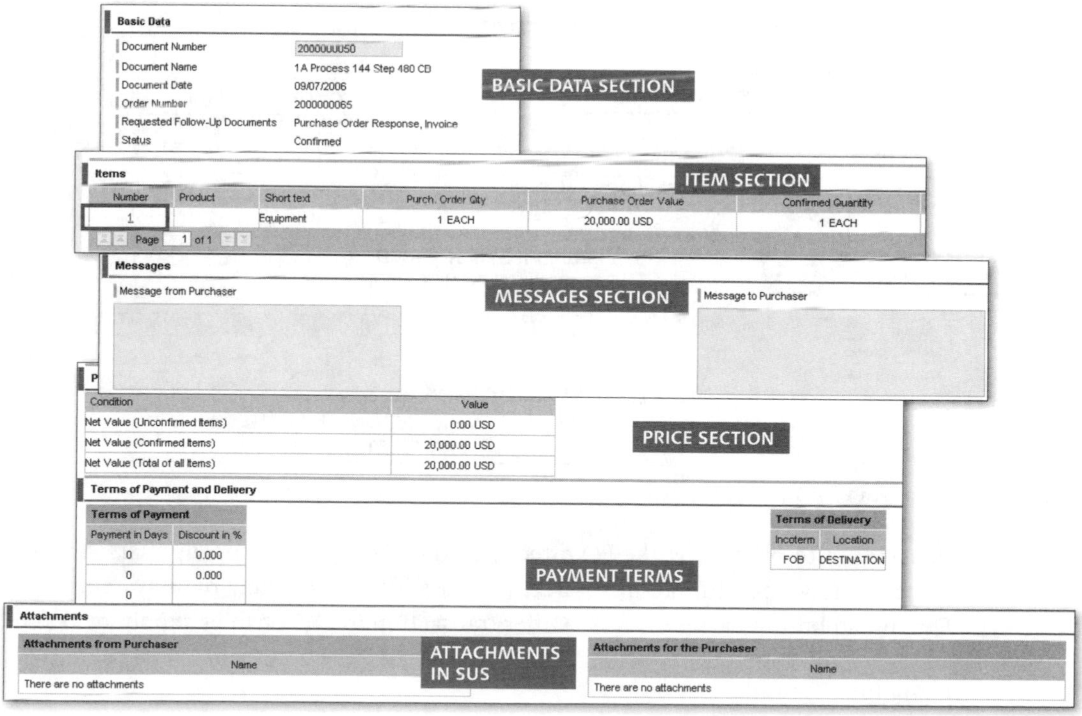

Figure 5.18 Details of PO Sections

While processing a PO in SUS, suppliers can accept the order partially by confirming some of the items or confirm the entire order. Additionally, they have the option to reject the items in the PO as well. Suppliers can also view the prices within the line items, and, if they disagree, change the price and then update the PO. The messages section in the PO enables the supplier to provide information to the purchaser. If additional documents need to be shared with the buying organization, the supplier can also attach documents in the Attachment section. Figure 5.19 shows an example of the supplier processing PO number 2000000040 in SUS.

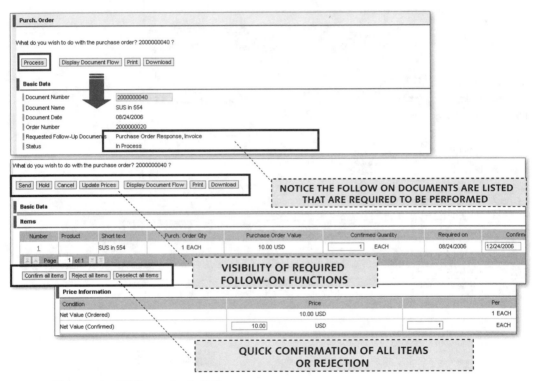

Figure 5.19 PO Processing in SUS

In addition to processing the PO directly in the SUS application, suppliers can also print or download the PO from SUS for possible use in their own systems. The Download button in the Purchase Order transaction in SUS enables suppliers to save an electronic copy of the PO. Figure 5.20 illustrates the XML version of the downloaded PO.

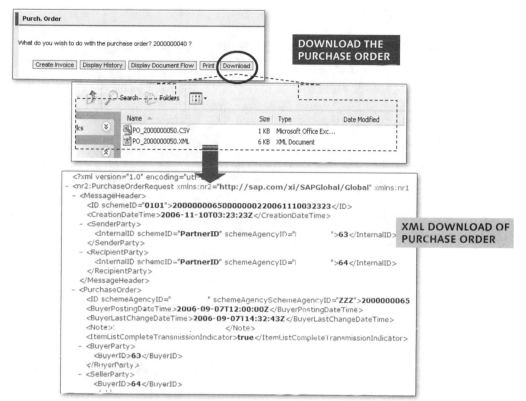

Figure 5.20 Suppliers Can Download POs

Purchase Order Response

Similar to the Purchase Order response transaction in SAP EB, SAP SRM enables suppliers to create a PO confirmation/acknowledgement using SUS. Once the supplier acknowledges the PO in SUS, the purchaser can review it in SAP EB. The PO response application was discussed in Chapter 3. You can see the PO response illustrated in Figure 5.21.

Invoice Entry

Organizations can empower suppliers to enter invoices directly in the SUS application instead of having their internal accounts payable staff create invoices and send them to the purchasing organization. This reduces the number of data entry tasks that need to be performed in-house. Additionally, most small suppliers are unable to transmit invoices electronically. By allowing suppliers to create invoices in SUS, buying organizations can reap the benefits of automatically receiving these invoices in SUS directly. Confirmations are processed in the SUS as seen in Figure 5.22

Figure 5.21 Response

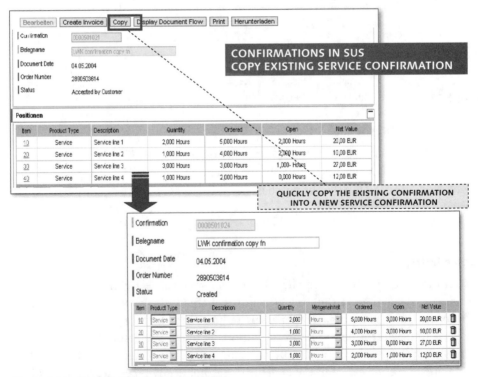

Figure 5.22 Confirmation Processing in SUS

Similar to the invoice entry functionality within SAP EB, SAP SRM lets suppliers create invoices in SUS. Invoices can be created with or without a reference to an existing purchase order. As illustrated in Figure 5.23, to create an invoice, a supplier uses the With ref. to Order link to create an Invoice with reference to a PO. To create an Invoice without any reference to a PO, suppliers need to use the With ref. to Contact Person link. If orders are being sent from SAP EB to SUS, then suppliers will be able to select the PO and directly create an invoice against it. This, however, depends on whether a confirmation or PO response is required before the invoice can be created.

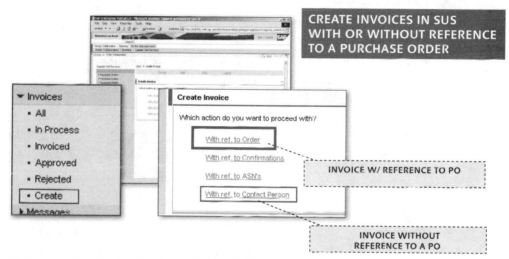

Figure 5.23 Creating Invoices in SUS With or Without PO Reference

When creating invoices, suppliers can also enter costs for unplanned delivery in the Unplanned Delivery Costs field within the invoice (illustrated in Figure 5.24). Unplanned costs are typically not known at the time of the creation of the purchase order. Therefore, this lets suppliers invoice the complete costs for the goods and services performed.

However, it is likely that this will create an invoice block if the total invoice value exceeds any tolerances created for posting an invoice. Figure 5.24 illustrates an example of creating an invoice in SUS. In our example, the supplier has selected PO number 20000000081 and is creating an invoice using the Create Invoice button as seen in Figure 5.23. At this point, he can invoice against all of the line items within the PO or create a partial invoice.

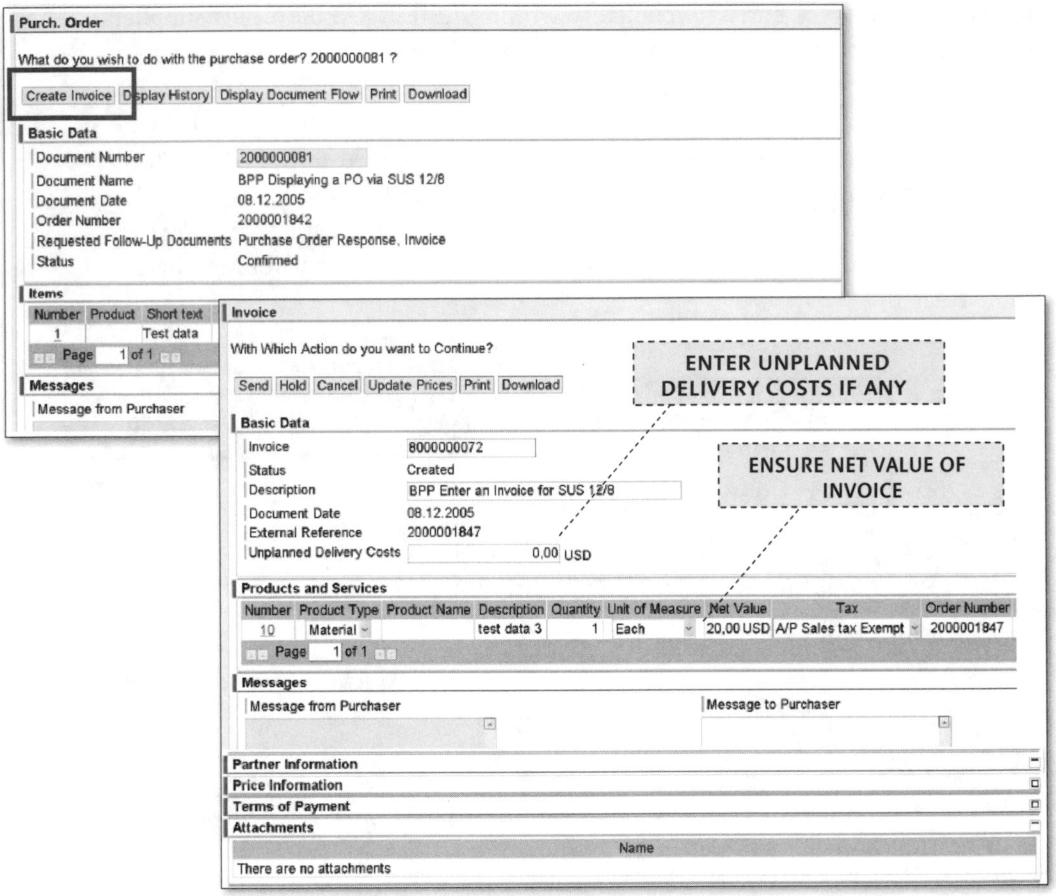

Figure 5.24 Creating an Invoice with PO Reference

At first, many organizations are hesitant to allow vendors to invoice via the SUS application, fearing that they lose control internally. However, SAP SRM provides many standard workflow templates to facilitate the process of approvals prior to invoices being posted in the system. An approval can be triggered in the SAP EB system for any documents posted in SUS.

For example, Figure 5.25 illustrates the approval of an invoice created in SUS. The invoice can always be Approved or Rejected, as shown in Figure 5.24, by the buying organization.

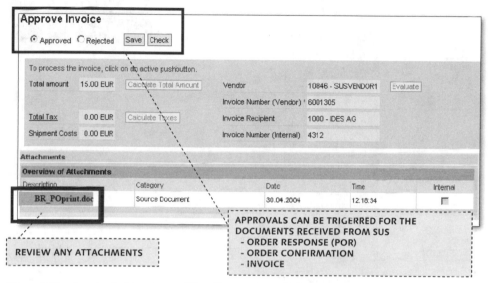

Figure 5.25 Approval of Invoice or Other Documents in SAP EB

As mentioned earlier, the EB-SUS scenario does not support the Extended Classic scenario. Many organizations that implement SAP SRM still process invoices in the SAP backend (ERP) system. Therefore, an invoice entry by a supplier in SUS would not be possible in an EB-SUS scenario, because invoices are sent to EB instead of the SAP backend.

Organizations that have implemented the Extended Classic scenario and want to receive invoices in SAP ERP via SUS need to customize their configurations for the interfaces in the SAP NetWeaver PI scenario (illustrated in Figure 5.26). In SAP NetWeaver PI, development will be required to the outbound and inbound Invoice Request map so that instead of sending the invoice from SUS to SAP EB, it is sent from SUS to the SAP ERP backend.

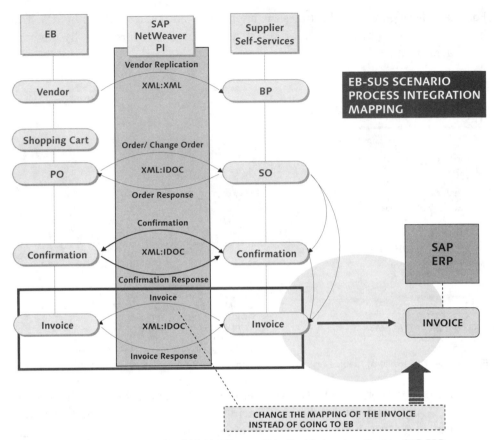

Figure 5.26 Changes Required in SAP NetWeaver PI to Enable Invoices Sent to SAP ERP

5.3.2 Plan-Driven Procurement Scenario with Supplier Integration (MM-SUS)

The *plan-driven procurement scenario* supports the procurement of direct materials or planned orders with integration to SUS, also called the *MM-SUS scenario*. In the supplier integration scenario, the SUS application is directly integrated with materials management in SAP ERP. This scenario is applicable for organizations that want to collaborate with suppliers on direct materials and delivery schedules using the SUS application.

Organizations that implement this scenario do not necessarily have to implement SAP EB, because the document exchange in this scenario occurs only between the materials management in SAP ERP and SUS systems. Figure 5.27 illustrates the processes of the MM-SUS scenario. The MM-SUS scenario enables suppliers to create an Advance Shipping Notice (ASN) in SUS and send it electronically to the SAP ERP backend.

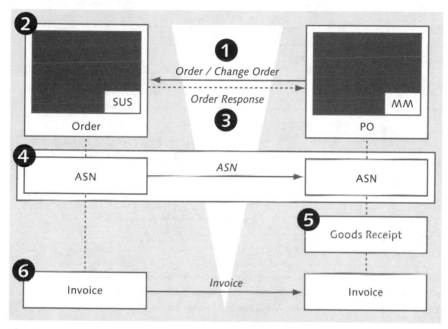

Figure 5.27 Plan-Driven Procurement Scenario (MM-SUS)

> **Note**
>
> The MM-SUS scenario (Classic Scenario) has a limitation around procurement and collaboration of services in SAP SRM releases prior to SAP SRM 7.0. Therefore, you cannot display POs that have item category "D" in the MM-SUS standard scenario. The self-service procurement scenario using MM-SRM and SUS in the standard SAP SRM system is only available beginning with SAP SRM 7.0 and SAP ERP 6.0 and Enhancement Package 4.

In the MM-SUS scenario, organizations have the ability to exchange orders created in SAP ERP systems with their suppliers. These orders are typically generated based on planned demand. Once a PO is generated, it is transferred to the SUS application via the SAP NetWeaver PI layer. Suppliers have the same ability to search and process these purchase orders in SUS as discussed in the EB-SUS scenario.

Figure 5.28 illustrates a material-based PO created in materials management in SAP ERP and the corresponding PO (2000000031) in the SUS application.

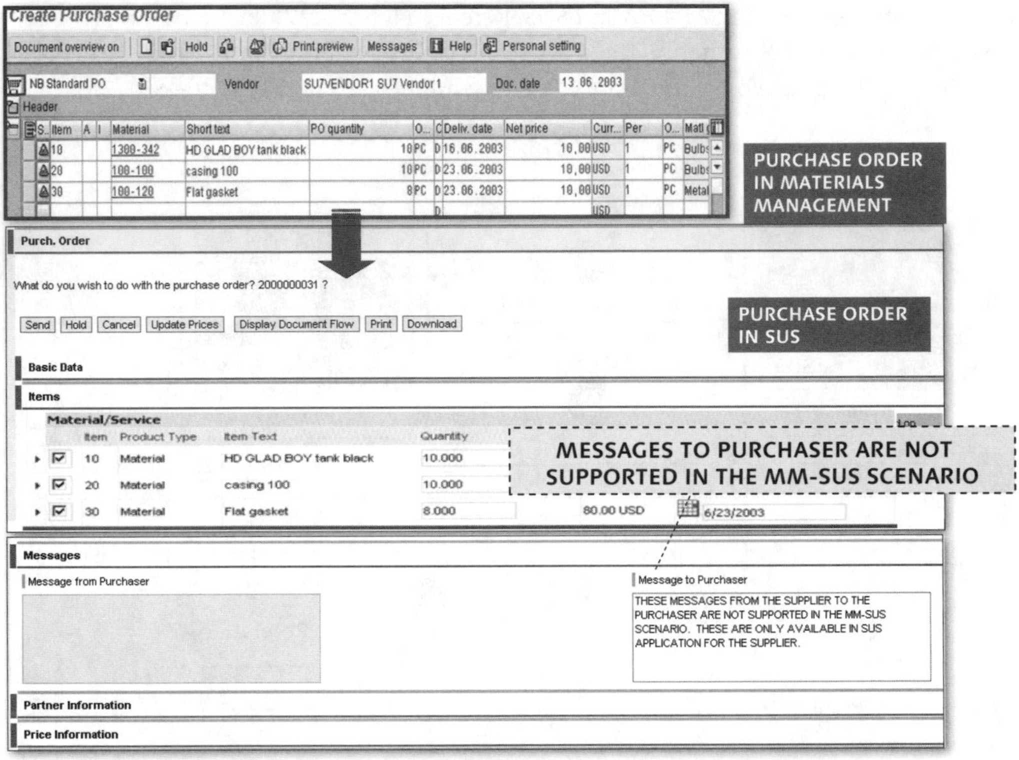

Figure 5.28 Purchase Order in Materials Management in SAP ERP with Corresponding Order in SUS

After the supplier agrees to the goods or services in the PO, he can complete the PO response transaction in SUS. The buying organization accepts the PO.

> **Note**
>
> In the standard MM-SUS scenario, if a supplier enters text into the Message to Purchaser window, it is not transferred to the materials management in SAP ERPPO. This functionality is only available in the EB-SUS scenario. However, there is an OSS note (761150) that customers can use to customize a workaround so that the order acknowledgement (ORDRSP) out of SUS transfers the supplier messages to the PO text on the header in the materials management in SAP ERP PO.

In the MM-SUS scenario, the supplier can create *Shipping Notifications* (also called *ASNs*) to indicate that the goods are being shipped. Shipping Notifications in the MM-SUS scenario are the same as *Confirmation* in the EB-SUS application. Within the

SUS application, there are two buttons (Confirmation and ASN). *Confirmation* triggers a Service Entry Sheet (SAP SRM 7.0) and *ASN* to a Shipping Notification / Inbound Delivery in SAP ERP. The service confirmation in SUS generates a Service Entry Sheet in "held" status in SAP ERP.

Depending on your scenario, the supplier processes either of the two documents. When processing the ASN in SUS, it defaults to the line items and quantities corresponding to the accepted PO (sales order) during the PO response process. Subsequently, the supplier can select the line items and quantities to be confirmed.

The ASN is completed in SUS; it is then transferred to the SAP ERP system via SAP NetWeaver PI. The ASN automatically creates inbound deliveries and the confirmation control key "LA" is included on the incoming confirmation line items. In Figure 5.29, a confirmation (SUS ASN) is posted in SAP ERP. Inbound deliveries 180000111 and 180000112 are automatically created in materials management in SAP ERP for the confirmation performed in SUS.

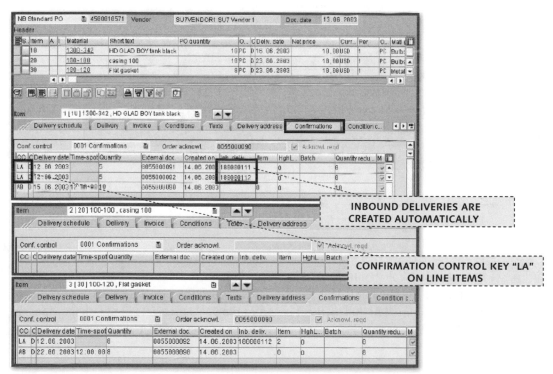

Figure 5.29 Confirmation in SAP ERP Based on Supplier-Posted ASN

225

Once the ASN has been posted in SAP ERP, you can create an invoice in SUS per the ASN. Invoices can be created with a reference to the PO or directly against the ASN in SUS. Figure 5.30 shows how to create invoices with a reference to ASNs in SUS. In SUS, the invoice will default to the line items and quantities that have been confirmed in the ASN. The SUS application can post complete or partial invoices. For partial invoices, at a later time, an invoice can be posted for the remaining amounts.

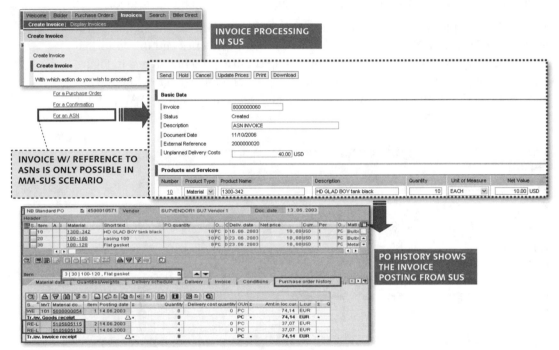

Figure 5.30 Creating Invoices for ASNs in SUS

5.3.3 Payment Status

The supplier collaboration solution lets suppliers review the *status* of an invoice submitted for payment. This functionality is provided by *SAP Biller Direct*, a new SAP application. SAP Biller Direct is part of the SAP Financial Supply Chain Management (SAP FSCM) application. The SAP Biller Direct application enables customers and suppliers to submit invoices, make payments, manage accounts, and settle and reconcile transactions via the Internet.

This application supports both customers and suppliers in either the Buy-Side or Sell-Side of SAP FSCM. Procurement functions fall under the Buy-Side functionality in SAP Biller Direct, which enables suppliers to view accounts payable information via the Web. It also allows your suppliers to perform Web-based self-service account inquiries and examine payment status.

Figure 5.31 shows the Sell-Side and Buy-Side of SAP Biller Direct. The Sell-Side provides capabilities used by customers and the Buy-Side provides capabilities for suppliers. This frees up an organization's accounts payable department from managing supplier questions about payment status, whether they come in by phone, e-mail, or fax. With SAP Biller Direct, suppliers can view payment information online, examine invoice and payment history, and view available supplier credit. Figure 5.32 illustrates the look and feel for the SAP Biller Direct application. Each supplier has access to only his own accounts and can view information on any bills, payments, or credits.

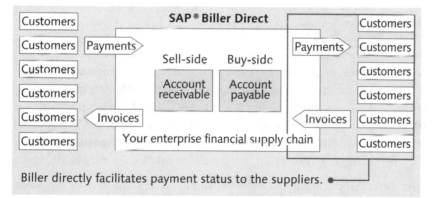

Figure 5.31 Biller Direct — Buy-Side

Figure 5.32 shows the Bill History and Payments Overview and Payments History information, which you can access by clicking on the Bills button. Remember, an invoice received from a supplier becomes a bill within SAP Biller Direct; the buying organization then makes payments for any open bills for a supplier.

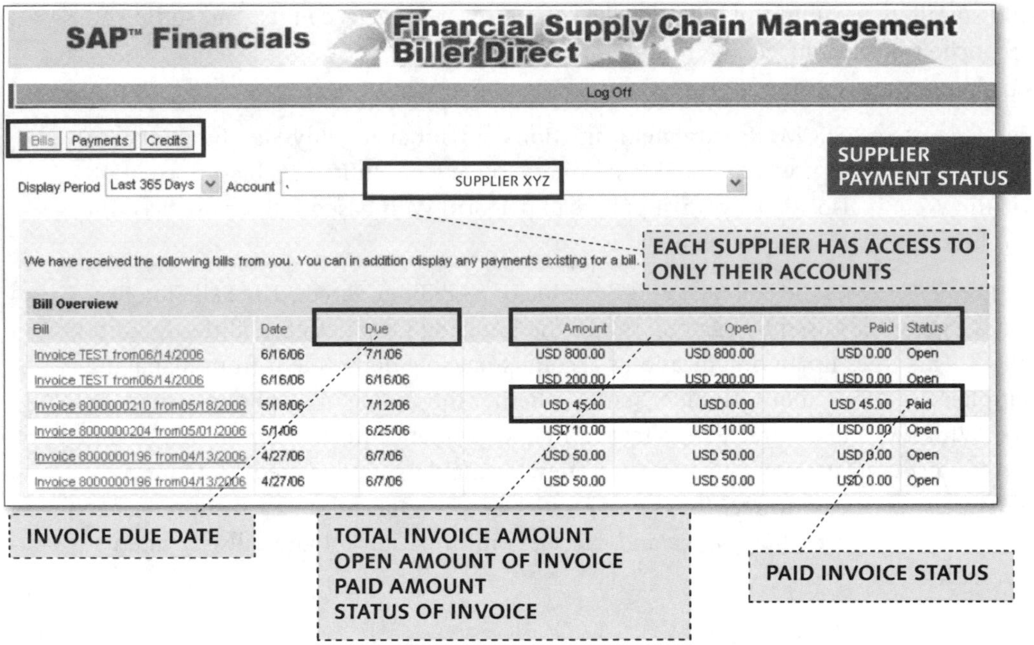

Figure 5.32 SAP Biller Direct — Vendor Payment Status

The Payment Status screen lets suppliers see the bills received (invoice), including information on due dates, open amounts, and payment status. Additionally, suppliers can get information on the actual check that was posted by the buying organization for bill payment. For example, Figure 5.33 shows that for the supplier Invoice 8000000210, a Check (1000000297) was posted in the amount of USD $144.00. This information provides for self-service for suppliers and reduces the need for manual follow-up with the accounts payable department about invoice payments.

The SAP Biller Direct application is new and its Buy-Side solution has not been implemented at many organizations. Prior to being integrated into SAP Biller Direct, a separate application, Payer Direct, existed for the Buy-Side. This application is no longer supported. If you have short project timelines, exercise caution when implementing this application.

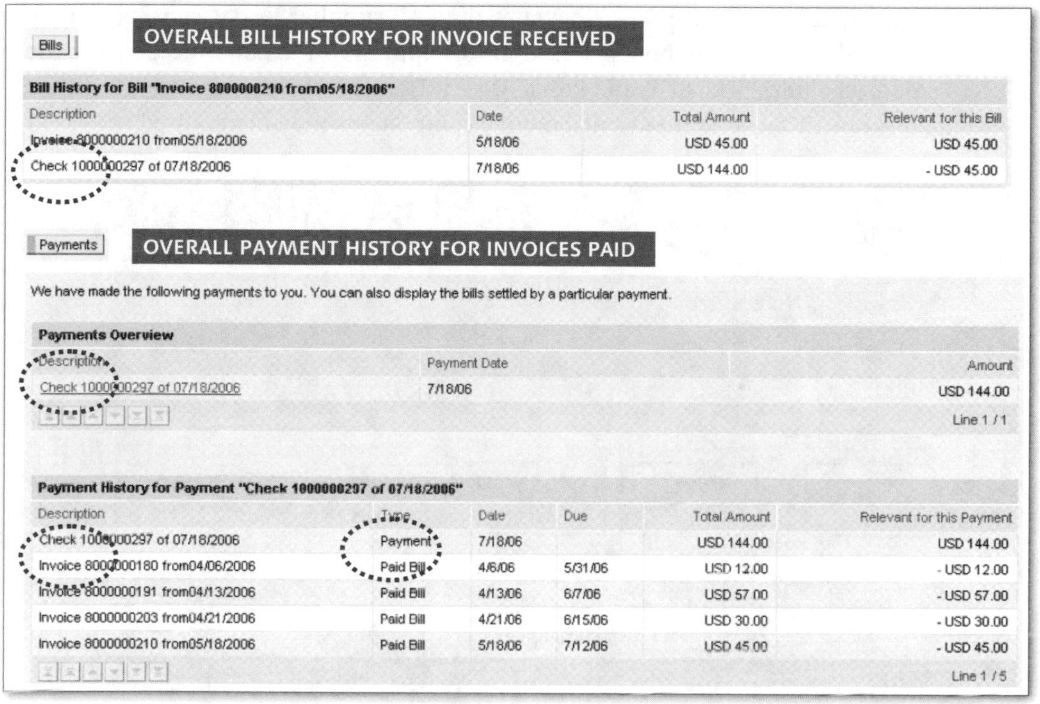

Figure 5.33 Detail on Bill Payment and History

5.4 Supplier Collaboration: Inventory and Replenishment

SAP SRM integrates with SAP SCM to provide automation and greater supply chain visibility for organizations and suppliers for collaboration of inventory and replenishment of orders. This software does not utilize supplier self-service component. Instead, this capability is provided by the following solutions.

5.4.1 SAP NetWeaver Portal Business Package for Supplier Collaboration

To provide a single collaborative solution for supplier management, SAP developed the Supplier Collaboration business package in the SAP NetWeaver Portal. The portal business package provides a unified solution for the supplier who does not need to understand the various SAP applications that provide the underlying capabilities.

In this scenario, the supplier logs in to a supplier portal and all of the relevant information is pulled from all SAP systems and is displayed via the supplier collaboration business package. Figure 5.34 illustrates the SAP supplier portal concept. The different collaborative components used in this application include the Collaboration Folders (cFolder), SUS, SNP, and Purch. Direct. Depending on your business requirements, one or more of these collaborative components may be required.

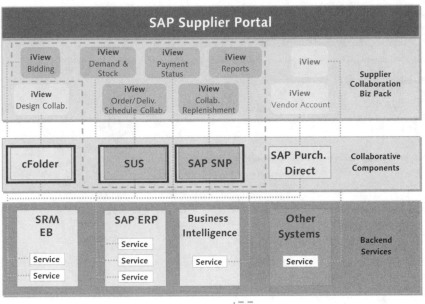

Figure 5.34 Supplier Portal or Supplier Collaboration

5.4.2 Supply Network Planning

Some organizations may find distinguishing between order collaboration and collaborative replenishment confusing. Figure 5.35 illustrates the difference between collaborative order management and collaborative replenishment.

In Figure 5.35, the Order Management process is enabled by supplier self-services and the inventory management process is enabled by supply network planning (SNP). The SNP functionality is not part of SAP SRM; instead, it is within SAP SCM. Therefore, organizations that want to use the processes illustrated in Figure 5.35, such as supplier managed inventory, will have to install and configure SNP independently from SAP SRM.

SUPPLIER SELF-SERVICES (SUS) SAP SRM		SUPPLY NETWORK PLANNING (SNP) SAP SCM	
	Order Management	**Inventory & Replenishment**	
Process Focus	ORDER MANAGEMENT	INVENTORY MANAGEMENT	
Supported Processes	• Supplier self registration • Bid invitations & auctions • Manage sales orders • Manage delivery schedules • Enter services rendered • Create invoices	• Supplier managed inventory • Manage delivery schedules • Create/change order • Packaging & printing	
	Demand & stock visibility, display financial status, reporting & alert handling		
Supplier Role	Sales assistent	MRP planner	
Product Categories	• Indirect Materials • Direct materials • Services	• Direct materials	
Underlying components	• SUS • Supplier Collaboration (business package)	• SAP SNP • Supplier Collaboration (business package)	

Figure 5.35 Supplier Collaboration Order Management (SUS) vs. Collaborative Replenishment (SNP)

Section 5.3 discussed the Order Management functionality. Organizations that are interested in the functionality identified under collaborative replenishment should review SAP SCM, specifically SNP.

5.5 Design Collaboration Using SAP PLM

SAP SRM enables engineering and product development teams in buying organizations to collaborate with their strategic suppliers providing those products. Sourcing of engineered materials requires efficient collaboration between buying organizations and their suppliers. Early communication between engineering, purchasing teams, and suppliers provides an environment that optimizes product costs during the early design phase and considerably shortens time-to-market.

The design collaboration capabilities are provided using the cFolders functionality in SAP PLM and the Bidding Engine in the SAP SRM application. Figure 5.36 illustrates the integration point between the SAP PLM and SAP SRM solutions.

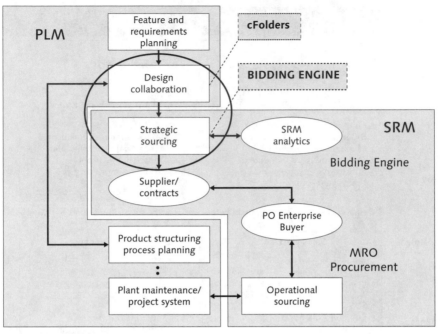

Figure 5.36 SAP SRM and SAP PLM Integration Points

SAP PLM contains a Web-based cooperation platform, referred to as cFolders. This platform promotes communication and collaboration between groups and people who need to work together but are regionally dispersed. Figure 5.37 illustrates cFolders in SAP PLM.

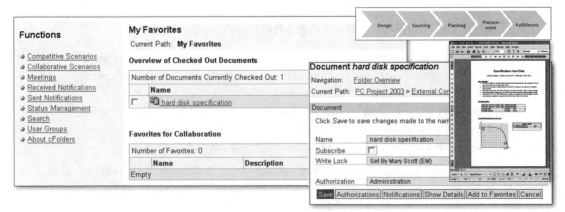

Figure 5.37 cFolders in SAP PLM (Figure Credit: SAP America)

cFolders is integrated with SAP SRM for customers who want to extend design collaboration capabilities to strategic sourcing and procurement for engineered goods (bills of material [BOMs]) and services.

The following bullets identify some of the benefits of using the SAP SRM design collaboration solution:

▶ Optimize product costs in the early design phase by bringing engineering and sourcing teams closer together.

▶ Increase process efficiency and shorten time-to-market through better communication between engineering, purchasing teams, and suppliers.

▶ Ensure the right deals with the right companies while accelerating the ability to develop and deliver new products.

5.6 Design Collaboration Using SAP SRM

In SAP SRM, the design collaboration process can be triggered in two ways:

▶ Via the Bidding Engine by the professional purchaser
▶ Via cFolders by an engineering professional

Either of these two scenarios leads to collaboration between purchasing and engineering departments when creating a bid invitation that is sent to a select group of suppliers. The overall bidding process is the same as discussed in Chapter 6. However, in this scenario, the supplier reviews the technical specifications in the cFolders application using a link provided in the bid invitation. Suppliers and buyers collaborate easily.

5.6.1 Design Collaboration via Bidding Engine by Purchasing Professional

Let's discuss the process of design collaboration when the collaboration is triggered by a purchasing professional using the Bidding Engine.

The following describes the process steps illustrated in Figure 5.38:

❶ The purchasing professional initiates a bid invitation from within the Bidding Engine application, based on requirements gathered from the engineering department.

❷ The purchaser creates a collaboration project within the cFolders application in SAP PLM and invites engineers to add product specifications within cFolders for the particular good or service required.

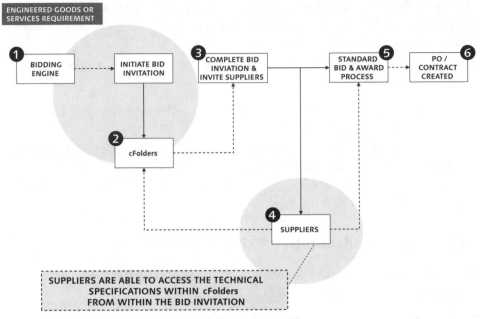

Figure 5.38 Sourcing Process Triggers Collaboration in cFolders

❸ Once all of the information is added in the cFolders project, the purchasing professional can complete the bid invitation and invite suppliers to participate in the bid invitation. Invited suppliers receive the notification about the bid invitation via email.

❹ Suppliers can initiate a corresponding bid and access technical specifications and other documents available within the cFolders application using a link available in the bid invitation.

❺ The standard bid and award process starts at this point, as described in Chapter 4 (Strategic Sourcing and Contract Management).

❻ Once all bids are received, the purchaser and the engineer can evaluate the bids based on the criteria defined in the bid invitation and create either a PO or a contract.

5.6.2 Design Collaboration via a cFolders Project by an Engineering Professional

Let's discuss the process of design collaboration when the collaboration is triggered by an *engineering professional* using the cFolders application.

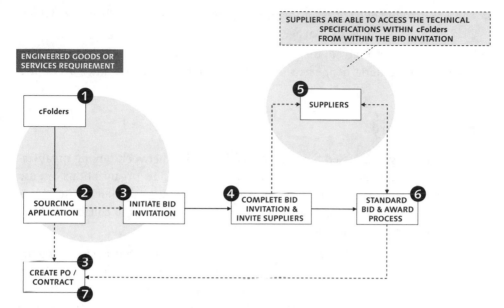

Figure 5.39 Engineering Process Triggers Collaboration in cFolders

Now you can review a description of the steps of the process illustrated in Figure 5.39:

❶ An engineer with access to the SAP PLM application can create a collaboration project requirement in cFolders and upload any technical product information related to the goods or services that are required from a supplier.

❷ The purchasing professional receives the requirement from cFolders as an open shopping cart in the Sourcing application in SAP SRM, with a link to the respective cFolders collaboration.

❸ The purchasing professional reviews existing sources of supply to source the goods or services required by engineering. If a source is found, the purchaser can inform the engineer to create a PO or contract. If no suitable sources are found the purchaser can initiate a bid invitation.

❹ The purchaser can add information and evaluation attributes to complete the bid invitation and invite suppliers to participate in the bid invitation. Invited suppliers receive the notification about the bid invitation via email.

❺ Suppliers can initiate a corresponding bid and access technical specifications and other documents available within the cFolders application using a link available in the bid invitation.

❻ The standard bid and award process now starts, as described in Chapter 4 (Strategic Sourcing and Contract Management).

❼ Once all bids are received, the purchaser and the engineer can evaluate the bids based on the criteria defined in the bid invitation and create either a PO or a contract.

5.7 Summary

In this chapter, we discussed the need for collaboration between buying organizations and their supplier communities. You learned about how organizations can use the capabilities of SAP SRM to progress supplier enablement. Supplier self-service is a core functionality within SAP SRM that enables organizations to collaborate both indirect and direct materials and services with suppliers.

Using SUS, suppliers and buying organizations can exchange business documents such as POs, PO Change, and Acknowledgments. In addition, using the MM-SUS business scenario, organizations can collaborate on direct material POs and allow suppliers to perform ASNs electronically using SUS and automatically integrate those ASNs within the materials management in SAP ERP application.

We also discussed the portals-based supplier collaboration solution that allows organizations to further collaborate with suppliers. Using SAP applications such as SNP and SAP PLM, organizations can share planning and forecast information, allow suppliers to manage inventory levels, and involve strategic suppliers to collaborate on engineering and design documents.

In Chapter 6, we'll address catalog and content management. The chapter starts off by discussing the need for catalogs and explaining how organizations can build a robust catalog strategy. Then, we'll move on to the SAP Catalog and Content Management (SAP CCM) solution, which enables organizations to create and manage internal (in-house) catalogs.

PART III
SAP SRM Implementation,
Integration, and Upgrades

"Catalogs are a key necessity for all successful e-procurement and supplier relationship management projects. The mantra for catalogs is: If you cannot find it, you cannot buy it; the quality of the content is a key to finding products and services in a catalog solution." — *Source unknown*

6 Catalog and Content Management — Crafting Your Catalog Strategy

In 2000, the financial firm, Commerce One, stated: "e-Commerce, in its simplest form, comes down to one core component: *content*. If there are no supplier catalogs, there is no e-commerce."

e-Procurement evolved from automating procurement processes into an end-to-end supplier relationship management solution. Catalog management has seen a similar evolution in the past few years. In the late 1990s, some of the e-procurement market leaders such as Ariba, Requisite, and Ascent used electronic catalogs to elevate the value that organizations obtained by implementing e-procurement solutions.

At some point in the last few years, the "*e*" was dropped from e-catalog, just as it was from many other applications that simply added the "*e*" to indicate "electronic." In this chapter, we will simply use the term "*catalog.*" Let's define the terms *catalog* and *catalog management*:

▶ **Catalog**
A catalog provides users with a list of products and services in an organized and searchable format. This usually refers to the presentation of the content to end users.

▶ **Catalog Management**
This is the process of consolidating and presenting goods and services offered for online purchase. The term usually refers to the authoring and management of content that needs to be presented to end users for searching.

Catalog content plays a vital role in procurement decision-making. On the one hand, buyers require high-quality, up-to-date, and comprehensive content to make the right purchasing decisions more quickly and cost-effectively. On the other hand, suppliers want to ensure that the catalog content is easy for customers to search and navigate.

Catalog solutions have seen an evolutionary growth from e-catalog to catalog management to the recent trend of master data management (Figure 6.1 illustrates this trend). The question is whether the catalog application your organization is using has caught up to this trend. SAP is in the process of doing so, as discussed in Section 6.2.9, Set up the Open Catalog Interface (OCI) for SRM.

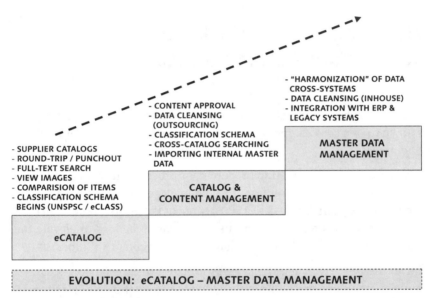

Figure 6.1 e-Catalog Evolution

In the early stages of e-procurement, organizations falsely assumed that accurate, appropriately formatted, buyer-specific content was a given. The reality, however, is that content management is not so simple. Quality content doesn't just happen.

Moreover, supplier-managed content is just one piece of overall content management. Organizations need the capability to present consolidated harmonized content from disparate legacy and enterprise resource planning (ERP) systems. Therefore, a more robust and complete solution is needed that addresses many of the following needs:

▶ Management of data across the enterprise applications, not just a quick upload of supplier data

▶ Cleansing data across disparate legacy and ERP systems

▶ Maintenance of a harmonized product data repository

- Consolidation of multiple ERP instances into a single system of record
- Integration with existing business processes enterprise backend

According to Forrester Research, master data management (MDM) is one of the key trends emerging in catalog and content management strategies for organizations.

Enterprises have long struggled with creating, maintaining, integrating, and leveraging enterprise master data. Furthermore, poor MDM gets in the way of successfully completing CRM, ERP, SCM, and other enterprise application initiatives. It can make it impossible to achieve promised returns on investment (ROI). To address these needs and support the move to services-oriented architecture (SOA), IT organizations are increasingly seeking cost-effective platforms that can support multiple master data entities outside of the core applications that use them.

This chapter is presented in two major parts. First, you will learn to build your catalog strategy. Then you will learn about catalog content management in SAP SRM.

6.1   Building a Robust Catalog Strategy

Before we dig into the SAP solution for catalog management, you need to understand catalogs and the different options available when building a catalog strategy for your SRM implementation. Once these are understood, all the concepts can be applied directly in the SAP Supplier Relationship Management (SRM) application.

In the beginning, many organizations are unaware of the options available to them when it comes to creating catalog strategies that complement their overall SAP SRM implementations.

Therefore, the various types of catalogs will be discussed in detail. This section provides an overview and should be discussed in further detail with your project teams. During the blueprint phase of the project, it is important that organizations discuss their true catalog needs in detail.

6.1.1   Types of Catalogs

Catalogs can be categorized into different types: supplier hosted, broker hosted, and buyer internally hosted.

Supplier Hosted Catalogs

These catalogs are hosted and managed by your supplier. Therefore, the supplier is responsible for hosting and maintaining the catalog and its contents. The supplier offers you access to specific content and company specific pricing, for example,

Office Depot, Dell, and Grainger. While supplier catalogs may be attractive, organizations need to keep in mind that every supplier is different, and this can sometimes be a training issue for casual users.

Broker Hosted Catalogs

These catalogs are hosted and managed by content aggregators, brokers, or the marketplace. These catalogs combine content from a number of suppliers. The content aggregator or broker is responsible for setting up the catalog and maintaining its contents, for example, ICG Commerce and SciQuest. This option provides organizations with access to many catalogs quickly, but the associated costs are prohibitive for many organizations. The benefit for the suppliers is that suppliers only publish content to the broker once to make it available to the entire buying community.

Buyer Internally Hosted Catalogs

These are hosted and managed by your organization. This catalog is hosted, managed, and maintained within your own company's firewall. A catalog tool is installed, set up, and maintained within your organization. Typically, organizations upload supplier data into this catalog, and internal master data from ERP systems is also uploaded into this catalog. Unlike the supplier hosted catalogs, the broker catalogs usually have licensed subscription fees for accessing content and are usually expensive.

> **Example**
>
> The Requisite catalog, SAP Catalog Content Management (CCM), and SAP NetWeaver Master Data Management (MDM) options provide the most control of what users see in the catalog. This requires dedicated support and maintenance staff for keeping the catalog content current.

Figure 6.2 provides a comparison between and illustrates how companies use the different catalog types. The internally hosted catalog can be accessed using a shopping cart within the firewall of your company. However, the supplier hosted and broker hosted catalogs exist outside of the company firewall, and the users accessing these catalogs need authorization to access the Internet to search the products and services offered.

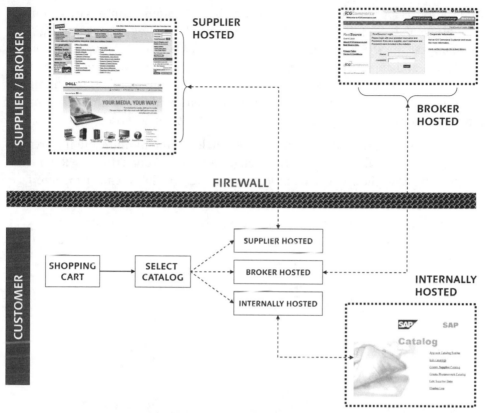

Figure 6.2 Accessing Supplier Catalogs

6.1.2   What are RoundTrip and Punch-Out?

The terms *RoundTrip* and *Punch-out* are synonymous. When the early e-procurement solutions were marketed in 1998, SAP and Commerce One used "RoundTrip," and Ariba used "Punch-out." This difference in terminology remains. RoundTrip allows suppliers to maintain branded content on their own websites (supplier hosted) or use a broker hosted system and extend their electronic catalogs to buying organizations.

A buyer can use a Web browser to connect to the supplier's website to select and configure products from the supplier's custom catalog. The supplier provides buyer specific items and pricing. An example of a RoundTrip catalog supplier is Office Depot. Customers can access the Office Depot catalog directly from their shopping carts and search for thousands of products offered by Office Depot.

After products are selected in the supplier catalog, the RoundTrip service automatically brings the required product details back into the buying application (e.g., the shopping cart in SAP SRM). At this point, the order is routed through the normal requisition and approval processes and eventually converted into a purchase order that is sent back to the supplier for order fulfillment. This provides organizations real-time up-to-date access to the suppliers' content while maintaining control of business processes and approvals within the SAP SRM application.

In SAP, the initial connection to the supplier catalog authentication and final return of the order information to SAP SRM are all facilitated via RoundTrip. The RoundTrip function in SAP is the SAP Open Catalog Interface (OCI). The Open Catalog Interface incorporates external product catalogs into the SAP SRM solution.

The flow illustrated in Figure 6.3 highlights the RoundTrip buying process:

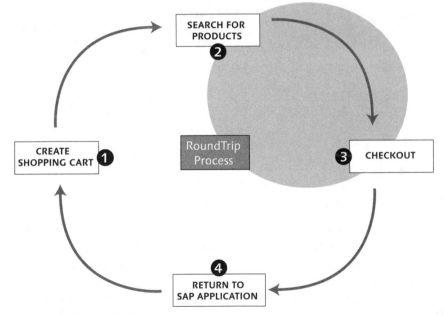

Figure 6.3 RoundTrip Buying Process

❶ The end user searches for products and services by clicking on a link to launch the supplier catalog and jumps directly to the supplier's website.

❷ Upon automatic authentication by the supplier, the end user can search and configure products using the website's resident capabilities. The end user can then select one or more items from the catalog.

❸ When the end user is ready to order the items from the supplier, he clicks on the "Complete order" or "Checkout" (or similar) button on the supplier's website.

❹ The order request with information on one or more line items is sent back to the buying application (SAP SRM). The system automatically brings selected product details back into the buying application. Organizations can configure what information is brought back from the supplier catalog to the buying application.

At this point, the RoundTrip process is completed. The shopping cart can be routed through the usual approval workflow and is eventually converted into a purchase order. Once the purchase order is created, it can be sent to the supplier via a standard format (email, XML, EDI, paper, fax, etc.).

6.1.3   A Single Catalog Solution Might Not be Enough

The key to an effective catalog strategy is to drive the largest possible amount of spending via negotiated catalogs. After all, cost savings and compliance are two key reasons to implement the catalog solution in the first place. And users will only want to use catalogs if they know that they can get to the majority of products and services via the available catalogs. For this reason, it is important to onboard as many supplier catalogs as you can, which is only possible when using a hybrid approach between the different types of catalogs. Organizations may only want to use the RoundTrip option to access catalogs, because it requires the least amount of effort for internal staff on the project and ongoing maintenance. But this strategy is not effective because each supplier needs to be onboarded separately. This wastes time and does not produce the expected results.

Figure 6.4 illustrates how companies can use a hybrid approach to meet their overall catalog and content management needs. When choosing the right catalog strategy for your organization, understand the cost and implementation effort required for each of catalog option.

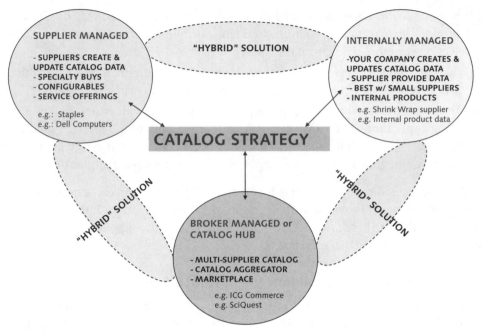

Figure 6.4   Adopting a Hybrid Catalog Strategy

Figure 6.5 illustrates this via a matrix. Organizations that want to use the strategy to internally manage the catalog content should be aware that there are high setup and implementation costs for this strategy.

	CATALOG STRATEGY	COST	IMPLEMENTATION EFFORT
1	**INTERNALLY MANAGED** - SETUP & MANAGE CATALOG INHOUSE	HIGH	HIGH
2	**BROKER MANAGED** - CATALOG HOSTING & MANAGEMENT SERVICES	MEDIUM	MEDIUM
3	**SUPPLIER MANAGED** - CONNECT TO SUPPLIER WEBSITE	LOW	LOW

Figure 6.5   Cost and Implementation Effort Matrix

However, this strategy provides the most control for the company in terms of making sure only select products are available to the end users. It also keeps the pricing for these products in check, because any updates to the catalog can be reviewed by the catalog manager or the buyer.

In comparison, the supplier managed catalog strategy is fairly low in terms of cost and implementation effort. The supplier manages all the content for the catalog and maintains the product and price information on its website. This strategy enables companies to quickly set up access to multiple supplier catalogs with minimum effort from your organization. However, it also provides a minimum amount of control over when updates are made to the supplier catalog content (e.g., new product additions or price updates).

Figure 6.6 provides a list of some supplier-hosted catalog providers that already provide RoundTrip or Punch-out capabilities and have successfully integrated with the SAP SRM application. Organizations need to reach out to their supplier communities as a part of the supplier survey (onboarding process) to determine whether their suppliers are RoundTrip (OCI) compliant.

Figure 6.6 Some RoundTrip Capable Supplier Catalogs

Brokers

The following is a list of some of the leading aggregators or brokers (catalog providers who host integrated catalogs for multiple suppliers in a single location). These catalogs are also accessed using RoundTrip capabilities. Many of these catalog providers started either as marketplace or industry vertical providers (e.g., SciQuest software provides solutions for the higher-education market). The value of a broker is that the organization can get access to many supplier catalogs. However, most catalog brokers charge a lot for their catalog solutions. These include:

▶ SciQuest

▶ ICG Commerce

▶ Perfect Commerce

▶ Ariba

▶ SAP Supplier Network (hubwoo)

Most of these catalog solution providers also provide access to a supplier network solution, which enables companies to access thousands of suppliers and send and receive purchase orders (POs), invoices, and other documents by using a web browser or the latest XML-based or EDI integration technologies. All of these services have extra costs.

6.1.4 Connect with Your Suppliers for Onboarding

One of the biggest pitfalls for organizations when implementing the catalog solution is that they forget to involve their business partners (suppliers) until much later in the project. Suppliers need to be informed and communicated with early in project implementation. This allows the organization to determine which suppliers are ready for integration. The suppliers can project their resource requirements internally to meet the project deadlines for requirements gathering, analysis, testing, and go-live preparation.

Remember, your organization is not the only one that Dell Computers or Office Depot is integrating with. These suppliers have ongoing internal projects and integration projects with other customers as well. Getting on a supplier's timeline ensures a smoother implementation process.

The process of communicating with suppliers and getting them integrated into your overall solution is loosely termed as *supplier onboarding*. Each supplier that needs to be integrated into the SRM application may have unique requirements; therefore, each supplier needs to be onboarded individually. Some integrations are simpler than others based on the supplier and the requirements.

While many organizations order goods and services on supplier websites, the orders are placed directly on the supplier websites, not integrated to application supplier catalogs and websites to order goods and services. For example, when ordering from Office Depot, the order is placed directly on the supplier's website.

Once suppliers are onboarded in the SAP SRM application, they expect to continue to receive their orders electronically. Therefore, many organizations also use the SAP SRM implementation as a step toward implementing electronic means of communicating purchasing documents (e.g., POs and invoices) such as EDI or XML.

Figure 6.7 illustrates an approach for supplier onboarding that has been used by a large educational and health care organization. There are a number of steps involved in onboarding a supplier, and it could take between eight to ten weeks or more to get a supplier catalog onboarded.

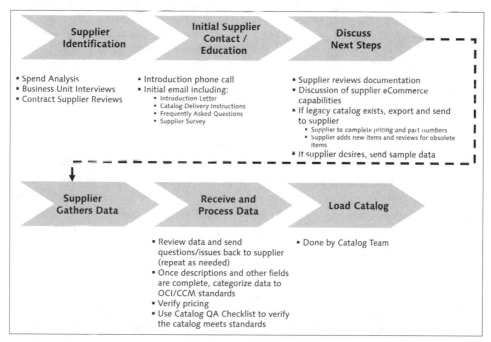

Figure 6.7 Example Supplier Onboarding Approach (Source: Client Organization)

6.1.5 Standardize Commodities

Garbage in is garbage out when it comes to master data and categorization. Organizations that take the time to cleanse and standardize the different master data elements are better able to report and analyze spending data. When it comes to catalog management, organizations must review their product masters and categorization. The product master is categorized poorly in many organizations. The same product could be created multiple times, or even categorized in entirely different commodities. Classifying products and services with a common coding scheme facilitates efficient commerce between buyers and sellers.

Many organizations that embark on SAP SRM also look at the project as an opportunity to standardize their products and services into industry relevant classifications, creating master data that is not only relevant to their internal organizations but also easier for exchange with their supplier communities.

> **Example**
>
> An end user in a health care organization wants to purchase gloves. He searches the available catalogs, selects the desired gloves available from a supplier catalog, and adds them to the shopping cart. Once the relevant information is completed, an order can be generated to the supplier. In this example, the supplier classifies the gloves under the category "Lab Supplies," but your organization categorizes this item purchase internally as "Patient Examination Products." There is a discrepancy between how your suppliers analyze your purchasing activity and the way your organization analyzes it. During contract re-negotiations or new contract discussions with other suppliers, there will be a situation of comparing apples to oranges if you and your suppliers cannot easily analyze the procurement activity.

This example shows where a standard taxonomy comes into play, as large corporations can get a harmonized view of purchases by using standardized codes for purchases. Purchasing departments should incorporate the codes in purchasing systems to help employees throughout the company find and purchase supplies and also to help themselves analyze the expenditures of supplies of the company. This would enable them to analyze the specifics in the buying process at the level of detail that most suits the business needs in a timely and precise manner.

They can cut the time it takes to find the products needed in half or less by searching by commodity code through brokers, online exchanges, business partners, and others across the globe. Organizations can spot buying patterns across departments or business units to leverage better conditions from suppliers and realize overall savings.

During the supplier onboarding process, organizations need to review the products and categories that will be available in the catalogs provided by the prospective suppliers. Then they need to review how they will treat the products once they're returned from the supplier catalog into their internal shopping cart (as described in the RoundTrip process). What categorization or taxonomy will your organization use once the product is returned from the catalog? Are you going to use the supplier's categorization? Are you going to use your own categorization? Are they the same? All these are important questions to answer. Organizations implementing SRM will find themselves mapping their supplier categories to their internal categories unless they follow a common categorization standard.

Organizations that lack a standardized categorization in their current environment should look toward the industry for standardization and classification. Standards and initiatives include the United Nations Standard Products and Services Code (UNSPSC), RosettaNet, eCl@ss, North American Industry Classification System (NAICS), and Standard Classification of Transported Goods (SCTG). These ease the information exchange between customers and suppliers by providing a framework to identify products and services in a global market. These classification systems provide a hierarchical system for grouping materials, products, and services.

UNSPSC is a commonly used classification schema widely used in the United States by customers and suppliers. e-Cl@ss is a classification schema that is more widely used by organizations and suppliers across Europe. Large suppliers such as Office Depot, Fisher Scientific, Grainger, Dell, and catalog brokers such as SciQuest, ICG commerce, and others already use the UNSPSC for classifying products and services with a common coding scheme. Therefore, if you're doing business with these suppliers, you can quickly benefit from using an industry classification such as UNSPSC.

UNSPSC is a hierarchical convention that is used to classify all products and services. It is the most efficient, accurate, and flexible classification system available today for achieving companywide visibility of spending analysis, enabling procurement to deliver cost-effective demands and allowing full use of electronic commerce capabilities. Organizations can get an introduction to UNSPSC and how it can be used at *www.UNSPSC.org*.

Organizations can review their current classification schemes for products and services to see how they can convert to an industry classification, and get the following benefits:

▶ Searching tool for quickly and efficiently finding products and services
▶ Analysis tool for analyzing spending consistently
▶ Standardizing for consistent naming and coding conventions

Thus far in this chapter, we've discussed how an organization should create a catalog strategy. In the next section, we will delve into catalog and content management and how organizations can use SAP SRM to manage their catalog content.

6.2   Catalog and Content Management Using SAP SRM

SAP has provided support for different catalog solutions integrated with SAP SRM. Each solution provided more mature capabilities and integrated solutions for management of catalog content. Beginning with Requisite in 1999 (now a part of Click Commerce), then CCM in 2004, and now the SRM-MDM Catalog since 2007.

Today the SAP SRM 7.0 release is delivered with an integrated SRM-MDM catalog, release 3.0, which provides the application for all catalog and content management. The SRM-MDM catalog is based on the SAP NetWeaver® Master Data Management component (SAP NetWeaver MDM). SAP NetWeaver MDM harmonizes and manages enterprisewide master data such as materials, vendors, and customers.

On the other hand for the SRM-MDM catalog, SAP delivers preconfigured content, which supports the processes relevant for procurement in SAP SRM and ERP applications, for example, the ability to transfer product (material) data from the SAP SRM system to the SRM-MDM catalog for users to quickly search what they need to purchase, or the ability to quickly upload content from suppliers to create an internally hosted catalog.

Many customers are already live with the SRM-MDM catalog. With each new SAP SRM implementation, they upgrade more customers. Overall, the SRM-MDM catalog solution has gained more customer satisfaction because of the maturity and user interface of this application in comparison to the previous CCM catalog.

> **Note**
>
> SAP acquired the MDM technology by acquiring a company called A2i in 2004. Unlike most SAP solutions, which are developed in a native ABAP technology, the MDM solution is based on C++. SAP is in the process of porting this into possibly ABAP, but it will take a while. Currently, the SRM-MDM solution uses the C++ technology for the core and SAP NetWeaver Java technology for the user interface of the catalog.

In the rest of this chapter, we'll provide an overview of the SRM-MDM catalog.

6.2.1   The SRM-MDM Catalog 3.0

The SRM-MDM catalog provides your organization with the ability to create, maintain, and manage catalog content in-house. The SRM-MDM catalog serves as an internally hosted catalog to the procurement organization.

> **Note**
>
> The SRM-MDM 3.0 catalog is based on SAP NetWeaver MDM 7.1 technology. Based on the roadmap, SAP plans to release the next version SRM-MDM 7.01 (or 4.0) at the end of 2009 along with the EhP 1 of the SRM 7.0 business suite. At that point, the SRM-MDM catalog version will be aligned with the SRM version.

So, how does the SRM-MDM catalog work? Figure 6.8 provides a high-level overview of the pieces that make up the SRM-MDM catalog and how they function together. Each of the four components are explained below.

How does it work?

Figure 6.8   SRM-MDM Catalog

1. The SRM-MDM repository

The core technology, about 80%, of the SRM-MDM catalog is leveraged from the MDM solution. SAP provides a repository specifically created for the management of Catalog items. This built-in repository contains data models that are relevant for the SRM processes. This repository is housed on the MDM server.

2. The front-end clients

Individuals who manage and approve the content in the catalog use windows based frontend clients to access the following key functions:

- Importing data via the Import Manager to upload and extract content within the SRM-MDM catalog.

- Enriching new or existing content via the Data Manager and also to possibly approve content.

3. The search user interface (UI)

SAP has created a WebDynpro-based search UI that is used by end users to search the content in the catalog. This search UI has been specifically designed for the SAP SRM application and is not available in the standard SAP NetWeaver MDM application. An end user only needs a web browser to use this catalog search UI.

4. **Integration via OCI technology**

Integration of the SRM-MDM catalog and SAP SRM shopping cart and other applications is done via the OCI technology. This is the same integration that is used when connecting the SAP SRM application with online supplier catalogs (supplier hosted catalogs).

> **Note**
>
> Chapter 13, Section 13.2.4, SRM-MDM Business Scenario, provides an illustration of the integration of SRM-MDM catalog together with the SRM server, MDM, and the SAP NetWeaver Process Integration (PI).

Now that we have an idea of how the SRM-MDM catalog works, let's review how it looks. Figure 6.9 and 6.10 provide an illustration of the user interface (UI) of the SRM-MDM 3.0 catalog that is used by end users to search goods and services to be purchased.

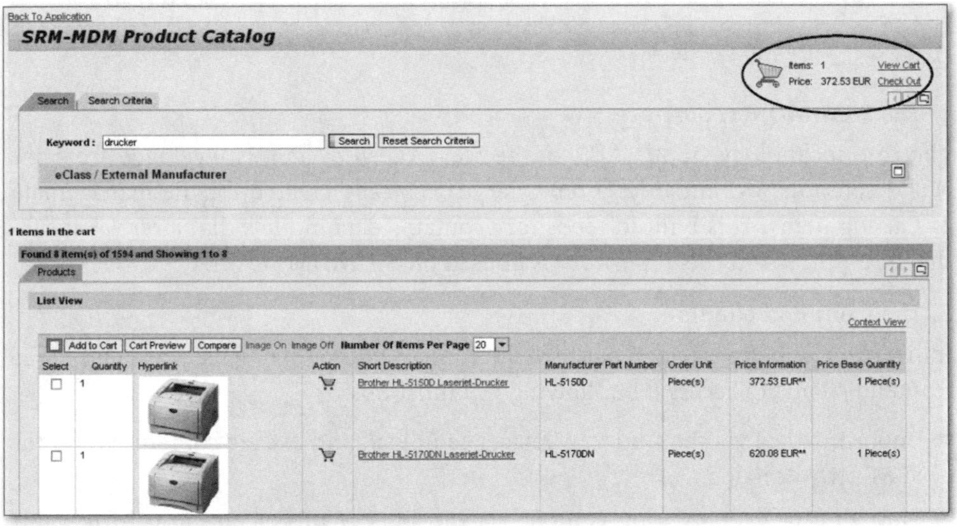

Figure 6.9 SRM-MDM Catalog 3.0 User Interface

Figure 6.9 illustrates the Search screen that is presented to the end users in the SRM-MDM catalog. The keyword search for "drucker" provides a list of all catalog items where the word "drucker" is found. Users can then select the appropriate item(s) and add to their shopping carts by either clicking the Add to Cart button or alternately clicking the shopping cart icon in the action column.

Note

The "Mini" shopping cart enhancement in the SRM-MDM 3.0 catalog provides a preview of the number of items and the total price of items in your cart, simulating a typical experience of online shopping for end users. The "Check Out" option transfers the items from the catalog into the SRM shopping cart application via OCI.

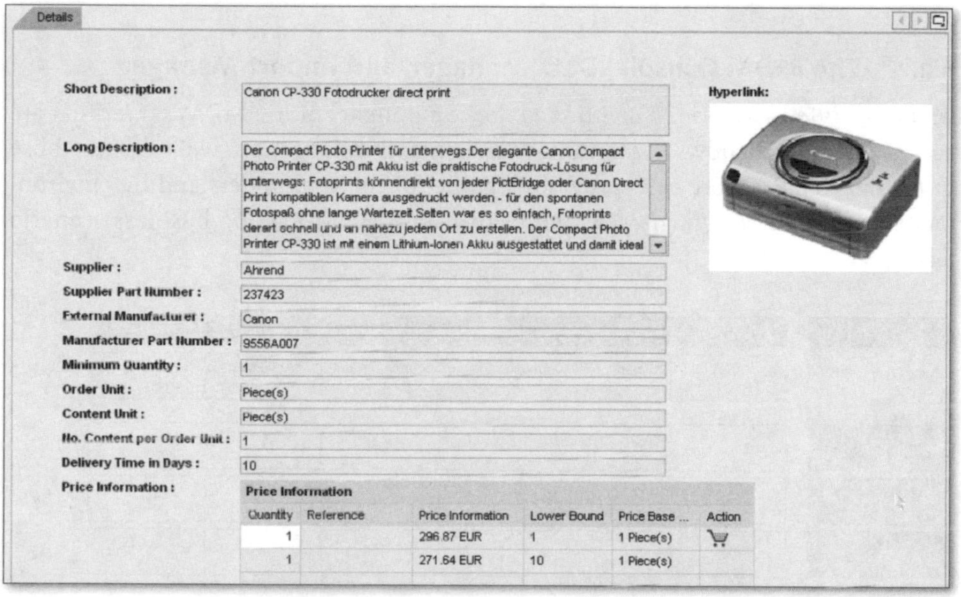

Figure 6.10 SRM-MDM Catalog – Item Detail

Users can also look at the details of each item in the catalog. Figure 6.10 illustrates the detail of a catalog item. The amount of information visible to the end user can be configured as part of the catalog setup.

Now that we have an overview of the relevance of SRM-MDM catalog for procurement, let's review some of the capabilities in further detail.

Note

Customers who upgrade to SAP SRM 7.0 from a previous release can continue to use SAP MDM Catalog Management 2.0 in combination with SAP SRM 7.0. SAP MDM Catalog Management 2.0 SP04 is supported on SAP SRM 7.0. However, this option is only supported for upgrade to customers who are currently using SAP SRM 4.0 or SAP SRM 5.0 with Catalog 2.0. New SAP SRM 7.0 customers have to use the SRM-MDM 3.0 catalog.

> **Note**
>
> Customers that have been using either the Requisite catalog application or the SAP CCM application need the ability to migrate their existing content into the SRM-MDM catalog. Unfortunately, SAP does not provide a migration utility to conduct this task. However, what many customers can do is easily export the content from their existing applications in .csv/Microsoft Excel format and then simply upload into the SRM-MDM catalog using the Import Manager.

6.2.2   The MDM Console, Data Manager, and Import Manager

In the overview, we briefly mentioned the components of the MDM server that are accessed using Windows based front-end clients. In this section, we'll discuss those in further detail. Figure 6.11 provides a guide for users to understand the environment or module in which each step of the SRM-MDM Catalog business scenario takes place.

MDM Module	Process Steps					
	Manage Catalog Repository	Import and Map	Enrich Product Content	Approve Product Content	Enable Web Catalog	Search for Catalog Items
MDM Console	X				X	
Import Manager		X				
Data Manager	X		X	X	X	
Search UI and Configuration					X	X

Figure 6.11 MDM Modules and Setup of the SRM-MDM Business Scenarios

MDM Console

The MDM Console is used by the catalog administrator. Using this console, the administrator can perform the following functions:

▶ Administer and monitor the MDM server
▶ Create and maintain the structure of the MDM repository/repositories
▶ Control access to the MDM repositories via user administration

The MDM repository contains the master data and schema of the actual catalog items. For SRM, a pre-configured repository is provided; however, customers can make copies of that repository and make changes suitable for their business requirements.

Records are not entered or managed using the MDM console but instead with the MDM Data Manager.

MDM Data Manager

The MDM Data Manager is the main application that is used for making changes to the catalog content that has been loaded in the SRM-MDM catalog. At a high level, it allows catalog managers to perform the following functions:

▶ Store, manage, and update master data consisting of text, images, URL, etc.

▶ Create taxonomies, families, and relationships for content

MDM Import Manager

The Import Manager uploads content into the SRM-MDM catalog. Once data is imported via the Import Manager, it is then available for validation and approval in the MDM Data Manager.

Using the Import Manager, you can import the following content:

▶ Data from suppliers such as product catalogs and hierarchies such as UNSPSC/ eCl@ss in either XML, .csv, or Microsoft Excel format.

Content based on the integration scenarios between the SRM-MDM catalog and SRM or ERP, as described in Section 6.2.6, Integration Scenarios between SRM and ERP. The SRM-MDM catalog allows users to search and compare products and services in the published catalogs that have been made available using the Import and Data Manager applications.

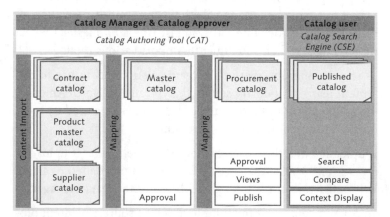

Figure 6.12 SAP CCM – CAT and CSE Functions

MDM allows organizations to create and manage unified catalogs, using tools that import data from internal and external sources, maintain consistent product schemas, and index products for faster search capabilities. This process is illustrated in Figure 6.13.

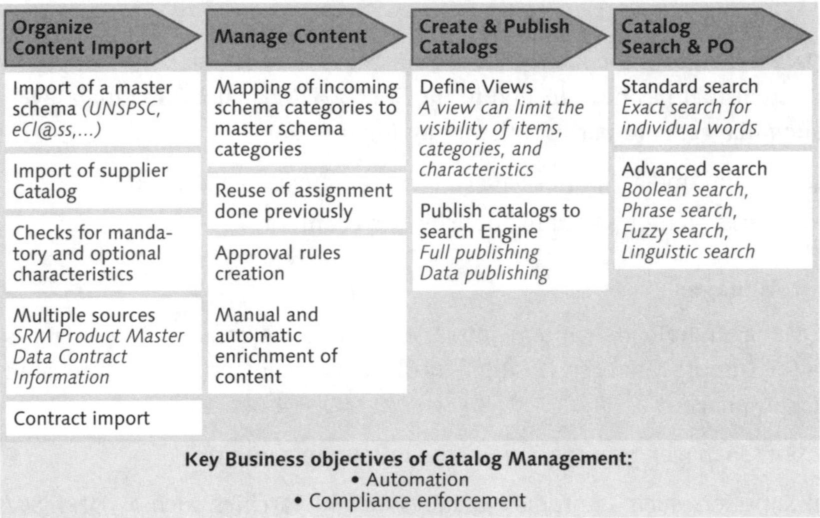

Organize Content Import	Manage Content	Create & Publish Catalogs	Catalog Search & PO
Import of a master schema *(UNSPSC, eCl@ss,...)*	Mapping of incoming schema categories to master schema categories	Define Views *A view can limit the visibility of items, categories, and characteristics*	Standard search *Exact search for individual words*
Import of supplier Catalog	Reuse of assignment done previously	Publish catalogs to search Engine *Full publishing Data publishing*	Advanced search *Boolean search, Phrase search, Fuzzy search, Linguistic search*
Checks for mandatory and optional characteristics	Approval rules creation		
Multiple sources *SRM Product Master Data Contract Information*	Manual and automatic enrichment of content		
Contract import			

Key Business objectives of Catalog Management:
- Automation
- Compliance enforcement

Figure 6.13 Process in MDM

Each of the processes seen in Figure 6.13 is discussed individually in the following subsections.

6.2.3 SAP NetWeaver MDM — Organize Content Import

The main aim of the import process is to collect data from all possible sources into the MDM catalog. This could simply be a catalog file that you receive from your supplier or product information from your internal systems. Upload a master schema (categorization) for the catalog and then subsequently import various catalogs.

The master schema is the classification that your organization wants to use to categorize the catalog content using an industry standard. Typically, in North America, the UNSPSC schema is widely used. In Europe, the eCl@ss schema is used by most of the suppliers to categorize content to uniform taxonomy.

The master schema is uploaded into the MDM catalog. The schema that is uploaded can be in different formats (e.g., UNSPSC). Once the schema is uploaded, the catalog can be edited to view the structure of the uploaded schema in the Data Manager.

The MDM catalog can contain content from multiple different sources: content provided by external suppliers, material master data from an SAP backend or product master in SAP SRM, and contract data (illustrated in Figure 6.14).

The following subsections explain further the different types of catalogs that can be uploaded into SAP CCM.

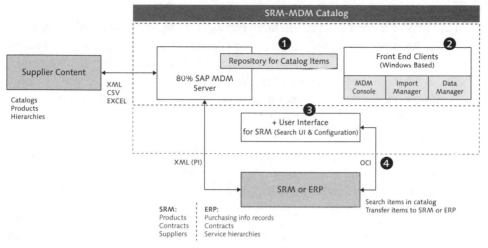

Figure 6.14 Uploading Data into MDM Catalog from Multiple Sources

Vendor Supplied Content

Based on a predefined template, these are also called *upload supplier content*. Suppliers can provide a list of their products in a predefined template format provided. This product listing usually contains product attributes such as prenegotiated contract price, description, picture (where allowable), manufacturer's part number, supplier's part number, and quantity in its container.

The format is typically in the form of a .csv, Microsoft Excel, or XML file. Select the Supplier Catalog and then click Upload to upload as a .csv or XML file. If the supplier catalog is imported using the XML format, the SAP NetWeaver Process Integration application is required.

SRM Product Master

Once the product master is transferred from the SAP EB system into the catalog, a product catalog is created in SAP NetWeaver MDM. The replicated products are available in the catalog within each product category hierarchy.

6.2.4 SAP NetWeaver MDM — Manage Content

Content management in SAP NetWeaver MDM provides the capability to enrich the catalog content to make minor changes directly in the MDM catalog. In addition, organizations can also create approval rules that can be used after catalog data has been uploaded.

- **Enrich Item Data**

  In the master catalog and procurement catalog, managers can manually enrich the product information by adding missing characteristics or characteristic values. SAP NetWeaver MDM allows mass editing of items, so catalog managers can select a set of items and then perform functions such as change, delete, or copy. If required, the catalog manager can manually create additional items and characteristics directly in SAP NetWeaver MDM.

- **Approvals**

  SAP NetWeaver MDM provides an approval capability for organizations to review uploaded content and determine whether the information is appropriate before it can be published and made available to end users. Rules can be defined to determine automatic and manual approval of items.

The default status for all catalogs is delivered as to be approved. Organizations can change this option in *Customizing*. Designated approvers can now search for all items that are assigned to them and have an approval status "to be approved." They can approve or reject single items or all selected items at once. In addition, item history is available to view the changes made to a particular item over time. Approvers can view information such as who uploaded the item, when the approval status was changed, or who approved the item.

6.2.5   SAP CCM — Search

The catalog search process, illustrated in Figure 6.15, allows end users to search the published catalog views. Users have access to specific catalog views based on the catalog authorization in the SRM Organizational Structure. In SRM, users can access the MDM catalog from one of the following applications:

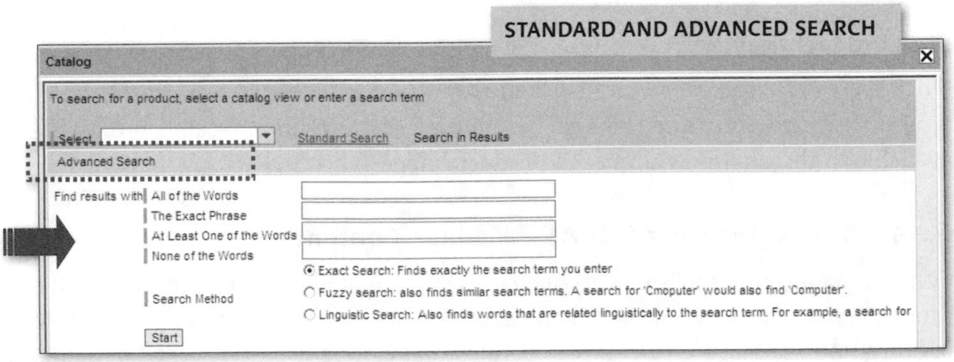

Figure 6.15   Standard and Advanced Search

- ▶ Shopping carts
- ▶ POs
- ▶ Contracts

From a process perspective, the end user selects the MDM catalog from one of these applications to launch the SRM-MDM application. Once the user is able to search and find the goods or services in the catalog, he can return to the SAP SRM application along with all the items selected in the MDM catalog.

At this point, he can access the process the shopping cart, PO, or contract further or send it for the next step.

6.2.6 Integration Scenarios for SRM and ERP

SAP provides predelivered business scenarios for the SRM-MDM catalog.

The search within the catalog repository is integrated with the following SAP SRM and SAP ERP business scenarios:

- ▶ Self-Service Procurement
- ▶ Service Procurement
- ▶ Contract Management
- ▶ ERP (Enterprise Resource Planning): Purchase Requisition (as of mySAP ERP 2005)
- ▶ ERP: Purchase Order (as of mySAP ERP 2005)
- ▶ ERP: Work Order (SAP PM: Plant Maintenance / SAP PS: Project System)

The following scenarios exist:

1. **Initalization of catalog tables with Master Data from SAP SRM or SAP ERP**

Organizations can upload the master data from their SAP SRM or SAP ERP systems into the SRM-MDM catalog, which serves as basic data for the catalog. The following data can be transferred and stored in the look-up table of the catalog:

- ▶ Currencies in ISO-Codes along with currency descriptions
- ▶ Units of Measures (UOM) in ISO-Codes along with descriptions
- ▶ Product Groups along with descriptions. Product groups are loaded as a flat representation, not in a hierarchical representation.
- ▶ Purchasing Organizations (only from SAP ERP) along with descriptions

> **Note**
>
> Use the MDM Generic Extraction Transaction (MDMGX) to set up the necessary communication parameters and start the extraction process.

2. Integration processes from SAP SRM or SAP ERP

Just as there are predelivered processes for the initialization data, there is other master data that can be imported into the SRM-MDM catalog using standard extractors delivered by SAP (Figure 6.16), as follows:

▶ **Transfer of product data from SAP SRM**
Organizations can transfer the product data that exists in their SAP SRM systems and import it into the SRM-MDM catalog to make it available for searching in catalogs for end users. This product data can be those products created manually in the SRM system or product data (materials) that was initially replicated from an SAP ERP backend into SAP SRM and then transferred to the SRM-MDM catalog. The material master from SAP ERP provides requesting departments a vehicle to request goods and services from an inventory or an internal provider, respectively.

> **Note**
>
> Use the report BBP_CCM_TRANSFER_CATALOG in the SRM system to initiate the transfer of product data. This process does require the use of SAP NetWeaver PI.

▶ **Transfer of material master from ERP**
Organizations can transfer the material master data that exists in their SAP SRM systems and import it into the SRM-MDM catalog to make it available for searching in catalogs for end users.

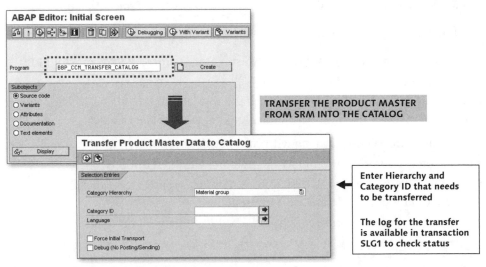

Figure 6.16 Product Data Transfer

Using a standard transaction in the SAP ERP system, project teams can choose to transfer product items from either info records or contracts. You can transfer data by material, vendor, purchasing organization, or receiving plant.

▶ **Transfer of contracts from SRM**

Organizations can transfer contracts created in SAP SRM into the SRM-MDM catalog for users to search. This process is initiated by using a check field on the contract header that indicates that the contract should be distributed to the SRM-MDM catalog. In Figure 6.17, the Distribute Contract to Catalog check box is selected. This marks the catalog for distribution to the catalog.

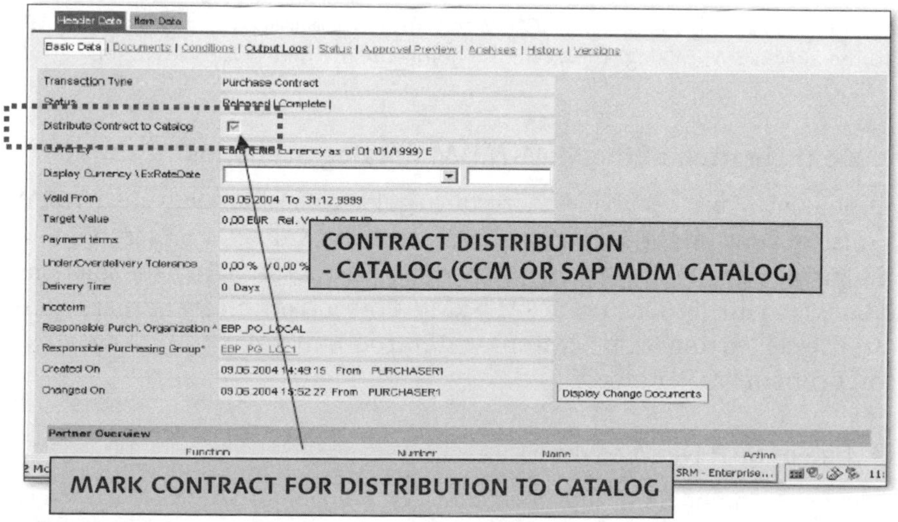

Figure 6.17 Contract Distribution to the SRM-MDM Catalog

▶ **Importing supplier information from SRM**

Although this scenario is not heavily utilized on SAP SRM projects, you can transfer/import the supplier list from the SAP SRM system to the SRM-MDM catalog. These suppliers are then available within the supplier's look-up table in the catalog.

An alternate approach is to only import suppliers that might be relevant to for the catalog scenario in your procurement process.

Note

The reports ROS_SUPPLIER_SEND_TO_CATALOG and ROS_SEND_UPD_VENDOR2CAT trigger the import and update of the supplier data respectively. This process requires the use of SAP NetWeaver PI/XI.

These reports are from the Supplier Registration component in SAP SRM.

▶ **Importing services with hierarchies from SAP ERP and SAP SRM**

As of the SAP SRM 7.0 release, organizations can also import the Service information from the SAP ERP system to the SRM-MDM Catalog. The Material Services Specification (MSS) structure is transferred to the SRM-MDM repository structure using SAP NetWeaver PI.

Organizations can also transfer service hierarchy from within an RFx (Bid Response) to the SRM-MDM Catalog. This can be triggered via the Publish to Catalog button in the RFx.

Note

In SAP ERP, you can use Transaction MECCM to transfer the Service Hierarchies from SAP ERP to the SRM-MDM catalog. This process requires the use of SAP NetWeaver PI.

6.2.7 Configuration of the SRM-MDM Catalog Scenarios

The SAP Solution Manager provides a structured guide on how to configure the SRM-MDM catalog based on the scenarios relevant for your SAP SRM project. Once in the Solution Manager (Business Process Repository), choose SRM from the solutions/applications, and use the menu path SAP SRM • CONFIGURATION STRUCTURES • SAP SRM 7.0 • BASIC SETTINGS FOR SRM-MDM CATALOG AND SAP SRM • SCENARIOS • CATALOG CONTENT MANAGEMENT.

6.2.8 Use of SAP NetWeaver PI

A common question on SRM implementations is the need of SAP NetWeaver Process Integration (PI) (previously called XI) when using SAP SRM and the SRM-MDM catalog. The SRM-MDM catalog uses SAP NetWeaver PI for all the scenarios listed in Section 6.2.10, Customizing the Web Service Call Structure in SAP SRM to Access Supplier Catalogs and SRM-MDM Catalog.

In general, SAP NetWeaver PI is a mandatory component for the integration scenarios together with SAP SRM or SAP ERP. So, the question is whether your implementation scope includes the transfer of product data, service hierarchies, or contract data into the catalog from either SAP SRM or SAP ERP. If yes, then the SAP NetWeaver PI application is needed.

> **Note**
>
> The SAP NetWeaver MDM application provides the ability to upload XML files without the need of the SAP NetWeaver PI server. This would serve useful if your suppliers provide data in the XML format instead of .csv/Microsoft Excel.

6.2.9 Set up the Open Catalog Interface (OCI) for SRM

The Open Catalog Interface (OCI) determines the data exchange between the SAP SRM and external catalog applications. OCI enables the transmission of selected goods and services from an external catalog to SAP SRM. The external catalog can be located either behind your firewall or on the Internet.

In Section 6.1.1, Types of Catalogs, we discussed the general process of using OCI-compliant supplier catalogs, also called RoundTrip suppliers. In this section, we'll discuss the technical information related to the OCI interface and its setup in the SRM system. Figure 6.18 illustrates OCI integration.

The catalog interface consists of two separate and distinct sections: the inbound section and the outbound section.

Inbound Section

The inbound section in OCI consists of the information being sent from the catalog application (supplier catalog, SAP CCM) to SAP SRM. This section contains data on the items selected in the catalog, such as the item descriptions, quantities ordered, and prices.

The inbound data identifies the information coming back from the supplier catalog's website and needs to be mapped to the shopping cart or PO fields in SAP SRM. Figure 6.19 provides a subset of the inbound and outbound OCI parameters available for SAP SRM release 4.0. A complete list of these is available in the SAP OCI document available on the Service Marketplace.

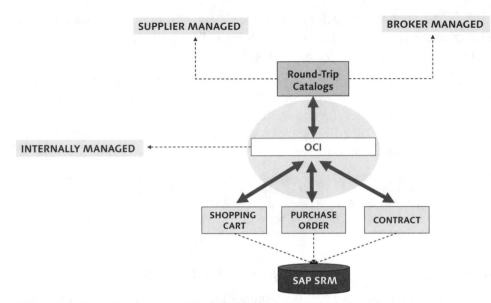

Figure 6.18 Integrate Internal and External Catalogs Using OCI Interface

INBOUND DATA *

- ITEM DESCRIPTION
- SAP PRODUCT NUMBER
- ITEM QUANTITY
- UOM
- PRICE
- CURRENCY
- DELIVERY TIME (LEAD TIME)
- LONG TEXT
- SRM VENDOR NUMBER
- VENDOR PRODUCT NUMBER
- SRM MANUFACTURER NUMBER
- SRM MATERIAL GROUP
- ITEM / SERVICE FLAG
- CONTRACT NUMBER
- CONTRACT ITEM
- URL FOR ATTACHMENTS
- SCHEMA
- CUSTOMER FIELD 1
- CUSTOMER FIELD 2
- ...

OUTBOUND DATA *

- CATALOG URL
- USERNAME
- PASSWORD
- SAP CLIENT
- CATALOG ID
- SAP LANGUAGE
- HOOK_URL
- ~OKCODE
- ...

* A COMPLETE LIST IS AVAILABLE IN THE
SAP OCI DOCUMENT IN THE APPENDIX

Figure 6.19 Sample List of OCI Inbound and Outbound Parameters

During the development and testing phase of integrating with a supplier catalog, there can be issues that result from the information coming back from the catalog. Project teams can quickly troubleshoot the root cause by reviewing the technical OCI Inbound parameters that are being passed back to the SRM application. You can do this by viewing the source code on the supplier's website at the time of checkout (as illustrated in Figure 6.20).

```
                    <B>Press button below to continue shopping or to process your Order Request and re
                    </FONT></TR><BR>
<FORM action=HTTP://                  ~ )0/scripts/wgate/bbppu99403a3b2f/?~target=_top&~forcetarget
target=_top name=retmarket>
<A HREF="http://_____.com/shopping_cart.asp" Onclick="return ('http://
()" onMouseOver="MM_swapImage('retshopping','','/images/aa/global/back_to_shopping_cart_ov2.gif
SRC="/images/aa/global/back_to_shopping_cart_2.gif" BORDER="0" width="115" height="16" alt="con

<input type="hidden" name="NEW_ITEM-DESCRIPTION[1]" value="01115"/>
<input type="hidden" name="NEW_ITEM-MATNR[1]" value=""/>
<input type="hidden" name="NEW_ITEM-MATGROUP[1]" value="MEEQ PN"/>
<input type="hidden" name="NEW_ITEM-QUANTITY[1]" value="1.000"/>
<input type="hidden" name="NEW_ITEM-UNIT[1]" value="EA"/>
<input type="hidden" name="NEW_ITEM-PRICE[1]" value="0.010"/>
<input type="hidden" name="NEW_ITEM-PRICEUNIT[1]" value="1"/>
<input type="hidden" name="NEW_ITEM-CURRENCY[1]" value="USD"/>
<input type="hidden" name="NEW_ITEM-LEADTIME[1]" value=""/>
<input type="hidden" name="NEW_ITEM-VENDOR[1]" value="200012"/>
<input type="hidden" name="NEW_ITEM-VENDORMAT[1]" value="1401360"/>
<input type="hidden" name="NEW_ITEM-MANUFACTCODE[1]" value="carborundu"/
<input type="hidden" name="NEW_ITEM-MANUFACTMAT[1]" value="01115"/>
<input type="hidden" name="NEW_ITEM-SERVICE[1]" value=""/>
<input type="hidden" name="NEW_ITEM-EXT_PRODUCT_ID[1]" value=""/>
<input type="hidden" name="NEW_ITEM-LONGTEXT_1:132[1]" value="longtext_1:No Description"/>
<input type="hidden" name="NEW_ITEM-CUST_FIELD1[1]" value=""/>
<input type="hidden" name="NEW_ITEM-CUST_FIELD2[1]" value=""/>
<input type="hidden" name="NEW_ITEM-CUST_FIELD3[1]" value=""/>
<input type="hidden" name="NEW_ITEM-CUST_FIELD4[1]" value=""/>
<input type="hidden" name="NEW_ITEM-CUST_FIELD5[1]" value=""/>
<input type="hidden" name="NEW_ITEM-DESCRIPTION[2]" value="01881"/>
<input type="hidden" name="NEW_ITEM-MATNR[2]" value=""/>
<input type="hidden" name="NEW_ITEM-MATGROUP[2]" value="MEEQ PN"/>
<input type="hidden" name="NEW_ITEM-QUANTITY[2]" value="1.000"/>
<input type="hidden" name="NEW_ITEM-UNIT[2]" value="EA"/>
<input type="hidden" name="NEW_ITEM-PRICE[2]" value="0.010"/>
<input type="hidden" name="NEW_ITEM-PRICEUNIT[2]" value="1"/>
```

> **OCI INBOUND PARAMETERS**
> **SOURCE INFORMATION FROM THE SUPPLIER**
> **CATALOG (WEBSITE)**

Figure 6.20 Example of Inbound Parameters on Supplier Website

Outbound Section

The outbound section in OCI consists of the information being sent from SAP SRM to the catalog application (supplier catalog, SAP CCM, etc.). This is typically information such as the supplier's URL, user authentication parameters for login, and other session parameters required to maintain a link between the SRM and catalog application. If an internal catalog is used (e.g., SAP CCM), it is still accessed using the OCI mechanism.

6.2.10 Customizing the Web Service Call Structure in SAP SRM to Access Supplier Catalogs and SRM-MDM Catalog

In SAP SRM, the catalog outbound call structure is set up in Customizing (as illustrated in Figure 6.21). Organizations can determine whether to set up the standard or integrated call structure for the catalog. The parameters and setup are the same for both call structures. The difference is that the standard call structure opens the defined catalog in a new window and the integrated call structure opens the catalog within the same window. As of SAP SRM 4.0, the Hook_URL, OkCode, Target, and Caller parameters are no longer mandatory for maintenance. The system provides default values automatically.

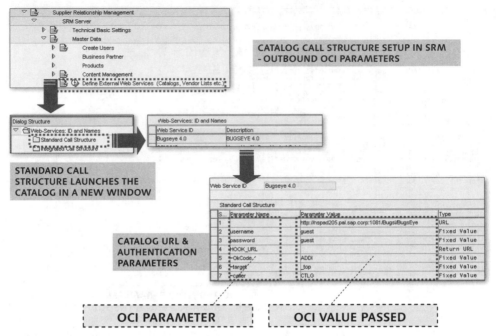

Figure 6.21 Catalog Customizing in SAP SRM

SAP provides a standard Business Add-In (BAdI) BBP_CAT_CALL_ENRICH for organizations to enhance or modify the OCI interface parameters. This might be especially useful if the supplier catalog contains information that is captured using the customer specific parameters in the OCI inbound call structure. Project teams can then use the BAdI to move that data to specific fields within the SAP SRM document (shopping cart or purchase order).

The OCI interface also processes data in HTML and XML as input. Most organizations select the HTML method, because it does not have additional infrastructure requirements. For XML-based integration for OCI, you need to have SAP NetWeaver PI set up with your SAP SRM system. Most suppliers support the standard HTML OCI interface, so organizations don't need to worry about XML for catalog integration.

To become RoundTrip enabled, suppliers must make a few modifications to their websites; many of the larger suppliers are already OCI compliant. Table 6.1 provides a list of some of these supplier catalogs that are already OCI compliant. These changes include preparing the website to send and receive OCI requests for buyer authentication, session initiation, and shopping cart transmission back to SAP SRM.

Web Service Call Structure for the SRM-MDM Catalog

The following call structure should be configured in the SAP SRM system to access your SRM-MDM catalog.

Seq	Parameter Name	Parameter Value	Type
10		http://<J2EE host>:<J2EE port>/ SRM-MDM/SRM_MDM	0 URL
20	Username	<username>	2 Fixed Value
30	Password	<password>	2 Fixed Value
40	Server	<MDM host>	2 Fixed Value
50	Port	<Slave1 port>:<Slave2 port>:<master port>	2 Fixed Value
60	Catalog	SRM-MDM-Catalog	2 Fixed Value
70	Uilanguage	SY-LANGU	1 SAP Field
80	Datalanguage	SY-LANGU	1 SAP Field
90	Namedsearch	Office_Supplies	2 Fixed Value
100	Mask	Office_Supplies	2 Fixed Value

Table 6.1 Web Service Call Structure for SRM-MDM Catalog

6.3   Relevant URL Links

There is a lot of additional information available on the SAP Service Marketplace. Table 6.2 provides you with some relevant content.

Link Type	URL Location
Blog	www.sdn.sap.com/irj/scn
Help	http://help.sap.com/srm7.0/etc.

Table 6.2 Additional Relevant Content

6.4   Relevant OSS Notes

Table 6.3 provides you with a list of important OSS Notes available on the SAP Service Marketplace that are relevant for organizations implementing the SRM-MDM catalog discussed in this chapter.

Note	Description
1077701	SRM-MDM Catalog FAQ
1177780	SRM-MDM Catalog 3.0 Configuration
1250442	Service Hierarchy Import into SRM-MDM Catalog
1153525	Shopping lists for named users
1147662	Left-hand and wild card search
1287412	Pre-requisites for OCI integration in SRM 7.0
1147103	SRM-MDM Catalog: Portal Deployment Restriction
1249323	Exception "Exit-Plug" while transferring catalog data to SRM
1276845	Release info SRM 7.0: Installation and upgrade information
1177779	SRM-MDM Catalog 3.0 Installation
1138862	SRM-MDM Catalog performance

Table 6.3 OSS Notes in the SAP Service Marketplace

6.5   Summary

In this chapter, you've been introduced to the concept of catalogs and content management. A well thought-out catalog and content strategy is important for any SRM initiative. Organizations should ensure that they do not pick a catalog strategy in a vacuum.

Internally managed, supplier managed, and broker managed catalogs each provide unique advantages. Broker managed catalog providers such as SciQuest and ICG Commerce are different than supplier managed catalogs because the broker hosts catalog data for multiple suppliers and typically charges an annual fee for accessing catalog data. Typically, these providers also offer other services such as order collaboration and document transmission.

We also discussed the capabilities of the catalog and content management solution SRM-MDM. A separate license is not required for SAP NetWeaver MDM if it is only used for catalogs within SAP SRM.

In Chapter 7, you'll learn about the different implementation scenarios available for SAP SRM and the details of each scenario. Chapter 7 will also equip you with the information to decide which implementation scenario to choose for your SRM implementation.

Is there a checklist to provide to clients when they are deciding to implement SAP Supplier Relationship Management (SRM)? Is there any tool out there that can be shared in advising customers about which scenario is best for their businesses?

7 Choosing Implementation Scenarios

One of the biggest decisions in any SAP SRM implementation, and one that continuously haunts project teams, is the selection of the appropriate implementation scenario. Even when you thoughtfully select the appropriate scenario, the questions still abound during and after implementation. The key reason is that, although SAP has provided flexibility for how organizations deploy the SRM solution using the different implementation scenarios, each scenario imposes known and hidden restrictions that organizations realize during their implementations. This chapter defines the available scenarios and provides the reasons for using one scenario over another.

7.1 Overview — SAP SRM Implementation Scenarios

SAP provides three main implementation scenarios (also sometimes called technical scenarios) that deploy the different SAP SRM business scenarios. These are:

- Classic
- Extended Classic
- Standalone

In addition, organizations can also implement a combination of these scenarios in parallel - based on the level of integration needed with the backend financial and materials management systems. The combination approach is loosely termed the decoupled scenario.

The selection of the implementation scenario is a key decision that determines the available functionality, unique configuration, and restrictions in the SAP SRM application.

For organizations and project teams, the selection of implementation scenarios in SAP SRM is a two-fold decision driven by business requirements and by implications for the technical environment. Additionally, certain SAP SRM functionality is only available based on the scenario implemented. Unfortunately, there is no one answer that fits all environments. This decision is entirely based on the organization's business requirements, business processes being implemented as a part of the current or future project(s), the current SAP environment (e.g., existing SAP landscape, new SAP implementation, or no SAP implementation), along with factors that are critical to the success of the project and user acceptance.

Most successful projects determine their implementation scenario during their blueprint phase of the project. This is when the project teams understand and share the "true" requirements and functionality so that a good choice can be made.

Figure 7.1 provides a quick overview of the business processes that exist within the three different implementation scenarios and where each of the main processes occurs.

	Classic	Extended Classic	Standalone
Create Shopping Cart	SAP SRM	SAP SRM	SAP SRM
Approval Workflow	SAP SRM or SAP ERP	SAP SRM	SAP SRM
Purchase Requisition	Optional: SAP ERP	N/A	N/A
Purchase Order Creation	SAP ERP	SAP SRM and copy of PO in SAP ERP	SAP SRM
Create Stock "Reservation"	Optional: SAP ERP	N/A	N/A
Confirmation Entry* or Goods Receipt	SAP SRM or SAP ERP	SAP SRM or SAP ERP	SAP SRM
Invoice Entry	SAP SRM or SAP ERP	SAP SRM or SAP ERP	SAP SRM (Acct. info sent to Backend system)

* A confirmation in SAP SRM is transferred to SAP backend and a Goods Receipt (G/R) is created.
  Backend system = SAP ERP or non-SAP system

Figure 7.1 Quick Glance at the SAP SRM Implementation Scenarios

> **Note**
>
> We use the term backend system generically to illustrate how the SAP SRM application can be integrated with SAP and non-SAP applications. For the vast majority of organizations, this backend system correlates to their SAP R/3 or enterprise resource planning (ERP) system. For purposes of this book, the term backend system is used interchangeably with the SAP backend, SAP R/3, or SAP ERP system.

Some examples of why organizations might use a backend system include:

- Checking the accounting information in SAP SRM against the information that exists in the backend system.
- Creating a purchasing document in the backend system, such as a purchase order (PO) or stock reservation.
- Creating an invoice (financial document) in the backend system.

> **Note**
>
> At a high level, the most applicable scenario for your organization may depend on the system in which your purchasing department wants to work and, consequently, where you want the follow-on documents to be created.

Now, let's move on to developing a good understanding of the various implementation scenarios and why an organization might select a specific scenario.

7.2 The Classic Scenario

The *Classic* scenario is by far the most widely adopted scenario among organizations that have implemented SAP SRM. When Enterprise Buyer was rolled out as a solution in 1999, the only scenario that was available for organizations was the Classic approach.

SAP, along with its partner Commerce One, targeted customers with an installed base of SAP R/3. The obvious selling point was simpler and tighter integration of Enterprise Buyer with SAP R/3 Materials Management and Financial Accounting software.

In the Classic scenario, Enterprise Buyer is connected to a backend system for materials management, SAP ERP Financials Financial Accounting, and SAP ERP Financials Controlling. All materials management documents, such as POs, reservations, purchase requisitions, goods receipts, and service-entry sheets are in the backend system. Accounting and controlling systems with the relevant documents are also connected. The SAP Enterprise Buyer (EB) system communicates all relevant business documents to the backend systems, where they are then processed further.

This scenario relies strongly on the SAP ERP backend system(s), because all materials management documents are located there. There may be one SAP EB system communicating with multiple SAP ERP systems within this scenario. All financial checks and postings are made in the SAP ERP system. The Classic scenario approach is illustrated in Figure 7.2.

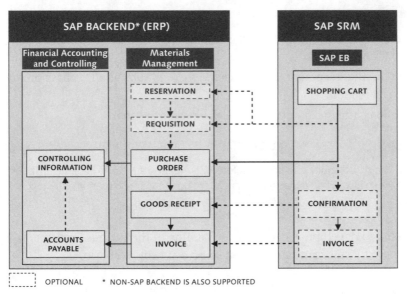

OPTIONAL   * NON-SAP BACKEND IS ALSO SUPPORTED

Figure 7.2 Classic Scenario Implementation in SAP SRM

In the classic scenario, the process begins in SAP SRM with the creation of a shopping cart and ends with the entry of an invoice. The process, illustrated in Figure 7.2, is as follows:

1. Create a shopping cart in SAP EB system with one or multiple line items.

2. Based on configuration and workflow customizing, the system determines whether an approval is required for one or more line items in the shopping cart.

> **Note**
>
> In this scenario, organizations may either choose to use the approval/workflow capabilities that exist in SAP EB or use workflows or release strategies in their backend SAP ERP systems.

3. Once all the required approvals are complete in SAP SRM, based on the configuration and customizing setup in SAP EB, the system creates one of the following documents in materials management: requisition, PO, or a reservation. Any changes required to these documents are entered within the SAP ERP backend system. The following functions take place in the materials management system:

   ▶ Source of Supply (Info Records, Contracts, etc.)

   ▶ Tax Determination

   ▶ Pricing Determination

   ▶ Output Determination

4. A goods receipt (referred to as a confirmation in SAP EB) and an invoice can be entered in SAP EB. Based on workflow customizing, once all approvals are complete, the system will then trigger the appropriate postings within the backend system. Alternately, companies could also choose to enter the goods receipt and invoice directly in the SAP backend (ERP) system.

Standard integration between SAP EB and the SAP backend ensures seamless status updates of the documents in both systems. So, you can see whether an invoice is posted against your original shopping cart or PO.

> **Tip**
>
> If a confirmation or invoice entry is performed in SAP EB, the corresponding goods receipt and invoice documents are distributed to the SAP backend system via means of Application Linking and Enablement (ALE) technology. A distribution model needs to be set up in Customizing, and — based on the release of your SAP ERP system — you need to select the appropriate IDoc Message Type(s).

Now we will discuss which organizations should consider the Classic scenario.

7.2.1 Which Organizations Should Look at This Scenario?

From here, you might ask which organizations should consider the classic scenario. Some of these include:

▶ Organizations that have an existing (possibly large) installed base of users within the SAP ERP environment and buyers in the organization who don't want to use multiple systems.

▶ Organizations that already have users within their purchasing departments using SAP R/3 MM/IM to procure goods and services and prefer options within the application.

▶ Organizations that want their purchasing professionals to continue to work and use the functionality offered in the SAP R/3 MM environment.

▶ Organizations that want to integrate with suppliers and utilize materials management in the SAP ERP system (Supplier Self-Services [SUS])-MM).

▶ Organizations that have already setup and want to continue to handle all supplier communication transmissions (EDI, fax, email, print, etc.) via existing channels in the SAP ERP system.

> **Note**
>
> Beginning with SRM 6.0, SAP has provided a support OSS note whereby organizations can implement the Extended Classic scenario and yet continue to handle document transmission with the backend ERP system.

However, there are some restrictions of the Classic scenario, which are examined next.

7.2.2   Restrictions of the Classic Scenario

Unfortunately, organizations implementing SAP SRM will find that restrictions exist when implementing a particular scenario. Therefore, project teams need to clearly understand their business requirements during the blueprint phase and review the following restrictions to make an appropriate decision. These restrictions are:

- ▶ For the integration of external requirements (plan-driven procurement) does not completely support a Classic scenario, the following restrictions exist:
  - ▶ You cannot procure direct materials using the Classic scenario.
  - ▶ When you procure services, you cannot use the Classic scenario to process limits without an expected value. Additionally, the service packages transferred to SAP SRM are not grouped together in SAP SRM.
- ▶ The integration of the procurement card is not possible in the Classic scenario in the standard release.
- ▶ The service-procurement scenario deployment with SUS cannot be integrated with the supplier self-services application. This scenario is also known as the EB-SUS scenario. Therefore, the POs are created in SAP EB and sent to the supplier self-services application.

7.2.3   Impact on the SAP SRM Organizational Structure

The implementation scenario has an impact on the organizational structure setup, and project teams need to be aware of how to set up the organizational structure when the Classic scenario is activated. The organizational structure is described in detail in Chapter 8.

7.2.4   Impact of Classic Scenario When Integrating Enterprise Buyer with Supplier Self-Services

Organizations that have implemented the SUS application to collaborate orders with their suppliers need to be aware that the implementation scenario in EB has an impact on the standard functionality that is available. For example, the Classic scenario does not allow for a PO to be sent to SUS from materials management in SAP ERP. Figure 7.3 illustrates the Classic scenario approach when SUS is integrated with SAP EB. As you can see, the supplier enablement is not supported in SUS when using the Classic scenario.

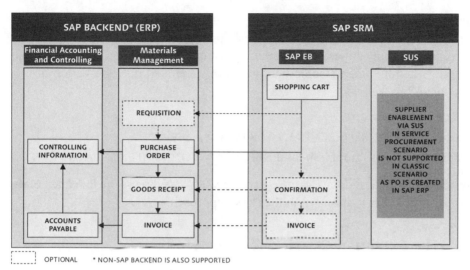

Figure 7.3 Supplier Self-Services Integration with SAP EB (Classic Scenario)

7.2.5 Technical Extras

Because SAP SRM is a separate system from the SAP backend system, there are standard functions and programs that are delivered by SAP to communicate between the two systems. It is often helpful to know the function modules and Business Application Programming Interface (BAPIs) that communicate the PO information between SAP EB to the SAP backend system.

Figure 7.4 illustrates the function module BBP_REQREQ_TRANSFER and BAPI BAPI_PO_CREATE that are used in SAP EB and SAP backend to create the PO.

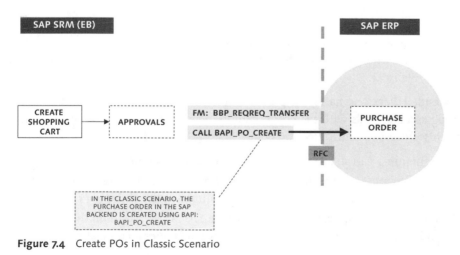

Figure 7.4 Create POs in Classic Scenario

Often, there are situations during projects where ambiguous errors are received when creating a PO in SAP ERP using the shopping cart. Some errors can be deciphered, and for many others, troubleshooting is required. The following step-by-step approach is helpful when troubleshooting errors generated during creation of the PO in the SAP backend:

1. Create a shopping cart.
2. Execute FM: BBP_REQREQ_TRANSFER in debug mode.
3. Using break-points, troubleshoot the BAPI BAPI_PO_CREATE that creates the PO.

Now that you understand the classic scenario in SRM, let's discuss the Extended Classic scenario and how it differs from the classic approach.

7.3   The Extended Classic Scenario

The *Extended Classic* scenario came into existence when SAP customers requested additional flexibility within their SAP EB implementations. Moreover, the Classic scenario required that the purchasing buyers work in the confines of the materials management environment. In the Extended Classic scenario, the entire procurement process takes place locally in SAP EB and a copy of the data is replicated to the backend system. In essence, this scenario is an extension of the Classic scenario.

SAP introduced the Extended Classic scenario in 2002 with the release of SAP Enterprise Buyer 3.5. The use of this scenario is growing rapidly because of its inherent flexibility. It is being adopted by many organizations that are undertaking a new SAP SRM implementation or are upgrading their existing SAP Enterprise Buyer systems.

Because POs are created locally within SAP EB, if the data in the shopping cart is insufficient to generate a complete PO, the data is supplemented manually within SAP EB before transferring to the backend system. The Extended Classic scenario is illustrated in Figure 7.5.

In the Extended Classic scenario, the process begins in SAP SRM with the creation of a shopping cart and ends with the entry of an invoice. The following list walks you through this process, as illustrated in Figure 7.5:

1. Create a shopping cart in SAP EB with one or multiple line items.
2. Based on configuration and workflow customizing, the system determines whether an approval is required for one or more line items in the shopping cart.
3. Once all the required approvals are complete in SAP SRM, based on the configuration and customizing setup in SAP EB, the system creates a complete or incom-

plete PO locally in SAP EB. If an incomplete PO is created, a purchasing professional intervenes, completes the PO (e.g., a source of supply or price needs to be assigned) and transmits it to the supplier. The following functions take place in SAP EB:

- ▶ Source of Supply (vendor lists, contracts, etc.)
- ▶ Tax Determination (external System, EB, custom rules)
- ▶ Pricing Determination (IPC, interlinkages, etc.)
- ▶ Purchasing Documents Output Determination (XML, email, etc.)

4. In the Extended Classic scenario, the PO is created in SAP SRM, and a read-only copy of that PO is sent to the backend materials management system. The PO in SAP EB is the leading PO. Therefore, all subsequent changes to the PO can be made in the SAP SRM system only.

5. Once the goods or services are received from the supplier, the end user can confirm the goods or services received either in the SAP EB or materials management in SAP ERP. If a confirmation is created in SAP EB, a corresponding goods receipt is created in the backend materials management system. Therefore, organizations have the flexibility to choose where to perform a goods receipt.

6. An invoice can also be entered within the SAP EB system and corresponding invoice documents are created in the SAP backend system. Most organizations, however, continue to enter an invoice in the SAP ERP backend system.

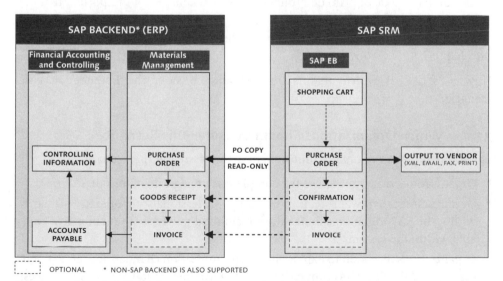

Figure 7.5 Extended Classic Scenario Implementation in SAP SRM

The PO in the backend system is a read-only copy that enables goods receipt, service entry, and invoice verification in the backend system. This PO cannot be changed in the SAP R/3 or ERP systems. If you wish to make any changes to the PO, you must do so in the SRM system. Once you save these changes, they are transferred to the backend purchase order. Therefore, in this scenario, the purchasing professionals operate primarily within SAP SRM instead of the SAP backend.

Most organizations that have a backend SAP ERP system continue to enter invoices within the backend system. Even though SAP has provided increased support and functionality for invoice processing within SAP EB, organizations tend to continue processing invoices in SAP ERP because of their existing business processes, central focus, and enterprise accounts-payable functions. Review Chapter 5 to learn about invoice functionality in SAP EB, and also read the "What's New" section to see the Invoice Management Solution (IMS) that has been released by SAP with SAP SRM 5.0.

In the Extended Classic scenario, the Purchasing Group is the key determinant for the resulting purchasing organization (POrg) on the PO sent to the supplier. If your company has multiple purchasing organizations, then the POrg will be determined based on the Purchasing Group used in the shopping cart.

However, in materials management in SAP ERP, the PO determines the POrg's value based on the plant in the PO line item. This also causes an issue if, for example, there are multiple company codes, and where the POrg determined in SRM is not assigned to the company code or plant determined in SAP backend. So, it's important that the POrg determined in SRM is the same as in SAP ERP so that the follow-on functions such as invoice entry are consistent. Review the OSS Notes referenced at the end of the chapter.

Now let's discuss which organizations should consider the Extended Classic scenario.

7.3.1   Which Organizations Should Consider This Scenario?

The following types of organizations might be interested in this scenario:

▶ Organizations that want to use the complete sourcing capabilities of SAP EB.

▶ Organizations that want their purchasing professionals to operate primarily within the SAP EB and maximize the streamlined purchasing functionality available within the system.

▶ Organizations that want to explore new communication channels for their suppliers (e.g., XML). SAP SRM provides standard XML integration via the SAP Process Integration (SAP NetWeaver PI).

▶ Organizations that don't have a business requirement to create a resulting requisition or reservation from the shopping cart.

7.3.2 Restrictions of the Extended Classic Scenario

Unfortunately, organizations implementing SAP SRM will find that restrictions exist when implementing this scenario. Project teams need to understand their business requirements during the blueprint phase and review the restrictions that exist in the scenarios to make an appropriate decision.

▶ **Purchase Requisitions**
In the Extended Classic scenario, after a shopping cart is created, the subsequent document cannot be a purchase requisition.

▶ **Material Reservations**
In the Extended Classic scenario, after a shopping cart is created, the subsequent document cannot be a material reservation. A Business Add-In (BAdI) to control the Extended Classic scenario can be used for achieving this functionality.

▶ **P-Card Functionality**
For organizations that want to use procurement cards (p-cards) as a mechanism of payment in SAP SRM, the Extended Classic scenario does not offer a solution. In the standard design, this functionality is only provided in the Standalone scenario.

> **Note**
>
> In SAP SRM 7.0, P-Card functionality is available within the Extended Classic scenario.

▶ **Shop with Limit Restriction**
In the Extended Classic scenario, when creating shopping carts with more than a one-item limit, separate POs will always be created for each item when ordering, regardless of the data (i.e., vendor, document type, purchasing group, company, location, performance period) in each item. For example, when a shopping cart with a two-limit position is ordered, two POs will be created rather than one PO for two items.

▶ **Integration with SUS for Confirmation and Invoice Entry**
With SUS, the Extended Classic scenario has partial supplier involvement for all the operational procurement scenarios. The scenario works for collaboration of purchase order, purchase order response, and change order but not for confirmation and invoice entry. If the Extended Classic scenario is activated in EB and you

send a purchase order from EB to SUS, you cannot send the confirmation and invoice with reference to this PO back from SUS to SAP EB. Additionally, this scenario is only supported for free text items. The material-based scenario is not supported in Extended Classic and only supported for the MM-SUS integration (described in Chapter 5).

7.3.3 Impact on the SRM Organizational Structure

The implementation scenario has an impact on the organizational structure setup, and project teams need to be aware of how to set up the organizational structure when the Extended Classic scenario is activated. The organizational structure is described in detail in Chapter 8.

7.3.4 Impact of Extended Classic Scenario When Integrating Enterprise Buyer with SUS

Organizations that have implemented the SUS application to collaborate with their suppliers on orders need to be aware that the implementation scenario in SAP EB impacts the standard functionality that is available. For example, if the Extended Classic scenario is implemented, only the PO can be communicated between SAP EB and SUS. The follow-on documents such as PO confirmation or invoice entry cannot be communicated between SAP EB and SUS.

Figure 7.6 illustrates the Extended Classic scenario approach when SUS is integrated with SAP EB. In Figure 7.6, a PO is created in SAP EB and is communicated to the SUS system as an order (sales order for the suppliers). At the same time, because you're in Extended Classic, a read-only copy of the PO is also sent to the materials management system.

7.3.5 Purchase Order Consistency Check

As of SAP SRM 7.0, a new consistency check has been introduced in the application that is useful for organizations implementing the Extended Classic scenario. In previous SRM releases, organizations faced visibility issues when the PO was created in the SRM system and if there were any errors in the backend system. With SAP SRM 7.0, organizations can configure the SRM system to perform a consistency check (simulation) before replicating the PO from SAP SRM to SAP ERP. In Customizing, an option exists to either issue an error or a warning if the consistency check is unsuccessful.

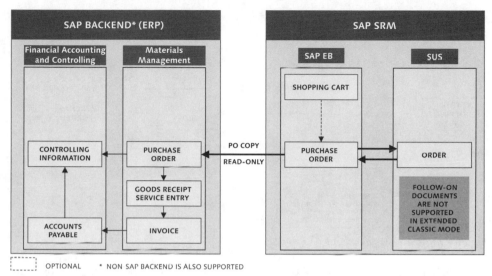

Figure 7.6 Supplier Self-Services Integration with SAP EB (Extended Classic Scenario)

In case of an Error Message, all simulation issues must be resolved prior to the PO being transmitted to the backend SAP ERP system. This also means that the PO will not be sent to the supplier.

Alternately, in case of a Warning Message, the PO is transmitted to the backend SAP ERP regardless of any issues that might exist. The PO is sent to the supplier as well.

7.3.6 Technical Extras

Because SAP SRM is a separate system from the SAP backend system, there are standard functions and programs that are delivered by SAP to communicate between the two systems. It is often helpful to know the function modules and BAPIs that communicate the PO information between SAP EB to the SAP backend system. Figure 7.7 illustrates the function module BBP_PD_PO_CREATE and BAPI BAPI_PO_CREATE1 that are used in SAP EB and SAP backend to create the PO.

> **Note**
>
> For SAP SRM 7.0, project teams need to execute the Transaction FIBF in the backend SAP ERP system. This activates the application SRMNTY in Table TBE11. This enables notification to the SRM system when follow-on documents to the PO are created in the backend system.

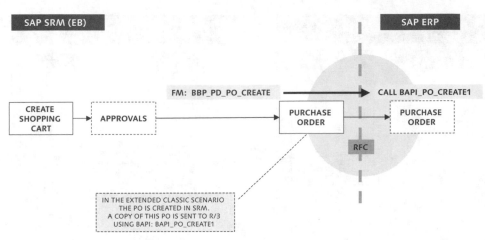

Figure 7.7 Create POs in Extended Classic Scenario

Now that you understand the Extended Classic scenario in SRM, let's discuss the Standalone scenario and how it is different from the other two implementation scenarios.

7.4 The Standalone Scenario

The *Standalone* scenario was initially introduced by SAP with EB 2.0 release in 2001. The primary reason SAP provided this implementation option was to cater to organizations with non-SAP enterprise applications. This new approach added benefits for organizations that had an SAP ERP environment but also had divisions or companies within its enterprise that were not yet running SAP. For large, global organizations, this provided a mechanism to provide its users with an enterprisewide procurement application that could integrate with SAP and non-SAP applications. The Standalone scenario probably has the smallest installed customer base but nevertheless has key benefits.

This scenario handles the entire procurement process in SAP EB. The shopping cart and follow-on documents, such as POs, goods receipts, and invoices, are created locally, and the whole procurement process is covered by SAP EB. Validations and approvals are handled directly within SAP EB.

All accounting validations are handled by one or more accounting backend systems. At the same time, a commitment can be created in the Financial Accounting and Controlling backend system. Auxiliary account assignment checks, such as cost center checks and budget checks, are also carried out in the backend system. The Standalone scenario approach is illustrated in Figure 7.8.

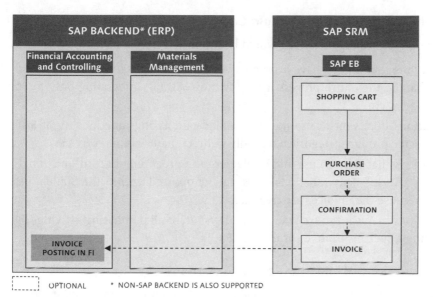

Figure 7.8 Standalone Scenario Implementation in SAP SRM

In the Standalone scenario, the process begins in SAP SRM with the creation of a shopping cart and ends with the entry of an invoice. All of the purchasing and accounts payable documents are created in SAP EB. The following bullet points walk you through this process as illustrated in Figure 7.8:

1. Create a shopping cart in SAP EB with one or multiple line items.

2. Based on configuration and workflow customizing, the system determines whether an approval is required for one or more line items in the shopping cart.

3. Once all the required approvals are complete, the system creates a complete or incomplete PO locally in SAP EB. If an incomplete PO is created, then a purchasing professional intervenes, completes the PO, and transmits it to the supplier.

4. Once the goods or services are received from the supplier, the end user can confirm the goods/services received and a confirmation is created locally in SAP EB.

5. An invoice can be entered at this point by a user in the accounts payable department. Once the invoice is entered, and unless any further approvals are required, the accounting information is transferred to the financial accounting and controlling system and all follow-on processes such as payments are processed there.

Now we will discuss which organizations should consider the Standalone scenario.

7.4.1 Which Organizations Should Consider this Scenario?

The following types of organizations would be interested in this scenario:

▶ Organizations that do not have a productive materials management system and want to handle the entire process locally within SAP EB, integrating only to an accounting system.

▶ Organizations that want to use the streamlined purchasing functionality of SAP EB for specific product categories, typically indirect materials and services.

▶ Organizations that want to use and implement the procurement card functionality within SAP EB. This functionality is only supported within the Standalone scenario because the invoices are created locally.

▶ Organizations that want to free the backend system of all purchasing activities by transferring a specific group of users to SAP EB.

7.4.2 Restrictions of the Standalone Scenario

Unfortunately, organizations implementing SAP SRM will find that restrictions exist when implementing this scenario. Project teams need to clearly understand their business requirements during the blueprint phase and review the following restrictions imposed by the scenarios to make an appropriate decision:

▶ Any functionality relating to integration with an SAP backend (ERP) system, such as the creation of purchase requisitions, POs, and material reservations, is not possible in the Standalone scenario because there is no backend materials management system connected in this scenario.

▶ The plan-driven procurement scenario cannot be integrated with the SUS application. This scenario is also known as the MM-SUS scenario. Therefore, the purchase orders are created in the SAP backend and sent to the SUS application. In the Standalone scenario, no POs are sent to the SAP backend.

7.4.3 Impact on the SRM Organizational Structure

The implementation scenario impacts the organizational structure setup, and project teams need to be aware of how to set up the organizational structure when the Standalone scenario is activated. The organizational structure setup is nearly the same as in the Extended Classic scenario. However, no back-end organization units are set up, only an attribute for the accounting system. The organizational structure is described in detail in Chapter 8.

7.4.4 Impact of Standalone Scenario When Integrating Enterprise Buyer with SUS

Organizations that have implemented the supplier self-services (SUS) application to collaborate orders with their suppliers need to be aware that the implementation scenario in SAP EB impacts the standard functionality that is available. Figure 7.9 illustrates the Standalone scenario approach when SUS is integrated with SAP EB.

Unlike the Classic and Extended Classic scenarios, the Standalone scenario provides a complete integration with SUS and allows collaboration between SAP EB and SUS with respect to the PO, confirmation, and invoice documents.

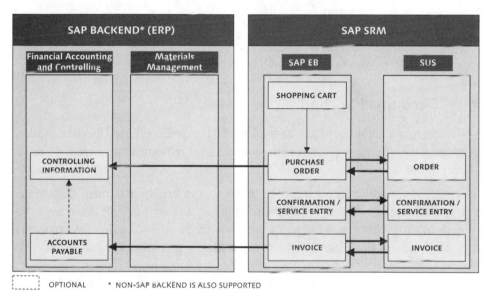

OPTIONAL   * NON-SAP BACKEND IS ALSO SUPPORTED

Figure 7.9 Supplier Self-Services Integration with SAP EB (Standalone Scenario)

7.4.5 Technical Extras

Because SAP SRM is a separate system from the SAP backend system, there are standard functions and programs that are delivered by SAP to communicate between the two systems. It is often helpful to know the function modules and BAPIs that are used to communicate the PO information between SAP EB and the SAP backend system. Figure 7.10 illustrates the function module BBP_PD_PO_CREATE that is used to create a PO in SAP SRM (EB). Because there is no backend integration for purchasing documents, there is no need to use a BAPI for creating a PO in SAP ERP as you do in the Classic or Extended Classic scenarios.

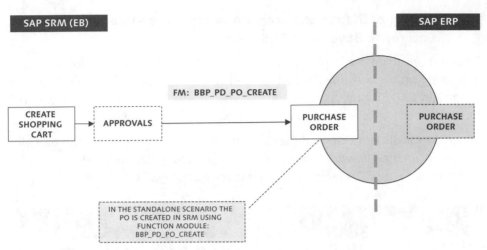

Figure 7.10 Create Purchase Orders in Standalone Scenario

7.5 Decoupled Scenario

In addition to the three scenarios defined in the previous sections, there is another option available for organizations with business requirements that warrant a combination of these scenarios.

One example would be an organization that wants to use the Extended Classic scenario but also has a business requirement to create a reservation in materials management in SAP ERP from a shopping cart. Such a business requirement can only be satisfied if both the Classic and Extended Classic scenarios are combined. This scenario is sometimes referred as the *Decoupled* scenario. The majority of companies implement a Classic, Extended Classic, or Standalone scenario. However, business requirements eventually drive a parallel use of multiple scenarios.

SAP EB supports the functionality of implementing a combination of the scenarios in parallel. In the standard system, this determination is made based on the product category (material group) of the ordered item. We explain the decoupled scenario using Figure 7.11.

In Customizing, organizations can decide whether the requisition or purchase order is to be created in the SAP ERP or SAP SRM system. As a standard, SAP provides the capability to make this decision based on the product category; however, that will usually not be suitable for most organizations as a decision criterion, for example, the medical devices product category.

Your organization could stock some items in inventory for which you want to create a reservation in materials management in SAP ERP. For all other non-stock items, a purchase order needs to be created and transmitted to an external vendor via the SAP EB system. Therefore, the product category is not usually a good criterion. This is where organizations can make use of the BAdI BBP_DETERMINE_LOGSYS and customize their own rules pertinent to their business requirements.

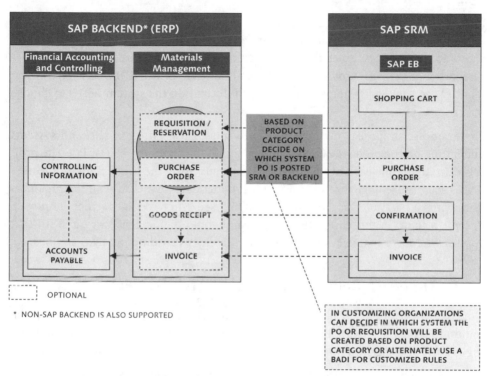

Figure 7.11 Decoupled Scenario in SAP EB

7.5.1 Running Scenarios in Parallel

The Classic, Extended Classic, and Standalone scenarios can be run in parallel. Here are some examples for when an organization might want to host multiple scenarios in the same SAP EB system:

▶ If the Extended Classic scenario was an appropriate fit for your organization but you wanted to use the reservations functionality in SAP ERP for products (materials) that were stocked within a plant.

▶ The organization might have non-SAP back-end systems in addition to SAP, and the organization wants to roll out a single procurement front end using Enterprise Buyer. This suits customers who already might a productive materials management back-end system, but wish to handle the procurement of some supplies locally and others within the back-end system.

7.5.2 Technical Extras

In the standard system, the determination of which back-end system is used based on the product category (material group) of the ordered item. If your organization wants to use business rules that are different than the standard delivered product category method, SAP provides a BAdI called BBP_DETERMINE_LOGSYS. Here, you identify the backend systems and enter the information the system needs to choose the correct one.

For example, suppose your organization wants to use different backend systems depending on the product category of the item in the shopping cart or PO. The project team can define each of these backend systems using the Implementation Guide (IMG) activity Define Backend System for Product Category. However, the organization wants a particular backend system to be used whenever a specified employee orders an item. In this case, the project team would define a rule in the BAdI that applies whenever that user orders an item, thereby overriding the IMG settings.

7.6 Things to Remember and to Watch Out For

Now that we've discussed all the implementation scenarios, you will have to select the option that best meets the business requirements of your organization. The following is a list of things to remember when selecting your implementation scenario:

▶ In the Classic scenario, the PO is created and modified in the SAP backend. In the Extended Classic and Standalone scenarios, the PO is created in SAP SRM.

▶ Requisitions and or Material Reservations can only be created in the SAP backend if the Classic scenario is implemented (unless BAdIs are implemented).

▶ The Classic, Extended Classic, and Standalone scenarios can all coexist in the same installation. Organizations need to use standard-delivered BAdIs for enabling multiple scenarios, the decoupled scenario.

▶ In the Extended Classic scenario, the PO cannot be changed in the SAP backend system; changes are only supported in the SAP EB system.

▶ In the Extended Classic scenario, all the purchasing documents (PO, contracts, etc.) can only be transmitted to the vendor from the SAP SRM system. If the organization wants to output via the SAP backend, then it must use the Classic Scenario or customize.

▸ PCards can only be used in the Standalone scenario. If other scenarios are used, organizations will have to customize using BAdIs and other developments.

▸ If the Extended Classic scenario is implemented, then during the cutover phase, the legacy purchasing documents (POs, contracts, etc.) need to be converted into the SAP EB system instead of the SAP ERP system. Organizations will find challenges in creating shopping carts (converting from requisitions) and contracts in SAP SRM. SAP does not provide any standard programs to create these documents. Organizations will have to use eCATT or other tools such as Mercury.

Keep these in mind during your implementation. Now let's review some relevant OSS Notes.

7.7   Relevant OSS Notes

Table 7.1 provides a list of important OSS Notes available on the SAP Service Marketplace that are relevant for organizations implementing one of the implementation scenarios discussed in this chapter. For example, OSS Note 861889 provides an explanation of the limitations in SAP SRM when creating Limit and service POs in an Extended Classic implementation.

Note	Description
861889	Limitations on limit and service POs in case of Extended Classic scenario
543544	SUS: Extended Classic scenario for SAP EB not supported
505030	Restrictions for the integration of external requirements
900825	Shopping cart commitments
946201	Using backend P Org/ P Grp directly in Extended Classic scenario local PO
752586	Customer fields in Extended Classic scenario
627542	Grouping not supported in Classic scenario
841277	Limit items not created in the backend system
841141	Valuated goods receipt in SAP SRM

Table 7.1   OSS Notes in the SAP Service Marketplace

7.8   Summary

In this chapter, you've been introduced the three main implementation scenarios: Classic, Extended Classic, and Standalone. Choosing an implementation scenario is an important decision for any organization as it forms a basis for the functionality that is available and the limitations for the business scenario selected.

In Chapter 8, you will learn about the concept and relevance of the organizational structure in SAP SRM. We'll answer questions such as: "Why do we need an organizational structure?" and "Why can't we use the organizational structure in SAP ERP HCM?" We'll also discuss how the organizational structure acts as a security mechanism to control what users can see and do, using the concept of attributes.

An organizational structure is a hierarchical view of information about your company's divisions, departments, and positions. These positions, together with the individuals that fill them, create the reporting structures defined within your company.

8   Organizational Structure

Structure, whether hierarchical or linear, exists within every corporation. In SAP, the organizational structure is contained within the SAP ERP Human Capital Management (HCM) application. Organizational management is the structural foundation upon which all other Human Resources (HR) and Payroll processes are based. The organizational management (OM) component is the central component that represents the enterprise's organizational structure and enables the administration and planning of this structure. Additionally, the organizational management structure provides the framework on which to build the security and authorization accesses for SAP end users. This structure also represents the task-related, functional structuring of the enterprise used to enable SAP Business Workflow.

The organizational structure in SAP SRM has largely been designed based on the OM functionality in SAP ERP, known as SAP ERP HCM. SAP SRM primarily facilitates procurement and strategic sourcing; therefore, the OM functionality available in SAP SRM does not make use of the complete SAP ERP OM functionality. For example, in SAP ERP, OM facilitates the hiring of employees. Although SAP SRM contains transactions for personnel management (e.g., PP01), there is no core functionality when using these transactions. In SAP SRM, this functionality has been enhanced to provide for the unique needs of procurement that are not captured within the core SAP ERP organizational structure.

Let's look at an example of typical scenarios and the questions that arise on SAP SRM projects.

Scenario

We already have SAP ERP HCM and maintain a large organizational structure. Why do we need another structure for SAP SRM? Can't we just use the one in SAP ERP HCM? Do we have to use the organizational structure that is in SAP ERP HCM? Can we maintain a separate organizational structure in SAP SRM? If we maintain a separate organizational structure in SAP SRM, what happens after go-live? That is, who maintains the organizational structure in SRM? Is this the responsibility of the HR team or the procurement team?

This chapter contains information that will enable managers and consultants to answer these questions and chart a successful SAP SRM implementation.

Let's start by highlighting the key differences between the organizational structure used in SAP ERP vs. the organizational structure used in SAP SRM (see Figure 8.1). It is important for you to understand these differences because this is one of the confusing aspects of SAP SRM projects. Many individuals mistakenly consider the organizational structure in SRM to be the same as in SAP ERP or disregard the organizational structure's importance. In SAP SRM, the organizational structure is one of the most critical elements of control that enables approval hierarchies and procurement attribute maintenance.

Organizational Structure in SAP ERP HCM	• … is primarily used to maintain the overall enterprise relationship between the **departments**, **positions**, **jobs** and **employees.**
	• … is purely structured around employee reporting hierarchy – actual approval responsibility for operational procurement could be very different.
	• … the structure further drives Human Resource functions key for the enterprise (e.g. Payroll, Time & Expense, etc.)
	• … the hierarchy built in Org Management (OM) is utilized extensively for organizational reporting purposes (employee – manager relationship).

Organizational Structure in SAP SRM	• … is primarily setup to define the **operational** hierarchy within the organization; it additionally drives the **approval** hierarchy & **responsibility**
	• … provides a core element of **control** in SRM via use of "**attribute**" maintenance (**Purchase Organization**, Purchasing Group, Plant, etc.) not available in the SAP ERP HCM Organizations Structure.
	• … the structure further **drives the procurement functions** for the enterprise (Indirect and Direct procurement, Bidding, etc.)

Figure 8.1 Comparing the Organizational Structure in SAP ERP HCM and SAP SRM

Before proceeding further, it is important to gain an overview of the organizational structure in SAP SRM.

8.1   Overview of the Organizational Structure in SAP SRM

The organizational structure in SAP SRM provides the base platform for executing most of the business transactions in the system. Unless a basic form of the organizational structure is available with relevant attributes, users in the SRM system are unable to perform tasks such as creating shopping carts or approvals. Why do you need an organizational structure in SAP SRM?

► By design, SAP Enterprise Buyer (EB) requires at least a basic organizational structure setup.

► The organizational structure constructs the hierarchy in which the various organizational units of an organization are arranged, according to tasks and functions.

► The purchasing organizations and groups responsible for shopping carts and POs can be determined.

► Operational attributes necessary for procurement need to be defined, such as company code, plants, and material groups. These are typically part of materials management in SAP ERP.

► SAP Business Workflow determines which agents are responsible for approving documents based on the hierarchy or approval limits defined within the organizational structure elements.

► The organizational structure acts as an extension to the SAP user master (SU01). It also acts as a security mechanism to control the authorization an end user has to various cost centers, product categories, catalogs, and others.

Organizations implementing SAP SRM will learn that one of the first things they need to set up is the organization's structure. Prior to this setup, no business transactions can be executed in SAP SRM. Unfortunately, this is one area where one size does not fit all. Each organization usually has a varied organizational structure and an even more varied purchasing organization. In SAP SRM, the structure that needs to be set up needs to contain not just the hierarchy of the division and departments within an organization but also the structure of the purchasing department(s) within the organization.

Depending on the culture of an organization, purchasing can be a centralized or a decentralized function. This can strongly impact how you design the organizational structure in SAP SRM. Many organizations use the implementation of SAP SRM as an opportunity to seek centralized procurement. Therefore, they might change the organizational structure to accommodate the changes within the blueprint and realization phases. Figure 8.2 illustrates the organizational structure for a global company.

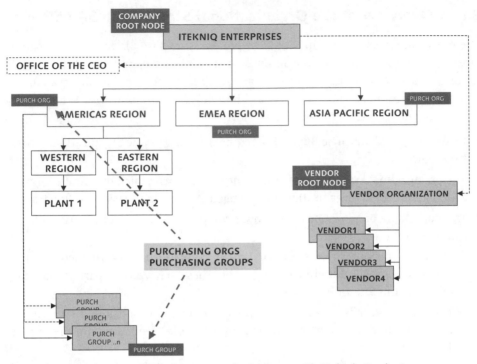

Figure 8.2 Sample Organizational Structure of a Company with Multiple Purchasing Organizations

Once the project teams have gathered an organizational structure with which to begin, the next step is creating this structure within the SAP SRM system. (Typically, this information is gathered from the HR department and then validated by individual departments with enhancement for procurement functions.)

Depending on the size of the organization and the scope of the implementation (whether SAP SRM is being implemented within a region or globally), creating this structure within SRM can be a daunting task. For example, in Figure 8.2, the company ITEKNIQ ENTERPRISES has three purchasing organizations: AMERICAS REGION, EMEA REGION, and ASIA PACIFIC REGION. Each of these would serve as the top organizational node for the organization's global regions. The example further expands the AMERICAS REGION into the WESTERN REGION and EASTERN REGION.

Creating a similar structure and all of the positions within the regions can be a large task. This is especially true because SAP SRM, just like other SAP solutions, is implemented in a three-tiered landscape (development, quality assurance [QA], and production). Therefore, you need an organizational structure in each of these environments (and individual clients). Not only is it challenging to create such a structure, but gathering the information needed to create the organizational structure is also a separate task. SAP provides best practices to assist organizations with options to transport the organizational structure from one environment to another; we discuss these in a later section of this chapter.

Figure 8.3 illustrates the transaction used in SRM for creating and managing the organizational structure. There are three different transactions with which you can access the organizational structure, as seen in Table 8.1.

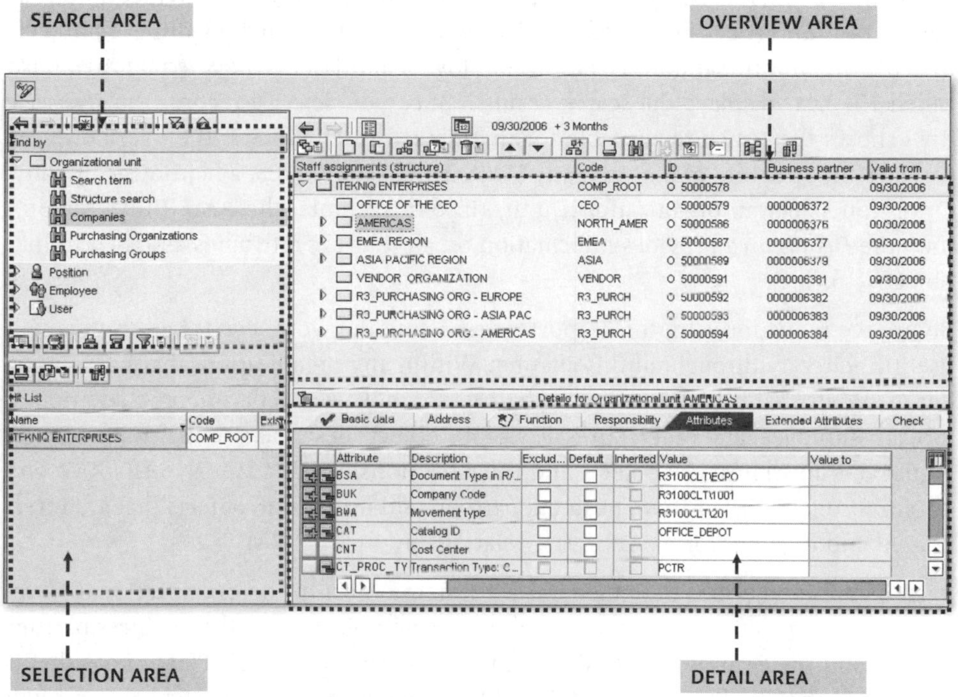

Figure 8.3 Organizational Structure in SAP SRM — PPOSA_BBP

Transaction Code	Description
PPOCA_BBP	Create the root organization nodes
PPOMA_BBP	Change the organizational structure/attributes
PPOSA_BBP	Display the organizational structure/attributes
PPOMV_BBP	Manage external partners in SAP SRM

Table 8.1 Transaction Code and Descriptions

Prior to the release of SAP SRM 1.0 (EB 3.0), you accessed the organizational structure transaction via the PPOMA_CRM; a scenario had to be selected before you could define user attributes. Since then, an independent transaction has been designed for SAP SRM </PPOMA_BBP>.

> **Note**
>
> Organizations using SAP SRM 5.0 or higher should also review Section 8.12, What's New in the Organizational Structure?, because the organizational model has been enhanced.

As Figure 8.3 illustrates, the organizational structure transaction is divided into four parts: The *Search Area* (also called Find by), which lets you search by different objects in SAP (Organizational unit, Position, Employee, and User). The *Selection Area* (also called Hit List) displays the search results. Once you select a record, the *Overview Area* shows the structure available for that object. In Figure 8.3, the overview area displays the structure of the company ITEKNIQ ENTERPRISES, a fictitious company. Once you select an organizational unit, (in our example, the AMERICAS region), then the *Details area* provides information on all relevant attributes assigned to that object.

Before we move forward, it is important to define the word *object*, because we will use it frequently throughout this chapter. Within any organization, there are different elements that bring structure to the organization — a department, a position, a job, an employee, and others. In SAP, various objects describe a similar relationship. Figure 8.4 illustrates SAP objects and their relationships relevant to SAP SRM. The organizational unit, position, business partner, and user are all objects that are interrelated and together form a complete relationship in SAP SRM.

Each of these objects is designated as a separate object in the organizational structure. The organizational object is "O," the position object is "S," the business partner is "BP," and the Central Person (CP) is linked to user object (US). Please note that it is coincidental that the position, CP, and US in Figure 8.4 are all called *Sachin Sethi*; usually, if the organization structure is brought from SAP ERP HCM into SAP SRM they would likely all have different names with the position "S" having a true position description.

Staff assignments (structure)	Code	ID	Business P	User ID	Valid from	Valid to	Assigned as
▽ ☐ Temporary Organization	Temp	O 50000632	111		03.09.2009	Unlimited	
▽ ⚇ Sachin SETHI	C-SSETHI	S 50000633			03.09.2009	Unlimited	03.09.2009
⚇ Sachin SETHI	Sachin	CP 50000634	112	C-SSETHI	03.09.2009	Unlimited	03.09.2009

Figure 8.4 Objects in an Organizational Structure Relevant to SAP SRM

The organizational structure transaction in SRM is similar to the transaction in SAP ERP HCM. However, in SRM, there are some additional features — such as searching by company, purchasing organization, and others — that are more relevant from a procurement point of view. Additionally, SAP SRM lets you maintain organizational attributes, a key functionality in SAP SRM that controls purchasing elements such as plants, catalogs, product categories, and others.

We explain the concept of attributes in detail later in this chapter. You can assign attributes to organizational units and positions relevant for purchasing. Figure 8.5 illustrates how you can perform different searches in the organizational structure in SAP SRM that are relevant to procurement. As you can imagine, a search by purchasing groups in the SAP ERP HCM organizational structure would not be relevant. However, in SAP SRM, it could be relevant to quickly search across all purchasing groups in the structure and either maintain or display the attributes within the purchasing groups.

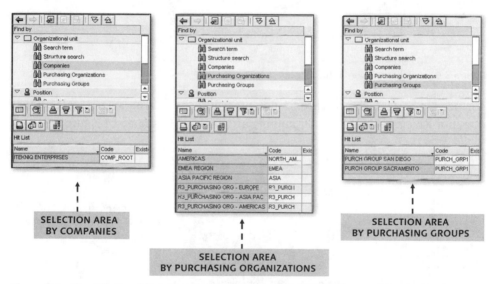

Figure 8.5 Organizational Structure Search by Purchasing Organizations and Purchasing Groups

Once a basic structure of the organizational plan is set up, it needs to be synchronized in such a way that the appropriate business partners are created for all of the organizational units created. This synchronization needs to take place on a regular basis via a background job. Unless an organizational unit is consistent, you can't assign positions or employees to that unit. You can use transaction BBP_BP_OM_INTEGRATE to synchronize the organizational structure, as illustrated in Figure 8.6.

Figure 8.6 Synchronization of the Organizational Structure

You need to perform the synchronization procedure for each organizational unit that does not have a business partner number assigned, as illustrated in Figure 8.7.

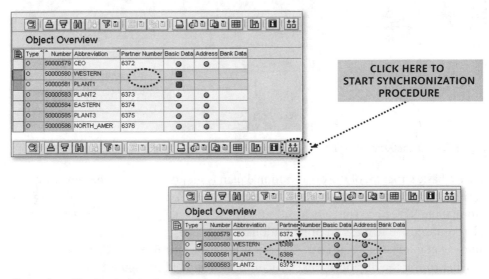

Figure 8.7 The Synchronization Procedure for an Organizational Plan

SAP provides a good step-by-step tutorial on how to create the structure of your organizational plan to reflect the structure and HR environment of your company. Project teams can access this tutorial via *http://help.sap.com/saphelp_erp2005/helpdata/en/fb/ 135990457311d189440000e829fbbd/frameset.htm*.

In the next section, we'll explain the Details area of the organizational structure, including the Basic data, Address, Function, Responsibility, Attributes, Extended Attributes, and Check areas.

8.2 The Details Area of the Organizational Structure

In Section 8.1, we briefly discussed the Search Area, Selection Area, and Overview Area of the organizational structure in Transaction PPOSA_BBP. In this section, we will discuss in greater depth the *Details area* of the organizational structure transaction. One of the reasons that this chapter puts greater emphasis on this section is that the attributes and functions for the entire organizational structure are maintained within this area. The Details area of the organizational structure contains configurable attributes organized within seven different tabs.

8.2.1 Basic Data Tab

The Basic data tab contains basic information about the selected object. For organizational objects, this is typically the name of the object; for position objects, the Basic data tab also lets you specify the validity period of the position. Because the SAP SRM user is a combination of the position, business partner, and user, a validity period assigned to the position indirectly assigns the validity period to the user record as well. Figure 8.8 illustrates the Basic data tab for an organizational unit and a position.

8.2.2 Address Tab

The Address tab displays basic information about the organizational unit object, such as the address and telephone numbers for the organizational unit. Addresses are maintained at an organizational unit level. If the organizational unit is also classified as a company, the address specified for the organizational unit becomes the default hierarchy address for all departments within that company. When internal (company) addresses are created in SAP SRM, such as delivery addresses that users can select in the shopping cart, those addresses can be created under this main address.

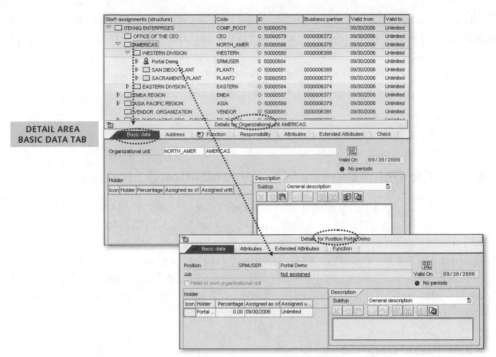

Figure 8.8 The Basic Data Tab in the Details Area of the Organizational Structure

An address is required for each organizational unit created in SAP SRM. Otherwise, the organizational unit is not considered consistent for employee assignment, as illustrated by the "Organizational unit 50000587 is not consistent" message, seen in Figure 8.9.

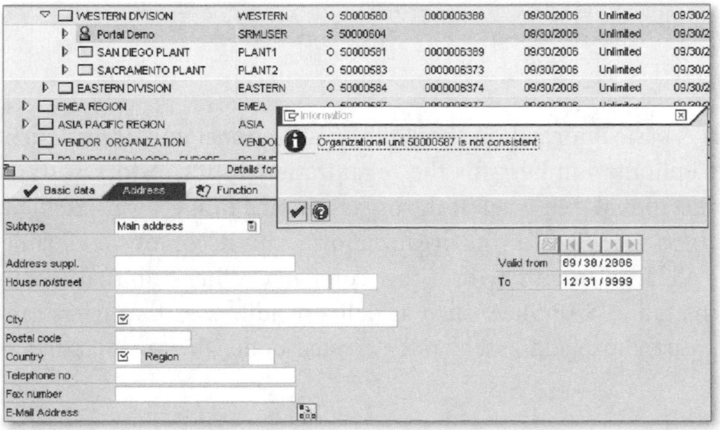

Figure 8.9 Organizational Units are Required to Have an Address in SAP SRM

Addresses are not required for positions and other objects in the organizational structure, as shown in Figure 8.10. In this figure, with the organizational unit ITEK-NIQ ENTERPRISES selected, the Details area shows an Address tab with an address of 1000 HELLO STREET. However, when the position Portal Demo is selected, the Details area does not show an Address tab (because, as we mentioned earlier, it isn't required).

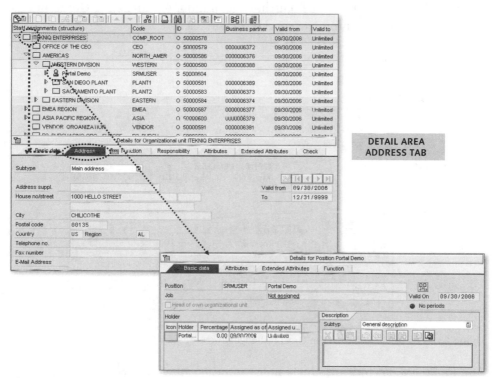

Figure 8.10 Address Maintenance in the Details Area

8.2.3 Function Tab

The Function tab has been a part of the organizational structure since the release of SAP SRM 3.0. This tab provides a structured way to identify an organizational unit as a Company, Purchasing Organization, or Purchasing Group. In Figure 8.11, the Details for Organizational Unit ITEKNIQ ENTERPRISES illustrates the Function section. Here, you can identify an organizational unit as a "Company" or "Purch. Organization" by selecting the appropriate checkbox.

To create purchasing documents, the elements of Company Code, Purch. Organization, and Purchasing Group are required in SAP ERP as well as in SRM. Company

Code 1001 has a secondary field with the value R3100CLT, which indicates the Remote Function Call (RFC) destination for the SAP ERP backend connected to the SAP SRM system. In the Classic scenario implementation of SAP SRM, a value is required in both the Company Code and backend system fields. Similar values are required for the elements Purch. Organization and Purchasing Group.

However, companies implementing the Extended Classic scenario don't have to enter a value for Company code, Purch. Organization, or Purchasing Group in this section. Selecting the appropriate checkbox is sufficient.

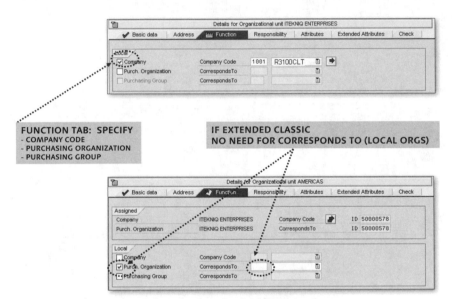

Figure 8.11 The Function Tab in the Organizational Structure

At a minimum, one organizational unit within the structure needs to be set up as a company. This attribute identifies an organizational unit as an independent legal entity. This flag can also be set for subsidiaries.

> **Note**
>
> You can only assign the ship-to and bill-to addresses to organizational units that are flagged as a Company. If there is more than one bill-to address in the organization, then you need to set multiple organizational units as Company, and they cannot be within the same hierarchy because the attribute is inherited down the structure.

The Purch. Organization attribute identifies an organizational unit as a purchasing organization for the company. The Purch. Organization identification is inherited by subordinate Organizational Units and positions. Therefore, a second Purch. Organization cannot be set up within the same hierarchy. Within the organizational structure, the Purch. Organization must be set at either a level higher than Purchasing Group or at the same level.

Let's look at an example. In Figure 8.12, we have selected the WESTERN DIVISION under the AMERICAS region. Notice that the Assigned area on the Function tab contains the Purch. Organization AMERICAS, and the Corresponds To field contains ID 50000586. Here, 50000586 is the system-generated number for the Organizational Unit object, AMERICAS. All other subordinate Organizational Units automatically inherit their Purchasing Organization as AMERICAS (50000586).

In addition to marking an Organizational Unit as a Purchasing Organization, you need to define the Corresponds To field and the backend RFC destination. In the Classic scenario, you must enter the corresponding 3 to 4 character backend Purchasing Organization, as well as the corresponding RFC destination. If you're implementing the Standalone or Extended Classic scenario, you can leave this blank. The checkbox is enough for identification, because no backend is verified, as illustrated in Figure 8.12.

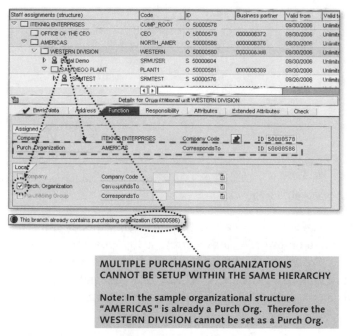

Figure 8.12 Purchasing Organization Inheritance

In the shopping cart and PO transactions, the Purchasing Organization and Purchasing Group name is shown exactly as the name of the Organizational Unit that is flagged as a Purchasing Organization and Purchasing Group. In our example, for instance, an end user sees the name of the Purchasing Group as PURCH GROUP SAN DIEGO in the Basic data section of the shopping cart transaction (illustrated in Figure 8.13). Therefore, determine the names of these organizational units accordingly. This also becomes a challenge when SAP ERP HCM integration is active, because SAP SRM project teams typically have less leverage to impact the names of organizational units. Remember that the Purchasing Group name in the shopping cart is derived from the Organizational Unit that has been selected as the Purchasing Group, as seen in Figure 8.13.

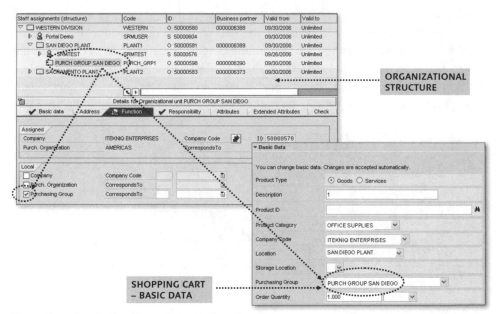

Figure 8.13 Purchasing Group Name in Shopping Cart

The Function tab is only available for Object type "O," an organizational unit. This sometimes can become an issue if project teams want to assign positions the attributes of Purchasing Groups. From an SAP ERP HCM perspective, the position makes best sense to identify with a Purchasing Group. If SAP ERP HCM integration is active, new Organizational Units might need to be created to accommodate the Purchasing Group attribute.

8.2.4 Responsibility Tab

The *Responsibility tab* is specifically designed for organizational units identified as a Purchasing Group. You can therefore assign this property only to objects of type "O."

In an enterprise, a Purchasing Group (sometimes referred to as a buyer) might be responsible for more than one commodity (product category), and might also be responsible for purchases made by individuals in different purchasing organizations. The Responsibility tab has been designed to set the product and organizational responsibility of a Purchasing Group.

Example

Buyer A might be responsible for the office supplies and furniture product categories. Therefore, when a user creates requests (shopping carts) to order goods or services belonging to these two product categories, buyer A will receive the open shopping carts to source to the appropriate vendor. The Responsible Purch. Organization and Purchasing Group attributes are determined based on a user's organizational unit assignment when he creates the shopping carts.

The attribute Product Category is used to define the product categories for which the purchasing group has procurement responsibility. If left blank, no restrictions are applied to that group. Additionally, because purchasing groups can be responsible for procurement on behalf of many departments within the organization, there might be multiple entries in the Purchasing Organization responsibility field. Figure 8.14 illustrates the assignment of the Responsibility tab.

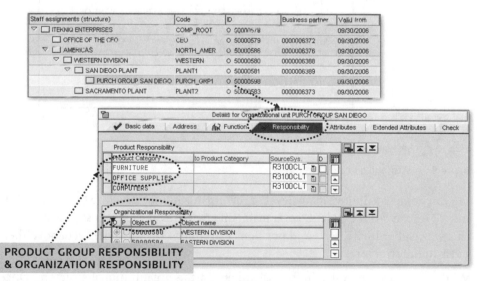

Figure 8.14 Product and Organizational Responsibility

In instances when more than one purchasing group is responsible for the same product category, the system defaults to the first entry in the table. However, users can change this in the shopping cart. This can be troublesome for organizations because users will have to perform this action every time. SAP provides BADI BBP_PGRP_FIND to enable organizations to determine the responsible purchasing group(s) in the shopping cart using their own business rules.

8.2.5 Attributes Tab

The Attributes tab in the organizational structure provides the elements of control for a user and position. In SAP SRM, users require organizational attributes in addition to their security roles so they can create purchasing documents such as shopping carts, POs, and others. Figure 8.15 provides an explanation of user attributes in SRM.

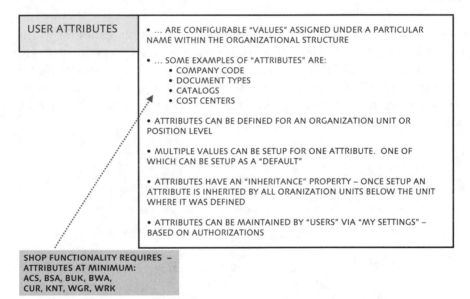

USER ATTRIBUTES

- ... ARE CONFIGURABLE "VALUES" ASSIGNED UNDER A PARTICULAR NAME WITHIN THE ORGANIZATIONAL STRUCTURE

- ... SOME EXAMPLES OF "ATTRIBUTES" ARE:
  - COMPANY CODE
  - DOCUMENT TYPES
  - CATALOGS
  - COST CENTERS

- ATTRIBUTES CAN BE DEFINED FOR AN ORGANIZATION UNIT OR POSITION LEVEL

- MULTIPLE VALUES CAN BE SETUP FOR ONE ATTRIBUTE. ONE OF WHICH CAN BE SETUP AS A "DEFAULT"

- ATTRIBUTES HAVE AN "INHERITANCE" PROPERTY – ONCE SETUP AN ATTRIBUTE IS INHERITED BY ALL ORANIZATION UNITS BELOW THE UNIT WHERE IT WAS DEFINED

- ATTRIBUTES CAN BE MAINTAINED BY "USERS" VIA "MY SETTINGS" – BASED ON AUTHORIZATIONS

SHOP FUNCTIONALITY REQUIRES – ATTRIBUTES AT MINIMUM:
ACS, BSA, BUK, BWA, CUR, KNT, WGR, WRK

Figure 8.15 Attributes in SRM

You can define attributes at any level of the organizational structure (for objects "O" and "S"). To avoid redundant work, maintain attributes at the highest possible level. This way, subordinate units and positions can inherit the attributes set above their levels in the structure.

Many attributes are available for assignment in the organizational structure. Once an attribute is assigned, it is inherited within the organization chain. Therefore, if all attributes are defined at the top-level root node of the organizational structure, every subordinate organizational unit, position, and employee will inherit applicable attributes. Examples of an inheritable attribute are Company Code (ACS) or Currency (CUR), given that there is only one company code in the organization and a single currency is used. Users are typically linked to a department or plant in the organizational structure. Maintaining attributes at the department or plant level automatically assigns the value of the respective attribute for all users in that department or plant.

Figure 8.16 illustrates the Attributes section for the organizational unit. In the Value field for the BUK attribute, a backend RFC destination and SAP ERP ACS is assigned; in our example this is 1010. Other attributes, such as Catalog ID (CAT), have also been assigned.

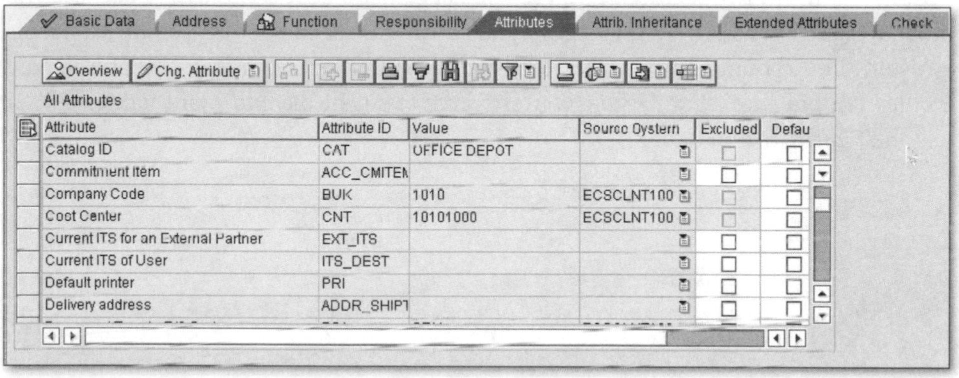

Figure 8.16 Attribute Assignment in the Organizational Structure

The value of this attribute, OFFICE DEPOT, illustrates that for the AMERICAS organizational unit, the OFFICE DEPOT catalog is provided. Therefore, all users that reside within the hierarchy of the organizational unit will inherit the CAT attribute value of OFFICE DEPOT and have the ability to use the Office Depot catalog in the shopping cart and other purchasing documents.

Depending on a user's security role, a different set of attributes might be required. For example, if a user is performing the role of a Contract Administrator, the attribute CT_PROC_TY (transaction type assignment for contracts) will be required so that the contract document type can be determined when a contract is being created.

Project teams will find that not all of the attributes available in SAP SRM are valid for their implementation. For example, the attributes TEND_TYPE and PM_WGR ACC_FUND_ACC_GRANT might not be relevant for your implementation because your scope for SRM might not cover the Bidding Engine or Plant Maintenance or be subject to a public sector overlay requiring Fund and Grant accounting objects.

Therefore, your project team should extract the list of all of the attributes available for your SRM release and select the ones that are relevant for your implementation. A list of organizational structure attributes is available in Appendix J.

In SAP ERP, users are aware of the Parameters (PIDs) available in their user master record. These let users seamlessly insert default information into fields commonly used in transactions, for example, ACS. In SAP SRM, users can change their own attributes with the SAP SRM User Settings application. These attributes are configured within the organizational structure in SRM, and allow users to control defaults within their shopping cart transactions.

Let's look at an example using Figure 8.17, which illustrates the User Settings application. If a user always assigns charge codes against a cost center, they can use the attribute *Account* assignment category and select *Cost Center* as the default value. As a result, the Account assignment category of Cost Center will always be preselected in the shopping cart. Similarly, if a user wants to set his *default* plant value, he can use the *Plant* attribute.

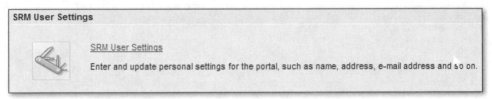

Figure 8.17 Users Can Define Defaults in the SAP SRM User Settings Application

8.2.6 Extended Attributes Tab

The Extended Attributes tab in the organizational structure was introduced with the release of SAP SRM 3.0. This provided more structure and simplified assignment of attributes to the various organizational units and positions. This tab lets you place restrictions on the following attributes:

- ▶ Product Categories and Locations
- ▶ PO Value Limits and Storage Locations

Product Categories and Locations

Product categories in SAP SRM are synonymous with material groups in SAP ERP. Project teams can restrict users to a specific list of product categories by assigning them on this tab. For example, if the IT department is responsible for the purchasing of computer equipment, then the category *Computer Equipment* should only be allowed in the organizational units and positions relevant to the IT department. If the Product Category field is left blank, then no product categories are available for users to select in the shopping cart.

Locations in SAP SRM are synonymous with plants in SAP ERP. Similar to enabling restrictions by product category, in SAP SRM, you can also enable location-based restrictions. For example, you can specify that only users working at a specific plant are able to select that plant as a location in their shopping cart transactions. Figure 8.18 illustrates attribute assignments on the Extended Attributes tab.

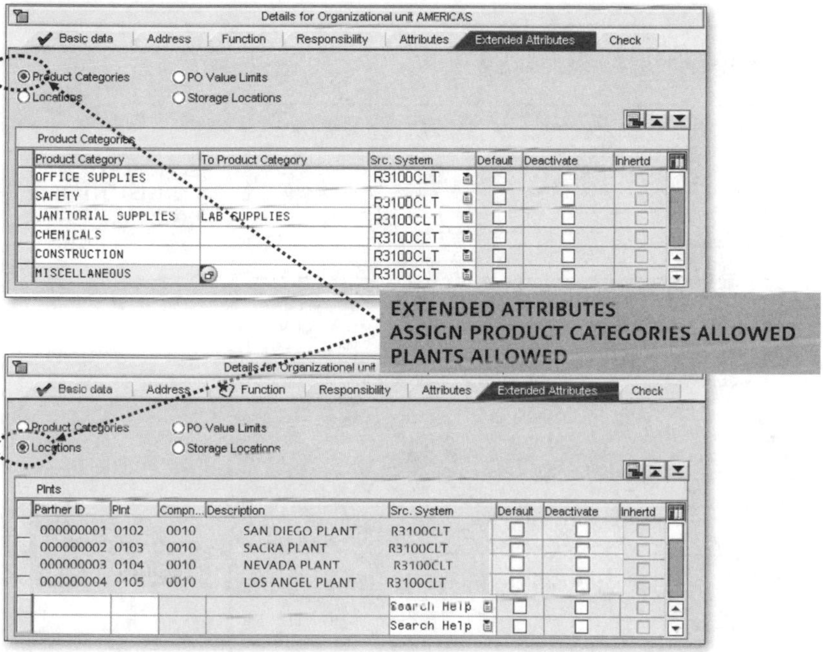

Figure 8.18 Extended Attributes — Product Category and Locations

PO Value Limits and Storage Locations

PO Value Limits let project teams who want to use approval workflow define value limits for the budget and spending limit approval workflows. Storage Locations are assigned in conjunction with Locations in SAP SRM. If direct material procurement is enabled in SAP SRM, users can select the appropriate storage locations within their shopping cart line items.

8.2.7 Check Tab

The Check tab lets you check the consistency of the selected object. Consistency means that the organizational structure expects that you have defined required elements before they are used in business transactions. If the required attributes are not defined, the check will be inconsistent. For example, an address is required for each organizational unit in the structure, as we explained in the Address tab section. If an organizational unit does not have an address defined, or other required attributes are not defined, then the Check tab for that organizational unit will show an inconsistency. Figure 8.19 illustrates the Check tab. With the EMEA REGION organizational unit selected in the Overview area, the Check tab in the Details area provides an analysis of consistency for the organizational unit.

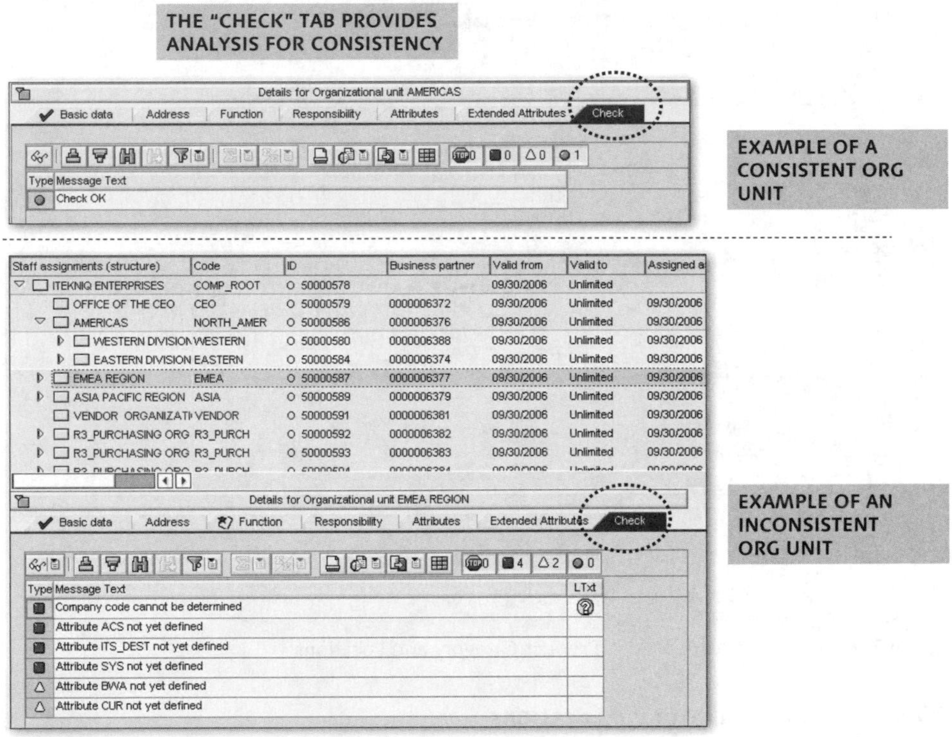

Figure 8.19 The Check Tab in the Organizational Structure

As you can see in Figure 8.19, when an object is not consistent, the system provides messages on the Check tab in the form of errors (red icons) or warnings (yellow icons). If all checks for that object are consistent, a message displays with a green icon.

The Check function within the organizational structure transaction PPOSA_BBP only provides a check for the selected organizational unit. It is recommended that project teams execute the standard report provided by SAP that allows a consistency check across the entire organizational structure. There are two options available for this check, Transaction BBP_ATTR_CHECK or report BBP_CHECK_CONSISTENCY. In Figure 8.20, we illustrate an example of report BBP_CHECK_CONSISTENCY.

In the Selection area, you can select how the check will be performed, at the level of Company, Department, or User. In the Check Type area, you can identify whether a check should be conducted for object consistency or to determine whether all attributes for the organizational object have been maintained for the business transaction, such as the shopping cart. This is important because although an object (organizational unit, position, or user) might be consistent, a user still might not be able to create a shopping cart if all of the required attributes are not maintained.

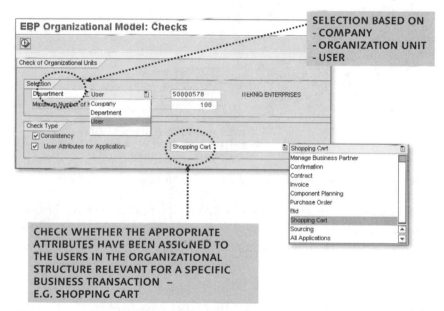

Figure 8.20 Transaction BBP_CHECK_CONSISTENCY

In Figure 8.21, you can see the results of the check; notice that the Consistency check section shows that the organizational unit is inconsistent because certain attributes are not defined. In addition, the User Attribute Check for Application: Shopping Cart section shows that the user SRMUSER does not have the required authorization to create shopping carts because the required roles for creating a shopping cart are missing.

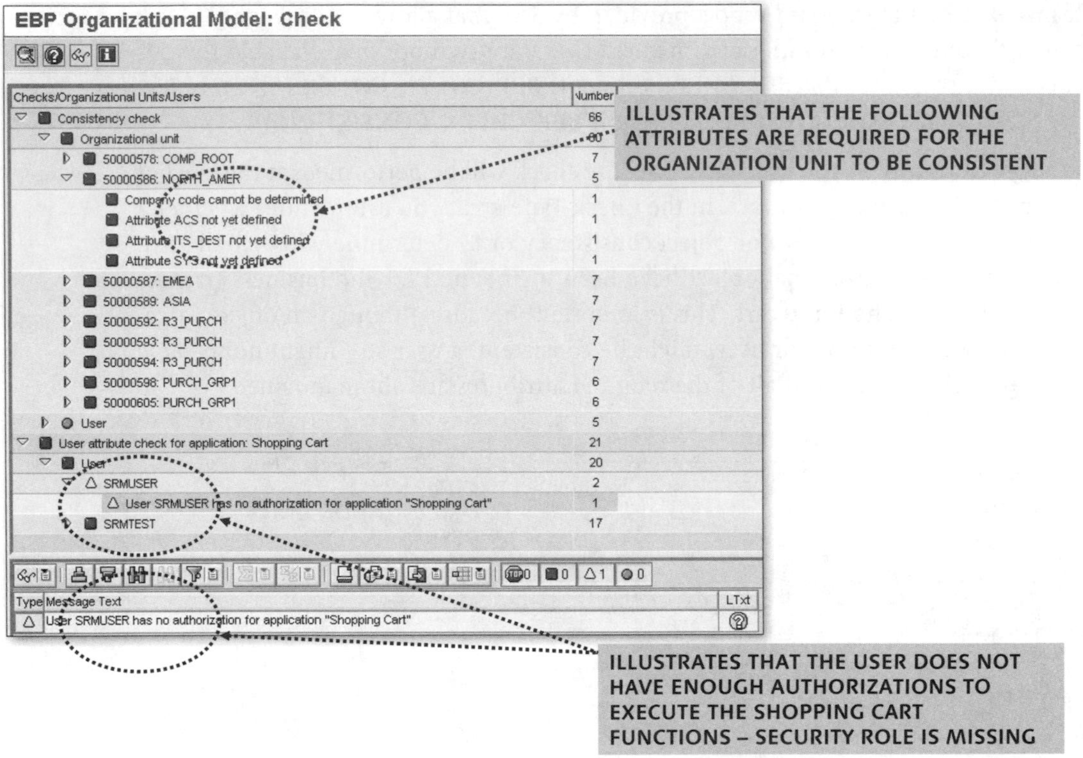

The figure shows a screen titled "EBP Organizational Model: Check" with annotations:

- **ILLUSTRATES THAT THE FOLLOWING ATTRIBUTES ARE REQUIRED FOR THE ORGANIZATION UNIT TO BE CONSISTENT**
- **ILLUSTRATES THAT THE USER DOES NOT HAVE ENOUGH AUTHORIZATIONS TO EXECUTE THE SHOPPING CART FUNCTIONS – SECURITY ROLE IS MISSING**

Figure 8.21 The Consistency Check Provides an Analysis of Possible Issues

Depending on the size of your organizational structure, the project team might need to maintain attributes using a program instead of performing maintenance manually. In the next section, we talk about the functionality available to reduce manual efforts in maintaining attributes.

8.3 Uploading Attributes via a Function Module

Maintaining attributes in the organizational structure can be a daunting task, especially given the interface of the Detail area in the organizational structure. In addition, many organizations want to provide financial controls by restricting which cost center users can display and use when shopping; this can be accomplished by using the *CNT attribute*. For any large organization, there could be hundreds of cost centers and the assignment of those at a user or department level in the organizational structure could be a maintenance-intensive task.

To help with this, SAP has provided a standard program B_UPLOAD_COST_CEN-
TER_ATTRIBUTE that lets you upload the cost center attribute into the organizational structure. The program can also be modified to flag the default cost center. For
example, in Figure 8.22, we've selected a text file in the File Name field under the
File for Upload section. In the Checks section of the program, we've selected Test
Mode, which indicates that we want to test the file upload without saving it to the
organizational structure.

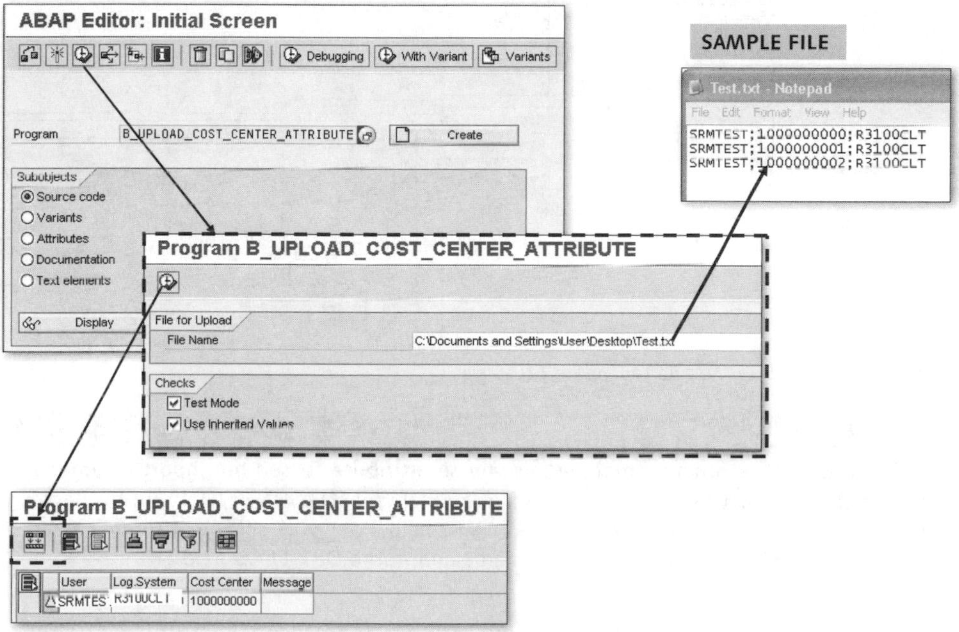

Figure 8.22 Program to Upload the Cost Center Attribute

The standard program only lets you update the cost center attribute. However, project teams can modify this program to enable updates of other attributes as well. As
an alternative, you can also use the function module BBP_UPDATE_ATTRIBUTES to
build a customized report. This function module lets you update most of the attributes in the organizational structure available on the Attributes tab. Figure 8.23
illustrates this function module.

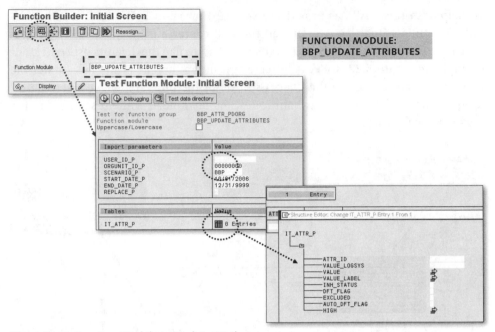

Figure 8.23 Function Module to Update Attributes

Note

In Figure 8.23, the Function module lets you set attributes based on import parameters such as the user ID (USER_ID_P) and organizational unit (ORGUNIT_ID_P). In the Tables section, you can set the attribute in the ATTR_ID field along with setting attribute characteristics, such as indicating an attribute as a default in the DFT_FLAG field.

In the next section, we'll discuss how project teams can customize attribute maintenance.

8.4 Customizing Attribute Maintenance

SAP delivers a set of attributes in SAP SRM with predelivered logic, such as whether an attribute can be inherited from the top organization level to subordinate levels, whether search help is provided for an attribute, and others. Project teams may, however, find it necessary to customize the standard delivered properties for attributes.

8.4.1 Customizing Delivered Standard Attributes

If necessary, you can customize the functionality of the delivered attributes in the standard system. You do this by using Transaction SM30 and table T77OMATTR, or by using Transaction OOATTRCUST. Figure 8.24 illustrates this transaction.

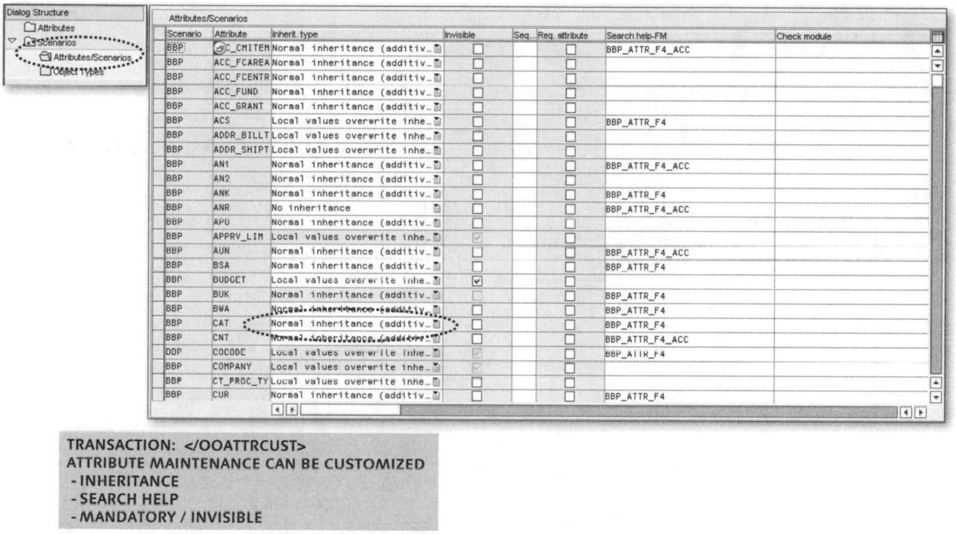

Figure 8.24 Changing Attributes and Scenarios

8.4.2 Create a New Attribute in the Organizational Structure

Organizations can define new attributes for use within their implementation and give users the ability to select these attributes within their "my settings" transaction. This gives organizations the power to use custom attributes in the organizational structure and gives users the flexibility to set these attributes individually. Figure 8.25 illustrates the process of creating new attributes:

1. Execute Transaction OOATTRCUST.

2. Click on New Entries.

3. Select the scenario BBP and create a new Z* attribute (for example, ZNEW, as illustrated in Figure 8.25).

4. Assign any maintenance attributes of inheritance or search and then save the new entry.

5. Make sure to assign which object types are allowed to maintain this attribute (i.e., Can this attribute be maintained at the organizational unit or position level or both?).

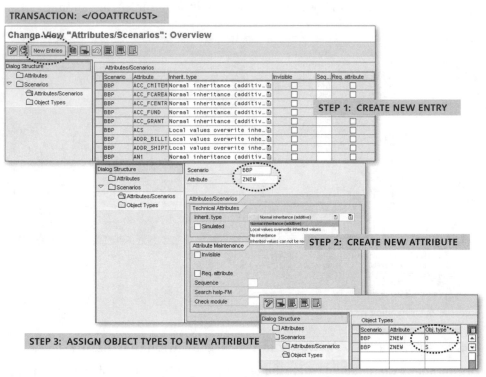

Figure 8.25 Creating New Attributes for Use in the Organizational Structure

8.4.3 Maintaining Attribute Rights by Role

SAP SRM lets you configure whether users assigned to a particular role are authorized to display or change an attribute in "my settings." Therefore, if the organization does not want users to be able to set the cost center attribute, they can limit this access using the IMG path SUPPLIER RELATIONSHIP MANAGEMENT • SRM SERVER • CROSS-APPLICATION BASIC SETTINGS • ROLES • MAINTAIN ATTRIBUTE ACCESS RIGHTS BY ROLE. This is illustrated in Figure 8.26.

In the standard system, these access rights are controlled using the SAP delivered roles. As most organizations copy standard roles into customer specific roles, this setting needs to be changed because the customer Z roles are not there by default.

Project teams will have to configure the attributes' definitions here based on each ZRole created (typically the Employee, Manager, and Purchaser Roles).

The organizational structure comprises the heart of the operational and strategic functions within SAP EB. Therefore, only a select group of personnel should be authorized to change and modify this transaction. As a best practice, always access this transaction in display mode via Transaction PPOSA_BBP. This also prevents problems caused by table locks, particularly when creating users. In addition, make sure that the organization admin closely tracks all changes made to the organizational structure — otherwise, things can get out of hand quickly. Chapter 11 provides information on how to secure the organizational structure in a decentralized maintenance environment where multiple groups maintain the organizational structure.

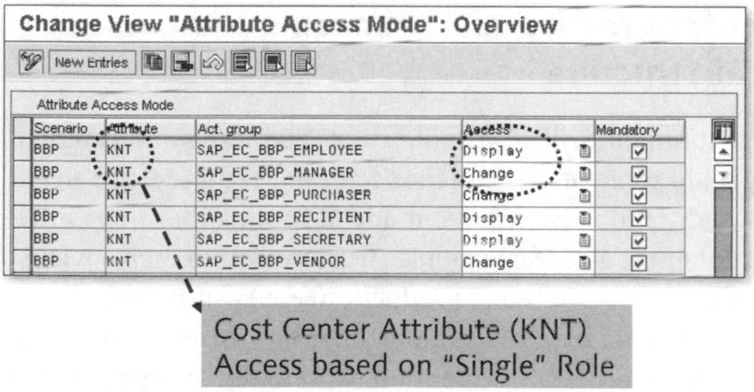

Figure 8.26 Maintain Attribute Access Rights by Role

In the next section, we'll discuss how to delete objects within the organizational structure, such as organizational units, positions, and business partners.

8.5   Deleting Organizational Objects in SRM

At times during the SRM implementation process, you may need to delete organizational structure objects. One example would be when you create the organizational structure from a legacy file using an upload program or possibly when integrating with SAP ERP HCM. It could happen, for example, that the structure was loaded incorrectly and needs to be deleted and reloaded.

The following process provides a guide to deleting objects from the Organizational Management and Personnel Planning in SAP SRM:

1. Execute report RHRHDL00 in Transaction SE38.

2. Enter the objects that need to be deleted, for example, "O" for organizational units, "S" for positions, and others. You can provide a range for the object numbers.

3. Make sure the Test checkbox is selected to verify the results the first time.

4. Once you are satisfied with the test simulation, deselect the Test checkbox and execute the deletion(s).

5. The objects listed will be deleted from the database.

In the next section, we will discuss how companies can use best practices for the creation and management of the organizational structure in SAP SRM.

8.6   Best Practices for Creating and Managing the Organizational Structure

As with any SAP implementation, the SAP SRM application is typically implemented within a three-tier landscape; in some implementations, it can get up to a five-tiered landscape with a sandbox and training environment added to the other three environments. Creating and maintaining an organizational structure within each environment (sandbox, development, quality, training, production, etc.) can be a resource-intensive activity. In addition, it is difficult to maintain all of the attributes and keep them in synch across each environment, not to mention the different clients possible in each environment.

8.6.1   Key Organizational Structure Challenges

It is important for readers to understand the challenges revolving around managing an organizational structure. Some of you might be familiar with the organizational structure in SAP ERP HCM and the number of changes that a typical HR department needs to make to keep up with constantly changing positions, jobs, and employee roles of an organization. The following bullets summarize some of the key challenges of managing an organizational structure in SAP SRM:

▶ Dual maintenance of organizational data (in SAP ERP HCM and SAP SRM).

▶ Maintenance as a result of frequent organizational changes.

▶ Creation and maintenance of organizational nodes and attributes.

▶ Sensitive data exposure within the organizational structure.

- Lack of well-defined financial approval structures (spending limit approval).
- Security (with large implementations).
- Keeping the organizational structure simple.
- Using the inheritance functionality for attributes from existing organizational nodes. Inheritance is configurable, but it can be difficult to decide on the best configuration.

From a best practices perspective, the following options are available:

- Transport the organizational structure from one environment to another (e.g., from quality to production).
- Integrate the SAP ERP HCM organizational structure with the structure in SAP SRM (only applicable if SAP ERP HCM is also implemented).

We will discuss these two best practices in detail in the next sections.

8.6.2 Transport the Organizational Structure

Creating and managing the organizational structure in SAP SRM can be a time-consuming activity. Although many organizations choose to maintain the organizational structure in each of the development, quality, and production environments individually, it is a best practice to transport the structure from one environment to another.

The challenge is that most companies are unable to define a clean organizational structure in the development environment and constantly use that as an experimental structure. Or, even if the development environment is strictly controlled for clean data, the complete structure is, nonetheless, often not defined because of the amount of time it takes to create the entire organizational structure.

The quality environment is a good environment to rebuild the structure. However, many project teams are unable to gather all of the data in time or spend the time creating the entire structure. However, it is a best practice that organizations create a production-like organizational structure in the quality environment and then transport that to the true production environment. Figure 8.27 provides a best practices guide to creating and maintaining key objects in the organizational structure within SAP EB. SAP provides a detailed document that explains the best practices defined in Figure 8.27, which can be downloaded from the SAP Service Marketplace (Transporting SAP EB Systems vers. 1.4.pdf).

	Development System	Quality Assurance of Consolidation System	Production System
Organizational model (organizational units only)	• Set up test organizational structure manually	• Set up company org structure manually • Transfer from a SAP ERP HCM backend using ALE	• Transfer from the Q system using ALE • Transfer from SAP ERP HCM backend using ALE
Attribute maintenance in org. model	• Manually	• Manually	• Transfer from the Q system using ALE
Product categories	• Download from Materials Management in SAP ERP backend using CRM middleware	• Download from Materials Management in SAP ERP backend using CRM middleware	• Transport from the Q system using transport request
User (SU01 user)	• Manually • CUA (Central User Administration) • Download from SAP ERP using reports	• CUA • Download from SAP ERP using reports • Manually	• CUA • Client copy • Download from the Q system using reports • Manually
SAP EB user (user in the organizational model)	• Manually • Download from SAP ERP using reports	• Transfer from SAP ERP HCM backend using ALE • Download from SAP ERP using reports	• Transfer from SAP ERP HCM backend using ALE • Download from Q system using reports • Download from SAP ERP using reports
RFC connections and logical systems	• Manually	• Manually	• Manually (if they have also been transported, they must be accepted.)
Other customizing settings	• Manually	• Manually, in some cases using transport requests	• Client copy, transport request

Figure 8.27 Best Practices for the Organizational Structure

8.7 Integration with SAP ERP HCM — A Key Decision

A number of corporations that have implemented SAP ERP have chosen to turn on only certain functionalities within the SAP suite (e.g., SAP ERP Financials, materials management in SAP ERP, inventory management, SAP Project Systems, etc.). That is, not everyone has SAP ERP HCM. It is also possible that your company uses a legacy system, or a competitive application like PeopleSoft, to manage SAP ERP HCM functions. This section is aimed at organizations that have implemented SAP ERP HCM or are planning to implement SAP ERP HCM along with the SAP SRM solution.

8.7.1 Need for SAP SRM Integration with the SAP ERP HCM Organizational Structure

On every project, the following questions come up: Why do we need to integrate the SAP ERP HCM organizational structure into SAP EB? What are the benefits?

The obvious benefit is to leverage existing efforts and implement standardization. If you have SAP ERP HCM, the organizational units, positions, employees, and others are already available in a standardized format. A previous or separate implementation team has taken the time to gather the organizational data, strategize on the structure, and align departments and positions closely with the reporting relationships within the corporation. What you need to do now is integrate this structure with the SAP EB system and identify what organizational structure maintenance is still required after the integration. We'll expand on this later.

Another key benefit is that the SAP ERP HCM system becomes the system of record and changes. For example, when an employee is relocated within the organization and the changes are entered and executed in the SAP ERP HCM system, the same changes are reflected within the SAP SRM system as well. Or, take the example of an employee who has been terminated.

The HR department is notified first and takes the necessary steps to ensure that the employee information is updated correctly within the SAP ERP HCM system. If the organizational structure is integrated within SAP ERP HCM and SAP SRM, this information is then also automatically updated in the SAP SRM organizational structure and authorization for the terminated employee will be restricted seamlessly in SAP SRM.

Another benefit revolves around frequent organizational changes, which are common in any large organization. Most organizational structure changes are not pleasant and a lot of time and effort is spent in restructuring and realigning various departments, positions, and employees. An integrated HR structure at least ensures that you maintain these changes only once, in the SAP ERP HCM system, and that the changes are propagated automatically to all other systems (e.g., SAP SRM).

8.7.2 SAP ERP HCM Integration Scenarios — When to Integrate

It is not always feasible for project teams to integrate the SAP ERP HCM organizational structure with SAP SRM. In this section, you'll learn the different scenarios where SAP ERP HCM integration is feasible, some with ease and others with difficulty. In Figure 8.28, we illustrate different levels of complexity for integrating the SAP ERP HCM organizational structure with SAP SRM. The figure also illustrates when it is ideal for organizations to integrate the SAP SRM structure with SAP ERP HCM. For example, the most complex scenario to implement is number 1 in Figure 8.28, where the organizational structure already exists in both the SAP ERP HCM and SAP SRM systems. In the paragraphs below, we'll discuss all four scenarios as illustrated in Figure 8.28.

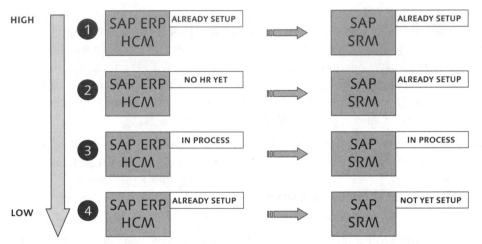

Figure 8.28 Feasibility of Integrating with the SAP ERP HCM Organizational Structure

Scenarios 1 and 2

Scenarios 1 and 2 illustrated in Figure 8.28 are quite complex to implement because an organizational structure has already been set up within the SAP EB system. In these scenarios, all of the organizational objects (O, S, P, etc.) have a different number range; for example, the organizational unit object (O) in ERP contains a number range that is entirely different than the available number range for the "O" objects in SAP SRM.

Integrating SAP ERP HCM in this scenario deletes the existing SAP EB organizational structure and overwrites it with the structure from SAP ERP HCM. In a production environment, this could have a large effect on existing users with functions already in place, such as shopping carts, POs, vendors, business partners, and others. The standard integration process of SAP ERP HCM to SAP SRM will not suffice in this scenario; a significant custom development effort would be required.

Scenario 3

Scenario 3, as illustrated in Figure 8.28, shows a situation where SAP is possibly being implemented across the entire enterprise. In this scenario, both SAP ERP HCM and SAP SRM could be in the process of being implemented and both have their individual timelines for completion. The SAP ERP HCM team and the SAP SRM team might each have goals and requirements of their own. One disadvantage in this scenario is that SAP ERP HCM is the leading system of record; therefore, SRM is always dependent on the timeline of the SAP ERP HCM implementation.

For example, in a project implementation schedule, if the SAP ERP HCM team is behind schedule, it directly impacts the SAP SRM timeline because it is dependent on the SAP ERP HCM organizational structure being available. Typically, the SAP ERP HCM data gathering process is slower than what is required for SAP SRM, because SAP SRM requires an organizational structure that supports the procurement organization. However, the SAP ERP HCM team has to gather data for the entire enterprise.

If your organization is implementing SAP ERP HCM and SAP SRM within the framework of this scenario, make sure the supply chain and SAP ERP HCM project teams work closely together. Define expected timelines upfront. One major issue in this scenario is that SAP SRM requires that an organizational structure is in place before it can begin its core transactions, such as shopping cart creation. In this scenario, project teams end up creating a manual organizational structure in SAP SRM independently to being the proof of concept process for all other pieces and wait until a sizable organizational structure is created in SAP ERP HCM to being the distribution process and utilize that as the organizational structure in SAP SRM.

The key advantage of this scenario is that both the SAP ERP HCM and SAP SRM teams have the opportunity to collaborate on requirements, and build an organizational structure strategy that is closely aligned to meet the needs of both business processes.

Scenario 4

The least complex scenario to implement and integrate SAP ERP HCM with SAP SRM is illustrated in scenario 4 in Figure 8.28. In this scenario, SAP ERP HCM has already been implemented within the company and SAP SRM (EB) is yet to be implemented or is currently being implemented. This provides an opportunity for the implementation teams to review the existing SAP ERP HCM organizational structure, understand the maintenance strategy, and better define the blueprint strategy for the SAP EB organizational structure.

From a timeline perspective, there is no pressure and no need to wait for data gathering efforts from the SAP ERP HCM teams. The SAP SRM team can review the existing organizational structure and determine possible gaps upfront. This allows for a better design and prevents surprises later.

The main disadvantage of this scenario is that the SAP ERP HCM and SAP SRM teams don't have much opportunity to collaborate on requirements. As the SAP ERP HCM organizational structure and business processes are already built and available in a production environment, there is less desire for change.

8.7.3 Distributing the SAP ERP HCM Organizational Plan

SAP provides a standard interface for the distribution of organizational structure objects from SAP ERP HCM into the SAP SRM system. However, organizations need to determine what organizational structure objects need to be distributed from SAP ERP HCM into SAP SRM; for example, should roles be distributed from SAP ERP HCM to SAP SRM? or, as another example, does address and bank information need to be distributed for employees? The process and setup of this distribution is covered in Chapter 21.

8.7.4 Maintenance of Organizational Structure After HR Integration

Integrating the SAP ERP HCM organizational structure with SAP SRM does not eliminate maintenance requirements within SAP SRM. On the contrary, there is still a significant amount of maintenance required in SAP SRM after the integration. For example, in the SAP ERP HCM organizational structure, there are no infotypes that are relevant for purchasing, such as purchasing organization, purchasing groups, plants, catalogs, and others. These attribute settings all need to be maintained in the SAP SRM organizational structure once it has been distributed from SAP ERP HCM.

Additionally, new organizational units are also necessary, such as the Vendor Root Organization, where all vendors are replicated from the backend SAP system. Further, for organizations implementing the Extended Classic scenario in SAP SRM, additional organizational units are required that represent the backend SAP purchasing organization and purchasing group.

If the Direct Material scenario is being implemented, then the organizational units are required to map the entry point for the requirements being transferred from the external system into SAP SRM.

Figure 8.29 illustrates some of the organizational units created manually in the SAP SRM organizational structure. If the supply chain project teams are able to persuade the SAP ERP HCM teams to create additional organizational units like the SAP ERP Purchasing Org in the SAP ERP HCM structure, then these could be distributed via the ALE model as well.

**ORGANIZATION UNITS DISTRIBUTED
FROM SAP ERP HCM**

Staff assignments (structure)	Code	ID		Business partner	Valid from	Valid to
ITEKNIQ ENTERPRISES	COMP_ROOT	O	50000578		09/30/2006	Unlimited
OFFICE OF THE CEO	CEO	O	50000579	0000006372	09/30/2006	Unlimited
AMERICAS	NORTH_AMER	O	50000586	0000006376	09/30/2006	Unlimited
WESTERN DIVISION	WESTERN	O	50000580	0000006388	09/30/2006	Unlimited
Portal Demo	SRMUSER	S	50000604		09/30/2006	Unlimited
SAN DIEGO PLANT	PLANT1	O	50000581	0000006389	09/30/2006	Unlimited
SACRAMENTO PLANT	PLANT2	O	50000583	0000006373	09/30/2006	Unlimited
EASTERN DIVISION	EASTERN	O	50000584	0000006374	09/30/2006	Unlimited
EMEA REGION	EMEA	O	50000587	0000006377	09/30/2006	Unlimited
ASIA PACIFIC REGION	ASIA	O	50000589	0000006379	09/30/2006	Unlimited
VENDOR ORGANIZATION	VENDOR	O	50000591	0000006381	09/30/2006	Unlimited
R3_PURCHASING ORG - EUROPE	R3_PURCH	O	50000592	0000006382	09/30/2006	Unlimited
R3_PURCHASING ORG - ASIA PAC	R3_PURCH	O	50000593	0000006383	09/30/2006	Unlimited
R3_PURCHASING ORG - AMERICAS	R3_PURCH	O	50000594	0000006384	09/30/2006	Unlimited

**ORGANIZATION UNITS CREATED
MANUALLY IN SAP SRM**

Figure 8.29 Organizational Structure — Manual Object Maintenance

The following is a list of several key attributes and master data elements that you must maintain in SAP SRM:

- Company Code
- Purchasing Organization
- Purchasing Groups
- Internal and External Web Catalogs
- Product Categories
- Plants and Storage Locations
- Technical System Links (backend financial system, materials management system, etc.)

8.7.5 Responsibility Matrix for Setting Up the Organizational Structure During an Implementation

During the blueprint and realization phase, typically the consultants on a project will be responsible for designing the organizational structure model and the actual creation of organizational units and attributes. Remember, the organizational structure is a key element; therefore, it is imperative that an appropriate knowledge transfer takes place between the consultants and business owners. As a best practice, business owners should set up the organizational structure in the quality and production environments. This ensures that the appropriate knowledge transfer has occurred.

8.8 Pros and Cons of Creating an Organizational Structure in SAP EB or Distributing from SAP ERP HCM

This section provides a comparison between maintaining the organizational structure in SAP SRM and distributing the organizational structure from SAP ERP HCM. Section 8.8.1 covers the pros and cons of creating an organizational structure in SAP SRM. Section 8.8.2 covers the pros and cons of integrating and using the SAP ERP HCM organizational structure.

CREATING AN ORGANIZATIONAL STRUCTURE IN SAP SRM	
PROS	• ...Allows the implementation team to have **better control** of the Organizational Structure setup. **Eliminates any dependencies.**
	• ... SAP SRM Org Structure requires a subset of overall SAP ERP HCM Org – **Minimize** Initial Setup & reduction of **complexity**
	• ... Allows flexibility to develop a custom structure if required for SAP SRM
	• ... Typically adheres to the timeline allocated for the project
CONS	• ... **Long-Term strategy** for many organizations is to integrate SAP ERP HCM Org with SAP SRM
	• ... **Dual maintenance** of Organizational Structure in SAP SRM and SAP ERP HCM
	• ... **Not synchronized** with the latest org changes in SAP ERP HCM (could have someone not working for the organization anymore in SAP, but still be able to order within SAP SRM)
	• ...FTE's required for **maintenance** of **ongoing** Organizational Structure and changes
	• ...If determined later to integrate with the SAP ERP HCM org structure, a large amount of re-work will be required. (see figure 11.28)

Figure 8.30   Creating an Organizational Structure in SAP SRM

8.8.1 Creating an Organizational Structure in SAP SRM

This section explains, with the help of Figure 8.30, the pros and cons of creating an organizational structure in SAP SRM. One of the main pros of creating the organizational structure in SAP SRM is that the project team has full control to create a structure that will serve the purposes of organizational procurement. The team is also in control of managing the overall timeline because there is no dependency on another team for the management of the organizational structure. However, for companies that also have implemented SAP ERP HCM, the long-term strategy and SAP best practice direct the integration of the SAP SRM organizational structure with SAP ERP HCM.

8.8.2 Integrating and Using the SAP ERP HCM Organizational Structure

This section explains, with the help of Figure 8.31, the pros and cons of integrating the organizational structure in SAP ERP HCM with SAP SRM. One of the biggest advantages of integrating the organizational structure in SAP ERP HCM with SAP SRM is that it reduces the duplication of efforts in the management of organizational structure objects. Because SAP ERP HCM is the system of record for changes in positions and employees (e.g., terminations or new hires), these objects can be managed in SAP ERP HCM and be distributed to SAP SRM in a timely manner. However, even after integrating to SAP ERP HCM, additional attributes need to be maintained in SAP SRM because they are only available in SAP SRM (e.g., a plant or purchasing organization attribute).

INTEGRATING & USING THE ORGANIZATION STRUCTURE IN SAP ERP HCM	
PROS	• ... No Duplication of Organization Setup • ... Less FTE 's required to maintain the Organizational Structure in SAP SRM. Need to concentrate on attribute changes only. • ...Real-Time synchronization of SAP ERP HCM Org structure with SAP SRM Org structure • ...Initial SRM implementation best suited for SAP ERP HCM-SAP SRM integration • ...If the corporation is using position based security, then Rolesand authorizations can be assigned directly in SAP ERP HCM and distributed to the SAP SRM system.
CONS	• ... Even after SAP ERP HCM Integration, attribute maintenance is still required in SAP SRM. SAP ERP HCM Integration does not eliminate SRM org maintenance. • ... Although SAP ERP HCM integration is available as standard solution, issues can result based on the SAP ERP HCM org design. • ... Possible risk to overall project timeline if resources are not dedicated or are unavailable • ...If SAP ERP HCM is being implemented at the same time as SAP SRM, there is a greater risk to project timelines. As SAP SRM cannot function without the Organizational Structure, the SAP SRM project team is highly dependent on the SAP ERP HCM Organizational Structure availability

Figure 8.31 Integrating and Using the Organizational Structure in SAP ERP HCM

8.9 Impact of the Extended Classic Scenario on SAP SRM Organizational Structure

In Chapter 7, we discussed the different implementation scenarios for SAP SRM, including the Extended Classic scenario. This section provides a brief description on how to set up the organizational structure in the Extended Classic scenario.

If you are implementing the Extended Classic scenario, the organizational structure needs to be set up a little differently. The key point to remember is that because all purchasing documents (shopping cart, PO, etc.) are created in the SAP SRM system, a local purchasing organization and local purchasing group are required in the organizational structure. However, because the PO is also sent to the SAP ERP backend, a small structure is needed for the backend purchasing organization and purchasing groups. In Figure 8.32, both the local purchasing organization and the backend SAP ERP purchasing organization are created. The local organization setup is illustrated in the shaded box for LOCAL PORG/PGRP and the backend ERP setup is illustrated in the shaded box for ERP PORG/PGRP.

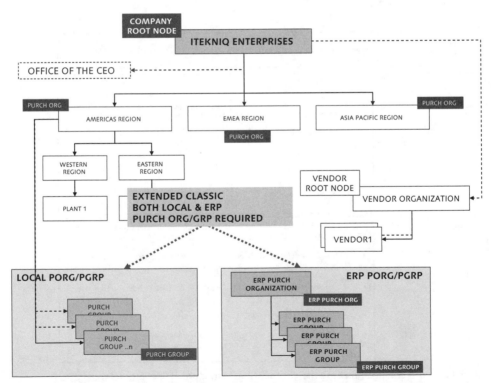

Figure 8.32 Sample Structure of an Organizational Plan for Extended Classic Scenario

In Figure 8.33, an organizational structure in SAP SRM matches the illustration in Figure 8.32. The AMERICAS organizational unit is a purchasing organization but does not have a value entered in the Corresponds To field, because it's not required for local purchasing organizations. However, the R3_PURCHASING ORG — EUROPE is also set as a purchasing organization but contains a value in the Corresponds To field. This indicates the ERP-based purchasing organization 101 and the appropriate RFC destination R3100CLT.

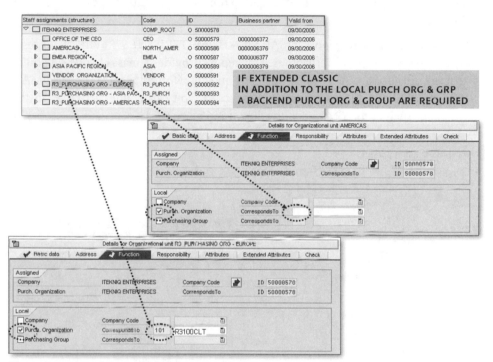

Figure 8.33 Sample Extended Classic Organizational Structure

8.10 System Refresh Procedure Steps

Enhancements, system rollouts, and new application releases drive the need to create new clients and/or refresh existing clients within the development and quality environments. New clients are often built using configuration, master, and transactional data from the production environment. Unlike SAP ERP, a SAP SRM client copy or refresh requires a number of post-refresh procedures. Some of these steps are executed by your BASIS team. Others require execution by the functional teams.

Once the system is refreshed, the organizational structure information needs to be reset based on the new system information (e.g., production environment copied onto a quality environment). A number of attributes in SAP EB contain references to the backend materials management or financial system, including PO document type, cost center, and material groups. For example, if the production system is copied over the QA system, then the cost center and material groups in the QA system organizational structure would still reference the backend destination of the production system. These will need to be changed to reflect the RFC and logical destinations of the QA system.

SAP provides a standard report in SAP EB, RHOMATTRIBUTES_REPLACE, to reset many of the system-specific attributes. This report provides a mass change capability so that all of the attributes can be changed quickly. Note that once the RHOMAT-TRIBUTES_REPLACE program has been executed, you can define attributes in the next screen, such as the CNT attribute shown in Figure 8.34.

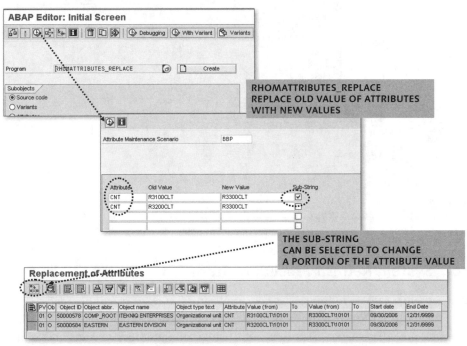

Figure 8.34 Report to Change the Organizational Attribute Values En Masse

In the Old Value field, enter the RFC destination for the source system and in the New Value field, enter the RFC destination of the copy system. Once all of the attributes are defined and the program is executed, the results page displays all of the corresponding objects where an attribute match was found and a mass change can be executed.

OSS note 447651 provides additional information on what to do when a system copy is done in SRM.

8.11   Things to Remember

Now that we've discussed the importance of the organizational structure in SAP SRM and also the impact of integrating the structure with SAP ERP HCM, we'd like to leave you with some key points to remember:

▶ When integrating with SAP ERP HCM, the organizational structure might be much larger than your SAP EB organizational structure needs to be. For example, you might only be rolling out SAP EB to a select group of users in the organization and do not require the entire population of positions and employees found in SAP ERP HCM.

▶ Maintenance of additional attributes such as commodities, cost centers, catalogs, and others will still be necessary in SAP EB, regardless of integration with SAP ERP HCM.

▶ Number ranges must be synchronized between the various environments. Remember, integrating with SAP ERP HCM becomes a challenge if organizational structures in SAP ERP HCM and SAP EB are already set up.

▶ Security needs to be built in so that SAP ERP HCM is the only source for modifications and changes.

▶ Changes made in the SAP EB organizational structure cannot be replicated into the SAP ERP HCM organizational structure.

8.12   What's New in the Organizational Structure?

As of SAP SRM version 5.0, an enhanced organizational (org) model called ERP-ORG has been provided. Because the org model was enhanced in the SAP ERP system, the same has been adopted for SAP SRM. This impacts both the SAP EB and supplier self-services (SUS) systems. There are two key differences in the organizational model in version 5.0, compared to previous releases:

▶ The organizational model has been split between internal and external business partner management. A new Transaction, PPOMV_BBP, has been created for managing external business partners (vendors, bidders, etc.), as opposed to managing them in PPOMA_BBP. Therefore, external business partners cannot be represented in a company's own organizational model that is using SAP SRM.

▶ For organizations using the integrated scenario with SAP ERP HCM, the creation of internal business partners, which were in previous releases created as a result of the HR ALE integration model, are now created in SAP SRM as they are created in the SAP ERP HCM-ORG in ERP system (assuming same client).

The standard Transaction, PPOMA_BBP, used to maintain the organizational structure also has been enhanced with a large detailed view for maintenance. You can access this view via the GoTo • LARGE DETAILED VIEW menu path.

Organizations that are upgrading from previous releases need to migrate the existing organizational structure. SAP provides a standard report, BBP_XPRA_ORGEH_TO_VENDOR_GROUP, to assist with this migration. The report deletes all of the organizational units and positions of vendors and bidders and groups them together into new organizational objects (vendor groups) that can be accessed in transaction. A vendor group is created for multiple vendors using the same attributes.

8.13 Summary

In this chapter, you were introduced to the concept of an organizational structure in SAP SRM, which is also a core component of control within SAP SRM. The organizational structure provides the necessary authorization for users to create shopping carts, POs, and other documents. Attributes, such as purchasing organization, purchasing group, plants, Web-based catalogs, cost center information, and others are all examples of master data elements that are assigned to positions and employees in the organizational structure. We also discussed the importance and need of integrating the organizational structure in SAP ERP HCM with SAP SRM and the best scenarios for this integration.

Chapter 9 discusses the integration of SAP ERP Financials with SAP SRM. Purchasing documents such as shopping carts and POs contain multiple integration points with master data in SAP ERP Financials; budget checks and real-time account validation are competitive selling points for the SAP SRM application.

Tight integration between SAP ERP and SAP SRM is a distinct advantage for customers. The integration of financial and procurement systems offers opportunities for both strategic and operational changes to improve overall efficiencies and reduce costs.

9 Integration with SAP ERP Financials and SAP Project System

ERP systems are the backbone of enterprise financial information management, handling all data associated with financial transactions. Company-wide control and integration of financial information are essential to strategic decision making of any company. According to SAP, SAP ERP centrally tracks financial accounting data within an international framework of multiple companies, languages, currencies, and charts of accounts. For example, when raw materials move from inventory into manufacturing, the system reduces quantity values in inventory and simultaneously subtracts monetary values for inventory accounts in the balance sheet. This chapter covers SAP SRM integration with SAP ERP Financials and SAP Project Systems (PS).

SAP SRM leverages the tight integration between the SAP ERP Financials software and SAP SRM, thereby creating a distinct advantage for the overall application. Real-time integration with SAP ERP Financials Financial Accounting software streamlines the entire supply chain process from the accounting perspective and creates a document audit trail that establishes the controls required by new compliance regulations such as the Sarbanes-Oxley Act (SOX). This integration also validates the finance master data when processing any procurement transaction. The integration real-time checks the available budget and real-time posts procurement transactions into financial accounting.

All accounting-relevant transactions made in SAP Logistics (LO) or SAP ERP Human Capital Management (HCM) software are posted in real time to Financial Accounting by means of automatic account determination. This ensures that logistical goods movements (such as goods receipts and goods issues) are exactly reflected in the value-based updates in accounting. Financial integration occurs at different levels:

enterprise structure, master data, and transaction data. Figure 9.1 illustrates at a high level the SAP components that integrate with SAP ERP Financials.

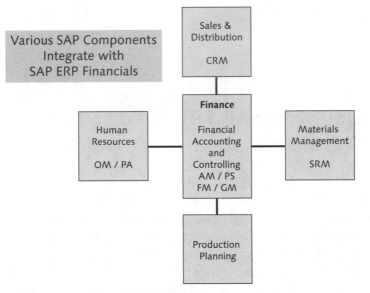

Figure 9.1 Integration with SAP ERP Financials

In the next section, we'll review the basics of SAP ERP Financials to lay a foundation for the later sections in this chapter.

9.1 Financial Accounting in SAP

The SAP ERP solution map provides a listing of all the core business processes within an organization. SAP provides solution maps so that organizations can easily visualize and plan for the different business processes covered within the SAP solution and also plan the processes required to successfully run their operations. Figure 9.2 illustrates the major business processes that exist in SAP ERP 6.0, and highlights the financial processes of SAP Financial Supply Chain Management (FSCM), Financial Accounting, Management Accounting, and Corporate Governance.

Figure 9.3 gives a more detailed view of the functionality required within each of the financial processes. Procurement integrates at a number of touch-points in SAP ERP Financials, such as SAP General Ledger, Accounts Payable, Fixed Assets Accounting, and Inventory Accounting.

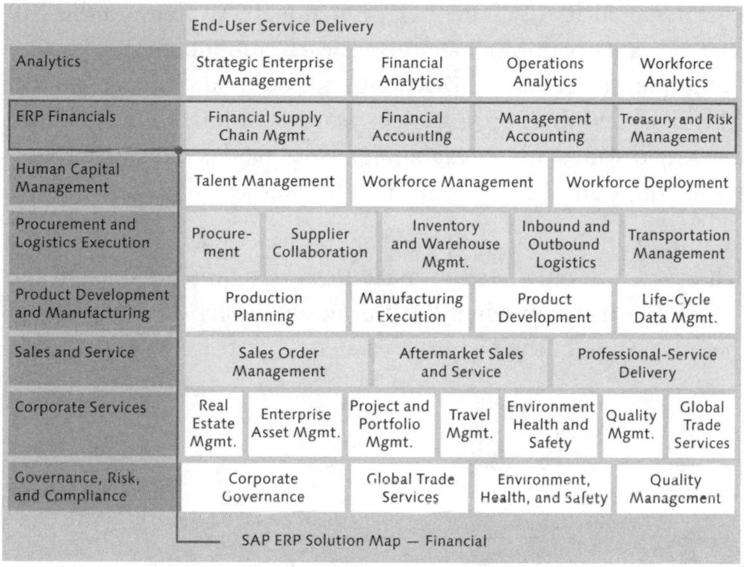
End-User Service Delivery
Analytics
Strategic Enterprise Management
Financial Analytics
Operations Analytics
Workforce Analytics
ERP Financials
Financial Supply Chain Mgmt
Financial Accounting
Management Accounting
Treasury and Risk Management
Human Capital Management
Talent Management
Workforce Management
Workforce Deployment
Procurement and Logistics Execution
Procure-ment
Supplier Collaboration
Inventory and Warehouse Mgmt.
Inbound and Outbound Logistics
Transportation Management
Product Development and Manufacturing
Production Planning
Manufacturing Execution
Product Development
Life-Cycle Data Mgmt.
Sales and Service
Sales Order Management
Aftermarket Sales and Service
Professional-Service Delivery
Corporate Services
Real Estate Mgmt.
Enterprise Asset Mgmt.
Project and Portfolio Mgmt.
Travel Mgmt.
Environment Health and Safety
Quality Mgmt.
Global Trade Services
Governance, Risk, and Compliance
Corporate Governance
Global Trade Services
Environment, Health, and Safety
Quality Management
SAP ERP Solution Map — Financial

Figure 9.2 SAP ERP 2005 Solution Map — Financials

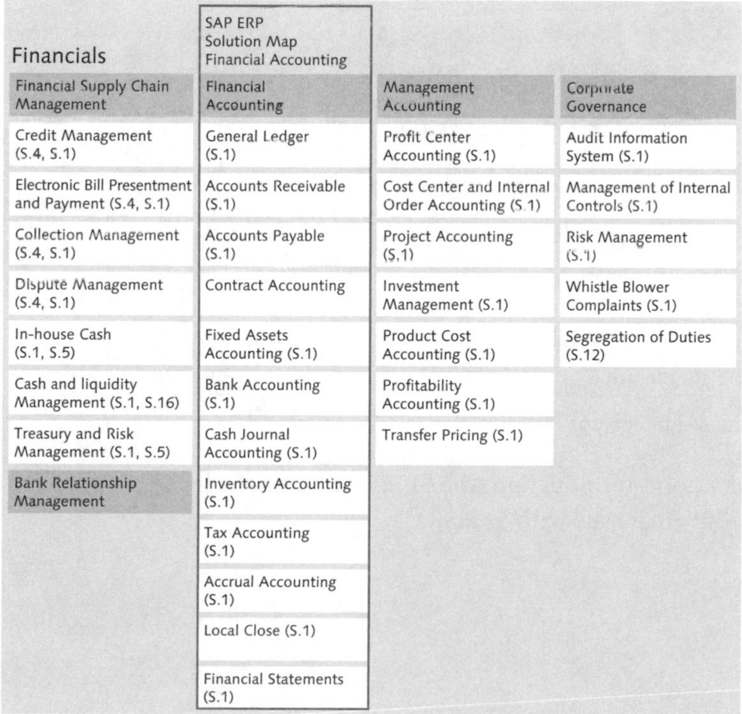
Financials
SAP ERP Solution Map Financial Accounting
Financial Supply Chain Management
Credit Management (S.4, S.1)
Electronic Bill Presentment and Payment (S.4, S.1)
Collection Management (S.4, S.1)
Dispute Management (S.4, S.1)
In-house Cash (S.1, S.5)
Cash and liquidity Management (S.1, S.16)
Treasury and Risk Management (S.1, S.5)
Bank Relationship Management
Financial Accounting
General Ledger (S.1)
Accounts Receivable (S.1)
Accounts Payable (S.1)
Contract Accounting
Fixed Assets Accounting (S.1)
Bank Accounting (S.1)
Cash Journal Accounting (S.1)
Inventory Accounting (S.1)
Tax Accounting (S.1)
Accrual Accounting (S.1)
Local Close (S.1)
Financial Statements (S.1)
Management Accounting
Profit Center Accounting (S.1)
Cost Center and Internal Order Accounting (S.1)
Project Accounting (S.1)
Investment Management (S.1)
Product Cost Accounting (S.1)
Profitability Accounting (S.1)
Transfer Pricing (S.1)
Corporate Governance
Audit Information System (S.1)
Management of Internal Controls (S.1)
Risk Management (S.1)
Whistle Blower Complaints (S.1)
Segregation of Duties (S.12)

Figure 9.3 SAP ERP Financials Financial Accounting

SAP ERP Financials is integrated across all the other functional SAP areas. In the SAP system, you define the relevant organizational units for each component that you are implementing. For example, for Sales and Distribution, you define sales organizations, distribution channels, and divisions (product groups). Similarly, for Purchasing, you define purchasing organizations, evaluation levels, plants, and storage locations. The organizational units are independent of each other at this stage.

To transfer data between the individual components, you have to assign the organizational units to each other. You only need to make these assignments once in the system. Whenever you enter data subsequently, it is automatically transferred. Figure 9.4 illustrates the integration of the finance area at an enterprise level.

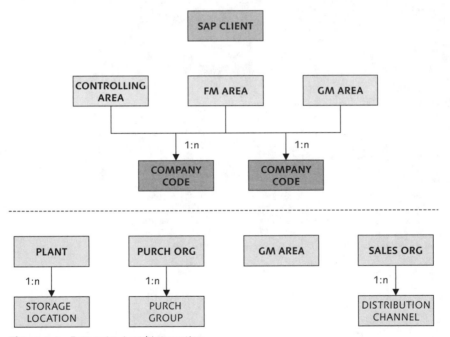

Figure 9.4 Enterprise-Level Integration

Now that you have a good introduction to SAP ERP Financials, let's dive into the integration of SAP ERP Financials with SAP SRM.

9.2   Integration of SAP ERP Financials with SAP SRM

SAP SRM provides real-time integration with *SAP ERP Financials*. Integration can happen at different levels: enterprise structure, master data, and at a business transaction level. The previous section briefly discussed enterprise-level integration in SAP. This section focuses on the integration touch points in SAP SRM where financial master data elements (cost center, SAP General Ledger account, etc.) interact with business transactions (shopping cart, purchase order, etc.)

9.2.1   Integration at the Master Data Level

Integration at the Master Data level means that the master data used in SAP SRM is integrated to master data in financial accounting via configuration within each individual area. To achieve optimum integration, master data must be designed thoughtfully and mapped in a meaningful manner. If designed correctly, it reduces reconciliation and maintenance issues.

From an accountant's point of view, whenever any purchase is made, it needs to be posted either as an expense, asset, or inventory in financial accounting based on the nature of the item purchased. A combination of attributes such as account assignment category and the characteristic of the item purchased (e.g., consumable, material, or service) directs the posting to the appropriate classification of this expense.

Some customers design the shopping cart approval workflow to include a finance validation to validate the buyer's choice of the appropriate account assignment. Getting this right the first time reduces the subsequent expense reclassification effort. The idea is to capture all the data correctly the first time and carry it through until the end of the process to reduce reconciliation and data re-entry.

In Figure 9.5, SAP SRM integrates at a Master Data level with the Controlling, Funds Management (FM), and Grant Management (GM) software within SAP ERP Financials. In SRM, users can utilize account assignments such as cost center, internal order, or funds in the shopping cart and PO documents.

These account assignments map to the cost center, internal order, and fund within Controlling and FM and GM software. Figure 9.6 illustrates how this mapping should be done in the account assignment customizing transactions in SAP SRM.

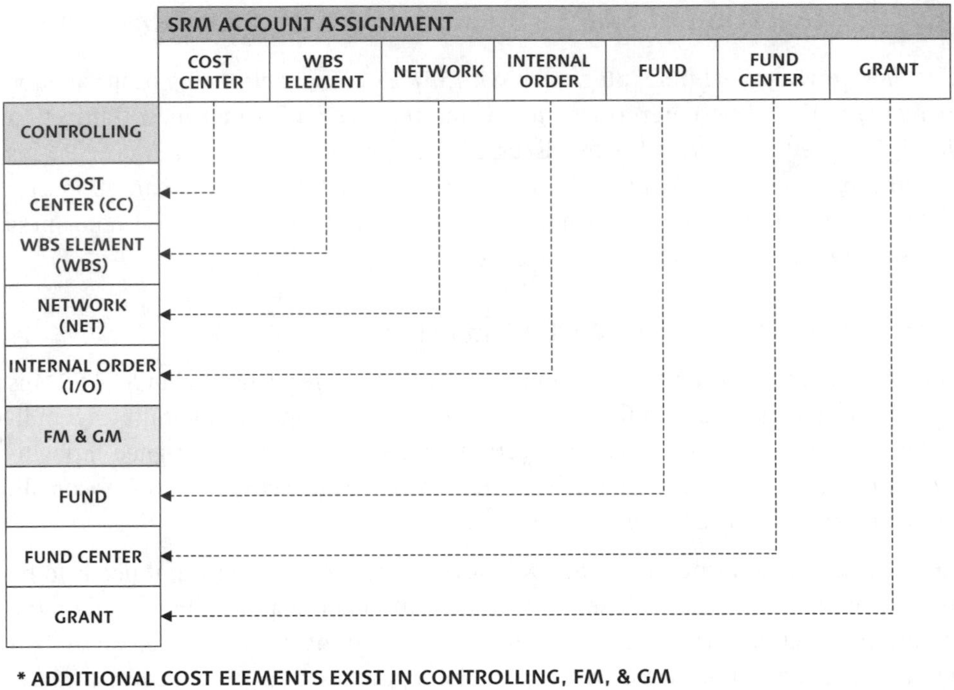

SRM ACCOUNT ASSIGNMENT						
COST CENTER	WBS ELEMENT	NETWORK	INTERNAL ORDER	FUND	FUND CENTER	GRANT

	COST CENTER	WBS ELEMENT	NETWORK	INTERNAL ORDER	FUND	FUND CENTER	GRANT
CONTROLLING							
COST CENTER (CC)							
WBS ELEMENT (WBS)							
NETWORK (NET)							
INTERNAL ORDER (I/O)							
FM & GM							
FUND							
FUND CENTER							
GRANT							

* ADDITIONAL COST ELEMENTS EXIST IN CONTROLLING, FM, & GM

Figure 9.5 SAP SRM Integration at Master Data Level with Controlling, FM, and GM

In Figure 9.6, the configuration setting in SAP SRM allows an organization to map the SAP SRM account assignment type to the SAP ERP account assignment. In SAP SRM, the Cost Center account assignment is delivered by SAP as "CC"; however, in SAP ERP, the Cost Center is delivered as "K." This mapping between the account assignments in SAP SRM and SAP ERP is done in the customizing section Account Assignment in SAP SRM. Additionally, project teams can choose to activate only a select few account assignments; for example, if asset procurement is not allowed via the shopping cart in SAP SRM, then leave the check box under the Active column blank for account assignment "AS," which is used for assets.

Again, from the accounting perspective, the purchase should be posted not only to the right type of classification but also to the correct SAP General Ledger account from the chart of accounts. How can the user make sure he picks the right SAP General Ledger account when making the purchase? With the kind of integration available between SAP SRM and the financial accounting, the user picks up the item to be purchased from the catalog and the backend configuration and integration posts it to the correct SAP General Ledger account. How does this happen?

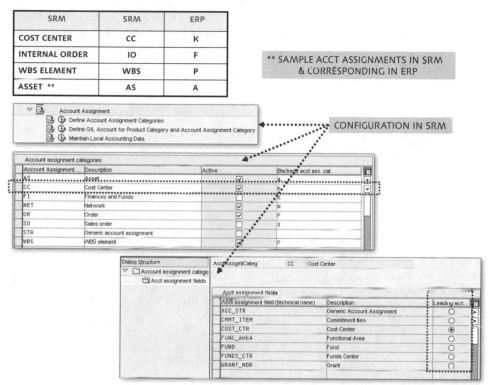

SRM	SRM	ERP
COST CENTER	CC	K
INTERNAL ORDER	IO	F
WBS ELEMENT	WBS	P
ASSET **	AS	A

** SAMPLE ACCT ASSIGNMENTS IN SRM & CORRESPONDING IN ERP

▽ ▣ Account Assignment
    ▣ ⊕ Define Account Assignment Categories
    ▣ ⊕ Define G/L Account for Product Category and Account Assignment Category
    ▣ ⊕ Maintain Local Accounting Data

CONFIGURATION IN SRM

Account assignment categories

Account Assignment ...	Description	Active	Backend acct ass. cat.	
AS	Asset	☑	A	
CC	Cost Center	☑	K	
FI	Finances and Funds	☑		
NET	Network	☑	N	
OR	Order	☑	F	
SO	Sales order	☐	X	
STR	Generic account assignment	☐		
WBS	WBS element	☑	P	

Dialog Structure
▽ ☐ Account assignment catego
    ☐ Acct assignment fields

AcctAssgmtCateg   CC   Cost Center

Acct assignment fields

Acct assignment field (technical name)	Description	Leading acc...	
ACC_STR	Generic Account Assignment	○	
CMMT_ITEM	Commitment Item	○	
COST_CTR	Cost Center	◉	
FUNC_AREA	Functional Area	○	
FUND	Fund	○	
FUNDS_CTR	Funds Center	○	
GRANT_NBR	Grant	○	

Figure 9.6   Account Assignment Category in SAP SRM

The use of product categories in SAP SRM allows the linking of the SAP General Ledger accounts from the company's chart of accounts to the product categories and catalogues in SAP SRM. Let's take an example of this mapping. A product category, *pencils and pens,* is mapped to an SAP General Ledger account, office supplies. When a buyer processes a shopping cart and chooses the product category, pencils and pens, the system automatically pulls up the SAP General Ledger account as *office supplies*.

This way, the users do not have to keep thinking about the choice of SAP General Ledger account, and the accountant doesn't have to validate whether every posting has been posted to the correct SAP General Ledger account. This ensures a great element of control and at the same time greatly reduces validation and subsequent reclassification work.

Figure 9.7 provides an illustration of the configuration that makes this integration available in SAP SRM. In Figure 9.7, the Category ID (or Material Group) STATIONERY is mapped to a Cost Center (CC) and an Asset (AS) in the AcctAssCat field. A corresponding SAP General Ledger account is mapped in the SAP General Ledger account no. field. An organization has the option of providing a different SAP General Ledger account per account assignment; for example, the CC is assigned to G/L 600100, and the AS is assigned to G/L 100255 in Figure 9.7.

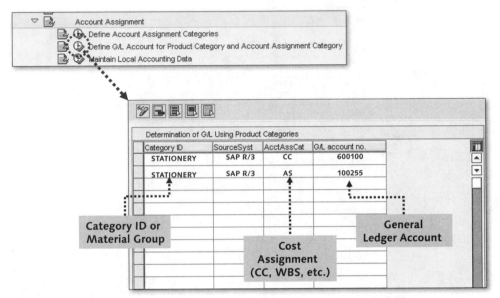

Figure 9.7 Product Category to SAP General Ledger Account Mapping in SAP SRM

The mapping illustrated in Figure 9.7 requires the purchasing team to work in conjunction with the finance team to determine the appropriate level or classification relevant for both procurement needs and financial budgeting. Many project teams find this classification agreement a difficult task. The procurement department needs classification for analysis of spending across the various commodities purchased. Finance needs the SAP General Ledger account classification from a budgeting perspective.

Allocate time during the design and configuration phase of the project to determine this activity. If no SAP General Ledger account is mapped in the SAP General Ledger account number field shown in Figure 9.7, then the user can enter any valid SAP General Ledger in the shopping cart. In the shopping cart, users with appropriate authorization can search for all available SAP General Ledger numbers in SAP ERP and select from this list of accounts.

Organizations using material-based (product-based) procurement in SAP SRM have the ability to control the SAP General Ledger account assignment via the valuation class within the material master in SAP ERP. For example, the material master record is linked to an SAP General Ledger account via valuation class configuration. A material master is linked to a valuation class, which in turn is linked to an SAP General Ledger account (illustrated in Figure 9.8).

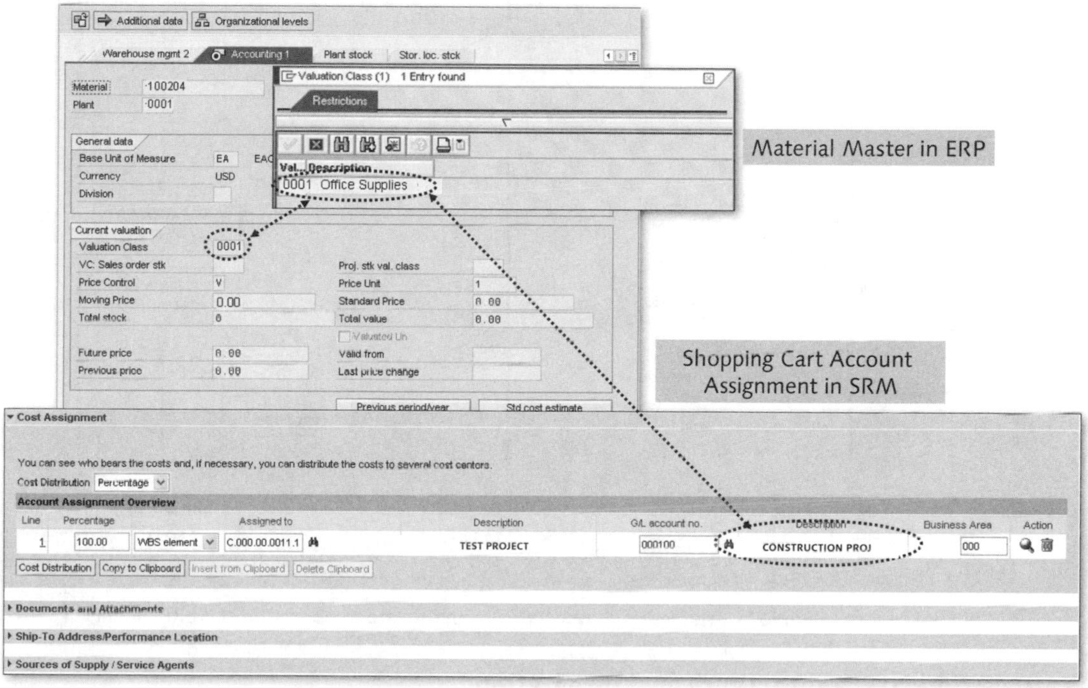

Figure 9.8 Material Master Valuation-Based SAP General Ledger Control

So, any time a business transaction relevant to financial accounting occurs for that material, a posting is made to the associated SAP General Ledger account in the SAP General Ledger. In the shopping carts, if organizations want to limit users from changing the SAP General Ledger account when using products, they can do so using the Business Add-In (BAdI) BBP_DETERMINE_ACCT.

Various financial functionalities are tightly integrated amongst themselves, so that once a posting updates any of the components, all the remaining functionalities are updated automatically when necessary. Figure 9.9 shows how the data is mapped in different functionalities.

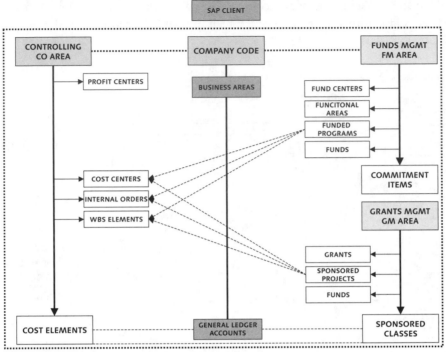

* For illustration purposes – does not reflect interaction between all master data and ledgers

Figure 9.9 Sample — Interaction of Master Data and Related Ledgers in SAP ERP Financials

9.2.2 Transaction Level Integration

Transaction level integration is the business transaction processed in one functional area that impacts or automatically updates or posts in another functional area in real time. For instance, when a PO is created in SAP SRM or in SAP ERP, a corresponding commitment is created in FM to commit the funds on the PO.

Different functionalities in financial accounting give multiple views of financial information that is used in various aspects of financial decision making.

> **Example**
>
> The SAP General Ledger is used for external financial reporting, whereas Controlling is used for internal management reporting, and so on. Each of these components has a different purpose and is updated differently for the same business transaction. Each also has its own master data, but it is tightly integrated with other submodules based on configuration.

The updates and postings in the different financial functionalities depend upon the extent of implementation and the type of transaction processed. Figure 9.10 illustrates the Transaction-level integration between SAP SRM and the different financial functionalities. In SAP SRM, when the Shopping Cart is created there is no corresponding posting in SAP ERP Financials. However, a requisition created in SAP ERP has a corresponding precommitment posting in FM.

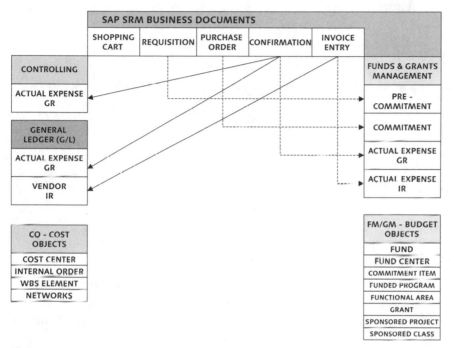

Figure 9.10 Integration at a Transaction Level

In SAP SRM, there are three main options of validating financial account assignment data while processing a business transaction (e.g., the shopping cart or PO):

▸ Locally within SAP Enterprise Buyer (EB)
▸ Real-time validation of SAP ERP Financials Financial Accounting data in SAP ERP
▸ No validation at all

In the shopping cart, a user can assign cost assignments at a Line-item level. If the system of financial record is SAP ERP and a Classic or Extended Classic scenario is being implemented, a real-time validation occurs in SAP SRM against the backend SAP system. If an invalid account assignment is used, the end user gets an error prior to order creation in the shopping cart. Figure 9.11 provides a view of the Cost Assignment section in the shopping cart. The PO in SAP SRM provides the same functionality.

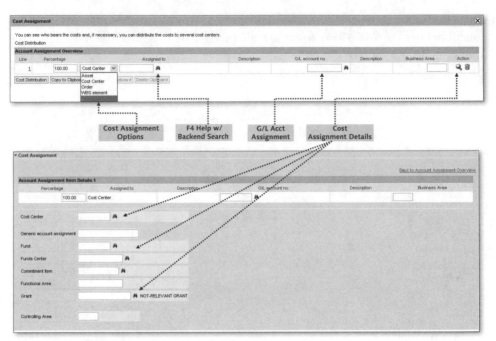

Figure 9.11 Cost Assignment Section in the Shopping Cart Line Item

In Figure 9.11, the magnifying glass icon lets you view the details of the cost assignment. Additionally, if organizations use the FM or GM functionalities in SAP ERP Financials Financial Accounting, shopping cart users might need to enter a Funds or Grant number on the details section of the cost assignment.

Cost assignments can be split across multiple lines and accounts in the shopping cart. For example, suppose a user creates a shopping cart to order a large multipurpose printer that will be used by multiple departments in the building. The cost for this printer will be shared across multiple departments. The cost assignment section in the shopping cart distributes the costs across multiple accounts. Costs can then be assigned based on a percentage basis, quantity basis, or by value.

Figure 9.12 illustrates how cost distribution can be done in the shopping cart in SAP SRM. In the Cost Distribution dropdown menu, a user can select to distribute costs by Percentage, By Qty, or By Value. Costs can then be distributed across multiple account assignments; in our example in Figure 9.12, we illustrate the cost distribution by Percentage and by using a Cost Center.

The value-based cost distribution is only available in SAP SRM. If the Classic or Extended Classic scenario is implemented, then the purchase order is also sent to SAP ERP. In materials management in SAP ERP, there is no capability to distribute based on value. When a shopping cart that is distributed by value is transferred to SAP ERP, the cost distribution is automatically converted into a percentage split in the materials management PO.

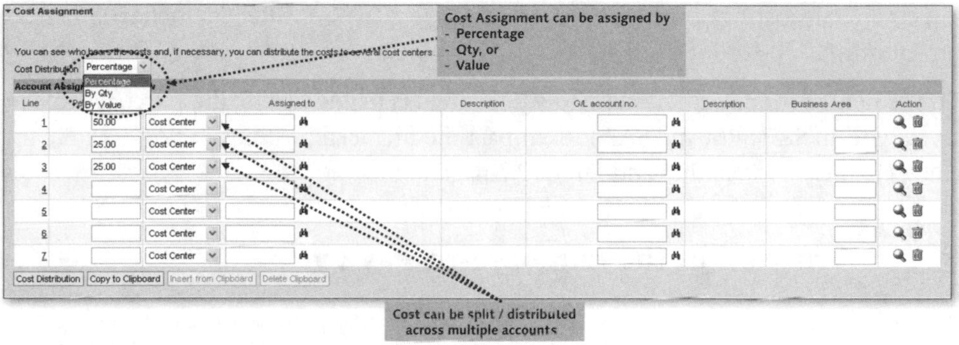

Figure 9.12 Cost Distribution in SAP SRM

9.2.3 Account Determination Based on Expense vs. Stocked Items

In SAP SRM, at the time of shopping cart creation, the system requires an account assignment category, account, and SAP General Ledger account. Unless valid accounting data is provided, the user cannot order the shopping cart. SAP SRM can be used for both *expense* and *direct material (stock)* procurement scenarios. Figure 9.13 illustrates what happens when a user in SAP SRM orders expense goods as opposed to goods to replenish stock.

Free Text Items including Catalogs	• Account Assignment Category is defaulted in the shopping cart from user's "my settings" or the Organization Structure in SAP SRM
	• The SAP General Ledger account assignment is determined based on the a Product Category, based on the account assignment mapping in the IMG in SAP SRM
Inventory Items	• Material based items, subject to inventory management
	• The "Order as Direct" button is used in the shopping cart to order products for replenishment
	• Account assignment information is not required in the shopping cart. This information is utilized from the accounting screen on the material master.
	• Account determination is handled in SAP ERP for the inventory management, GR/IR reconciliation account or other postings
Planned based requirements (MRP)	• Plan based requirements, such as demand based requisitions in MRP, PS, PP are transferred from ERP into SAP SRM for sourcing
	• In SAP SRM no account assignment information is passed, Account determination is handled in SAP ERP

Figure 9.13 Account Determination in SAP SRM and Materials Management in SAP ERP

As discussed in Chapter 7, SAP SRM can be implemented in different scenarios: Classic, Extended Classic, and Standalone. It is important to understand the differences in the financial postings when different implementation scenarios are used in SAP SRM. The next section describes the impact of SAP SRM implementation scenarios on financial postings in the different subledgers of SAP ERP Financials Financial Accounting.

In the next section, we'll discuss how documents created during the purchase to pay cycle within SAP SRM and SAP ERP impact the financial postings in SAP ERP Financials Financial Accounting and Funds Management.

9.3   Overview of the Purchase-to-Pay Cycle

In SAP SRM, the *purchase-to-pay* cycle starts with the step of creating a shopping cart and ends with the posting of an invoice. This process and its impact on the SAP ERP Financials component is illustrated in Figure 9.14.

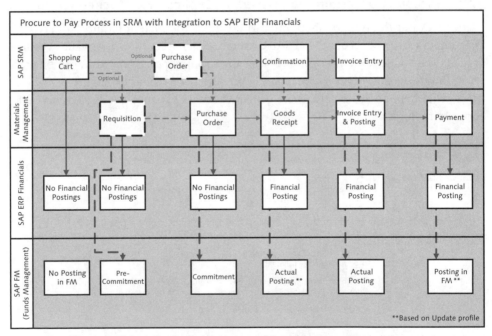

Figure 9.14   Purchase- to-Pay Process in SAP SRM with Integration to Finance

As illustrated in Figure 9.14, once a shopping cart is created, it is either routed for approval or converted into a purchase order. At this time, there are no postings that occur in financial accounting. In certain scenarios, there is an option of creating a purchase requisition in materials management in SAP ERP. If this option is chosen, a precommitment document is posted in FM. No other postings occur in any other financial functionality.

Moving a step further, when the shopping cart is converted into a PO, a commitment document is posted within FM, with no postings to other modules. At this stage, if a precommitment document was previously created via a purchase requisition, then it is liquidated.

Upon receipt of a PO, the vendor transmits the goods or services to your organization. At this time, in the purchase-to-pay process, a confirmation can be entered within SAP SRM for receiving and accepting the goods or services. Confirmations in SAP SRM are seamlessly converted into a goods receipt document in SAP ERP. At this time, postings are created in SAP ERP Financials Financial Accounting. The expense or inventory posting is made in SAP General Ledger and an expense posting is made in SAP ERP Financials Financial Controlling. In FM, the previously posted commitment (based on the PO) is liquidated against the actual expense posting.

At the time of goods receipt, the ownership of the goods passes from the seller to the buyer so the expense and the provision for the liability to pay the seller are posted in SAP ERP Financials Financial Accounting. All these entries are posted automatically in SAP ERP Financials Financial Accounting on a real-time basis when the user makes an entry for receiving the goods.

This reflects a tight integration between purchasing and accounting. Several other ERP vendors have not been able to achieve this kind of integration between purchasing and SAP ERP Financials Financial Accounting software. For example, organizations using the Ariba Buyer solution are unable to attain the tight integration with SAP ERP Financials as available in SAP SRM.

Confirmations in SAP SRM are not exactly the same as a Goods Receipt document in SAP ERP. The confirmation document allows a user to indicate the receipt of goods and services from a vendor.

Depending on the organization and configuration, subsequent approvals might be required. Once the System Status of the confirmation is Approved, a corresponding Goods Receipt document is created in SAP ERP. Figure 9.15 illustrates the system status.

> **Note**
>
> The confirmation document number in SAP SRM is a different number than the Goods Receipt document in SAP ERP.

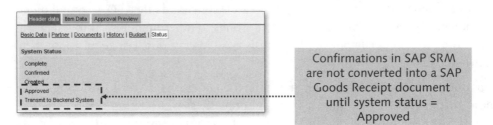

Figure 9.15 Confirmation Status in SAP SRM

The final step in the purchase-to-pay process in SAP SRM is the processing of vendor invoices. Once an invoice is entered in SAP SRM, it can be subject to subsequent approvals. If no approvals are required or once all required approvals are completed, the invoice is transferred to SAP ERP via standard ALE IDocs.

In SAP ERP, a three-way match of the invoice, goods receipt, and the PO can occur to check the accuracy of the quantity invoiced and the rate at which it is invoiced. If there is a match, the invoice is posted without any payment blocks. If there is a mismatch on either front, the invoice is posted with a block for payment.

The invoice posting creates posting in the various submodules of SAP ERP Financials. It posts a vendor liability in SAP General Ledger, and updates FM with the actual expense posting depending on the update profile configured in FM.

Once invoices are posted in SAP, the next step is to make a vendor payment for the goods/services rendered. In SAP ERP, the payment program transmits payment to the vendor by appropriate payment media (check, ACH, and others).

9.3.1 Classic Scenario: SAP SRM and Backend System is SAP ERP

In the Classic scenario implementation, the purchasing documents (requisition and PO) are created within the SAP ERP system. However, Goods Receipts (confirmation) and Invoices can be created in either SAP ERP or SAP SRM. Figure 9.16 illustrates the impact of the Classic scenario on financial postings in SAP.

As illustrated in the Figure 9.16, once the shopping cart is created in SAP SRM, no postings occur in either SAP ERP Financials Financial Accounting or in FM. Depending on the configuration in SAP SRM, an organization can choose to create requisitions as the follow-on document to shopping carts or skip the requisition and directly create a PO. If the purchase requisition is created, there is no posting in SAP ERP Financials Financial Accounting, but a precommitment document is posted within FM for organizations using the Public Sector solution.

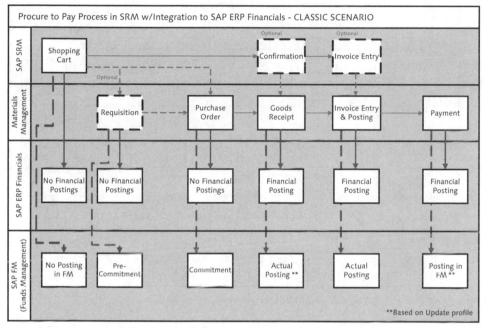

Figure 9.16 Classic Scenario Impact on Financial Postings

If business rules determine that a PO is to be created as a follow-on document, there are still no postings created in SAP ERP Financials Financial Accounting; however, for an organization using the Public Sector solution, a commitment document is posted within FM. The subsequent financial postings when creating confirmations, invoices, and vendor payments remain the same as described in Section 9.3, Overview of the Purchase-to-Pay Cycle.

9.3.2 Extended Classic Scenario: SAP SRM and Backend System in SAP ERP

In the Extended Classic scenario implementation, the Purchase Order document is created within SAP SRM. Once this document is complete (with approved status), a copy is transferred to the SAP ERP system. The system of record is SAP SRM. Goods receipts (confirmation) and invoices can be created in either SAP ERP or SAP SRM.

Figure 9.17 illustrates the impact of the Extended Classic scenario on financial postings in SAP.

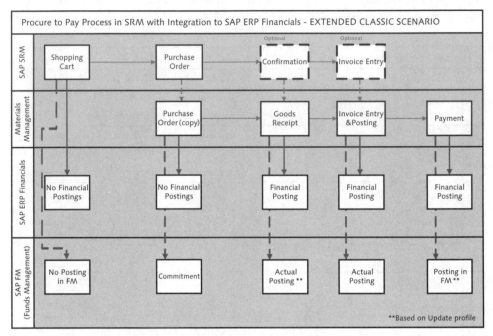

Figure 9.17 Extended Classic Scenario Impact on Financial Postings

As illustrated in the Figure 9.17, once the shopping cart is created in SAP SRM, no postings occur in either SAP ERP Financials Financial Accounting or FM. In this scenario, unlike the Classic, there is no option of creating purchase requisitions as follow-on documents to the shopping cart.

Therefore, the first time any document is posted in SAP ERP Financials Financial Accounting is at the time of posting the PO. In this scenario, the PO is created in SAP SRM and a copy is sent to materials management in SAP ERP. The posting of a PO creates a commitment document in FM.

The rest of the processes, from creation of the goods receipt to the payment of the invoice, remain the same as described earlier in this section.

9.3.3 Standalone Scenario: SAP SRM with Non-SAP Backend System

In the Standalone scenario implementation, the PO, confirmation, and invoice are created within SAP SRM. The SRM application is not integrated with the backend accounting system apart from the creation of payments. In this case, the only time a posting from SAP SRM into SAP ERP Financials Financial Accounting occurs is upon the posting of the vendor invoice so that it can be paid out of SAP ERP Financials Financial Accounting.

As illustrated in Figure 9.18, there is no financial posting when a shopping cart, confirmation, or PO is created in SAP SRM. However, when an invoice is posted in SAP SRM, a financial posting happens in SAP ERP Financials Financial Accounting and the actual posting happens in F. Also, when the payment is posted in SAP ERP, a corresponding financial posting is also done in SAP ERP Financials Financial Accounting and FM.

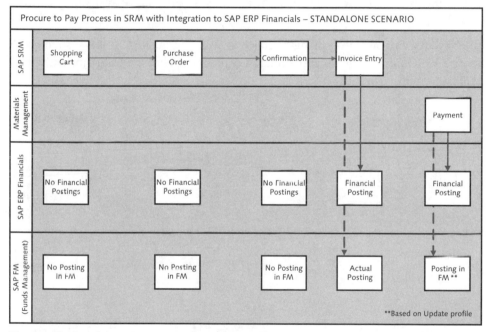

Figure 9.18 Standalone Scenario Impact on Financial Postings

In the next section, we will discuss the real-time budget check functionality in SAP SRM.

9.4   Budget Check in SAP SRM

Every time any purchasing activity (for example, creation of shopping carts or purchase orders) happens in SRM, the budget for the respective budget bearing object is checked in the SAP ERP Financials backend. If the budget is not sufficient, then

— based on the configuration — a warning or error message is issued at the time of commitment generation.

Budgeting is done in the SAP ERP Financials Financial Controlling component. In case, the industry solution for public sector companies is implemented, budgeting can also be done in FM for internal funding sources and in GM for external or sponsored funding sources.

Various organizations implement budgeting for controlling expenses. This control can be achieved via monitoring through reporting or by then having system-based controls check the budget at the time of posting and issue a warning or error message to the user if the budget is not sufficient (this is called active availability control [AVC]).

In SAP SRM, the budget availability check is available in the SAP EB system as of Release 2.0C and is triggered at the following points or with the following activities, as illustrated in Figure 9.19.

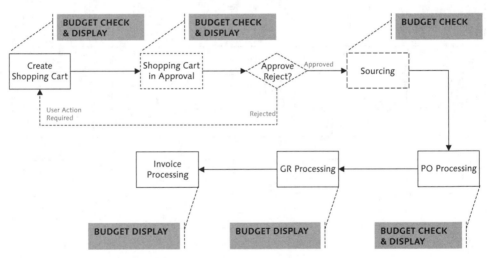

Figure 9.19 Budget Check in SAP SRM

In addition to the budget check, SAP SRM provides functionality for budget display in the various document types. The budget display functionality in SAP SRM provides an overview of the spent and available budget for an accounting object of a document. Users with appropriate authorizations are able to view the budget values and/or execute an SAP NetWeaver BW report for further details.

The budget display provides a simulation of the budget consumed for a particular budget object at the time of the document creation, such as the shopping cart.

The budget display function compares the total value in the shopping cart with the total budget allocated and subtracts the budget used amount read from the SAP ERP Financials Financial Accounting and SAP ERP Financials Financial Controlling backend. Figure 9.20 illustrates the budget simulation in the shopping cart.

In the shopping cart overview, a Budget link is available within the Additional Specifications area. When you click on this link, the Budget Overview section is displayed. The Budget Overview provides a simulated view of the budget availability and allows the end user to visually see the budget consumption based on the shopping cart or PO value. The Budget field provides the overall budget available for the cost assignment in the Assigned to field.

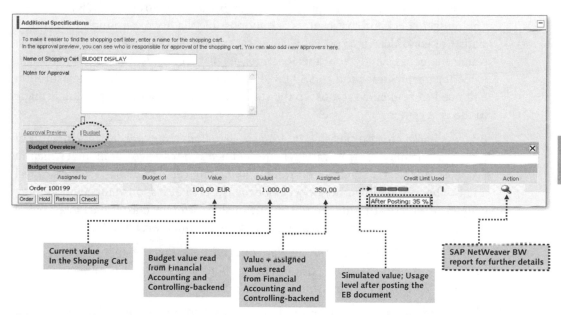

Figure 9.20 Budget Display in SAP SRM

In our example in Figure 9.20, there is a budget of 1.000,000 EUR and the shopping cart Value is 100,000 EUR. The Assigned field displays the total budget value, which includes the shopping cart value plus the budget read from the SAP ERP Financials Financial Accounting and SAP ERP Financials Financial Controlling backend system, in our case 350,000. The Credit Limit Used field provides a simulated view of the budget usage. If the budget is exceeded, this field will show a simulated value in red.

> **Note**
>
> The budget check illustrated in Figure 9.20 does not take into consideration shopping carts that are awaiting approval or in the sourcing cockpit. Because there is no posting in SAP ERP Financials Financial Accounting or FM for shopping carts, the budget check will not be 100% accurate until this shopping cart converts into a requisition or PO.

In SAP, budgets can be maintained in SAP ERP Financials Financial Controlling, FM, or GM. SAP SRM provides standard functionality for budget checks across all of these areas.

The budget checks in SAP ERP Financials Financial Controlling are available only if the cost object is an internal order or a Work Breakdown Structure (WBS) element. The budget check for cost centers is only possible via a workaround of creating a statistical job order for a cost center or cost center group and then entering the cost center budget as a budget for this job order. Availability control will need to be activated for the job order and an SAP ERP Financials Financial Controlling substitution will need to be defined to post to the statistical order every time a posting is made to the cost center.

Budget checks are also possible in FM and GM. Budgeting and implementation of budget availability controls can be better defined in these two submodules than in SAP ERP Financials Financial Controlling. Budgeting can be done at a granular level and can be broken down by the type of expense, area of responsibility, and funding sources. All these attributes can be defined using different master data available in FM. Budgeting by grants is possible at the same granular level in GM.

Project teams can influence the standard budget check functionality in SAP SRM by using the BAdI BBP_BUDGET_CHECK. In addition, Authorization for Budget Display controls the budget display using object BBP_BUDGET.

If your organization uses a non-SAP backend where financials are managed, you need to understand how commitments are handled for shopping carts and other purchasing documents. In this scenario, a commitment is simulated and the budget is checked using a remote function call (RFC). No commitment is written to the database. After the shopping cart is saved, it is transferred to the respective backend. A commitment is created depending on the setting used in the backend, for example, Purchase Requisition Commitment or Purchase Order Commitment.

In the next section, we'll discuss how SAP SRM integrates with Project Systems and finance. You will learn that structural cost assignments in project systems such as WBS elements and networks can be used for purchase activity in SAP SRM.

9.5   Integration with Project System

Both large-scale projects such as building a factory and small-scale projects such as organizing a trade fair require precise planning of the many detailed activities involved. To control all tasks in project execution, clear, unambiguous project structure is the basis for successful project planning, monitoring, and control. The SAP Project Systems (PS) component in SAP provides the functionality to plan, execute, monitor, and control the various phases within a project. A project in SAP can be structured in two different views:

- By structures, using WBS
- By process, using individual activities (Work Packages)

A user in SAP SRM can use structural cost assignments created in project systems (WBS and Networks) when requesting goods and services in the shopping cart or PO. Figure 9.21 illustrates this within the shopping cart transaction. In the Cost Assignment area of the shopping cart, a user can select the WBS element or Network account assignment in the account assignment dropdown menu. In our example, the WBS element C.000.00.0011.1 is used, which is a TEST PROJECT.

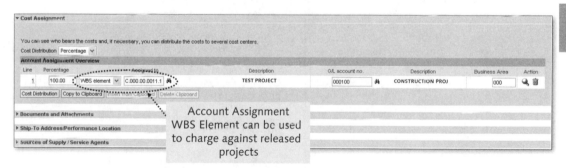

Figure 9.21 Cost Assignment — WBS for Project-Related Purchases

Organizations could have varying requirements when it comes to procurement of goods and services. Depending on the business requirement in project systems, there can be a few different methods of integrating PS with SAP SRM. Some options exist.

Let's describe each of these options aided by Figures 9.22, 9.23, 9.24, and 9.25. These figures contain the process flow, advantages, and disadvantages of each of the options listed for integrating PS with SAP SRM. These options are valid based on certain business requirements. It is entirely possible for project teams to define another option to fulfill the unique needs of their business processes.

▶ **Option 1:** Create purchase orders in SAP ERP directly, with no integration to SAP SRM
This is illustrated in Figure 9.22.

▶ **Option 2:** Create shopping carts in SAP SRM, with PO creation in SAP ERP (Classic scenario)
This is illustrated in Figure 9.23.

▶ **Option 3:** Create shopping carts and purchase orders in SAP SRM (Extended Classic scenario)
This is illustrated in Figure 9.24.

▶ **Option 4:** Create requisition in SAP ERP and PO in SAP SRM (External Procurement business scenario)
This is illustrated in Figure 9.25.

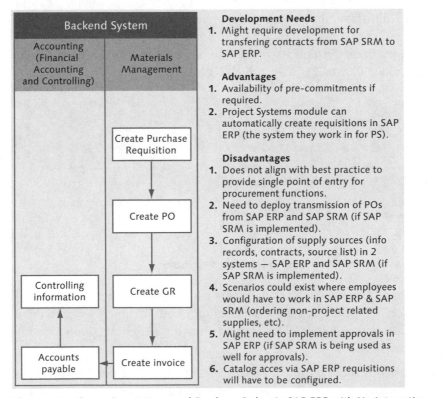

Development Needs
1. Might require development for transfering contracts from SAP SRM to SAP ERP.

Advantages
1. Availability of pre-commitments if required.
2. Project Systems module can automatically create requisitions in SAP ERP (the system they work in for PS).

Disadvantages
1. Does not align with best practice to provide single point of entry for procurement functions.
2. Need to deploy transmission of POs from SAP ERP and SAP SRM (if SAP SRM is implemented).
3. Configuration of supply sources (info records, contracts, source list) in 2 systems — SAP ERP and SAP SRM (if SAP SRM is implemented).
4. Scenarios could exist where employees would have to work in SAP ERP & SAP SRM (ordering non-project related supplies, etc).
5. Might need to implement approvals in SAP ERP (if SAP SRM is being used as well for approvals).
6. Catalog acces via SAP ERP requisitions will have to be configured.

Figure 9.22 Create Requisitions and Purchase Orders in SAP ERP with No Integration to SAP SRM

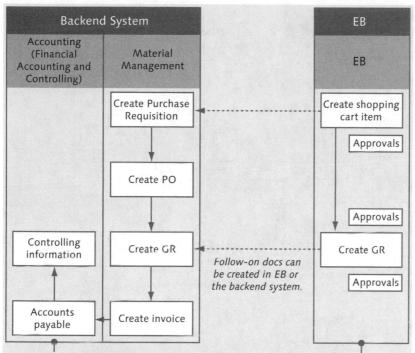

Figure 9.23 Create Shopping Carts in SAP SRM, with a PO Creation in SAP ERP

When using the Extended Classic scenario, a requisition cannot be created in SAP ERP. Therefore, a precommitment cannot be created in SAP, and it is impossible to display funds usage.

In the next section, we'll discuss the functionality gap in SAP SRM when implementing the Extended Classic scenario and the SAP Public Sector solution. You'll also learn about a workaround solution that companies can develop to overcome this gap in functionality.

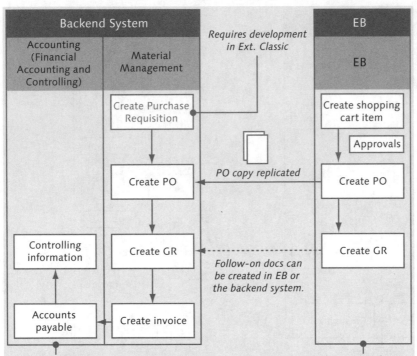

Development needs
1. To obtain FM encumbrances, development effort to create requisitions in ERP (non standard in extended classic scenario).

Advantages
1. Single user interface for all procurement functions.
2. No need to create approval processes in both SAP SRM and SAP ERP for procurement of goods/services.
3. Access to on-line catalogs.

Disadvantages
1. Work in two systems - SAP ERP for Project Systems and SAP SRM for Shopping Cart (Project System users).
2. Requires duplicate data entry (PS WBS/Network and in Shopping Cart line items).
3. No ability for pre-commitments if required.
4. Project Managers will have to utilize SRM system for Approvals.

Figure 9.24 Create Shopping Carts and POs in SAP SRM

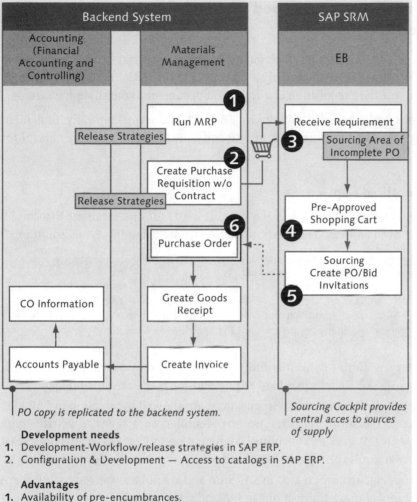

PO copy is replicated to the backend system.

Sourcing Cockpit provides central acces to sources of supply

Development needs
1. Development-Workflow/release strategies in SAP ERP.
2. Configuration & Development — Access to catalogs in SAP ERP.

Advantages
1. Availability of pre-encumbrances.
2. Construction requisitions will create encumbrances.
3. Supply Chain can piggyback on existing design (being implemented for IM-MRP).
4. Project Systems will automatically create requisitions in SAP ERP (the system they work in for PS).
5. No duplicate data-entry.

Disadvantages
1. No existing design in place to implement approvals in SAP ERP.
2. Supply Chain is planning to have catalogs available in SAP SRM only (Product Master will be available).
3. Scenarios could exist where employees would have to work in SAP ERP & SAP SRM (ordering non-project related supplies, etc.).
4. Changes to Purchase Orders will occur in SAP SRM.

Figure 9.25 Create Requisition in SAP ERP and a PO in SRM

9.6 Limitation of Extended Classic Scenario for SAP Public Sector Solution

In the Extended Classic scenario implementation, a shopping cart and a corresponding PO are both created in SAP SRM. Only a PO copy is sent to SAP ERP. There is no functionality for creating a requisition as a follow-on document to the shopping cart.

Organizations using the Industry Solution EA-PS (Public Sector) typically implement the FM and GM functionalities within SAP and activate the availability control for budget check.

9.6.1 Identified Gap

The following bullet points explain the *gap* that exists for organizations that implement SAP SRM in an Extended Classic scenario and are using the EA-PS solution:

> **Note**
>
> This gap does not apply to organizations using SAP SRM Public Sector solution with the EA-PS solution. SAP has released the SAP SRM Procurement for Public Sector (PPS) solution for SAP SRM, which identifies and closes this gap. The following section is only relevant for organizations that use SRM but not the SAP SRM PPS solution.

▶ Shopping carts do not consume budget in SAP ERP, only the documents transferred to SAP ERP, such as purchase requisitions or POs, consume budget.

▶ In Extended Classic, no purchase requisitions are allowed for creation in SAP ERP. Additionally, the shopping carts are not identified as a separate activity type within FM or GM availability control configuration in SAP ERP. Thus, no special availability controls can be configured for a shopping cart.

▶ As the shopping carts are created in SAP SRM and are not transferred to ERP, there is no visibility of these transactions in FM and GM reports.

9.6.2 Solution Approach

SAP does not offer any standard solutions for the identified gap; therefore, organizations implementing the Extended Classic scenario will need to develop a customized solution to meet their precommitment and AVC needs.

One approach for development is to use the earmarked funds document (funds reservation) document in SAP ERP for encumbrances based on the shopping carts created in SAP SRM. These funds reservations would provide the appropriate precommitment and visibility in FM.

The essential aspect of this customized solution is that the shopping cart and funds reservation in SAP ERP have to be kept in sync at the various stages and statuses of the documents in SAP SRM. Figure 9.26 illustrates what happens when the funds reservation is updated in SAP ERP at shopping cart creation, shopping cart change, approval, sourcing, PO creation, and PO change.

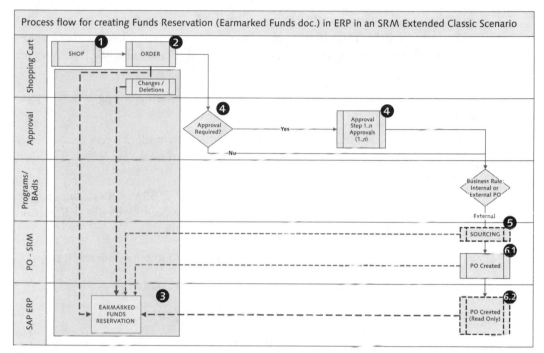

Figure 9.26 Process Flow for the Customized Solution Approach

Organizations planning to undertake this development need to be aware that the most important phase of this development is testing. There are numerous scenarios when the shopping cart and subsequent documents in SAP SRM are updated. The changes all need to be kept in sync with the corresponding funds reservation document in SAP ERP. The largest single amount of time in this solution is spent during the testing phase.

If you are interested in funds reservation/encumbrance as it relates to shopping carts and SAP SRM Extended Classic scenario, review Chapter 17. Here, you will find information about the planned functionality for shopping cart-based encumbrances in the Procurement for Public Sector (PPS) solution.

9.7   Integration with cProjects

SAP cProjects and SAP PS are both part of SAP's offering for Project Management. Customers can use them independently or integrated depending on project requirements. If both are integrated, then typically, cProjects manages project schedule and resources while cost and budget are managed in SAP PS.

Organizations that are use SAP SRM in a cProjects landscape need to be aware that the cProjects to SRM Integration is only available in an SAP SRM Standalone scenario. The integration between cProjects and SAP SRM is enabled via SAP NetWeaver PI.

The business reason for using the SAP SRM application when working with cProjects is twofold:

▶ When resource needs (external staffing/consultants) are identified in the project (cProject) to fulfill customer projects, the SAP SRM system can source this need and create a PO for the supplier.

▶ Once a resource is on-boarded for the project, the SAP SRM system can capture the time and expenses against this project using the Service Confirmation functionality.

Let's illustrate the above business objectives using the following figure and steps:

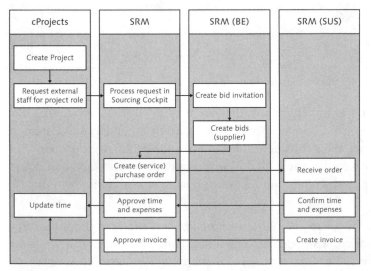

Figure 9.27   SAP SRM Integration with cProjects (Figure from SAP America – SRM RKT)

1. A project is created in cProjects.
2. The project manager requests a need for external staffing/consultant to fulfill a project role.
3. The request is transferred to the Sourcing application within the SAP SRM system. In SAP SRM, a requirement is created as an external requirement and this information is communicated back to cProjects.
4. In the SAP SRM Sourcing application, the professional buyer has the option to either create a PO directly or initiate an RFx (bid) to request quotes and source this staffing need. In either option, a PO is finally generated in SAP SRM locally. Status information for the PO is communicated back to cProjects.
5. If the organization is using the SUS application, then the PO is transmitted to SUS or directly to the supplier via EDI, fax, email, and others.
6. The supplier/external consultant cannot submit their time worked and pertinent expenses via the Service Confirmation functionality in SAP SRM or SUS. Once these are reviewed and approved by the project manager (or designee), then the time is updated in the cProjects project.

In the next section, we'll review relevant OSS notes that deal with the integration of SAP SRM with SAP ERP Financials.

9.8   Relevant OSS Notes

Table 9.1 lists important OSS Notes available on the SAP Service Marketplace that are relevant for readers when working with the Account Assignment, Budget Check, and Commitment in SRM. For example, OSS Note 815849 provides a FAQ on the system behavior when using the Account Assignments in SAP SRM.

Note	Description
815849	FAQ: Account assignment system response
520717	Budget Check in EBP
828231	Commitments in SRM
524670	Budget display in EBP
1002895	cProjects SRM integration

Table 9.1 OSS Notes and Descriptions

9.9 Summary

In this chapter, we reviewed the integration of SAP SRM with SAP ERP Financials, as well as the integration of SAP SRM with FM and GM. The real-time integration of SAP SRM with SAP ERP Financials is the core strength for the solution; SAP General Ledger validations and budget checks are examples of the close integration between the two solutions.

Chapter 10 will introduce you to the concept of workflow in SAP SRM. We will begin with a discussion of what workflow means and then delve into how SAP SRM uses workflow to promote seamless and efficient work processes.

The efficient flow of work processes within an organization can not only improve how business documents and actions are processed but can also provide the controls necessary for businesses today.

10 The Role of Workflow in SAP SRM

An efficient flow of work processes within an organization can create wonders in optimizing the entire process. It provides consistency, reduces wasted follow-up time, enables process standardization, and provides organizational audit and control. Software-based workflow, in its simplest terms, is the automated flow of work processes, whereby events, actions, and documents are routed to responsible users and groups for their review or action.

A simple workflow example in a procure-to-pay process could be the routing of a purchase order (PO) for a computer purchase to your departmental team for review and to your manager for approval or rejection, as shown in Figure 10.1.

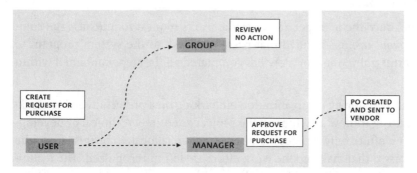

Figure 10.1 Example of Workflow in Procure-to-Pay Process

In many organizations, the routing of the requisition or PO as shown in Figure 10.1 is a paper-based nonautomated process. This process at times could take one to two weeks for completion. A supplier relationship management system automates such work processes to reduce the wasted time and retain an electronic audit trail that can be reviewed at any time. Automating this process using workflow can reduce the approval time to less than one day. This achieves an efficiency factor of more than 10 days.

Let's review Figure 10.2, which is similar to Figure 10.1 but depicts a technical process flow. In this example, multiple parts of a workflow work together to define a concise and legible process flow.

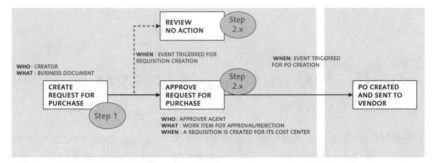

Figure 10.2 Event-Driven Workflow

The end user creating a purchase request is triggering an event (*when*). This event causes workflow to take action and determine *what* needs to be done next, which creates a new task of creating a work-item for the manager to approve or reject the request. The manager in this scenario then is the *who* and is responsible for executing the task. Each of the *whats, whens,* and *whos* need to be determined. In addition to tasks that need to be executed by users, there many tasks that execute in the background based on events.

In our example, once the manager approves the user's request to purchase the computer, a *Background Task* is executed that passes the task to the system program to create a PO. At this point, the workflow has completed all the steps contained within this process.

A common mistake made by an organization embarking on a project involving workflow is to treat the workflow activities on the project as entirely technical or development related. Too often, only development resources are allocated for this effort; the functional processes that make up the work effort are left unrecognized. The technical or development aspect of workflow only provide automation.

Unless the underlying core process are thoroughly reviewed and designed by the business, however, the workflow automation could be a waste. The functional knowledge experts need to build the process maps with detailed workflows of documents, events, and actions with the assistance of their workflow experts. Unless you can clearly define what a manager does with a time-entry workflow activity, the workflow itself is useless.

Workflow in SAP is an event-driven chain of process that answers the questions of who, what, and when as discussed in the example seen in Figure 10.2. Each link in the chain, once completed, leads to the next step or task and a request for action (user driven or system driven).

Figure 10.3 provides an overview of the activities that work together within the SAP Business Workflow. In SAP SRM, there are a number of Business Objects such as the shopping cart business object BUS2121 or the PO business object BUS2201. In these business objects, an Event such as ordering a shopping cart or changing a PO could trigger the start of workflow. At this point, the Attributes of the business object are checked, and the workflow system will Evaluate Starting Conditions to check whether a workflow Task should be generated.

> **Example**
>
> When a shopping cart is ordered, the workflow system evaluates the start conditions for the shopping cart business object BUS2121 to evaluate whether an approval task is required. The workflow system then makes a decision to generate either a user decision task or a background task. The user decision requires an action from an end user (for example, a department manager) and the background task assigns a specific status to the Business Object. At this point, the workflow process is complete until the next Event is triggered.

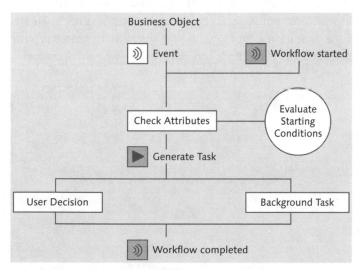

Figure 10.3 SAP Business Workflow (Source: SAP America)

This chapter will focus on the role of workflow specifically in SAP SRM. It will provide an understanding of how the various processes in SAP use workflow. SAP provides a number of standard workflow templates for SAP SRM that can be used out-of-the-box without any development. For detailed learning on workflow development, read the SAP PRESS book *Practical Workflow for SAP* by Alan Rickayzen. The second edition of this book has a fairly detailed chapter on workflow for SAP SRM and has a lot of valuable information around the new workflow in SAP SRM 7.0.

This chapter doesn't provide the same level of detail as *Practical Workflow for SAP*, because the content is better suited in the other book. Review this chapter to get an overview of the workflow functionality and get detailed information from the other book. We discuss the new workflow capabilities in SAP SRM 7.0 later in this chapter.

10.1 Workflow in SAP SRM

If you are familiar with business workflow in SAP, you will find some pleasant changes in the workflow delivered in SAP SRM. The workflow design is much more user-friendly and intuitive within SAP SRM. SAP has created many standard workflow templates for different processes existing in SAP SRM. Organizations can select the appropriate templates, activate them, and be ready to use automated workflow without writing a single line of code. In other words, SRM offers out-of-box workflows.

In addition to the standard templates, SRM offers a graphical start-condition editor that does not exist in the core SAP ERP system. This condition editor provides the ability to start a particular workflow template via configurable business rules. Figure 10.4 shows a preview of the condition editor. This figure shows that, unlike typical SAP ERP workflow, no development is required but only logic based on operators.

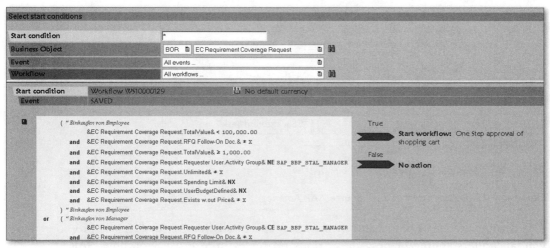

Figure 10.4 Graphical Workflow Editor in SAP SRM (SRM 5.0 & below)

> **Note**
>
> Beginning with SAP SRM 7.0, there are two different business workflows that are supported: Application-Controlled and Process-Controlled.
>
> The Application-Controlled workflow is what customers have been using in SAP SRM 5.0 and earlier releases. In this workflow, multiple workflow templates were provided and triggered using start conditions. This workflow going forward is only intended to be supported for customers who upgrade from an SAP SRM 5.0 or earlier release to SAP SRM 7.0.
>
> The Process-Controlled workflow was introduced with the controlled release SAP SRM 6.0 to a select group of customers and now is the workflow standard beginning with SAP SRM 7.0. With this release, the idea is to provide an environment whereby the workflow can be configured in a more flexible way and reduces the need for extensive custom development to model the process. Instead of the multiple templates, a single workflow template is used.
>
> The main SAP SRM workflow template is now WS 40000014, along with two subworkflows of "Approval" WS 40000016 and "Completion" WS 40000017.

So, we use the term *workflow* when the requirement in SAP SRM is configurable and does not necessarily require development. On the other hand, if the standard templates are not sufficient for your organization approval requirements, then development is inevitable. To allow organizations to enhance the standard delivered workflows in SAP SRM, SAP has provided a few workflow Business Add-Ins (BAdIs). These BAdIs enable the use of standard delivered workflow templates but still enhance them using additional business rules applicable to the organization.

> **Note**
>
> Organizations implementing SAP SRM 7.0 need to be aware that many of the available BAdIs available in previous releases of SAP SRM may not be supported. Review Appendix D for the supported 7.0 BAdIs.

Another distinguishing factor of workflow in SAP SRM is the ability for users to easily enhance the workflow process at runtime. A user can supplement the process by using a standard delivered anchor concept called *ad-hoc* approval. This anchor concept enables the addition of approval steps; users can add approvers and reviewers on the fly. Figure 10.5 provides an example of the ad-hoc approval functionality.

In the approval preview, the approval status shows Automatic Approval, under the Process Step field, which means that no system generated approvals have been determined. At this point, the end user can click the Add Approver or Add Reviewer buttons to add an approver. All standard delivered workflow templates are predelivered with the functionality of ad-hoc insertion. Organizations that want to leverage the standard workflow templates and don't want any additional custom development can use the ad-hoc functionality to provide flexibility to their users to add approval steps at any point in the approval process.

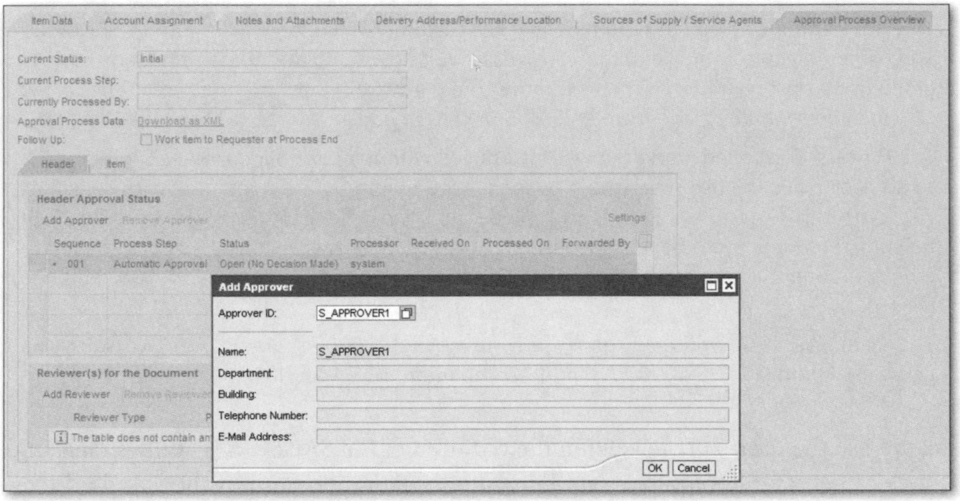

Figure 10.5 Ad-Hoc Approval Functionality; Anchor Concept in SAP SRM

The basic premise in SAP SRM is self-service for the end user; it empowers end users so that they not only can initiate the purchasing process but also determine the status of their purchasing documents at any given time. An example of the end user could be a requisitioner who creates a shopping cart to request office suppliers. Using the Approval Preview function in the Shop for and Check Status application, the requisitioner can review the status of the approval steps for his shopping cart. Workflow in SAP SRM contains a graphical Java applet for status visualization (in releases 5.0 and below). As of SAP SRM 7.0, the graphical viewer has been replaced by a textual table-based view.

The approval preview allows the end user to see the current status of the entire approval process and, if necessary, determine who to follow up with or review any roadblocks.

The ability to preview the approval workflow provides an additional opportunity for users to make changes to the approvers prior to executing the work item. Figure 10.5 provides an example of the approval preview status visualization applet. During the creation of a shopping cart, a preview of the approval is available.

After saving the shopping cart, one of the active approval workflows is started, depending on the start conditions. During the approval, the approver and the requisitioner can change the shopping cart. This starts a back-and-forth approval functionality where the shopping cart is sent between the requisitioner and the approver until approved or rejected.

Figure 10.6 illustrates the graphical view of the approval preview for two shopping carts and two PO documents. This graphical view is in releases 5.0 and earlier. In Figure 10.7, we illustrate the table view that is provided beginning SAP SRM 7.0.

In Figure 10.6, the first example, illustrated by 1, the shopping cart triggered a multi-level approval. The first level has approved and is shown as Shopping Cart Approved by, along with the name of the approver, date, and time. The next approver is shown under In approval since, along with date and time. In the third example, illustrated by **3,** the PO was approved by the first approver in the chain but rejected by the second approver and the final status of the shopping cart is shown as Result: Rejected. Beginning from SAP SRM 6.0, the graphical view is no longer supported.

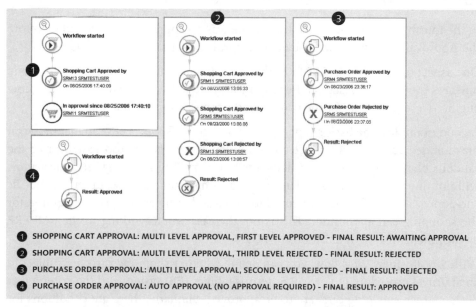

Figure 10.6 Example of Visualization of the Approval in SAP SRM (SRM 5.0)

Beginning with SAP SRM Release 4.0, a tabular view of approval preview is available as an alternate to the graphical Java applet view. The main aim of the graphical or tabular view in SAP SRM is to provide an end user with an easy-to-understand approval flow. Figure 10.7 illustrates the tabular view of the Approval Preview function. The view in Figure 10.7 shows the same example as shown in Figure 10.6 but in a table format. In the first example, illustrated by 1, the approval preview shows that Level 1 Approval approved the shopping cart and the shopping cart Status is Awaiting Approval by.

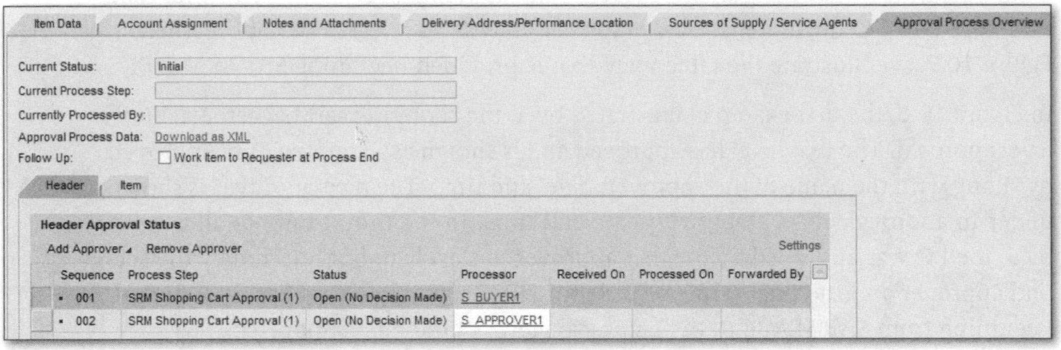

Figure 10.7 Example of Visualization in Table Format (SAP SRM 7.0)

In the fourth example, illustrated by 4, there was no approval needed, and therefore the Approval Preview shows Document Approved, which is a system status.

One aspect of workflow in SAP SRM that users find confusing is that there are many business transactions based on the workflow process. In other words, the workflow engine is a requirement for the core business transactions to function at all.

A good example is the basic shopping cart transaction "shop." Let's say that the organization decides not to introduce any shopping cart workflow processes during the sandbox phase to quickly build a demo environment. The shopping cart transactions will not function until the standard workflow environment is set up and a specific "no-approval" workflow is configured to indicate that no approvals are required for the shopping cart application. This is not the case when working in the SAP ERP environment creating requisitions or POs.

With SAP Business Workflow, you can define whether shopping carts are subject to an approval procedure in the SAP Enterprise Buyer (EB) system and the criteria that decide which shopping carts are to be approved. Similarly, there are conditions for approval of POs, confirmations, PO responses, invoices, contracts, and other business documents.

In the start conditions in Customizing, you can define which workflow is started under what conditions. As SAP offers multiple workflows for the same business transaction (e.g., shopping cart), a selection needs to be made to activate workflows used and inactivate workflows not being used. This way the system is able to provide flexibility in selection and use of approval workflows. Figure 10.8 illustrates this in a simple diagram.

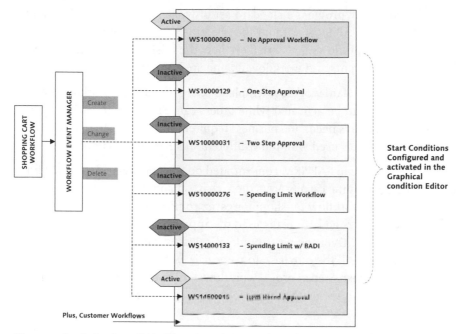

Figure 10.8 Activation of Workflow Templates to Trigger Required Workflows

Figure 10.8 shows that there are active and in-Active workflows within the system. The starting conditions were only activated for the WS14500015 and WS10000060 workflows. Therefore, when the shopping cart is created, changed, or deleted, the WORKFLOW EVENT MANAGER reviews the conditions defined to determine the active workflow template and rules to be triggered. This process of activation and in-activation is required to set up many of the business transactions in SAP SRM.

Now that we've reviewed the workflow functionality, let's learn about the standard workflow templates that are pre-delivered in SAP SRM.

10.2 Standard Delivered Workflows in SAP SRM

> **Note**
>
> The workflows described in this section are based on the templates provided in SAP SRM 5.0 and earlier releases. Customers that are either on SAP SRM 5.0 or upgrading to SAP SRM 7.0 and continue to use the "Application-Controlled" workflows can utilize these workflow templates. Organizations implementing SAP SRM 7.0 will not be able to use these templates as in 7.0; a single workflow template has been created to accommodate for the capabilities described here. We discuss the new workflow capabilities in SAP SRM 7.0 in Section 10.7, What's New in SAP SRM 7.0 Workflow.

As discussed earlier, SAP provides a standard set of workflow templates that can be used out-of-the-box in SAP SRM without the need for any development. Before we discuss the standard workflows, let's briefly review the business transactions in SAP SRM from which the events and workflow engine are triggered.

SAP provides a set of standard workflow templates ready for use. The workflow system requires some of these to be activated while others can be activated and configured based on the organization's needs and business requirements. Figure 10.9 presents the major workflow templates used within the different business transactions.

Until recently, workflow in SAP SRM concentrated on the approval templates within the requisitioning (shopping cart) process more than on any other process. Although there had been a basic workflow for shopping carts, confirmations, invoices, and others, SAP and its customers had not really used the approval workflows available in all the SAP SRM processes. Over the past couple of releases, however, approval workflows have expanded in all the purchase-to-pay cycles within SAP SRM. An example is the introduction of the n-Step approval workflow, which initially was used only for shopping carts. The approval template is available for other processes such as POs.

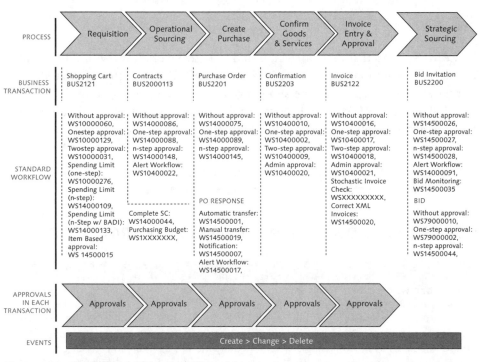

Figure 10.9 Standard Workflow Templates

The n-Step approval workflow enabled organizations to create a multilevel approval process, not restricted to just a single step or two steps. Using the n-Step workflow template, organizations can use their own business rules to determine how many approvers will be triggered in the approval chain: 1 through n. In Figure 10.9, for some applications, SAP still provides one-step and two-step templates as a standard.

Let's review the approval flow within the purchase-to-pay process. Figure 10.10 provides an illustration of this approval flow.

Approval Process Flow

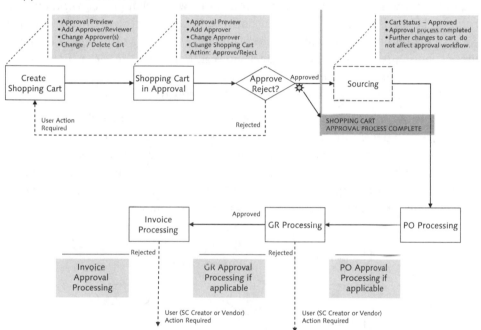

Figure 10.10 Self-Service Procurement Business Scenario Approval Process

In Figure 10.10, the functionality available in the shopping cart approval (Approval Preview, Add Approver/Reviewer, Change Approver(s), etc.) is also available during PO Processing, GR Processing, and Invoice Processing steps that are not shown in the figure.

Note
During the sourcing step, the shopping cart status is approved, and the approval process is complete for the shopping cart. Any changes that are done to the shopping cart in the Sourcing application do not affect the approval workflow.

10.2.1 Shopping Cart Workflows

In Figure 10.9, we provided a list of all the standard workflow templates pre-delivered in SAP SRM. In this section, we'll concentrate on the workflow templates predelivered for the Shopping Cart application.

We'll discuss each of the standard shopping cart workflows in detail, beginning with the No Approval workflow.

No Approval Workflow (WS10000060)

In SAP SRM, business documents such as shopping carts, POs, and confirmations require the workflow environment to be configured whether approval workflows are going to be used for that document or not. The No Approval workflow, also called workflow without approval, allows the creation of a shopping cart without the need for any subsequent approval or manager intervention. Once the requisitioner completes the shopping cart, the status of the document is changed to approved, and the control is passed to the follow-on function of sourcing or PO creation.

Most organizations use the No Approval workflow for purchases that are usually below a certain dollar threshold (e.g., all purchases of less than $500). Also, shopping carts that involve the purchase of direct materials for inventory or reservations are usually not subject to any approvals. Figure 10.11 illustrates the flow for the Without Approval workflow template (WS10000060). The Business Rules signify the workflow starting conditions that are defined as part of Customizing.

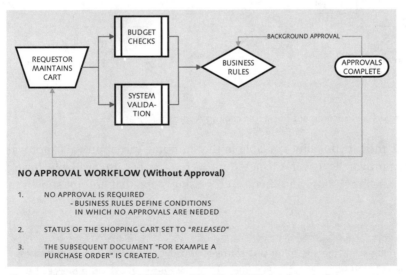

Figure 10.11 No Approval Workflow (Workflow Without Approval)

One-Step Approval Workflow (WS10000129)

The One-Step Approval workflow template (WS10000129) triggers the approval by a manager or supervisor of the shopping cart creator. When this approval template is used, only a single approver step is determined by the system. All additional approvers need to be added to the approval flow using the Add Approver functionality discussed earlier in this chapter. Figure 10.12 illustrates that, based on the workflow Business Rules, the One-Step workflow is started and the system determines the requestor's manager as the shopping cart approver. The manager or supervisor is determined based on the hierarchy defined in the organization structure in SAP SRM. The One-Step approval does not take into account any spending or approval limits.

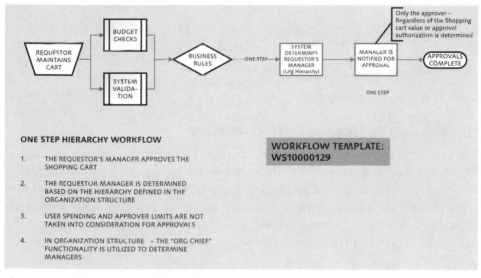

Figure 10.12 One-Step Approval Workflow

Two-Step Approval Workflow (WS10000031)

The Two-Step Approval workflow template (WS10000031) functions exactly the same as the One-Step Approval workflow except that the system determines two system approvers instead of one. Figure 10.13 shows that once the shopping cart is created and Business Rules are evaluated, the system determines two approvers: the first approver is the manager of the shopping cart requestor, and the second approver is the manager of the requestor's manager.

The requestor's manager and the manager's manager are determined based on the hierarchy defined in the organization structure in SAP SRM.

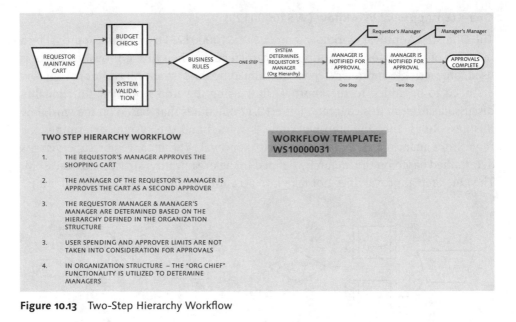

Figure 10.13 Two-Step Hierarchy Workflow

Spending Limit for Shopping Cart (WS10000276)

The Spending Limit for Shopping Cart approval workflow was introduced in SAP EB 3.0 and was well accepted within organizations, because they valued the ability to assign approval and spending thresholds to individuals within the organization. Most organizations have financial structures already in place, typically within the controller's office, that provide a spending authorization matrix based on structure within the organization (e.g., job levels or categories).

Figure 10.14 illustrates that once the BUSINESS RULES are evaluated and the SPEND-ING LIMIT APPROVAL workflow is started, the workflow system determines the approver based on the total value of the shopping cart and the spending limit of the approver. This workflow is also known as Single-Step Approval Over Limit because only a single approver is determined with the final authority for approval based on his approval limit.

In the Organizational Structure in SAP EB, each user is assigned a SLAPPROVER attribute. This attribute designates the Spending Limit Approver (SLA).

In addition, each requisitioner is assigned a spending limit, and each approver is assigned an approval limit. The limits can be assigned to users either directly in the user master Transaction (SU01) or via role assignments. SAP provides two object keys, BBP_APPROVAL_LIMIT and BBP_SPENDING_LIMIT, to capture the actual values for the approval and spending limit. These object keys are within the personalization tab that exists in the user master or user role.

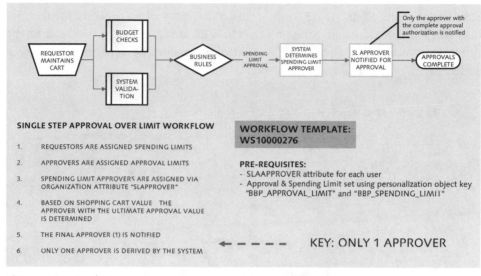

Figure 10.14 Single-Step Approval Over Limit (Value Limit) Workflow

Role Name	Spending and Approval Limit
Spending/Approval limit Role 1	$0.00
Spending/Approval limit Role 2	$2,500.00
Spending/Approval limit Role 3	$5,000.00
Spending/Approval limit Role 4	$25,000.00
Spending/Approval limit Role 5	$50,000.00
Spending/Approval limit Role 6	$100,000.00
Spending/Approval limit Role 7	$250,000.00
Spending/Approval limit Role 8	$500,000.00
Spending/Approval limit Role 9	$1,000,000.00
Spending/Approval limit Role 10	> $1,000,000.00

Figure 10.15 Example: Spending or Approval Limit Matrix for Single-Step Approval Workflow

Figures 10.15 and 10.16 illustrate an example of how the spending limit workflow works in SAP SRM. In Figure 10.15, a matrix has been provided that contains 10 roles. Each role has been assigned the same spending and approval limit. Therefore, the user assigned the role of Spending/Approval limit Role 3 has a spending limit of $50,000 and an approval limit of $5,000. Therefore, if this user creates a shopping cart with a total value of $5,000, no approval workflow will be required.

Now, let's review Figure 10.16. It illustrates a hierarchy of an organizational structure where the Requisitioner has an SLAPPROVER attribute as the HR Department Administrator who has an SLAPPROVER attribute as the HR Department Manager and so forth.

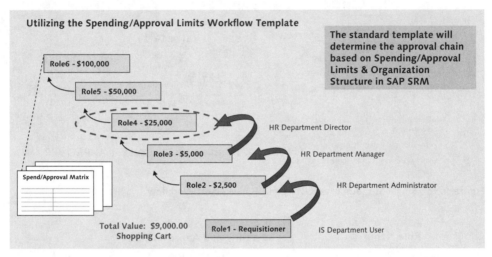

Figure 10.16 Example: Spending/Approval Limit Matrix for Single-Step Approval Workflow

The requisitioner has been assigned Role 1, which, according to Figure 10.15, assigns a $0.00 spending and approval limit to this user. Now, assume that the requisitioner creates a shopping cart with a Total Value of $9,000. Because the requisitioner has a $0.00 spending limit, an approval is required. The workflow system will evaluate the role hierarchy illustrated in Figure 10.16 and determine that only a user with Role 4 has the authorization to approve this shopping cart because users with Role 3 only have authorization to approve up to $5,000. Therefore, the HR Department Director will receive the shopping cart for approval action.

The spending limit workflow template gives organizations an avenue to not just rely on the organizational structure hierarchy but also use the financial authority matrix that is prevalent in many organizations.

The obvious shortcoming of this workflow template is that only one approver is eventually determined; this shortcoming can be overcome with the N-Step Spending Over Limit workflow template introduced in SAP EB 3.5 (illustrated in Figure 10.17).

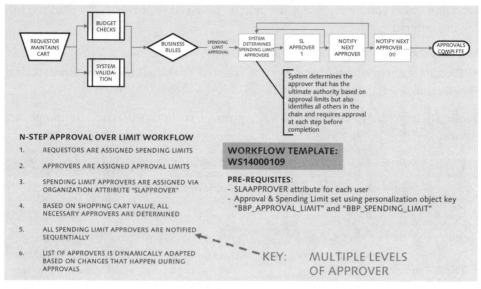

Figure 10.17 N-Step Approval Over Limit Workflow (Value Limit, N-Step)

N-Step Value Limit Approval Workflow (WS14000109)

The *N-Step Approval workflow* is based on the same concept as the Spending Limit Approval workflow template WS10000276. The SLAPPROVER attribute, the object key's BBP_APPROVAL_LIMIT and BBP_SPENDING_LIMIT are required to assign users' spending and approval limits. The difference is that the N-Step Approval Over Limit workflow provides a multistep approval.

If we use the same example illustrated in Figure 10.16 and use the N-Step Approval template, the $9,000 shopping cart will result in three approvers instead of just one. Basically, the shopping cart will require an approval from the HR Department Administrator and then the HR Department Manager. The final approver will be the HR Department Director.

Item Level Approval Workflow (WS14500015)

With each release of SAP SRM, new workflows have been introduced. Beginning with the SAP SRM 4.0 release, SAP has provided support for Shopping Cart Approval functionality at an item level instead of for the total as in previous releases. This is a direct result of development requests entered by many organizations that were already using SAP SRM and recognized the need to determine approvers for individual items within a shopping cart. In Item Level Approval, only approvers responsible for their respective items act on it. Organizations that use the Item Level Approval workflow most commonly use it for determination of approvers by one of the following criteria:

► Cost center–based approver at individual item level

► Product category–based approver for selected commodities such as safety and radiation, capital items, and others

Table 10.1 compares the Item Level Approval with the Classic Shopping Cart Approval.

Classic Shopping Cart Approval	Item Level Approval
All items in the shopping cart require approval from each approver determined.	Approvers are only responsible for select items in the shopping cart and act on those individually.
Approvers receive all items.	Approvers receive select items.
Either the entire shopping cart requires approval or none.	Certain items in the shopping cart might not require any approval and are presented as *status approved*.
The follow-on documents (e.g., requisition, PO) are not created until the entire shopping cart is approved.	As with the Classic approval, a follow-on document is created only after all the items in the shopping cart are approved.

Table 10.1   Item Level Workflow Compared to Standard Shopping Cart Workflow

Figure 10.18 illustrates the Item Level Approval in comparison to the standard Shopping Cart Approval. The approvers sequentially determined in the Classic Approval logic and in the Item Level Approval; approvers are determined based on the individual items.

To use the Item Level workflow, the template WS14500015 needs to be triggered in the workflow Customizing (TCode: /SWB_COND). This workflow can only be used if implemented in conjunction with the BAdI: BBP_WFL_APPROV_BAdI. The BAdI allows organizations to specify required business rules to determine approvers by cost centers and product categories.

Tip
One key aspect of this workflow that project teams need to be especially aware of is that the Item Level workflow is never restarted. In other words, the authorization levels of LOW and MEDIUM in BBP_WFL_SECURITY personalization object key do not have relevance in this workflow.

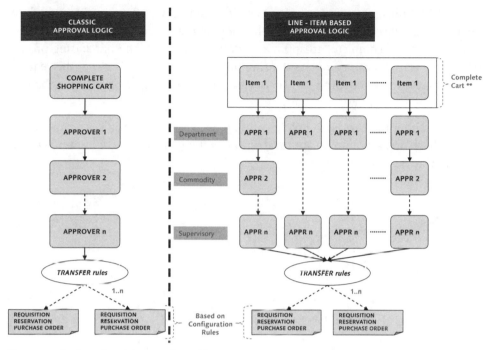

Figure 10.18 Item Level Approval Workflow

Shopping Cart Completion Workflow (WS14000044)

In the procurement process, there are a number of scenarios where the requisitioner is only able to define the need for a particular item, and is unable to determine the appropriate price and vendor. In such cases, the professional buyers need to intervene. The Shopping Cart Completion workflow (WS1000044) provides the functionality for buyers to intervene in such scenarios and complete the shopping cart with the appropriate information prior to other approvals, such as financial approval. The following scenarios can be considered for this workflow:

▶ Items with free text (vs. catalog or product based)
▶ Items where no price has been identified
▶ Items where no vendor has been identified

Figure 10.19 illustrates the Shopping Cart Completion workflow. In this workflow, the Business Rules determine whether the shopping cart is complete. If the shopping cart is not found complete, an approval workflow is sent to the purchasing professional (buyer) who can complete the shopping cart. Once this is done, the requisitioner receives the shopping cart for review and can accept or reject the changes made by the purchaser.

Once the shopping cart is complete, subsequent approval workflows can be triggered. Therefore, a secondary approval workflow template can be determined based on the business rules in the system.

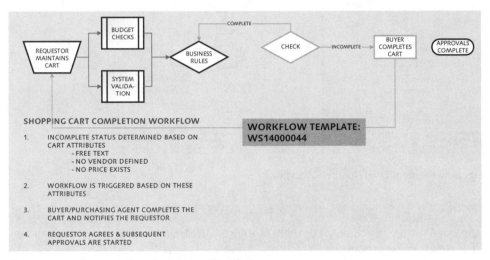

Figure 10.19 Shopping Cart Completion Workflow

User Defined Budget Workflow (WS10000129)

The User Defined Budget workflow template was provided as an alternate workflow for organizations that need to trigger approvals based on individual user budgets. These budgets have no relevance to the Budgeting functionality in SAP ERP Financials Financial Controlling or Funds Management (FM) within SAP ERP Financials. The user budget is set directly in SAP SRM. The system calculates the amount of budget spent for each user in a table (BBP_USRBDGT) and only when that exceeds the budget amount allocated for the user is an approval required. Figure 10.20 illustrates the User Defined Budget workflow.

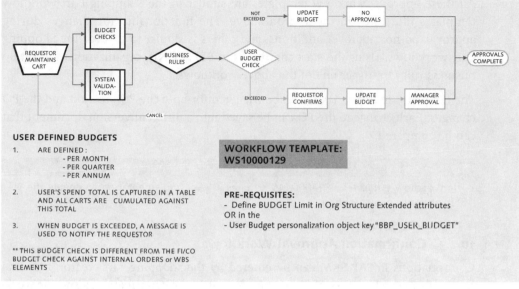

Figure **10.20** User Defined Budget Workflow

Now that you've learned about the workflow templates available for the Shopping Cart application, we can move on to discuss workflow templates available for the other applications such as PO and Confirmation. The core concept of how these workflows operate is similar to that used for the shopping cart.

10.2.2 Purchase Order Approval Workflows

Figure 10.21 illustrates three workflow templates that are predelivered in SAP SRM for approval of PO and PO changes (versions).

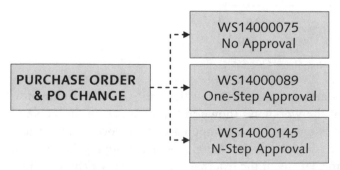

Figure **10.21** Approval Workflows for Purchase Orders and Changes (Versions)

All these approval workflow templates are similar to the Shopping Cart workflow templates illustrated in the section above. The functionality for changes during approval, ad-hoc approver additions, and others is similar to that for the Shopping Cart workflows. Using the start conditions in BBP_COND, organizations can set up business rules to trigger one of the above workflows.

The templates in Figure 10.21 can be triggered for both the PO creation and the PO changes. Each change to the PO can be saved into a different version document that can be compared.

> **Tip**
>
> The workflow template WS14000145 requires a BAdI implementation to enable the N-Step approval determination.

10.2.3 Confirmation Approval Workflows

Confirmations in SAP SRM can be entered by the shopping cart creator, a central receiver, or even by a vendor. Based on who enters the confirmation, a specific workflow template can be triggered. Figure 10.22 illustrates four workflow templates that are predelivered in SAP SRM for approval of confirmations.

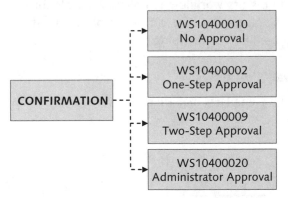

Figure 10.22 Standard Approval Templates for Confirmations

Organizations can use the start conditions in Transaction BBP_COND to set up business rules to trigger one of the workflows shown in Figure 10.22. In the standard solution, if a confirmation is created by the shopping cart creator, no approval is required. If the confirmation is created by the central receiver, an approval is required by the shopping cart creator. Finally, if the external vendor creates a confirmation, an approval of the confirmation is required by the shopping cart creator. This is illustrated in Figure 10.23.

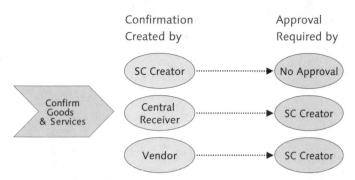

Figure 10.23 Confirmations in SAP SRM

10.2.4 Invoice Entry Approval Workflows

Most organizations that use SAP SRM still continue to use their SAP ERP system to post and process invoices. However, organizations that use the invoice-entry functionality in SAP SRM can benefit from the pre-delivered standard workflow templates. The standard workflow templates predelivered in SAP SRM for approval of invoices are displayed in Figure 10.24.

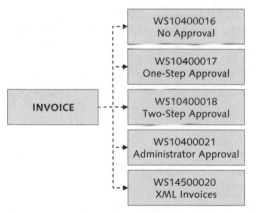

Figure 10.24 Standard Approval Templates for Approval of Invoices

Starting the approval workflows above depends on the completion status, invoice category (credit memo or invoice), role, and total value of the invoice. Organizations can use the start conditions in Transaction BBP_COND to set up Business Rules to trigger one of the workflows shown in Figure 10.24.

Invoices in SAP SRM can be entered by the shopping cart creator, an accounts-payable clerk, or even a vendor as illustrated in Figure 10.25. Based on who enters the confirmation, a separate workflow template can be triggered.

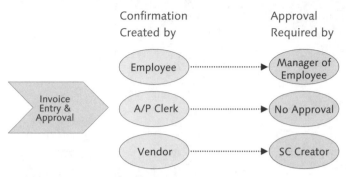

Figure 10.25 Approval of Invoices — Standard Logic

If your organization receives electronic invoices in SAP SRM via XML, a separate workflow template can be triggered to handle the erroneous invoices. Instead of just sending the erroneous XML invoices back to the vendor, those invoices can be processed by the responsible employee using the WS14500020 workflow template.

10.2.5 Purchase Order Response (POR) Approval Workflows

The *PO Response (POR)* document allows the vendor to provide a notification on the acceptance of the PO goods and service, the quantity, and prices. These confirmations can be entered in SAP SRM in a few different methods: manually by the professional purchaser; by the vendor using the SUS component, or electronically via XML.

The standard workflow templates predelivered in SAP SRM for approval of PO response are illustrated in Figure 10.26.

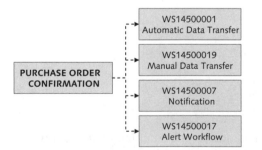

Figure 10.26 Purchase Order Confirmation Approval Workflow

The workflow template WS14500007 can be used as an alternative to the WS14500019 template. If the Notification workflow template is used, the professional purchaser can be notified that a PO response is awaiting approval. An email is sent automatically to the responsible purchaser, and using the link in the email, he can review the PO response and take appropriate action.

Using the start conditions in Transaction BBP_COND, an organization can set up Business Rules such that the POR data is either transferred to the PO automatically or manually by the purchaser. For example, a tolerance can be set up in the starting conditions such that only PO responses with a variance above the tolerance are sent to the buyer for approval. All other PO responses are automatically transferred to the PO using the Automatic Data Transfer workflow.

10.2.6 Contracts and Contract Changes (Version) Workflows

The standard workflows templates predelivered in SAP SRM for approval of contracts or contract changes (versions) are illustrated in Figure 10.27.

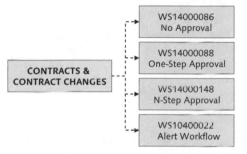

Figure 10.27 Contracts and Contract Changes (Version) Approval Workflows

The Workflow templates of No Approval, One-Step, and N-Step are similar in processing as the other Shopping Cart workflows. For example, the One-Step Approval requires approval by the manager of the responsible purchasing organization to which the contract is assigned. Similar to the Shopping Cart One-Step workflow, the entire contract needs to be approved and not just selected line items.

However, the Alert Workflow (WS10400022) is implemented in conjunction with SAP NetWeaver Business Warehouse (SAP NetWeaver BW) reporting and the Alert Monitor.

Tip
The Workflow template WS14000148 requires a BAdI implementation to enable the N-Step Approval determination.

10.2.7 Bid Invitations and Bid Workflows

The standard workflow templates predelivered in SAP SRM for approval of bid invitation and bids are illustrated in Figure 10.28.

The Alert Workflow is used only when using external bid invitations in the context of auctions. When an auction event is in progress, this workflow keeps the bid-invitation creator notified of any errors during the auction or about the completion of the auction.

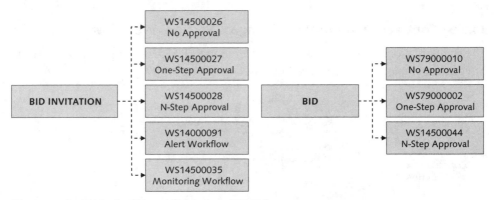

Figure 10.28 Bid Invitation and Bid Approval Workflows

The Monitoring Workflow monitors the status of the bid invitation. This workflow is started when the buying organization publishes a bid invitation. At this time, the Monitoring Workflow waits for the bid invitation to end. Once that happens, the system triggers a notification to the creator that the event has ended.

The No Approval, One-Step, and N-Step workflow templates work similarly to the Shopping Cart Approval templates explained in Section 10.2.1, Shopping Cart Workflows.

10.2.8 Procurement Card Workflows

SAP SRM provides the functionality to use a procurement card as a method of payment in the shopping cart. This allows organizations to streamline their processes of procurement and payment for small-dollar transactions. The following standard workflows are supplied by SAP in SAP SRM for approval of procurement card transactions.

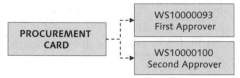

Figure 10.29 Approval Templates for Procurement Cards

The requisitioner is responsible for all approvals until the settlement value exceeds the limit specified in the customizing. All others are approved by the manager.

10.2.9 User Master and Vendor Master Workflows

Organizations that have many employees can reduce the work for their security team by allowing the employees to create their own user records. In this scenario, the employee can create a user record for himself but requires the approval of his manager. If the manager approves the request, the user record is released and the employee receives the login information in his email. In this scenario, the manager within the organization decides whether employees need access to the SAP SRM system. A standard workflow template called *New User* is provided for this scenario.

On the login page for SAP SRM, users can select the Change Password application. There are two approval templates available in SAP SRM for password changes. The Forgotten Password Without Approval workflow (WS10000224) allows the user to request for the password change and receives a new password in email. Alternatively, the Forgotten Password Approval (WS10000223) is used, and a workflow is sent to the person defined in Customizing for approving password changes. If approved, an automatically generated password is sent to the user via email or rejection email is sent.

The standard workflow templates predelivered in SAP SRM for approval of user master records and vendor records are illustrated in Figure 10.30.

Figure 10.30 User Master and Vendor Master Approval Workflows

Many organizations already have processes in place for creation of user master records and seldom use the workflows illustrated in Figure 10.30. These are applicable to a few unique scenarios.

So far, we have talked about the need for workflow in SAP SRM and the predelivered templates that are available to organizations out-of-the-box. In the next section, we'll learn about the different options available for approving or rejecting the work items generated by these different workflows.

10.3 Online and Offline Approvals

Assuming that you have selected the workflows that are relevant for use in your organization, we now need to learn how to take action when a work item is sent to an approver.

The term *work item* refers to a single workflow request on which the receiver needs to take an action. The action could be of approval, rejection, or simply forward to another individual.

There are a number of ways an action (i.e., approval or rejection) can be taken. Figure 10.31 illustrates three different ways in which an approval or rejection can be performed in SAP SRM. The most common option is via the SAP SRM Inbox. With the second option, an approver receives an email notification with the URL link to the work item. The third option is direct approval in the email client using the approval and rejection buttons.

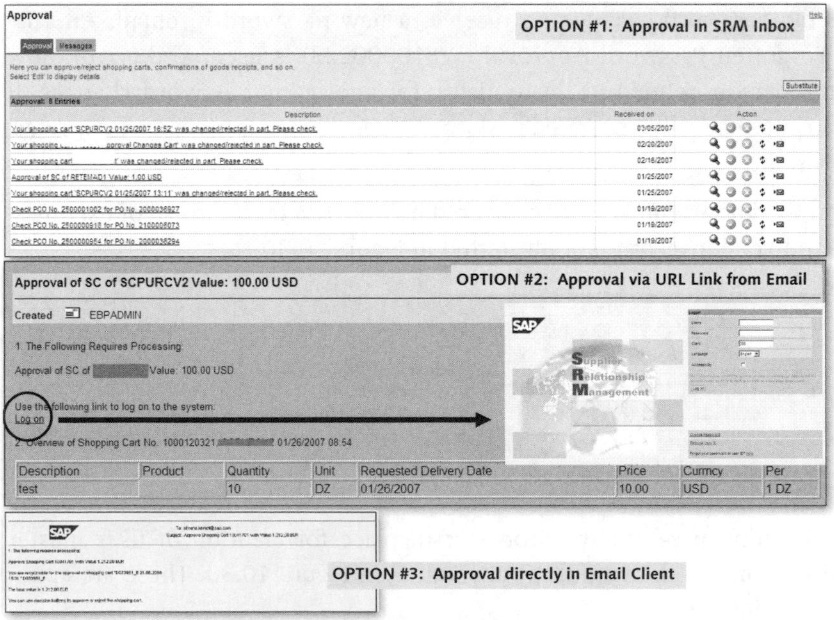

Figure 10.31 Options Available for Approval of Work Items

10.3.1 Approval in SAP SRM Inbox

To approve or reject a shopping cart, PO, or other documents, the user needs to have the approval role assigned. Based on the role assignment, an approver will have access to the Approval application, also called the SAP *SRM Inbox*. All users with the employee role also have the Approval inbox but do not have the authorization to approve or reject work items.

Figure 10.32 illustrates the overview screen of the Approval application, which has two tabs: Approval and Messages. The Approval tab contains a list of work items that require action (approve or reject) from the approver. The Messages tab contains notifications that the system generates to provide additional information but do not require an action from the approver.

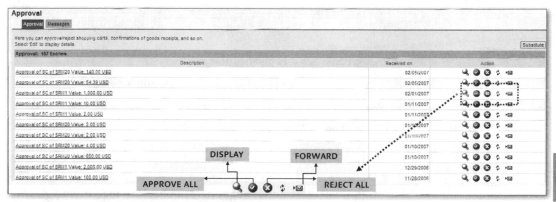

Figure 10.32 Approval Application (SAP SRM Inbox)

An approver has the option of directly taking an action on the approval work items in his inbox using the buttons that exist in the Action column. In Figure 10.32, the DISPLAY function is illustrated by a Magnifying Glass icon. The APPROVE ALL function is illustrated by a green check-mark icon. The REJECT ALL function is illustrated by a red x-mark icon and the FORWARD function is illustrated by an email icon.

The approver can take action directly in the overview window of the Approval application by clicking on the APPROVE ALL or REJECT ALL buttons. This is useful if the information visible in the overview screen is sufficient for the approver to make a decision. In most cases, the approver needs to see more information to be able to make an educated decision. This is one reason why some organizations restrict the APPROVE ALL and REJECT ALL buttons in the overview screen of the Approval application. This can be restricted using workflow Customizing.

To view additional information about the work item, the approver can click on the DISPLAY function illustrated by the magnifying glass. Figure 10.33 illustrates the detail screen of the Approval work item. The Approval detail looks similar to the shopping cart overview screen, because during approval of a shopping cart, the approver reviews the same information as the requisitioner.

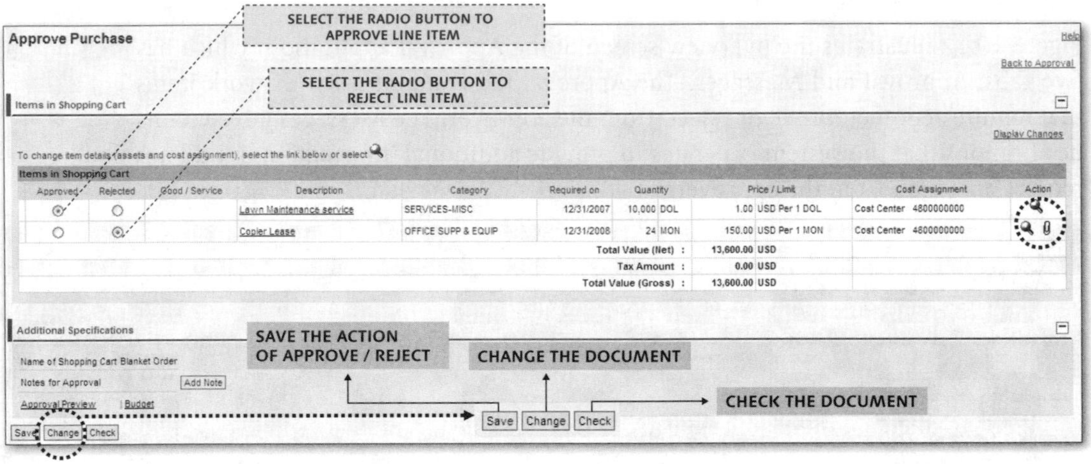

Figure 10.33 Approve Purchase — Work Item Details

As shown in Figure 10.33, the approver can select the Approved or Rejected radio buttons and click the Save button to complete the approval process. If the information available on this screen is not enough, he can click the magnifying glass to review the details of each line item in the shopping cart.

Alternately, if the approver needs to change information in the shopping cart (or other document approval), he can click on the Change button to begin editing. At this point, the approver can change information such as Quantity or Price, or click on the magnifying glass to change information in the details of the line item. An example is if the approver wanted to change the SAP General Ledger account for the item he is approving. The user will need to do this in the details of the line item.

Once all changes are complete, the approver can ensure that the correct radio button is selected for approved or rejected and click on the Save button to complete the action.

This completes the approval or rejection of a work item. If there are additional work items in the approver's inbox, the approver can continue to take action on the remaining work items.

10.3.2 Approval via URL Link from Email

Most users do not like logging into multiple inboxes. Similarly, the SAP SRM Inbox and the Approval application from the previous section would be considered as a separate inbox for an approver to check on a daily basis to see whether a work item is there to process, for example, a work item to approve a shopping cart.

Instead, an organization can use the Email Notification functionality in SAP SRM. SAP provides standard integration to email clients such as Microsoft® Outlook®, IBM® Lotus Notes®, and Novell® GroupWise®. Therefore, the work items that are sent to the SAP SRM Inbox can also be simultaneously sent to the email application used by the approvers. This way, the approvers get notifications in regular inboxes that they check regularly.

An added advantage of the approval notifications in SAP SRM is that the approver receives a work item with a brief description and a URL link to the actual work item. The email notification contains a brief description of the items within the shopping cart work item and the value of the shopping cart. The approver can click on the Log on link provided in the shopping cart to launch the SAP SRM approval inbox, as illustrated in Figure 10.34. A login is required once the URL is accessed.

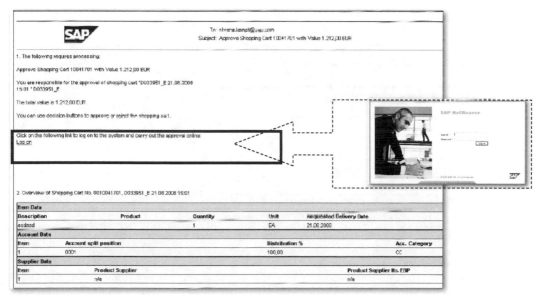

Figure 10.34 Approval Email with Login URL

Once the user logs into the SRM system, he is directly taken to the respective work item, where he can click on the Approve or Reject buttons as explained in the previous section.

Email is integrated with a standard report, RSWUWFMLEC. This report collects all the work items that require approval and sends them to the SAP Connect component. A second report, RSCONN01, can then be scheduled to take all the items waiting in the SAP Connect component and send them to the respective email addresses of the approvers.

10.3.3 Approval Directly in Email Client (Offline Approval)

The third option for approving shopping carts and other documents in SAP SRM as illustrated in Figure 10.31 introduces the concept of *offline approval*. In this option, an approver receives email notification in his email client such as Microsoft Outlook or IBM Lotus Notes as he did in the second option discussed. But in addition to the login URL in the email, the approver also receives two additional HTML links in the email: Approval per Email and Rejection per Email. Figure 10.35 illustrates a sample email containing these two links.

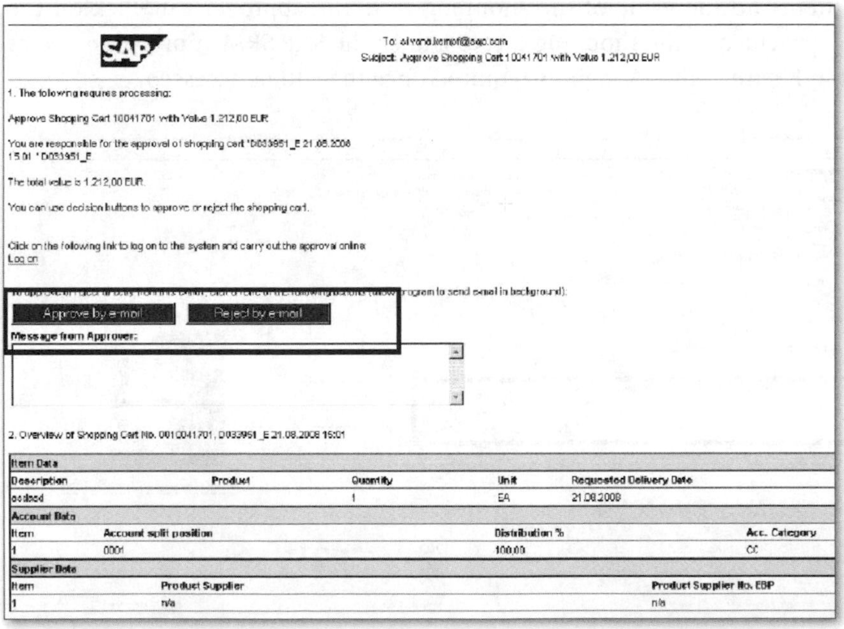

Figure 10.35 Offline Approval

The reason this option is sometimes also called offline approval is because in this option the approver does not have to log on to the SAP SRM system and can process the work item directly in the email by clicking on the Approval per Email or Rejection per Email links. Once the approver clicks on either of these links to complete his action, an email is generated with the action (approval or rejection) and sent to the SAP SRM system with the approval result.

This option is ideal for departments or individuals who are mobile and do not have access to the system all the time. They can then access their approval emails offline, take action (approve or reject), and then synchronize with the SAP system once they're back online.

> **Note**
>
> In this scenario, the approver needs to approve or reject the entire document and does not have the ability to approve or reject by line item.

In SAP SRM, the offline approval functionality is enabled using two reports, *RBBP_NOTIFICATION_OFFAPP* and RBBP_OFFLINE_EVAL, as described in Figure 10.36.

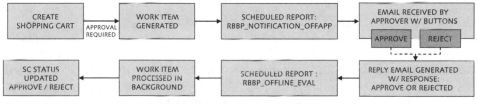

Figure 10.36 Offline Approval Process

Transaction SOST in SAP EBP contains a list of all work items that are either waiting to be sent to the external system or have already been sent (illustrated in Figure 10.37). This transaction can be monitored to see whether the email work items are being sent correctly.

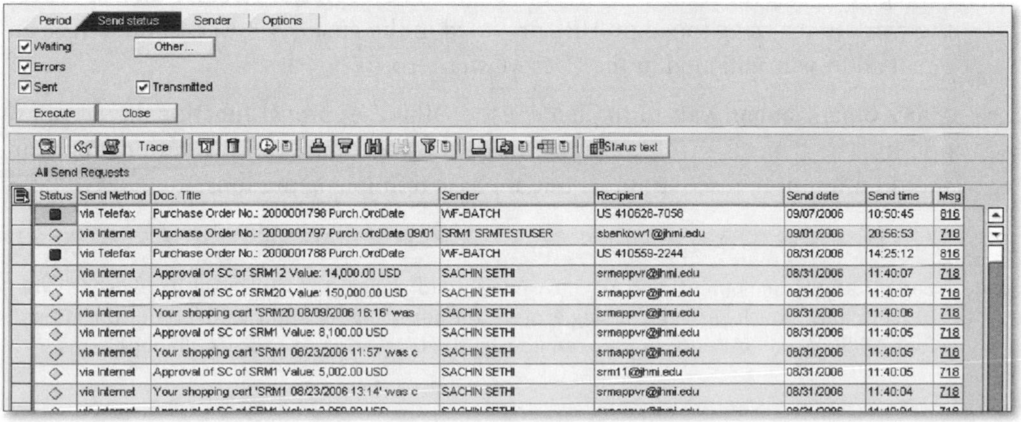

Figure 10.37 SAP Connect Transmission Log

An organization can choose to either include or exclude the email buttons Approve and Reject using a variant for the report, RSWUWFMLEC (displayed in Figure 10.38).

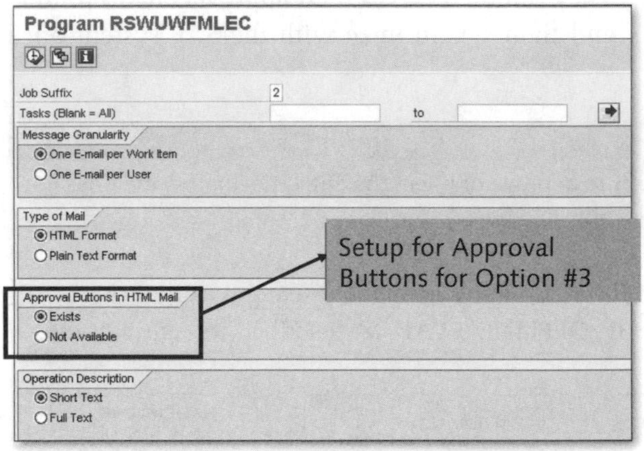

Figure 10.38 Report RSWUWFMLEC

Most organizations implement the three methods to approve in phases as discussed in Sections 10.3.1, Approval in SAP SRM Inbox, through this section, and shown in Figure 10.31. The option of Approval in the SAP SRM Inbox as discussed in Section 10.3.1, Approval in SAP SRM Inbox, is standard, out-of-the-box functionality. There is no additional effort required from the project team to implement.

The option of Approval via URL Link from Email as discussed in Section 10.3.2 provides the greatest approval flexibility because the approver can either process the work items in their SAP SRM Inboxes or wait until a work item is sent to them in his regular email client (Microsoft Outlook, IBM Lotus Notes, etc.). He then approves the work items using the login URL provided in the email. All users should have an email address maintained in the User Master record.

Many organizations wait to implement the Offline Approval functionality as a last option. The benefits of offline approval also bring complications; an organization should minimize those within its initial phase of implementations.

Note

Organizations implementing SAP SRM 6.0 should review the Universal Worklist (UWL) functionality, which provides a single place for accessing all approval/alerts/notifications for SAP SRM and SAP ERP. A user can go to a single location to process all work items.

10.4 Implementation Best Practices

This section provides some *best practices* to use during your SAP SRM project implementation. We'll start by discussing a five-step process for determining your workflow needs. Figure 10.39 provides an overall methodology and strategy to follow during the blueprint phase of the project.

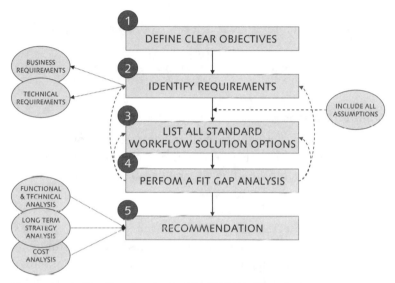

Figure 10.39 Five-Step Process for SAP SRM Workflow Projects

Define Clear Objectives

It is extremely important to define clear objectives for the project and the role of workflow. SAP Business Workflow provides rich functionality, but not all available functionality may be relevant for this project.

Identify Workflow Requirements

Project teams that do a good job of capturing most workflow requirements end up more successful than others. This is true especially if the standard workflow templates are not sufficient and workflow needs to be customized. The impact on timeline, resources, and cost is more tremendous when requirements are not captured completely and accurately. Some workflow requirements include:

▸ Ability for all approvers to modify, approve, or reject shopping carts
▸ Ability for all reviewers to display shopping cart requests, although without the ability to modify, approve, or reject the shopping cart

▶ If a shopping cart is rejected, the requisitioner receives a notification via email, informing him of the rejection. The requisitioner should have the opportunity to accept, modify, or resubmit the shopping cart.

▶ A modification that changes the shopping cart will trigger a notification to the requisitioner and a request to generate the reapproval process.

▶ All approvers and reviewers receive email notifications when shopping cart approvals are required.

▶ Ability to substitute another approver as a delegate approver for a period of absence

▶ Ability to add additional approvers to the approval process before and after the system-generated approvers

List All Standard Solution Options

List All Standard Solution Options should include all and any assumptions. Custom workflow development is a costly endeavor, especially in a rapidly changing solution like SAP SRM. In each new release, the workflow capabilities in SAP SRM have been enhanced greatly. Therefore, review and exhaust the capability of standard delivered workflow templates in SAP SRM. Implementing what your organization does is an easy user decision but not a strategic management decision. Instead, companies that have decided to implement SAP SRM need to take the time and opportunity to explore the best practices used at leading organizations. SAP-delivered workflows are a result of research and development of industry best practices. For most organizations, the implementation of SRM is not only a change in technology but also a change in the business processes existing in their entire value chain. Organizations are well advised to make use of the standard workflow templates delivered in SRM and if necessary add business rules using the delivered BAdIs.

Identify all the standard workflow templates for all the business documents relevant for workflow and list any assumptions when discussing with the business and technical implementation teams. Review the different sections in this chapter that describe the standard workflows delivered. Here are some assumptions that should be discussed:

▶ If spending limit and approval limit by dollar thresholds are required, they will remain common across the enterprise.

▶ A requisitioner will provide appropriate account assignment and product category information in the shopping cart to drive approvals.

Perform Fit-Gap Analysis

Custom workflow development is a costly endeavor, especially in a rapidly changing solution offering like SAP SRM. Over the past six years, the SAP SRM application has seen tremendous growth and with that has come a large array of enhancements. Organizations that opted for highly customized workflows had to upgrade these time-consuming and costly workflows.

Just as with any other development effort within the SAP environment, a fit-gap analysis should be conducted for the workflows in SAP SRM. Figure 10.40 shows how to do a fit-gap analysis for your project. In a fit-gap analysis, we list all of the possible options and then map each option against the following questions:

▶ Is the option an SAP standard functionality?

▶ What is the level of development effort required to achieve the option?

▶ What is the ongoing maintenance effort and cost for this option?

OPTIONS CONSIDERED	SAP Standard Functionality	Development Effort	On-going Maintenance
1 Utilize controlled Ad-Hoc approvals functionality • The ability for endusers to add approvers "on-the-fly" • Controls will have to be built to restrict the list of approvers available • Provides a mechanism to handle inconsistent approval requirements	Yes	N/A	N/A
2 Utilize modified Spending/Approval Limit workflow template in conjunction with Ad-Hoc approvals functionality • The ability for system-driven approvals based on user spending/approval limits • This template utilizes the SAP organizational hierarchy • Utilize Ad-hoc for any additional approvals that are required to adhere to varying departmental policies	Yes	Low	Low
3 Significant modifications/enhancements to the standard workflow templates in conjunction with Ad-Hoc approvals functionality • The ability to automate approvals based on cost center, dollar threshold, and commodity • Significant on-going effort to maintain business rules • Utilize Ad-hoc for any additional approvals that are required to adhere to varying departmental policies	No	High	High

Figure 10.40 Example of High-Level Fit-Gap Workflow Analysis

> **Note**
>
> The options identified above a just a few of many available to organizations during SAP SRM implementation. Each project may have an entirely different set of parameters that could drive a different set of options.

Recommendations

Eventually, each project team needs to determine the path of endeavor. A recommendation needs to be made using the information gathered in the four previous steps. Ideally, your recommendation along with the information gathered in the fit-gap analysis step should allow the management team to select an appropriate option for the implementation and long-term viability.

10.5 Security and Authorizations in Workflow

When we talk about workflow and agents (the individual(s) who receive work items), the audit departments pay close attention. They are interested in who can approve what, how the approvers are determined, and what authorizations they will have for changing or adding to the business documents. A common question asked by auditors is: "Can the approver determined by the SAP SRM system be changed by the end user or further approvers?"

SAP offers authorizations and BAdI(s) in SAP SRM to provide such flexibility for organizations. These allow changes to approvers or give specific users the ability to make such changes.

Transaction PFTC_CHG makes it possible to assign specific processors for workflow templates. In the standard system, if there is no specific processor assigned, then that workflow task is considered a General Task (i.e., one that anyone is allowed to process). Alternatively, specific processors can be assigned based on user, role, Organizational Unit, position, and others. Authorization can change and or insert an approver or reviewer.

Table 10.2 lists workflow templates that can be configured in Transaction PFTC_CHG for either change or insertion. Here you can configure who can be changed or inserted as an approver.

Workflow Template	Description	Change Approver	Insert Approver/ Reviewer
WS10000129	Approve shopping cart (one-step)	x	
WS10000031	Approve shopping cart (two-step)	x	
WS10000060	Workflow without approval (shopping cart)	x	
WS14000133	N-step approval of shopping cart	x	
WS14000109	N-step approval of shopping cart over value limit	x	

Table 10.2 Workflow Templates in SAP SRM

Workflow Template	Description	Change Approver	Insert Approver/ Reviewer
WS10000271	Approval of shopping cart		X
WS14000089	Approval of purchase order (one-step)	x	
WS14000075	Workflow without approval (purchase order)	x	
WS14000145	N-step approval of purchase order	x	
WS14000154	Reviewer workflow for purchase order	x	
WS14000002	Approval of purchase order		X
WS10400002	Approval goods receipt (one-step)	x	
WS10400009	Approval goods receipt (two-step)	x	
WS10400010	Workflow without approval (goods receipt)	x	
WS10400020	Approval of goods receipt by administrator	x	
WS10400008	Approval of goods receipt		X
WS10400017	Approve invoice (one-step)	x	
WS10400018	Approval invoice (two-step)	x	
WS10400016	Workflow without approval (invoice)	x	
WS10400021	Approval of invoice by administrator	x	
WS10400014	Approval of invoice		X
WS14000088	Approval of contract (one-step)	x	
WS14000086	Workflow without approval (contract)	x	
WS14000145	N-step approval of contract	x	
WS14500010	Approval of contract		X
WS14500027	Approval of bid invitation (one-step)	x	
WS14500026	Workflow without approval (bid invitation)	x	
WS14500028	N-step approval of bid invitation	x	
WS14500022	Approval of bid invitation		X
WS79000002	Approval of Bid (one-step)	x	
WS79000010	Workflow without approval (bid)	x	
WS14500044	N-step approval of bid	x	
WS14500040	Approval of bid		X

Table 10.2 Workflow Templates in SAP SRM (Cont.)

In addition to removing the classification of workflows as General Tasks (i.e., assigning specific processors of work-items), you can define whether a business transaction such as a shopping cart can be changed during the approval process.

Additionally, the standard workflow(s) can be influenced by Personalization Objects available for shopping cart workflows. In User Maintenance (SU01) on the Personalization tab, there are several Personalization Objects available for workflows: BBP_WFL_SECURITY, BBP_SPENDING_LIMIT, BBP_APPROVAL_LIMIT.

These objects can restrict the authorizations of users or define value limits for control of approval workflows. These objects can be assigned at a user or role level. The best practice calls for setup of this authorization within the user role instead of individual user personalization. This reduces overall maintenance and consistency across the user base. If several roles are assigned to the user, then the system uses the highest available authorization level during runtime.

For example, the BBP_WFL_SECURITY object can define the authorization level used in workflow action once something is changed in the shopping cart. Table 10.3 provides a listing of the different workflow authorization levels and the behavior of the shopping cart workflow during the approval process.

Authorization level	Effects on approval	Workflow behavior
NONE	Not possible to change a shopping cart during approval process	Workflow continues.
LOW	Possible to change the shopping cart	The entire approval workflow restarts after each shopping cart change is made.
MEDIUM	Possible to change the shopping cart	The system evaluates the workflow start conditions and starts the approval workflow again if the change necessitates a new approval. If this is not the case, the approval workflow continues.
HIGH	Possible to change the shopping cart	Workflow continues

Table 10.3 Workflow Authorization Levels and Behavior During Approval

The different authorization levels enable organizations to control the behavior of the shopping cart workflow. A user with the authorization level of NONE can view or display the shopping cart but cannot change it.

If the user has the authorization level Low, then changes to the shopping cart are allowed, but the workflow process restarts every time a shopping cart change is made, independently of which field of the shopping cart was changed. Organizations need to be careful when selecting the Low authorization level. Although it addresses the audit concerns of reapproval, it can be an unnecessary burden for the approvers and delay the procurement process just because an SAP General Ledger account change is made. Figure 10.41 illustrates the Authorization level object key that controls the approver's authorization level.

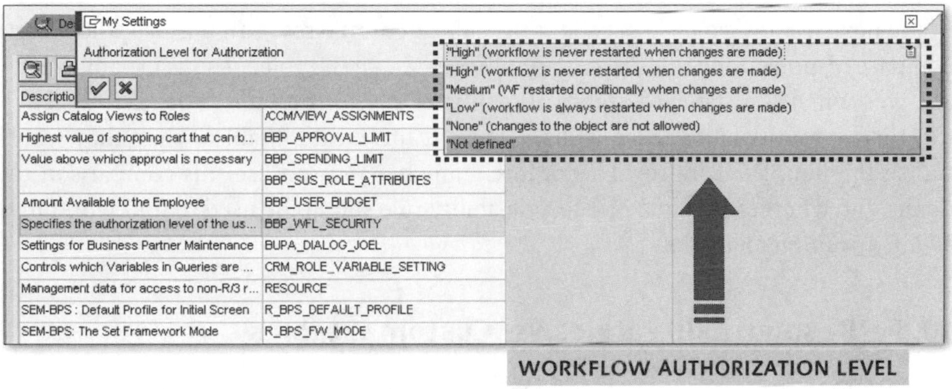

My Settings	
Authorization Level for Authorization	"High" (workflow is never restarted when changes are made)
✓ ✗	"High" (workflow is never restarted when changes are made)
Descriptio	"Medium" (WF restarted conditionally when changes are made)
Assign Catalog Views to Roles	/CCM/VIEW_ASSIGNMENTS	"Low" (workflow is always restarted when changes are made)
Highest value of shopping cart that can b...	BBP_APPROVAL_LIMIT	"None" (changes to the object are not allowed)
Value above which approval is necessary	BBP_SPENDING_LIMIT	"Not defined"
	BBP_SUS_ROLE_ATTRIBUTES	
Amount Available to the Employee	BBP_USER_BUDGET	
Specifies the authorization level of the us...	BBP_WFL_SECURITY	
Settings for Business Partner Maintenance	BUPA_DIALOG_JOEL	
Controls which Variables in Queries are ...	CRM_ROLE_VARIABLE_SETTING	
Management data for access to non-R/3 r...	RESOURCE	
SEM-BPS : Default Profile for Initial Screen	R_BPS_DEFAULT_PROFILE	
SEM-BPS: The Set Framework Mode	R_BPS_FW_MODE	

WORKFLOW AUTHORIZATION LEVEL

Figure 10.41 Authorization Level of the User in Approval

In the authorization level Medium, the workflow behavior depends on the type of changes made to the shopping cart. After each change, the workflow system evaluates the starting conditions in SAP SRM to determine if a new workflow needs to be triggered.

> **Example**
>
> A user creates a shopping cart of value $2,000. Based on the start conditions, a single-step approval workflow is triggered. During approval, the manager, changes the shopping cart value to $5,500. The workflow system re-evaluates the start conditions and determines that for all shopping carts worth more than $5,000 a two-step approval workflow is required. At this time, the workflow system starts this new approval and completes the old single-step approval.

The authorization level High allows users to make changes to the shopping cart and does not impact the further processing of the workflow. Approvers are not redetermined, so that if the user was the last in the chain of approvers, the workflow will complete after approval. If there were other approvers in the chain after this approver, the workflow continues. We have seen more organizations use the High authorization approval level than any of the other levels.

In addition to the personalization object key, a BAdI BBP_WFL_SECURE_BADI is available for organizations to develop business rules and override the settings of None, Low, Medium, or High authorization levels. With the BAdI BBP_WFL_SECUR_BADI, and method SET_SECURITY_LEVEL, you can change the workflow security level and override the value determined from role personalization. Using this BAdI, an organization can further determine whether to allow changes to the shopping cart or define how the workflow should behave once the changes are done. A list of BAdIs available in SRM is available in Appendix D.

In the next section, you'll learn about the concept of rule resolution in workflow and compare responsibility rules to commonly used Z tables. Project teams usually create Z tables when the standard approval templates do not provide sufficient capabilities for approval routing. Also, many project teams create Z tables when they want to use the item-level approval workflow template. You can use this comparison to determine whether a Z table or a responsibility rule should be used to find workflow agents for implementation.

10.6 Responsibility Rules vs. Custom Z tables

In workflow, the determination of agents (approvers or owners or recipients) can be derived in many different ways. A common method is agent assignment in the workflow template in SAP SRM. Transaction PFTC_CHG assigns specific processors for workflow templates as discussed in the security section above. But it is often not possible to just use agent assignment on projects, because it may not be possible to determine approvers for a particular workflow (e.g., shopping cart) using a role, position, job, organization unit, and others. It could instead be based on cost center ownership or even on the wish of each individual department in the company to determine its own approvers.

	RESPONSIBILITIES	CUSTOM TABLE
STANDARD SAP DELIVERED FUNCTIONALITY	YES	NO
DEVELOPMENT EFFORT REQUIRED	LOW	HIGH
LOAD EFFORT	HIGH	HIGH
MAINTENANCE COMPLEXITY	HIGH	LOW
MAINTENANCE: CENTRAL / DISTRIBUTED	CENTRAL	CENTRAL OR DISTRIBUTED
SECURITY	LOW	COULD BE HIGH
GLOBAL VISIBILITY	POOR	GOOD
TROUBLESHOOTING	POOR	GOOD
TRANSPORTABLE	PARTIALLY *	YES
LONG TERM IMPACT	LOW MAINTENANCE	HIGH MAINTENANCE

* ONLY THE RESPONSIBILITY RULE CAN BE TRANSPORTED AND NOT THE ACTUAL DATA (APPROVERS), THOSE NEED TO BE ENTERED IN EACH ENVIRONMENT/CLIENT

Figure 10.42 Responsibility Rules vs. Custom Tables

This is when the common question arises: "Can we just use a custom Z table to list all our approvers and have the workflow driven off the custom table?" Yes, just like any other ABAP program in SAP, workflows can use a custom table as well. SAP delivered workflows using a BAdI and customer-developed workflows. Custom tables might be the first thought but definitely not the best or only option when it comes to SAP Business Workflow.

Responsibility rules in SAP offer similar functionality to custom tables and are better suited for SAP Business Workflow. It is, however, always challenging to persuade project teams to use responsibility rules instead of a custom table. Figure 10.42 provides a comparison between the two to provide information that project teams can use to make educated decisions.

10.7   What's New in SAP SRM 7.0 Workflow

Beginning with SAP SRM 7.0, there are two different business workflows that are supported: Application-Controlled and Process-Controlled.

The Application-Controlled workflow is what customers used in SAP SRM 5.0 and earlier releases. In this workflow, multiple workflow templates were provided and triggered using start conditions. This workflow going forward is only intended to be supported for customers that upgrade from an SAP SRM 5.0 or earlier release to SAP SRM 7.0.

The Process-Controlled workflow was introduced with the controlled release SAP SRM 6.0 to a select group of customers and now is the workflow standard beginning with SAP SRM 7.0. With this release, the idea is to provide an environment whereby the workflow can be configured in a more flexible way and reduces the need for extensive custom development to model the process.

In earlier SRM releases, there were multiple workflow templates that existed as described in Section 10.2, Standard Delivered Workflows in SAP SRM. In SAP SRM 7.0, a unified template has been created. The main SAP SRM workflow template is now WS 40000014, along with two sub workflows of "Approval" WS 40000016 and "Completion" WS 40000017.

Figure 10.43 provides a high-level illustration of the difference in workflow architecture between "Application-Controlled" vs. "Process-Controlled" workflows.

The workflow in SAP SRM 7.0 builds on the concepts discussed throughout this chapter. It continues to support the functions of approval and rejection and builds on the concepts of "Completion" as described in Figure 10.19 in Section 10.2, Standard Delivered Workflows in SAP SRM.

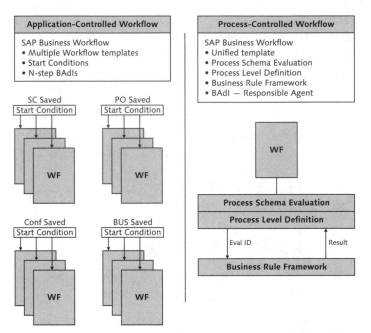

Figure 10.43 Application-Controlled vs. Process-Controlled Workflow

What is different from an end user perspective is the look and feel of the Approval function. For example, the Java applet-based graphical preview of the approval chain is no longer available; that is replaced by a tabular format of the approval process (illustrated in Figure 10.44).

Item Data	Account Assignment	Notes and Attachments	Delivery Address/Performance Location	Sources of Supply / Service Agents	Approval Process Overview

Current Status: Initial

Current Process Step:

Currently Processed By:

Approval Process Data: Download as XML

Follow Up: ☐ Work Item to Requester at Process End

| Header | Item |

Header Approval Status

Add Approver ◢ Remove Approver   Settings

Sequence	Process Step	Status	Processor	Received On	Processed On	Forwarded By
▪ 001	SRM Shopping Cart Approval (1)	Open (No Decision Made)	S_BUYER1			
▪ 002	SRM Shopping Cart Approval (1)	Open (No Decision Made)	S_APPROVER1			

Reviewer(s) for the Document

Add Reviewer Remove Reviewer   Settings

Reviewer Type	Processor	Received On	Processed On	Forwarded By

ⓘ The table does not contain any data

Figure 10.44 Approval Preview in SAP SRM 7.0

Another major shift is the use of the Universal Worklist for approvals. Basically, the SAP SRM Inbox in previous releases has been replaced by the Universal Worklist, an SAP NetWeaver Portal technology (illustrated in Figure 10.45). A user will have a central inbox, which is connected to several SAP systems (e.g., SAP SRM and SAP ERP). If there are approval items that originate from SAP SRM or an invoice approval work item that originates in SAP ERP, the approver can execute it from a central inbox – the Universal Worklist.

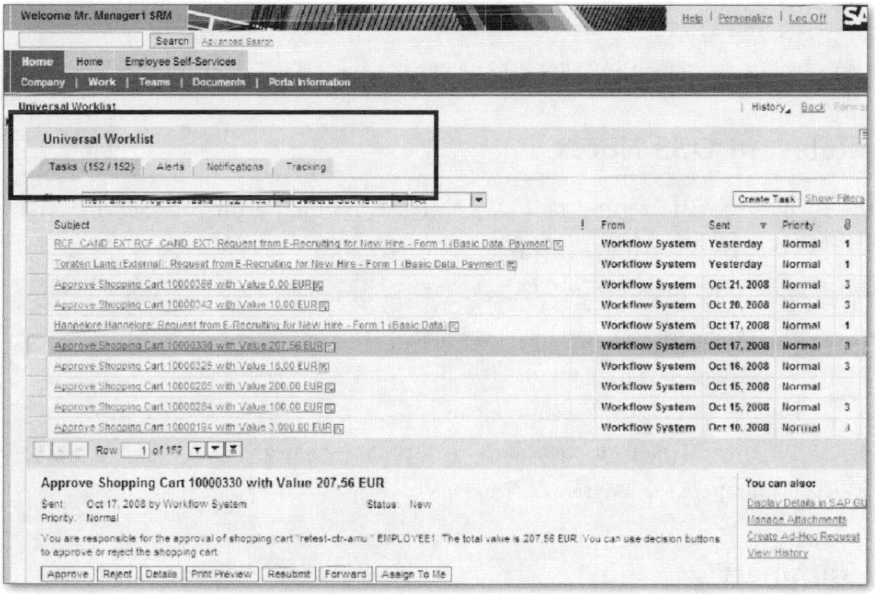

Figure 10.45 Universal Worklist in SAP NetWeaver Portal for SAP SRM 7.0

In the shopping cart and during approval, users are still able to add, Ad-Hoc approvers, and make changes to existing approvers.

One change is that during the approval of a shopping cart, the only time users are able to change the information in the cart is during the "Completion" step. Shopping carts should be completed prior to sending through the approval process. A "Completion" step allows the organization to include responsible owners that might have specific knowledge in completing the shopping cart with price, supplier details, and others.

A new functionality of "Inquire" allows the approver and the requester to go back and forth with a shopping cart document. For example, if the approver partly rejected a cart or, if in the "Completion" phase, the approver marked the item for "inquiry." Figure 10.46 illustrates the "Inquire" function in approval.

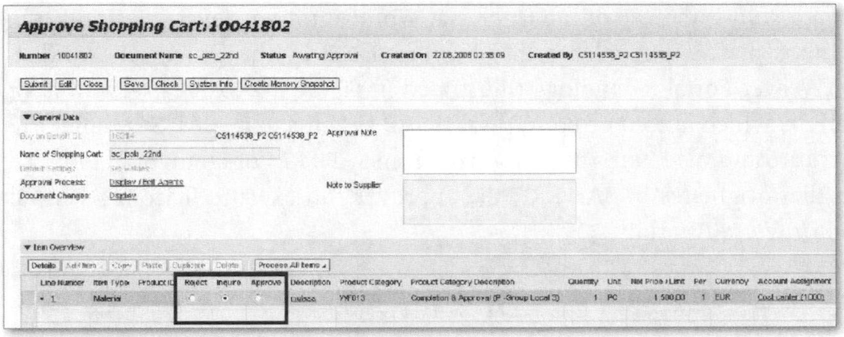

Figure 10.46 Inquire function in SAP SRM 7.0 Approvals

10.8 Relevant OSS Notes

Table 10.4 provides a list of important OSS Notes available on the SAP Service Marketplace that are relevant when managing workflow in SAP SRM.

Note	Description
547601	FAQ workflow, runtime environment, and troubleshooting
903200	Workflow tracing for problem detection
322526	Analysis for workflow problems
391674	How to build ad-hoc agents in customer workflows

Table 10.4 OSS Notes from the SAP Service Marketplace

10.9 Summary

In this chapter, you were introduced to the concept of workflow in SAP SRM. The chapter started with a discussion on the importance of workflow and how organizations can achieve efficiency by implementing workflow processes using SAP SRM. You are now aware that a number of workflow templates are predelivered in SRM and can be used in applications such as shopping carts, POs, contracts, and confirmations.

As of SAP SRM 6.0 (SRM 2007), there is a new functionality for workflow and considerable changes. A number of the existing SAP SRM workflow BAdIs and functions will become obsolete.

In Chapter 11, we'll discuss the role of security in SAP SRM and how SAP security administrators can manage roles and authorizations within SAP SRM. We'll also cover why and how security is different in SAP SRM and the impact of Organizational Structure in security.

As businesses grow, their information systems support whole communities of users: customers, suppliers, partners, and employees, all counting on the secure exchange of a wide variety of information. Managing the security of ERP information into and out of your organization has never been more critical — or more challenging.

11   Managing Security in SAP SRM

In today's environment, organizations are not just looking for a technical solution to thwart viruses, hackers, and information theft. They are looking for software companies to provide the most secure enterprise solutions, built on rigorous security standards and industry best practices, to help them manage governance, risk, and compliance. So let's start by defining *security*. The following are some security definitions:

► A secure system is a system that does exactly what we want it to do and nothing that we don't want it to do, even when someone else tries to make it behave differently — *www.wikipedia.com*

► In the computer industry, refers to techniques for ensuring that data stored in a computer cannot be read or compromised by any individuals without authorization — *www.Webopedia.com*

► A process of system screening that denies access to unauthorized users and protects data from unauthorized uses — *www.ask-edi.com*

► Work that involves ensuring the confidentiality, integrity, and availability of systems, networks, and data through the planning, analysis, development, implementation, maintenance, and enhancement of information systems' security programs, policies, procedures, and tools — *www.opm.gov*

The general idea of most of these definitions is that application security is required to restrict sensitive and important data within an organization. Based on an individual's job or responsibility, the security developer's need to determine what transactions they should access, display, or execute.

SAP provides an enterprise solution for integrating the various aspects of organizations: internal operations, external business networks, regulatory compliance, and other. In its annual report for 2005, SAP stated that SAP products include security features that are intended to protect the privacy and integrity of customer data.

Despite these security features, these products may be vulnerable to attacks and similar problems caused by Internet users, such as hackers bypassing firewalls and misappropriating confidential information. Such attacks or other disruptions could jeopardize the security of information stored in and transmitted through the computer systems of SAP customers and lead to claims for damages against SAP from customers. However, SAP technologies have not been significantly exposed to security attacks so far, and SAP provides extensive security functions, so the risk is unlikely.

The focus of this chapter is to discuss security as it relates to SAP SRM, but we'll start by briefly discussing the basic security concepts in SAP. In the SAP system, security is administered for objects (profiles and authorizations). Users are only authorized to display or change the areas of the system in ways made necessary by their respective job responsibilities.

11.1   Overview of Security in SAP

SAP has been implemented at more than half of the Fortune 500 companies, has approximately 44,500 installations at 32,000 customers in more than 120 countries, with more than 10 million users. Given this customer landscape, SAP is constantly striving to provide the best security practices available.

SAP is built on the *role-based security concept*. Each user within the organization is assigned one or multiple roles that are deemed necessary for the functions they are supposed to perform, based on assigned organizational responsibility. The core of application security in SAP is the authorization concept. The three pillars of authorization in SAP are *transactions*, *authorization objects*, and *roles*. Figures 11.1 and 11.2 illustrate this concept.

▶ **Transactions**
Transactions are what users execute to perform functions in SAP. For example: MEPO is the Transaction for purchase-order creation.

▶ **Authorization Objects**
An authorization object groups up to 10 fields that are related by AND. Authorizations allow users to perform an operation in the SAP system. For an authorization check to be successful, all field values of the authorization object must be appropriately maintained in the user master.

▶ **Roles**
Roles are ultimately assigned to a user. Transactions and authorization objects are

not directly assigned. Instead, authorizations are combined in an authorization profile that is associated with a role.

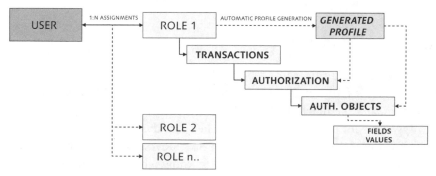

Figure 11.1 Security Hierarchy in SAP

Prior to SAP R/3 Release 4.0, companies had to go through the painstaking efforts of building user profiles and creating individual transactions with required authorizations, involving field- and value-level checks. SAP has since provided many standard roles for different functional areas, such as the SAP_MM_PUR_PURCHASEORDER role, available for users who need to create purchase orders (POs).

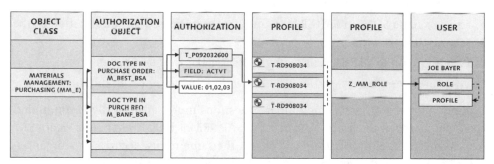

Figure 11.2 Authorization in SAP (for Colors, View Legend in SAP)

The best practice for creating specific user roles is to copy the standard delivered SAP roles into Z roles in the customer namespaces and then modify the transactions and authorizations to conform to the organization's needs and requirements.

However, most organizations still seem to disregard the delivered roles and start off their security project by building these roles from scratch. This can be a long and tedious process, although it ensures the highest form of security development because it is based precisely on the organization's requirements and needs.

Now that we've covered the security concept as it relates to SAP, let's move on to specifically discuss security in SAP SRM and some similarities and differences between security in SAP ERP and SAP SRM.

11.2 Security in SAP SRM

On most projects, the security teams seem to be aware of the security processes, setup, and best practices from an SAP ERP perspective, but SAP SRM is usually a new solution for them, and the functionality within SAP SRM is varied enough to create a steep learning curve for many security teams. The core advice for project managers is to involve and educate the security team on the SAP SRM solution, beginning with the blueprint phase. Security professionals need to know what questions to ask and what issues to worry about from a security perspective. If these professionals are not offered adequate training, security will lapse.

11.2.1 Common Questions About SRM Implementations

It is natural for questions to arise during SAP SRM implementations. Some include:

▶ Is SAP SRM another component or functionality in SAP ERP?

▶ Are there roles in SAP SRM as in SAP ERP?

▶ Can I execute SU53 in SAP SRM to provide the authorization information to the security team?

▶ When I log in to SAP SRM using my SAP User ID, why do I get an error?

▶ What are these BSP transactions, and how do I include them in the role?

It might help you answer some of these questions more satisfactorily if you understand some important issues. To start with, SAP SRM is built leveraging the core SAP NetWeaver technology platform and shares the same robust security that organizations have used in the enterprise SAP ERP application for years.

The first thing that security professionals and organizations who have been working on the core SAP ERP solution need to understand is that SAP SRM is an independent application offered by SAP. It is an entirely separate system, installed on its own box, with its own database, and with an independent architecture and landscape.

Organizations need to manage security within the SRM environment and its components independent of the security in the SAP ERP environment. The SAP ERP 2005 version is an exception to this rule, because SAP SRM can be installed within the SAP ERP system as an add-on component. Figure 11.3 illustrates this by using a simple diagram showing that SAP has many different applications and that application security is required in each system.

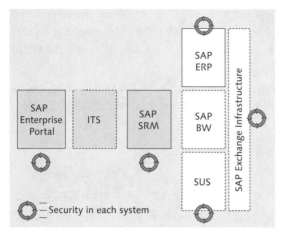

Figure 11.3 Security Requirements in SAP Solutions

11.2.2 Similarities Between SAP ERP Enterprise and SAP SRM

It is important for security professionals to realize that, although SAP SRM is a separate application from SAP ERP, it offers many similarities to SAP ERP. It is not a stretch to say that the security-development environment in both the applications is pretty much the same. Therefore, let's get the basic similarities out of the way:

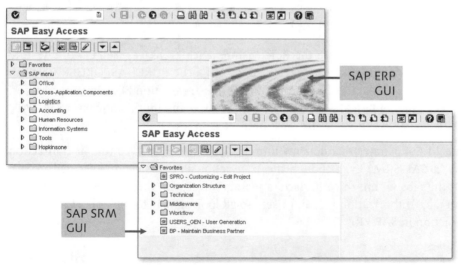

Figure 11.4 GUI in SAP ERP Enterprise vs. GUI in SAP SRM

▶ The configuration and setup GUI for SAP SRM looks just like the core SAP ERP GUI (called the SAP GUI), as illustrated in Figure 11.4. The distinction here is between what a configuration expert does vs. what an end user does. The end users working with SAP SRM use the web browser (Microsoft® Internet Explorer®, Mozilla® Firefox®, etc.) as their user interfaces to create transactions like shopping carts and POs in SAP SRM.

▶ The Role Maintenance transaction in SAP ERP and SAP SRM is the same and is accessed via Transaction PFCG, as illustrated in Figures 11.5 and 11.6.

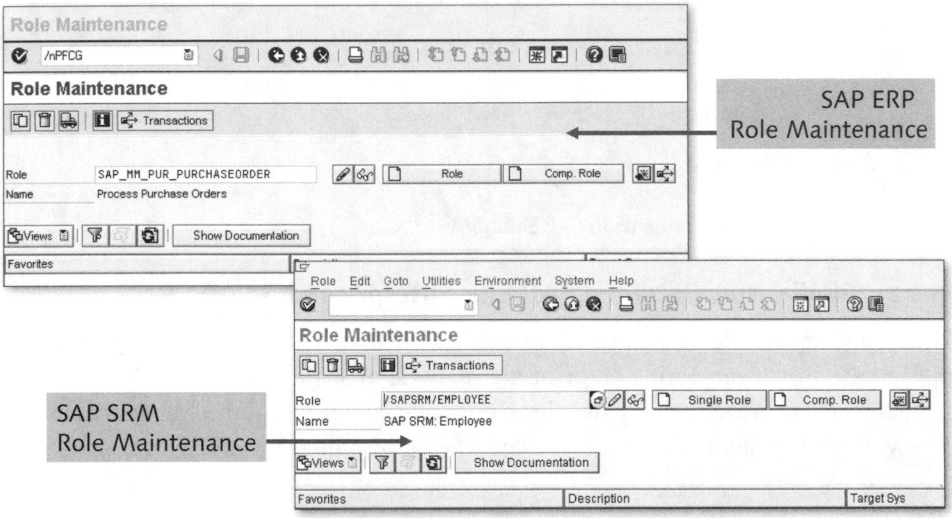

Figure 11.5   Role Maintenance in SAP ERP Enterprise and in SAP SRM

In Figure 11.5, we illustrate the Role Maintenance Transaction PFCG in SAP ERP Enterprise. Using this transaction, the SAP_MM_PUR_PURCHASEORDER Role can be maintained in SAP ERP. In SAP SRM, the same Transaction PFCG maintains roles. As an example, in SAP SRM, a security expert can maintain the purchaser role SAP_EC_BBP_PURCHASER using the same process as in SAP ERP.

Figure 11.6 illustrates that detail within the SAP SRM employee role in Transaction PFCG in SAP SRM. Even though the Transaction PFCG is being executed in SAP SRM, the tabs within this interface to maintain roles are the same as SAP ERP. The Menu tab, Authorization tab, and User tab all look similar to the Role Maintenance Transaction in SAP ERP.

> **Note**
>
> In SAP SRM 7.0, there are no longer any menu transactions with the roles provided by SAP. Therefore, in Figure 11.6, the Menu tab in the /SAPSRM/EMPLOYEE role does not contain any information. This role in SAP SRM only contains the actual authorizations. The menu of what an end user sees is entirely driven by the SAP NetWeaver Portal roles for SAP SRM.

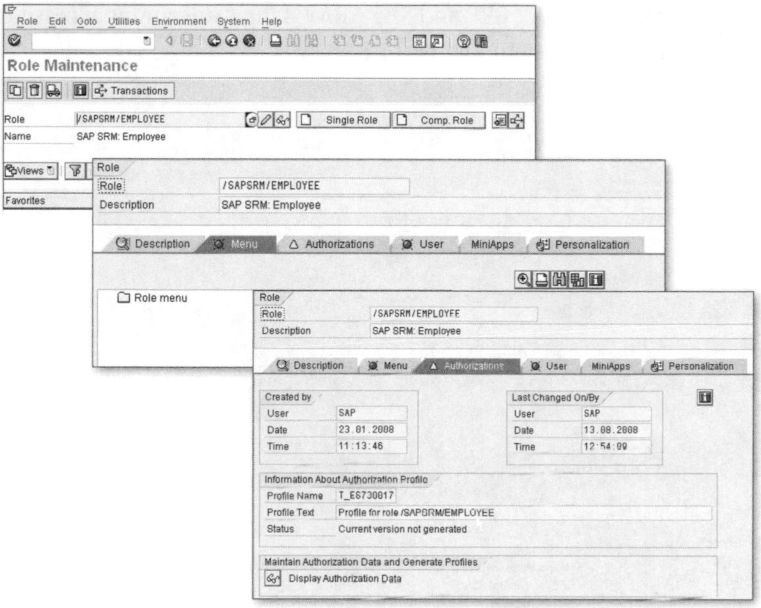

Figure 11.6 Detail of Maintenance of a Role in SAP SRM

▶ The User Management Maintenance Transaction in SAP ERP and SAP SRM is the same and is accessed via Transaction SU01, as illustrated in Figure 11.7. Notice that the Display User transaction in SAP ERP and SAP SRM look exactly the same. However, unlike SAP ERP, the Transaction SU01 alone does not create a complete SAP SRM user (this will be discussed in the next section).

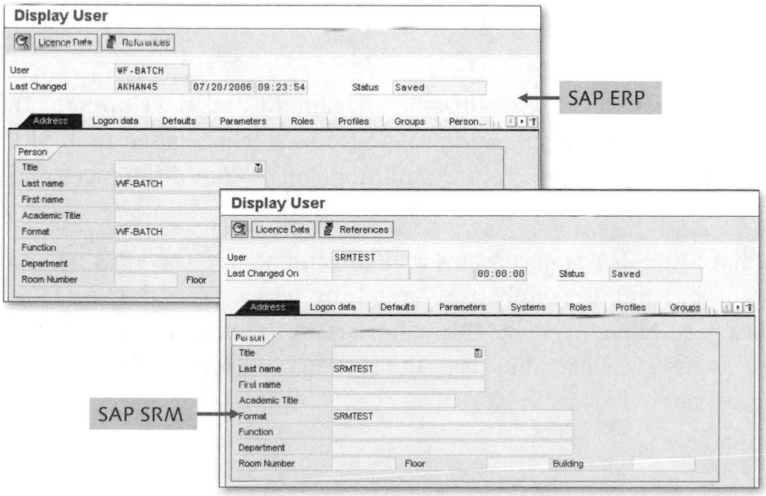

Figure 11.7 User Creation SU01 in SAP ERP and SAP SRM

► The User Information System in SAP ERP and SAP SRM is the same and is accessed via Transaction SUIM, as illustrated in Figure 11.8.

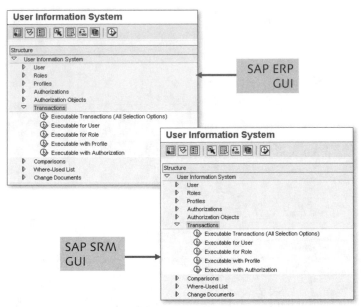

Figure 11.8 User Information System in SAP ERP and SAP SRM

11.2.3 Security Related Differences in SAP ERP vs. SAP SRM

The obvious question after reading the previous section is: What is the real difference in *security* between what's in SAP ERP vs. SAP SRM? All of the key transactions we reviewed in the section above are the same and are accessed the same way. Where is the learning curve?

Although, the core environment for security management and development in SAP SRM is similar to what consultants and project teams might be used to in SAP R/3 Enterprise or earlier releases, there are a number of unique differences and requirements.

The first thing is that SAP SRM project teams and consultants use the SRM GUI to configure the system, but end users only use a web browser to access the SAP SRM application, as illustrated in Figure 11.9. This is important to understand. Once the SAP SRM system is configured, all end users of the system can execute all their functions within the browser.

User access in SAP SRM provides each user with a list of the only transactions available for him to execute. Unlike SAP ERP, in SAP SRM, end users do not enter transaction codes to execute business functions.

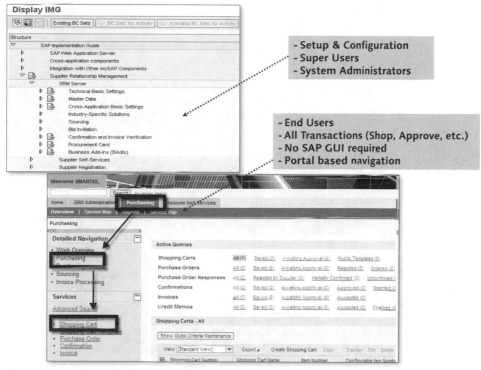

Figure 11.9 End Users Access SAP SRM via a Web Browser

To understand the security within SAP SRM, there are two main points to clarify.

First, let's discuss the user-creation process in SAP SRM. Unlike SAP ERP, where users can be created by using Transaction SU01, SAP SRM has just one step in its user-creation process. In SAP SRM, there is key user information that can only be stored as attributes in the organizational model.

Therefore, the user must be integrated in the organizational model. Figure 11.10 illustrates what a valid SAP SRM user looks like. As illustrated in the figure, the required relationship for users in SAP SRM is a Position, Business Partner, and User ID relationship. We will discuss the user creation concept in SAP SRM in more detail in Section 11.3, User Creation in SAP SRM for SAP EB (Internal).

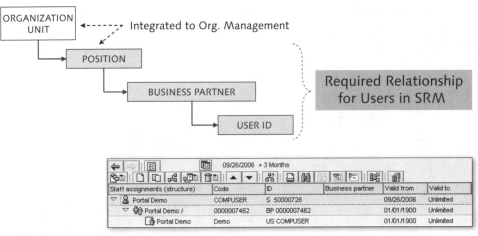

Figure 11.10 Valid Relationships for Users in SRM (SAP Enterprise Buyer [EB])

The second key to understanding security in SAP SRM is that the assignment of roles to user IDs in SAP SRM does not enable a user to perform functions such as creating shopping carts, creating POs, and others. For this, the user also must be a part of the Organizational Structure in SAP SRM. Each user is assigned a position, and each position is attached to an Organizational Unit, as illustrated in Figure 11.10.

The SAP SRM application only supports 1:1 assignments between users and their positions. When users are deleted objects, Position, Business Partner, and User are managed as a common SAP EB user object. Positions and Organizational Units are objects of the Organizational Structure in SAP SRM and are set up by the organization's management team.

Therefore, the two key points from our brief discussion above are:

▶ Users in SAP SRM cannot be created just by using Transaction SU01. Further processing is required.

▶ Users in SAP SRM need to be integrated into the Organizational Structure or they will not be able to perform their functions in SAP SRM.

However, there is a distinction between users who configure the SAP SRM system and end users who use the SAP system. The concept above does not necessarily pertain to user IDs required to configure the system.

Because of the nature of the SAP SRM application, there is a need for both internal and external users. Internal users are typically employees of the organization who work within the system firewall. External users are partners of the organization engaging in business with the organization, such as vendors and bidders. SAP SRM contains functionality within supplier self-services (SUS), Bidding Engine, and the Live Auction applications that might require your security teams to create external users. In the next section, we'll discuss the process of creating both internal and external users in SAP SRM.

11.3   User Creation in SAP SRM for SAP EB (Internal)

Users in SRM can be created in many ways. One of the prerequisites for mass user creation in SAP SRM is to have at least a basic Organizational Structure. Figure 11.11 illustrates a simple process flow.

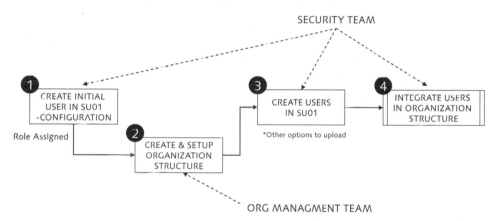

Figure 11.11   Simple Process Flow for User-Creation Requirement

In the flow seen in Figure 11.11, the security team in Step ❶ creates a configuration user in SAP SRM using the standard Transaction SU01. Let's assume that a configuration role has been assigned to this user, which allows him to create a simple Organizational Structure within the SAP SRM system in Step ❷. Users created in this manner are only used for configuration or user administration but cannot be used for creation or approval of shopping carts. In Step ❸, the security team can create users in SAP SRM using Transaction SU01 for user management and then in Step ❹ integrate the users in the Organizational Structure created.

In Step ❹, there are multiple ways to integrate users in the Organizational Structure. This aspect depends on which of the following options the organization uses:

▸ Using SAP SRM as a standalone system

▸ Using the HR Integration scenario

▸ Using Central User Administration (CUA) within SAP SRM

▸ Depending on the options above, the plan to create users can be different.

11.3.1 Using SAP SRM as a Standalone System

Do not confuse this option as the Standalone implementation scenario in SAP EB. The standalone system means that all the security is maintained only within the SAP SRM system. In SAP SRM, users are created via three main methods:

▶ Via the user self-service function in the web browser
▶ Via the Manage User Data administrator function in the Web
▶ Via Transaction USERS_GEN

Creating New Users via the Web Self-Registration Service

Let's review how to create new users via the Web self-registration service.

Users access the SAP SRM system via a URL in a Web browser. On the initial logon page, a user can either log in using his assigned user ID and password or can request for a new user ID by choosing the Request User ID link, as illustrated in Figure 11.12. This option is only available if organizations want to make the user creation process self-service. Users are required to enter a User ID, First name, Last name, E-mail address, and Approver. In addition, a user is also required to enter his manager's or supervisor's information. Once these required fields are entered, an approval email is sent to the user's manager for approval.

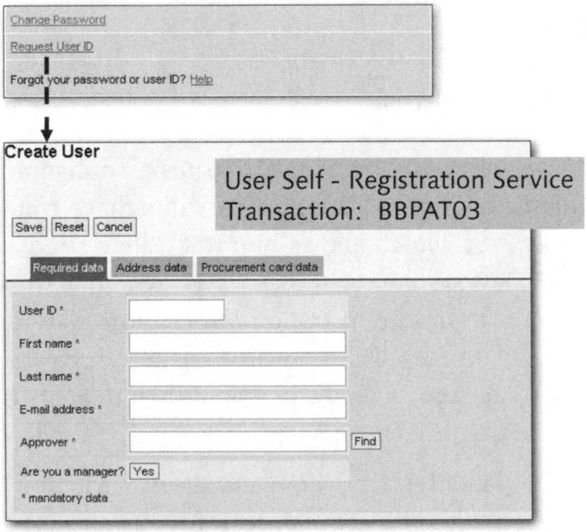

Figure 11.12 User Self-Registration Service — Transaction BBPUM02

A standard approval template is delivered for a manager's approval when new users are created. Organizations can choose to activate or deactivate this workflow. See Chapter 10 for details on workflow.

There are obvious issues that an organization can face if it chooses this method of creating users. Standardization is a big issue, and data integrity is another. Moreover, security teams dislike this option because most organizations have an existing user creation process and SAP seems like just another application that needs to be included within the existing security processes.

Creating New Users via the Manage User Data Web Service

The Manage User Data service is a Web-based transaction, which for all practical purposes, should only be executed in a Web browser. To get access to this service, the Role SAP_EC_BBP_ADMINISTRATOR has to be assigned to the user. Figure 11.13 illustrates this transaction. When a user is created using BBPUSERMAINT, a corresponding position, business partner, and user master record are created in SAP SRM. Therefore, the objects S, BP, and US are created, which completes the requirement for a user in SAP SRM, as shown in Figure 11.10. An Organizational Unit is required when creating users via this transaction. This unit will typically be provided by the functional team requesting the user creation, which then completes Step ❹ shown in Figure 11.11.

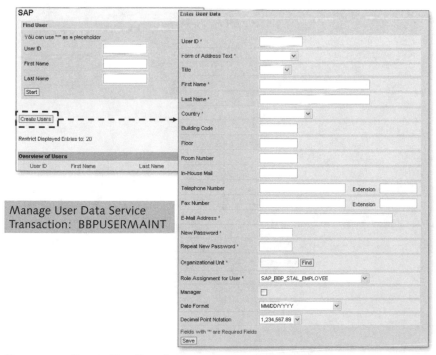

Figure 11.13 Manage User Data Service — Transaction BBPUM01

When creating the user initially, only one role can be assigned. Once the user record is created, then the user ID needs to be changed either in the Web or in Transaction SU01 to assign additional roles.

Most organizations shy away from the BBPUSERMAINT Web transaction, because it becomes a tedious function that only allows the creation of one user at a time. They use this transaction more for deletions (which is explained later), and end up using Transaction USERS_GEN because it allows more flexibility and the ability to create multiple users at one time.

> **Note**
>
> SAP SRM transactions for user administration have changed in release SAP SRM 5.0 onward. Transaction BBPUSERMAINT is now accessed via Transaction BBPUM01, and Transaction BBPAT05 is accessed using Transaction BBPUM02.

Creating New Users via Transaction USERS_GEN

Since SAP SRM 2.0 release, SAP has provided a standard transaction that allows creation of individual and mass users in SAP SRM. Transaction USERS_GEN is executed in the SAP GUI instead of the web browser. Figure 11.14 illustrates this transaction.

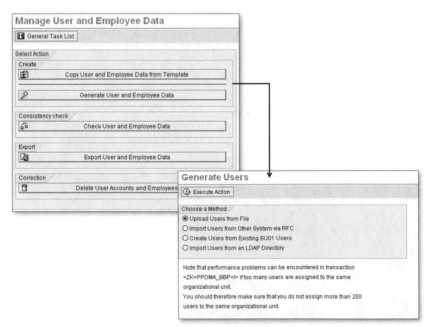

Figure 11.14 Generate Users Transaction (USERS_GEN)

This transaction is used for the initial creation of SAP SRM users, but once the users are created, they can be maintained in Transaction SU01 or the Manage User Data service in the portal.

In the Generate Users Transaction (USERS_GEN) illustrated in Figure 11.14, security administrators can Choose a Method to generate users. The various methods available are listed next and then explained in greater detail:

▶ Upload Users from File and Download Users to a File

▶ Import Users from Other System via Remote Function Call (RFC)

▶ Create Users from Existing SU01 Users

▶ Import Users from a Lightweight Directory Access Protocol (LDAP Directory)

Upload Users from File and Download Users to a File (ASCII)

Organizations can use the Upload Users from File method to create users from a flat file (ASCII) that contains details about the users, including the User ID, Last Name, Organizational Unit, and E-Mail Address as illustrated in Figure 11.15.

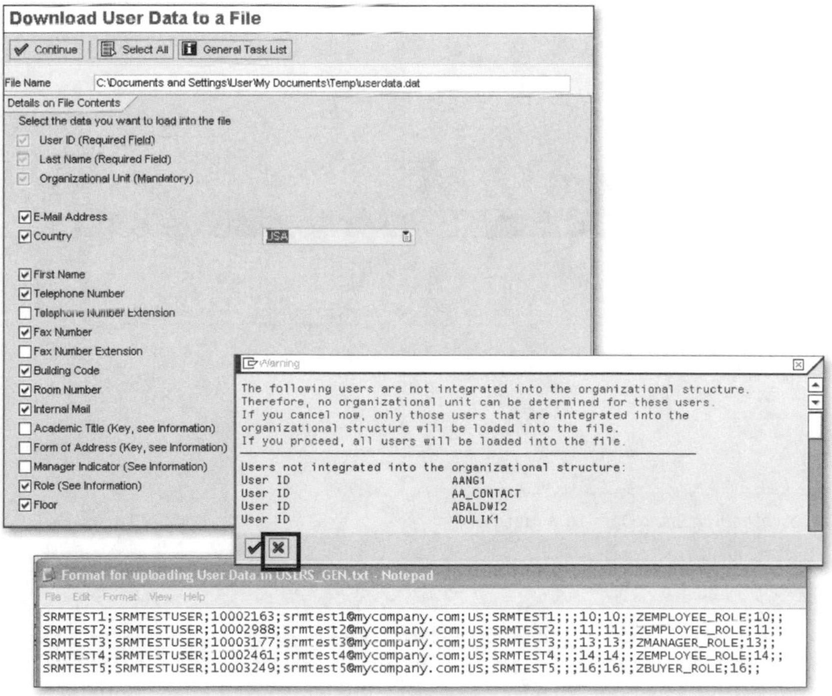

Figure 11.15 Uploading User Data via a Flat File

The data fields in the upload file should contain a separate row for each user record and the fields separated via a semicolon. The order of the data fields in the file have to be in the order specified in the Details on File Contents section as illustrated in Figure 11.15.

Security administrators can select the Download Users to a File method to create a download of the file, because it then provides the appropriate format for an Upload file that can then be used as an input file for the Upload Users from File method. Figure 11.16 illustrates an example of how a file can be generated using the Download User Data to a File method.

This method allows selecting the data fields that you want to download into the file. In our example in Figure 11.16, if users are not integrated into the organizational structure, a Warning is displayed, indicating that certain users are not integrated in the Organizational Structure and whether those users should be included in the downloaded file.

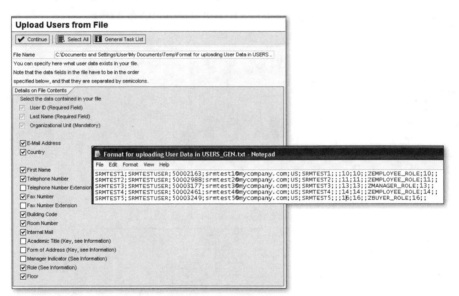

Figure 11.16 Downloading User Data to a Flat File

> **Note**
>
> The Organizational Unit is required for each user record. This information needs to be provided by the SAP SRM functional team creating the Organizational Structure. This is an iterative process because the Organizational Structure within SAP SRM continues to change as additional data is gathered by the organization. Organizational Units could be added and deleted. Therefore, this upload file would change over time.

In the standard system, if the user record contains an email address, the system creates a password and sends it to the user's email address.

Import Users from Other Systems via RFC

It is possible to create users in SAP SRM by importing user information from another SAP ERP system via RFC as shown in Figure 11.17. Assuming that the appropriate RFC destinations were already created in Transaction SM59, the users can be uploaded from the corresponding system.

If the user record in the standard system contains an email address, the system creates a password and sends it to the user's email address. Some security administrators like this functionality because the users are automatically notified and the security team can expend less effort reaching out to users. Many security administrators are wary of this functionality, however, because they do not want passwords sent via email, especially if incorrect email addresses are captured in the system.

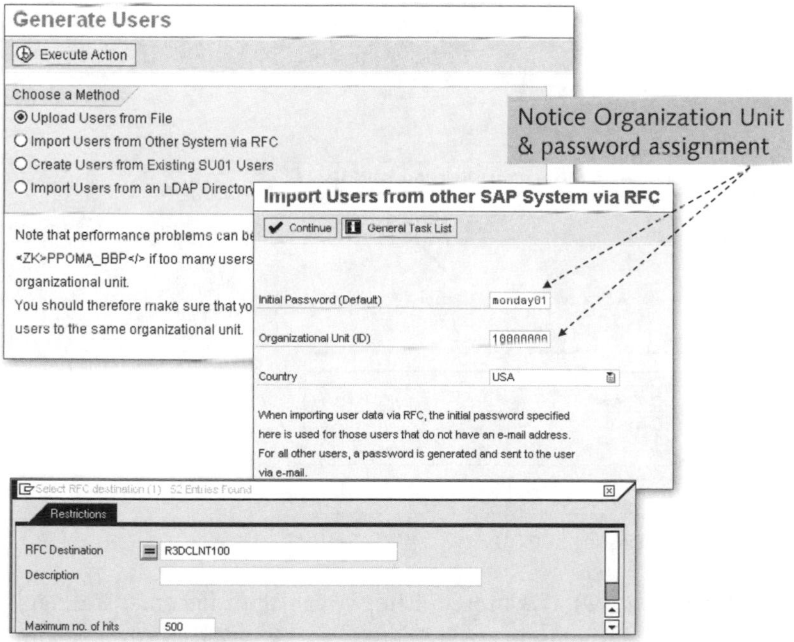

Figure 11.17 Importing Users from Another SAP System via RFC

Enter a default Initial Password and Organizational Unit (O) as a prerequisite, which then becomes a default Organizational Unit where all the users are created. Once the user creation is complete, a record from Position (S) to Business Partner (BP) to

User (US) is created, which can then be moved within the Organizational Structure. This can be a tedious process depending on how large the Organizational Structure is for the organization.

A subsequent step is required after this function to assign any additional roles to the users. The standard transaction assigns the BBP*EMPLOYEE role to the user records as a default. Thus, role assignment can be done via Transaction PFCG.

Create Users from Existing SU01 Users

Using this method, organizations can convert existing SU01 users into SAP SRM users. This is especially useful if the user record is already created in SAP SRM or possibly created using the CUA application. In Figure 11.18, we illustrate how users created in SU01 can then be integrated within the Organizational Structure.

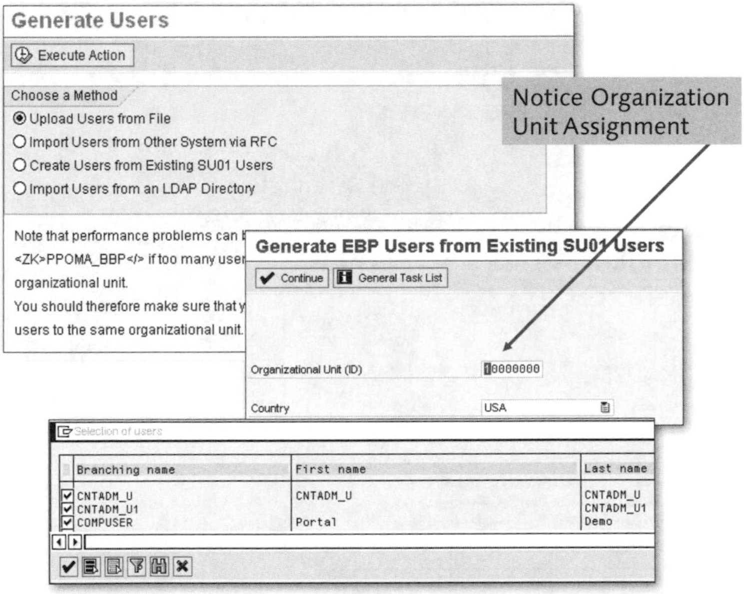

Figure 11.18 Create Users from Existing SU01 Users

Enter an Organizational Unit (O) as a prerequisite, which then becomes a default Organizational Unit where all the users are created. Once the user creation is complete, a Position-Business Partner-User relationship is created, which can then be moved within the Organizational Structure. This can be a tedious process depending on how large the Organizational Structure is for the organization.

Import EBP Users from an LDAP Directory

In this method, LDAP users are imported into SAP SRM to create Transaction SU01 records. A secondary step assigns the individual Organizational Units to the users to integrate in the Organizational Structure. The second step is similar to the method Create Users from Existing SU01 Users.

Most large organizations use a corporate LDAP Directory to maintain all the users in the organization and their appropriate authorizations. Using the Import EBP Users from an LDAP Directory method, an organization can quickly create users in SAP SRM from an existing data source.

Create New Users with Sequential Number

Create New Users with Sequential Number is useful when mass-creating a number of users for testing purposes. Uses include performance or stress testing, when you need a thousand users created in the system. This method allows creation of users quickly by providing a basic convention and having the program create sequential users in SAP EB. For example, if you wanted to create 1,000 users beginning with the name as SRM, of eight-characters in length, you would need to enter the following using this method:

- Leading Initial: SRM
- Number part: 1 to 1,000
- Length: 8

This would result in the creation of 1,000 user records such as SRM00001, SRM00002, and so on sequentially to SRM01000.

11.3.2 Using SAP ERP HCM Integration Scenario

Many organizations are planning to use the SAP best practice of integrating the Organizational Structure between SAP ERP HCM and SAP SRM. In the last section, we described the scenario where the Organizational Structure was maintained independently in SAP SRM with no integration with the Organizational Structure. In this section, we'll cover the scenario where the Organizational Structure is maintained in SAP ERP and periodically distributed to SAP SRM.

What impact does this have on security? When distributing the Organizational Structure from SAP ERP, an organization has the option of distributing the Organizational Unit, Positions, and also the employees, as illustrated in Figure 11.19.

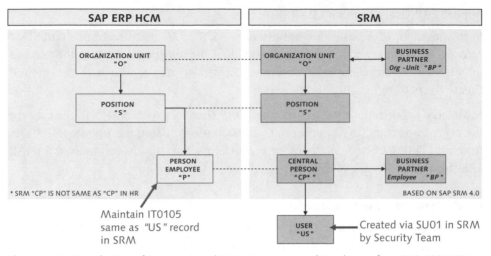

Figure 11.19 Distribution of Organizational Units, Positions, and Employees from SAP ERP HCM into SAP SRM

The HR integration scenario follows SAP best practices, because it reduces maintenance across a multitude of functions. The Organizational Structure is only being maintained primarily in SAP ERP, and dual maintenance is reduced in SAP SRM. HR is usually the system with data of record for the organization. From a security perspective, this scenario reduces the maintenance of user records dramatically. When HR integration occurs, the only prerequisite for security teams is to create the standard user record in SAP SRM prior to the distribution of the employees from the HR system.

Figure 11.19 illustrates that the User record Object US needs to be created in SAP SRM. One additional important point is that the Info Record IT0105 for the employee Object P in SAP ERP HCM has to be exactly the same as the User ID in SAP SRM. Once the value in IT0105 in HR matches the User ID in SAP SRM, a business partner record is created. The process of distributing the Organizational Structure was discussed in detail in Chapter 8.

If the organization is planning to use position-based security, then security roles can be assigned directly to the Position in SAP ERP. Using the distribution model, the roles can be transferred to SAP SRM along with the Organizational Unit, position, and employee. This further reduces the maintenance effort required for the security teams. However, in this scenario, the roles have to be created in SAP SRM because the Web services transactions and corresponding authorization objects are only available in SAP SRM.

> **Note**
>
> When HR Integration is active, all employee personal data must be managed in the HR personnel management transactions, and therefore the SAP SRM Transactions BBPUSER-MAINT and USERS_GEN are deactivated. Users are only allowed to change certain fields for default assignment under the Settings section (Transaction BBPAT05 or BBPUM02 depending on SAP SRM release).

Figure 11.20 illustrates how USERS_GEN can be used in SAP SRM even if HR Integration is active. This is not a best practice. However, organizations might find the need for this option if the HR Organizational Structure does not have certain positions and users that are required in the SAP SRM Organizational Structure.

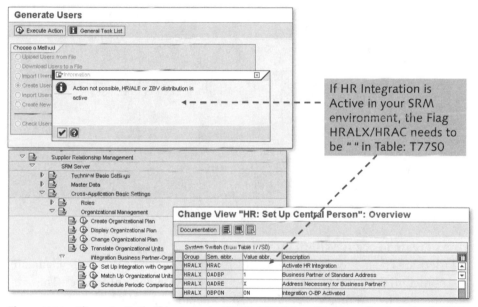

Figure 11.20 Alternate Method to Activate USERS_GEN When HR Integration is Active in SRM

11.3.3 Using CUA Within SAP SRM

CUA allows security teams to create and manage SAP users centrally within one system and distribute the user records to all the connected systems via ALE. SAP SRM can be operated together within a CUA environment, but there are certain restrictions. In this section, we'll explain how SAP SRM can be used with CUA. Central user administration in SAP SRM can be integrated in two scenarios:

▶ HR integration is active, as described in the last section

▶ Users are managed in SAP SRM using the User Management Transactions Manage Users (BBPUSERMAINT or BBPUM01), as explained in Section 11.3, User Creation in SAP SRM for SAP EB (Internal)

When HR integration is active, all employee personal data must be managed in the HR personnel management transactions, and therefore the SAP SRM transactions Manage Users and My Settings are deactivated. Figure 11.21 illustrates how CUA can be used in this scenario. Let's review these steps now:

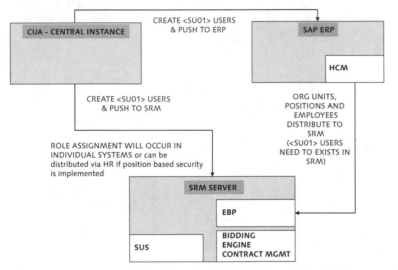

Figure 11.21 CUA in SAP SRM When SAP ERP HCM Integration is Active

1. **Users Created Locally Within CUA System**
   All users are created locally within the CUA-CENTRAL INSTANCE system and are distributed to the SAP ERP and SAP SRM SERVER system via ALE IDocs. This creates the user record object US in both SAP ERP and SAP SRM.

2. **HR Data Distribution from SAP ERP to SAP SRM**
   Once the users are distributed in the SAP SRM SERVER, the Organizational Units, Positions, and Employee data can be distributed from SAP ERP HCM into SAP SRM. This creates the required business partner (BP) to User (US) relationship record required in SAP SRM. It is important that the IT0105 Infotype in the Employee record in SAP ERP contains the user value that is exactly the same as the User ID in SAP SRM.

It isn't possible to create external users in SAP SRM within a CUA environment. SAP SRM 4.0, SUS 3.0 is currently not integrated with the CUA.

So far, we've concentrated on the creation of users in SAP SRM that are internal to the organization. Because the SAP SRM solution is tightly integrated with external business partners such as vendors and bidders, we'll discuss in the next section the process of creating users that are external to your organization.

11.4   User Creation in SRM for SAP EB (External)

SAP SRM contains business scenarios where an external business partner needs to access and perform functions within SAP SRM. Therefore, it is necessary to create user records for external business partners, for example, company data for vendors and bidders, and master data for individual contact persons from the external vendor. In SAP SRM, the following applications require external business partner access:

▶ **Bidding Engine**
Bidding Engine in SAP SRM is used for external vendors to submit competitive bids on goods and services required by the purchasing organization. A contact person is created as a bidder for each vendor that needs to receive bid invitations and create bids in SAP SRM.

▶ **Supplier self-service**
In Chapter 5, we discussed how organizations can use the SUS component in SAP SRM to drive supplier enablement. Using SUS, business partners external to your organization can collaborate in the procurement cycle to streamline the procure-to-pay process.
In SAP SRM, there are two ways external business partners can gain access:

▶ **Self-Registration**
Master data for external business partners (such as bidders and vendors) can be created based on a registration application from an employee of the business-partner company. Once the user completes the self-registration, the purchaser or system administrator receives a work item with a link to the Manage Business Partners application. The responsible employee can see the data that the requesting user entered and can complete it. Once external users have been created or maintained, contact persons receive emails containing their User IDs and passwords.

▶ **User Creation via SAP SRM**
User Creation via SAP SRM is accomplished by using the administrator service Manage Business Partners (BBPMAININT). In SAP SRM, a separate transaction, Manage Business Partner Transaction BBPMAININT, creates bidders, as illustrated in Figure 11.22.

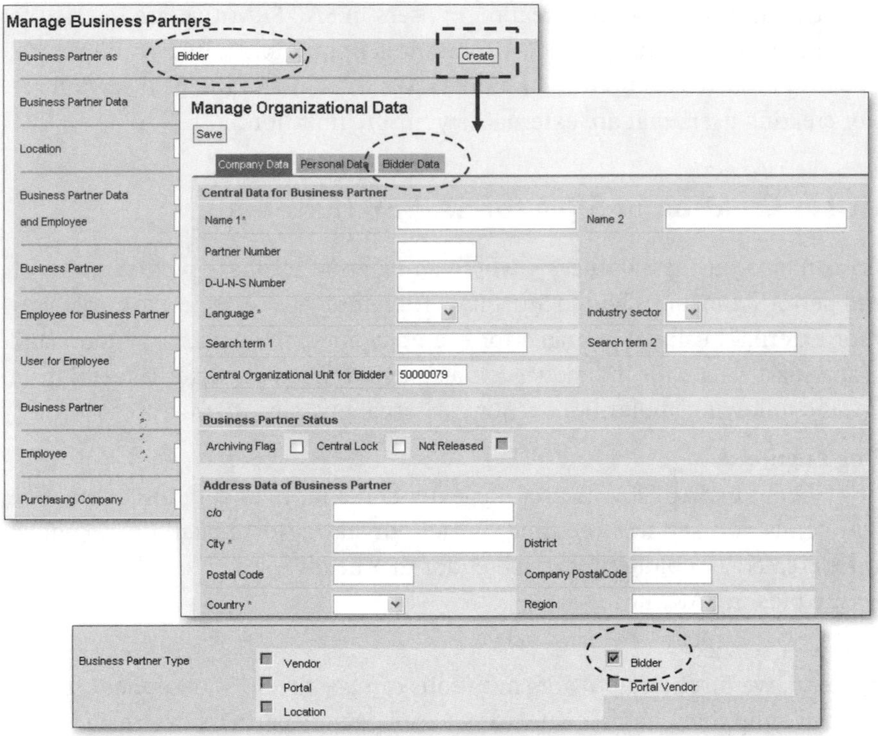

Figure 11.22 Manage Business Partners in SAP SRM — Transaction BBPMAININT

Once bidders and/or contact persons are created in SAP SRM, editing their user data is also done via the BBPMAININT transaction. To maintain the bidders in the BBPMAININT transaction, Business Partner and Employee numbers are required, as illustrated in Figure 11.23.

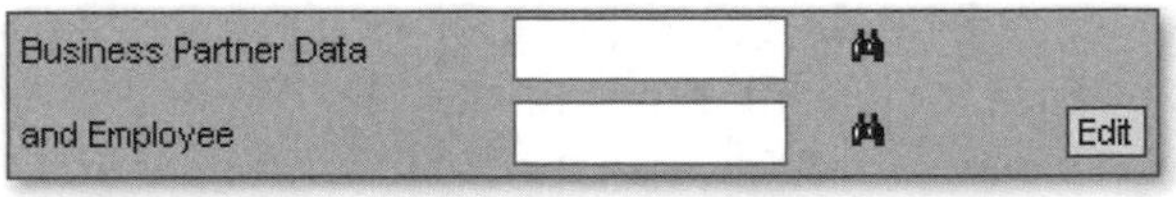

Figure 11.23 Edit Business Partners (Bidders) using BBPMAININT

> **Note**
>
> Both Bidding Engine and SUS require the vendor contact persons to gain access to these applications hosted inside of your organization firewall. Additional security might be required to enable SAP Enterprise Portal to provide access or require SSL certificates for authentication. Most organizations today implement the Bidding Engine and SUS applications via the SAP Enterprise Portal.

In this section, we discussed the process of creating users within SAP SRM. Equally important is the discussion on how to delete users in SAP SRM, which is the subject of the next section.

11.5 Deleting Users in SAP SRM

You sometimes need to delete users in the SAP SRM system. A user could have been created incorrectly, for example, or test users might need to be removed from the system. As we discussed earlier, a complete user in SAP SRM is a combination of the objects Position (S), Business Partner (BP), and User (US). When security administrators use the User Management Transaction SU01 to delete a user, the only object that is deleted is the US object. The remaining objects S and BP are incorrectly left undeleted. Therefore, deletion of users in SAP SRM using the Transaction SU01 is not correct.

Deletion of users in SAP SRM should only be carried out using the administration service Manage User Data (Transaction BBPUSERMAINT). When you do this, all the relationships for the US object are deleted, as well as the BP and US objects. Figure 11.24 illustrates the Manage User Data application (BBPUSERMAINT), which also allows you to delete users in SAP SRM.

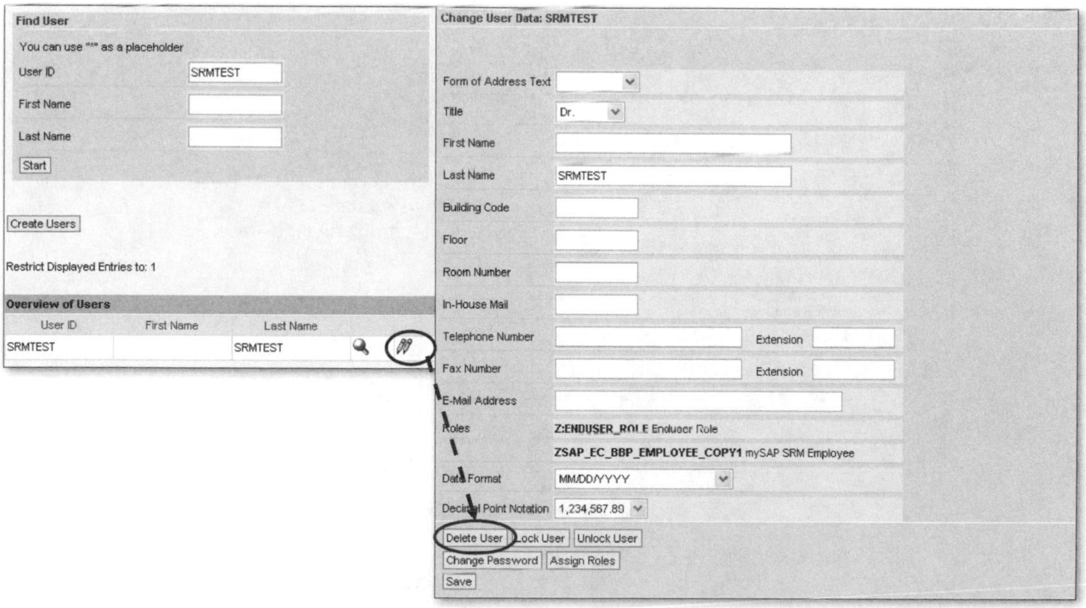

Figure 11.24 Deleting Users via Manage User Data — Transaction BBPUSERMAINT

In the example illustrated in Figure 11.24, the SRMTEST User ID can be deleted by clicking the change button (pencils) in the Overview of Users and then clicking on the Delete User button in the Change User Data section.

> **Tip**
>
> SAP recommends that users in SAP SRM be deleted using the transaction illustrated in Figure 11.24.

As users in SAP SRM need to be integrated into the Organizational Structures, it's often necessary to check users to ensure their consistency. In the next section, we discuss the process of checking users in SAP SRM.

11.6   Checking Users in SAP SRM

SAP delivers a standard transaction, USERS_GEN, to check the consistency of users in SAP SRM. This same transaction also makes it possible to repair any defective users. Figure 11.25 illustrates how the user check can be conducted. Once the Check Users radio button is selected, the Execute Action button begins the process of checking users. In the subsequent Check and Repair SAP EB Users screen, we can either Check Individual Users or Check Multiple Users as illustrated in Figure 11.25.

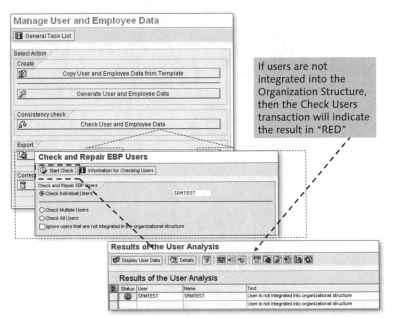

Figure 11.25   Check Users in Transaction USERS_GEN

In the example illustrated in Figure 11.25, we check an individual user, SRMTEST. The result of the user analysis is that the user SRMTEST is not integrated within the Organizational Structure and therefore is not consistent. This user needs to be repaired prior to executing any SAP SRM transactions for shopping cart, approvals, and others. However, this user cannot be repaired unless integrated into the Organizational Structure.

Figure 11.26 illustrates the scenario where the same user, SRMTEST, has been integrated into the Organizational Structure via the Transaction USERS_GEN option to create users from existing SU01 users. When the check user's function is executed again, the user analysis shows that the SRMTEST user is now consistent. If the users are displayed with green Traffic Light icons in the list of results, then this indicates consistency. The Organizational Unit where the user is being integrated is also needs to be consistent. This can be checked in Transaction CRM_OM_BP_INTEGRATE. Only when the Traffic Light icon for the entire Organizational Unit is green is the Organizational Unit consistent.

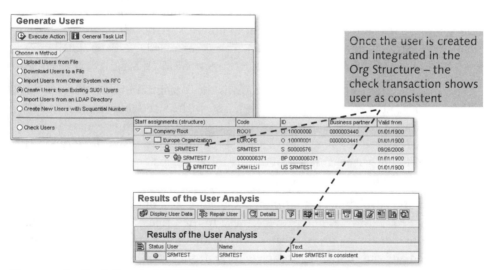

Figure 11.26 Check Users in SAP SRM — Example of a Consistent User

The Check Users function should be executed on a periodic basis in the SAP SRM environment. When users are found to be inconsistent, this transaction also provides a mechanism to repair the users.

> **Tip**
>
> If you have HR/ALE distribution active, users cannot be repaired in SAP SRM using the USERS_GEN transaction. To repair the user data, you must redistribute using HR/ALE replication.

In the next section, we will discuss roles and authorizations within SAP SRM and the best practices organizations can use to manage this security.

11.7   Roles and Authorizations in SAP SRM

SAP SRM comes delivered with a large number of predefined role templates that organizations can use directly or customize for their organization's requirements. Each user in the SAP SRM system is assigned one or more roles that provide authorization to execute specific transactions.

When talking about roles and authorizations, it's important to understand that along with a role assignment, users in SAP SRM are also required to be integrated in the Organizational Structure. This allows them to inherit specific attributes that further enhance or restrict their access in SAP SRM. This is discussed in greater detail in Section 11.8, Impact of Organizational Structure in SAP SRM on Security.

SAP best practice for using roles in SAP SRM is that organizations use the standard delivered roles and create customer specific Z roles. The standard roles are predelivered with appropriate menus that can be used right away. Security teams can verify whether the delivered roles meet the business requirements. If not, they can create roles tailored to the particular needs of the organization, assign transactions to them, and generate an authorization profile.

For sandbox and development environments, the quickest option is to create Z roles for standard SAP SRM roles and provide these to the project team. Once the standard system is functional, project teams can decide on which transactions need to be eliminated and can choose to just delete those from the user menu or go through a detailed authorization check activity.

End users in SAP SRM access SAP SRM using a standard web browser to access the portal, so they are not executing the transactions directly. Rather, they use the services available in their user menu in the Web and execute only those services (more information regarding this further in this section). The key lesson here is that users cannot execute the Transaction SU53 in the Web, which is widely used in SAP ERP to get details on the authorizations missing for an end user. Security administrators therefore need to use other tools to get information on missing user authorizations.

Figure 11.27 Example of a User Menu in SAP SRM

> **Note**
>
> In SAP SRM 7.0, there are no longer any menu transactions with the roles provided by SAP in the SAP SRM system. The SAP SRM system roles contain the necessary authorizations for an end user, and the SAP NetWeaver Portal role drives the visibility of transactions of a user and his navigation. For example, the SAP NetWeaver Portal will determine that an end user can see the "Shopping Cart" application once they log on to the portal. However, whether the user can actually shop for a particular plant, purchasing organization, and others will be controlled via the SAP SRM role authorizations along with the organization structure in SAP SRM. Figure 11.28 provides an illustration for authorizations within an SAP SRM Employee role. This is the SAP SRM role, not the portal role. Figure 11.31 illustrates a subset of the roles in SAP SRM and corresponding role in the SAP NetWeaver Portal.

SAP provides a standard list of roles that are predelivered with the SAP SRM application. These are available to customers once the SAP SRM system is installed. Table 11.1 provides a list of standard roles delivered in SAP SRM release 5.0 and SAP SRM 7.0. This includes the most-used roles on SAP SRM project implementations. In addition, there are other roles in SAP SRM. These roles are used in conjunction with the SAP NetWeaver Portal roles that provide the end user navigation and role menu illustrated in Figure 11.27.

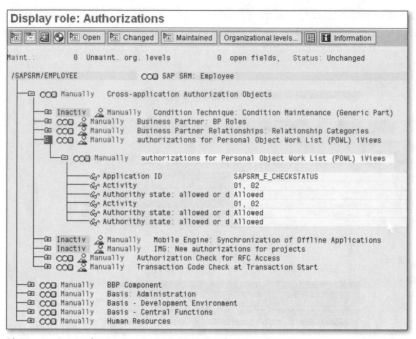

Figure 11.28 Authorization in SAP SRM Employee Role

Role Name in SAP SRM 7.0	Role Name in SAP SRM 5.0	Role Description
/SAPSRM/EMPLOYEE	SAP_BBP_STAL_EMPLOYEE	SAP SRM Employee
/SAPSRM/MANAGER	SAP_BBP_STAL_MANAGER	SAP SRM Manager
	SAP_BBP_STAL_PURCHASER	SAP SRM Professional Purchaser
/SAPSRM/BIDDER	SAP_BBP_STAL_BIDDER	SAP SRM Bidder
/SAPSRM/SUPPLIER	SAP_BBP_STAL_VENDOR	SAP SRM Vendor
/SAPSRM/RECIPIENT	SAP_BBP_STAL_RECIPIENT	SAP SRM Goods Recipient
SAPSRM/ADMINISTRATOR	SAP_BBP_STAL_ADMINISTRATOR	SAP SRM Administrator
/SAPSRM/SECRETARY	SAP_BBP_STAL_SECRETARY	SAP SRM Purchasing Assistant
/SAPSRM/ACCOUNTANT	SAP_BBP_STAL_ACCOUNTANT	SAP SRM Accountant
/SAPSRM/OP_PURCHASER	SAP_BBP_STAL_OPERAT_PURCHASER	SAP SRM Operational Purchaser
/SAPSRM/ST_PURCHASER	SAP_BBP_STAL_STRAT_PURCHASER	SAP SRM Strategic Purchaser
/SAPSRM/PLANNER	SAP_BBP_STAL_PLANNER	SAP SRM Component Planner

Table 11.1 List of Standard Roles in SAP SRM 7.0 and 5.0

This list of standard roles can be found in the Role Maintenance transaction, Transaction PFCG. For all SAP SRM roles, search for /SAPSRM/* as illustrated in Figure 11.29.

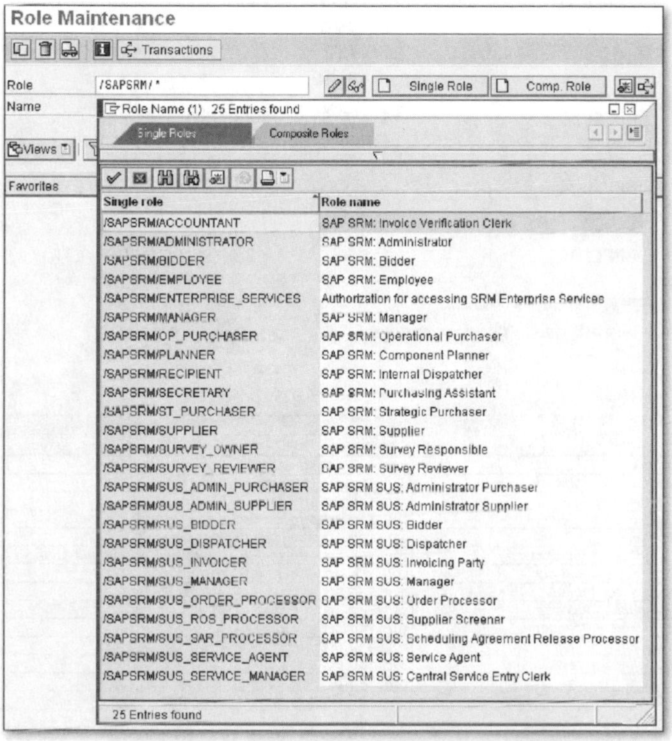

Figure 11.29 List of Standard Delivered Roles in SAP SRM

The Application Security Guide for SAP SRM contains detailed information on the standard roles in SAP SRM and the corresponding transactions and authorization objects within the roles. This information is useful for all project teams, because it is one of the first tasks conducted to gather security requirements on the project. Figure 11.30 illustrates the level of detail provided in the Application Security Guide, available for download from the SAP Service Marketplace.

If organizations decide to create their own roles, the best practice is to always use the standard delivered roles (/SAPSRM/*), which contain the authorizations. Copying the delivered role maintains the synchronization in the menus built for SAP SRM roles; otherwise, users will get the same menu entry multiple times in the browser. Figure 11.27 illustrates the standard menu for the Employee role in the SAP NetWeaver Portal.

Roles/Technical Names	Services (Menu Entry)	Transaction	Authorization Group	Authorization Objects	S_RFC	S_TCODE
Employee	Request	BBPSC18	AAAB	B_BUPA_RLT (02,03)	ARFC	BBP_BGRD_APPROVAL
SAP_EC_BBP_EMPLOYEE	Shop	BBPSC02		B_BUPR_BZT (ACTVT02; RELTYP BUR010)	BBP_ATTR_MAINT	BBP_CTR_DISP
SAP_BBP_STAL_EMPLOYEE	Shop (one screen)	BBPSC03		S_ME_SYNC (38)	BBP_BD_META_BAPIS	BBP_CTR_DISPNR
SAP_BBP_MULTI_EMPLOYEE	Check Status	BBPSC04		S_PRO_AUTH (03)	BBP_BS_POD	BBP_CTR_EXT_PO
	Confirm Goods/Services	BBPCF02		S_RFC	BBP_BS_RQD	BBP_CTR_WF_APP

Figure 11.30 Sample Role — SAP_BBP_STAL_EMPLOYEE and Corresponding SAP SRM Authorization Objects

SAP SRM 7.0		
PFCG	**Enterprise Portal**	
/SAPSRM/ACCOUNTANT	Invoicer	com.sap.pct.srm.core.ro_invoicer
/SAPSRM/ADMINISTRATOR	SRM Administrator	com.sap.pct.srm.core.ro_srmadministrator
/SAPSRM/BIDDER	Bidder	com.sap.pct.srm.core.ro_bidder
/SAPSRM/EMPLOYEE	Employee Self-Service	com.sap.pct.srm.core.ro_employeeselfservice
/SAPSRM/MANAGER	Manager	com.sap.pct.srm.core.ro_manager
/SAPSRM/OP_PURCHASER	Operational Purchaser	com.sap.pct.srm.core.ro_operationalpurchaser
/SAPSRM/PLANNER	Component Planner	com.sap.pct.srm.core.ro_componentplanner
/SAPSRM/RECIPIENT	Goods Recipient	com.sap.pct.srm.core.ro_goodsrecipient
/SAPSRM/SECRETARY	Purchasing Assistant	com.sap.pct.srm.core.ro_purchasingassistant
/SAPSRM/ST_PURCHASER	Strategic Purchaser	com.sap.pct.srm.core.ro_strategicpurchaser
/SAPSRM/SUPPLIER	Supplier	com.sap.pct.srm.core.ro_supplier
/SAPSRM/SURVEY_OWNER	Supplier Survey Cockpit	com.sap.pct.srm.core.ro_survey_owner
/SAPSRM/SURVEY_REVIEWER	Supplier Survey Cockpit	com.sap.pct.srm.core.ro_survey_reviewer
/SAPPSSRM/MANAGER	Manager	com.sap.pct.srm.gp.ro_manager
/SAPPSSRM/BIDDER	RFx Respondent	com.sap.pct.srm.gp.ro_bidder
/SAPPSSRM/EMPLOYEE	Employee Self-Service	com.sap.pct.srm.gp.ro_employeeselfservice
/SAPPSSRM/PROCUREMENT	Procurement	com.sap.pct.srm.gp.ro_procurement
/SAPPSSRM/REQUISITIONING	Requisitioning	com.sap.pct.srm.gp.ro_requisitioning
	Operational Purchaser (ERP)	com.sap.pct.srm.suite.ro_operationalpurchaser_erp
	Operational Purchaser (ERP/SRM)	com.sap.pct.srm.suite.ro_operationalpurchaser
	Strategic Purchaser (ERP)	com.sap.pct.srm.suite.ro_strategicpurchaser_erp
	Strategic Purchaser (ERP/SRM)	com.sap.pct.srm.suite.ro_strategicpurchaser
	Invoicer	com.sap.pct.srm.onecint.ro_invoicer
	Supplier	com.sap.pct.srm.onecint.ro_supplier

Figure 11.31 Roles in SAP SRM and Corresponding Role in SAP Portal (Subset)

In SAP SRM, the Employee role is the most widely used role, because it contains transactions that create shopping carts (which employees use to request goods and services). There are three different layouts of the shopping cart transaction, as shown in Table 11.2.

Shopping Cart Type	Transaction Code
Wizard Based	BBPSC02
Extended form — professional users	BBPSC01

Table 11.2 Types of Shopping Cart Forms and Corresponding GUI Transactions

However, the Transaction BBPSC01 is not available in the /SAPSRM/EMPLOYEE role. In the standard delivery, it is only available in the Operational Purchaser role /SAPSRM/OP_PURCHASER. When organizations copy the standard Employee role, they will be unable to get access to the Extended Form BBPSC01 transaction unless they emerge from the Purchaser role.

11.7.1 Authorization Objects in SAP SRM

Beginning with SAP SRM release 4.0, the authorization check has been changed and new authorization objects have been added that include authorization parameters and authorization fields. In previous SAP SRM releases, users were only able to create/edit/display business documents (PO) according to their organizational unit dependencies (which means only one purchasing organization) inherited within the Organizational Structure in SAP SRM.

Document Checks Using Authorization Objects in SAP SRM determines whether a user can access a specific document (e.g., PO) and what functions (display, change, and so on) the user can carry out.

The Application Security Guide for SAP SRM contains detailed documentation on the standard roles in SAP SRM and the corresponding transactions and authorization objects within the roles. Authorization objects that have been extended or newly created for SAP SRM 5.0 are also included in this guide, which is available from the SAP Service Marketplace. A list of authorization objects relevant for SAP SRM is available in Appendix G of this book.

SAP SRM 5.0 Tip

From SAP SRM Release 4.0 onward, users have the ability to use [F4] help for available account assignments in the Shopping Cart and PO transactions. Both the number and the description of an account assignment object or SAP General Ledger account are displayed for backend systems. In SAP SRM Release 5.0, organizations can customize whether a user is allowed to use [F4] help. This can be restricted in the single role, SAP_EC_BBP_EM-PLOYEE (or the customer specific employee role created for your organization), and by changing the values for authorization object BBP_FUNCT. Un-check entry BE_F4_HELP.

11.8 Impact of Organizational Structure in SAP SRM on Security

The Organizational Structure is the heart of SAP SRM. Users cannot process any of the SAP SRM functions such as creating shopping cart, approvals, or processing POs until an Organizational Structure is created. It is important for security professionals to understand the organizational structure in SAP SRM because the Organizational Structure contains attributes that provide an additional level of security in addition to the SAP roles and integrated authorizations.

11.8.1 Organizational Structure as a Security Mechanism

The Organizational Structure in SAP SRM acts as a security mechanism to control the authorization a user has to various operational attributes such as company codes, cost centers, plants, and others. Sometimes, we refer to it as an extension to the SAP user master.

Typically, in SAP ERP, organizations secure the purchasing values such as Purchasing Organization, Plant, and others, using the SAP role assigned to the end user, making use of fields and values in the authorization objects. In SAP SRM, many of these are controlled within the SAP SRM Organizational Structure. Table 11.3 lists user attributes that are relevant from a security perspective that are maintained and controlled via the SAP SRM Organizational Structure.

Attribute	Description
BSA	Purchase Order document type
BUK	Company Code assigned to users
CAT	Catalog ID — Name of catalog an organization or user is allowed to access
CNT	Account Assignment (Cost Center) object allowed
ITS_DEST	The URL used to access the SAP SRM Web frontend
PURCH_GRP	Purchasing Group assignment to users
PURCH_ORG	Purchasing Organization assignment to users
ROLE	All roles that can be adopted by a person within an Organizational Unit
SLAPPROVER	Indicates the approver used in shopping cart workflows based on spending limit
SPEND_LIM	Spending limit assigned for a user. Once this limit is exceeded, approval workflow is triggered.
WRK	Plants that users are allowed to access and assign for procurement

Table 11.3 Examples of Attributes Within the Organizational Structure in SAP SRM

Figure 11.32 illustrates an example of attributes assigned in the Organizational Structure. In our example, the SLAPPROVER attribute is selected in the Attributes tab, which contains a value of the approver who will get the approval notification for shopping carts. In addition to the SLAPPROVER attribute, security teams need to be aware of all the possible attributes that are planned for use within the SAP SRM environment. They also must be aware of how the controls are going to be implemented within the organizational structure for audit compliance.

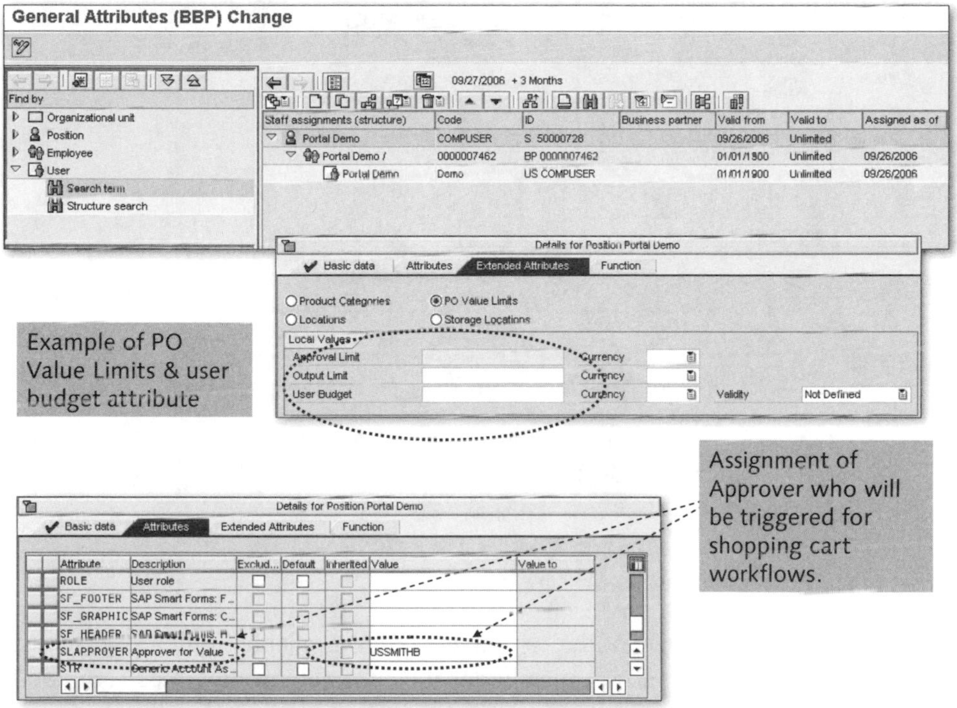

Figure 11.32 Attribute Assignment Within SAP SRM Organizational Structure

Most security teams are sensitive to the accessibility of any user ID and password information within the SAP system outside of security transactions. In SAP SRM, the catalog management configuration contains explicit access information with user name and password information that can be accessed by anyone having access to the IMG, as illustrated in Figure 11.33.

Catalogs are a key functionality in SAP SRM. Users can access catalogs within their shopping carts and view products and services offered by various vendors. The CAT attribute in the Organizational Structure controls who gets access to which catalogs within SAP SRM. Security teams need to work with their functional project teams to decide which individuals need access to this setting.

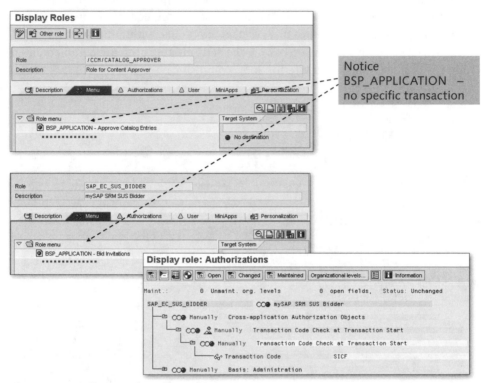

Figure 11.33 Definition of Catalogs Within SRM IMG

In SAP ERP, users are aware of the parameters (PIDs) available in their user master record. These allow users to seamlessly default information into fields commonly used in transactions, for example, the company code. In SAP SRM, instead of using PIDs within the user master record, users can set attributes in the My Settings transaction, Transaction BBPAT05. These attributes are configured within the Organizational Structure in SAP SRM, and allow users to control defaults within their shopping cart transactions.

For example, if a user always assigns the charge codes against a cost center, he can use attribute Account assignment category and select Cost Center as a default value. This way, in the shopping cart, the Account Assignment category Cost Center will always be preselected. The same can be done if a user wants to set his default plant value; he can use the Plant* Attribute as illustrated in the Settings transaction (also called Change Settings) shown in Figure 11.34.

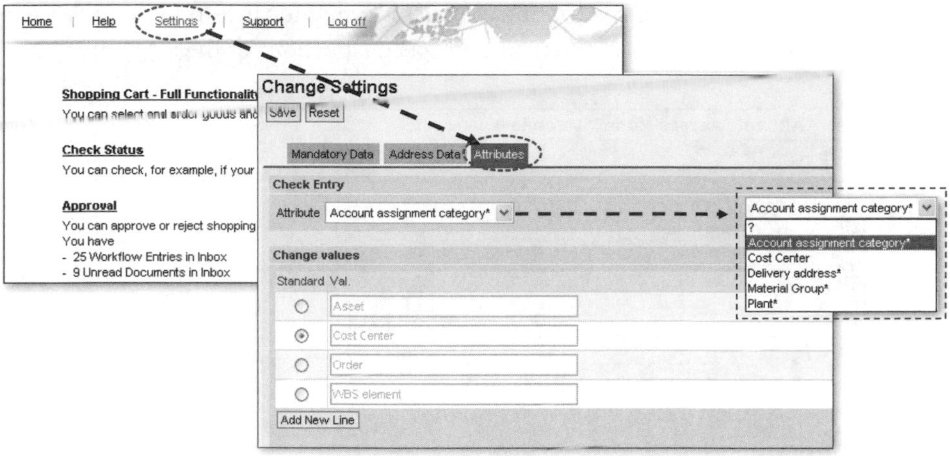

Figure 11.34 Settings Service — Transaction BBPAT05

You can configure SAP SRM to specify whether a user assigned to a particular role is authorized to display or change an attribute in My Settings. Therefore, if the organization wants a user to set the Cost Center attribute, it can enable this access in the IMG.

The menu path is SUPPLIER RELATIONSHIP MANAGEMENT • SRM SERVER • CROSS-APPLICATION BASIC SETTINGS • ROLES • MAINTAIN ATTRIBUTE ACCESS RIGHTS BY ROLE.

In Figure 11.35, the Cost Center Attribute KNT contains the Access of Display and Change depending on the role assignment in the Act. Group column. All users with the role assignment of SAP_EC_BBP_EMPLOYEE can display the Cost Center, and users with the SAP_EC_BBP_MANAGER role have the access to change the Cost Center.

Security administrators should keep in mind that if customer-specific roles have been created, then those should be used instead of the standard SAP SRM roles supplied by SAP as illustrated in Figure 11.35.

In the next section, we will discuss how an organization can secure the Organizational Structure maintenance in SAP SRM. This can be especially useful for large organizations that might have a decentralized organization, such as one divided by geographical regions including Americas, EMEA, and Asia Pacific. Imagine a global organization that has a single SAP SRM instance. For such an organization, it's often impractical for a single department to maintain the Organizational Structure. Therefore, it is especially important to secure Organizational Structure maintenance transactions such that only specific groups are able to maintain specific portions of the structure.

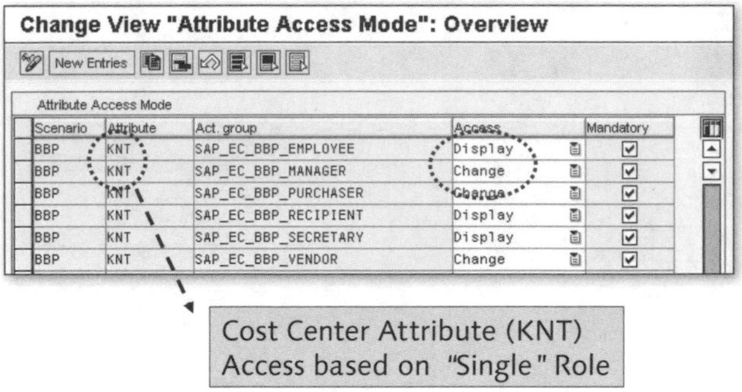

Figure 11.35 Maintain Attribute Access Rights by Role

11.8.2 Securing the Organizational Structure in a Decentralized Environment

In most SAP SRM implementations, project and security teams forget that in addition to developing and managing security for all end user roles, there needs to be a tight security on who should access and manage the Organizational Structure. This is true especially if the Organizational Structure is going to be maintained in a decentralized environment after go-live.

The core issues are as follows:

▸ The Organizational Structure in SAP EB is currently wide open to anyone who has authorization to access the Organizational Structure.

▸ Display and Change of the Organizational Structure need to be separated based on the Department/Organizational Unit.

The Organizational Structure can be secured using Transaction OOSP to create authorization profiles and Transaction OOSB to assign appropriate profiles to users who need to maintain the Organizational Structure, as illustrated in Figure 11.36.

Users in SAP require roles to execute transactions and access data in the SAP system (SAP and SRM are synonymous here). In SAP, roles are either assigned directly to a user record or to a position object in the Organizational Structure. So far in this chapter, we have discussed how security roles are assigned to users directly via the Role Maintenance transaction, Transaction PFCG. In the next section, we'll go over the concept of position-based security in SAP and how it works with SAP SRM.

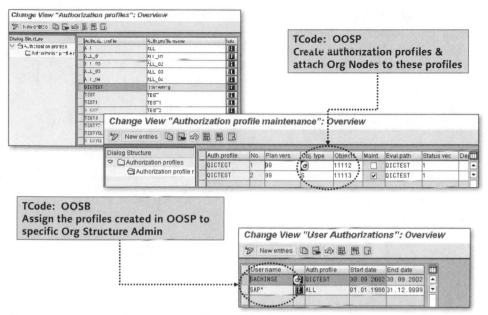

Figure 11.36 Securing the Organizational Structure

11.9   Position-Based Security in SAP SRM

Let's start by answering the most commonly asked question: Does position-based security work in SAP SRM? The answer is yes. Now, let's go into what that really means.

Position-based security simplifies the process of assigning roles to users in an organization. In position-based security, roles are assigned to a position in the Organizational Structure and then are applicable to any user who occupies that position. Because of this, position-based security is relevant only for organizations that implement the SAP ERP HCM application.

For example, a manager in a department has a particular SAP role. When this manager leaves the department, the same role will be assigned automatically to the new manager hired into that position. The role assignment process will occur automatically in SAP with no action required by the security teams.

When role assignment is based on positions, the activity to assign roles is no longer triggered by routine turnover of employees but instead by changes to processes, to positions, or to the department. Organizations either implement role-based security or position-based security, which also requires role assignment. Figure 11.37 provides a quick comparison between role-based and position-based security.

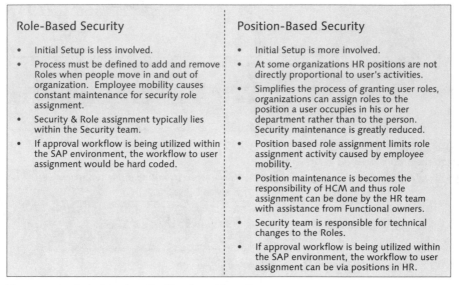

Role-Based Security	Position-Based Security
• Initial Setup is less involved.	• Initial Setup is more involved.
• Process must be defined to add and remove Roles when people move in and out of organization. Employee mobility causes constant maintenance for security role assignment.	• At some organizations HR positions are not directly proportional to user's activities.
	• Simplifies the process of granting user roles, organizations can assign roles to the position a user occupies in his or her department rather than to the person. Security maintenance is greatly reduced.
• Security & Role assignment typically lies within the Security team.	• Position based role assignment limits role assignment activity caused by employee mobility.
• If approval workflow is being utilized within the SAP environment, the workflow to user assignment would be hard coded.	• Position maintenance is becomes the responsibility of HCM and thus role assignment can be done by the HR team with assistance from Functional owners.
	• Security team is responsible for technical changes to the Roles.
	• If approval workflow is being utilized within the SAP environment, the workflow to user assignment can be via positions in HR.

Figure 11.37   Role-Based vs. Position-Based Security

Position-based security is relevant for SAP SRM implementations when the HR organization structure is integrated into SAP SRM and the organization is implementing position-based security in SAP. Chapter 8 discussed in detail the process of integrating the Organizational Structure in SAP ERP HCM with SAP SRM. In the SAP ERP HCM integration scenario, the Organizational Units, positions, and employees' objects are distributed from SAP ERP HCM into SAP SRM. In addition to distributing these objects, SAP roles assigned to those positions can also be distributed to SAP SRM.

The HR Organizational Structure is distributed from SAP ERP into SAP SRM via a standard report, RHALEINI (or via Transaction PFAL). As part of customizing, organizations can maintain distribution filter(s) indicating the type of information that is to be distributed from the Organizational Structure in SAP ERP into SAP SRM. For example, the payroll or bank account information for a user in the HR master has no use in SAP SRM and therefore is not distributed. However, the roles assigned to the position in which a user resides can be distributed via the object type AG in the filter definition. This is illustrated in Figure 11.38.

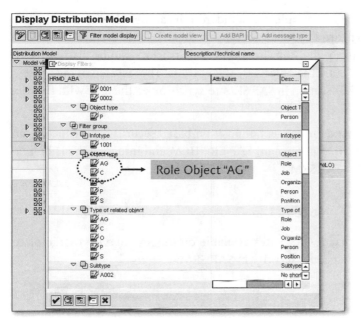

Figure 11.38 Distribution of Role Object (AG) Using ALE Distribution

In Figure 11.38, Infotype 1001 contains multiple object types: O for Organizational Unit, P for Person, S for Position, C for Job, and AG for Role. All the objects included in this filter are distributed from SAP ERP HCM into the SAP SRM Organizational Structure.

Figure 11.39 provides a sample process for distributing the positions and roles from SAP ERP into SAP SRM when position-based security is implemented. As illustrated, the role object AG is assigned to the position object S in the Organizational Structure in SAP ERP HCM. One or more roles can be assigned to a single position.

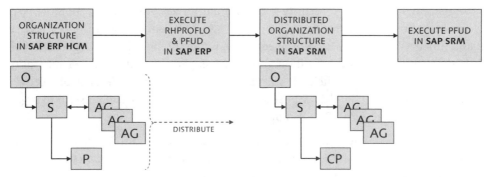

Figure 11.39 Process Flow for Roles Distribution from SAP ERP into SAP SRM with Position-Based Security

Once all role assignments are complete, a standard job can be scheduled to execute the position to a role-synchronization process using the RHPROFLO and PFUD Transactions in SAP ERP. At this point, the Organizational Structure can be distributed to SAP SRM using a filter to send the objects O, S, P, and AG. The last step in the process is to execute the PFUD Transaction in SAP SRM to synchronize the user with the role assignment in SRM.

In this section, we discussed the concept of position-based security. This concept can benefit for organizations that implement SAP ERP HCM and integrate the HR Organizational Structure with SAP SRM.

11.10 Relevant OSS Notes

Table 11.4 lists the important OSS Notes available on the SAP Service Marketplace that are relevant when managing security in SAP SRM.

Note	Description
501797	Check all SAP EB users
419423	Repairing incorrect SAP EB users
402592	SAP SRM in the environment of a Central User Administration
548862	FAQ: SAP EB user administration
644124	EBP: Managing access rights to attributes per user role
857745	Generation of User Authorizations in SAP EB/CRM/SRM environment

Table 11.4 Important OSS Notes and Descriptions

11.11 Summary

In this chapter, we reviewed the role of security in SAP SRM and how security administrators can manage security roles and authorizations within SAP SRM. We discussed why and how security is different in SAP SRM and shared the key lesson that a functional user in SAP SRM needs to be integrated within the Organizational Structure with a link to the position and business partner (a user master record in Transaction SU01 is not sufficient). You also learned about the difference of role- vs. position-based security and how position-based security is especially useful to organizations using the SAP ERP HCM application.

In Chapter 12, we'll cover the importance of master data within SAP SRM. You will learn about the different types of master data elements in SAP SRM and the strategy for maintaining master data on your SAP SRM project.

U.S. businesses lose more than $600 billion each year from operational and staffing costs directly related to dealing with poor data quality and management. The need to clean, manage, process, and maintain master data is more than a best practice. It is imperative for business success.
— The Data Warehousing Institute

12   Dependency of Master Data in SAP SRM and SAP ERP

SAP SRM is tightly integrated with SAP ERP and other SAP ERP solutions. The various applications and components of SAP ERP HCM, SAP ERP Financials, materials management in SAP ERP Operations, and other SAP software all provide critical master data elements that form the basis for an integrated solution. Many organizations manage their master data in various IT and business systems. Discrepancies between vendor, products, business partners, and other master data across the various systems lead to delays in processing time and incorrect decision making. Harmonization of this data enables organizations to reduce costs and improve efficiency within their business processes.

In Figures 12.1 and 12.2, an overview of the different types of master data exists in SAP SRM and SAP ERP. Because master data can exist in both the SAP SRM and backend systems, the figure also identifies elements that are maintained, replicated, or distributed from the backend, and used in SAP SRM.

Master data elements such as vendors, locations, products, and product categories can be maintained in either the SAP SRM system or the SAP back end. However, an organization with SAP ERP backend maintains this master data in SAP ERP and replicates it to the SAP SRM system. SAP provides transactions and middleware to download this master data.

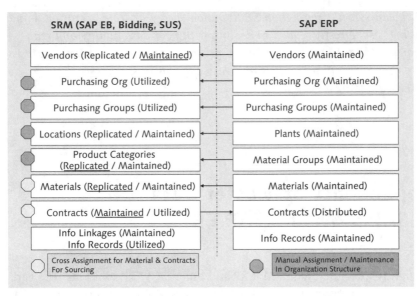

Figure 12.1 Master Data in SAP SRM and SAP ERP – I

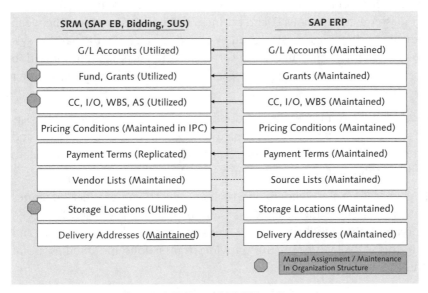

Figure 12.2 Master Data in SAP SRM and SAP ERP — II

There also are objects such as SAP General Ledger accounts, account assignments, purchasing organizations, and purchasing groups, which could be maintained in SAP ERP but are used in SAP SRM.

A real-time validation occurs within the SAP backend to check whether the master data used in SAP SRM is correct. An SAP General Ledger account is an example of such a validation. An error message is displayed in the SAP SRM shopping cart if the SAP General Ledger account used is not valid in the SAP backend. Similarly, if an incorrect purchasing group is used in the SAP SRM organization structure, a validation check occurs and an error is provided prior to purchase order (PO) creation.

The Organizational Structure in SAP Enterprise Buyer (EB) contains many of the master data objects seen in Figures 12.1 and 12.2. The Purchasing Organization, Groups, Locations, Storage locations, and Delivery Addresses are all manually referenced in the Organizational Structure. These provide a mechanism for user defaults and attribute inheritance in business transactions, for example, a shopping cart, a PO, or a contract.

In the upcoming sections of this chapter, we'll discuss each of these master data elements.

12.1   Middleware

Products and categories can either be created manually in the SAP SRM system or be replicated from the SAP backend system. The middleware is a set of programs that exist partly in the SAP EB system and partly in the SAP backend. This software is predelivered in the SAP system and is responsible for the replication of many master data objects.

Figure 12.3 shows how the middleware functions within SAP and SAP EB. Essentially, a plug-in is installed within the SAP ERP Basis layer and an adapter on the SAP EB system communicates with this plug-in. Install the plug-in corresponding to your SAP SRM release.

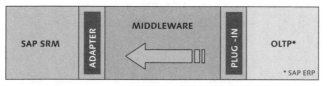

Figure 12.3   Middleware Function in SAP SRM

The two main master data objects transferred from the SAP backend into SAP SRM are:

- Material Masters
- Material Groups

Tip

In SAP SRM, the product master corresponds to the materials in SAP ERP, and the product categories correspond to the material groups. In SAP SRM, both materials and services are stored as products. However, you can distinguish materials from services using the product type.

The data in SAP SRM is downloaded from the backend system using two mechanisms:

- **Initial Download**
  The initial download allows for downloading all the required data (based on filter settings) for products (materials) and product categories (material groups).
- **Ongoing Delta Download**
  Subsequently, a delta download occurs, whereby during the normal processing and operation the online transaction processing (OLTP) system sends the updated data for materials automatically. As an example, when a Material Master record is changed in the SAP ERP system, and if that material record is subject to the filter settings, the record is automatically sent from SAP ERP into SAP SRM via the qRFC mechanism.

During the setup and configuration of SAP SRM, filters can be configured in SAP SRM to identify which products and categories should be downloaded from SAP ERP. These could be based on number ranges, material types, and others. Suppose, for example, that an organization wants to use SAP SRM only for indirect goods and services procurement, and wants to continue the procurement of raw materials within the SAP ERP system. In that case, a filter should be set up within SAP SRM that restricts the replication of raw material–type products from SAP ERP into SAP SRM. Figure 12.4 shows an example of a material filter in SAP SRM.

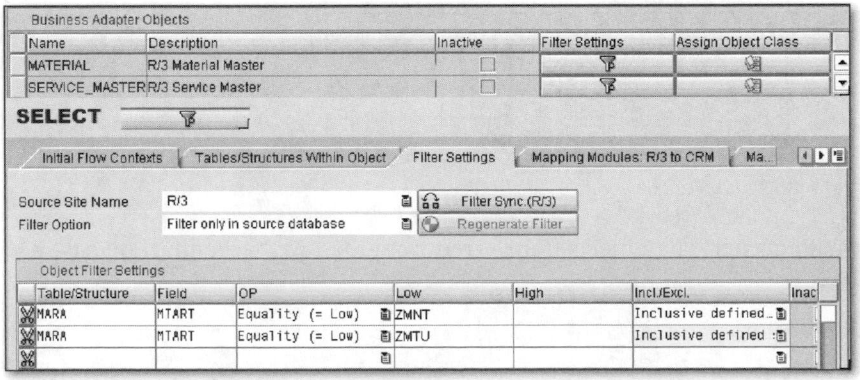

Figure 12.4 Material Filter in Transaction R3AC1

However, the delta download is only available for business objects and is not available for product categories, considered as a Customizing object. After the initial download, as new product categories are created in the backend system, they need to be replicated manually using the initial download mechanism. The relevant Customizing objects in SAP SRM include:

▶ DNL_CUST_BASIS3: Basis CRM online
▶ DNL_CUST_PROD0: Material number conversions
▶ DNL_CUST_PROD1: Product categories
▶ DNL_CUST_SRVMAS: Customizing: Service master

The relevant Business Adapter Objects in SAP SRM are:

▶ MATERIAL SAP ERP: Material Master
▶ SERVICE_MASTER SAP ERP: Service Master

The initial download is triggered in SAP SRM using the Transaction R3AS. Once the parameter Load Object is specified with the customizing or business objects, and the sender (SAP backend) and receiver (EB/CRM) systems are specified, the download can be triggered.

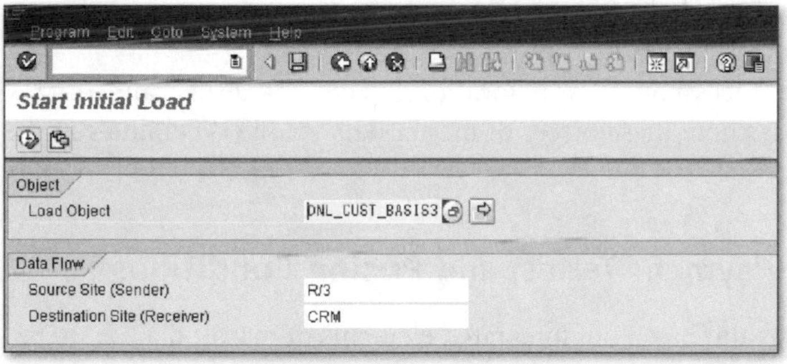

Figure 12.5 R3AS — Start Initial Download

The Load Object can contain more than one Customizing or business object for download. Distinguish which objects have dependencies; only independent objects can be downloaded in parallel. For example, the MATERIAL business object cannot be downloaded before the DNL_CUST_PROD0 Customizing object is downloaded.

Once the objects have been downloaded, they can be accessed in the following Transactions:

▶ COMMPR01 (product master or materials)
▶ COMM_HIERARCHY (product categories or material groups)

Products and categories are stored internally in the SAP SRM system as Global Unique Identifiers (GUIDs). End users do not come in contact with GUIDs, but configuration, technical, and support analysts need to be aware of their function. Most components, programs, and Business Add Ins (BAdIs) use and access information in the SAP SRM system with the use of GUIDs. In addition to products and categories, other objects in SAP SRM such as shopping carts, POs, vendor masters, and others are all stored as GUIDs as well.

SAP provides documentation on the set up and replication of the middleware objects, which can be downloaded from the SAP Service Marketplace. In addition, Chapter 18 walks through the setup in SAP SRM to download the products and categories from SAP ERP into SAP SRM.

> **Note**
>
> The middleware concept in SAP SRM was a legacy of the SAP Customer Relationship Management (SAP CRM) application. SAP CRM, just like SAP SRM, has master data needs that integrate back to the SAP ERP core system (e.g., sales organizations, sales materials, etc.) The middleware for SAP SRM was detached from the SAP CRM solution since the release of SAP SRM 4.0. This provided efficiencies and simplicity to the SAP SRM solution because the SAP CRM middleware objects were eliminated. In addition, this also made the download object Plant (DNL_PLANT) and the CRM-specific download objects (DNL_CUST_BASIS3 and DNL_CUST_BASIS5) obsolete.

The next section introduces concepts of locations, payment terms, and pricing conditions, and discusses how these pieces of master data enable capabilities in the SAP SRM solution.

12.2   Locations, Payment Terms, and Pricing Conditions

This section covers some unrelated but integrated elements of master data: *locations*, *payment terms*, and *pricing conditions*. Locations and payment terms are mandatory master data elements that are needed for the procurement functionality in SAP SRM. Locations define physical entities within an organization. Payment terms, though unrelated, are required to define the legal terms of agreement between the customer and the supplier.

12.2.1   Locations

In SAP SRM, the term *location* is synonymous to the term *plant* in SAP ERP. The function of a location in SAP SRM is to define a physical entity of an organization. A standard program replicates the locations (plants) existing in the SAP backend into SAP SRM.

SAP provides the BBP_LOCATIONS_GET_ALL program/report to download the relevant plants from the backend SAP ERP systems. Once the program is executed, the results can be viewed in Transaction SLG1.

Once the locations have been replicated within the SAP SRM system, an attribute assignment needs to be maintained in the Organizational Structure. The location attribute is maintained in the Extended Attributes tab in the Organizational Structure. This allows the end users to have access to one or many locations while creating shopping carts or POs.

The location(s) are available for end users in the basic data section of their shopping carts. In the Classic or Extended Classic scenario, the location is sent to the SAP ERP PO as a plant.

> **Note**
>
> In SAP ERP, the plant determines the purchasing organization on a PO. However, in SAP SRM the purchasing group determines the purchasing organization on a PO. Locations (plants) only define a user's location. This is of great significance if multiple purchasing organizations are used within the purchasing process.

12.2.2 Payment Terms

The procure-to-pay process in SAP uses the payment terms to determine the payment terms agreed on between the vendor and the purchasing organization. These can be created locally in SAP SRM (Standalone scenario) or can be replicated from the SAP backend (Classic or Extended Classic scenario).

SAP provides the BBP_UPLOAD_PAYMENT_TERMS program/report to download the payment terms (see Table 12.1). The BBP_PAYTERM table in SAP SRM can verify and analyze the payment terms. Additionally, the payment terms can also be created manually in SAP SRM by using this table. However, there is no procedure to replicate these from SAP SRM to the SAP backend. Also, ensure that the terms of payment texts are maintained in the tables.

SAP ERP Backend	SAP SRM
T052	BBP_PAYTERM
T052U	BBP_PAYTERM_TEXT

Table 12.1 Maintenance of Payment Terms Texts

The terms of payment are available on the PO in SAP SRM and can be changed during PO creation or processing. In the Classic or Extended Classic scenario, the terms are sent to the SAP ERP PO.

12.2.3 Pricing Conditions

In SAP SRM, *pricing* for POs have the following priority:

- Manual price
- Contract price
- Catalog price
- Price from product linkage or from product

An organization using an SAP backend that wants to transfer the pricing conditions from the SAP ERP backend can use the standard report, EBP_GET_BACK END_PRICES, in SAP SRM. Figure 12.6 illustrates this report. Product ID is a required field in this report. Additionally, an organization can choose to replicate prices based on an Average value of all prices or Use first price.

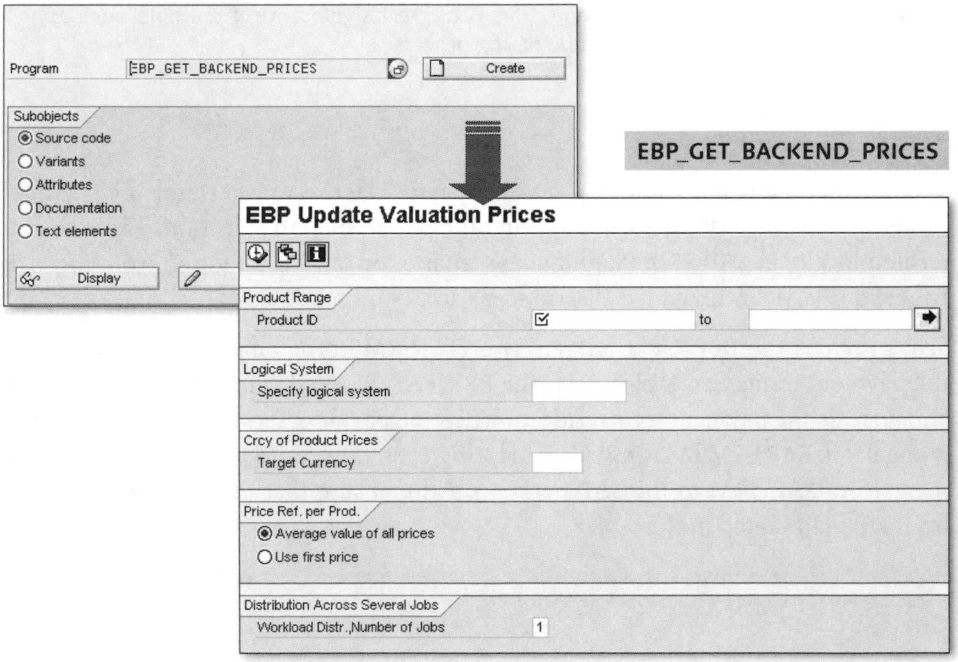

Figure 12.6 Transfer of Conditions from SAP Backend to SAP SRM

12.3 Interlinkages

In this section, we talk about the master data element *interlinkage*. At the basic level, an interlinkage creates a relationship between a product, vendor, and price in SAP SRM. This creates a vendor-specific price for a particular product.

12.3.1 Interlinkages and Info Records

In SAP ERP, an Info Record is used significantly within the material procurement scenario. However, in SAP SRM there are no Info Records that are created locally or replicated from the SAP backend. In the SRM Standalone scenario, the Info Record is not available for use. Only in the Classic or Extended Classic Scenario, if the Info Records are maintained in the SAP backend, can they be used for sourcing of shopping carts in SAP SRM.

Interlinkages in SAP SRM are similar to Info Records in SAP ERP. They are based on a product and vendor relationship and provide a mechanism to determine vendor-specific pricing for products while creating purchasing documents in SAP SRM. The product linkage is created manually in Transaction COMMPR01. Interlinkages are not as robust as Info Records and provide only minimal functionality. Most SAP SRM projects do not use Interlinkages as master data.

In the next section, we introduce the concept of a vendor list, contract, and catalog in SAP SRM and how they are related. Vendor lists create the relationship between a product or product category and a vendor. This way, organizations can create lists of preferred vendor relationships as sourcing criteria, which can be used when creating shopping carts, POs, and other documents.

12.4 Vendor Lists, Contracts, and Catalogs

This section uncovers the relationship between vendor lists, contracts, and catalogs. The key between all of these master data elements is that all of them can be used as fixed sources of supply in the different purchasing documents. On most projects, there always seems to be confusion on the relationship between these applications. Figure 12.7 clarifies this confusion by illustrating the interaction between a vendor list, contract, and catalog.

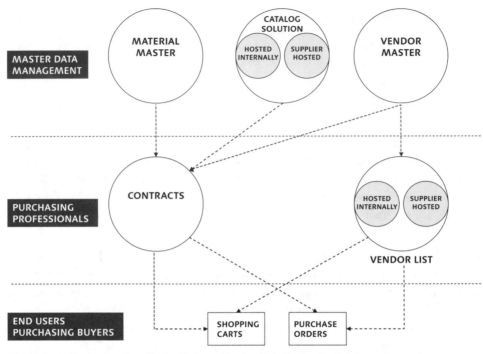

Figure 12.7 Understanding Master Data — Vendor List, Contracts, Catalogs

In most organizations, the material master and vendor master applications end up as the responsibility of the master data management team. For organizations that have in-house catalog applications, the support and management of the catalog are best handled by the master data management team as well. Using these master data objects, professional purchasers can create contracts and vendor lists in SAP SRM. Both contracts and vendor lists can be created using a material master or catalog item, and the vendor (business partner) is a required object.

Once contracts and vendor lists are created, they can be used as sources of supply in the shopping carts and POs by end users or purchasing buyers. In addition, catalogs can be directly used in shopping carts and POs.

12.4.1 Vendor Lists

Vendor lists in SAP SRM correspond to source lists in SAP ERP. The vendor list provides a mechanism to create a sourcing relationship between a product or product category and a vendor. The purchasing organization can create preferred lists of vendors valid for a particular product or product category. Users can employ these vendor lists when searching for sources of supply for their purchases.

Product-based vendor lists take precedence over product category–based vendor lists. The following information is required when creating a vendor list:

▶ A product or product category

▶ A vendor or backend contract

The vendor list is integrated into every application that contains a vendor search help and in which you can display sources of supply such as the following:

▶ **Shop and Shop with Value Limit**
You can specify that only vendors maintained in the vendor list can be selected or just have them highlighted in the sources of supply overview.

▶ **Sourcing Application**
Professional purchasers can assign vendor lists as a source of supply when completing open requirements but is not limited to these. If the Open Partner Interface (OPI) is connected, sourcing can be extended to cover external vendor lists.

▶ **Bidding Engine**
Strategic purchasers can search for bidders via defined vendor lists for a product or product category.

In the vendor list, one or more vendors can be assigned as preferred sources of supply, and can be marked as active or inactive. This provides the flexibility to have access to the preferred suppliers for a particular product or product category and activate them when desired (illustrated in Figure 12.8). For example, if the active supplier is unable to provide the goods for a defined period of time due to backordering, the professional purchaser can activate an inactive supplier already available as a substitute in the list.

Using hierarchically arranged product categories (e.g., eCl@ss and UNSPSC), a buyer can create a vendor list for a hierarchy subtree (i.e., combine multiple product categories). This vendor list is then valid for several product categories. Once the vendor list is released, all requirements that contain the hierarchical product category can use this vendor list as a source of supply.

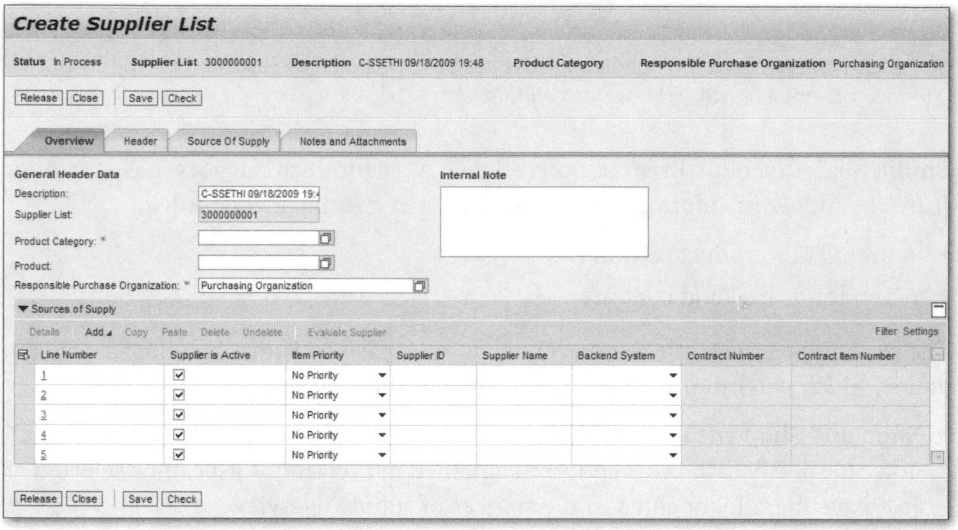

Figure 12.8 Creating Vendor Lists

Figure 12.9 illustrates an example of a hierarchy-based vendor list. In this example, a product category of 008* shows how a wildcard-based category can create a vendor list. Once this vendor list is created and released in SAP SRM, purchasing professionals can use a wild card search of 008*, and all vendor lists that have been created for this hierarchy of categories is available.

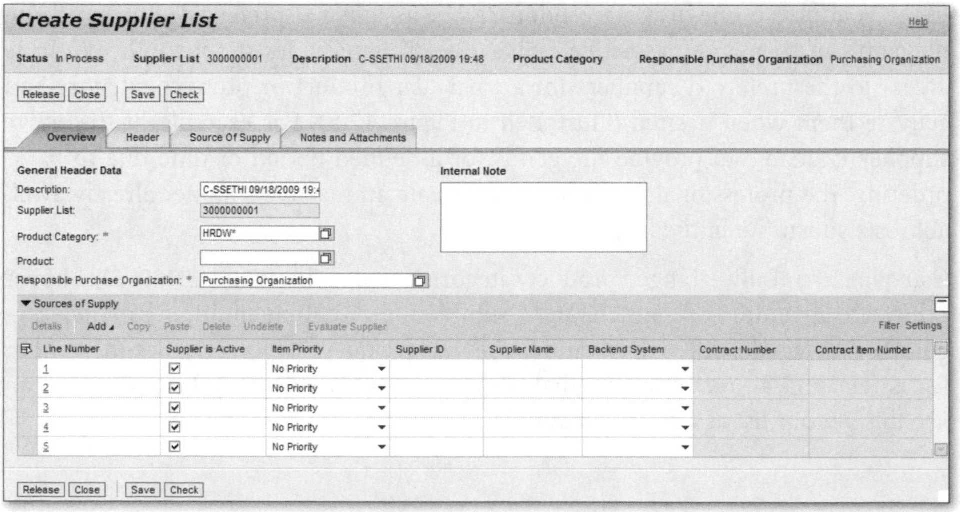

Figure 12.9 Vendor List Hierarchy by UNSPSC

If a purchasing organization is not specified in the vendor list, all purchasing organizations in the SAP SRM system use this business partner as a source of supply within the Shopping Cart and Sourcing transactions.

The Classic scenario also allows contracts that exist in the SAP backend to be used within the SAP SRM vendor list. Local contracts used in Extended Classic or Standalone scenario are not supported in the vendor list as of SAP SRM 4.0.

> **Note**
>
> Vendor lists in SAP SRM do not provide any functionality for validity based on dates like source lists in materials management in SAP ERP. An active or inactive radio button activates various sources of supply. Additionally, a vendor list requires at least one active source record.

12.4.2 Contracts

SRM provides the functionality to create value- and quantity-based *contracts* that determine price and act as sources of supply in shopping carts and POs. Additionally, Global Outline Agreements (GOAs) for the entire organization can be created in SAP SRM.

Contracts and GOAs can also be distributed from SAP SRM to one or more backend systems, and can be used locally. Contracts were discussed in detail in Chapter 6.

12.4.3 Catalogs

SRM provides the functionality for requisitioners and purchasers to access online and hosted catalogs to search for goods and services quickly and efficiently. These catalogs also make it possible for the organization to maintain compliance by offering access to selected products and services that have been prescreened by the purchasing organization.

Catalogs and the concept of content management were discussed in detail in Chapter 6.

12.5 Delivery Addresses

In this section, we'll discuss the need of delivery addresses in SAP SRM. When we talk about procurement of goods and services, one of the key pieces of information that needs to be communicated to a vendor is a delivery address. In SAP SRM, delivery addresses can be created by the SAP SRM administrator and are available for use by end users in the different purchasing documents such as shopping carts and POs.

12.5.1 Addresses for Business Partners

In SAP SRM, you can maintain a *ship-to address* during the creation of a shopping cart on item level and transfer this ship-to address to the SAP backend system. System behavior for ship-to addresses changed with SAP SRM 3.0 (EB 3.5) release. Since then, a default ship-to-address is required for the shopping cart user in the Organizational Structure. Then users have the ability to overwrite the default delivery address in the shopping cart (illustrated in Figure 12.10). Review OSS Note 701321.

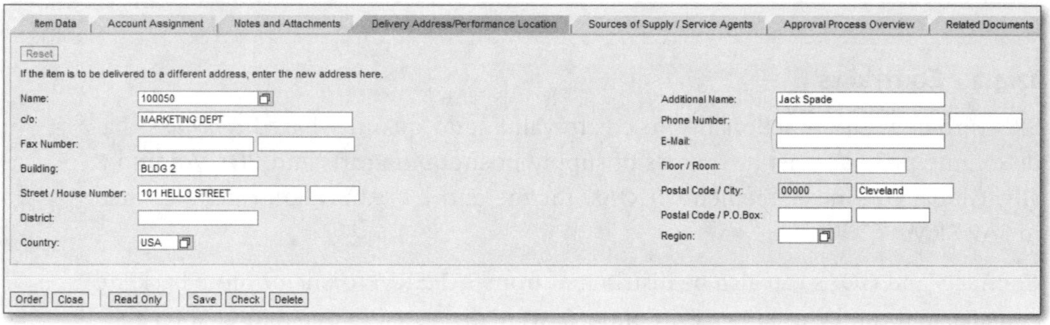

Figure 12.10 Delivery Address in Shopping Cart

In the standard solution, if the shopping cart line items have a delivery address (default or manually created), then the delivery address of the backend purchase order is the same as the shopping cart. If no delivery address is specified in the shopping cart line item, the address in SAP ERP is defaulted based on the plant data that was transferred from the shopping cart.

Project teams can create standard delivery addresses in SAP SRM, which users can select from while creating their shopping carts. This simplifies the need for users to re-enter the standard delivery addresses manually. In SAP SRM, addresses can be created for Organizational Units (in the Organizational Structure in PPOMA) that are marked as COMPANY under the Function tab.

> **Note**
>
> You can only assign ship-to addresses for companies where the attribute IS_COMPANY is set in the Organizational Structure.

This allows the flexibility to create separate delivery addresses for one company vs. another (a company in SAP SRM is not the same as the company code). The company could be any logical separation of the organization. Figure 12.11 shows the Organizational Structure transaction in SAP SRM where the Function tab indicates an organization unit as a Company. SAP SRM creates one or more delivery addresses for each organization unit marked as a Company. This is illustrated in Figure 12.11.

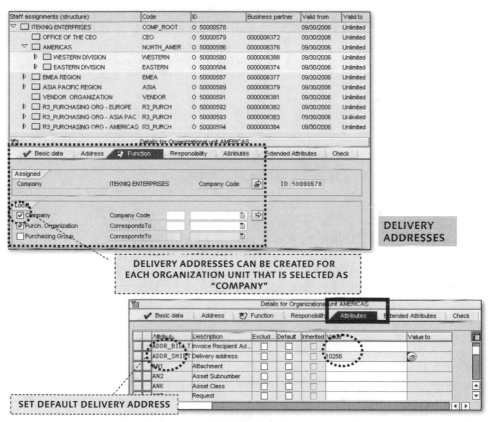

Figure 12.11 Assigning Organizational Units as Company

In SAP SRM, addresses can be created using the Maintain Internal Addresses application (BBPADDRINTC), or in SAP SRM 7.0 as shown in Figure 12.12.

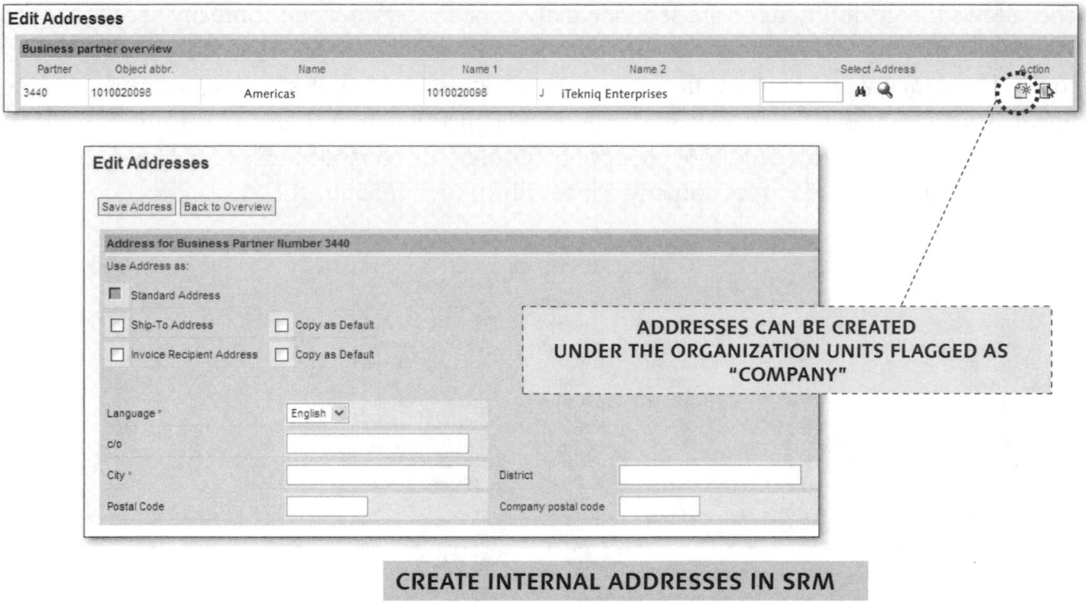

Edit Addresses

Business partner overview						
Partner	Object abbr.	Name	Name 1	Name 2	Select Address	Action
3440	1010020098	Americas	1010020098	J iTekniq Enterprises		

Edit Addresses

Save Address | Back to Overview

Address for Business Partner Number 3440

Use Address as:

☐ Standard Address

☐ Ship-To Address   ☐ Copy as Default

☐ Invoice Recipient Address   ☐ Copy as Default

ADDRESSES CAN BE CREATED
UNDER THE ORGANIZATION UNITS FLAGGED AS
"COMPANY"

Language *   English ▾

c/o

City *   District

Postal Code   Company postal code

CREATE INTERNAL ADDRESSES IN SRM

Figure 12.12 Creating Internal Addresses

12.6 External Business Partners in SAP SRM

Business partners in SAP SRM can be internal to the organization or external to the organization. Vendors and bidders are considered external business partners.

12.6.1 Vendors

Similarly to products and categories, *vendors* can be maintained either in the SAP backend or the SAP EB system locally. The vendor in SAP SRM is attached within the Organizational Structure and receives a corresponding business partner record similar to the Organizational Units. In SAP SRM, the concept of a business partner is introduced and a number of master data objects existing in the SAP backend correspond to a business partner in SAP SRM.

Vendors, plants, and bidders are all examples of business partners. In SAP SRM, the vendor master record is also referred to as a *business partner*. In SAP SRM, an internal or external business partner is created for every person, organization, or group of people who could be involved in a business transaction (e.g., a PO or bid invitation).

Figure 12.13 illustrates the Manage Business Partner application (Transaction BBP-MAININT) in SAP SRM.

> **Note**
>
> In SAP SRM 7.0, business partners can be managed within the SAP NetWeaver Portal application. The SRM Administrator role in the portal can manage business partners for external and internal partners. Within this role, there is a separate application defined for creation of business partners of type, Supplier, Bidder, Invoicing Party, Purchasing Company, Employee, and others.

This application allows the creation and management of business partners in SAP SRM. For example, a vendor can be flagged with status of Central Lock in the Business Partner Status section of this application.

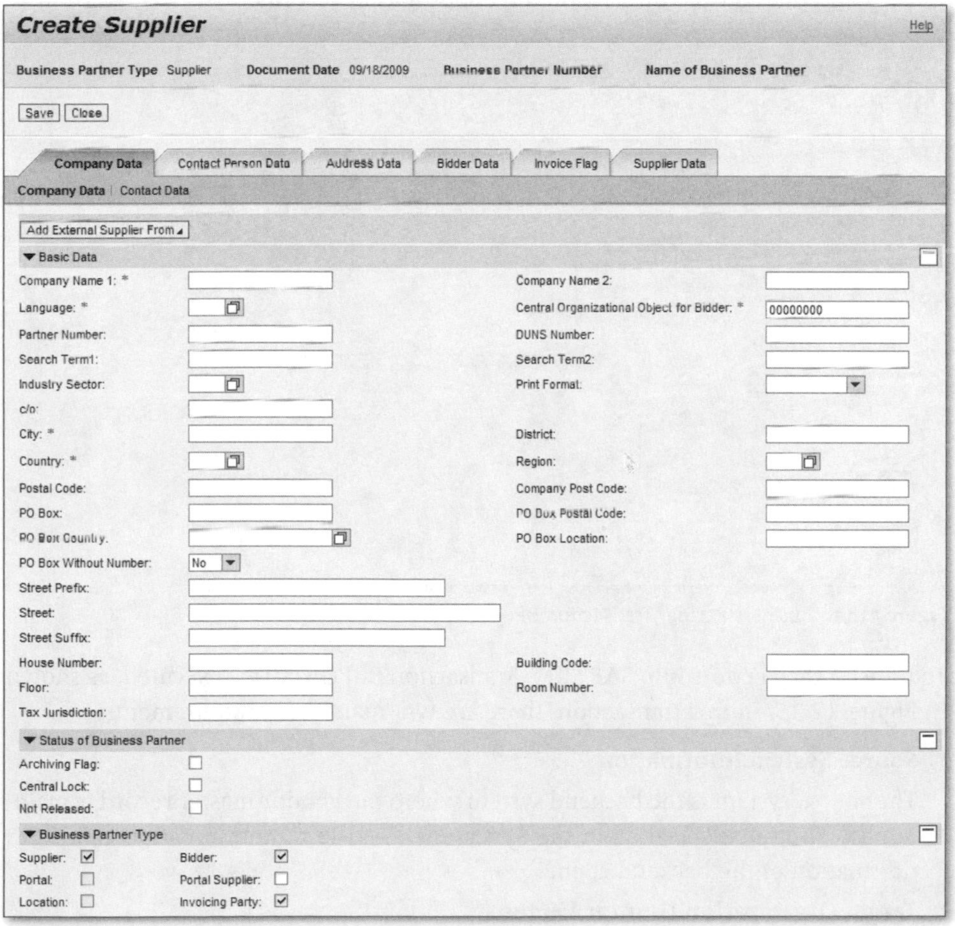

Figure 12.13 Managing Business Partner (Vendor) Transaction

Business partners, internal and external, can also be accessed via the Business Partner transaction (Transaction BP) as shown in Figure 12.14. In Transaction BP, the Display in BP role field contains the type of business partner: Bidder, Business Partner (Gen), Financial Services BP, Organization Unit, and Vendor.

Several organizations using SAP SRM maintain the vendor master in the backend SAP system and replicate them within the SAP SRM system. The core reasoning here is the existing processes for vendor maintenance in the enterprise system. SAP delivers a standard set of programs and transactions to replicate the vendor master from the backend SAP ERP system to SAP SRM. There are two different transactions that are available for the transfer of the vendor master: initial transfer of vendor master records and the update/comparison of vendor master records.

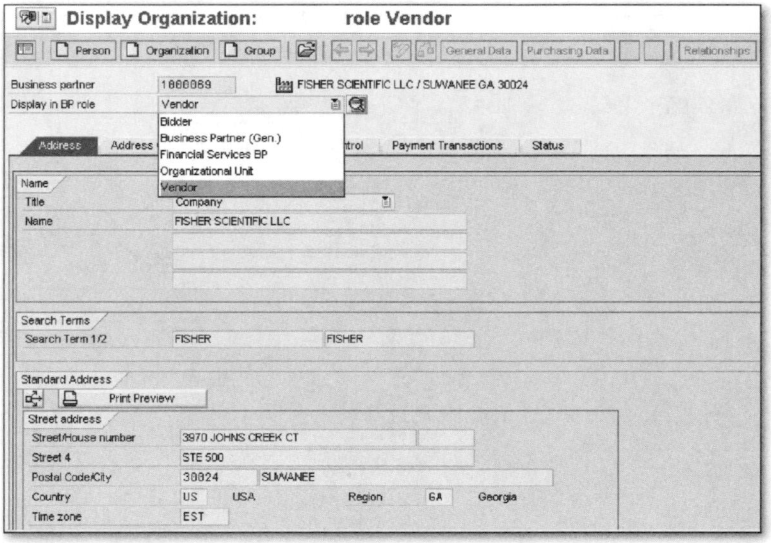

Figure 12.14 Business Partner Transaction BP

To transfer the vendors into SAP SRM, Transaction BBPGETVD is executed, as shown in Figure 12.15. In this transaction, there are two mandatory requirements:

▶ **Source System Information**

The source system is the backend system where the vendor master record is maintained. The value specified in the System field is the remote function call (RFC) destination of the backend client.

▶ **Target Organization Unit for Vendor**

The second mandatory element, Object ID, is the value for the Vendor Root Organization in the Organizational Structure, as shown in Figure 12.16.

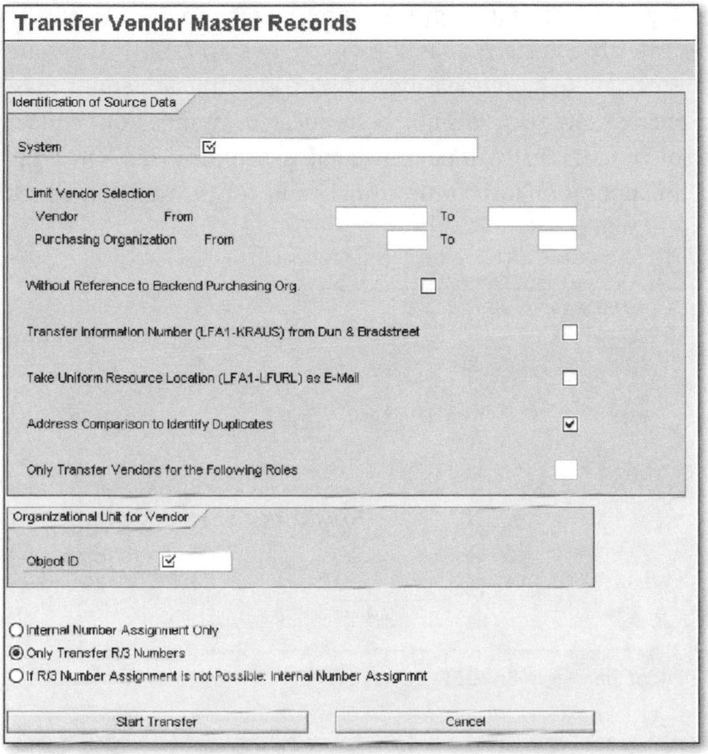

Figure 12.15 Vendor Master Replication Transaction BBPGETVD

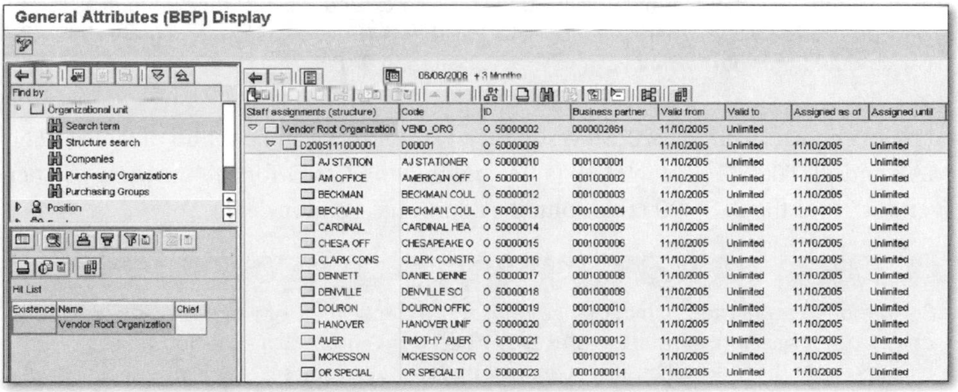

Figure 12.16 Vendor Root in the Organizational Structure — Object ID

To limit the selection of vendors for replication, additional fields are available in Transaction BBPGETVD. Once the values are maintained, it must be decided whether to keep the backend number assignment or internally assign within SAP SRM.

Prior to the actual transfer of the vendor records, a summary is provided to ensure that the appropriate records are transferred, as shown in Figure 12.17. If there are discrepancies in the master data (e.g., purchasing view or incomplete vendor master), the program lists the vendors that will not be replicated (number of vendors lost). The total number of vendors that will be replicated is also provided. Once the transmission is started, an application log captures the results for the transfer, which can be viewed in Transaction SLG1.

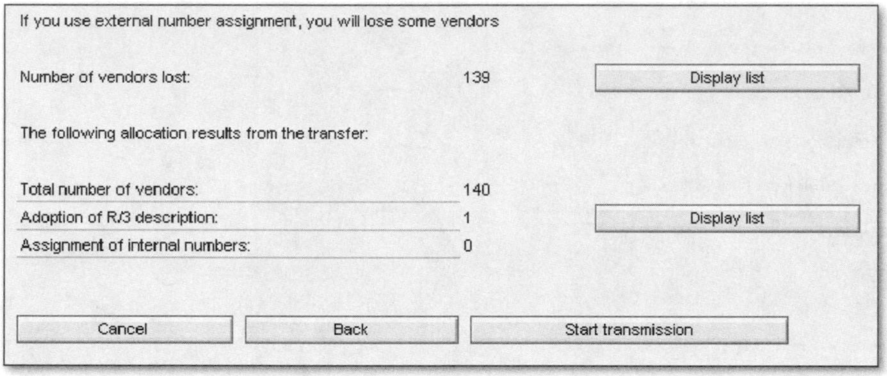

Figure 12.17 Summary of Vendor Transfer in BBPGETVD

> **Note**
>
> Only purchasing-relevant vendors are available for replication into SAP SRM. Therefore, in many implementations, the organizations have to extend their existing vendor masters with purchasing views. Therefore, accounts payable (A/P) vendors can remain in the ERP backend and only purchasing vendors are replicated in SAP SRM.

At the technical level, the SAP SRM supplier/vendor data can be found in tables VEN-MAP and BUT000. The VENMAP table contains the GUID for the business partner (vendor), and the BUT000 table contains additional vendor details.

> **Note**
>
> Set the business partner number range prior to the replication of vendors or the creation of any other business partners in SAP SRM. Because vendors, organization units, plants, bidders, and others, are all business partner objects, review and set up the business partner number range before any records are created. (IMG: SUPPLIER RELATIONSHIP MANAGEMENT • CROSS-APPLICATION COMPONENTS • SAP BUSINESS PARTNER • BASIC SETTINGS • NUMBER RANGES AND GROUPINGS)

Once the number ranges are defined (see Figure 12.18), they can be assigned to the groupings to indicate internal vs. external. Grouping 0001 indicates Internal Number Assignment. This number range will be used for internal Organizational Structure (PPOMV_BBP) business partners and vendors created locally in SAP SRM.

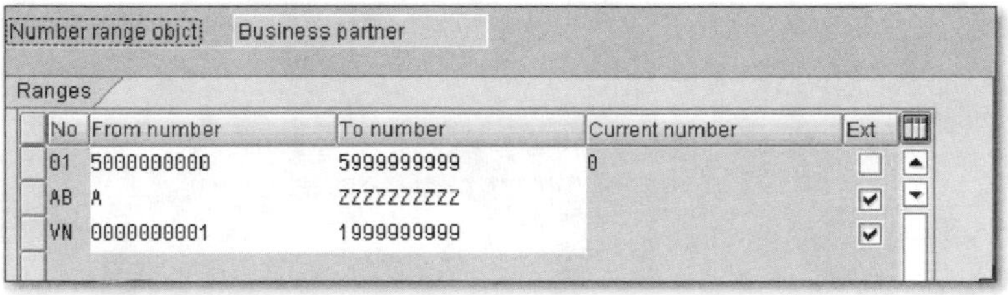

Number range objct	Business partner				
Ranges					
No	From number	To number	Current number	Ext	
01	5000000000	5999999999	0	☐	▲
AB	A	ZZZZZZZZZZ		☑	▼
VN	0000000001	1999999999		☑	

Figure 12.18   Business Partner Number Range

Grouping 0002 indicates External Number Assignment (see Figure 12.19). This number range will be used for external vendors that will be replicated from SAP ERP. Typically, the SAP ERP number range for vendors will either be numeric or alphanumeric.

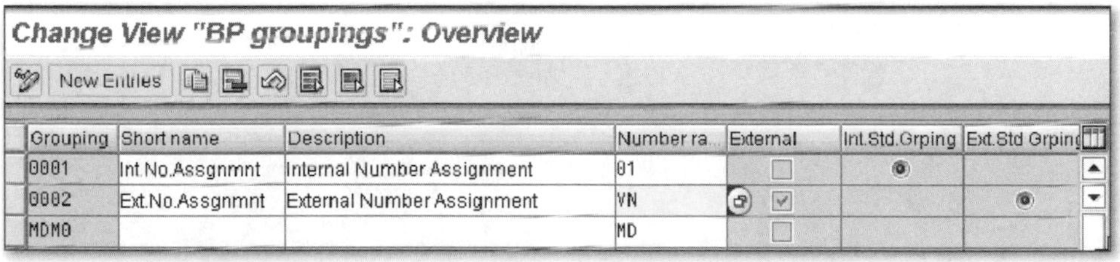

Change View "BP groupings": Overview

⚙ New Entries 🗋 🗐 🖉 🗟 🗟 🗟

Grouping	Short name	Description	Number ra.	External	Int.Std.Grping	Ext.Std Grping	
0001	Int No.Assgnmnt	Internal Number Assignment	01	☐	◉		▲
0002	Ext.No.Assgnmnt	External Number Assignment	VN	☑		◉	▼
MDM0			MD	☐			

Figure 12.19   Business Partner Groupings

The vendor master can also be created manually in SAP SRM using Transaction BBPMAININT, as shown in Figure 12.20. SAP does not provide a reverse process to transfer the vendor master records created in SAP SRM back to SAP ERP. However, the replicated vendor records (i.e., those created in ERP and replicated to SRM) that have been modified in SAP SRM can be updated in SAP ERP via a standard SAP NetWeaver PI/XI scenario in SAP SRM 5.0 release.

Once the vendor records have been replicated into SAP SRM, any updates to the vendor master in SAP ERP can be updated in SAP SRM either using the Update transaction or a synchronization job can be scheduled. The update transaction, Transaction BBPUPDVD, compares the SAP ERP vendor record to the SAP SRM record and replicates any changes.

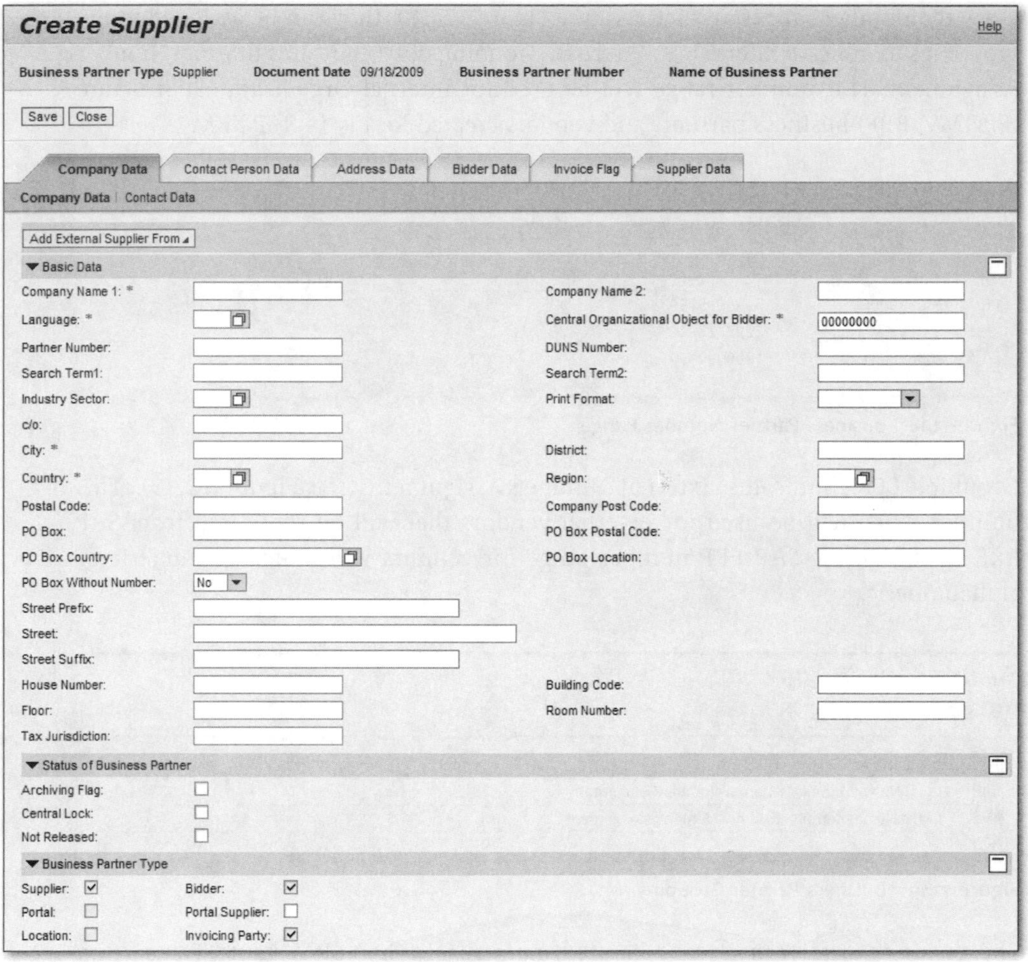

Figure 12.20 Create Vendor Master Record in SAP SRM Transaction BBPMAININT

As an alternative, using customizing for vendor synchronization, you can define the systems between which you wish to automatically synchronize the vendor master data. This can be done in the IMG: SUPPLIER RELATIONSHIP MANAGEMENT • SRM SERVER • TECHNICAL BASIC SETTINGS • SETTINGS FOR VENDOR SYNCHRONIZATION. SAP provides the BBP_VENDOR_SYNC program to automatically synchronize the backend suppliers with the SAP SRM system, if the master data in the backend system is different from the replicated data in SAP SRM.

Subsequently, a job is scheduled automatically that synchronizes the newly created or changed vendor master data in the backend and updates regularly in the SAP EB

System. In addition to updates to the vendor master records, the Create New Vendors Also check box transfers new vendor master records in SAP SRM as they are created in the ERP backend (Figure 12.21).

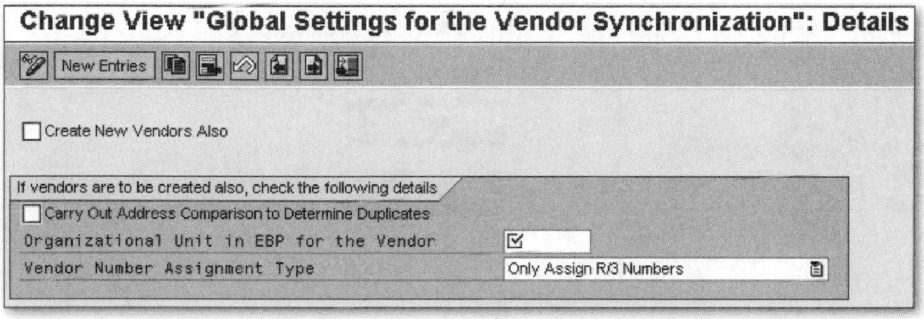

Figure 12.21 Vendor Synchronization

> **Note**
>
> Table 12.2 contains information about the synchronization job.

BBP_VDSYNC_CUST	information about the last synch
BBP_NEWVD_LOG	new vendors added
BBP_SNEW_SYNCVD	new vendor added

Table 12.2 Synchronization Jobs

Vendor Replication in Extended Classic Scenario

In the Extended Classic scenario, local purchasing organizations and purchasing groups are required to create shopping carts and POs. In this scenario, when the vendors are replicated from the SAP backend using BBPUPDVD program (vendor replication) or the vendor-synchronization programs, the vendor update in SAP SRM is only for the SAP ERP purchasing organization. Because the local purchasing organizations are required in SAP SRM for the Extended Classic or Standalone scenario, these replicated vendors (business partners) need to be extended to the local purchasing organizations.

Organizations can use Transaction BBP_UPDATE_PORG for extending the vendors to the local purchasing organization (illustrated in Figure 12.22). Also see OSS Note 390546.

477

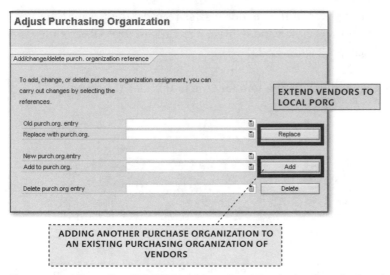

Figure 12.22 Extending SAP ERP Vendors to Local Purchasing Organizations in SAP SRM

12.6.2 Bidders

A *bidder* is synonymous with an external vendor partner and is a subset of the vendor record in SAP SRM. The vendor in SAP SRM is a business partner (supplier or a service provider). A contact person or service agent is created in SAP SRM for the external vendor organization that needs to engage in bidding or request-for-proposal functions with the purchasing organization. A contact person represents an end user in the vendor or bidder organization. Once a contact person (user ID) is created, vendors can log in via a predefined URL, access Bid Invitations, and enter their bids.

SAP security administrators need to be aware that bidders cannot just be created via the standard Transaction SU01 (Create User), instead Transaction BBPMAININT creates bidder records (Manage Business Partners).

In Transaction BBPMAININT, the bidder's user ID, password, email address, and other details are specified. Once the record is saved, SAP SRM creates an automated email containing the system access details that can be sent to the vendor. An example is shown in Figure 12.23. In our example illustrated in Figure 12.23, this email contains the User and Password information for the bidder. External partners (bidders) can click on the links specified in the email to access your SAP SRM system.

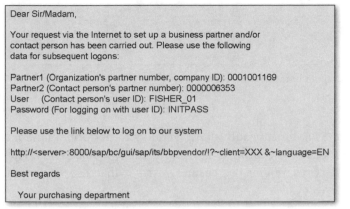

Dear Sir/Madam,

Your request via the Internet to set up a business partner and/or
contact person has been carried out. Please use the following
data for subsequent logons:

Partner1 (Organization's partner number, company ID): 0001001169
Partner2 (Contact person's partner number): 0000006353
User   (Contact person's user ID): FISHER_01
Password (For logging on with user ID): INITPASS

Please use the link below to log on to our system

http://<server>:8000/sap/bc/gui/sap/its/bbpvendor/!?~client=XXX &~language=EN

Best regards

  Your purchasing department

Figure 12.23 Example of Bidder Registration Email

SRM uses role-based authentication and therefore requires appropriate roles assigned
to each user in the system. During the creation of a bidder, the system administrator can assign a default role for the bidder. However, only a single role assignment
is allowed. If additional role assignment is required, a further manual step will be
required.

SRM also provides a self-registration functionality for external business partners.
This functionality was described in detail in Chapter 5.

Although bidders are external users, they still reside within the Organizational Structure in SAP SRM. Position, business partner, and user records are created for each
bidder contact person/service agent with the vendor organization in SAP SRM, as
shown in Figure 12.24. In our example, the business partner is FISHER SCIENTIFIC
and the user record for the bidder is FISHER_01. The user specified in Figure 12.23
is FISHER_01. Therefore, when this user was created, an email is generated for the
external business partner, in our example, FISHER_01.

However, if HR integration is active (i.e., the Organizational Structure is distributed
from SAP ERP HCM to SAP SRM), the vendor position, business partner, and user are
only available in SAP SRM and not in SAP ERP HCM. Therefore, these objects have
to be created locally in the SAP SRM Organizational Structure. SAP ERP HCM Integration with SAP SRM distributes the organization (O), position (S), and employee
(P), and others automatically. These objects are then only maintained in the SAP ERP
HCM system.

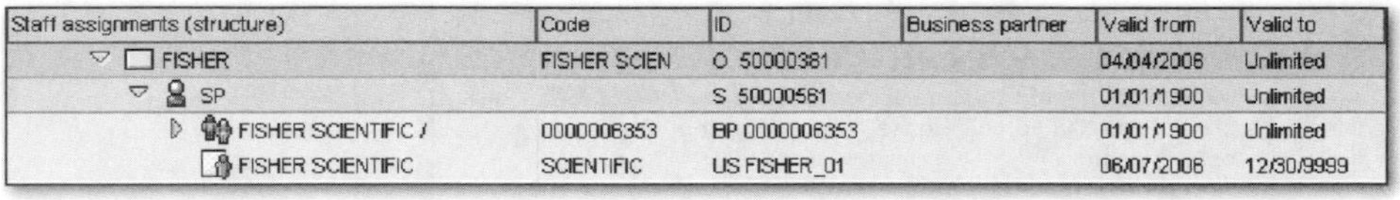

Staff assignments (structure)	Code	ID	Business partner	Valid from	Valid to
▽ ☐ FISHER	FISHER SCIEN	O 50000381		04/04/2006	Unlimited
▽ 🔲 SP		S 50000561		01/01/1900	Unlimited
▷ 🔲 FISHER SCIENTIFIC /	0000006353	BP 0000006353		01/01/1900	Unlimited
🔲 FISHER SCIENTIFIC	SCIENTIFIC	US FISHER_01		06/07/2006	12/30/9999

Figure 12.24 Business Partner and Contact Person Record for a Vendor

12.6.3 Portal Vendor

The supplier self-services (SUS) functionality allows vendors to perform a number of collaborative functions such as PO processing, confirmation, invoice entry, and payment status inquiry. A portal vendor is a business partner that also exists as a business partner record in SUS.

The portal vendor is created in a similar fashion as a bidder. In the Manage Business Partner transaction, a field for *Portal Vendor* flags a vendor to be enabled for SUS.

12.7 Relevant OSS Notes

Table 12.3 provides a list of important OSS Notes available on the SAP Service Marketplace that are relevant for master data in SAP SRM.

Note	Description
744359	ECS: Deactivate transfer of delivery address to backend
427906	Transfer of the delivery address to the backend system

Table 12.3 OSS Notes

12.8 Summary

This chapter introduced many master data elements within SAP SRM. We discussed business partners, replication of products and categories, contracts, vendor lists, and other topics. Master data is a key functionality for any enterprise software, and clean and harmonized master data is essential for enabling the true benefits of SAP SRM.

Chapter 13 will introduce the architecture of SAP SRM. We will review the different business-process scenarios and how each scenario might have a unique requirement from the architecture.

SAP SRM leverages the powerful capabilities of the SAP NetWeaver tech-nology platform to integrate seamlessly with both third-party and SAP applications. The SAP SRM application uses functionalities within the SAP NetWeaver technology platform, such as BW and MDM, to create a power-ful strategic, operational, and analytical supplier relationship management application.

13 Architecture and Technology of SAP SRM

SAP SRM is built on the core SAP NetWeaver technology, the application and inte-gration technology platform of SAP. SRM was one of the first SAP products that was launched on the SAP NetWeaver technology platform and it has leveraged the power of SAP NetWeaver ever since. The SAP SRM application harmonizes both internal and external processes. The SAP NetWeaver technology platform provides the flex-ibility in the SAP SRM application to integrate the self-service, sourcing, catalog management, and supplier collaboration processes that drive the efficient processes within supplier relationship management.

The business scenarios in SAP SRM provide a range of functionalities, including global spend analysis, self-service procurement, strategic sourcing, content and mas-ter data management, and collaborative supplier processes, such as order collabo-ration. These business scenarios are made possible by the software infrastructure delivered by SAP NetWeaver.

> **Note**
>
> SAP NetWeaver is not a single product but rather a single technology platform. SAP NetWeaver provides a technology platform where a number of different components are included. Figure 13.1 illustrates the components within the SAP NetWeaver technology platform and how SAP SRM leverages the power of SAP NetWeaver.

For an organization to leverage the full opportunity within the SAP SRM applica-tion, SAP NetWeaver integration is a must. SAP NetWeaver applications such as SAP NetWeaver Portal, SAP NetWeaver Business Warehouse (SAP NetWeaver BW), and SAP NetWeaver Process Integration (SAP NetWeaver PI) are key components of the SAP SRM application. Figure 13.2 provides a simple illustration of the components that are used in SAP NetWeaver for SAP SRM.

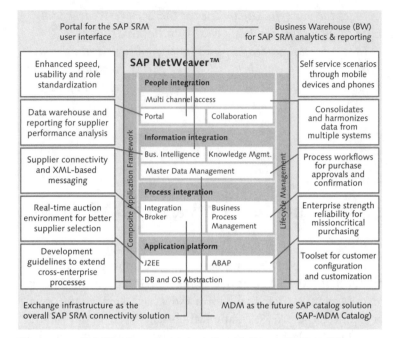

Figure 13.1 SAP SRM Leverages Integration Platform of SAP NetWeaver

SAP Business Suite / Solutions	SAP applications						SAP NetWeaver					
	SAP ERP	SAP SCM	SAP CRM	SAP SRM	SAP SEM	SAP KW	Web AS	Business Warehouse	Enterprise Portal	Process Integration	Mobile Infrastructure	Master Data Management
SAP Business Suite	√	√	√	√	√	√	√	√	√	√	√	√
SAP CRM	√	√	√		√	√	√	√	√		√	
SAP SRM				√			√	√	√	√	√	√
SAP SCM	√	√	√	√		√	√	√	√	√		
SAP PLM	√		√	√		√	√	√	√			
SAP ERP	√			√	√	√	√	√	√	√	√	

Figure 13.2 SAP and NetWeaver Components Used in SAP SRM

SAP SRM is a separate application, independent of the SAP ERP application offered by SAP. It is common for people to forget that SAP SRM is installed and implemented within its own three-tiered architectural landscape, independent from the SAP ERP landscape. However, it's still an SAP system; the GUI for SAP SRM is the same as for native SAP ERP, with an IMG for core configuration. The difference lies in the user interface for SAP SRM: An end user only requires a web browser to access all the transactions.

13.1 SAP SRM Functionalities and Matrix

The overall SAP SRM application is based on several different SAP functionalities, integrated to provide a comprehensive application. Some components are core to the SAP SRM system; others are integrated with the SAP SRM server to provide the application.

13.1.1 Definition of Functionalities

Before we discuss the integration of these functionalities further, understand the terminology and brief definitions of some of the components that make up the SAP SRM application:

▶ **SAP SRM or SRM Server**
This software has many names, which creates confusion for users. Figure 13.3 illustrates by example the different terminology for SAP SRM. SAP Supplier Relationship Management Server (SAP SRM Server) comprises SAP Enterprise Buyer (EB), SAP Bidding Engine, and Supplier self-service (SUS).

▶ **SRM-MDM Catalog**
The SRM-MDM Catalog software replaces the earlier catalog SAP Catalog Content Management (CCM) offered since 2004. It is built on the SAP NetWeaver MDM technology. However, it is available as part of the SAP SRM core license.

> **Note**
>
> Starting from SAP SRM 5.0, the SAP-MDM Catalog has been introduced based on the SAP NetWeaver MDM Solution. All customers implementing or upgrading to SAP SRM 7.0 will need to use the SRM-MDM Catalog.

▶ **ITS and WebDynpro**
The Internet Transaction Server (ITS) is the link between the Internet and SAP applications. It enables users to access SAP transactions (including SAP SRM)

using a web browser. ITS is a required functionality to access most of the transactions in SAP SRM. Since SAP SRM 4.0, ITS has been integrated within the Web AS layer.

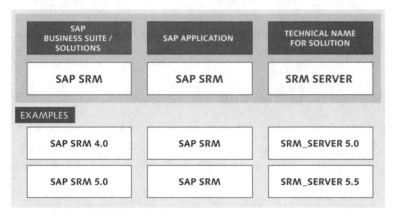

Figure 13.3 SAP SRM Terminology

▶ Beginning with the SAP SRM 6.0 controlled release and now generally available SAP SRM 7.0, ITS technology is no longer used. Instead, WebDynpro technology is used. The overall user interface of SAP SRM is redone with WebDynpro-based screens.

▶ **IPC**
The Internet Pricing Configurator (IPC) is a tool for product configuration and pricing in the Internet. In SAP SRM, it is a required functionality if the Extended Classic scenario is implemented.

▶ **TREX**
TREX is the search and classification engine used across many SAP applications. It is a technical component of SAP NetWeaver that provides applications with a wide range of functions for intelligent search, retrieval, and classification of textual documents. The TREX engine is primarily used for catalog and contract management solutions in SAP SRM.

▶ **Process Integration (PI) (previously Exchange Infrastructure [XI])**
As a part of SAP NetWeaver, SAP NetWeaver PI provides message-based integration of all internal and external systems. It is a required functionality for organizations that want to use SUS, the SRM-MDM master-data inclusion scenario, transmission of purchasing documents via XML from SRM server, and other functionalities.

In general, there has been a shift in terminology for the SAP NetWeaver components since the SAP NetWeaver 2004 release, which is integrated in the SAP SRM 5.0 release and higher. This is illustrated in Figure 13.4.

Previous SAP NetWeaver "components" providing certain capabilities	Usage Type with SAP NetWeaver 2004s	Short name
SAP NetWeaver BW	Business Warehouse	BW
SAP BW + SAP Web AS (Java)	BI Java Components	BI Java
SAP NetWeaver AS (SAP Web AS) + certain Java components	Development Infrastructure	DI
SAP NetWeaver AS (SAP Web AS)	Mobile Infrastructure	MI
SAP NetWeaver Portal (SAP EP)	Enterprise Portal	EP
SAP NetWeaver PI	Process Integration	PI
SAP NetWeaver AS (SAP Web AS)	Application Server ABAP	AS ABAP
SAP NetWeaver AS (SAP Web AS)	Application Server Java	AS Java

Figure 13.4 SAP NetWeaver Components Terminology Shift

13.1.2 SAP SRM Server Components — Overview

The SAP SRM Server contains a combination of a few different components, such as SAP EB, Bidding Engine, and SUS. Figure 13.5 provides a simple view of the components that make up the core SAP SRM server. Depending on your implementation, these components can be installed on one or more servers and within separate clients. For example, SAP EB and SUS can be installed on a single server but are always installed within separate clients.

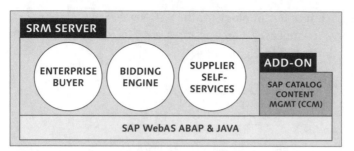

Figure 13.5 Main Components of the SAP SRM Server

In addition to the components above, there are a number of other integrated SAP components that make up the SAP SRM application. These components are typically installed separately and require their independent environment and landscape, such as the SAP NetWeaver Portal, SAP NetWeaver BW, SAP NetWeaver PI, and more.

> **Note**
>
> SAP SRM 7.0 is based on SAP NetWeaver 7.01 Technology and consists of various components listed in Table 13.1.

ABAP Components	JAVA Components	Others
SAP SRM Server 7.0	Live Auction Cockpit	NetWeaver Business Client
SAP SRM Plus 7.0	SRM MDM Catalog	SAP GUI for Windows core
SAP SRM Extended Functionality 7.0	TREX	
SAP SRM Extension Plus 7.0	Portal Content	
	Portal Content – Supplier	
	BW Content	
	PI Content	
	SRM Java Toolbox	

Table 13.1 ABAP and Java Functionalities in SAP SRM

Depending on the business scenario being implemented, one or more of these functionalities are mandatory. The next section discusses the business scenario and functionality matrix in greater detail.

With SAP SRM 5.0, organizations can no longer use SAP Exchange Interface (XI) 3.0 because it is not compatible. An organization upgrading to SAP SRM 7.0 and already using SAP NetWeaver PI will need to upgrade the SAP NetWeaver PI functionality as well. An organization that may have created custom interfaces within SAP NetWeaver PI will need to pay special attention to the interfaces when upgrading the SAP NetWeaver PI environment.

13.1.3 Business Scenario-Based Component Matrix

As described throughout this book, the SAP SRM solution is implemented based on the many business scenarios, such as self-service, strategic sourcing, and others. Each of these business scenarios requires one or more of the functionalities illustrated in Table 13.1. To assist organizations in determining what components are required, SAP provides a standard functionalities matrix.

This matrix allows the functional and technical teams to determine easily the technology components required for implementing specific functional business scenarios. Based on the project blueprint, the functional teams should be able to determine the *business scenarios* that are going to be required to meet the requirements gathered during blueprinting.

Based on these scenarios, the technical teams should be able to use the matrix to determine all the components that might be required to support these business scenarios.

This scenario matrix is available in the following SAP Guide at HTTP://SERVICE.SAP. COM/INSTGUIDES • INSTALLATION AND UPGRADE GUIDES • SAP BUSINESS SUITE APPLICATIONS • SAP SRM • SAP SRM SERVER 7.0.

Application Operations Guide – SAP SRM Powered by SAP NetWeaver

An organization using SAP SRM can use the functionality matrix to determine which SAP SRM and SAP NetWeaver components are required or are optional, based on the business scenario being configured. For example, the SAP SRM Server is a required component for implementing SAP SRM no matter what business scenario. In another example, if your organization is planning to implement the spend analysis business scenario, the SAP NetWeaver BW component and BW Content are required.

13.2 SAP SRM Architecture Based on Business Scenario

In Section 13.1, we discussed how SAP SRM contains a number of business scenarios, and to implement each of the business scenarios, the technical teams need to determine the SAP SRM and SAP NetWeaver components that need to be installed in the landscape. In this section, we'll further detail the architecture needs based on the business scenario that needs to be implemented for SAP SRM.

Use the SAP SRM Master Guide in addition to the business scenarios discussed in this section to get additional detail of the integration of the components illustrated in these scenarios. The Master Guide can be found at *http://service.sap.com/instguides*.

13.2.1 Self-Service Procurement Business Scenario

In Chapter 3, we discussed in detail the self-service procurement scenario in SAP SRM and described the functions that employees in an organization would execute. For example, they could create and manage their own requisitions for procuring indirect materials, operational and strategic MRO materials, and services. Figure 13.6 illustrates the different SAP SRM components that are typically required to support the processes within the self-service procurement scenario.

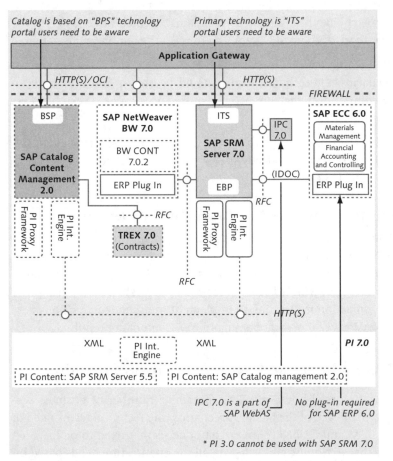

Figure 13.6 SAP SRM 7.0 — Self-Service Procurement (Illustration — SAP)

Beginning from SAP SRM 5.0, the IPC application has been integrated within the SAP Web AS. So, organizations don't require a separate installation for IPC. Organizations implementing SAP SRM in the Extended Classic scenario are required to use the IPC.

13.2.2 Plan-Driven Procurement Business Scenario

In Chapter 3, we discussed the capabilities of the plan-driven procurement scenario in SAP SRM. Within this scenario, organizations typically either integrate the requirements generated in the SAP ERP planning functionalities (MRP, PM, etc.) with SAP EB for sourcing or the SUS functionality. If planning requirements from SAP ERP are sent to SAP EB for sourcing and procurement, the SAP ERP or ERP system needs to be connected with the SAP EB system using standard remote function call (RFC) and IDoc connections, as illustrated in Figure 13.7.

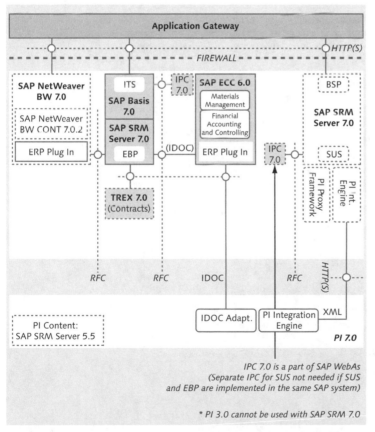

Figure 13.7 SAP SRM 7.0 — Plan-Driven Procurement (Illustration – SAP)

An organization can also integrate the planning requirements in SAP ERP with the SUS functionality. This scenario was explained in Chapter 5. From an architecture and technology standpoint, SAP NetWeaver PI is required in this scenario to communicate between the business document in the SAP ERP system and SUS. The SAP ERP system uses the IDoc Adapter to communicate with the SAP NetWeaver PI system, as illustrated in Figure 13.7.

13.2.3 Service Procurement Business Scenario

From the SAP SRM 4.0 release, SAP continuously enhanced the functionality for the procurement of services using SAP SRM. More organizations are now interested in using the service procurement business scenario. Users can create service requests in SAP EB and use SAP NetWeaver PI to communicate those to the SUS functionality. Vendors or suppliers can then review these service requests in SUS and provide responses.

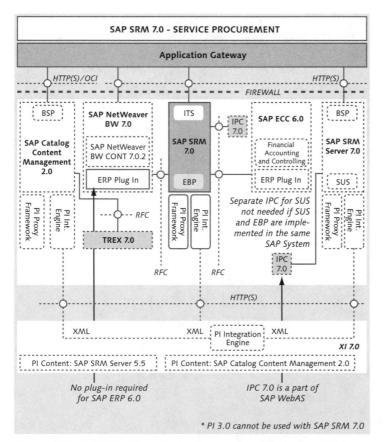

Figure 13.8 SAP SRM 7.0 — Service Procurement (Illustration – SAP)

Figure 13.8 illustrates the integration between SAP SRM, SAP ERP, and SAP NetWeaver components in the service-procurement scenario. Beginning with SAP SRM 5.0, the IPC application has been integrated within Web AS; therefore, organizations do not require a separate installation for IPC. Organizations implementing SAP SRM in the Extended Classic scenario are required to use the IPC.

13.2.4 SRM-MDM Business Scenario

SAP introduced the SRM-MDM catalog in 2005. Chapter 6 explains the capabilities of SRM-MDM in detail. At a basic level, SRM-MDM acts as the catalog solution for applications within SAP SRM, enabling end users to use catalogs to search and order goods and services maintained by an organization. The user interface in SRM-MDM is powered by Java technology.

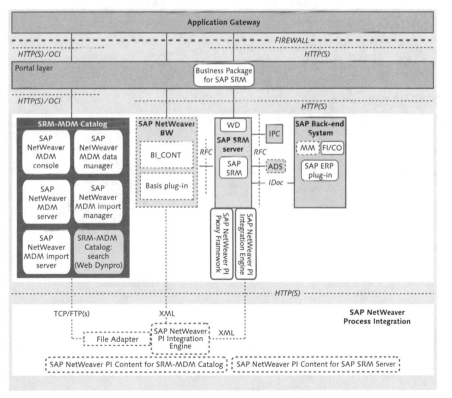

Figure 13.9 SAP SRM 7.0 — SRM-MDM Catalog (Illustration – SAP)

The PI Integration Engine is a requirement if specific scenarios are implemented for SAP CCM. For example, Figure 13.9 illustrates that master data and contract data can be integrated between SAP EB and SRM-MDM using the PI Integration Engine. Review Chapter 6 for additional details.

13.2.5 Strategic Sourcing Business Scenario

In many ways, the strategic sourcing business scenario uses all of the SAP SRM and SAP NetWeaver components. In addition to the components described in the sections above, strategic sourcing also introduces the Live Auction Cockpit (LAC) functionality in SAP SRM. An organization using the SAP Bidding Engine can utilize LAC to perform real-time online auctions.

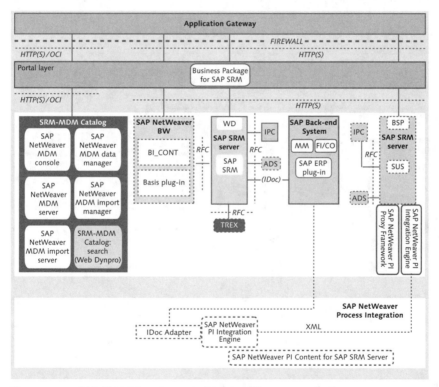

Figure 13.10 SAP SRM 7.0 — Strategic Sourcing (Illustration – SAP)

LAC is an integral part of SAP Bidding Engine and replaces the previous reverse auction functionality. Depending on your SAP SRM implementation design, some of the components illustrated in Figure 13.10 might not be required. However, this figure provides a comprehensive illustration of the different components that work together to enable the strategic sourcing business scenario.

13.2.6 Spend Analysis Business Scenario

A key objective for organizations implementing SAP SRM is to analyze their overall spending. Too many organizations fall under the trap of implementing operational procurement and forget to realize the true value of SAP SRM as they overlook spend analysis. Leaders in the market analyze their spending to find ways to strategically source, use contract management, and reduce maverick spending, for example.

In SAP SRM, the SAP NetWeaver BW solution provides reporting and spend analysis. In SAP NetWeaver BW, SAP provides prebuilt reports and queries for SAP SRM that can be activated and used out-of-the box. In the spend-analysis business scenario, both the SAP ERP and SAP SRM systems are connected. SAP NetWeaver BW integrates with both SAP ERP and SAP SRM to extract master data and transactional data to populate the reports and queries available in SAP NetWeaver BW. Figure 13.11 illustrates the architecture for spend analysis in SAP SRM.

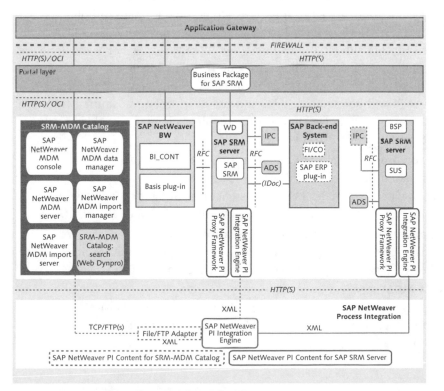

Figure 13.11 SAP SRM 7.0 — Spend Analysis (Illustration – SAP)

In most of the business scenarios described in this chapter, the SAP NetWeaver PI integration engine is used as an underlying architecture layer. This is because SAP NetWeaver PI is an integral part of the underlying technology platform for all SAP applications including SAP SRM. The next section will provide you with an understanding of when SAP NetWeaver PI becomes a mandatory functionality in SAP SRM.

13.3 SAP SRM Business Scenarios Using SAP NetWeaver PI

SAP NetWeaver PI is highly integrated within the overall SAP SRM application. However, it is not a required functionality for all business scenarios. Organizations need to review the business scenarios that they want to implement and use the information in this section to determine whether they need the SAP NetWeaver PI component installed and configured. The following bullet points will help readers determine situations when the SAP NetWeaver PI component will become mandatory in their SAP SRM implementations:

- **Output of purchasing documents from SAP SRM in XML format**
  In general, if there is a need to input or output any document (inbound or outbound) in the SAP SRM system using XML technology, SAP NetWeaver PI becomes a required functionality. If, for example, the Extended Classic or Standalone scenario is being implemented, then this requires transmission of POs from SAP SRM. If there is a requirement to transmit POs to suppliers in XML format, SAP NetWeaver PI will be required. If documents need to be transmitted from SAP SRM in EDI format, SAP NetWeaver PI is required along with a third-party EDI adapter (e.g., Seeburger EDI Adapter).
- **Plan-driven procurement with supplier integration**
  An organization that has a requirement to exchange planning documents (POs with material items) from the SAP ERP system to the SUS functionality will require SAP NetWeaver PI. This scenario is also called the SUS-MM deployment.
- **Service procurement with supplier integration**
  An organization that has a requirement to exchange service orders with suppliers using the SUS functionality is also called the SUS-EB deployment.
- **SAP SRM-MDM scenario**
  If an organization just uploads supplier catalog files into the SRM-MDM Catalog in formats other than XML, SAP NetWeaver PI is not required. However, it is required when:

▶ Contract distribution is made from SAP SRM to the SRM-MDM catalog

▶ Product master data from SAP SRM is included in the SRM-MDM catalog

The SRM-MDM scenario also requires SAP NetWeaver PI if the contract distribution or product master distribution scenario is implemented.

If any of these described scenarios are used, then a separate business system is configured on the PI Integration Server. SAP EB, SUS, and materials management in SAP ERP are all separate business systems when it comes to integrating with the SAP NetWeaver PI application. The Integration Server within SAP NetWeaver PI contains a business system for all the other applications that need to interact with SAP NetWeaver PI.

In the next section, we'll discuss a change in the User Interface architecture. This is especially important for an organization that is upgrading from a previous SAP SRM release and currently has large ITS architecture requirements to support the SAP SRM application.

13.4 User Interface ITS to WebDynpro in SAP SRM

Up to SAP SRM 5.0, the user interface was based on ITS technology; an organization had no choice but to have an independent landscape for SAP ITS. This caused organizations not only to support additional software but also bear the cost of a separate environment (development, QA, production). Furthermore, some organizations had their core SAP SRM servers installed on UNIX platforms and ITS functionality installed on Microsoft® Windows® platform to minimize costs, thus maintaining and supporting different operating platforms.

From SAP SRM 6.0, ITS technology is no longer used to Web enable SAP SRM. A new portal-based WebDynpro technology is utilized. ITS technology is obsolete for SAP SRM functions from SAP SRM 6.0 onward.

SAP SRM 7.0 utilizes SAP WebDynpro technology for all application screens with SAP SRM. The User Interface for SAP SRM is powered by the SAP NetWeaver Portal and SAP WebDynpro. The major benefit of WebDynpro is that end users can influence the appearance of the SAP SRM screen to a certain degree. For example, a user can hide or display individual fields/elements on the shopping cart screen (iView) via a right-click. This can be done without the need of an application developer, which was not possible in previous SAP SRM releases that used the ITS user interface.

13.5 SRM Sizing

Just like any other SAP application, the SAP SRM application needs to be sized accordingly for optimum efficiency. SAP SRM is a Web-based solution. Unlike the standard SAP GUI used on SAP projects, end users access the SAP SRM application using an Internet browser. Not only are organizations faced with SAP SRM server optimization, but they need to be fully aware of the requirements for Internet connectivity, secure socket layer (SSL), wireless connectivity, and others.

Project teams that do not spend the appropriate time conducting accurate sizing may have issues in the performance of the application once the application is rolled out to the user community. The system might not have the optimum hardware and capacity required to support the users involved or the processes and documents generated in your SAP SRM environment. Project teams need to clearly understand the business scenarios and the components that are planned within the scope of their SAP SRM implementation to correctly size the application.

Often, there is misunderstanding between the functional teams and the technical teams while determining all the functionalities that are required for implementing a particular business scenario. This is where the detailed functionality matrix comes in handy for reference. SAP publishes the procedure shown in Figure 13.12 for sizing the SAP SRM solution.

Typically, the SAP Basis or technical team on the project is responsible for downloading the sizing questionnaire from the SAP Service Marketplace as illustrated in Step 2 in Figure 13.12. The functional teams are responsible for providing the business scenarios and information about the number of business documents expected from their daily and yearly operations.

For instance, if the SAP SRM business scenario is a self-service procurement, then it is important for the sizing questionnaire to capture the number of requisitioners and buyers, shopping carts and POs expected, and others. This information collectively is used by SAP or another sizing partner to determine the hardware requirement for your SAP implementation.

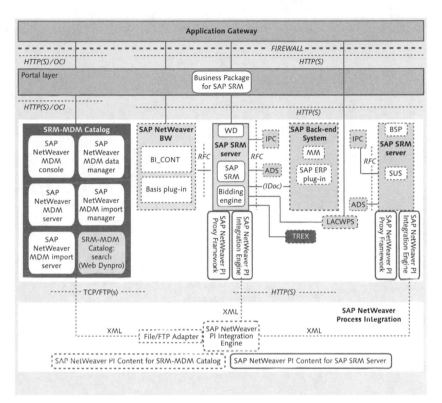

Figure 13.12 SAP SRM Sizing Procedure

13.6 Summary

This chapter covered the architecture and technology that power the SAP SRM application. We also discussed the importance of the various SAP NetWeaver functionalities such as SAP NetWeaver BW and SAP NetWeaver PI and how they enable a holistic SAP SRM application. Project teams can use the architectural illustrations provided in this chapter to map out the technology requirements on their projects, based on the selection of business scenarios.

In Chapter 14, you'll learn about upgrades to your SAP SRM system. The chapter will explain why organizations need to upgrade and describe approaches for SAP SRM upgrades.

SAP is continuously enhancing its SAP SRM solution, and over the last nine years there have already been more than eight product releases. This chapter provides an overview for organizations on what it means to undertake an SAP SRM upgrade initiative.

14   Upgrade — A How-To Approach

What is an upgrade? An upgrade is a new or enhanced version of a software product that has major enhancements or improvements to its features or functionality. Usually, an upgrade is denoted by a version number.

If your organization currently in the process of implementing SAP SRM, be ready. You are going to upgrade in the next two to three years. Based on an SAP SRM upgrade presentation by Kodak at the annual ASUG conference in 2006, the company already has upgraded SAP SRM three times since it first installed SAP SRM in 2000. Kodak implemented Enterprise Buyer Professional (EBP) 2.0B in Dec 2000, EBP 3.0 in June 2002, and SRM 4.0 in December 2005.

Although SAP SRM has consistently evolved over the last nine years (as illustrated in Figure 2.1 in Chapter 2), SAP SRM is still a relatively new application for many companies. Many organizations still operate only portions of the overall SAP SRM suite, with the majority using only SAP Enterprise Buyer (EB).

Organizations that implemented the core SAP ERP solution are more accustomed to a four- to five-year window of upgrades, but they realize that in order to continually stay competitive and optimize their business processes they need to leverage the major enhancements and improvements provided in the software upgrades provided by SAP. In the next section, we'll answer the question that many companies ask: Why should we upgrade?

14.1   Why Upgrade?

This is the million dollar question. As an organization, if we just made a large investment in the SRM implementation, then is there justification for an upgrade two to three years in the future, given that SAP supports the releases for a number of years. The answer eventually boils down to the age old decision of "build vs. buy."

Luckily, standard software upgrades from SAP are already included within the maintenance and support fees of the SRM application. However, the organization should confirm this with its SAP account representative. Licenses and contracts are specific for each company, and it is important to understand what is covered in the software upgrades.

Therefore, the true costs in an upgrade are the implementation costs and possible hardware costs, which can be significant. An upgrade project is similar to a new implementation, such that a project methodology is still required. The environments for sandbox, development, and test are still required. A dedicated technical, functional project management team is still needed. In other words, the upgrade project needs to be executed like an SAP project. Organizations that have experience with the initial implementation will realize the time commitment they can expect.

Many organizations that have implemented SAP ERP for a while have circumvented the upgrade path and chosen to customize the required functionality in-house. This is partly due to the large undertaking the core SAP ERP solution upgrade requires and partly to the fact that the product releases are spread-out over a number of years. Organizations that required functionality not available within their SAP releases went ahead and developed it internally; they could not afford to wait for the next available SAP release. The SAP SRM application has evolved at a rapid pace over the last several years.

SAP has released a new version of the SAP SRM application almost every year. Customers have seen advantages and disadvantages from SAP's rapid release strategy. The advantage is that SAP has incorporated customer requirements and new functionality and marketed them quickly, providing organizations with the ability to leverage the best practices developed by SAP in the new release. The disadvantage is that customers would have to upgrade to the newer SAP SRM release to attain the major enhancements. Figure 14.1 provides a comparative look at the software releases by SAP for the core SAP ERP solution vs. SAP SRM over the last six years. It can be clearly seen that SAP has released a new version of SAP SRM almost every year.

The complexities involved in an implementation for SAP SRM could be similar to those of an SAP implementation, but the impact to the organization may be vastly different. SAP SRM focuses on procurement and strategic sourcing; a typical SAP implementation could involve SAP ERP Financials Financial Accounting, SAP ERP HCM, Sales, and Distribution, to name a few solution areas.

The impact to the organization is huge, involving everything from requirements gathering, gap analysis, organization change, training, and deployment. This is one reason why some organizations have been able to undertake an SAP SRM upgrade two to three times over the last five to six years rather than upgrading their core SAP ERP system once at most. Another reason why many organizations have upgraded SRM multiple times is because of the enhanced functionality that SAP has provided with every new release. It is more beneficial for organizations to upgrade and benefit from this new functionality.

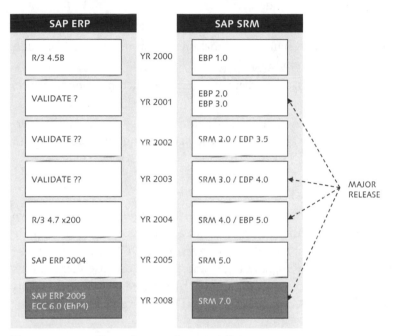

Figure 14.1 SAP SRM Solution Release Timeline

There are probably as many reasons to upgrade as there are companies. However, let's take a look at the top eight identified reasons in the bulleted list below:

▶ The maintenance and support is ending for your current release of SAP SRM. As an example, the Requisite catalog that was previously bundled with the SAP SRM application will no longer be supported past 2006. This would require companies to either upgrade to the new SAP catalog solution of Catalog Content Management (CCM) or SAP NetWeaver MDM or have a separate contract maintenance and support with Requisite.

▶ The business functionality your organization needs is available in the newer release of SAP SRM, and you recognize the limitations of your current environment.

▶ The total cost of ownership (TCO) of your existing SAP SRM solution is reduced greatly by the upgrade. For example, an organization operating on SAP SRM 3.0

or earlier typically has a separate Internet Transaction Server (ITS) infrastructure for each of its SAP SRM sandbox, development, quality, and production environments. Beginning with SAP SRM 4.0, a separate ITS infrastructure is no longer required; an internal ITS is available within the SAP SRM Server.

▶ Your organization is upgrading the backend SAP ERP application, and therefore the entire landscape is being upgraded.

▶ Minimize customizations, thus reducing the need to implement enhancements.

▶ The upgrade release provides significant functionality improvements for additional rollouts to your user community.

▶ The upgrade release increases user acceptance (error reduction, user interface, process time improvements).

▶ The upgrade strategy is in line with the organization's strategy to constantly leverage enhancements in software and technology to gain a competitive advantage in the industry.

14.1.1 Decision Methodology

An upgrade is an important and major undertaking for any organization. There have been a number of organizations that started to build a business case for an upgrade but then were unable to quantify the return on investment (ROI). Therefore, these organizations either stopped the upgrade effort and jumped on an enhancements initiative or strategically decided to wait for another year based on either the effort involved or the value foreseen. A detailed assessment is important.

14.1.2 Working with a Decision Methodology

Figure 14.2 illustrates a five-step decision methodology that has been successful at many organizations. Let's review these steps next:

▶ Step ❶: **Create a List of All Enhancements**
These could be requirements gathered from the user community to post to your initial SAP SRM implementation, issues that were put on a parking lot for review after go-live, or optimization/user acceptance opportunities.

▶ Step ❷: **Prioritize the List**
Once an exhaustive list of enhancements has been created, prioritize it. One strategy is to create high, medium, and low priority groupings, and then to divide all the enhancements within these groups.

▶ Step ❸: **Review SRM Delta Guide**
As a new SRM release is introduced, SAP provides customers with release notes and delta guides. The resources enable project teams to understand the function-

ality in the new release and act as a metric for comparison with the existing releases. This step can either be performed after the first two or can be performed independently.

Figure 14.2 Upgrade Decision Methodology

▶ **Step ❹: Comparison Analysis**
Once steps ❶, ❷, and ❸ are complete, comprehensive gap and comparison analyses should be conducted. A gap analysis is required to understand the enhancements/requirements that may not be available in the new release. A comparison analysis is necessary to identify the opportunities existing for an upgrade, especially when 75% to 80% of the enhancements might be available in the new product release.

▶ **Step ❺: Recommendation**
The results obtained from Step ❹ can then become the basis of your recommendation for a management decision.

14.2 Answer the Question: Technical or Functional?

An upgrade is an important and major undertaking for any organization and is not a trivial effort. At the end of the day, it's another SAP implementation. Most organizations struggle with the scope definition in upgrades. It is important to define scope and not to allow it to slip. To define scope, understand the goal and objectives of the upgrade.

An important question to ask is: Are you planning to do a purely technical upgrade or a functional upgrade? At first, it's a confusing question for many, but as we delve further, answering this question provides a framework for defining the overall scope of the project.

A technical upgrade focuses purely on upgrading the core release and architecture of the product. These are more focused and shorter-duration projects. One example is a situation where SAP stops providing support for a particular release of SAP SRM; there is end to maintenance. An organization will then want to upgrade to the release that is supported within the maintenance strategy offered by SAP.

Although the organization might not want to spend the money and resources on the upgrade, it would be a strategic decision to just upgrade the product release. The focus of a technical upgrade is not new functionality or enhancements; instead, it's to migrate to the newer product release as quickly as possible.

A functional upgrade, on the other hand, involves a technical upgrade plus with an additional goal of mining the new functionality offered and revisiting existing business processes. Figure 14.3 provides a simple view of the difference between a technical and functional upgrade. A functional gap analysis is a common practice, and business processes are outlined that might require blueprinting.

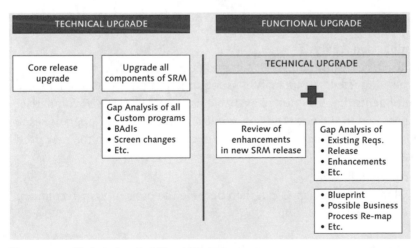

Figure 14.3 Technical or Functional Upgrade

Managing scope on a functional upgrade is typically tough. During the upgrade, the project team realizes new benefits and functionality and constantly struggles to focus on the scope boundaries. In the next section, we'll discuss why it's important for project teams to understand what they have in their existing SAP SRM environment. Unless you understand what you already have, it is difficult to decide what you want in an upgrade.

14.3 Understand Your Current Environment

Understanding your current SAP SRM environment is important to adequately analyze the potential impact of the newer release. Typically, once the consultants who implemented the initial SAP SRM release have gone, so does the technical know-how. Organizations that manage this situation well, using project methodology for the ongoing knowledge transfer, usually can eliminate this issue.

As the SAP SRM solution has gone through a change in branding, many organizations may be more familiar with their SAP EB release instead of the SAP SRM release. Figure 14.4 provides a quick correlation between the SAP SRM and SAP EB releases.

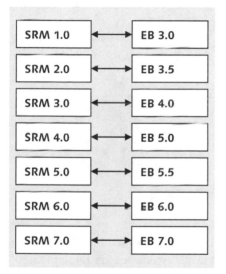

SRM 1.0	←→	EB 3.0
SRM 2.0	←→	EB 3.5
SRM 3.0	←→	EB 4.0
SRM 4.0	←→	EB 5.0
SRM 5.0	←→	EB 5.5
SRM 6.0	←→	EB 6.0
SRM 7.0	←→	EB 7.0

Figure 14.4 Overview of Corresponding EB and SRM Releases

Based on this, an organization may find that its existing implementation is two to four releases behind the current market release of SAP SRM. Many new functional enhancements have been made to the SAP SRM/EB application in addition to the technology enhancements provided in the new releases.

Depending on the scope of your SAP SRM implementation, much functionality could exist within your environment. This is one reason why there is not a one-size-fits-all solution for upgrades. See Figure 14.5 for a comparison of two different SAP SRM implementations. One has a small implementation scope, and another has a large scope.

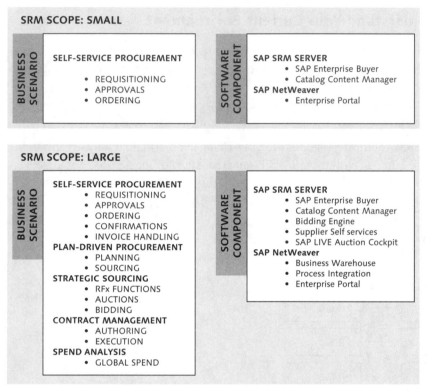

Figure 14.5 Scope Comparison for Two SAP SRM Implementations

It is evident from this example that the small scope contains only a single business-scenario implementation. Therefore, the underlying software functionalities used are limited. However, in the larger scope, as more business scenarios are implemented, additional software functionalities are required.

This example illustrates that the level of effort in an upgrade project for an SAP SRM implementation will depend on the current environment. It is important to realize the dependency on the software components; more components means upgrading each of the components individually. Out of each component arises an independent opportunity for issues.

In an upgrade, the project team(s) understands the current environment well, in addition to the vision of the future. Figure 14.6 illustrates the specific components used in an organization's current SAP EB environment and shows the changes in the technology landscape between the SAP SRM 4.0 application and SAP SRM 7.0.

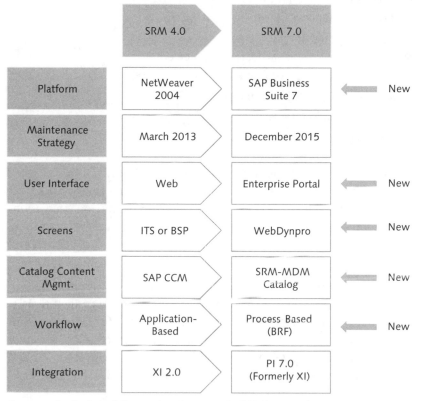

Figure 14.6 Technical Comparison Between SAP SRM 4.0 and SAP SRM 7.0

What is clearly evident is the technology shift and demands that the SAP SRM 7.0 application puts forward on customers. The ITS and BSP-based user interface in SAP SRM 4.0 is now changed to WebDynpro-based screens. The User Interface is based on SAP NetWeaver Portal and hence a mandatory requirement. The SRM-MDM catalog begins a strategic shift for SAP for the catalog management solution of choice. Although the SRM-MDM catalog was introduced in SAP SRM 5.0, organizations had a choice of SAP CCM or SAP NetWeaver MDM, it's a must have in SAP SRM 7.0. The architecture needs for SAP SRM have decreased in some areas over the years but also increased in other areas such as SAP NetWeaver Portals, which all can require an independent architecture, including SAP's TREX search engine and SAP NetWeaver Process Integration functionality. Section 14.4, Expected Changes in New SRM Release, discusses some of the new changes in SAP SRM 7.0

> **Note**
>
> SAP SRM 7.0 is a major release with considerable changes in technology for SAP SRM. The main technology changes include:
>
> ▸ Major User interface changes
>
> ▸ ITS technology phased out with WebDynpro
>
> ▸ SAP NetWeaver Portal becomes a mandatory requirement
>
> ▸ New Workflow introduced (Process Controlled)
>
> ▸ Personal Object Worklist (POWL) introduced
>
> ▸ Service Procurement enhanced for Hierarchies
>
> ▸ Central Contract Management concept introduced

The organization in our example could be using Requisite BugsEye, a third-party software solution for managing electronic catalogs, as its catalog solution for SAP SRM. SAP has announced that it will no longer support Requisite Catalog integration; therefore, organizations must decide whether to support the product internally, pay additional maintenance fees to SAP, or align themselves with the future content and catalog strategy supported by SAP.

A detailed discussion is required to determine whether you want to replace the SAP BugsEye solution and replace with CCM and to review the pros and cons. If CCM is implemented, it requires additionally the implementation of TREX for search and SAP NetWeaver PI for integration. Not all CCM implementations require SAP NetWeaver PI; however, specific scenarios in CCM require the use of SAP NetWeaver PI. The product master replication scenario in CCM is an example where SAP NetWeaver PI is used as the standard middleware component.

A number of organizations that installed Enterprise Buyer release 3.0 or earlier also ventured into new methods of electronic communication like XML. However, they used SAP's earlier XML solution, Business Connector. The current strategy for SAP is to support integration of all types. That includes internal integration between other SAP systems (e.g., SUS and EB) and external (e.g., between business partners) via SAP NetWeaver PI. Organizations that are planning to upgrade to the newer release of SAP SRM need to analyze the impact of SAP NetWeaver PI on their environment. SAP offers standard business content in NetWeaver PI for integration with supported business scenarios in SAP SRM. The next section highlights some of the major changes that have been introduced in SAP SRM compared to previous releases.

14.4 Expected Changes in New SRM Release

During the analysis or blueprint phase of the project, a gap analysis of the SAP SRM releases will provide the project team with the major changes that need to be reviewed and addressed.

Figure 14.7 provides a quick overview of some changes between SAP SRM 4.0 and previous releases.

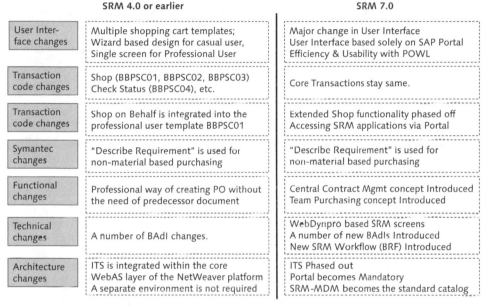

Figure 14.7 Overview of Changes Between SAP SRM 4.0 and Earlier Releases

Compared to SAP SRM 4.0, the following major noteworthy changes have been introduced in the SAP SRM application:

▶ SAP SRM 7.0 uses a WebDynpro-based User Interface technology, along with the SAP NetWeaver Portal, instead of the ITS User Interface technology used in SAP SRM 4.0. The SAP NetWeaver Portal is a mandatory functionality for SAP SRM 7.0. Review the Portal chapter regarding Enhancement Pack 1 for SAP SRM 7.0 which aims to remove the requirement for the SAP NetWeaver Portal to use SAP SRM 7.0.

▶ The User Interface (UI) has completely changed. In addition to providing usability enhancements in the SAP SRM application, new navigational designs have been introduced to enable quick access to information using Personal Object Worklists (POWL).

- ▶ Additionally, the UI and Portal environment makes it easier for employees to easily personalize without the need for custom development as in previous releases.

- ▶ A single interface and layout introduced for all SAP SRM applications like Shop for, Purchase Order, Contracts, and others.

- ▶ A new Process-Controlled Workflow lets organizations manage approvals without the need for custom development to a certain extent vs the Application-Controlled Workflow in previous releases.

- ▶ Sourcing and Bidding Engine functions have been enhanced. SAP NetWeaver Portal harmonizes roles for purchasing users with access to both SAP SRM and SAP ERP applications of shopping cart and POs. All necessary procurement functions can be executed from a single screen.

- ▶ SRM-MDM is now the catalog application for SAP SRM. All organizations implementing SAP SRM 7.0 have to use the SAP NetWeaver MDM catalog.

- ▶ SAP has introduced many new BAdIs in the newer SRM releases, allowing organizations to reduce the core modification to the SAP release and instead building business logic using release-supported BAdIs (similar to User Exits).

Organizations upgrading to the SAP SRM 5.0 release need to convert their existing Organizational Units for vendors into vendor groups. In previous releases of SAP SRM, a single organization-management transaction was used: PPOMA_BBP. This maintained both internal and external organization units and business partners. Vendors were maintained within a single hierarchy using this transaction.

Beginning with the SAP SRM 5.0 release, a new transaction, PPOMV_BBP, was developed to create and maintain vendor organization units. The concept of vendor groups (VG) has been introduced and is used for grouping; it is no longer obligatory to have one VG per vendor, as was previously the case for organizational units. If several vendors (who previously were assigned to an organizational unit) have identical attributes, they are now assigned directly to a common VG. During the upgrade, organizations can execute the report: BBP_XPRA_ORGEH_TO_VENDOR_GROUP to create vendor groups.

Delete all organizational units and organizational plans of the vendors from the internal organizational plan (Transaction PPOMA_BBP) and group these according to their attributes in new organizational objects (Transaction PPOMV_BBP).

After an upgrade to SAP SRM 5.0, this report must be executed in each client for each central organizational unit for vendors (root organizational unit). This applies both to SAP EB and SUS. So far, we have discussed why organizations need to upgrade their

SAP SRM systems. The next section highlights some of the tools that project teams can use during their upgrade initiative.

14.5 Upgrade — Tools and Resources

A common question that comes up regarding upgrade projects is: Where do I start? Let's take a look at what you can do to ease your upgrade process.

14.5.1 SAP Documentation

SAP provides invaluable documentation for the execution of your upgrade project. Figure 14.8 provides an overview of the major documentation provided by SAP within the upgrade phase.

The Upgrade Master Guide, available at the SAP Service Marketplace, is the starting point for upgrading the business scenarios of the SAP SRM solution. It provides scenario-specific descriptions of preparation, execution, and follow-up of an upgrade. It also refers to other documents, such as the Component Upgrade Guides and SAP Notes. Only specific components may be valid for the SAP SRM upgrade within your organization.

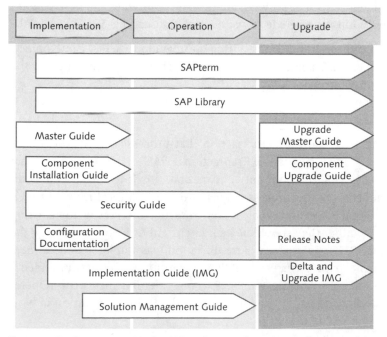

Figure 14.8 Documentation for SAP Software Life Cycle — Focus: Upgrade

> **Tip**
>
> If your organization does not use the plan-driven procurement business scenario in SAP SRM, then those aspects of the upgrade guide can be skipped.

The Component Upgrade Guide describes the technical upgrade of an SAP component, taking into account the combinations of operating systems and databases. It does not describe any business-related configuration.

Release notes are documents that contain short descriptions of new features or changes in SAP functionalities since the previous releases. Release notes about ABAP developments enable the SAP system to generate delta and upgrade IMGs.

The master guide, component guide, and release notes will all help to get you started in the right path. In addition, there are standard tools used for the application of support packs and notes, all of which are valuable utilities that are used within the upgrade process.

14.5.2 Modified Objects

During an upgrade, existing objects of the SAP standard system are overwritten with the objects redelivered in the new release. To help customers retain the development objects modified in their existing (previous) release, SAP provides the newly modified objects redelivered in the upgrade adjustment of Transactions SPDD and SPAU.

Organizations can use these transactions during an upgrade to select these objects and modify them manually. Transactions SPDD and SPAU are commonly used by the BASIS teams in the upgrade process.

Transaction SPDD

Transaction SPDD is a standard SAP transaction that processes ABAP Dictionary objects. The process of reconciliation of Transactions SPAU and SPDD objects can waste time. Contrary to what is commonly understood, this is not purely a technical or development activity. This process begins with the technical team but then requires your functional experts to analyze and research the reason for existing changes and decide whether they should be kept as current or be overridden by the new changes from SAP. For instance, if a modification was implemented to meet a business requirement in your current SAP SRM environment but has provided a standard solution in the SAP SRM upgrade SAP to meet that business requirement, your functional experts need to provide direction to the technical team on how to move forward with the SAP update.

Transaction SPAU

Transaction SPAU is a standard SAP transaction that allows you to adjust programs, function modules, screens, interfaces, documentation, and text elements after an upgrade. One common example in SAP SRM upgrades is HTML template changes. Organizations that implemented SAP SRM early on struggled with the user interface, and for user acceptance changed many standard HTML templates provided by SAP. Transaction SPAU would identify those template objects and request an action to accept changes in the SAP upgrade or analyze the existing templates. Other examples would be standard programs, screen and menu painter, and text elements.

Basically, when your upgrade is complete, you check Transactions SPDD and SPAU, which will indicate all standard SAP objects changed in previous version (e.g., customer modifications like HTML screens or OSS notes, etc.). Typically, the basis team will provide the SPAU list, and the SRM upgrade team will have to determine in each object change whether to accept a new version (RESET TO ORIGINAL). For organizations that have made many modifications in their SAP SRM system, this activity will be one the most important post upgrade tasks.

Implementing an OSS note via SAP note assistant
The table below outlines the simple steps required to implement an OSS note using SAP note assistant (SNOTE).

Step	Icon	Description
1		Download note
2		Set process status to 'in process'
3		Read note instructions
4		Implement note (popup will appear allowing you to read note)
5		View implementation log, add comments of your own
6		Set status to 'complete'

Other icons

	De-implement note
	Note browser (view all in system for your user)

Figure 14.9 Implementing an OSS Note via SAP Note Assistant

Note Assistant (SNOTE)

SNOTE is a standard SAP transaction provided to automate the process of applying SAP OSS Notes. This tool (shown in Figure 14.9) allows you to download SAP Notes into your SAP environment and then automatically implement the corrections contained in the notes into your SAP system. The Notes assistant works well when there is code insertion or deletion into existing ABAP objects. However, notes that contain HTML or Java scripting corrections cannot be implemented via the SNOTE transaction; they have to be implemented manually. This tool is useful to quickly apply OSS Notes that earlier required a lot of manual development effort.

eCATT

SAP users have long used the Computer Aided Test Tool (CATT) heavily during the testing and conversion phases of a project implementation. CATT scripts frequently upload master data or make changes to master data records. In an upgrade, this tool comes in handy as it can be used for testing transactions, reports, and business scenarios. The SAP SRM system is based on the SAP NetWeaver platform, and transactions run on the SAP Web Application Server (Web AS), for which the CATT tool does not work. However, the extended Computer Aided Test Tool (eCATT) can be used in SAP SRM and other Web Application Server 6.20 or higher systems for the same. In SAP, eCATT can be executed using the standard transaction SECATT.

In the next section, we will discuss the best practices to keep in mind during your upgrade project.

14.6   Best Practices — Upgrade Impact

Upgrade projects are notorious for getting out of hand when it comes to scope. Therefore, it is extremely important that your project management team create clear boundaries on the goals of your upgrade and the overall scope. Is your upgrade project a purely technical upgrade? Or is it both a functional and a technical upgrade? A purely technical upgrade would have a strict guideline for the project that only current functionality will be implemented (i.e., new functionality will be out of scope). The system will be upgraded to the newer release of the software but only functionality existing in the "current production environment" will be tested and supported.

A functional upgrade, on the other hand, is initiated with the expectation that the software release will be upgraded to make use of the rich functionality in the new release of the product. One example is that in your current environment the SAP SRM service procurement business scenario has not been implemented. However, in the upgrade, your organization would like to roll out this new functionality.

It is important for an organization to understand the impact of an SAP SRM upgrade project. Users, training, change management, system architecture, and maintenance and support all are important areas for impact analysis.

14.6.1 Upgrade Assessment — Process-Based Impact to User Community

Each upgrade release brings new enhancements and changes to the core application. Ideally, the changes in the new SAP SRM release should be for the better, but as with any change, it has to be managed. An assessment is required to define the processes that are used in your SAP SRM implementation and map any new changes to those processes, so user impact can be determined.

The SAP SRM application map provided by SAP is a good place to start; it provides an overview of all the business scenarios within the new SAP SRM release. The impact of these process changes will be different for each organization, depending on the functionality implemented in their current SAP SRM environment.

Figure 14.10 shows an example of a self-service procurement process chain. During your upgrade assessment, the project team should map out all the subprocesses (new and existing) that will promote a change within the current processes. The sample depicted in Figure 14.10 shows an example of an SAP SRM implementation that does not include Invoice Entry and Approval within the existing implementation and future scope of the SAP SRM upgrade. Therefore, there are no subprocesses listed as being affected by the upgrade. Each subprocess needs to be further broken down and listed as either an enhancement or a new functionality.

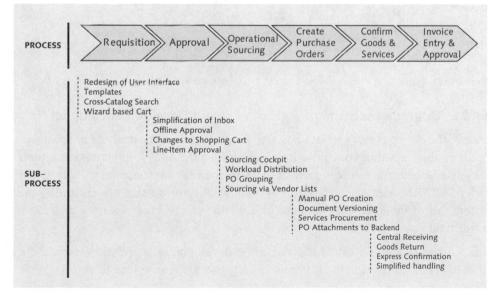

Figure 14.10 Sample — Processes Impacted by the Upgrade

Typically, SRM upgrades have a considerable impact on end users. SAP has enhanced the user interface for SAP SRM in almost each new product release. Depending on your current SRM release, an upgrade to SAP SRM Release 5.0 or 6.0 could be a major change in user interface (apart from functionality). User acceptance and usability impacts need to be assessed along with impacts on training and user guides.

Figure 14.11 shows an example of user impact during an SAP SRM upgrade. In our example, the suppliers were originally collaborating with the organization using a custom-developed application. The upgrade scope included the implementation of SUS, and hence had a considerable impact to the supplier community as well.

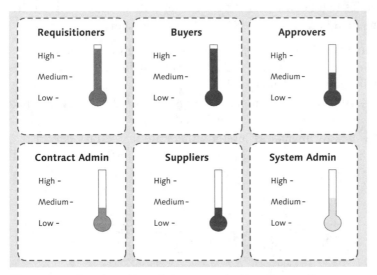

Figure 14.11 Sample — Upgrade Impact to the User Community

14.6.2 Upgrade Assessment — Technical and Development Impact

One of the core processes within any SAP SRM upgrade is the analysis of the development objects within your system. In your initial SAP SRM implementation, there may have been many customized changes to the user interface (especially in the older SAP SRM releases such as 2.0), workflows, business rules–driven BAdIs, and others. All of these are development objects that are affected when an upgrade is performed.

The functional teams work closely with the development teams to determine the plan of action to upgrade the different objects that are customized in your environment. These are typically activities conducted during the blueprint and build phases of the upgrade project. The following key areas require the functional and development teams to work together to determine the appropriate action to take when it comes to upgrading objects such as HTML templates, Workflows, and BAdIs.

HTML Templates

Since SAP SRM 3.0, the user interface has changed. If your organization made changes to the HTML templates for SAP EB, you will need to analyze these one at a time and determine whether you still require those customizations or the new user interface (which is dramatically user friendly) is sufficient for the user acceptance. If customizations are still required, then the development team needs to customize each of the existing HTML screen changes in the new screens provided by SAP. This can waste time.

Workflows

In the earlier SRM releases, many organizations customized the standard SAP delivered *workflow* templates to meet their business requirements for approvals. As of SAP SRM 7.0, new workflow functionality has been introduced. Organizations will find that their needs might have been met by SAP and they can do away with their existing custom development. Or, if changes are required, they will be able to use new BAdIs to enhance the delivered workflow capabilities.

BAdIs

SAP has built upon their strategy to deliver a standard SRM application that can be used across various industry organizations, and it has been able to deliver on this strategy by allowing companies to adapt their business requirements into the standard SAP application by using BAdIs. A BAdI is a standard exit within SAP programs whereby organizations can change SAP programs without carrying out any system modifications. During an upgrade, organizations will need to review the existing BAdIs that they are using and check to see if those have been changed by SAP in the new release. A change could be that the BAdI has been enhanced or it could be completely replaced with a new BAdI. The functional and development teams need to work on this activity together.

Table 14.1 provides an abridged list of the backend purchasing documents related BAdIs introduced in SAP SRM 5.0. A complete list of BAdIs in SAP SRM is available in Appendix D. Also, this appendix provides a more detailed understanding of BAdIs and new changes that have been introduced to BAdIs in the SAP SRM 4.0 and 5.0 releases. This is especially important because any new business logic that needs to be developed should be done using the new BAdIs. Also, the existing code should be moved into the new BAdIs for appropriate support.

BAdI Description	SAP SRM 5.0	Earlier Releases
Purchase Order in Backend system	BBP_CREATE_BE_PO_NEW	BBP_CREATE_PO_BACK
Purchase Requisition in Backend system	BBP_CREATE_BE_RQ_NEW	BBP_CREATE_REQ_BACK
Reservation in Backend system	BBP_CREATE_BE_RS_NEW	BBP_CREATE_RES_BACK
Grouping of Shopping cart items for follow-on documents	BBP_BS_GROUP_BE	BBP_SC_TRANSFER_BE, BBP_RESERVATION_GRP
Determine target objects in Backend system	BBP_TARGET_OBJTYPE	BBP_TARGET_OBJECTS

Table 14.1 New BAdIs in SAP SRM 5.0 for Follow-On Documents

OSS Notes

Anyone who has gone through an SAP upgrade before knows the importance of OSS Messages and application of SAP Notes (corrections). When you encounter a problem during your upgrade, it is possible that other organizations might have experienced the same. This is where the SAP Service Marketplace (also known as *SAP OSS*) is of great help. Before you spend hours troubleshooting the issue, search your issue on the SAP Service Marketplace. If you are unable to find a similar issue, create a Customer Message with SAP. Figure 14.12 provides a simple template to manage your OSS Messages.

Short text	Long Description	Working in Previous Release	System ID	Installation	Message Number	Component	Priority	Status	Created on	Changed on	Reporter name
EBP 30: upgraded vendors are not updated in new tables	After the upgrade the Vendors are not updated in the new tables. When the shopping cart is created the vendors are not displayed as a search result in the Preferred Vendor search.	Yes	EBS	XXXXXXXXX	12567	SRM-EBP-ADM	Medium	In Processing by SAP	1/1/2006	1/1/2006	MIKE

Figure 14.12 Template to Manage OSS Messages

14.6.3 Upgrade Assessment — Impact on End User Training

Training is serious business. Depending on your current and upgrade release, there might be major design and functional changes. Capturing those changes and adequately training users is not an easy task. SAP SRM 7.0, for example, introduces a completely revamped SRM release from a user interface perspective and any organization upgrading to SAP SRM 7.0 will have to focus heavily on the end user training and change management element.

During the initial SAP SRM implementation, many organizations embarked on Web-based e-training (e.g., video, sound, and multimedia). The upgrade brings changes, making the existing training content obsolete. Now, organizations are faced with a new question: Do we continue to develop extensive multimedia-rich training only to see it become obsolete in a few years? The SAP SRM application has changed almost every new release from a new player to a key player. Today, SRM is a best-of-class e procurement solution, but there are no guarantees that major changes will not happen in the upcoming releases.

Organizations upgrading will find themselves faced with major rewrites of their existing training materials. A best practice is to build delta training guides targeting your largest audience. Typically, the Requisitioners and Approvers are by far the biggest SAP SRM user segments in most organizations, and also the most dispersed. Building the training material can be a daunting task; the best practice is to begin this activity during the development phase of your upgrade.

Go-Live Strategy — Some Thoughts

Although each implementation has its own goals and objectives and no two upgrades may be the same, the following thoughts will help you with your go-live strategy.

▶ As a best practice, all end users in the current system should go live with an upgrade at the same time. Sometimes, this might be a challenge to implement when a single SAP instance is being used across a global user base.

▶ A phased roll-out by plant, geographical region, or functional areas creates the need to support two or more production systems and makes huge demands on technical and functional dependencies.

▶ Once the project phase is in integration testing, parallel roll-outs of the existing release would have to be stopped.

- The project cutover should typically occur over a holiday period or long weekend. Organizations that operate on a 24 hour/7 day schedule are unable to sustain long system downtime. Many organizations aim to achieve a two-day downtime period during their upgrades.
- Although you are implementing an SAP SRM upgrade, it impacts your entire environment. The SAP ERP system, the SAP NetWeaver BW system, and the SAP NetWeaver Portal system are just examples of what might be affected in the overall SAP SRM solution by an upgrade. Ensure the availability of the dependent systems.

Project teams need to be aware of the changes and enhancements that are available in the new SAP SRM release. This is especially relevant if, for example, your organization has built a number of custom function modules or remote function call (RFC) programs to achieve some business requirements. In the new SAP SRM release, it could be that SAP has provided standard Business Application Programming Interfaces (BAPIs) that accommodated those business requirements. It is important for your project team to be aware of such new functionality, and secondly, it needs to be clear within your project charter whether conversion of existing custom code to new BAPIs is within the scope of your upgrade project. If your project timeline is aggressive, it is advisable not to undertake such activity; instead, define a separate project focused toward similar efforts.

In an assessment for the SAP SRM upgrade, an organization should also consider using SAP NetWeaver Portals for the overall user interface. SAP recommends that portals be used as the single user interface to provide access to the various components integrated within SAP SRM (shopping carts, SAP NetWeaver BW reporting, SAP ERP, etc.). Again, this becomes a scoping question. Implementation of SAP NetWeaver Portal is typically a strategic direction for the organization and would be advisable to be implemented and as a separate project.

In the next section, we'll discuss some of the lessons gathered from implementing SRM upgrade projects.

14.7 SAP SRM 7.0 – Major Changes

Throughout this chapter, you've been introduced to new capabilities for SAP SRM 7.0 and the possible impacts for organizations. In this section, you will learn about specific changes and enhancements that are a part of the SAP SRM 7.0 release.

Table 14.2 provides a list of major changes that have been introduced as a part of SAP SRM 7.0 release.

Functionality	Description
SAP NetWeaver Portal	With SAP SRM 7.0, the SAP NetWeaver Portal is a mandatory component. As opposed to previous SRM releases where a portal was a nice to have, with SAP SRM 7.0, the entire end user interface is based on the portal and hence a must.
	The portal contains an entirely new Business Content for SAP SRM 7.0. For organizations that have the backend ECC 6.0 EhP04, the portal contains a harmonized role that integrates transactions from SAP SRM and SAP ERP seamlessly.
Universal Work List (UWL)	The portal offers new functionality for approvals and notifications – via the SAP Universal Work List (UWL).
	UWL allows users to see their consolidated task lists from SAP SRM and other systems, for example, SAP ERP. For example, a manager can access a shopping cart and an invoice approval from a single application in the portal. (In this example, the Shopping Cart was from SAP SRM and Invoice from SAP ERP.)
End User Interface	The ITS-based User Interface (UI) in SAP SRM 5.0 and earlier releases has been replaced by a new portal-based ABAP WebDynpro UI in SAP SRM 7.0.
	This new UI offers numerous personalization and customization options without a need for custom development.
Personal Object Work Lists (POWL)	With the introduction of Personalized Object Work Lists, users can generate basic reports from personalized criteria, and store them for repeated use. Also enables enhanced user efficiency.

Table 14.2 New Changes in SAP SRM 7.0

Functionality	Description
SAP Workflow	SAP SRM 7.0 introduces an entirely new workflow — process-controlled workflow framework has been introduced. However, the old application-controlled workflow is still supported for customers upgrading to SAP SRM 7.0.
SAP Netweaver BW Content	SAP NetWeaver BW has also been upgraded and organizations implementing SAP SRM 7.0 need to migrate to SAP NetWeaver BW 7.0 from BW 3.5, which results in improved performance and end user experience.
OCI	For organizations that want to implement the new Service Hierarchy functionality in SAP SRM 7.0, new fields, which handle the transfer of hierarchical data, have been added to the Open Catalog Interface (OCI).
Solution Enhancements	In SAP SRM 7.0, all the SAP SRM screens have been developed in WebDynpro. Henceforth, organizations that now want to make changes to visibility of fields and changes can do so without the need for costly and lengthy modifications. WebDynpro allows personalization of screen element changes by the end user. For modification of business logic, a number of new BAdIs are available.
SAP ERP	Organizations that have an ECC 6.0 backend with EhP 04 (Enhancement Pack 04), can make use of tighter integration between SAP SRM and SAP ECC for transferring: ▶ Purchase Requisitions ▶ Services ▶ Confirmations ▶ Purchase Orders ▶ Contracts

Table 14.2 New Changes in SAP SRM 7.0 (Cont.)

The following figures illustrate the major change in the layout of SAP SRM 7.0 and previous releases. Figure 14.13 shows the Check Status application in SAP SRM 5.0. When users need to check the status of their ordered carts, they use the "Find Shopping Cart" section to find the cart and then search.

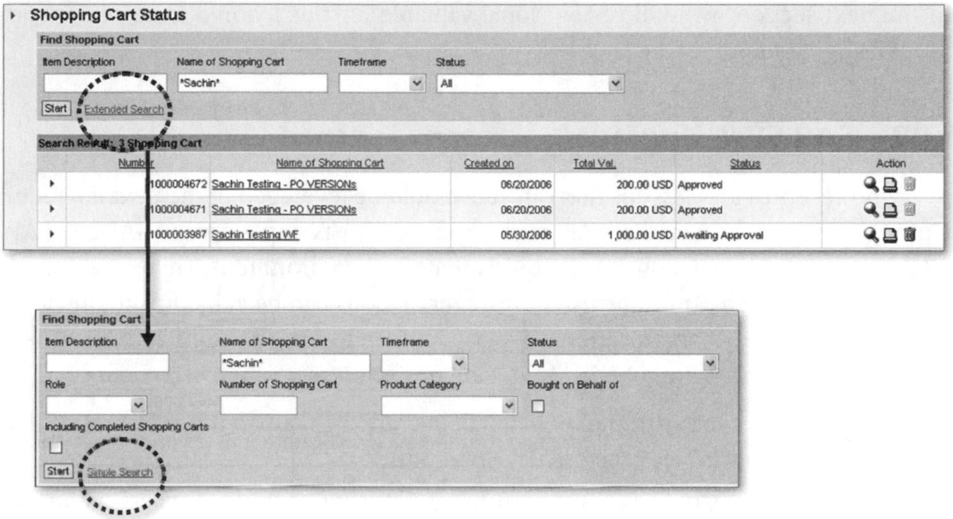

Figure 14.13 Shopping Cart Status in SAP SRM 5.0

Alternately, in SAP SRM 7.0, as illustrated in Figure 14.14, predefined search queries can be defined by end users, which automatically determine the search criteria based on defined fields. When a user logs in to the portal into their workspace, SAP SRM automatically executes the "Active Queries" to show the results.

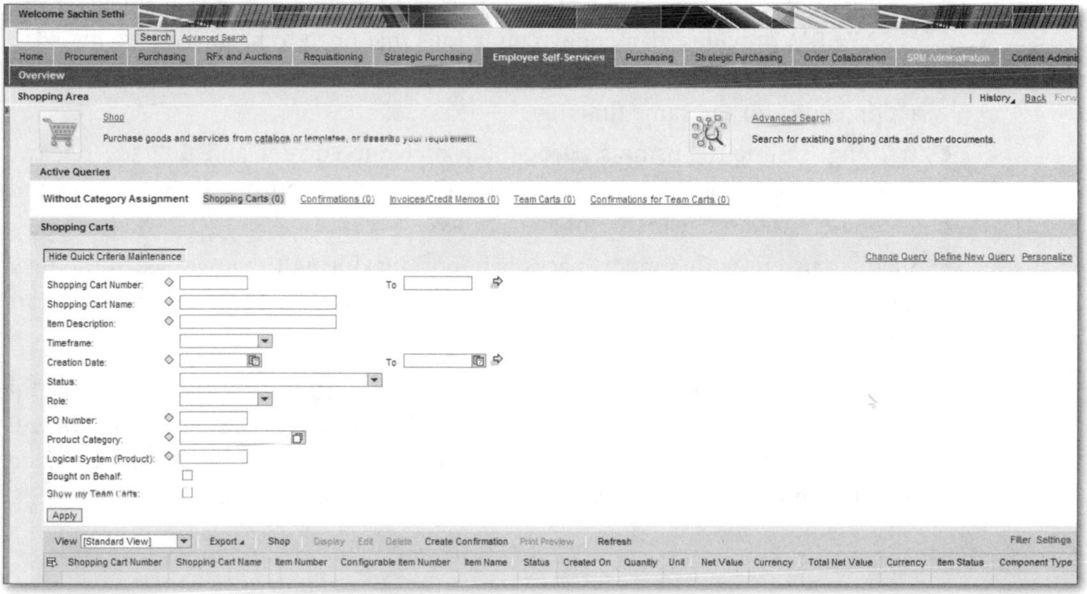

Figure 14.14 POWL-Based Query for Shop for Application in SAP SRM 7.0

In the next section, we will review some valuable lessons learned from real world SAP SRM upgrades.

14.8   SAP SRM Upgrade — Lessons Learned

Every project provides lessons that can and should be leveraged in the next upgrade. Unfortunately, in the world of SAP, each organization has implemented SAP and SAP SRM to accommodate its business requirements and environment. Therefore, a one-size-fits-all approach cannot be used. However, lessons can be gained from previous experiences or other organization's experiences. Here are the top lessons learned from our experience with SAP SRM upgrade projects:

▶ Keep an eye on the functionality being delivered in the upcoming releases of the product; aim toward less custom development.

▶ Do not treat an upgrade as a technical effort. Enlist your business users for analysis from the beginning.

▶ Define your scope. A new release from SAP offers hundreds of new functionalities; define the overall scope of the project upfront.

▶ Do not forget the external systems; new software releases provoke changes in all areas of the product.

▶ Programs that contain variants need to be reviewed.

▶ Do not underestimate the role of security in your upgrade effort. Each new release of SAP SRM provides many new transactions that need to be analyzed with existing user authorizations. The SAP SRM application is notorious for changing transaction codes for the same function.

▶ Training is serious business. Depending on your current and upgrade release, there might be major design and functional changes. Capturing those changes and adequately training users is not an easy task.

▶ Staying current with support packs is important during the upgrade. In the new release, especially ramp-up, SAP provides corrections via OSS Notes and support packs.

The next section provides an upgrade assessment questionnaire that can be useful for organizations prior to beginning their upgrade initiatives. This questionnaire will help to answer questions that are typically not intuitive and prompt organizations to think through the different areas relevant for any upgrade project.

14.9 Upgrade Assessment — via a Questionnaire

An upgrade is an important and major undertaking for any organization. Asking the right questions upfront not only provides a clear picture of the various opportunities, challenges, and risks involved but also saves a great deal of time in planning and execution.

The following list of questions can be used as an assessment for your e-procurement upgrade and enhancement project. To answer the following questions, input will be required from different functional and technical teams in your organization. Once you are able to complete this assessment, your project team can analyze the answers in the different section to create a starting point for building your upgrade vision and scoping document:

1. **Goal**
   - What is the reason for the upgrade?
   - Current release going out of support
   - Would like to leverage features available in new release
   - Due to internal infrastructure standardization
   - System consolidation
   - Other

2. **Current Implementation**
   - What is the current release of SRM/EBP implemented?
     - Release xxxx
   - Which of the following components of SRM are implemented?
     - Enterprise Buyer (EB)
     - Bidding Engine
     - Contract Management
     - Supplier self-services
     - Requisite BugsEye
     - Requisite Emerge
     - SAP CCM
     - Internet Transaction Server
     - Other xxxx
   - When was the current implementation installed or upgraded to?
     - Year xxxx

- Which integration scenarios are currently implemented?
  - Classic
  - Extended Classic
  - Standalone
  - If a combination of above scenarios exist, please advise the functionality used for the scenario xxxx
- Which functional scenarios are implemented?
  - Self-Services Procurement
  - Plan-Driven Procurement
  - Strategic Sourcing
  - Auction/Bidding
  - SAP ERP HCM Integration to SRM
  - Plant Maintenance Integration
  - SAP NetWeaver BW for Spend Analysis
  - XML PO to Suppliers
- Do you have any custom workflow implemented?
  - Yes No
- What type of workflow (e.g., cost-center based)?
- Which catalogs are used and how many?
- Any internal catalog?
- Number of suppliers in internal catalog
- Number of roundtrip catalogs — xxx
- Is P-card function implemented?
  - Yes No
  - In SAP SRM or SAP ERP x
- How many Business Add-Ins (BAdIs) have been used?
- Please provide a list of possible
- Have you customized the frontend user experience (modified standard SAP HTML templates)?
  - Yes No
- If yes, could you please advise if minor or major?
- Is SAP SRM system integrated to multiple SAP ERP backend systems?
  - Yes No

▶ Is SAP SRM system integrated to non-SAP ERP backend systems?

  ▶ Yes No

▶ Do you have multicurrency, multilanguage implemented?

  ▶ Yes No

▶ If yes, what currencies and languages?

▶ How many sites are using SAP SRM?

  ▶ xxx

▶ How many users are using SAP SRM?

  ▶ xxx

▶ Please list any major limitations/shortcomings/problems in current system.

  ▶ xxx

▶ How many environments in current SAP SRM system landscape?

3. **Additional Functions/Features in Upgrade**

▶ Please list new functions and features you are planning to include in the upgrade.

  ▶ xxx xxx xxx xx

▶ Please list functions and features you are planning to enhance in the upgrade.

  ▶ xxx

▶ Please list functions and features you are planning to discontinue after the upgrade.

  ▶ xxx

▶ Are you planning to replace your internal catalog with SAP CCM?

  ▶ Yes No N/A

▶ Are you planning to use SAP Business Connector with SAP NetWeaver PI?

  ▶ Yes No N/A

▶ Please explain the planning and study already done for scope of the upgrade activity.

▶ Are you planning to increase any environment for SAP SRM system? Introduce Pre-production, add QA, etc.

  ▶ Yes No N/A

▶ Do you currently use the SAP NetWeaver Portal?

  ▶ Yes No

▶ Do you plan to utilize the SAP NetWeaver Portal with SAP SRM?

  ▶ Yes No

- ▶ If you currently do not integrate with SAP ERP HCM for Organizational Structure, do you plan on integrating that in the upgrade?
  - ▶ Yes No
- ▶ Will there be additional sites/users rolled out as part of the upgrade?
  - ▶ Yes No

14.10 Relevant OSS Notes

Table 14.3 lists important OSS Notes available on the SAP Service Marketplace that are relevant for organizations upgrading to SAP SRM 7.0.

Note	Description
1223493	SAP SRM 7.0: Release & Information Note
1224654	SRM-MDM Catalog 3.0 Upgrade from SRM-MDM Catalog 2.0
1261825	SAP SRM: Used Roles Matrix

Table 14.3 OSS Notes from SAP Service Marketplace

14.11 Summary

The goal of this chapter was to provide you with an understanding of how to approach SAP SRM upgrade projects. It is important for project teams to continuously consider the scope-creep threat in an upgrade project. Also, it is vital to treat an upgrade project as another SAP implementation. Depending on the SAP SRM release, new enhancements and changes at various areas of the product could affect the application usability, architecture, training, and possibly change management.

Now, we can proceed to Chapter 15, which addresses performance reporting via SAP NetWeaver BW.

Every organization strives to find tangible information — amid mountains of data — that provides true competitive differentiation. This information allows you to make timelier, more accurate, and fiscally advantageous decisions that drive improved corporate performance.

15 Performance Reporting via SAP NetWeaver BW

Organizations implement SAP applications all the time; sometimes, it takes years to complete an initial SAP ERP implementation. Scope is adjusted, resources are strapped, the timeline is always adjusted, and what gets scrapped are performance reporting measures. These were the same performance measures that were discussed in the beginning of the project and probably were a key factor for implementing the application.

Often, organizations plan to implement performance reporting but lag in the delivery of that reporting. Part of the issue is that when requirements are gathered, the functional teams bombard the performance reporting teams with the existing requirements and customized reports that they have available in the legacy systems.

The performance reporting team seeks to meet the desired needs by struggling in a dark cloud for a few months, trying various methods to produce the requested customized reports that were deemed go-live critical. Not until after the project realization phase does realization dawn that the overall business processes will be changed as part of the new application implementation, and the customized reports may be nice to have rather than critical.

A business-intelligence survey by IDC found that: "...only 15% of managers agree with the statement that most reports developed in their organizations deliver the right data to the right people at the right time."

Unfortunately, what both the functional and performance reporting teams forget during this process are the real needs of the new business environment. What are the key performance indicators (KPIs) that are required to realize the immense value of the application that was implemented? Most e-procurement and supplier relationship management (SRM) implementations face the situation described here.

Many organizations are bound by industry and governmental requirements and drive the desired reporting. Those situations aside, our argument applies to non-regulated reporting needs.

Performance reporting in a supplier relationship environment is also multifaceted. There are many business partners who need to analyze data and cannot operate efficiently without proper reporting mechanisms. In an organization, the departments need to report on purchases made and compare against open budgets and actual expenses.

Professional purchasers need to analyze spending based on contracted and noncontracted sources, and review maverick procurement. Strategic buyers need to view supplier history and performance to negotiate better contacts and select the best sources of supply. The key requirement for all these business partners, internal and external to the organization, is to analyze data for better decision making.

According to Research Vice-President Frank Buytendijk at Gartner Research: "...if you ask organizations what they want to use business intelligence (BI) for, better decision making is the top answer. The pressure from cost cutting and compliance has put a greater focus on BI..."

SAP SRM does not provide many standard reports, only a few reports that don't serve any strategic or operational needs. However, the SAP NetWeaver technology platform integrates SAP's business intelligence functionality, SAP NetWeaver Business Warehouse (SAP NetWeaver BW) with SAP SRM to deliver a multitude of out-of-the-box reports that organizations can use in standard delivery.

15.1 SAP NetWeaver BW with SAP SRM

This section describes SAP NetWeaver BW in general and how it integrates with the SAP SRM solution. At the very basic level, SAP NetWeaver BW acts as the reporting functionality for SAP SRM. There are no reports available within the different functionalities of SAP SRM (EB, SUS, etc.). In SAP Enterprise Buyer (EB), there are a few administrator reports but none that are practically useful for end users.

The standard content in SAP NetWeaver BW, however, fills the gap for reports in SAP SRM. SAP provides over 100 standard reports that are available using SAP NetWeaver BW.

15.1.1 Business Intelligence within SAP NetWeaver BW

Before we move further, let's define the term *business intelligence* from an industry and an SAP perspective. You can review two definitions here:

▶ "Business intelligence is a broad category of applications and technologies for gathering, storing, analyzing, and providing access to data to help enterprise users make better business decisions." — searchSAP.com

▶ "SAP Business Information Warehouse (now SAP NetWeaver BW) provides data-warehousing functionality, a business intelligence platform, and a suite of business intelligence tools that enable businesses to attain these goals." — SAP Service Marketplace

Most organizations might be familiar with the product name *SAP BW*, which has been around for many years. The information-warehouse software is now part of the SAP NetWeaver BW suite and functions as the core reporting functionality for all SAP applications, including SAP SRM.

All SAP technology components are now integrated within SAP NetWeaver, including SAP NetWeaver Portal, SAP NetWeaver Master Data Management (MDM), SAP NetWeaver Process Integration (PI), and SAP NetWeaver BW. Figure 15.1 illustrates how the business intelligence functionality is integrated within SAP NetWeaver.

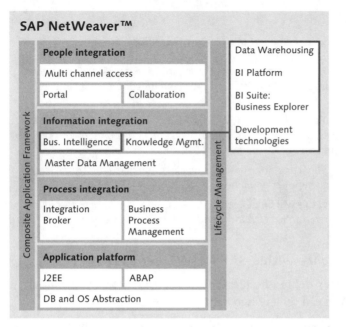

Figure 15.1 Business Warehouse Within the SAP NetWeaver Platform

15.1.2 Basic Reporting Concepts

Before we move forward, understand the following terms and definitions, because we'll use this terminology within this chapter. Get acquainted with these terms so you can speak knowledgeably when discussing and providing requirements to the performance reporting teams for your project. The following terms are not an all-inclusive list of terms within SAP NetWeaver BW but rather a set of key concepts:

- ▶ DataStore Layer
- ▶ InfoCube Layer
- ▶ MultiProvider Layer
- ▶ DataSources
- ▶ DataStore Objects
- ▶ InfoSources
- ▶ InfoCubes
- ▶ Structures
- ▶ Web Templates
- ▶ Queries

15.1.3 SAP SRM Integration with SAP NetWeaver BW

Now that you understand at a high level what the SAP NetWeaver technology platform looks like and where SAP NetWeaver BW is integrated within the SAP NetWeaver technology platform, let's see how SAP SRM leverages the functionality provided by SAP NetWeaver BW.

The first thing that should be clarified is that SAP NetWeaver BW is installed and implemented on an independent environment separate from SAP SRM. The standard SAP technology of remote function call (RFC) connects the two systems. Therefore, create a connection between the SAP SRM and SAP NetWeaver BW systems, as illustrated in Figure 15.2.

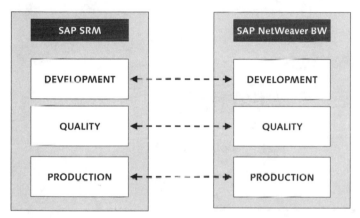

Figure 15.2 Typical Landscape for SAP SRM and Business Intelligence Integrated

Why is this important? First, when the business intelligence analyst questions about the requirement, understand that you're not talking about the SAP ERP environment, because SAP SRM is a separate system. Often, project teams new to SAP SRM assume that the source system will be SAP ERP.

15.1.4 Source System

Simply put, the main job of the business intelligence system is to connect to all the systems in the enterprise landscape and collect data from the different places (sources). Figure 15.3 provides an example of what sources could be important in a typical SAP SRM–BW implementation. In this figure, SAP ERP is a source system for SAP NetWeaver BW, and SAP SRM is another source system. Basically, the SAP NetWeaver BW functionality can pull data from any of these sources to create an appropriate report, which provides information collected and aggregated from both of these source systems in a single analytic report.

One example of this scenario is in SAP SRM the organization that creates shopping carts and purchase orders (POs). The goods receipts and invoices are entered and posted in the SAP ERP system. In this scenario, if a department manager wanted to know about the open items that still need to be received in the system, he could use an Open Items (Confirmations) report, which could provide information on the following:

▸ Cost center that ordered the goods or services
▸ The PO number
▸ The open PO value outstanding
▸ The open delivery value
▸ The open PO quantity

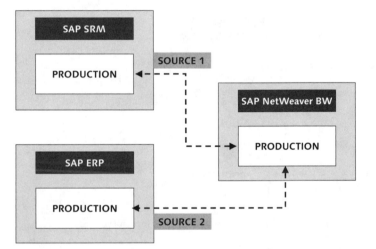

Figure 15.3 Example of Source Systems from an SAP NetWeaver BW Perspective

Note
Confirmations in SAP SRM are similar to goods receipt entries in SAP ERP.

In such a report, the source system for the PO information is SAP SRM. The source system for the delivery, confirmation, or goods receipt information is SAP ERP. This report then is not truly valuable unless the information is aggregated from both these sources and presented to the end user in a single format to analyze. This is where the power of SAP NetWeaver BW comes to play, and its integration with SAP applications provides an edge over the competition.

The transactional source systems are the DataSources that define the structures and the data used for reporting in SAP NetWeaver BW. Figure 15.4 illustrates the sample scenario described above. In this illustration, the invoice entry is not used in SAP SRM. We do not need to activate the DataSource, which transfers invoice data from SAP SRM to SAP NetWeaver BW, because it does not contain any data.

> **Note**
>
> Organizations should be aware that competitors are gaining ground on SAP. SAP NetWeaver BW competitors such as *Cognos* (Cognos 8 MR1 release) are stepping up their integration with SAP applications to provide an alternate application for SAP customers.

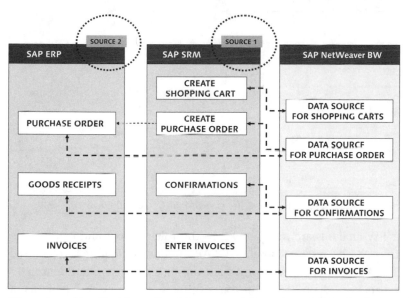

Figure 15.4 Simplified Operational Procurement Example — Self-Service Business Scenario in SAP EB

15.1.5 Accessing Reports from SAP NetWeaver BW in SAP SRM

There are two key methods for users to access the analytics and reports created in the SAP NetWeaver BW system in SAP SRM.

Directly Integrated in the User's LaunchPad in SAP SRM

A simple way to integrate reports from SAP NetWeaver BW into SAP SRM is via a user's LaunchPad. The LaunchPad is the menu provided to end users within their browsers once they've successfully logged on.

The role-based concept in SAP SRM provides all users with roles and within each role there are specific Web services and transactions that they can execute, for example,

Shopping Cart-Full functionality, or approval. These are typically presented to end users via a menu in their Web browsers, as illustrated in Figure 15.5.

These are specifically for organizations not using the SAP NetWeaver Portal for SAP SRM. SAP SRM 7.0 uses the portal as a frontend, so all SRM applications and SAP NetWeaver BW reports are presented using the portal role concept.

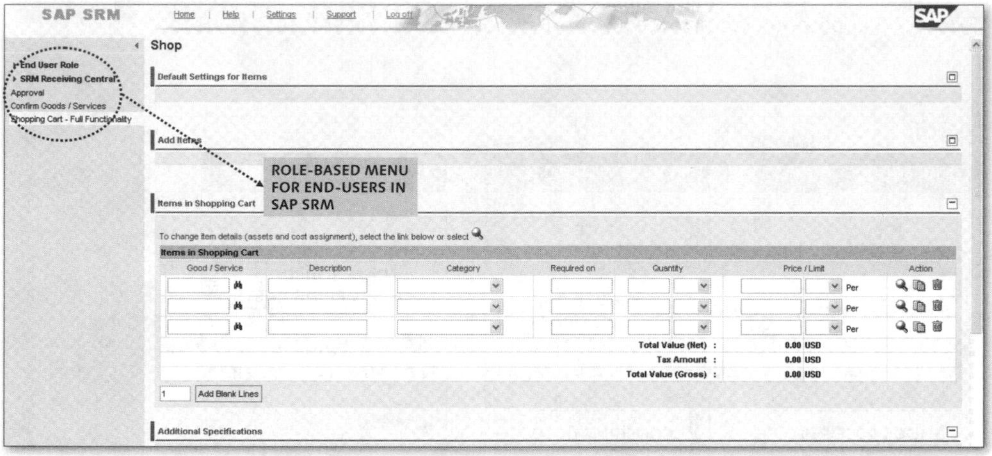

Figure 15.5 SAP SRM — Role-Based User Menu (Release SAP SRM 4.0 and Lower)

SAP NetWeaver BW analyses are integrated into the role concept and can be executed directly from the browser's LaunchPad. SAP provides predefined, role-based models in SAP NetWeaver BW for SAP SRM that contain a set of standard templates for reporting and analysis. Figure 15.7 illustrates this concept. Some key benefits of this option are as follows:

▸ A user can analyze the reports without leaving SAP EB.

▸ The option is suitable for organizations not using the SAP NetWeaver Portal.

▸ Standard roles in SAP NetWeaver BW and SAP SRM can provide out-of-the box solutions for accessing these reports quickly.

▸ Allows usage of predefined templates for reporting and analysis.

To illustrate this via an example, let's review the manager role (SAP_BIC_SRM_MAN-AGER) in SAP NetWeaver BW provided for the SAP SRM operational procurement business scenario. This SAP NetWeaver BW role contains standard templates and queries that a manager using SAP SRM may want to access from a reporting and analysis perspective. The manager may want an overview of the purchasing history within his department or cost center and additionally may want to also know who requisitioned those purchases.

SAP provides three standard Web templates for use within the SAP NetWeaver BW manager role. For each of these templates, a set of standard queries is available for use within SAP SRM. Figure 15.6 illustrates the scenario of the manager role within SAP NetWeaver BW.

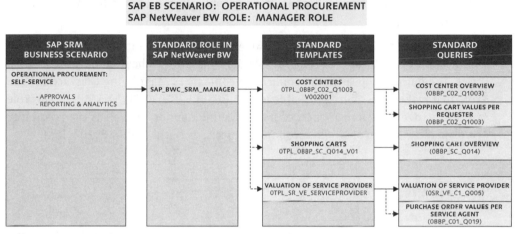

Figure 15.6 Standard SAP NetWeaver BW Manager Role for Use with SAP SRM

Figure 15.7 illustrates the access of queries within the SAP SRM user LaunchPad.

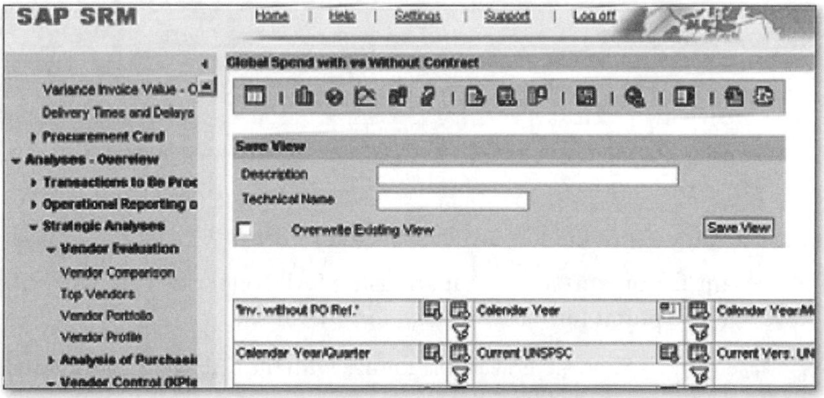

Figure 15.7 Analyses Within LaunchPad in SAP EB (Release SAP SRM 4.0 and Lower)

> **Note**
>
> A number of standard SAP NetWeaver BW roles are provided for use with various SAP SRM business scenarios.

Some of these reports are also directly accessible for professional purchasers to make decisions during sourcing, PO processing, or during contract management. An example is a scenario in which a buyer needs to determine the best source of supply for a particular shopping cart in the *Sourcing* application. The buyer may want to compare different vendors for past performance. The buyer can launch an SAP NetWeaver BW report directly from within the *Sourcing* application, allowing him to streamline the sourcing process.

To have buttons displayed to launch SAP NetWeaver BW reports from the different application contexts of reporting for SAP EB, special roles have to be assigned to a user. The buttons appear in the application contexts as Magnifying Glass icons. One role that makes these buttons visible is SAP_EC_BBP_BUDGET_EXAMPLE. This role offers the overview information of the budgeting queries, as well as the possibility of displaying details of single accounting objects, as illustrated in Figure 15.8.

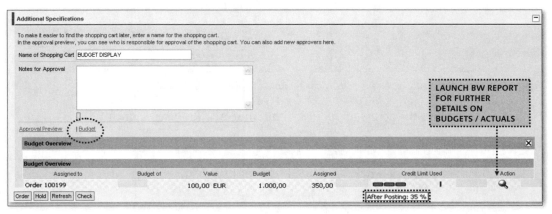

Figure 15.8 Launching BW Budget Report from Budget Overview in SAP SRM Shopping Cart

Using Business Packages Provided in SAP NetWeaver Portal

This option is relevant for organizations that are using SAP NetWeaver Portal, with SAP SRM to leverage the portal Business Package for SAP SRM.

The Business Package for SAP SRM 4.0 is available for use with the SAP NetWeaver Portal 60.2 release, and can be downloaded free from *www.sdn.sap.com*. This Business Package contains worksets and iViews defined for all the standard SAP SRM roles, so organizations using SAP SRM can quickly incorporate SAP SRM transactions within the portal.

So, basically, what project teams can do is use the standard roles in the SAP NetWeaver Portal to access the standard queries provided by SAP for SAP SRM. These standard queries are available in the portal as iViews. If an organization uses the roles in SAP

NetWeaver Portal and SAP SRM applications out-of-the-box, without modification, this software provides end users with a seamless and effortless access of standard queries within the SAP NetWeaver Portal.

However, it is unlikely that organizations are going to use the roles without modification. The standard roles delivered by SAP are based on best practices but are not always practical for different organizations.

Example

There are two different standard roles for purchasing professionals: Operational Purchaser and Strategic Purchaser. Your organization might not differentiate between the two roles, and maybe the professional purchasers in your organization are responsible for all the transactions or activities that form these two roles. In this example, the project teams can no longer use the standard roles available in SAP NetWeaver Portal, SAP SRM, or SAP NetWeaver BW. A new role would have to be developed and integrated across the three applications.

SAP provides the business-package roles illustrated in Figure 15.9 along with the backend roles (SAP SRM and SAP NetWeaver BW) to which the business-package roles are mapped.

ENTERPRISE PORTAL ROLE	SRM ROLE	BW ROLE
EMPLOYEE / USER	SAP_BBP_STAL_EMPLOYEE	NO STANDARD BW ROLE EXISTS FOR THIS SRM ROLE
MANAGER	SAP_BBP_STAL_EMPLOYEE	SAP_BWC_SRM_MANAGER
	SAP_BBP_STAL_MANAGER	
PURCHASING ASSISTANT	SAP_BBP_STAL_EMPLOYEE	SAP_BWC_SRM_PURCHASING_ASSIST
	SAP_BBP_STAL_SECRETARY	
OPERATIONAL PURCHASER	SAP_BBP_STAL_EMPLOYEE	SAP_BWC_SRM_OPER_PURCHASER
	SAP_BBP_STAL_PURCHASER	
STRATEGIC PURCHASER	SAP_BBP_STAL_EMPLOYEE	SAP_BWC_SRM_STRAT_PURCHASER
	SAP_BBP_STAL_STRAT_PURCHASER	
CONTENT MANAGER	SAP_BBP_STAL_EMPLOYEE	NO STANDARD BW ROLE EXISTS FOR THIS SRM ROLE
	SAP_BBP_STAL_CONTENT_MANAGER	
COMPONENT PLANNER	SAP_BBP_STAL_EMPLOYEE	NO STANDARD BW ROLE EXISTS FOR THIS SRM ROLE
	SAP_BBP_STAL_PLANNER	
GOODS RECIPIENT	SAP_BBP_STAL_EMPLOYEE	SAP_BWC_SRM_RECIPIENT
	SAP_BBP_STAL_RECIPIENT	
ACCOUNTANT	SAP_BBP_STAL_EMPLOYEE	SAP_BWC_SRM_ACCOUNTANT
	SAP_BBP_STAL_ACCOUNTANT	
ADMINISTRATOR	SAP_BBP_STAL_EMPLOYEE	NO STANDARD BW ROLE EXISTS FOR THIS SRM ROLE
	SAP_BBP_STAL_ADMINISTRATOR	

Figure 15.9 SAP NetWeaver Portal Roles Mapped to SAP SRM and SAP NetWeaver BW Roles

For purposes of illustration, in Figure 15.9, the SAPSRM roles only show composites; single roles and multiple roles are not displayed but are available for use. To implement this option, the following prerequisites need to be completed:

▶ SAP SRM 4.0 is installed.

▶ SAP NetWeaver BW 3.5 is installed.

▶ SAP NetWeaver Portal 6.0 is installed.

▶ SAP NetWeaver Portal Plug-In is installed on the SAP NetWeaver BW server.

- Single Sign-On is configured for SAP SRM and SAP NetWeaver BW.
- SAP SRM 4.0 Business Package is imported in SAP EP.
- All relevant Business Content in SAP NetWeaver BW is activated.

> **Note**
>
> Although the Business Packages provide out-of-the-box integration with SAP SRM, organizations spend considerable time customizing Business Packages to meet their own role and security requirements. Business Packages reduce the overall time to integrate SAP SRM within the SAP NetWeaver Portal application, but the organization-specific effort should not be underestimated.

Now let's discuss the importance of the standard content available in SAP NetWeaver BW for SAP SRM. SAP provides prebuilt reports and queries that organizations can use for SAP SRM, available by importing the content relevant to your SAP SRM release.

15.2 Standard SAP NetWeaver BW Business Content for SAP SRM

One of the key competitive advantages that SAP software has over other data-warehousing software in the marketplace is that SAP provides a large amount of predelivered content for SAP SRM. People in an organization who are responsible for managing a department's budget, or audit personnel, procurement buyers, and others, typically have many reporting requirements.

Building these reports manually can waste time. This is where the standard content in SAP NetWeaver BW becomes a business advantage. SAP provides more than 100 standard reports that organizations can use directly out-of-the-box. Organizations can either use these reports and queries as delivered or they can use them as a starting point to further meet business requirements.

When we talk about SAP NetWeaver BW Content, we're referring to the software functionality in SAP NetWeaver BW that provides the content for all SAP applications, including standard content for SAP SRM. The SAP NetWeaver BW functionality has to be installed to use any of its functionality. As of SAP NetWeaver BW 3.1, SAP's application has been split into two different software functionalities: a business warehouse functionality and a business intelligence functionality.

15.2.1 Key Benefits for Standard SAP NetWeaver BW Content

There are several benefits for organizations implementing SAP SRM to the standard SAP NetWeaver BW Content provided by SAP, which include:

► Out-of-the-box reports, data models, extractors, and transformations

► A good starting point for extending the reports for use within your business needs and requirements

► The standard reports provided, based on best practice researched from customer needs

► Shorter project implementation timeline

► Ability to use standard reports and analysis until actual requirements are determined, based on new business processes implemented

15.2.2 Release Compatibility for SAP SRM and SAP NetWeaver BW

Because SAP NetWeaver BW and SAP SRM are separate applications, they have their own independent release roadmaps. SAP is continually trying to get the release strategy for all functionalities into uniformity, but until that actually happens, organizations have to deal with different release roadmaps.

At the beginning of the project, release compatibility is accessed between SAP SRM and SAP NetWeaver BW. Since release 3.1 of SAP NetWeaver BW, the software functionalities are divided; review whether the appropriate SAP NetWeaver BW content is available for the SAP SRM release. Figure 15.10 illustrates the release compatibility between SAP SRM and SAP NetWeaver BW as of SAP SRM 5.0.

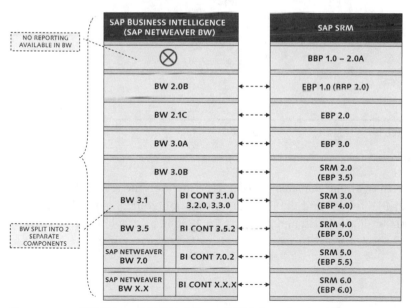

Figure 15.10 SAP SRM and SAP NetWeaver BW Release Compatibility

15.2.3 Business Intelligence Content Delivered for SAP SRM

SAP provides standard business content that is delivered for many different SAP solutions including SAP SRM. The term *business content* is synonymous with the pre-delivered objects such as roles, templates, queries, data models, extractors, transformations, and others. Business content is delivered as an add-on to the core SAP NetWeaver BW application. Therefore, for SAP SRM, SAP provides a specific add-on that is compatible with your SAP SRM release, as illustrated in Figure 15.9.

Figure 15.11 illustrates a timeline for the variously named SAP NetWeaver BW and BI applications over the past several releases, including the BW Content available for each release.

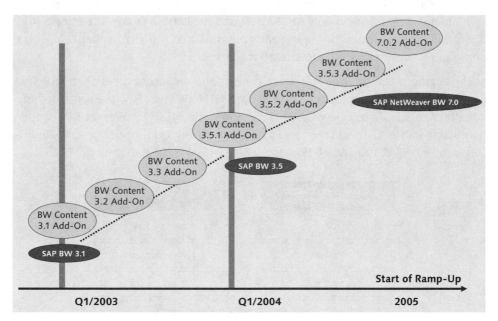

Figure 15.11 Business Intelligence Product Release Timeline (Source: Service-SAP.com)

SAP provides a list of all the available content dependent on the SAP SRM release or SAP NetWeaver BW release and the BW Content add-on your organization is planning to implement. This is illustrated in Figure 15.12, and a complete listing is available on the SAP Service Marketplace.

SRM Release	BW Tech Release	available since BI Content Release	Area	Query Name	Query-id	Backend	Target (ODS / Info-/Multi-cube)
SRM 2.0	3.0B	3.0B	eProcurement Account Assignment-Total Records	Purchase Values per Cost Center	0BBP_C02_Q007	MM* and SRM	0BBP_C02
SRM 2.1	3.0B	3.0B	eProcurement Account Assignment-Total Records	Purchase Values per Order	0BBP_C02_Q009	MM* and SRM	0BBP_C02
SRM 2.3	3.0B	3.0B	eProcurement Account Assignment-Total Records	WEB: My Cost Center - Current Procurement	0BBP_C02_Q1001	MM* and SRM	0BBP_C02
SRM 2.2	3.0B	3.0B	eProcurement Account Assignment-Total Records	SRM Manager - Cost Center Overview	0BBP_C02_Q1003	MM* and SRM	0BBP_C02
SRM 2.0	3.0B	3.0B	Goods/Services Confirmation-Single Documents	Overview of Return Deliveries	0BBP_CONF_Q013	MM* and SRM	0BBP_CON
SRM 2.0	3.0B	3.0B	Invoice - Single Documents	Invoices per Contract	0BBP_INV_Q012	MM* and SRM	0BBP_INV
SRM 2.0	3.0B	3.0B	Purchase Order - Single Documents	Purchase Orders per Contract	0BBP_PO_Q011	MM* and SRM	0BBP_PO
SRM 2.0	3.0B	3.0B	Shopping Cart - individual documents	Shopping Carts per Shopping Cart Number	0BBP_SC_Q001	SRM	0BBP_SC
SRM 2.0	3.0B	3.0B	Shopping Cart - individual documents	Shopping Carts per Shopping Cart Number with	0BBP_SC_Q002	SRM	0BBP_SC
SRM 2.0	3.0B	3.0B	Shopping Cart - individual documents	Shopping Carts per Requester	0BBP_SC_Q003	SRM	0BBP_SC
SRM 2.0	3.0B	3.0B	Shopping Cart - individual documents	Shopping Carts per Product / Product Category	0BBP_SC_Q004	SRM	0BBP_SC
SRM 4.0	3.5	3.5.2	FI-SL only; FI Global Spend Data for SRM	Top 15 Suppliers	0SR_FICO1_Q0004	** FI Special Ledger	0SR_FIC01
SRM 4.0	3.5	3.5.2	FI-SL only; FI Global Spend Data for SRM	Invoice Values per Category (Top 5)	0SR_FIC01_Q0006	** FI Special Ledger	0SR_FIC01
SRM 4.0	3.5	3.5.2	FI-SL only; FI Global Spend Data for SRM	Top 15 Categories	0SR_FIC01_Q0007	** FI Special Ledger	0SR_FIC01
SRM 4.0	3.5	3.5.2	FI-SL only; FI Global Spend Data for SRM	Invoices per Account	0SR_FIC01_Q0008	** FI Special Ledger	0SR_FIC01
SRM 4.0	3.5	3.5.2	FI-SL only; FI Global Spend Data for SRM	Invoice Values with PO and Contract Ref. (Con	0SR_FIC01_Q0009	** FI Special Ledger	0SR_FIC01
SRM 4.0	3.5	3.5.2	Contract Management	Contract Details	0SRCT_DS1_Q002	MM* and SRM	0SRCT_DS1
SRM 4.0	3.5	3.5.2	Contract Management	Expiring Contracts	0SRCT_DS1_Q004	MM* and SRM	0SRCT_DS1
SRM 4.0	3.5	3.5.2	Contract Management	Contracts per Product Category (current)	0SRCT_DS1_Q005	MM* and SRM	0SRCT_DS1
SRM 4.0	3.5	3.5.2	Contract Management	Contracts per Purchasing Organization / Purch	0SRCT_DS1_Q006	MM* and SRM	0SRCT_DS1
SRM 4.0	3.5	3.5.2	Contract Management	Contract Alerts	0SRCT_DS1_Q007	MM* and SRM	0SRCT_DS1
SRM 4.0	3.5	3.5.2	Contract Management	Contracts per Product and Vendor	0SRCT_DS1_Q008	MM* and SRM	0SRCT_DS1
SRM 4.0	3.5	3.5.2	Contract Management	Scheduling Plan Details	0SRCT_DS1_Q009	MM* and SRM	0SRCT_DS1
SRM 6.0	7.0	7.0.2	Procurement Account Assignment	Cost Center Overview	0SR_C02_Q002	MM* and SRM	0SR_C02
SRM 5.0	7.0	7.0.2	Auctions	Auctions Analysis	0SR_LAC1_Q0001	SRM	0SR_LAC1
SRM 5.0	7.0	7.0.2	Auctions	Auction Items Analysis	0SR_LAC1_Q0002	SRM	0SR_LAC1
SRM 5.0	7.0	7.0.2	Auctions	Bidders Analysis	0SR_LAC1_Q0003	SRM	0SR_LAC1
SRM 5.0	7.0	7.0.2	Procurement Overview (multicube aggregate)	Procurement Value Analysis	0SR_MC01_Q0001	MM* and SRM	0SR_MC01
SRM 5.0	7.0	7.0.2	Procurement Overview (multicube aggregate)	Procurement Values per Service Provider	0SR_MC01_Q0002	MM* and SRM	0SR_MC01
SRM 5.0	7.0	7.0.2	Procurement Overview (multicube aggregate)	Supplier Information	0SR_MC01_Q0003	MM* and SRM	0SR_MC01
SRM 5.0	7.0	7.0.2	Procurement Overview (multicube aggregate)	Key Performance Indicators	0SR_MC01_Q0004	MM* and SRM	0SR_MC01
SRM 5.0	7.0	7.0.2	Procurement Overview (multicube aggregate)	Price Trend Analysis per Product	0SR_MC01_Q0005	MM* and SRM	0SR_MC01
SRM 5.0	7.0	7.0.2	Procurement Overview (multicube aggregate)	Number of Suppliers per Country	0SR_MC01_Q0006	MM* and SRM	0SR_MC01
SRM 5.0	7.0	7.0.2	Procurement Overview (multicube aggregate)	ABC Analysis for Suppliers (Lorenz Curve)	0SR_MC01_Q0007	MM* and SRM	0SR_MC01
SRM 5.0	7.0	7.0.2	Procurement Overview (multicube aggregate)	ABC Supplier	0SR_MC01_Q0008	MM* and SRM	0SR_MC01
SRM 5.0	7.0	7.0.2	Procurement Overview (multicube aggregate)	Success of an SRM Project	0SR_MC01_Q0009	MM* and SRM	0SR_MC01

Figure 15.12 Standard Queries Based on SAP SRM, SAP NetWeaver BW Release, and BW Content Add-On

15.2.4 Operational Procurement Scenario

As discussed in Chapters 3, 4, and 5, there are many business scenarios in SAP SRM, with operational procurement scenario being a key engine for the rest. Figures 15.13 and 15.14 provide a list of reports available in SAP SRM 7.0 using BW Content 3.5 to support the operational procurement scenario.

Figure 15.13 illustrates the queries that are available for the MANAGER, OPERA-TIONAL PURCHASER, and ACCOUNTS PAYABLE ACCOUNT roles in SAP SRM. For each of these roles, there is a set of queries that can be activated in the standard delivered content. For example, the MANAGER role contains the query 0BBP_C02_Q1003_V002 for the Cost Center Overview. Department managers responsible for a particular cost center can run this report to see all the shopping carts that have been created where their cost center(s) have been charged.

In addition to the roles in Figure 15.13, additional queries are available for the PRO-CUREMENT MANAGER, PURCHASING ASSISTANT, and the GOODS RECIPIENT roles, as illustrated in Figure 15.14. For example, a purchasing manager might be interested in analyzing the number of POs created based on a purchasing organization or purchasing group. They can use the 0BBP_PO_Q005_V02 query for PUR-CHASE ORDER PER PORG or PGROUP.

ROLE	WEB TEMPLATES	QUERIES
MANAGER SAP_BWC_SRM_MANAGER	COST CENTER INFORMATION 0TPL_0BBP_C02_Q1003_V002001	COST CENTER OVERVIEW 0BBP_C02_Q1003_V002
		OVERVIEW OF PROCURMENT VALUES PER REQUESTER 0BBP_C02_Q1003_V001
	SHOPPING CART INFORMATION 0TPL_0BBP_SC_Q014_V01	OVERVIEW OF SHOPPING CARTS 0BBP_SC_Q014_V01
	EVALUATION OF SERVICE PROVIDERS 0TPL_SR_VE_SERVICEPROVIDER	EVALUATION OF SERVICE PROVIDERS 0SR_VE_C1_Q005
		PROCUREMENT VALUES PER SERVICE PROVIDER 0BBP_C01_Q019
OPERATIONAL PURCHASER SAP_BW_SRM_OPER_PURCHASER	DEADLINE MONITORING 0TPL_0BBP_DS1_Q013_V002	DEADLINE MONITORING BBP_DS1_Q013_V002
	HELD PURCHASE ORDERS 0TPL_0BBP_PO_Q007_V02	HELD PURCHASE ORDERS BBP_PO_Q007_V02
	SHOPPING CART INFORMATION 0TPL_0BBP_SC_Q004_V02	SHOPPING CART INFORMATION 0BBP_SC_Q004_V02
	CONTRACT UTILIZATION 0TPL_0BBP_CT_Q004	CONTRACT UTILIZATION 0BBP_CT_Q004
		VENDOR EVALUATION 0BBP_C01_Q032
ACCOUNTS PAYABLE ACCOUNTANT SAP_BW_SRM_STRAT_PURCHASER	INVOICE VERIFICATION / MONITOR PAYMENTS 0TPL_BBP_DS1_Q002	OPEN ITEMS (INVOICES) 0BBP_DS1_Q004
		EXCESSIVE INVOICES 0BBP_DS1_Q005
		INVOICES PER VENDOR 0BBP_INV_Q002

Figure 15.13 Operational Procurement Scenario Queries

ROLE	WEB TEMPLATES	QUERIES
PROCUREMENT MANAGER SAP_BW_SRM_PROC_MANAGER	EVALUATION CONTROLLING 0TPL_SRVE_CONTROL_01	SUBMITTED INVOICES FOR EVALUATION 0SRVE_IS1_Q003_V001
		SUBMITTED EVALUATIONS FOR GR / SERVICE CONF. 0SRVE_IS2_Q003_V001
		SUBMITTED EVALUATIONS FOR VENDORS 0SRVE_IS3_Q003_V001
	BID INVITATION PER PRODUCT CATEGORY 0TPL_SR_BIDC01_Q005	BID INVITATION PER PRODUCT CATEGORY 0SR_BIDC01_Q005
	UTILIZATION PER PURCHASING GROUP 0TPL_BBP_PO_Q005_V02	PURCHASE ORDER PER PORG / PGROUP 0BBP_PO_Q005_V02
		SHOPPING CARTS PER PORG / PGROUP 0BBP_SC_Q005_V02
		CONTRACTS PER PORG / PGRP 0SRCT_DS1_Q006
	PROJECT SUCCESS OF AN EBP IMPLEMENTATION 0TPL_BBP_C01_Q039	
PURCHASING ASSISTANT SAP_BW_SRM_PURCHASING_ASSIST	SHOPPING CART OVERVIEW 0TPL_BBP_SC_Q003_V0302	SHOPPING CARTS PER REQUESTER 0BBP_SC_Q003_V02
		SHOPPING CART STATUS 0BBP_SC_Q003_V03
		SHOPPING CARTS TO BE APPROVED 0BBP_SCA_Q003_V001
GOODS RECIPIENT SAP_BW_SRM_RECIPIENT	EVALUATE GOODS RECIEPTS 0TPL_SRVE_IS2_Q001	MANDATORY EVALUATION OF GR / SERVICE CONF. 0SRVE_IS2_Q001_V01
		OPTIONAL EVALUATION OF GR / SERVICE CONF. 0SRVE_IS2_Q002_V01
	GOODS RECEIPTS 0TPL_BBP_DS1_Q002009	OPEN ITEMS (CONFIRMATIONS) 0BBP_DS1_Q002
		DELIVERY DELAYS 0BBP_DS1_Q009
		QUANTITY RELIABILITY (10 WORST VENDORS) 0BBP_C01_Q032_V001
		TIMELINESS (10 WORST VENDORS) 0BBP_C01_Q032_V002

Figure 15.14 Operational Procurement Scenario Queries

The terms reports and queries are used interchangeably in this chapter. There is a difference, however. One easy way to differentiate this is that a query contains a specific structure, designed for a specific requirement, and usually built from a single SAP NetWeaver BW InfoCube.

A report (also known as template), on the other hand, can be constructed using one or more queries. For example, as a part of the PROCUREMENT MANAGER role, a Web report — UTILIZATION PER PURCHASING GROUP — is available. This report is built using three queries: 0BBP_PO_Q005_V02 and 0BBP_SC_Q005_V02, and 0SRCT_DS1_Q006. For content information on SAP SRM 5.0, also read Section 15.4, Delivered Reports in SAP SRM 7.0.

High-level Activities for Integrating SAP NetWeaver BW Reports in SAP SRM

Before users can use the reports in SAP SRM, the performance reporting teams need to configure the SAP NetWeaver BW system and activate the relevant DataSources in SAP SRM. Figure 15.15 illustrates at a high level the prerequisites for using SAP NetWeaver BW reporting within SAP SRM.

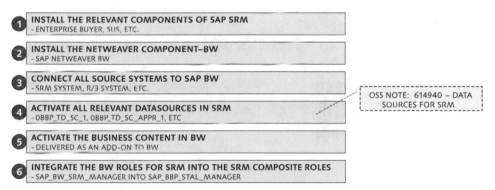

Figure 15.15 High-Level Activities for Integrating SAP NetWeaver BW Reports within SAP SRM

15.2.5 Some Standard SAP NetWeaver BW Reports for SAP SRM

As we've already discussed, there are many standard reports and queries available for SAP SRM in SAP NetWeaver BW. Now, let's look a few examples of the reports available. An organization can use these reports to analyze the procurement activity within the company. For example, a department manager can use the Overview of Approved Shopping Carts report to quickly analyze the shopping carts where all approval activity has been completed.

Overview of Approved Shopping Carts

This query provides information to a department manager concerning all the shopping carts that have been approved, along with who approved them, and the number of approval steps required to approve a shopping cart for a particular purchase amount. This is especially valuable for organizations auditing the approval process for purchase of goods or services. Figure 15.16 illustrates this query.

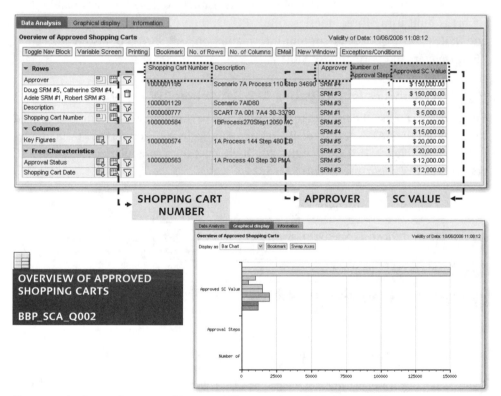

Figure 15.16 Query: Overview of Approved Shopping Carts (BBP_SCA_Q002)

Shopping Carts per Catalog

Many organizations implement SAP SRM but do not follow up with the appropriate analysis of the value achieved after the initial project implementation. For example, catalogs may be implemented but value analysis forgotten when it comes to checking whether those catalogs are actually being used by the organization. This query shows an overview of the shopping carts that were created from a particular catalog. In addition, the Vendor and Product Category fields are available in this report, so the professional purchaser can analyze whether particular purchases in a product category should have originated from a vendor catalog onboarded by the organization. Figure 15.17 illustrates this query.

Catalog	Shopping Cart Number	Description	Vendor	Shopping Cart Date	Approval Status	Product Category	SC Quantity	SC Value
GE_MEDI	1000001150	7a8S3441 0catalog shopping	GE MEDICAL SYSTEMS	09/25/2006	Approved	PATIENT SUPPL & DISP	1.0 EA	$139.26
FISHER_SCI	1000000691	2A Process 450 Step 20340 tk	FISHER SCIENTIFIC	09/05/2006	Approved	LAB SUPPLIES & EQUIP	80.0 EA	$28.00
GRAINGER	1000000365	3E Process 10 Step 27080 tk	1690077	08/30/2006	Approved	OFFICE SUPP & EQUIP	1.0 EA	$72.99
	1000000774	SCART 2 002 2A430-20120	1690077	09/07/2006	Approved	OFFICE SUPP & EQUIP	10.0 EA	$211.60
Result							11.0 EA	$284.59
#	1000000365	3E Process 10 Step 27080 tk	STO VENDOR	08/30/2006	Approved	DURABLE MED EQUIP	35.0 EA	$350.00
	1000000397	3C Process 30 Step 25310 tk	UNIVERSITY OF	08/30/2006	Approved	SUDAWARDS	80,000.0 EA	$80,000.00
	1000000402	SRM20 08/30/2006 14:13	MENTOR INC	08/30/2006	Not assigned	LAB SUPPLIES & EQUIP	10.0 EA	$280.00
	1000000421	3D Process 30 Step 26730 MC	STO VENDOR	08/30/2006	Approved	DURABLE MED EQUIP	1.0 EA	$10.00
	1000000428	1A Process 805 Step 6989 tk	ABBOTT DIAGNOSTICS	08/30/2006	Approved	PATIENT SUPPL & DISP	*	$46.54
						DURABLE MED EQUIP	1.0 BOX	$60.00
	1000000494	SRM1 08/31/2006 13:00	CARDINAL	08/31/2006	Approved	PATIENT SUPPL & DISP	2.0 CV	$0.16
	1000000511	test - delete	CARDINAL	08/31/2006	Approved	PATIENT SUPPL & DISP	1.0 CV	$120.00
	1000000513	1B Process 190 Step 11180 tk	CHARLES RIVER LABS	08/31/2006	Approved	LIVE ANIMALS	1.0 EA	$54,000.00
	1000000540	1A Process 1080 Step 9080 tk	OWENS AND MINOR	08/31/2006	Approved	BANDAGE DRESSING	600.0 BOX	$50,000.00
	1000000687	1A Process 1030 Step 8570 JH	OWENS AND MINOR	09/05/2006	Approved	PATIENT SUPPL & DISP		$345.00

Figure 15.17 Query: Shopping Carts per Catalog (BBP_SCA_Q006)

Maverick Buying Analysis

Maverick Buying Analysis allows purchasing professionals in an organization to review the purchases that do not conform to a strategic contract. The report provides information on POs that have resulted from contracts and the value of the POs that have not resulted from contracts. Additionally, the vendor data is available so that maverick purchases can be identified.

An organization often will be able to analyze procurement activity to spot additional contract opportunity. Perhaps many goods or services are being ordered from a particular vendor, and there is an opportunity to enter into a contract. Figure 15.18 illustrates this query.

Purchase Order Detail by Line Item

Every organization needs reporting on the details of the purchases being made. The Purchase Order Detail by Line Item report or query provides detail information about the PO with line item and accounting details. Figure 15.19 illustrates this query.

Contracts per Product and Vendor

Organizations that use the Contract Management functionality in SAP SRM can use the Contracts per Product and Vendor query to get an overview of the value-based and quantity-based contracts for particular vendors and products. This report can allow a strategic purchaser to analyze the total releases for the contracts open in the system. Figure 15.20 illustrates this query.

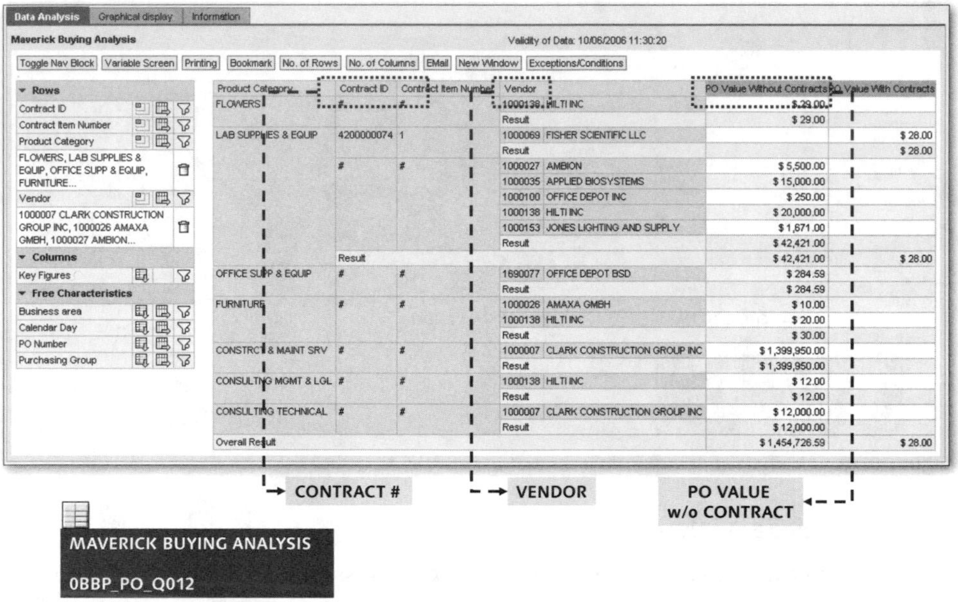

Figure 15.18 Query: Maverick Buying Analysis (0BBP_PO_Q012)

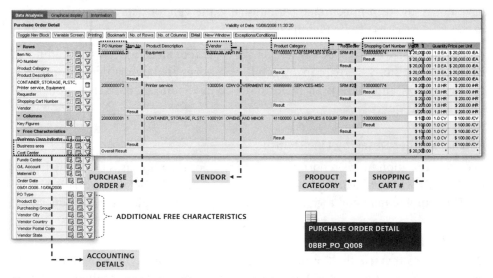

Figure 15.19 Purchase Order Detail by Line Item (0BBP_PO_Q008)

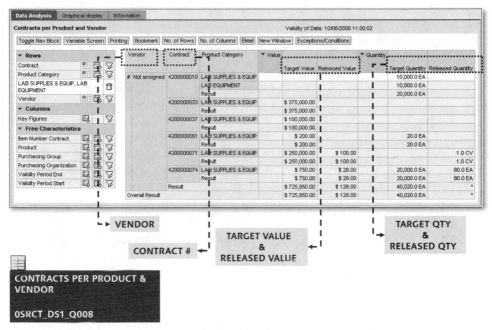

Figure 15.20 Query: Contracts per Product and Vendor (0SRCT_DS1_Q008)

In the next section, we'll evaluate the impact of SAP SRM implementation scenarios on extracting and developing content in SAP NetWeaver BW.

15.3 SAP SRM Implementation Scenario Impact on SAP NetWeaver BW Reporting

As we've already discussed, SAP SRM can be implemented in different scenarios: Classic, Extended Classic, and Standalone. Based on the scenario implemented in SAP SRM, the SAP NetWeaver BW DataSources may change. For example, in the Classic scenario, the shopping cart is only created within SAP SRM; therefore, transactional data for shopping carts can only be extracted from SAP SRM. However, data for other purchasing documents such as POs, goods receipts, and invoices needs to be extracted from SAP ERP. In this example, at least two different source systems are needed to extract data into SAP NetWeaver BW to provide reporting. Therefore, understand the implication of SAP SRM implementation scenarios on SAP NetWeaver BW.

Regardless of the implementation scenario, the DataSources (seen in Table 15.1) from SAP SRM and the SAP ERP backend are needed to load the various DataStores in SAP NetWeaver BW to enable reporting in the operational procurement business scenario for SAP SRM.

SYSTEM	DATASOURCE	DATASOURCE USE
SRM	0BBP_TD_SC_1	Header and item-level information for shopping carts (e.g., product, product category, etc.)
SRM	0BBP_TD_SCA_1	Shopping cart approval information such as: approver of a shopping cart, the time of approval, and the approved value of a shopping cart
SRM**	0SRM_TD_PO	Information on header, item, and schedule line from SAP SRM and ERP POs
SRM**	0SRM_TD_PO_ACC	Header and item-level information on PO data with associated account assignment data
SRM**	0SRM_TD_CF	Header, item, and account assignment information from confirmations in SAP SRM
SRM**	0SRM_TD_IV	Header and item-level data on invoices created or parked in SAP SRM
SRM	0BBP_TD_CONTR_2	Header and item-level data for contracts created in SAP SRM
SRM	0SRM_REL_CT	Release Information for the contract usage
ERP	2LIS_02_HDR	Header information for a purchasing document (e.g., POrg, Vendor, etc.)
ERP	2LIS_02_ITM	Item-level information for a purchasing document (e.g., Pgroup, Plant, etc.)
ERP	2LIS_02_SCL	Schedule line information for a purchasing document (only if scheduling agreements are used)
ERP	2LIS_02_ACC	Accounting information for a purchasing document (e.g., cost center, WBS element)
ERP	2LIS_06_IV	Header and item-level information for an invoice document (e.g., invoice number, terms of payment)

Table 15.1 Relevant DataSources in SAP SRM and SAP ERP

> **Note**
>
> The DataSources 0SRM_TD_PO, 0SRM_TD_PO_ACC, 0SRM_TD_CF, and 0SRM_TD_IV are only available as of SAP SRM 5.0 release and SAP ERP 2005 release.

All master-data texts that are relevant for account assignment are not located in SAP EB but in the SAP ERP backend system. If, for example, a cost center is uploaded and only SAP EB is connected, it is only possible to display the cost center number in a report (for example, 1000) and not the corresponding text. To get the master data text into SAP NetWeaver BW, you either have to connect your SAP ERP backend to SAP NetWeaver BW to upload this part of the master data.

Figure 15.21 illustrates the overall data model in business reporting: extraction of data from the various DataSources, into the ODS (Operational Data Store) DataStores, to the InfoCube, to multiproviders, and finally to be made available for end user reporting.

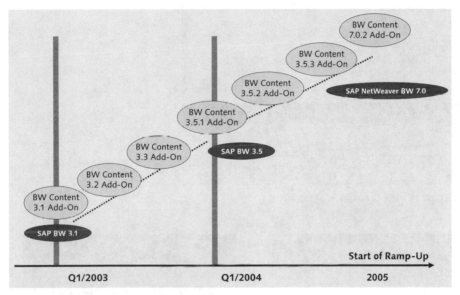

Figure 15.21 Overall Data Model

15.3.1 The Classic Scenario

In the Classic scenario, the shopping cart document is created in SAP SRM. Based on business configuration, a purchase requisition or a PO is subsequently created in the SAP ERP backend. Follow-on documents such as goods receipt (confirmation) and invoices can be entered in SAP SRM or the SAP backend. However, the transactional data for POs, goods receipts, and invoices is extracted from SAP ERP. Figure 15.22 illustrates this scenario.

In this implementation scenario, both SAP SRM and SAP ERP need to be connected to the SAP NetWeaver BW system as source systems, as illustrated in Figure 15.22. Figure 15.23 illustrates the data flow and mapping between the DataSources and DataStores based on the Classic implementation scenario of SAP SRM.

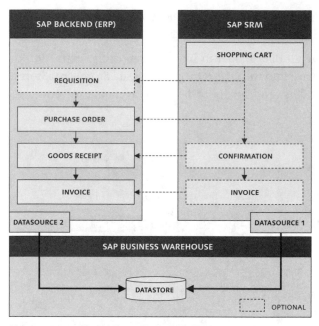

Figure 15.22 Classic Scenario in SAP SRM

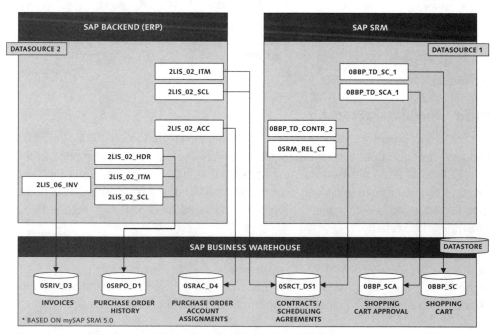

Figure 15.23 DataSource and DataStore Mapping in Classic Scenario

15.3.2 The Extended Classic Scenario

In the Extended Classic scenario, the shopping cart and the PO documents are created in SAP SRM. Subsequently, once the PO status is completed in SAP SRM, a copy of this PO is transferred to the SAP ERP backend system.

The PO in the SAP backend is a read-only document; changes to this document are only allowed in SAP SRM. Follow-on documents such as goods receipt (confirmation) and invoices can be entered in SAP SRM or the backend. However, the transactional data for goods receipts and invoices is extracted from SAP ERP. Figure 15.24 illustrates this scenario.

> **Note**
>
> In the Extended Classic scenario, the complete procurement process can take place locally within the SAP SRM system: shopping cart, purchase order, confirmations, and invoices. However, most organizations continue executing the goods receipt and invoice functions within their SAP backend systems.

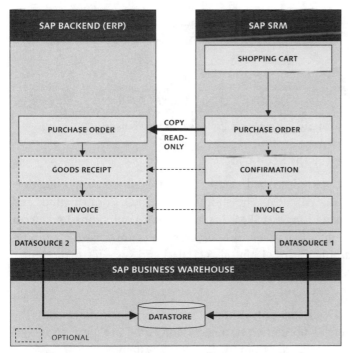

Figure 15.24 Extended Classic Scenario in SAP SRM

In this scenario, both SAP SRM and ERP need to be connected to the SAP NetWeaver BW system as source systems, as illustrated in Figure 15.24.

Figure 15.25 illustrates the data flow and mapping between the DataSource and the DataStore based on the Extended Classic implementation scenario of SAP SRM.

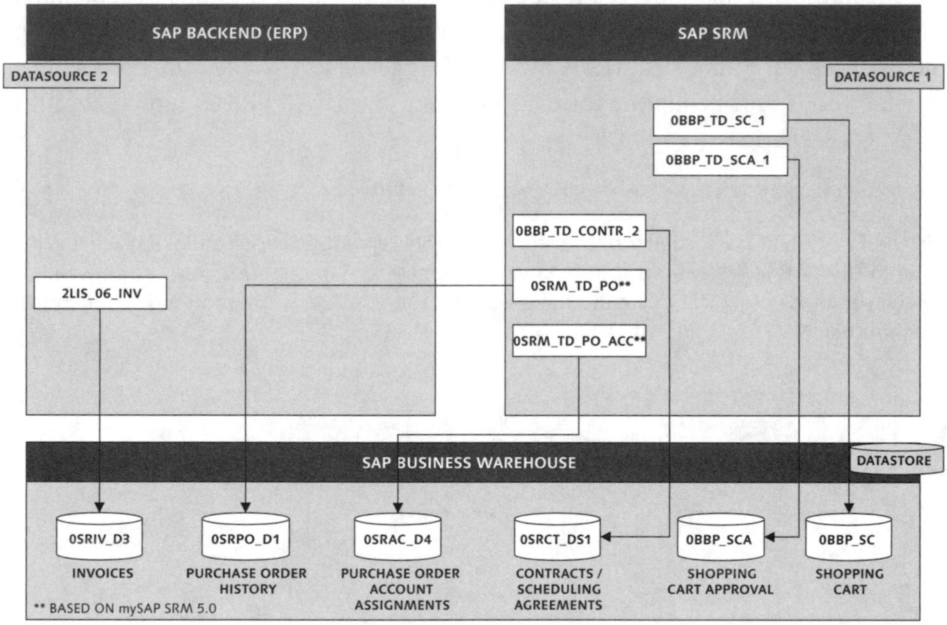

Figure 15.25 DataSource and DataStore Mapping in Extended Classic Scenario

15.3.3 The Standalone (Lean) Scenario

In the Standalone scenario (also described as *Lean* scenario), all the purchasing documents are only created in SAP SRM. The shopping cart, PO, confirmation, and invoice documents are created in SAP SRM. In this scenario, all validations occur within the SAP SRM system, while accounting processes such as financial accounting and controlling are still handled within the SAP backend system. Invoice entry is completed in SAP SRM and posting of the invoice happens in the SAP backend. Figure 15.26 illustrates this scenario.

In the standalone scenario, only the SAP SRM system needs to be connected to the SAP NetWeaver BW system as the source system, as illustrated in Figure 15.26. All transactional data is extracted directly from the SAP SRM system.

Figure 15.27 illustrates the data flow and mapping between the DataSources and DataStores based on the Standalone implementation scenario of SAP SRM.

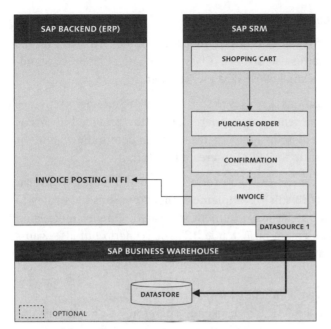

Figure 15.26 Standalone Scenario in SAP SRM

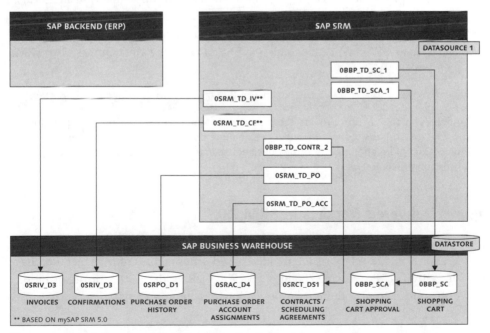

Figure 15.27 DataSource and DataStore Mapping in Standalone Scenario

15.3.4 The Decoupled Scenario

SAP SRM can also be implemented in a decoupled mode. In simple terms, this means that a combination of the scenarios listed above (Classic, Extended Classic, or Standalone) can be implemented in a single SAP SRM environment.

A common reason why organizations do this is to separate the procurement activities within SAP SRM and the SAP backend. The standard application provided by SAP is based on product category. Based on this, the organization can determine whether it wants to create a PO locally within SAP SRM or create it within the SAP backend.

However, most organizations do not use the product category option but instead use available Business Add-Ins (BAdIs) to implement their own business rules to determine in which system a purchasing document is created. One example is an organization that wants to implement an Extended Classic scenario but also wants to use the functionality to create material-based shopping carts in SAP SRM that create *reservations*.

Because SAP SRM does not have the functionality to create reservations, those documents can only be created in the SAP ERP backend. Therefore, a Classic scenario would have to be implemented for creation of reservations from a shopping cart. In our example, project teams can use the available BAdI to implement business rules so that when a material is used the Classic scenario is enabled, but otherwise, the Extended Classic scenario is enabled. This is considered a decoupled mode. From an SAP NetWeaver BW perspective, data is captured from the DataSources, SAP SRM, and SAP ERP.

> **Note**
>
> The figures in this section provide the mapping information focused on the operational procurement business scenario. Review the documents available at the SAP Service Marketplace for information on the other business scenarios such as strategic sourcing and plan-driven procurement.

15.4 Delivered Reports in SRM 7.0

SAP provides a series of reports via the standard content for SAP SRM in SAP NetWeaver BW. These reports are divided based on user roles of Manager, Purchasing, and Strategic Purchasing (Figures 15.28, 15.29, and 15.30). An organization, however, can customize these roles per its business requirements.

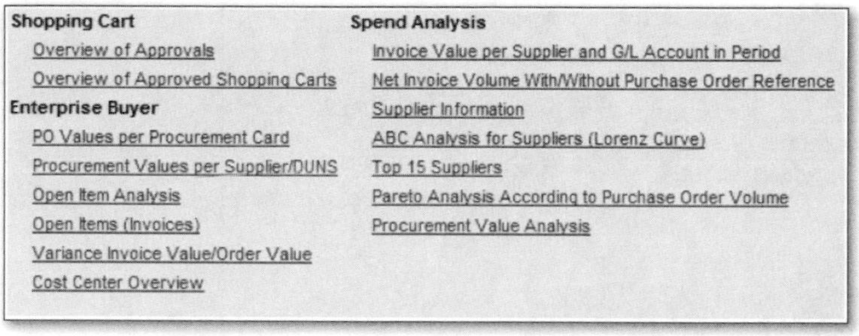

Shopping Cart

Overview of Approvals

Overview of Approved Shopping Carts

Enterprise Buyer

PO Values per Procurement Card

Procurement Values per Supplier/DUNS

Open Item Analysis

Open Items (Invoices)

Variance Invoice Value/Order Value

Cost Center Overview

Spend Analysis

Invoice Value per Supplier and G/L Account in Period

Net Invoice Volume With/Without Purchase Order Reference

Supplier Information

ABC Analysis for Suppliers (Lorenz Curve)

Top 15 Suppliers

Pareto Analysis According to Purchase Order Volume

Procurement Value Analysis

Figure 15.28 Reports for Manager

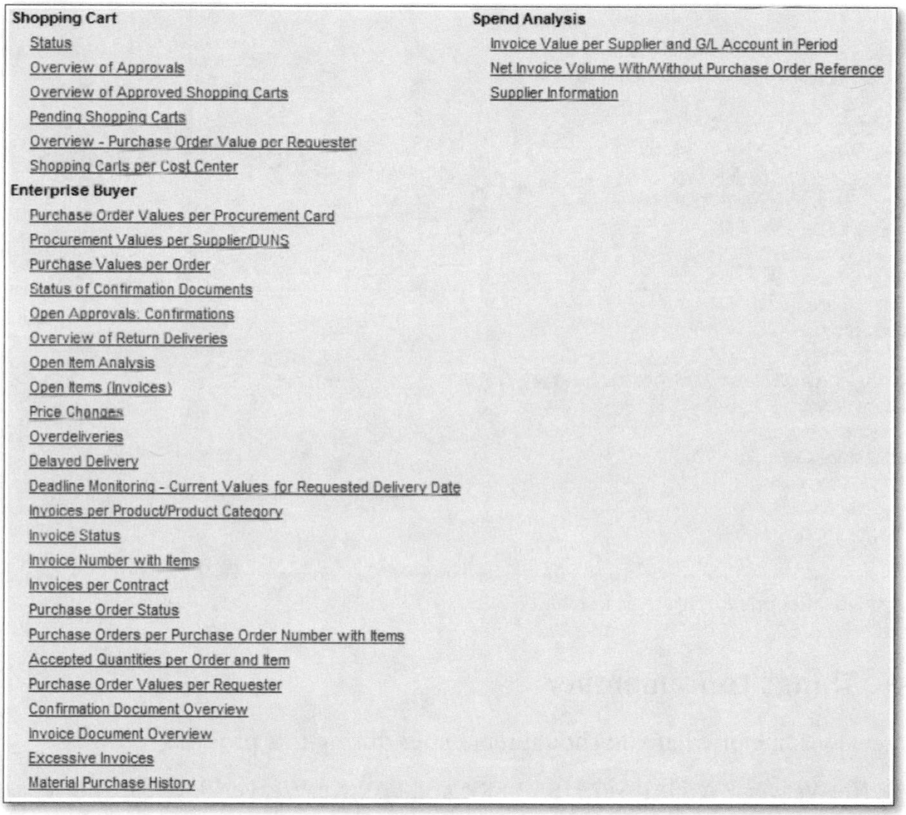

Shopping Cart

Status

Overview of Approvals

Overview of Approved Shopping Carts

Pending Shopping Carts

Overview - Purchase Order Value per Requester

Shopping Carts per Cost Center

Enterprise Buyer

Purchase Order Values per Procurement Card

Procurement Values per Supplier/DUNS

Purchase Values per Order

Status of Confirmation Documents

Open Approvals: Confirmations

Overview of Return Deliveries

Open Item Analysis

Open Items (Invoices)

Price Changes

Overdeliveries

Delayed Delivery

Deadline Monitoring - Current Values for Requested Delivery Date

Invoices per Product/Product Category

Invoice Status

Invoice Number with Items

Invoices per Contract

Purchase Order Status

Purchase Orders per Purchase Order Number with Items

Accepted Quantities per Order and Item

Purchase Order Values per Requester

Confirmation Document Overview

Invoice Document Overview

Excessive Invoices

Material Purchase History

Spend Analysis

Invoice Value per Supplier and G/L Account in Period

Net Invoice Volume With/Without Purchase Order Reference

Supplier Information

Figure 15.29 Reports for Purchaser

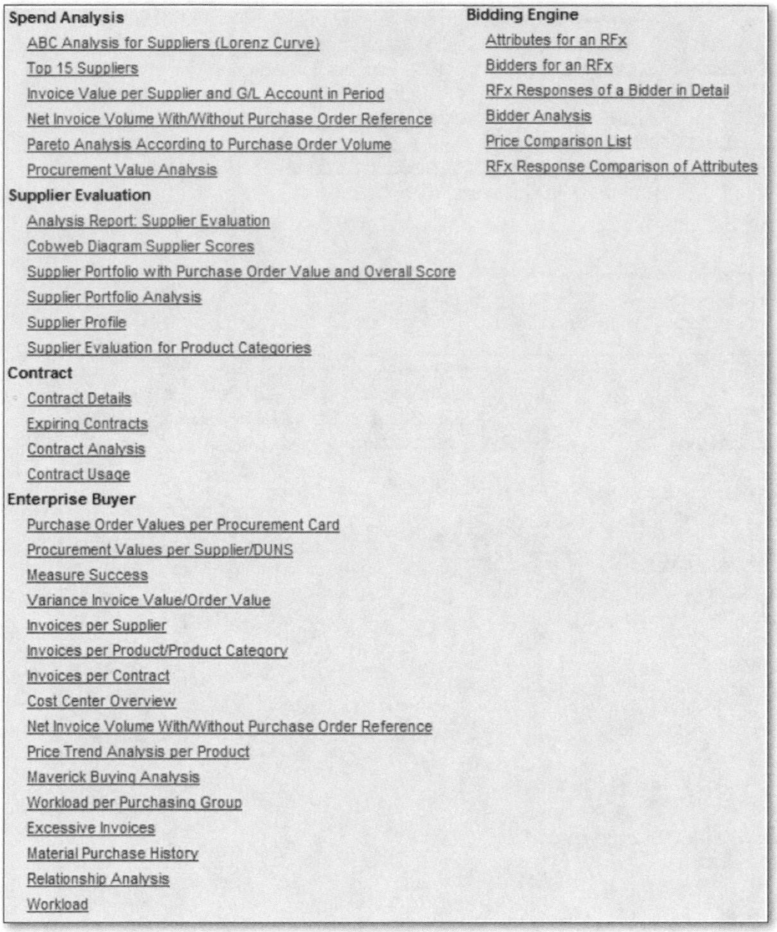

Spend Analysis

ABC Analysis for Suppliers (Lorenz Curve)

Top 15 Suppliers

Invoice Value per Supplier and G/L Account in Period

Net Invoice Volume With/Without Purchase Order Reference

Pareto Analysis According to Purchase Order Volume

Procurement Value Analysis

Supplier Evaluation

Analysis Report: Supplier Evaluation

Cobweb Diagram Supplier Scores

Supplier Portfolio with Purchase Order Value and Overall Score

Supplier Portfolio Analysis

Supplier Profile

Supplier Evaluation for Product Categories

Contract

Contract Details

Expiring Contracts

Contract Analysis

Contract Usage

Enterprise Buyer

Purchase Order Values per Procurement Card

Procurement Values per Supplier/DUNS

Measure Success

Variance Invoice Value/Order Value

Invoices per Supplier

Invoices per Product/Product Category

Invoices per Contract

Cost Center Overview

Net Invoice Volume With/Without Purchase Order Reference

Price Trend Analysis per Product

Maverick Buying Analysis

Workload per Purchasing Group

Excessive Invoices

Material Purchase History

Relationship Analysis

Workload

Bidding Engine

Attributes for an RFx

Bidders for an RFx

RFx Responses of a Bidder in Detail

Bidder Analysis

Price Comparison List

RFx Response Comparison of Attributes

Figure 15.30 Reports for Strategic Purchaser

15.5   Things to Remember

Let's review some of what you should remember during this process:

▸ SAP NetWeaver BW, SAP SRM, SAP ERP, and SAP NetWeaver Portal are all separate systems, installed on their individual landscapes.

▸ Security roles are independent in each system; there are roles in SAP NetWeaver Portal, roles in SAP NetWeaver BW, roles in SAP SRM, and roles in SAP ERP.

▸ Functional teams need to allocate enough time to test the reports generated by the performance reporting teams. It is not just a matter of checking that the reports execute; data within the reports must be correct.

- The standard content provided by SAP provides a good starting point, but the standard queries are not typically sufficient, and modification is generally required by organizations. However, it is much easier to modify these delivered queries than to develop them from scratch.

- Do not forget about customized fields created in the different system (e.g., custom fields created for the shopping cart and PO documents in SAP SRM). These need to be extracted as well in the queries. If organizations are not able to report on the customized fields, then it defeats the purpose of creating them. Let your performance teams know up front that you need to report on customized fields.

- When testing the queries, review each characteristic and its values. Many of the custom queries are delivered with incorrect data. For example, the product characteristic may be delivered with the GUID value instead of the actual product number, or the purchasing group characteristic may be delivered with the organization unit value instead of the name of the purchasing group.

15.6   Relevant OSS Notes

Table 15.2 lists important OSS Notes available on the SAP Service Marketplace that are relevant for organizations implementing the SAP NetWeaver BW solution for SAP SRM.

Note	Description
352814	Loading data from SAP EB into SAP NetWeaver BW
401367	Calling the SAP NetWeaver BW Web Reports via the SAP EB LaunchPad
520131	Activation of SAP SRM roles for SAP NetWeaver BW and SAP SRM decisions
614940	DataSources for SAP EB
955804	SAP SRM 5.0/6.0 — SAP NetWeaver BW Content data model changed
1237150	SAP SRM 7.0 – The SAP NetWeaver BW content enhancement

Table 15.2   OSS Notes from SAP Service Marketplace

15.7   **Summary**

In this chapter, we introduced the SAP NetWeaver BW reporting solution. The majority of the organizations implementing SAP SRM need to implement SAP NetWeaver BW because there is a lack of reporting in SAP SRM by itself. SAP provides all reporting and analytics capabilities in SAP NetWeaver BW for use in SAP SRM. Standard content for SAP SRM can be imported into SAP NetWeaver BW to provide out-of-the-box reports.

In Chapter 16, you will be introduced to the concept of the SAP NetWeaver Portal and you will learn how this SAP NetWeaver functionality can become a key application for your SAP SRM implementation.

SAP NetWeaver Portal provides the default user interface for all SAP SRM applications. Using the portal, organizations can now have unified and harmonized access across the entire SAP business suite and information within.

16 SAP NetWeaver Portal and SAP SRM

SAP NetWeaver Portal is a functionality within the SAP NetWeaver technology platform that unifies information and applications to give users a single entry point for all end user business scenario needs. Organizations implementing SAP SRM today also need to implement the SAP NetWeaver Portal as a part of their SAP SRM deployment strategy. The latest SAP SRM 7.0 release supports a totally new user interface, which is built on top of the SAP NetWeaver Portal technology. This new user interface harmonizes multiple user interfaces across the entire SAP business suite. In this chapter, we'll review the integration of SAP SRM 7.0 with the SAP NetWeaver Portal.

> **Note**
>
> The Enterprise Portal terminology was widely used in previous releases such as Enterprise Portal 6.0. Throughout this book and this chapter, it's referenced as SAP NetWeaver Portal or SAP NetWeaver Portal 7.0.

Target audiences for this chapter are:

- Project Manager, Solution Leads
- SRM Implementation Consultants
- Functional process owners curious about the role of SAP NetWeaver Portal in SAP SRM
- Portal Consultants responsible for integrating SAP SRM into SAP NetWeaver Portal
- Portal system architects

SAP SRM leverages the SAP NetWeaver Portal functionality, seen in Figure 16.1, for many capabilities. First, the portal provides the frontend to all SAP SRM applications; users can access all SAP SRM components via a single harmonized view. This provides the enhanced benefit of efficiency for end users, increasing productivity. Second, the simple navigation capabilities in the portal ensure a consistent user experience regardless of the process or information the user is accessing. The collaboration capabilities in the portal allow users to access an integrated inbox, which can receive work items from multiple applications. This integrated inbox is called the Universal Worklist, which we'll cover later in this chapter. Users can also seamlessly access analytical reports that assist in their operational and strategic decision making.

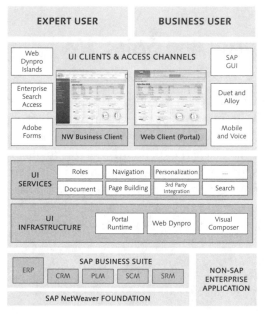

Figure 16.1 SAP SRM Uses the Power of SAP NetWeaver Portal

> **Note**
>
> With SAP NetWeaver Portal 7.0 release, SAP now offers two User Interface (UI) clients to access the SAP Business Suite. Organizations can use either the SAP NetWeaver Business Client (NWBC) or the more commonly used SAP NetWeaver Portal. The desktop-based NWBC client is an SAP integration platform that provides end users with a seamless integration of portal-based transactions, classic SAP GUI-based transactions, and new applications developed in WebDynpro (ABAP and Java). An FAQ on the SAP Community Network provides an introduction, comparison, and recommendation between the two clients. Search for the following document at *www.sdn.sap.com*: FAQ: SAP NetWeaver Business Client and the UI Client for SAP NetWeaver Portal.

Until recently (prior to the SAP SRM 2007/6.0 release), components within SAP SRM, such as SAP Enterprise Buyer (EB), Catalog Content Management (CCM), and supplier self-services (SUS) were available via an independent Web interface. Organizations did not necessarily require SAP NetWeaver Portal for deployment. However, beginning with SAP SRM 7.0 (including the restricted release SAP SRM 6.0), the SAP SRM application has been completely revamped and SAP NetWeaver Portal has become the user's frontend for accessing all applications within SAP SRM. Thus, the statement: SAP NetWeaver Portal is no longer a nice to have, instead a necessity to implement the SAP SRM solution. By using SAP NetWeaver Portal's SSO approach, users can simply log on to a single application and access all the other applications they need for their respective functions without the need for secondary log-ons.

An organization that is currently on an SAP SRM release 5.0 or under needs to consider the impact of the SAP NetWeaver Portal within its upgrade strategy. The SAP SRM 7.0 release cannot be implemented or utilized without the SAP NetWeaver Portal. The SAP SRM 7.0 application is based on SAP NetWeaver 7.01 SP Stack 02 (see OSS Note: 1276845).

> **Note**
>
> SAP has announced that with the release of Enhancement Pack 1 for SRM 7.0, there will be an opportunity for organizations to implement SAP SRM without the mandatory requirement of the SAP NetWeaver Portal. The support of a new navigation frame enables users to run an installation of SAP SRM without a portal.
>
> Obviously, as Enhancement Pack is still on the drawing board, we don't really know what will finally be delivered, but the announcement from SAP does provide a glimpse into how the SAP customer base reacted to the SAP NetWeaver Portal requirement for SAP SRM 7.0. For those customers opposed to using the SAP NetWeaver Portal, this would be good news.

SAP provides an integrated approach for SAP SRM applications and the SAP NetWeaver Portal. Since SAP SRM Release 2.0, SAP has provided portal users with role-based access to business applications relevant to their specific work-related tasks and other information. Organizations implementing SAP SRM can quickly integrate with the SAP NetWeaver Portal by using standard business packages provided by SAP. These business packages contain SAP SRM specific roles, worksets, and iViews that allow organizations to access SAP SRM business processes from within the SAP NetWeaver Portal.

16.1   SRM Business Packages for SAP NetWeaver Portal

According to SAP, business packages provide users (both buyer and suppliers) with an integrated workplace and user-friendly role-based access to all tasks that are part of the procurement process in SAP SRM, available via iViews in SAP NetWeaver Portal 7.0. In other words, the business package provides predefined portal content and roles for SAP SRM–related business processes.

In addition, the content also has predefined integration with SAP SRM and other SAP applications to attain log-on-free access via SSO; you only need to log on once to the SAP NetWeaver Portal.

There are many benefits from using business packages as opposed to manually creating content and then providing role-based access for created content in the SAP NetWeaver Portal environment.

- **Faster Implementation Benefits**
    - SAP provides predefined, role-specific content.
    - There is no development required (however, changes are inevitable).
    - A production environment is set up quickly.
- **Built-in Business Processes Benefits**
    - You have access to harmonized roles across the business suite.
    - You can seamlessly integrate analytics from SAP NetWeaver BW and services from other SAP and non-SAP applications.
    - You can leverage the work done by SAP.
- **Maximum Flexibility Benefits**
    - Use worksets as required.
    - Use iViews as required.
    - Use roles as required.

> **Note**
>
> The various elements within a Business Package are referred to as Content; roles, worksets, pages, and iViews are the content of a business package.

Although, each project has its own unique set of requirements, a typical process to implement business packages is illustrated in Figure 16.2.

Figure 16.2 Process for Implementing the SAP NetWeaver Portal Business Packages

16.1.1 Download the Business Package

Portal administrators can install the Business Packages for SAP SRM 7.0 via the Solution Manager, similar to other software packages. To download the packages, simply log on to the SAP Service Marketplace Software Distribution Center (*www.service.sap.*

com/swdc) and navigate to SELECT DOWNLOAD • SUPPORT PACKAGES AND PATCHES • ENTRY BY APPLICATION GROUP • SAP APPLICATION COMPONENTS • SAP SRM • SELECT THE RELEVANT SRM RELEASE • ENTRY BY COMPONENT.

> **Note**
>
> SAP creates business packages for specific releases of SAP SRM. Therefore, download the appropriate business package that is relevant to your SAP SRM release. For example, for SAP SRM 7.0, the business package for SAP SRM contains content that is WebDynpro based. Whereas for SAP SRM 5.0, the content is ITS based, which is a different technology. Once the business package is downloaded, it can be imported in your portal system and available for role assignment.

Table 16.1 provides a guide to choosing the right business package for your implementation. Also, SAP offers multiple business packages for your SAP SRM release that are business scenario specific. For example, there is a separate package for the core SAP SRM functionality, and a specific Portal Content for the SAP NetWeaver MDM Catalog. Implement all the packages that are relevant for your project scope.

SAP SRM release	Portal Business package	Technical Requirements
SAP SRM 4.0	Business package for SAP SRM 4.0 — 6.02	Enterprise Portal 6.0, SP 4 SAP SRM 4.0 BW 3.5 CCM 1.0
	Business package for supplier collaboration	Enterprise Portal 6.0, SP 4 SAP SRM 4.0 (SUS) BW 3.5
SAP SRM 5.0	Business package for SAP SRM	Enterprise Portal 7.0 (NetWeaver 2004s) SAP SRM 5.0 SAP BI Content 7.0.2
	Business package for supplier collaboration	Enterprise Portal 6.0, SP 4, or 7.0 SAP SRM 4.0 (SUS), SRM 5.0 BW 3.5
SAP SRM 6.0	*Controlled SAP SRM Release only available to specific customers. Not GA release.	*Controlled SAP SRM release only available to specific customers. Not GA release.

Table 16.1 Business Package Compatibility

SAP SRM release	Portal Business package	Technical Requirements
SAP SRM 7.0	Portal Content SRM Includes content for core SRM and harmonized ERP processes	SAP NetWeaver Portal 7.01 SAP SRM 7.0 SAP NetWeaver BW Content 7.03, 7.04, and 7.05
	Portal Content MDM Catalog	SAP NetWeaver Portal 7.01 SRM-MDM 3.0 SAP SRM 7.0
	Portal Content Supplier	SAP NetWeaver Portal 7.01 SAP SRM 7.0

Table 16.1 Business Package Compatibility (Cont.)

After all the required Business Packages have been downloaded, the SAP NetWeaver administrator can install these using the Java Support Package Manager (JSPM). The JSPM is a new tool based on the SAP Software Delivery Manager (SDM) used previously. SAP has provided an OSS Note relevant for the installation of SAP SRM 7.0 Business Packages (see Section 16.4, Relevant OSS Notes and Links).

Once the business package has been installed successfully, its content is now available with the SAP NetWeaver Portal, and the administrator assigns this content using available roles to the user community. Figure 16.3 illustrates how the Portal Content looks once the Business Package "Portal Content SRM" has been installed. This package contains not just SAP SRM content but also SAP ERP content that harmonizes views to the backend systems.

Additional information about the Business Package for SAP SRM 7.0 is available within the Solution Manager: SAP SRM • CONFIGURATION STRUCTURES • SAP SRM 7.0 • BASIC SETTINGS FOR SAP SRM • BUSINESS PACKAGE FOR SRM 7.0.

> **Note**
>
> If you are new to the SAP NetWeaver Portal, when using the SAP delivered Business Packages, always copy the content relevant for your project scope to a Customer namespace. This is important, because otherwise, when a new version of the Business Package is installed, the existing content will be overwritten. So, it's necessary that a customer namespace is used. Also, create customer-specific content in the Customer namespace in the Portal Content Directory (PCD).

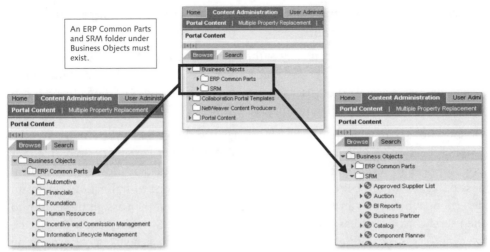

Figure 16.3   SAP SRM 7.0 Content Within the SAP NetWeaver Portal Functionality

As you learn about the business packages available for SAP SRM and the content within these packages, understand portal security and how it differs from other SAP applications. Now that you understand the business packages for SAP NetWeaver Portal, let's move on to portal security.

16.2   Portal Security

Security in the portal environment is independent of the security maintained within the individual applications that are being integrated. Therefore, in addition to the roles and authorizations maintained in SAP SRM or SAP ERP, security must be maintained in the SAP NetWeaver Portal system.

The SAP NetWeaver Portal is a separate functionality with its independent architecture, therefore objects such as users, roles, and so on, are required to be created in SAP NetWeaver Portal just as in any other SAP system. Security in SAP NetWeaver Portal is two-fold, as explained in the following sections.

16.2.1   User Authentication and SSO

As mentioned earlier, the user in the SAP NetWeaver Portal is a separate object than the user in SAP SRM. Organizations can choose one of the following options:

- Create distinct users within SAP NetWeaver Portal
- Upload users from SAP SRM or another SAP system
- Authenticate the users via a corporate LDAP environment

16.2.2 Provide Roles and Authorizations for Accessing Content in Portal Environment

Roles can be either created manually in the portal or uploaded from SAP SRM or SAP ERP. Alternatively, roles can be assigned to user groups in the LDAP and the portal can authenticate against these user groups when users log on. Additionally, roles can be automatically created by importing the business package for SAP SRM.

Organizations that implement SAP SRM 7.0 have no choice but to use SAP NetWeaver Portal; others on SAP SRM 5.0 can use the SAP NetWeaver Portal if desired. In either case, the best practice approach is to use the content provided by SAP within the business packages for SAP SRM. Portal administrators can work with functional teams to determine which roles and portal content are relevant and then assign these roles to the users. Once a role has been assigned to a user in the SAP NetWeaver Portal, the user can access the different SAP SRM applications as long as he has a corresponding UserID, role, and appropriate authorization available in the SAP SRM system.

The role of portal security is to identify what applications and processes should be visible to the end user in the portal. The role of security within SAP SRM is to then check whether the user accessing an application from the portal has the appropriate authorizations to access those applications in the SAP SRM system.

For example, an end user in the SAP NetWeaver Portal may have been assigned a role: SRM Employee. This role contains iViews that allow users to access the shopping-cart application in SAP SRM. Once a user clicks on this application, the security in SAP SRM takes control. In SAP SRM, a corresponding role and additional authorization objects then determine whether the user can create a shopping cart using a particular catalog. The controls within SAP SRM determine what the user can do within the Shopping Cart application.

> **Note**
>
> Security teams need to understand that they could be required to create users and roles in the SAP NetWeaver Portal functionality. For this reason, organizations train their security teams on the SAP NetWeaver Portal and define a process for the creation of users and roles within the SAP SRM and SAP NetWeaver Portal systems. It is not uncommon to find that the security group has not had appropriate training up front, and therefore a constant catch-up occurs through the implementation.

In Chapter 11, we discussed standard SAP SRM roles. For each standard delivered role in SAP SRM, a corresponding role is provided in the SAP NetWeaver Portal business package. Table 16.2 provides an example of the SAP SRM 7.0 role matrix. A complete list of roles can be found in the Business Package for SAP SRM document available when downloading the Business Package on the SAP Service Marketplace.

SAP NetWeaver Portal Role for SAP SRM	PFCG Role in SAP SRM 7.0	PFCG Role in SAP SRM 5.0
Employee Self-Service com.sap.pct.srm.core. ro_employeeselfservice	/SAPSRM/EMPLOYEE	SAP_EC_BBP_EMPLOYEE
Manager com.sap.pct.srm.core. ro_manager	/SAPSRM/MANAGER	SAP_EC_BBP_MANAGER
Employee Self-Service ** com.sap.pct.srm.gp.ro_ employeeselfservice	/SAPPSSRM/EMPLOYEE	

Table 16.2 Business Package Roles in SAP NetWeaver Portal and PFCG Roles in SAP SRM

In Table 16.2, the "Employee Self-Service **" role is listed twice. One role is for the SAP SRM core system and another is used by organizations using the Procurement for Public Sector (PPS) solution, discussed further in Chapter 21.

Figure 16.4 illustrates what the end-user sees in the SAP NetWeaver Portal when assigned the Employee Self-Service role. In this role, the user has access to the Shop for application along with other search options.

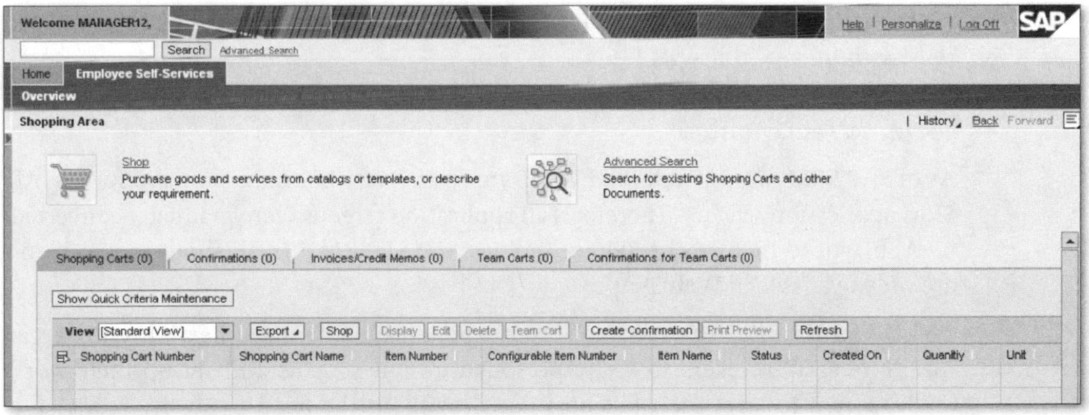

Figure 16.4 The Employee Self-Service role Within the SAP NetWeaver Portal

Although SAP provides standard content for SAP SRM in the business packages, an organization needs to change the contents of this business package to meet its requirements. For example, if the portal role "Employee Self-Service" is used, it provides access to the Shop for, Check status, Inbox, Confirmation, and Invoice applications.

If the organization does not plan to perform the Accounts payable business process (Invoice Entry) in SAP SRM, then this access needs to be removed from the Employee role in the SAP NetWeaver Portal. Therefore, the role and worksets in the portal will need to be changed to remove the Invoice iView to represent appropriate user access. Similarly, other changes might be required; therefore, organizations should not look at the business package approach to involve zero work effort. Instead, they should consider the content available via the business package as a good starting point.

Business packages provide organizations with a starting point to quickly integrate the SAP solutions, such as SAP SRM, within their portal solution. However, business packages do not provide a complete solution. Project teams need to enhance the contents of these packages and integrate other components and applications that are not available as business packages. A well thought-out SAP NetWeaver Portal strategy is critical for any enterprise implementing SAP.

16.3 What's New in SAP SRM 7.0

The SAP NetWeaver Portal 7.0 introduces new user interface technology and concepts that are utilized throughout the SAP SRM application. In this section, we'll review these new concepts.

16.3.1 WebDynpro

As of SAP SRM 6.0, SAP adopted WebDynpro as a user interface standard for all SAP SRM application screens. Therefore, all application screens were gradually converted to WebDynpro from ITS or BSP technology. In SAP SRM 7.0, all application screens are only available in WebDynpro.

WebDynpro provides a consistent user experience and creates flexibility for organizations to allow users to easily personalize their screens and set up their work environment to meet their business needs, without the need to always "code" the SAP SRM application.

In the SAP SRM application, there are two powerful capabilities that are powered by the SAP NetWeaver Portal and WebDynpro. These are user worklists applications known as the Personal Object Worklist and Universal Worklist.

16.3.2 Personal Object Worklist

Personal Object Worklist (POWL) is a new WebDynpro application in the SAP NetWeaver Portal that enhances user productivity. POWL provides the user with an overview of various business objects that are relevant for their daily work stream, grouped according to their status, and can be referred to as active queries that a user can define using selection parameters, without the need of any development, as illustrated in Figures 16.5 and 16.6.

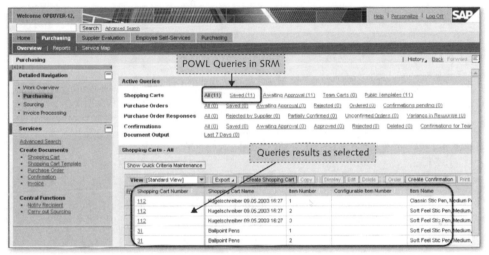

Figure 16.5 Personal Object Worklist overview

As a user, you can make changes to these queries. For example, you can easily change the Shopping Cart query, as illustrated in Figure 16.6. Additionally, you can define new queries as the need arises.

In previous releases of SAP SRM, the user had to click multiple actions to get to the results, which is now available at the instance of login to the SAP NetWeaver Portal. This improves user productivity and enhances the user adoption for the SAP SRM application.

Now let's discuss another powerful application, the Universal Worklist, which replaces the traditional inbox for SAP SRM and the SAP Business Suite.

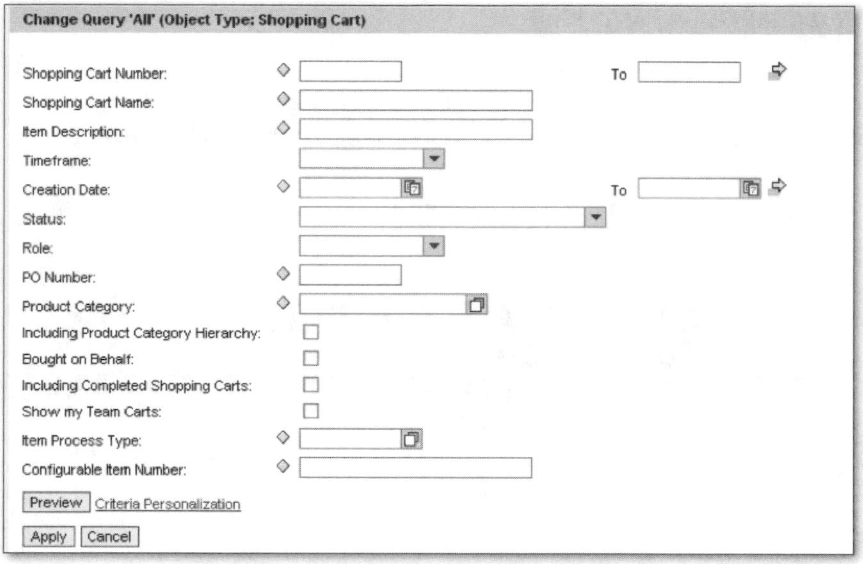

Figure 16.6 Change Mode in the Shopping Cart Query in POWL

> **Note**
>
> Organizations can maintain user authorizations to enable or disable their ability to change/display queries or refresh active queries only or all active queries. This authorization can be restricted using the object CA_POWL.

16.3.3 Universal Worklist

The Universal Worklist (UWL) is a key technology within SAP NetWeaver that is vital for the simplification of end user experience and productivity. It acts as a central inbox for end users to access all workflow alerts, tasks such as approvals and notifications across SAP SRM, SAP ERP, and other systems. In short, users can now go to a single location and process all work items or seamlessly navigate to the application where the task can be completed. Each of the work items in the UWL can be processed in one or more of the following ways:

- Approve
- Reject
- Forward
- Resubmit
- Assign To Me

Figure 16.7 provides an illustration of the UWL in the SAP NetWeaver Portal.

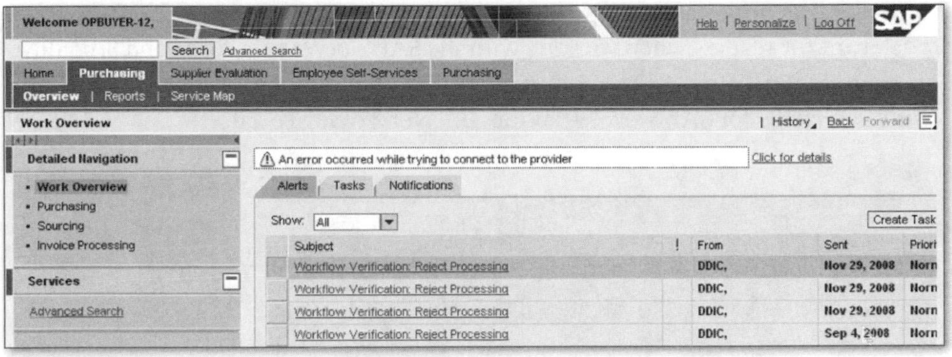

Figure 16.7 Universal Worklist in the SAP NetWeaver Portal

SAP provides a good definition of how the Universal Worklist (UWL) supports an end user:

► It aggregates workflow task items from multiple systems in one universal list (e.g., SAP SRM, SAP ERP, ESS, etc.).

► It displays additional information, as required, from document and object repositories, including attachments and other details.

► It helps you personalize work items.

► It enables you to assign another user to your work items as a substitute in case of absence.

Practical Usage

Imagine yourself as a department manager who is responsible for many employees within your department and possibly other cross-organizational areas. Depending on the activity of the employees, you may need to perform approval/rejection tasks as a manager. For example, purchase of goods/service requests, employee leave requests, approval of supplier invoices, and others. Now, using the UWL, you can perform all your approval tasks directly within the single inbox, instead of performing these tasks in separate applications:

► Procurement (SAP SRM)

► Human resources (SAP ERP HCM)

► Accounts payable (SAP AP)

16.4   Relevant OSS Notes and Links

Table 16.3 lists important OSS Notes available on the SAP Service Marketplace that are relevant for readers when working with the SAP NetWeaver Portal and SAP SRM. For example, OSS Note 1232945 provides recommendations on how to install the Business Package for SAP SRM 7.0 in the SAP NetWeaver Portal.

Note	Description
1232945	BP for SRM 7.0: Installing the Business Packages
1178470	BP for SRM 7.0: Additional Upgrade / Migration information
1178469	BP for SRM 7.0: Additional Installation information
1260119	BP for SRM 7.0: Problem accessing a catalog
1173659	UWL Configuration

Table 16.3   OSS Notes and Descriptions

16.5   Summary

In this chapter, we've reviewed how the SAP NetWeaver Portal functionality can be used with SAP SRM to provide a single user interface for the entire organization. Users can log on once into the portal and automatically get secure access to all the SAP SRM components without logging on again. Organizations can use standard business packages available for SAP SRM to quickly provide role-based application access to users.

Chapter 21 will introduce the SAP Procurement for Public Sector (PPS) solution, which was previously called the Government Procurement (GP) solution. The PPS solution has been specifically designed for government and public-sector companies dealing with regulatory requirements. But first, let's review some customer case studies, in Chapter 17.

Continuous and leveraged learning is a valuable opportunity that customers and consultants can gain by understanding what others have done in the industry and how sharing best practices can enable a stronger solution design for your SAP SRM initiative.

17   Customer Case Studies

The following statement is a common one: "No two SAP projects are alike. Each project brings new and unique organizational, cultural, and business process challenges." SAP SRM projects are no different. However, there is considerable opportunity to learn from similar implementations at other organizations.

SAP publishes customer case studies, which are available for review by customers at *www.sap.com* or from your SAP account executive. In this chapter, we'll review case studies that are specific to SAP SRM implementations so you can learn what others have done in the industry when implementing SAP SRM. To provide a relevant reading, we've included implementations of Self-Service, Catalog Management, Operational Procurement, Strategic Sourcing, and E-Sourcing.

The case studies described in the next section cover the following:

- New SAP ERP and SRM Implementations Case Study
- Existing SAP Customer with New SRM and E-Sourcing Implementations

> **Note**
>
> The actual customer names have been changed for confidentiality in the case studies described in the next section.

17.1   Case Study #1: New SAP ERP and SAP SRM Implementation

The customer illustrated in this case study will be referred to as "Pioneer Industries," a global leader in manufacturing of consumer goods and supplies with revenues of over $20 billion. As a global leader, Pioneer has locations across North America,

Europe, the Middle East, and Asia Pacific. Prior to implementing SAP SRM, Pioneer utilized its own software for managing their indirect procurement and inventory management package. As with many large organizations, Pioneer has grown with acquisitions and therefore a number of companies with the Pioneer umbrella use a variety of software packages to manage procurement and financials.

17.1.1 Project Scope: SAP ERP and SAP SRM

Pioneer decided to standardize on a global procurement platform along with a global financial system. So, SAP ERP and SAP SRM were selected as the global applications for procurement and sourcing.

The core business objective was to implement a standardized "global" platform to manage procurement and gain visibility into global spending. As with other SAP and SRM projects, the blueprint and design phase is key to ensure a solid design is defined that satisfies requirements for all business units.

Budgeting and other project timelines in the organization limited the initial wave/rollout of SAP and SAP SRM application to North America. However, a global blueprint needed to be completed with resources dedicated from all regions to ensure that the requirements were gathered completely and a global template was built (Table 17.1).

Process/Function	Tool Used
Requisitioning	Shopping Cart in SAP SRM
Approvals	Workflow in SAP SRM using Universal Worklist (Portal)
Sourcing & Processing of Requisitions	Sourcing application in SAP SRM
Strategic Sourcing - RFx events	Bidding Engine in SAP SRM
Contract Management	Contract Management in SAP SRM

Table 17.1 Various Processes and Tools Used in the Project Scope

Based on the ASAP methodology, Table 17.2 illustrates the high-level project timeline that was developed.

Project Phase	Timeline
Project Planning	1 month
Blueprint	3.5 months
Realization	5 months
Realization: Testing & Training	3 months
Preparation / Cutover	1.5 months
Go-Live	Big Bang

Table 17.2 High-Level Project Timeline

17.1.2 Key Challenges Prior to Implementing SAP SRM

As previously mentioned, the business had grown considerably in the last year, including acquisitions of smaller companies. There were a handful of challenges that needed to be addressed before implementing SAP SRM. These included:

▶ Inconsistent purchasing policies across regions

▶ Manual procurement processes in many locations

▶ Maverick procurement practices across the organization

▶ Lack of visibility to leverage supplier contracts

17.1.3 SAP SRM Application Design and Implementation Scenario

Based on the business requirements, a solution was designed so that SAP SRM would be the only system that would be used for requisitioning of all goods and services (both indirect and direct). Any planned demand, based on MRP, will automatically create requisitions in SAP ERP and sourced in SAP SRM when required.

The implementation scenario that was used was the Decoupled scenario, a combination of the Extended Classic and Classic Scenarios. The Extended Classic scenario was implemented because the procurement organization could use and leverage a single user interface to a global procurement system. In addition, the Classic scenario was implemented for the creation of reservations in SAP ERP for inventory related requests. Figure 17.1 illustrates the implementation scenario at a high level.

Some important things to know and think about regarding this case study are as follows:

▶ All procurement and sourcing activities were performed in the SAP SRM system. Because Pioneer did not have an SAP system in place prior to implementing SAP SRM, the organization was interested in using SAP SRM and had no business requirement that drove it to using the SAP ERP system for procurement.

▶ Shopping carts in SAP SRM were used as the only mechanism to request both indirect and direct goods and services.

▶ For catalog management, external catalog suppliers were on-boarded for a number of commodities including office supplies, industrial goods, lab supplies, marketing and gifts, computer supplies, consulting services, and so on.

▶ In addition, the SRM-MDM Catalog enabled an internal catalog for Pioneer where supplier catalogs were created and managed. Examples were packaging material catalog, services, and facilities.

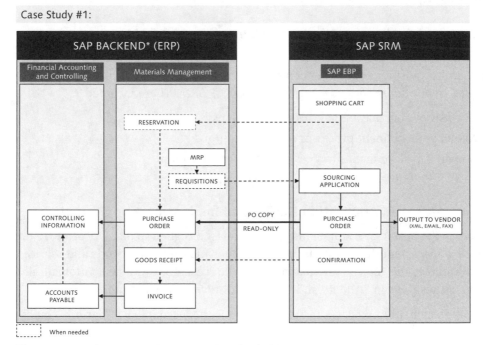

Figure 17.1 Implementation Scenario in Case Study #1

▶ Material Masters were created in SAP ERP for products that needed to be in inventory. These were replicated to SAP SRM so that end users could request them using the shopping cart. The Order as Direct functionality requested any goods that needed to be received into inventory.

▶ All the MRP demand created in SAP ERP system was transferred to the SAP SRM system for sourcing, automatically via contracts, or manually by a purchaser in the Sourcing application in SAP SRM.

▶ No manual requisitions were created in the SAP ERP system.

► Based on business requirements, Pioneer required that Reservations were created for products that were in their inventory. End users that needed to request products from the warehouse or inventory used the Shopping Cart capability to order a material in the shopping cart, and if stock was available in the inventory (MM-IM), then a reservation was created automatically.

► Pioneer's organizational policies aligned to an organizational hierarchy and dollar threshold for approvals to purchase goods and services. So, each supervisor or manager had a dollar value limit for approval. As the SAP ERP HCM solution was not in scope for this implementation, an independent organization structure was created in SAP SRM to represent the organizational hierarchy for Pioneer. In addition, the Spending Limit/Approval Limit workflow functionality was configured in SAP SRM to enable the dollar threshold approval requirement.

► The SAP Enterprise Portal was used as a single entry point for access to all SAP SRM applications. In addition, the Universal Worklist (UWL) was used for approvals of all goods and services.

► The SRM Contracts Management functionality created contracts for both product and product category. Product-based contracts automatically sourced the MRP demand in SAP SRM. In addition, the Product Category contracts sourced indirect goods and services.

► All purchase orders (POs) were created in SAP SRM and a copy of those POs was sent to the SAP ERP system for accounts payable functions.

► POs were transmitted from SAP SRM using various formats of email, electronic fax, and XML. For specific suppliers, the XML format was utilized for exchanging POs and receiving PO acknowledgments. The SAP NetWeaver Process Integration (SAP NetWeaver PI) application was used.

► SAP NetWeaver BW was used as the reporting and analytics tool for operational and strategic spend reporting.

17.1.4   SAP Landscape and Environment

There are various tools that were used in this case study's implementation process. They include:

► SAP SRM
► SRM-MDM Catalog
► SRM Contract Management
► SAP ERP
► SAP NetWeaver Portal
► SAP NetWeaver BW

17.2 Case Study #2: Existing SAP Customer with New SAP SRM and E-Sourcing Implementation

The customer illustrated in this case study will be referred to as "Global Services Inc (GSI)." GSI is a global leader and provider of professional services and consulting with revenues of over $3 billion. GSI already used SAP ERP software. The organization used materials management in SAP ERP operations for procurement of indirect goods and services. Although materials management in SAP ERP was the functionality for procurement and sourcing, the organization had limited success to rollout requisitioning and approval capabilities in SAP ERP to the larger user population in GSI due to lack of user adoption and ease of use. Procurement was largely centralized with end users sending emails and paper requests to the purchasing departments when goods and services were needed.

In addition, GSI had many departments that were procuring goods and services outside of the procurement policies and also negotiating contracts with suppliers.

17.2.1 Project Scope: SAP ERP and SAP SRM

GSI decided to implement the SAP SRM application as a global platform for procurement and sourcing. A key driver for using SAP SRM was the ability of the organization to decentralize the requisitioning and procurement of goods and services via the Shopping Cart functionality in SAP SRM.

Strategic sourcing activities for contract management and negotiation were to be centralized using the SAP E-Sourcing application in a hosted platform. GSI decided that it was extremely important for them to get visibility of all procurement contracts in the organization and manage those in a central location moving forward (Table 17.3).

Process/Function	Tool Used
Requisitioning	Shopping Cart in SAP SRM
Approvals	Workflow in SAP SRM
Sourcing and Processing of Requisitions	Sourcing application in SAP SRM
Contract Management	E-Sourcing and integrated to SAP ERP as outline agreements
PO creation	SAP ERP

Table 17.3 Various Processes and Tools Used at GSI

Based on the ASAP methodology, Table 17.4 shows the high-level project timeline that was developed.

Project Phase	Timeline
Project Planning	0.5 months
Blueprint	2 months
Realization	4.5 months
Realization: Testing and Training	2 months
Preparation / Cutover	0.5 months
Go-Live	Rollout based on multiple waves

Table 17.4 High-Level Project Timeline for GSI

17.2.2 Key Challenges Prior to Implementing SAP SRM

GSI had a handful of challenges to overcome before implementing SAP SRM. These challenges are common throughout industries, and include:

▸ Highly manual effort for requesting goods/services
▸ No visibility for end users on the status of their purchase requests
▸ Manual procurement processes in many locations
▸ Approval processes were 100% manual with no reporting mechanism
▸ Maverick procurement practices across the organization
▸ Lack of visibility to leverage supplier contracts

17.2.3 SAP SRM Application Design and Implementation Scenario

Based on the business requirements, the application was designed so that SAP SRM would be used as the only system for requesting all goods and services. GSI was a services organization and therefore didn't have a large environment for inventory management. Because of this, inventory management was never configured in the existing materials management in SAP system.

Requisitioning was to be rolled out as a decentralized process to every user in the organization.

SAP E-Sourcing was identified as the solution for managing all contracts (procurement) within the organization. To limit the implementation scope, the initial rollout for contracts would primarily gather contracts internally from different sources within the organization and then create a limited agreement in SAP E-Sourcing so that visibility can be gained around contracts. As a subsequent wave of the project, the agreements from E-Sourcing were integrated with SAP ERP for operational sourcing.

The implementation scenario (Figure 17.2) used was the Classic scenario. All requisitioning was done using a shopping cart in SAP SRM, but the eventual PO created in SAP ERP. In addition, the SAP E-Sourcing application was implemented for management and integration of contracts.

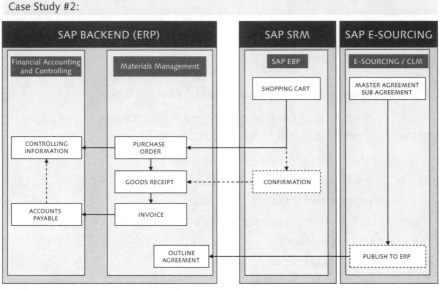

Figure 17.2 Implementation Scenario in Case Study #2

Some important things to know and think about regarding this case study are as follows:

▶ Because GSI had used SAP ERP for many years, the procurement organization (buyers) was fairly comfortable with the PO capabilities in materials management in SAP ERP operations, and wanted to continue to leverage their experience. The Classic scenario provided the ability for GSI to rollout SAP SRM to end users as the core application and buyers could continue to utilize the SAP ERP application for the materials management functions.

▶ Shopping carts in SAP SRM were used as the only mechanism to request goods and services.

▶ For catalog management, GSI selected a catalog hub to on-board many catalog suppliers quickly. GSI subscribed to the catalog service with SciQuest. There was a cost to using this service, but GSI enabled its goal of on-boarding many supplier catalogs quickly.

- GSI did not want to manage any internal catalogs and henceforth no internal catalog system was implemented.

- No manual requisitions were created in the SAP ERP system. A shopping cart was required prior to creation of any POs.

- GSI as an organization had an approval policy for purchases to be approved by the individual cost center owner. Although other approval best practices were discussed, the organization wanted to approve purchases based on cost centers. In addition, the purchase requests would often have more than one cost center, especially ones created by the administrative groups. This business requirement demanded a cost center–based approval design in SAP SRM.

- The approval design was highly complex with a need for continuous maintenance. Due to the business requirements, a cost center table was defined in SAP SRM that would be used for workflow at a shopping cart line item level.

- The organization structure hierarchy was not needed for the approval of shopping carts and henceforth a fairly flat representation of the organization structure was defined in SAP SRM. Also, GSI did not use the SAP ERP HCM functionality and thus the organization structure was created directly in SAP SRM.

- The buyer community moved away from the creation of the requests to strategic sourcing activities of negotiating better prices on commodities. Because end users created the actual shopping carts and used catalogs from SciQuest, many orders could be automated without the need for buyer intervention.

- Buyers/Purchasers only intervened on purchases that were largely free-text, capital, or orders where the PO was large enough for the buyer to ensure the supplier of choice.

- All POs were created in SAP ERP. Subsequent functions of goods receipts were done in SAP SRM by requestors. All accounts payable functions for invoice receipt and payments were continued within the SAP ERP system as before.

- POs were transmitted from SAP ERP using existing formats of email and fax.

- The SAP NetWeaver Portal was used as a single point of entry for accessing SAP SRM applications and for the buyers to access the materials management transactions.

- In a parallel project stream, the purchasing organization gathered all the contracts in the organization pertaining to procurement of goods/services and then created mini-agreements in the E-Sourcing application. The reason they were "mini" were because only selective pieces of information were entered in the agreements in SAP E-Sourcing in the initial phase. The goal was to have a repository of all contracts within E-Sourcing.

▶ Once the repository was created, a subsequent wave of the project enabled the integration of SAP E-Sourcing with SAP ERP to publish agreements in E-Sourcing as Outline agreements in SAP ERP. These outline agreements were then utilized to source requirements originating from SAP SRM.

▶ The purchasing department ensured contract compliance and gained visibility to global contracts. In addition, they captured the validity of contracts and notified when contracts were expiring. Also, the organization had a single platform to create, change, and manage all procurement contracts in the organization.

▶ SAP NetWeaver BW was used as the reporting and analytics tool for operational and strategic spend reporting. The data for reporting was gained from SAP SRM, SAP ERP, and also E-Sourcing. All users accessed the reports via the SAP NetWeaver Portal application.

17.2.4 SAP Landscape and Environment

The following were used in the GSI SAP implementation:

▶ SAP SRM
▶ SAP E-Sourcing
▶ SAP ERP
▶ SAP NetWeaver Portal
▶ SAP NetWeaver BW

17.3 Summary

In this chapter, we discussed case studies for customer implementation of SAP SRM. These case study implementation scenarios were illustrated with new implementations, enhancements, and upgrades. Also, the technical scenarios such as Classic and Extended Classic were discussed. Now, let's move on to discuss SAP E-Sourcing in Chapter 18.

E-Sourcing fills the void that existed in SAP's on-demand As a Service strategy. SAP software has the ability to provide a solid strategic sourcing solution to its large SAP customer base.

18   SAP E-Sourcing

If you read any of the analyst advisory reports in the area of sourcing and procurement, such as Aberdeen, Gartner, Hackett, one aspect is similar – the value proposition of strategic sourcing. This has been the case for the last few years. Pressures of cost reduction across organizations are requiring procurement managers to take a hard look at their spending and determine ways to consolidate the supplier base, negotiate better terms and prices, and reduce costs. What a lot of procurement managers are asking for are tools that help them gain visibility on contracts, spending, and the ability to conduct RFx, bids, and auctions to negotiate better contracts and reduce spending.

This is where SAP E-Sourcing provides significant value. In 2006, SAP acquired a company called Frictionless. With Frictionless came what is now rebranded as the SAP E-Sourcing application: a Web-based user interface, with extremely rich functionality in Strategic Sourcing.

> **Note**
>
> E-Sourcing provides a totally new line of business for SAP. The market for E-Sourcing is different than traditional SAP customers. About 70% to 80% of the customers use a "hosted" solution for SAP E-Sourcing, to quickly deploy within the procurement organization and gain quick return on investment (ROI).

Target audiences for this chapter are:

▶ Project Manager, Solution Leads
▶ SRM Implementation Consultants
▶ Functional process owners with interest in Strategic Sourcing

SAP E-Sourcing provides a single platform for the following sourcing and contract management capabilities:

- ► Category and Project Management
- ► Request for Information/Quote/Proposal (RFI/RFQ/RFP)
- ► Forward and Reverse Auctions
- ► Contract Lifecycle Management including contract generation
- ► Supplier Management and Spend Analysis
- ► According to SAP, E-Sourcing helps attain bottom-line savings and accelerates the deployment time so value can be realized faster with a quicker user adoption. Together with SAP SRM, SAP E-Sourcing now enables a complete sourcing and procurement process for an organization with multiple deployment options and capabilities.

Before we move on to further detail on the various capabilities of the solution, let's look at the user interface of SAP E-Sourcing using Figures 18.1 and 18.2.

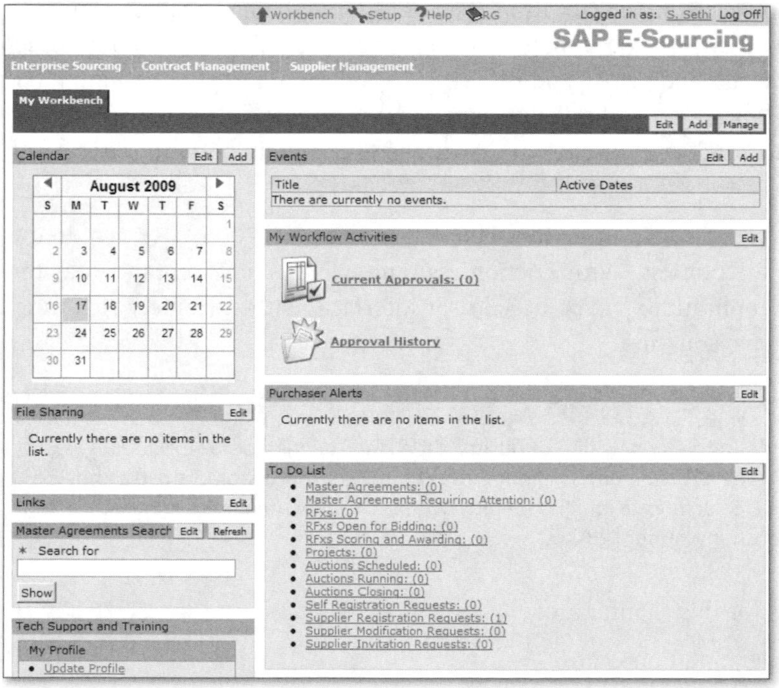

Figure 18.1 SAP E-Sourcing Workbench (Version 5.1)

Figure 18.1 illustrates the landing page or *workbench* in E-Sourcing. The capabilities are divided into three main sections: Enterprise Sourcing, Contract Management, and Supplier Management. Enterprise Sourcing contains the Project Management,

RFx, and Auctioning capabilities as illustrated in Figure 18.2. Contract Management contains the Master Agreement and Contract authoring capabilities. Supplier Management provides the ability for supplier registration and management.

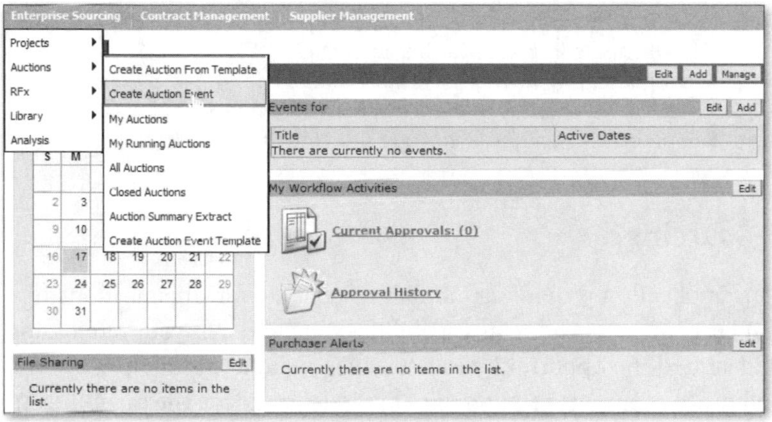

Figure 18.2 Enterprise Sourcing Capabilities (version 5.1)

SAP SRM is a separate application built on the SAP NetWeaver platform with capabilities for operational procurement, Bidding, Auctions, and Contract Management. SAP E-Sourcing is definitely not a replacement but provides an option for customers to quickly leverage some capabilities. Table 18.1 provides an illustration of this discussion.

Capability	SAP SRM	SAP E-Sourcing
Project Management		X
RFx and Bidding	X	X
Auctions	X	X
Clause Libraries		X
Contract Management	X	X
Contract Management – Legal and Authoring using Microsoft Word		X
Supplier Registration	X	X
Supplier Collaboration – orders, confirmations, invoices, etc.	X	

Table 18.1 Functionality Available in SAP SRM and SAP E-Sourcing

As of SAP E-Sourcing 5.1 release, there is no standard integration available between E-Sourcing and SAP SRM. There are a few customers that have built a custom integration. SAP has advised that in 2010 there will be integration between SAP E-Sourcing 6.0 and SAP SRM. Currently, for E-Sourcing 5.1, there is an integration package available for SAP E-Sourcing and SAP ERP, which we'll discuss further in Section 18.2, SAP E-Sourcing 5.1 Architecture. SAP E-Sourcing integration with SAP ERP is valuable for organizations implementing SRM in a Classic scenario or those that are not implementing SAP SRM at all and integrating SAP with E-Sourcing to gain quick strategic sourcing capabilities.

18.1   SAP E-Sourcing

The SAP E-Sourcing application provides a number of benefits for organizations that want to quickly on-board strategic sourcing capabilities. Imagine that your purchasing organization has identified the opportunity to better negotiate terms and prices for a particular commodity (i.e., computer equipment), but it doesn't have the capability in-house to conduct an electronic bid or auction event to invite suppliers to participate.

SAP E-Sourcing provides the ability for an organization to use these capabilities quickly in an on-demand option. They can now conduct the actual bid/auction event to quickly gain savings without waiting for a long project to implement these capabilities in-house.

SAP E-Sourcing enables the following capabilities:

▶ **Category and Project Management**
  ▶ Using SAP E-Sourcing, purchasing organizations can manage their internal sourcing activities, track tasks and milestones, monitor project status, and capture opportunities for savings.
  ▶ In most organizations, purchasing teams doing these activities use Microsoft Excel spreadsheets or other to-do lists. Using SAP E-Sourcing, they manage projects using a process methodology, capture supporting documents in project repository, and collaborate with key stakeholders.

▶ **RFx, Auction, and Bid Optimization**
  ▶ Using SAP E-Sourcing, organizations can identify and qualify supplier capabilities using RFI processes and utilize templates to create RFI and RFQ events quickly.
  ▶ Execute simple and complex sourcing (RFx, Auction) activities in an automated Web-based system that captures all the interaction between the customer and the supplier organization during a sourcing event.

▶ Utilize robust scorecard and evaluation capabilities for sourcing events using weighted scoring, comparisons, and historical analysis.

▶ Negotiate with your suppliers through an online, real-time bidding and auction solution.

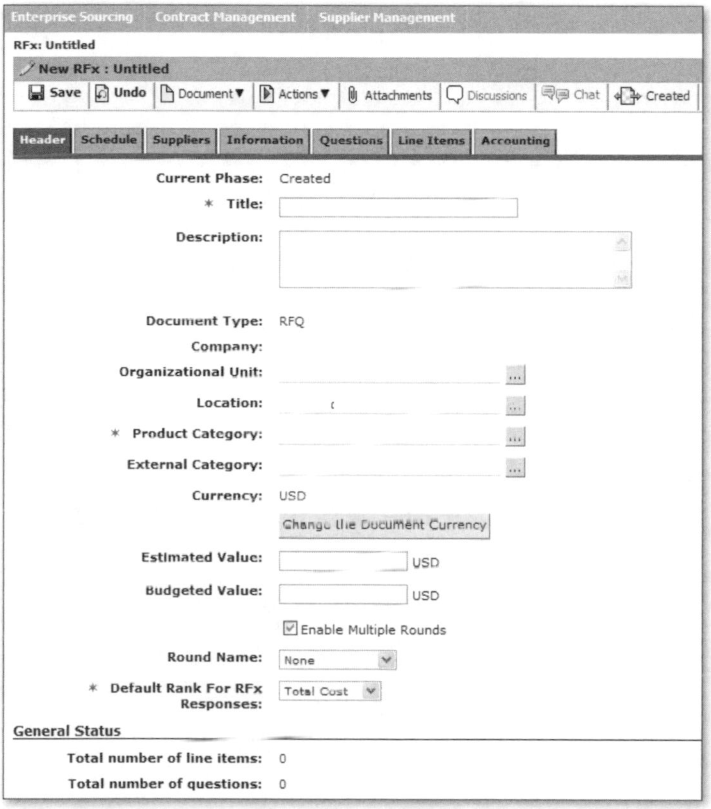

Figure 18.3 RFx Screenshot from SAP E-Sourcing 5.1

▶ **Contract Lifecycle Management**

▶ Using the contract functionality of SAP E-Sourcing (branded as SAP Contract Lifecycle Management [SAP CLM]), organizations can manage procurement and other contracts within the enterprise in a single repository.

▶ An organization can manage the entire process of contract creation — from a draft to completion and generation of the final Microsoft Word-based document with continuous version control.

▶ An organization can utilize templates, contract libraries, and clause libraries to enforce and utilize legal terms and conditions while drafting, negotiating, and generating contracts.

▶ An organization can utilize approval workflows to route the contract documents for approval within and outside the organization. SAP CLM provides capabilities for managing compliance by capturing audit trail of creation, editing, approvals, and changes to all documents.

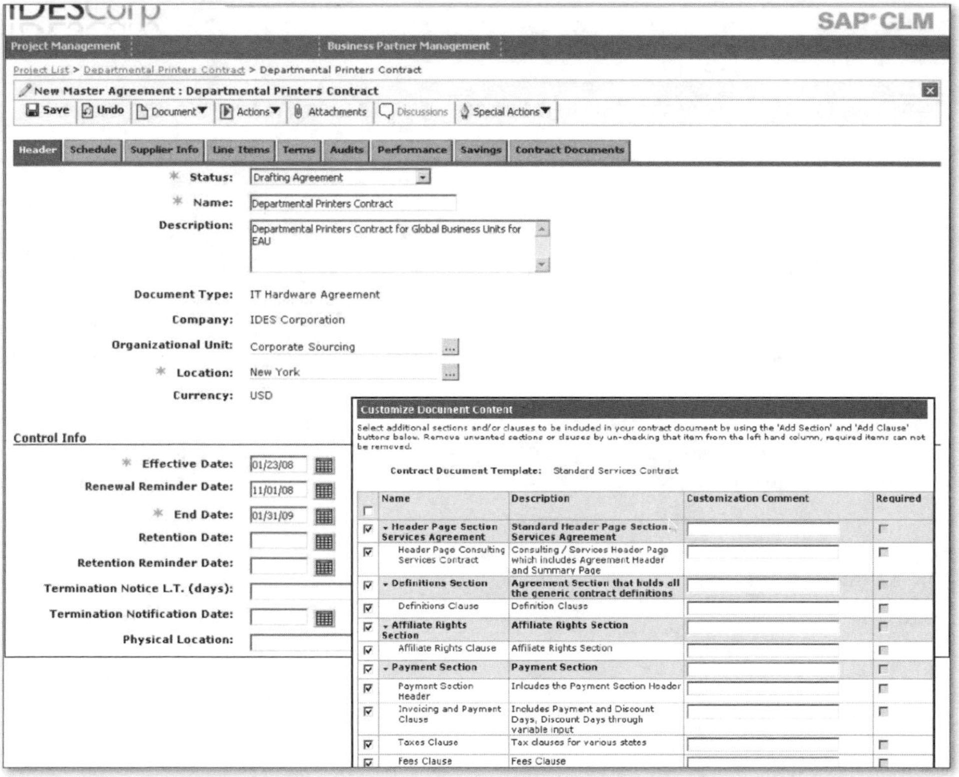

Figure 18.4 Contract Screenshot from SAP E-Sourcing

Note

SAP CLM uses SAP E-Sourcing as the base platform for contract management and repository. Plus, it leverages the search and classification capabilities of SAP Knowledge Management (KM) and TREX. In addition, for creating the actual contract in Microsoft Word, SAP CLM uses the Microsoft .NET framework along with IIS technologies.

The Contract Generation server is used to actually generate the final Word-based contract. Keep in mind, organizations don't have to actually generate the Word contract – it's an option, not a requirement.

▶ **Supplier Management**

  ▶ SAP E-Sourcing provides capabilities for supplier registration and management.

  ▶ Suppliers can manage their profiles, participate in category surveys, respond to RFx/auction events, view supplier scorecards, and view their active contracts — all through a single, Web-based application.

Customers have the following three choices when it comes to implementing SAP E-Sourcing:

▶ On-demand

▶ Hosted

▶ On-premise

> **Note**
>
> It's important to understand that customers can integrate SAP E-Sourcing with their SAP ERP system in either the Hosted or the On-Premise options. These are discussed further in Section 18.3.

18.1.1 On-Demand

On-Demand is good for customers who want to try out the E-Sourcing capabilities before any significant investment. Customers can pay an event-based fee and conduct a bid/auction event to invite suppliers and possibly negotiate on a particular commodity.

18.1.2 Hosted

Many E-Sourcing customers use a Hosted option; 90% of these are Frictionless customers who are now SAP E-Sourcing customers.

The ROI can be easily justified using a Hosted option because organizations can participate in strategic sourcing events (RFx, Auction, etc.) and gain value by negotiating better spending with suppliers in particular commodities. This option is good for customers that want a strategic sourcing tool and don't want the hassle of building an in-house infrastructure and support team to manage the tool. The Hosted platform allows the purchasing department to quickly get their requirements configured in a Hosted approach and still be able to conduct all RFx, Auctions, and Contract Mgmt capabilities in SAP E-Sourcing.

The Hosted option allows the organization to utilize its own master data for suppliers, materials, product categories, and so on.

18.1.3 On-Premise

The On-Premise option is the traditional approach for SAP customers, where they have to install and implement in-house. It is also not unusual for customers to start from the Hosted option and then build a roadmap to bring the application within their organization using the On-Premise option. Apart from moving away from a subscription-based program, On-Premise provides more flexibility for an organization when it comes to upgrading or not upgrading the E-Sourcing application. Also, from an integration perspective, an On-Premise platform provides more flexibility for the organization.

SAP E-Sourcing is a 100% Java application. Customers implementing it On-Premise need to understand the support requirements for their IT administrators. SAP E-Sourcing 5.1 release is implemented on the SAP NetWeaver Java platform.

18.2 SAP E-Sourcing 5.1 Architecture

Customers using SAP E-Sourcing/CLM in a hosted environment often do not need to worry about architecture and system landscapes — the hosting provider takes care of these. However, organizations that either have an On-Premise solution or plan to migrate from a Hosted scenario need to be aware of the E-Sourcing/CLM landscape. Figure 18.5 provides a high-level illustration of the system landscape for SAP E-Sourcing 5.1/CLM 2.0.

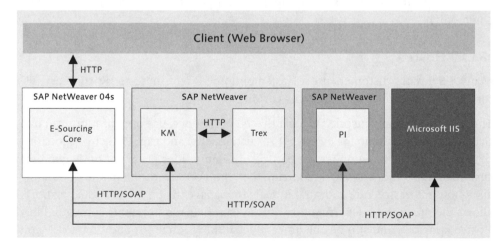

Figure 18.5 SAP E-Sourcing 5.1/CLM2.0 System Landscape (Credit: SAP)

In Figure 18.5, KM, Trex, and Microsoft IIS applications are only used for SAP CLM. SAP NetWeaver PI (previously XI) is used for integration scenarios of SAP E-Sourcing/CLM with SAP ERP.

In the next section, you'll learn about the integration packages that are available for customers who want to use SAP E-Sourcing integrated with their SAP ERP or SAP SRM systems.

18.3 SAP E-Sourcing Integration with SAP ERP and SAP SRM

As we mentioned in the introduction, SAP E-Sourcing is what was formally known as Frictionless. Because of this, the application is not built on a traditional SAP ABAP or SAP NetWeaver technology platform. However, SAP believes that it's beneficial for customers to select SAP E-Sourcing over other strategic sourcing applications, due to the opportunity to integrate E-Sourcing with the core SAP ERP system. So, SAP has provided specific points of intersection where SAP E-Sourcing integrates with the overall operational sourcing and source-to-contract scenarios in the backend SAP ERP system and also SAP SRM. In this section, we'll outline those areas.

> **Note**
>
> As of SAP E-Sourcing 5.1 release, there is no core integration between SAP E-Sourcing and SAP SRM. However, customers have built custom integration using the SAP NetWeaver PI API's. According to SAP, the SAP E-Sourcing 6.0 release will provide standard integration between SAP SRM and SAP E-Sourcing. SAP E-Sourcing 6.0 is supposed to be generally available in 2010 along with the next release of the SAP Business Suite. Integration is expected with the Contract Management capabilities. You can learn more at the SAP E-Sourcing 6.0 blog on SDN: *www.sdn.sap.com/irj/scn/weblogs?blog=/pub/wlg/12885*

18.3.1 SAP E-Sourcing Integration Package

Strategic sourcing activities such as RFx and auctions when completed need to be converted into an award document, such as a PO or contract. This can be done within SAP E-Sourcing. However, a contract's value is limited if it isn't being utilized within the operational procurement process. So, it's key for you to take the output documents (such as POs or contracts) and integrate them with the core SAP system (SAP ERP or SAP SRM). This is where the integration package comes into play.

The SAP E-Sourcing/ERP Integration package enables integration between SAP ERP and SAP E-Sourcing. It provides standard APIs for both replication of master data and integration of purchasing documents (RFQ, PO, Outline Agreement).

> **Note**
>
> The integration package requires the use of SAP NetWeaver PI content for predelivered data maps and interfaces.
>
> As mentioned earlier, this integration is available for both Hosted and On-Premise options for SAP E-Sourcing. Step-by-step guides are available on SAP Service Marketplace for either of the integrations.
>
> The integration process begins with the download of a zip file from the SAP Service Marketplace that contains necessary content for SAP E-Sourcing, SAP NetWeaver PI (XI), and SAP ERP.
>
> If your E-Sourcing solution is hosted, then some of the content upload (JAVA files) work needs to be completed by the Hosting team and the SAP NetWeaver PI (XI) integration tasks need to be completed by your organization internally.
>
> You should start with the integration guides, which provide a detailed process on what is needed.

The following business processes are supported via this integration package:

▶ **Master data replication and synchronization**

Organizations can replicate master data elements from the SAP ERP system to the SAP E-Sourcing application so that the resulting PO and contracts from SAP E-Sourcing reference a single master data element. For example, when you conduct an auction event and then award the contract to Supplier A. However, if Supplier A is different in SAP E-Sourcing and ERP, then you would have downstream integration impacts. Therefore, the core master data has to be the same between SAP ERP and SAP E-Sourcing for a seamless integration of processes. Table 18.2 provides a list of master data elements that can be replicated.

Master Data	Replicated how?
▶ Vendor Master	▶ ALE and IDoc integration
▶ Material Master	▶ ALE and IDoc integration
▶ Company Code	▶ Flat file import into E-Sourcing
▶ Purchasing Organization	▶ Flat file import into E-Sourcing
▶ Plants	▶ Flat file import into E-Sourcing
▶ Unit of Measure (UOM)	▶ Flat file import into E-Sourcing
▶ Payment Terms	▶ Flat file import into E-Sourcing

Table 18.2 Master Data Replication Between SAP ERP and E-Sourcing

▶ **Replication of SAP E-Sourcing supplier to SAP ERP**
When executing RFx events, new suppliers can be on-boarded that do not currently do business with the organization. In such events, a new supplier can be created in SAP E-Sourcing and replicated to the SAP ERP system. The Supplier/Vendor Master in SAP ERP is fairly extensive and captures a lot of information about a supplier. The data that is exchanged between SAP E-Sourcing and SAP ERP is limited to a basic subset of fields.

▶ **Integration of an RFQ from SAP ERP to SAP E-Sourcing**
In SAP ERP, an RFQ can be generated and then be transferred to the SAP E-Sourcing application. In SAP E-Sourcing, an RFP can be created and post the RFP process a resulting PO or contract (outline agreement) can be created that can then be integrated back to the SAP ERP system.

▶ **RFx or Auction award in SAP E-Sourcing to a PO or Contract in SAP ERP**

▶ **E-Sourcing Master Agreement to a Contract (Outline Agreement) in SAP ERP**
Organizations that use the Master Agreement functionality in SAP E-Sourcing can integrate them with an Outline Agreement in SAP ERP. This enables operational procurement activities to utilize the negotiated agreements out of SAP E-Sourcing.

▶ There are several things to keep in mind when evaluating SAP E-Sourcing for yourself or your business:

1. Although SAP E-Sourcing provides analytics, organizations that use SAP ERP and SAP SRM probably also use SAP NetWeaver BW for reporting. In this scenario, they may want to continue to report using SAP NetWeaver BW, with additional integration of SAP NetWeaver BW with data from the SAP E-Sourcing application to provide a single reporting platform for the procurement organization.

2. The SAP E-Sourcing application does not contain financial information, such as account assignments. This information has to be entered after the creation of a PO or contract (outline agreement) in the SAP ERP system.

3. The integration package provided by SAP only supports the integration with a single SAP ERP backend.

4. For detailed list of considerations, review the integration package OSS Note listed in the next section.

18.4   Relevant OSS Notes and Links

Table 18.3 lists important OSS Notes available on the SAP Service Marketplace that are relevant for readers when working with the SAP Solution Manager and SAP SRM.

Note	Description
1313088	Integration of SAP E-Sourcing 5.0/5.1 and SAP ERP

Table 18.3 OSS Notes and Descriptions

18.5   Summary

In this chapter, we discussed at a high level the capabilities of the SAP E-Sourcing solution. You also learned about the integration points between SAP E-Sourcing and the SAP ERP backend, which integrates strategic sourcing activities to be leveraged within the operational procurement activities. In Chapter 19, we'll discuss SAP Solution Manager and SAP SRM.

What used to be nice to have a few years ago is now a must-have. SAP Solution Manager applications are now required functionalities for organizations that want to implement new SAP solutions or are in the process of upgrading their existing SAP solutions. It is now the default SAP application management platform to manage your entire SAP solution landscape.

19   SAP Solution Manager and SAP SRM

When SAP released Solution Manager in early 2003, it was a product that customers received with mixed feelings. It was not clear how this new software from SAP would help customers manage their SAP landscape. What was definitely not clear was whether it was going to be a technical application, which would benefit, be used, and maintained by the BASIS organization, or if it would actually have significance to the rest of the organization. Most customers implementing SAP and SAP SRM projects up until 2006 were largely unaware of this new application management solution from SAP. It was not until SAP made the SAP Solution Manager a mandatory requirement for new product installations that customers became aware of its existence.

Today, however, it's a different story. The SAP Solution Manager product is highly robust and extremely useful to manage the technical and business aspects of your enterprise SAP solutions.

> **Note**
>
> Even as organizations begin to understand the value of the SAP Solution Manager, basic functions such as Installation, Applying Patches, accessing configuration documentation, and so on, are only possible today using the SAP Solution Manager. A number of organizations are introduced to the Solution Manager when the IT organization made them realize that it is mandatory – without it, SAP SRM and other solutions could not be installed.

Target audiences for this chapter are:

▶ Project Manager, Solution Leads
▶ SRM Implementation Consultants

▶ Functional process owners curious about the role of the SAP Solution Manager in SAP SRM

▶ BASIS/SAP NetWeaver architects responsible for setup of the SAP Solution Manager

SAP Solution Manager acts as a centralized, robust application management and administration solution. SAP Solution Manager combines tools, content, and direct access to SAP to increase the reliability of solutions and lower total cost of ownership. The SAP Solution Manager has many capabilities, including:

▶ SAP Business Suite implementation and upgrades

▶ Change control management

▶ Testing

▶ IT and application support

▶ Root cause analysis

▶ Solution Monitoring

▶ Service-level management and reporting

▶ Service processing

▶ Administration

Figure 19.1 provides a high-level view of the capabilities that exist within the SAP Solution Manager.

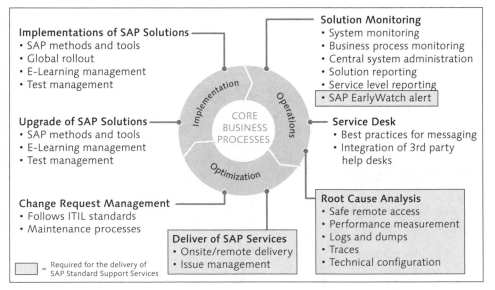

Figure 19.1 SAP Solution Manager Capabilities

SAP Solution Manager is a separate application independent of SAP SRM. It's typically installed on a separate hardware and configured so that it can connect and work with other SAP Solutions, including SAP SRM, SAP ERP, SAP NetWeaver Portal, and so on.

In this chapter, we will focus on discussing the SAP Business Suite implementation and upgrade capability of the Solution Manager as it relates to SAP SRM. You'll learn how the SAP Solution Manager can help your SAP SRM project, and gain knowledge of how to set it up for your project.

> **Note**
>
> Readers interested in detailed knowledge of the SAP Solution Manager can read *SAP Solution Manager Enterprise Edition* by Marc O. Schäfer and Matthias Melich.

19.1 Solution Manager Relevance to SAP SRM

The SAP Solution Manager provides content that accelerates implementation. It provides a central access to tools, methods, and content such as configuration documentation, release notes, and templates, which can be used during evaluation, implementation, and operational processing of your SAP systems.

The SAP Solution Manager assists SAP SRM customers in some of the following areas of their solution implementation:

- Installation of the SAP SRM solution and components such as SRM-MDM Catalog
- Installation and ongoing maintenance of support/enhancement packs
- Access to standard implementation content for business processes
- Ability to document and modeling customer-specific business processes
- Roadmaps for new implementation and upgrades
- Project Management activities such as distribution of customizing tasks to the project teams and tracking of configuration progress
- Act as a single point of configuration for business processes running on different systems such as SAP SRM, SAP ERP, SAP NetWeaver MDM catalog
- Setup of test cases using standard objects in the SAP Solution Manager and assignment to testing users
- Accelerators for upgrade projects

The SAP Solution Manager provides tools and content to assist your project team throughout all phases of your SAP SRM project cycle, as illustrated in Figure 19.2.

Many organizations today use the SAP Solution Manager for accessing best practices, roadmaps, and documentation during the business blueprint phase and also for configuration of SAP SRM during the Realization phase.

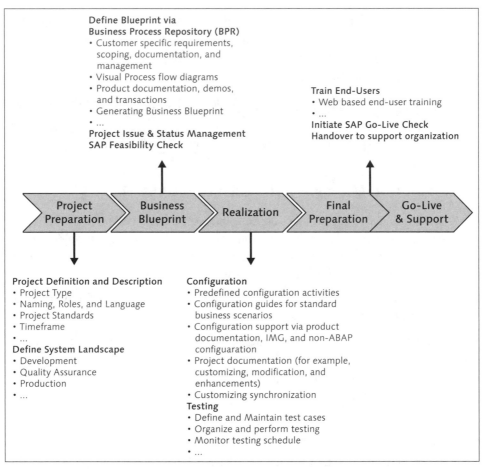

Figure 19.2 SAP Solution Manager Value in Phases of an SAP SRM Project

19.1.1   Installation and Maintenance of the SAP SRM Application

An installation key is required to implement SAP SRM. This key is only available via the SAP Solution Manager. So, even if the customer is not planning to use the SAP Solution Manager for its other capabilities, it's necessary to install SAP SRM and its components.

In Chapter 20, we'll discuss the role of the SAP NetWeaver Portal and the SAP SRM business packages delivered in the portal. For customers to make use of the business packages, they need to be downloaded and installed. This can only be done via the SAP Solution Manager, so this capability in the SAP Solution Manager makes it a mandatory application for implementing the SAP SRM solution.

19.1.2 Standard Implementation Content for SAP SRM

SAP Solution Manager provides standard content that is valuable for both project managers and implementation teams. Project managers have access to Roadmaps that cater to new SAP SRM implementation and upgrades. These roadmaps include an ASAP-based project plan and links to other accelerator documents. In addition, during the project preparation phase, project managers define the project scope and the teams within the SAP Solution Manager for use within the subsequent phases of the project.

Implementation teams and consultants, on the other hand, have access to content that is valuable throughout the business blueprint and configuration activities. Figure 19.3 illustrates some of the content that is included in the SAP Solution Manager for blueprint and configuration activities.

Implementation Content for Business Blueprint and Configuration includes:
- Links to IMG and Transactions in Satelite Systems
- Configuration Documentation
- IMG Documentation from the Satelite System
- Notes
- Business Scenario and Process Descriptions
- Business Process Swimlane Diagrams

Structured By:
- Business Scenarios and Business Processes

Figure 19.3 Implementation Content for SAP SRM 7.0

> **Note**
>
> Organizations can download the business content for SAP SRM using from the SAP Service Marketplace. Download the ST-ICO 150 at *http://service.sap.com/swdc*. Once the content is downloaded, it can be uploaded into the SAP Solution Manager. You cannot upload the content that is just relevant for your project scope; you must upload the entire SAP Solution Manager Content for SAP SRM and then enable the business scenarios relevant for your project scope.

In SAP SRM 7.0, there are many business scenarios that organizations can implement based on the scope of their projects. Project teams can then enable those business scenarios and use the content provided within the SAP Solution Manager to configure these business scenarios and the processes within. Business Scenarios include various Business Process descriptions and guided configuration support for SAP SRM and its components. Figure 19.4 illustrates the business scenarios that are delivered in the SAP SRM 7.0 content.

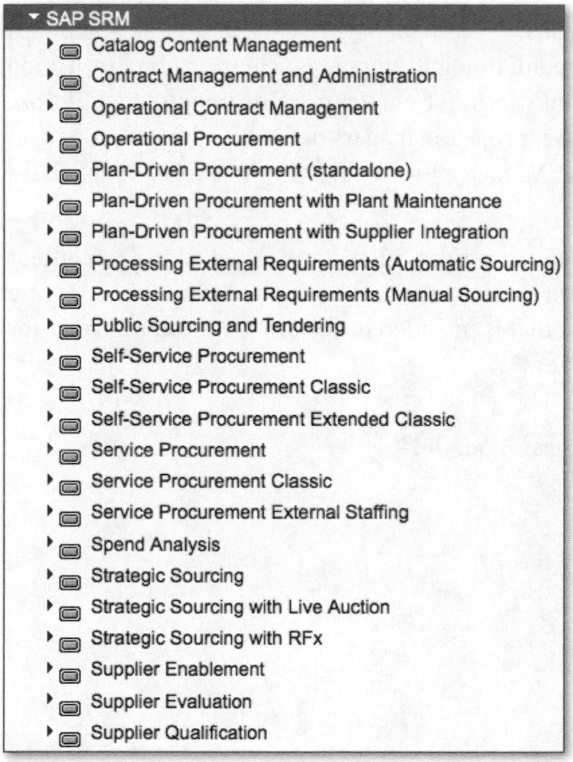

▼ SAP SRM
- ▸ Catalog Content Management
- ▸ Contract Management and Administration
- ▸ Operational Contract Management
- ▸ Operational Procurement
- ▸ Plan-Driven Procurement (standalone)
- ▸ Plan-Driven Procurement with Plant Maintenance
- ▸ Plan-Driven Procurement with Supplier Integration
- ▸ Processing External Requirements (Automatic Sourcing)
- ▸ Processing External Requirements (Manual Sourcing)
- ▸ Public Sourcing and Tendering
- ▸ Self-Service Procurement
- ▸ Self-Service Procurement Classic
- ▸ Self-Service Procurement Extended Classic
- ▸ Service Procurement
- ▸ Service Procurement Classic
- ▸ Service Procurement External Staffing
- ▸ Spend Analysis
- ▸ Strategic Sourcing
- ▸ Strategic Sourcing with Live Auction
- ▸ Strategic Sourcing with RFx
- ▸ Supplier Enablement
- ▸ Supplier Evaluation
- ▸ Supplier Qualification

Figure 19.4 Scenarios in SAP Solution Manager for SAP SRM 7.0

Within each of the business scenarios, there are multiple business processes that need to be configured to enable the business scenario. For example, if your project scope includes the use of Contract Management, then your team can configure the business processes outlined within the Operational Contract Management business scenario, as illustrated in Figure 19.5.

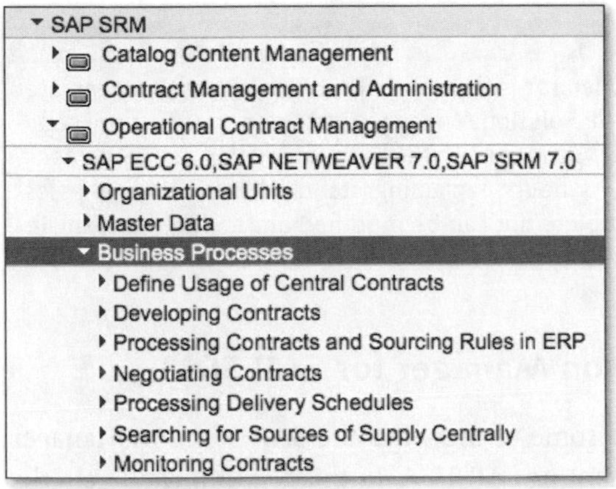

Figure 19.5 Business Processes Within Operational Contract Management

The business processes provide a chronological order for configuring the SAP SRM application. Figure 19.6 illustrates the process step Create Contract. The SAP Solution Manager guides the project team to follow the different steps outlined by providing seamless connectivity to the system where the configuration activity needs to be done, along with providing documentation regarding the activity. According to Figure 19.6, we need to complete two IMG steps to set up Contracts in SAP SRM.

1. Define Transaction Types.
2. Define Number Ranges for Purchase Contracts.

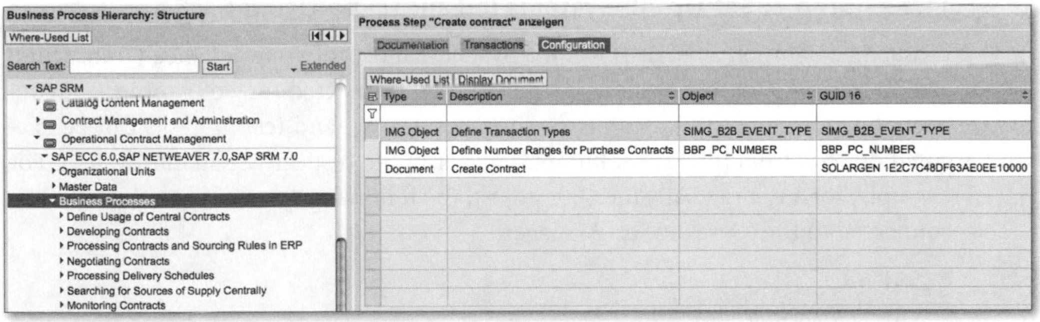

Figure 19.6 Configuration of Business Process "Create Contract"

Similarly, other business processes and scenarios in SAP SRM can be enabled using the SAP Solution Manager.

An example of an SAP SRM project accelerator is the ability for organizations to generate a business blueprint document via the SAP Solution Manager. Customer-specific and scope relevant blueprint documentation can be generated without the need for the implementation team members to spend countless hours explaining standard business processes within SAP SRM. Instead, the generated blueprint can be modified and tailored to explain processes that may deviate from the standard.

19.2 Configuring the Solution Manager for SAP SRM

In the previous section, we discussed some of the ways the SAP Solution Manager can assist organizations when implementing SAP SRM. In this section, we'll help the project teams to set up and configure the SAP Solution Manager for your SAP SRM 7.0 project. The following steps are an overview, and it's important to work with your solution architect and SAP Solution Manager experts for additional details.

19.2.1 Step 1: Upload Content for SAP SRM 7.0

Once SAP Solution Manager has been installed, ensure that the SAP SRM 7.0 content has been uploaded into the SAP Solution Manager. This content provides all the possible standard SAP SRM business scenarios available to the organization and can be then tailored specifically to your company's scope and business processes.

19.2.2 Step 2: Set Up All Systems in Landscape Using SMSY

In the SAP Solution Manager, use the System Landscape Maintenance (Transaction SMSY) to set up all the systems that need to be connected for your project. A connection is required so that configuration, monitoring, and testing tasks can be executed directly from the SAP Solution Manager in the respective satellite system. For example, for a typical SAP SRM 7.0 project, the following systems would need to be connected to the SAP Solution Manager:

▶ SAP SRM
▶ SAP NetWeaver Portal
▶ SAP ERP
▶ SAP NetWeaver MDM

Note

Users need to be created in the individual systems like SAP SRM and SAP ERP. These users should ideally have SAP_ALL and SAP_NEW access. In addition, the authorization object for trusted RFC (S_RFCACL) needs to be added to this user.

When setting up each of the satellite systems, the setup assistant guides the administrator to set up necessary RFC destinations and logical components.

19.2.3 Step 3: Create a Project (SOLAR_PROJECT_ADMIN)

Once all the relevant systems are set up within your landscape, we are ready to create a project within the SAP Solution Manager. A project provides the ability to plan and define the core business processes relevant to the scope of your SAP SRM project.

Create the project using the Project Administration Transaction SOLAR_PROJECT_ ADMIN. Figure 19.7 illustrates the Create or Maintain Project transaction.

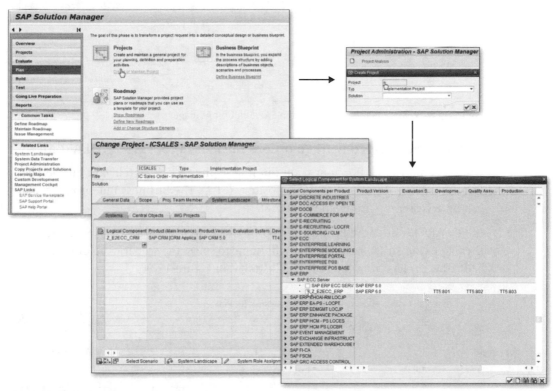

Figure 19.7 Create or Maintain Project

While creating a project, you can also define the project team members, project milestones, and standards, as illustrated in Figure 19.8.

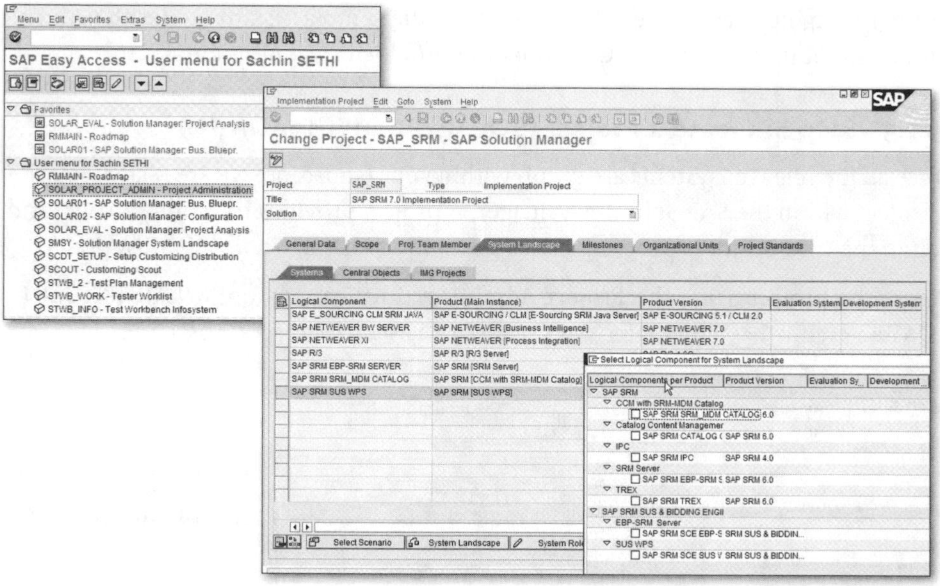

Figure 19.8 Maintaining a Project Within SAP Solution Manager

19.2.4 Step 4: Document Your Core Business Processes (SOLAR01)

Once a project is set up, your team can import the SAP SRM relevant business scenarios from the Business Process Repository (BPR). The Business Blueprint Structure can be accessed via Transaction SOLAR01.

In SOLAR01, under the Business Blueprint Structure, select Business Scenarios, and then go to the Structure tab in the right frame to select the scenarios relevant for your SAP SRM project from the BPR, as illustrated in Figure 19.9.

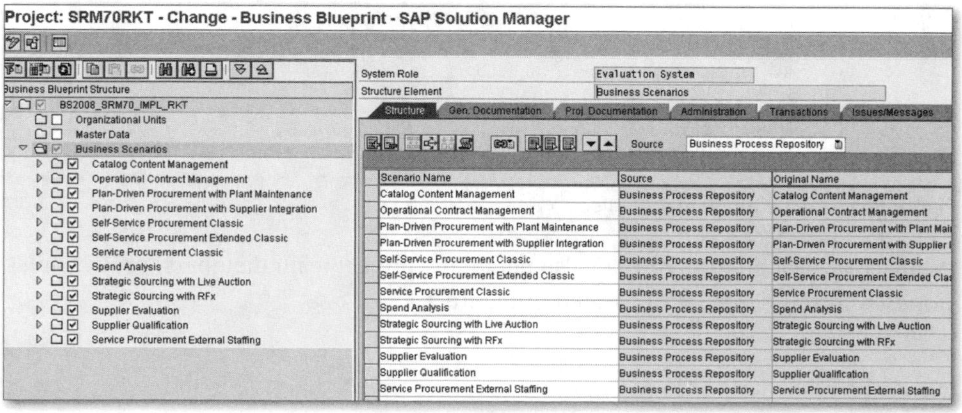

Figure 19.9 Selecting Business Scenarios for SAP SRM

> **Note**
>
> Only select scenarios that are not grayed out, because they correspond best to the system landscape you have set up.

In this business blueprint transaction, you can get access to standard SAP documentation in the Gen. Documentation tab, and have the ability to upload project-specific documentation, including documentation of custom code and interfaces.

19.2.5 Step 5: Configure Your Project (SOLAR 02)

The next step is to configure the scenarios selected in the previous step via the project configuration transaction, Transaction SOLAR02.

Execute Transaction SOLAR02 in the SAP Solution Manager, and maintain the following:

1. Click the Configuration node in the left frame.
2. Select the Structure tab on the right hand frame.
3. Select the Change Configuration Structure button. This will refresh the screen in change mode.
4. Place your cursor on the first line below Configuration Element and press the F4 key. Choose SAP SRM and select the checkbox for SAP SRM 7.0.
5. Click on the Save icon.
6. Repeat the bullets above to enable other systems in your list for configuration similarly.

We are now ready to configure our SAP SRM system, using Transaction SOLAR02 in the SAP Solution Manager.

Before we proceed, understand how the content is structured within the SAP Solution Manager. Figure 19.10 provides a visual illustration to the content structure.

The Implementation Content in the SAP Solution Manager is split into two main groups for SAP SRM:

▶ **Basic Configuration:** Contains the basic configuration like setup backend destinations, master data replication, and other technical settings for SAP SRM.
▶ **Business Scenarios:** Provides the scenarios that can be optionally configured by an organization based on their project scopes. Each business scenario contains business processes and further process steps relevant to the business scenario (as illustrated in Figures 19.5, 19.6, and 19.7).

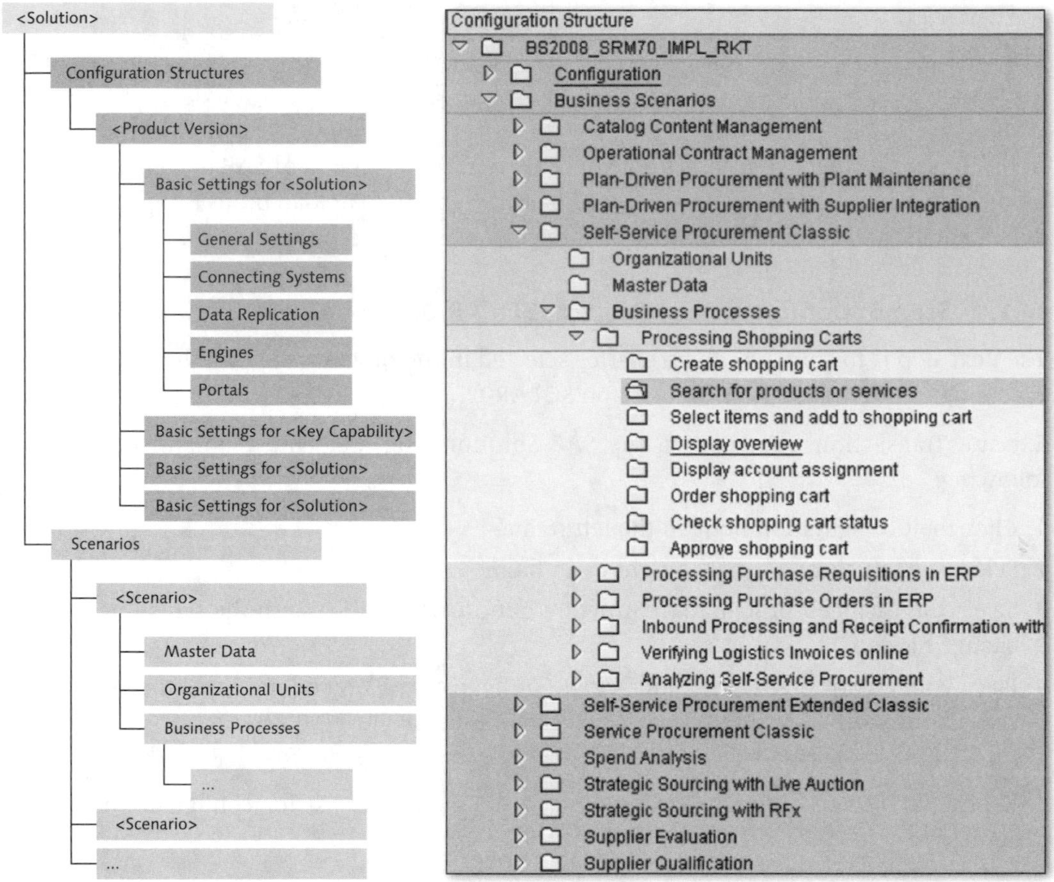

Figure 19.10 Implementation Content Structure

To begin configuring your SAP SRM application, in Transaction SOLAR02, select either the Basic configuration node or the Business Processes and select the Configuration tab on the right hand frame. All relevant configuration objects will be available in chronological order. These could include IMG activities, or even documentation such as OSS Notes for assistance. Figure 19.11 illustrates the Business Process: Processing Shopping Carts, and the relevant configuration objects to search for products and services in SAP SRM.

Transaction SOLAR02 also provides the ability for the project teams to test transactions within each process step under an SAP SRM scenario once it is configured. This can be done via the Transactions tab.

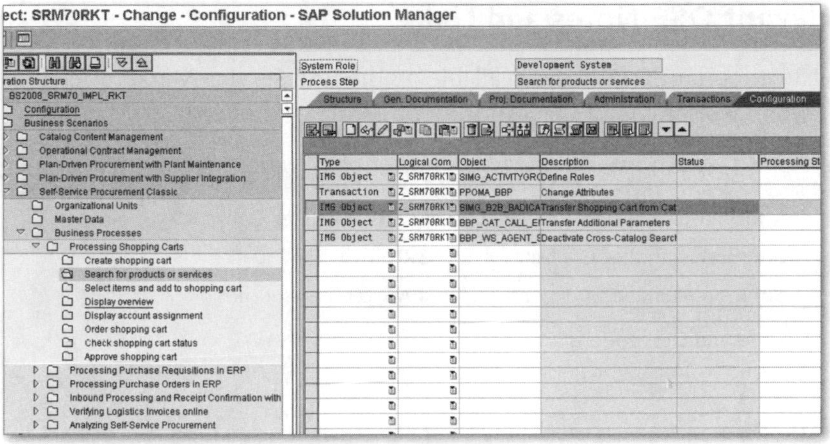

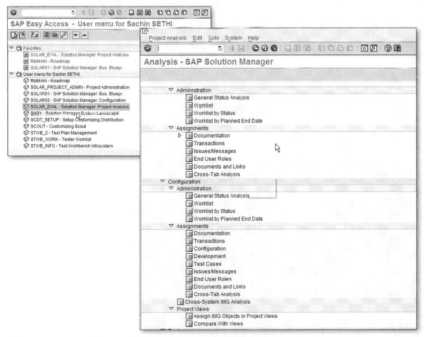

Figure 19.11 Implementation Content Structure

19.2.6 Step 6: Evaluate and Report on the Project (SOLAR_EVAL)

At various points during your SAP SRM project, the project manager can analyze the status of the blueprint, configuration, and testing. This can be done via the Transaction SOLAR_EVAL, as illustrated in Figure 19.12.

Figure 19.12 Analysis and Evaluation of the SRM project

19.3   Relevant OSS Notes and Links

Table 19.1 lists important OSS Notes available on the SAP Service Marketplace that are relevant when working with the SAP Solution Manager and SAP SRM.

Note	Description
1230438	Information about SAP SRM 7.0 Solution Manager Content
983603	Solution Manager Content for SAP SRM 6.0
1001556	Solution Manage Content for SAP SRM 6.0 (cookbook)

Table 19.1   OSS Notes and Descriptions

19.4   Summary

In this chapter, we discussed how the SAP Solution Manager can be used as a valuable tool in your SAP SRM project. Project teams can get access to solution documentation; best practices–based methodologies, configuration guides, and a single access point to set up all the business scenarios that are relevant for their SAP SRM projects. The SAP Solution Manager Business Scenarios, Business Processes, and Process Steps guide the user on relevant configuration activities along with providing them access to necessary OSS notes and guides that make their configuration process streamlined and highly efficient.

Now, let's move on to Chapter 20, where we'll discuss procurement in the public sector.

PART IV
Industry Solutions

Government entities responsible for maintaining public funds and public trust must adhere to strict regulations and guidelines. For them, the standard procurement solution offers only partial functionality. These organizations require a procurement solution that specifically addresses their unique needs and requirements.

20 Procurement for Public Sector

In the first edition of this book, we introduced the concept of *Government procurement*. Government procurement (GP) as a generic term describes the procurement activities of government entities such as federal, state, and local governments. In addition, it covers activities of other public entities or enterprises and generally covers procurement of all goods and services including construction services. The types of transactions covered in this procurement are purchase, lease, rental, and hire purchase.

Over the last few years, SAP has extended the solution that was initially designed for government entities to a larger sector for the public sector. Now, the solution is known as *Procurement for Public Sector (PPS)*.

This chapter presents an overview of the SAP Procurement for Public Sector (PPS) solution and briefly describes the highlights of the functionality within this solution offering. SAP PPS is still a relatively newer solution; however, many public sector organizations have implemented this solution. The current release of SAP PPS is 2.0.

20.1 SAP SRM and SAP Procurement for Public Sector

SAP PPS is a relatively new solution that focuses on the procurement processes of government organizations and other public sector entities. It is primarily an SAP SRM–based solution that fully integrates with the funds management (FM) and materials management functionalities in SAP ERP.

> **Note**
>
> SAP SRM is the foundation for SAP Procurement for Public Sector (PPS). Therefore, to use the PPS solution the SAP SRM solution is mandatory to be implemented. SAP PPS is not the same as the SAP Public Sector solution (IS-PS/EA-PS). Rather, SAP PPS builds on the SAP SRM solution and enhances the standard capabilities when integrated with the SAP EA-PS solution.
>
> It is presumed that organizations that implement the SAP PPS solution will also implement the SAP IS-PS/EA-PS solution. Also, organizations implementing EA-PS will be using the SAP Funds Management functionality and the PPS solution provides standard integration of shopping cart with Funds Management. A capability that needed to be custom developed for SAP SRM in the past releases.

The SAP PPS solution delivers a wide range of functionality for professional purchasers and contracting personnel and augments SAP SRM 7.0 standard capabilities. It also eliminates the need to operate and maintain multiple procurement solutions and associated interfaces.

The SAP PPS solution combines the SAP SRM, SAP ERP, SAP Records Management, and SAP NetWeaver applications to collaborate and support public sector customers.

Public sector organizations can use the capabilities of the GP solution to maintain Federal Acquisition Regulations (FAR) clauses and detailed FAR document and contracts, and integrate these with the enhanced sourcing and procurement capabilities within SAP SRM.

According to Wikipedia, the free online encyclopedia, FAR consists of a series of regulations issued by the U.S. federal government concerning the requirements for contractors selling to the government, the terms under which the government obtains ownership, title, and control of the goods or services purchased, and rules concerning specifications, payments, and conduct and actions regarding solicitation of bids and payment of invoices.

Therefore, it is imperative that the procurement and sourcing solution used by government and public sector organizations provide extensive capabilities for adhering to FAR regulatory requirements. The core functionality in GP was defined based on the requirements generated by the U.S. Defense Logistics Agency (DLA).

Figure 20.1 illustrates at a high level the various applications that make up the overall PPS solution. In addition to functional enhancements made to SAP SRM, shown in Figure 20.1, the Document Builder is a major component of the PPS solution.

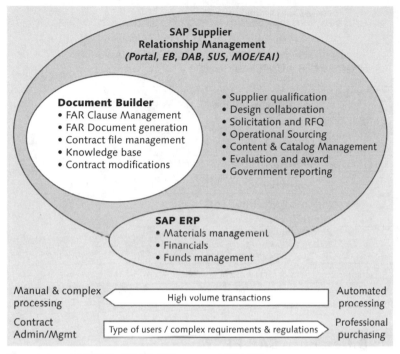

Figure 20.1 SAP SRM, SAP NetWeaver, and SAP ERP

Document Builder is available to organizations as part of the SAP PPS add-on to SAP SRM 7.0. The purpose of Document Builder is to allow creation of complex documents that can be used for many different business documents such as contracts and POs. Organizations can create and manage FAR regulatory documents using the capabilities within Document Builder. Figure 20.2 illustrates the technical components within the SAP PPS solution.

> **Note**
>
> SAP PPS was developed to work in an Extended Classic scenario.
>
> The SAP NetWeaver Process Integration (SAP NetWeaver PI) application is mandatory if organizations want to use the Document Builder–based delivered integration with SAP SRM.

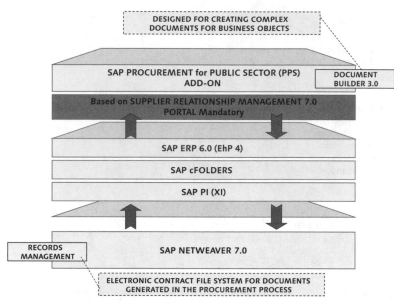

Figure 20.2 SAP PPS Solution Landscape

20.2 What Is Different in SAP PPS?

As discussed earlier, SAP SRM provides the underlying foundation for SAP PPS. In many cases, SAP PPS extends or augments the standard functionality provided in SAP SRM. Based on various documents from SAP, Table 20.1 describes some of the key highlights of the SAP PPS solution. Although the PPS solution is quite extensive, we will highlight just a selection of its capabilities.

Table 20.1 provides a comparison of the functionality available in the SAP SRM application and corresponding enhancements within SAP PPS.

Provided by SAP SRM	Procurement for Public Sector (PPS)
	▶ Introduction of SAP Document Builder application, a solution for creating complex documents for business objects.
	▶ Web-based user interface, with integration to SAP SRM.

Table 20.1 Key Highlights for SAP PPS Solution

Provided by SAP SRM	Procurement for Public Sector (PPS)
Document Number generation: In SAP SRM, a standardized system-generated document numbering scheme is used. For example: POs have a 10-digit sequential numbering scheme of 2000000000 — 2xxxxxxxxx	▸ Configurable customer-defined document numbering (Long Procurement Number or Smart Number) is introduced. ▸ Ability to assign a second, customer-defined document ID number to Bid Invitations, Contracts, and PO in SAP SRM. ▸ Complies with US FAR, DFARS, European Union, Canadian, and other numbering schemes, as well as local government and other public schemes. ▸ This document is available for search in SAP SRM and SAP ERP documents.
SAP ERP Integration of Shopping Cart: In SAP SRM, the shopping cart is integrated with the SAP ERP system to create subsequent documents for Requisition or PO. However, for the shopping cart, there is no integration with commitments in FM.	▸ When PPS is used, an approved shopping cart posts a commitment in SAP ERP for integration with funds management automatically. ▸ The commitment and budget information, along with documents can be reviewed from the shopping cart header.
Movement types in SAP SRM: Confirmations (goods receipt) or Service Entry allow movement types 101 and 102 for SAP backend system.	▸ New movement types 107 and 109 have been added to MM, to allow receipt of items at the vendor facility, before shipping, that also allows FM to be affected.
Sourcing: Sourcing application is available and customized rules can be created using BAdIs.	▸ Automated sourcing of requirements to contracts (with customer defined rules). ▸ User warning and error messages have been improved.
Document Status and History: Standard PO History provides a fairly basic view of follow-on documents (Goods Receipt and Invoice). Primarily document numbers are available as a history.	▸ An *Extended History* tab has been added to the SAP SRM Purchase Order transaction to display the complete transactional history including: ▸ GR posted in backend ERP ▸ Invoice posted in backend ERP ▸ Payment history from ERP ▸ Extended History can be viewed at both the header and line-item level. The SAP SRM document provides direct links to the backend SAP ERP documents.

Table 20.1 Key Highlights for SAP PPS Solution (Cont.)

Provided by SAP SRM	Procurement for Public Sector (PPS)
Bidding Engine: Bid Invitations can be manually created in the Sourcing application.	▶ Bid Invitations can be created automatically based on the requirements received from external planning systems. ▶ Document Builder introduction. ▶ Choice to auto-publish (0-step workflow) or manually publish after workflow approval.
Goods Receipt: Confirmation of goods is entered once goods are received at buyer's location.	▶ New concept of acceptance of goods at production or delivery facility of the vendor (termed Origin Acceptance). ▶ This provides an ability to create a Goods Receipt for items that are still at the vendor distribution facility. Often, a functionality requirement for government organizations (e.g., U.S. Department of Defense). ▶ Ability to trigger FM integration before physical receipt of items. ▶ New movement types 107 and 109 have been created for this capability.
Invoice Payment Plans: Standard SAP SRM Extended Classic scenario does not provide any capability for Invoice plans as in SAP ERP.	▶ With SAP PPS solution, a billing document can be automatically generated based on the payment plans defined in the SAP SRM PO. ▶ A new screen has been created for SAP PPS to provide payment plan at item level of an SAP SRM PO. ▶ Payment plans are often valuable for managing procurement of Rent, Maintenance, Construction contracts, and Down Payment type scenarios.
Contract Management: Contracts do not encumber any funds and no financial postings are possible for contracts.	▶ Introduced new functionality for reservation of funds in SAP ERP based on SAP SRM Contracts (Guaranteed Minimum). ▶ Ability to manually record a funds reservation (via earmarked funds) on an SAP SRM contract header. ▶ Consumption of reservation amount is based on obligations of POs issued against the contract.

Table 20.1 Key Highlights for SAP PPS Solution (Cont.)

Figure 20.3 illustrates an example of the customer-defined, configurable, document numbering (also called *Smart Number*) available in SAP SRM with the SAP PPS add-on. In the PO document, this number is illustrated in the Doc. Name field. A secondary number that is system generated is displayed in the Number field as shown in Figure 20.3.

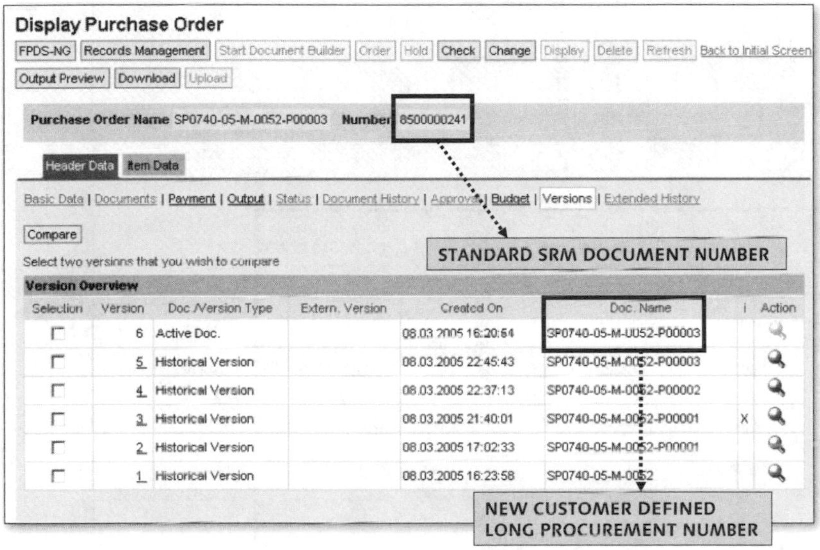

Figure 20.3 Long Document Number in the Purchase Order (Figure Credit: SAP America, SAP SRM 5.0)

Figure 20.4 illustrates the creation of commitments in SAP ERP via a shopping cart in SAP SRM. Also, users can see the detail directly in SAP SRM.

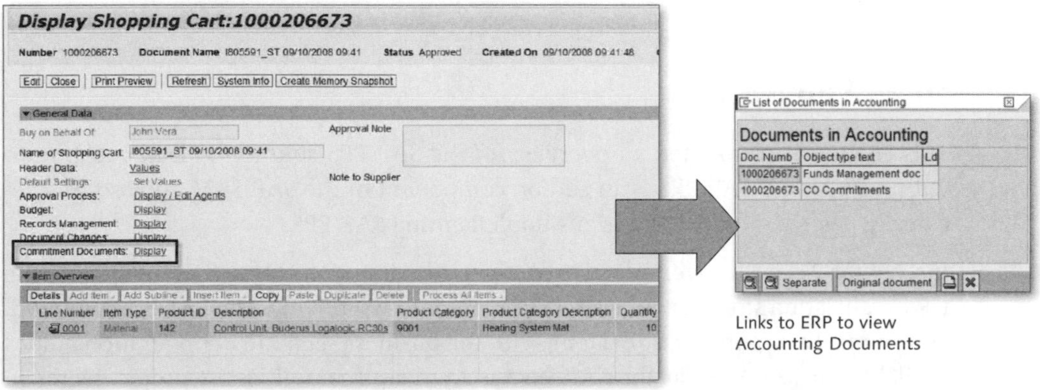

Figure 20.4 Shopping Cart Commitments in SAP ERP (Figure Credit: SAP America)

Figure 20.5 illustrates an example of the enhanced history available in the PO document within the Payment History area. Without the GP add-on, the PO in SAP SRM only provides a basic view of follow-on documents (Goods Receipt and Invoice). The PO document using the GP add-on solution displays the complete transactional history, including Goods Receipt, Invoice, Payments, Credits, and even Clearing Documents, with subtotals and totals.

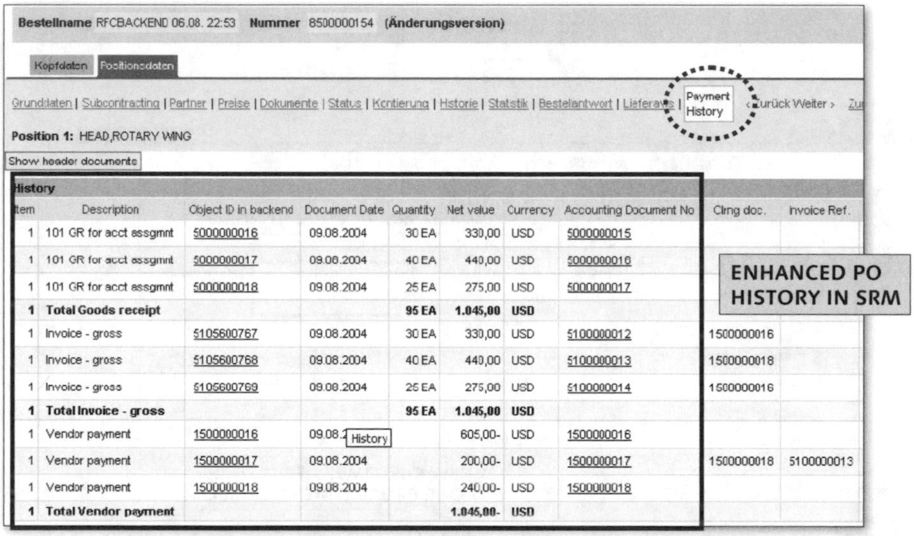

Item	Description	Object ID in backend	Document Date	Quantity	Net value	Currency	Accounting Document No	Clrng doc.	Invoice Ref.
1	101 GR for acct assgmnt	5000000016	09.08.2004	30 EA	330,00	USD	5000000015		
1	101 GR for acct assgmnt	5000000017	09.08.2004	40 EA	440,00	USD	5000000016		
1	101 GR for acct assgmnt	5000000018	09.08.2004	25 EA	275,00	USD	5000000017		
1	**Total Goods receipt**			**95 EA**	**1.045,00**	**USD**			
1	Invoice - gross	5105600767	09.08.2004	30 EA	330,00	USD	5100000012	1500000016	
1	Invoice - gross	5105600768	09.08.2004	40 EA	440,00	USD	5100000013	1500000018	
1	Invoice - gross	5105600769	09.08.2004	25 EA	275,00	USD	5100000014	1500000016	
1	**Total Invoice - gross**			**95 EA**	**1.045,00**	**USD**			
1	Vendor payment	1500000016	09.08.2 History		605,00-	USD	1500000016		
1	Vendor payment	1500000017	09.08.2004		200,00-	USD	1500000017	1500000018	5100000013
1	Vendor payment	1500000018	09.08.2004		240,00-	USD	1500000018		
1	**Total Vendor payment**				**1.045,00-**	**USD**			

Figure 20.5 Enhanced PO History in SAP SRM (Figure Credit: SAP America, SAP SRM 5.0)

> **Note**
>
> Although most of the enhanced procurement functionality has been created for Public Sector procurement, SAP is also including some of this within the standard SAP SRM application.

20.3 Summary

This chapter has provided an overview of the SAP PPS solution and its integration within SAP SRM. SAP PPS is an add-on component of the SAP SRM application specifically designed for organizations implementing SAP PPS.

In Chapter 21, we'll cover selective configuration in SAP SRM such as integrating the HR organization structure with SAP SRM, workflow setup in SAP SRM, catalog setup, and so on. This configuration, along with the business scenario configuration guides available for SAP SRM at the SAP Service Marketplace, will assist project teams in implementing their SAP SRM applications.

PART V
Selected Configuration in SAP SRM

In this chapter, we'll cover selected configuration settings found in SAP SRM, such as SAP ERP HCM integration, workflow, and MRP integration. You will find these settings useful because most of them are not generally covered in other SAP resources.

21 Selected Configuration in SAP SRM

The purpose of this book was to arm you, the reader, with information we have gained over the years implementing SAP SRM, and that is generally unavailable in print. In the final chapter of this book, we want to give you some selected configuration settings in SAP SRM that you will find useful. Let's begin with SAP ERP Human Capital Management (SAP ERP HCM).

> **Note**
>
> The configuration settings covered in this chapter are meant to provide a guide on how to approach your configuration but will need to be modified to meet the requirements of your specific project implementation.

21.1 Integrate Organizational Structure with SAP ERP HCM

This section provides a set of steps required to distribute the organizational structure from SAP ERP HCM to the SAP Enterprise Buyer (EB) system.

21.1.1 Prerequisites for Integration

The distribution of HR data into SAP SRM expects that the following activities have already taken place:

▶ You have reviewed the following OSS Notes: 550055 and 390380 (Composite SAP Note: HR/ALE distribution in EBP/CRM; check the Related Notes section).

▶ In SAP ERP, the HR data has been created (Orgs, Positions, Jobs, Employees) — check the filter information below to ensure that the required information exists.

▶ In SAP ERP, an ALE distribution model has been created with Filters defined, as listed below, and distributed to the appropriate SAP SRM system and client.

► For users that need to be created in SAP SRM, in the SAP ERP system, the corresponding Employees have been assigned Infotype 0105. In SAP SRM, the users (SU01) have been created — at least the ones that contain a corresponding Infotype 0105.

► Prior to the distribution process, make sure that no additional updates or changes are being performed on the Organization Objects (O, C, S, P,) within the SAP ERP HCM system, because the system will try to lock these objects during distribution.

The customizing table T77S0 has been set up as seen in Figure 21.1.

Change View "HR: Set Up Central Person": Overview

Group	Sem. abbr.	Value abbr.	Description
HRALX	HRAC	X	Activate HR Integration
HRALX	OADBP	1	Business Partner of Standard Address
HRALX	OADRE	X	Address Necessary for Business Partner?
HRALX	OBPON	ON	Integration O-BP Activated
HRALX	OBWIG	X	Ignore Business Partner Warnings
HRALX	ONUMB	1	Business Partner Number Assignment (Org. Unit)
HRALX	OPROL	BUP004	Roles: Functional Description
HRALX	OSUBG		Business Partner Subgroup (Organizational Unit)
HRALX	PBPHR	ON	Employees Are Replicated from HR System
HRALX	PBPON	ON	Integration Employee/BP Activated
HRALX	PCATS		Integration P-BP for CATS Activated
HRALX	PNUMB	1	Business Partner Number Assignment (Employee)
HRALX	PPROL	BUP003	Roles: Employee Description
HRALX	PQUAL		Import Qualifications
PLOGI	PLOGI	01	Integration Plan Version / Active Plan Version
PLOGI	PRELI	99999999	Integration: default position

Figure 21.1 Integration Setup with Organizational Management

21.1.2 Filtering of Objects to be Distributed from SAP ERP into SAP SRM

The technical setup of the distribution model between SAP ERP and SAP SRM in BD64 requires the following filters for message type HRMD_ABA (OSS Note: 312090).

Filter Group for Organization Objects

► Infotype:
  ► 1000   Existence of Org objects
  ► 1002   Description of Org objects
► Objects:
  ► C   Jobs

- ► S   Position
- ► O   Organization

Filter Group for Employees:

These subtypes are required; otherwise, the Business Partner in SAP SRM will not be created.

- ► Infotype:
    - ► 0000   Actions — IT0000
    - ► 0001   Organization Assignment
    - ► 0002   Personal Data — IT0002
- ► Objects
- ► Person or Employee

Filter Group for Relationships

- ► Infotype:
    - ► 1001   Relationship between objects
- ► Objects:
    - ► AG   Role
    - ► C   Jobs
    - ► O   Organization
    - ► P   Person
    - ► S   Position
- ► Type of related object (SCLAS):
    - ► AG   Role
    - ► C   Jobs
    - ► O   Organization
    - ► P   Person
    - ► S   Position
- ► Subtypes:
    - ► A002   Reports to
    - ► A007   Describes
    - ► A008   Holder
    - ► A012   Manages
    - ► B002   Is line supervisor of
    - ► B007   Is described by

- ▸ B008   Holder
- ▸ B012   Is Managed by

Filter Group for Employees

This is required; otherwise, the Business Partner in SAP SRM will not be created.

- ▸ Infotype
- ▸ 0006 Address
- ▸ Subtypes
- ▸ Permanent Residence

This creates the relationship between the SAP ERP Employee and the SAP SRM User. As a standard, the relationship is only created if both Infotype 0105 (in SAP ERP) and UserID (in SAP SRM) exist.

- ▸ Infotype:
  - ▸ 0105   Communication
- ▸ Subtype:
  - ▸ 0001   SY-UNAME
  - ▸ 0010   Email Address

Filter group for Employees — Relationship:

- ▸ Infotype:
  - ▸ 1001
- ▸ Object type:
  - ▸ P
- ▸ Type of related object:
  - ▸ S
- ▸ Subtype:
  - ▸ B008

Filter Group for Relationship with Linked Objects

(See OSS Note 312090)

- ▸ Infotype:
  - ▸ 1001   Relationship between objects
- ▸ Objects:
  - ▸ O   Organization
  - ▸ S   Position

▶ Type of related Object (SCLAS):

  ▶ O   Organization

  ▶ S   Position

▶ Subtypes:

  ▶ A003   Belongs to

  ▶ B003   Incorporates

> **Note**
>
> In SAP SRM, employees will only be created if their status is Active, and at least the following valid infotypes have been maintained in SAP ERP HCM: Info Type 0000, 0001, 0002, and 0006 (with subtype 1). Sometimes organizations may want to restrict the sensitive data in infotype 0006 for distribution. Look at the option for setting constants for these fields using Transaction BD62 and BD79.

21.1.3 Activating Change Pointers

You can activate change pointers in the SAP ERP HCM system to avoid distributing the entire structure when you make changes to the HR-ORG model, and instead distribute only the changes you have made. Follow these steps:

1. In SAP ERP, go to Tcode and follow this path: </SALE> • Modeling and Implementing • Master Data Distribution • Replication of Modified Data • Activate Change Pointers — Generally.

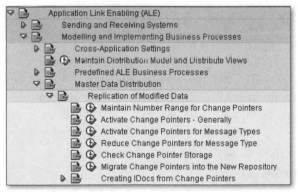

Figure 21.2 ALE Model — Activation of Change Pointers

2. Set the button for activating change pointers as shown in Figure 21.3. This is a transportable configuration; therefore, the system will request a transport number.

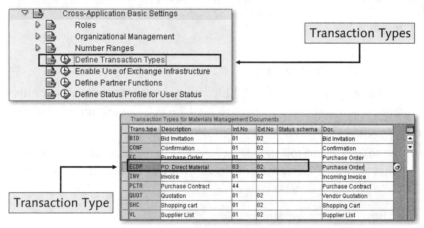

Figure 21.3 Activation of Change Pointers

3. Select Activate change pointers for Message Types, and select the message type for which the change pointer should be activated, as seen in Figure 21.4.

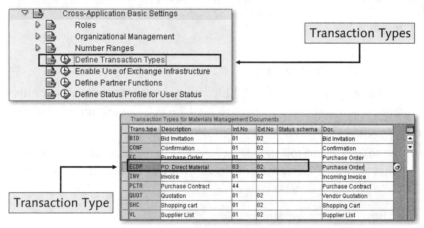

Figure 21.4 Change Pointer Activation Based on Message Type

4. Set the active indicator for message type HRMD_ABA, as shown in Figure 21.5.

This is a transportable entry; therefore, create a transport request. You can combine it with the earlier transport. Then, save your entries.

Job Scheduling for Transferring Changes or Deletions from SAP ERP HCM to SAP EB

You must schedule a report so that master data changes from the SAP ERP HCM system can be distributed to the SAP EB system. This report reads the change pointers activated previously and generates IDocs from it. You schedule this report in the SAP ERP system. To do so, the following steps are required:

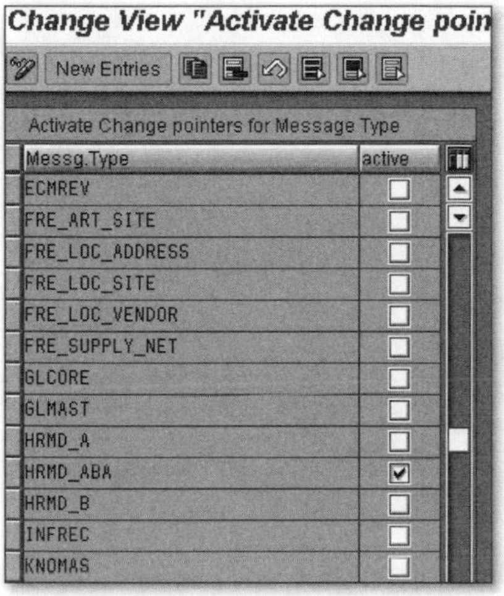

Figure 21.5 Select Appropriate Message Type

1. Define variants for the program RBDMIDOC, as seen in Figure 21.6, and schedule the report on a periodic basis (e.g., once a day).

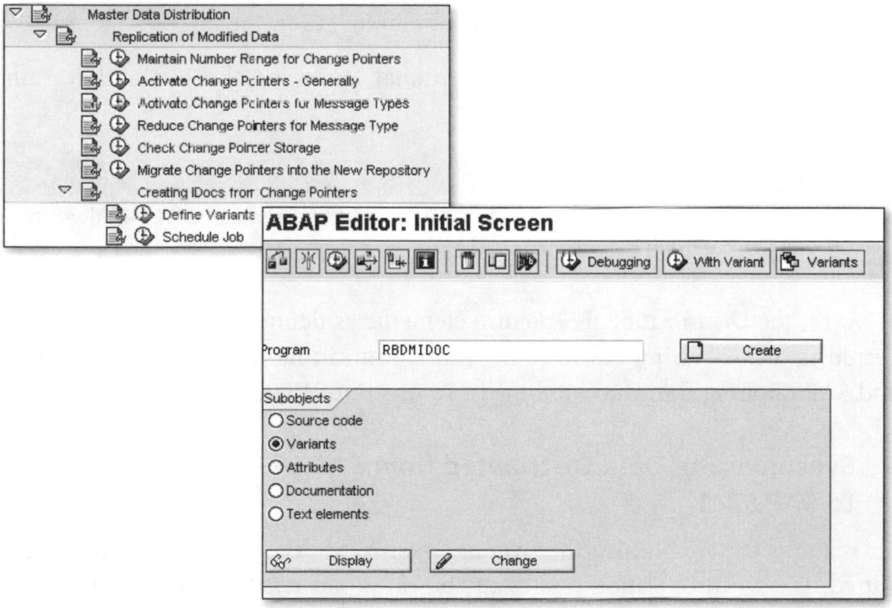

Figure 21.6 Define a Variant for Program RBDMIDOC

2. The variant you create should be for the message type selected in the previous steps. As such, enter HRMD_ABA, as seen in Figure 21.7.

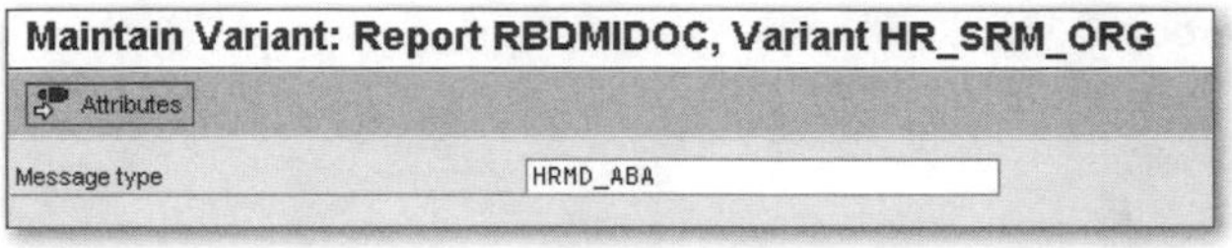

Maintain Variant: Report RBDMIDOC, Variant HR_SRM_ORG

Attributes

Message type	HRMD_ABA

Figure 21.7 Maintain Variant for RBDMIDOC

3. Once you've created a variant, you can schedule a periodic job to run this report on a regular basis. Typically, a daily run is sufficient.

4. Change pointers can be manually executed using Transaction codes BD21 and BD22.

21.1.4 Distribute the SAP ERP HCM Organizational Model (Initial Distribution)

For distributing the SAP ERP HCM organizational model, follow these steps:

1. Execute Transaction SA38 or SE38.

2. Start the report RHALEINI, and specify the data that should be distributed. Be careful with this transaction because you can distribute the organization model in INITIAL or UPDATE mode; the INITIAL mode completely deletes and recreates the Organizational Structure or positions or employees in the target system.

One approach is to distribute all Organizational Units via the Evaluation Path O-S-P.

> **Tip**
> All subsequent replications or distributions (if any) should be done in UPDATE mode; otherwise, the existing data will be overwritten.

At this point, the Organizational Structure elements as defined in the ALE filter are transferred to SAP EB using the IDoc Interface. You can monitor the IDocs in SAP ERP and SAP EB using the IDoc Monitor in Transaction WE02.

21.1.5 Synchronizing Data Distributed from SAP ERP HCM to SAP SRM

The next step is to synchronize the overall Organizational Structure that has been distributed. The synchronization creates any business partners that have been missed and also provides a report for the organizational objects that have issues and need to be fixed:

1. In SAP SRM, execute Transaction BBP_BP_OM_INTEGRATE.

2. Select the options shown in Figure 21.8. This will synchronize all of the objects in the structure.

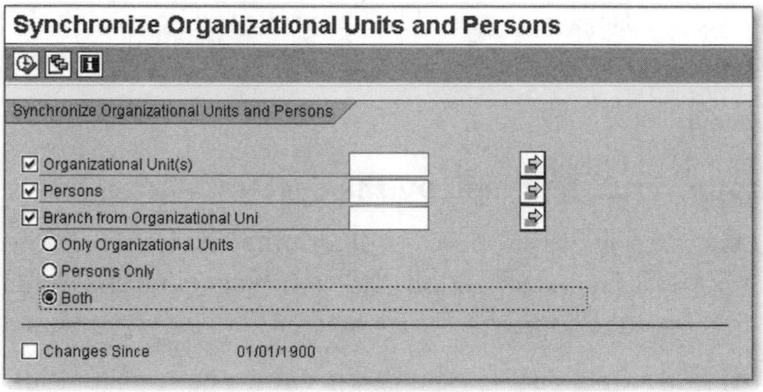

Synchronize Organizational Units and Persons

Synchronize Organizational Units and Persons

- ☑ Organizational Unit(s)
- ☑ Persons
- ☑ Branch from Organizational Uni
  - ○ Only Organizational Units
  - ○ Persons Only
  - ◉ Both

☐ Changes Since   01/01/1900

Figure 21.8 Synchronize the Organizational Structure

3. Click on the Execute icon and a results table is displayed, as shown in Figure 21.9.

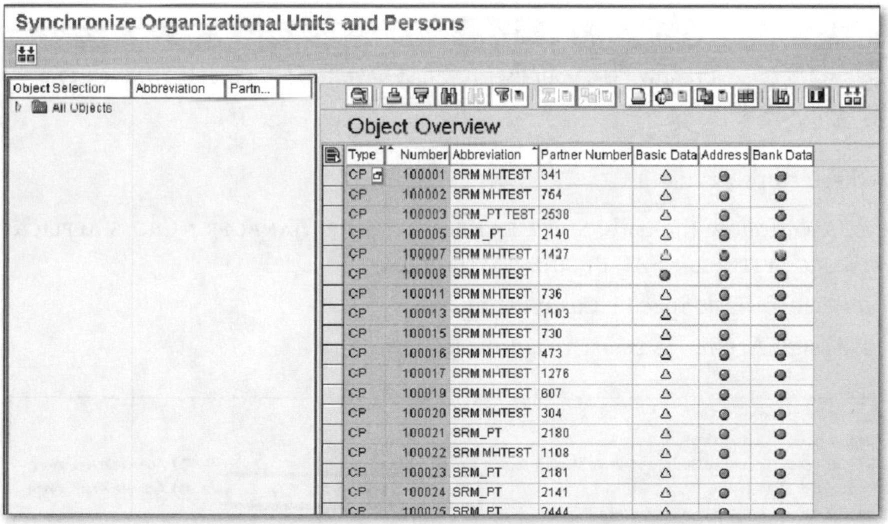

Synchronize Organizational Units and Persons

Object Overview

Type	Number	Abbreviation	Partner Number	Basic Data	Address	Bank Data
CP	100001	SRM MHTEST	341	⚠	◉	◉
CP	100002	SRM MHTEST	764	⚠	◉	◉
CP	100003	SRM_PT TEST	2538	⚠	◉	◉
CP	100005	SRM_PT	2140	⚠	◉	◉
CP	100007	SRM MHTEST	1427	⚠	◉	◉
CP	100008	SRM MHTEST		◉	◉	◉
CP	100011	SRM MHTEST	736	⚠	◉	◉
CP	100013	SRM MHTEST	1103	⚠	◉	◉
CP	100015	SRM MHTEST	730	⚠	◉	◉
CP	100016	SRM MHTEST	473	⚠	◉	◉
CP	100017	SRM MHTEST	1276	⚠	◉	◉
CP	100019	SRM MHTEST	607	⚠	◉	◉
CP	100020	SRM MHTEST	304	⚠	◉	◉
CP	100021	SRM_PT	2180	⚠	◉	◉
CP	100022	SRM MHTEST	1108	⚠	◉	◉
CP	100023	SRM_PT	2181	⚠	◉	◉
CP	100024	SRM_PT	2141	⚠	◉	◉
CP	100025	SRM_PT	2444	⚠	◉	◉

Figure 21.9 Synchronization of Organizational Units and Persons

Items with green lights are all set, items with red lights indicate an error, and items with yellow lights indicate that you need to take corrective action. Use the Synchronize icon to fix incorrect objects. This activity can take some time, depending on the number of objects with a *yellow* or *red* status.

21.2 Workflow: Restriction for Changing and Adding Approvers in the Shopping Cart

In the Shopping Cart Approval Preview function, a user can change the approver that is determined by the system. Also, a user can add an approver ad hoc, using the Add Approver button. This section provides the configuration necessary to control this functionality.

21.2.1 Changing the Approver Determined by the System

As a standard in SAP EB, users can change the approver determined by the workflow starting conditions in the Approval Preview function. This can be an audit issue for an organization that does not want the approver to be changed.

To provide some control over this functionality, you can perform the configuration outlined below. Once completed, only a user with a specific role, for example, the Manager role, will be available (in a list) to change the system-derived shopping cart approver. The key to this configuration is to limit the agent assignment on Workflow Task TS10008126.

Tip
To assign roles to a workflow task, your user ID must have the proper authorization to assign roles to user groups.

Follow these steps next:

1. In the IMG, follow the path: SUPPLIER RELATIONSHIP MANAGER • CROSS-APPLICATION BASIC SETTINGS • SAP BUSINESS WORKFLOW.

2. Select Perform Task-Specific Customizing.

3. Select Assign Agents, as seen in Figure 21.10.

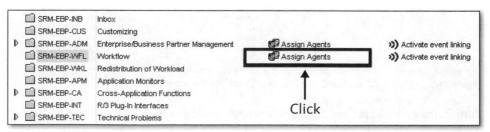

Figure 21.10 Selecting Assign Agents

4. Find and select Workflow Task TS10008126.

5. Click on Attributes.

6. Mark task TS10008126 as General forwarding allowed, as seen in Figure 21.11.

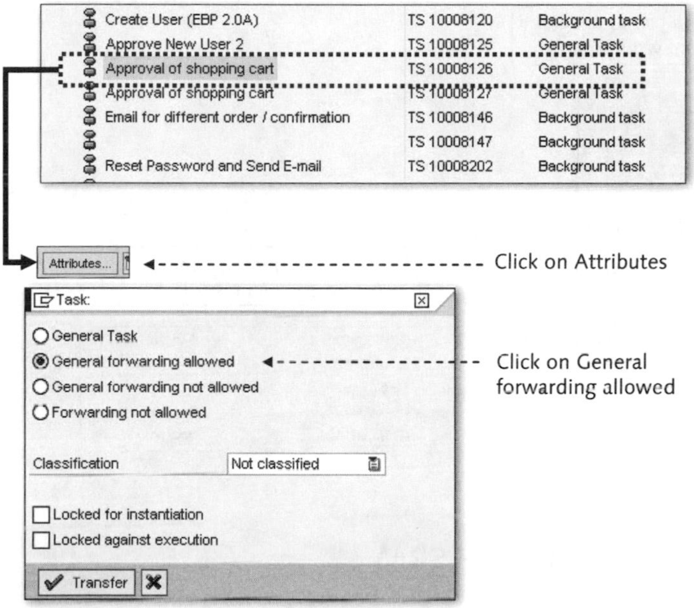

Figure 21.11 Configuring General Forwarding Allowed

7. Assign the restriction on who should be selected in the approval preview, as shown in Figure 21.12. (In our example, it's by Role restriction of Manager.)

8. Once the Manager role is assigned, in the Approval Preview function, only users with the Manager role will display for selection and change.

21.2.2 Adding an Ad-Hoc Approver

In the Shopping Cart Approval Preview, a user can also add an approver in addition to the system-generated approver(s). As a standard in SAP EB, a user can add any valid user ID as an approver. If this is not desired, then follow the same steps as shown in Section 21.2.1, but use Workflow Task WS10000271 instead.

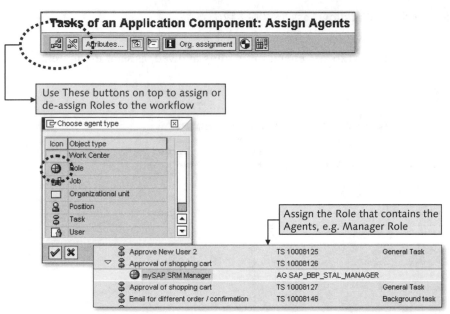

Figure 21.12 Assigning a Role Restriction

21.3 MRP Integration with SAP SRM

In this section, we'll examine the configuration required to integrate the MRP requisitions from SAP ERP into the SAP SRM system. Configuration is required in the SAP EB and SAP ERP systems for:

▶ Number ranges
▶ Document types
▶ Organizational structure
▶ Sourcing decision
▶ MRP tables
▶ Jobs

Let's move on to the integration now, for which you will need to follow these steps:

1. Define Number Range for Local Purchase Orders in SAP EB, as shown in Figure 21.13.

2. In SAP ERP, create a number range similar to the one shown in Figure 21.13 and mark it as an External Number Range, because the POs will be sent from SAP EBP.

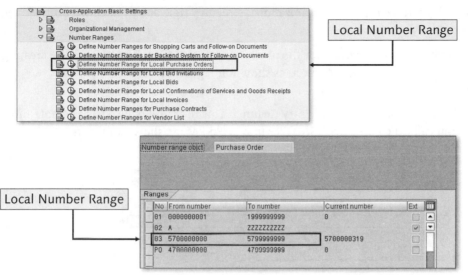

In ERP create a similar Number Range — External Number Range

Figure 21.13 Defining a Local Number Range in SAP EB

3. Create a transaction type document type in SAP EB. Specify as ECDP for direct procurement.

4. In the SAP ERP system, create a similar document type ECDP, as seen in Figure 21.14.

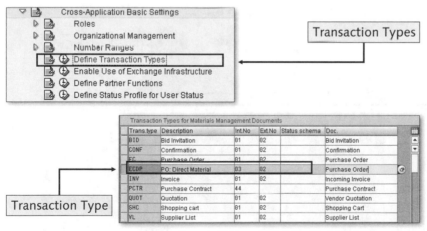

In ERP create a similar Document Type: ECDP

Figure 21.14 Create a Document Type ECDP

Now, let's move on to the organizational structure Transaction PPOMA_BBP. See the steps below:

1. Create an Entry channel for the planning system (MRP). Basically, you're creating an Organizational Unit object, as shown in Figure 21.15.

2. Create an SAP SRM User.

3. Place this user within the Entry Channel. This user will be used as a remote function call (RFC) user from SAP ERP into SAP SRM, as shown in Figure 21.15.

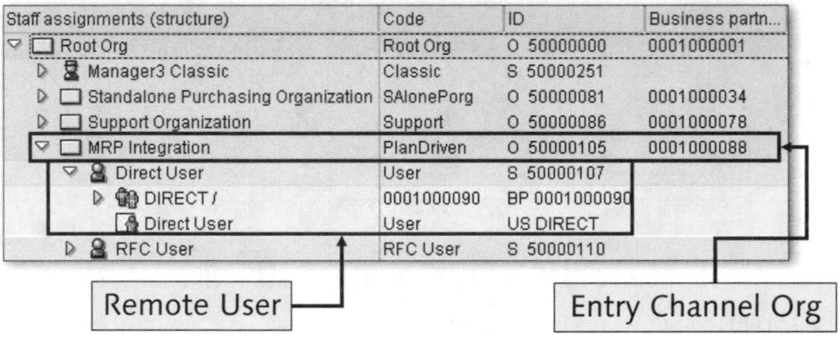

Figure 21.15 Creating an MRP Entry Channel and Remote User

4. Define the organizational responsibility for the entry channel you created. This should state which Purchasing Group will be responsible for this entry channel, as shown in Figure 21.16.

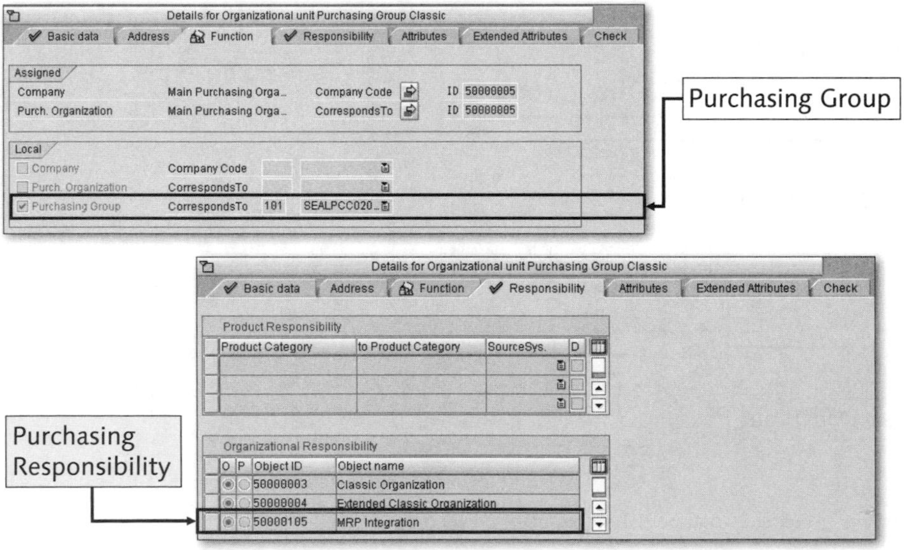

Figure 21.16 Purchasing Group Responsibility

5. Assign the Attribute of creating a Direct Material Purchase Order for this entry channel. Assign attribute DP_PROC_TY as ECDP. You can see this in Figure 21.17.

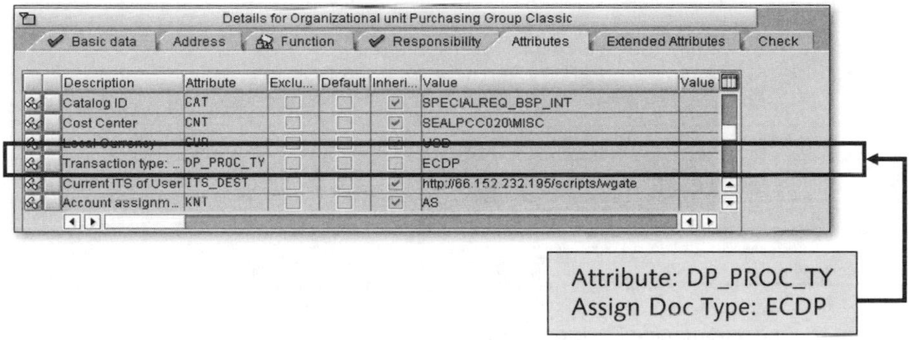

Figure 21.17 Assigning Attribute to Create Direct PO

6. At any time, you need to download the plants and Replicate Plants from SAP ERP, as seen in Figure 21.18. In the example, the Category is R3MATCLASS.

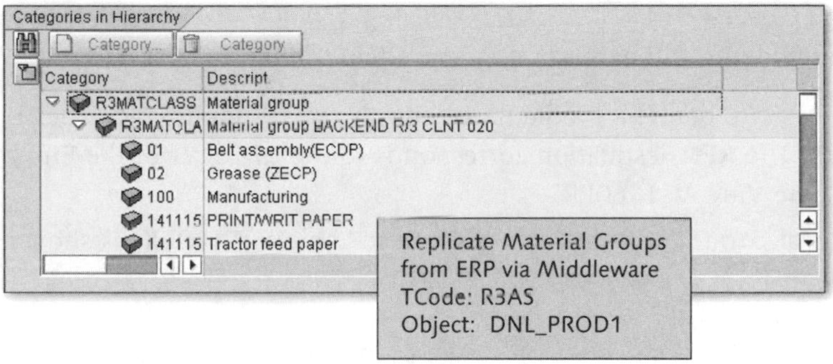

Figure 21.18 Replicate Plants and Material Groups

7. Define how Sourcing will be carried out in EBP — either via the Sourcing application or via the Purchase Order application. This can be seen in Figure 21.19.

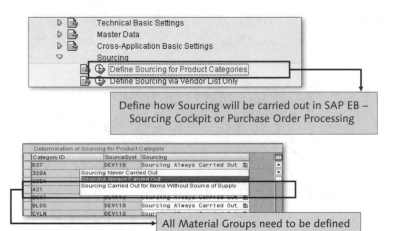

Figure 21.19 Define the Sourcing Decision

Let's take a look at what these options mean:

▶ **Sourcing Never Carried Out**
All external requirements will be sent as Incomplete POs in SAP EB.

▶ **Sourcing Always Carried Out**
All external requirements will be sent into the Sourcing Application in SAP EB.

8. In the SAP ERP system, define a profile name and the corresponding RFC destination to SAP EB. The RFC destination corresponds to the RFC user of the Entry Channel. Define the View V_T160PR.

9. Define the Material Group to Profile combination in Table V_T160EX, as shown in Figure 21.20.

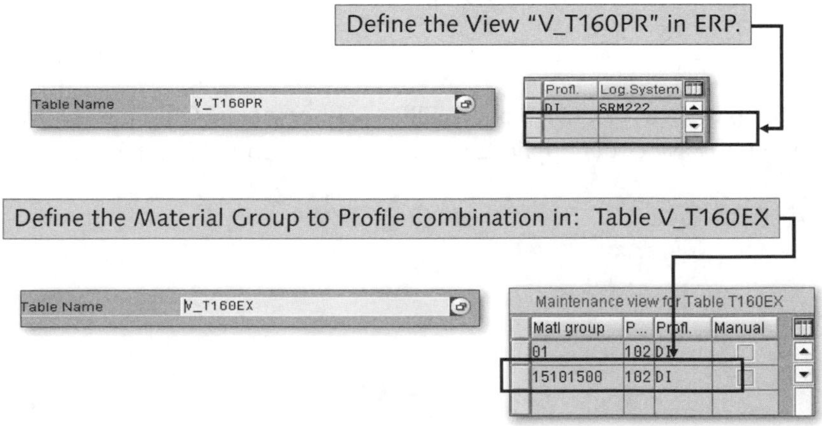

Figure 21.20 Define RFC Destination and Material Group Profile

10. When you're finished configuring these settings, you can begin to schedule the program that transfers the requirements from SAP ERP into SAP SRM. Report RPRSEL01 reads Table EPRTRANS from SAP ERP to see what needs to be transferred to SAP EBP.

21.4   Other Configuration with SAP SRM

There are many valuable configuration guides that exist on the SAP Service Marketplace, SAP SRM Community, and SAP SRM Wiki. This section provides useful links to some of those configuration guides.

Configuration	URL access
E-Sourcing / CLM	*http://Service.sap.com* • Release and Upgrade Info • SAP SRM • SAP E-Sourcing 5.1/SAP CLM 2.0 • Integration SAP ERP/Hosted SAP E-Sourcing: Config. Guide.pdf
	Integration SAP ERP/On-Premise SAP E-Sourcing: Config. Guide.pdf
SRM 7.0 new features	*http://Service.sap.com* • Release and Upgrade Info • SAP SRM • SRM 7.0 • Additional Configuration Material for SAP SRM 7.0.pdf
Workflow Guide 7.0	*http://Service.sap.com* • Release and Upgrade Info • SAP SRM • SRM 7.0 • Workflow Guide – SAP SRM 7.0

Table 21.1   Useful Links for Configuration Guides

21.5   Summary

In this chapter, you learned to integrate SAP SRM organizational structure with SAP ERP HCM and also learned how to change approvers for the shopping cart and how to integrate MRP.

These integration issues are important as you move forward in your procurement enhancement journey with SAP SRM. The key solution configuration information in this chapter was not intended to be comprehensive in scope. Rather, it was to be a guide for key setup and configuration areas in SAP SRM.

21.6   Book Conclusion

We are also now at the end of this book. We hope you found this to be a practical and useful resource that you will return to from time to time, when you need solutions or advice. We intended this to be a practical guide and tried to keep a real-world focus throughout.

From gaining an overview of SAP SRM and understanding how it fits into the overall SAP landscape, you learned information about detailed functionality and capability of this solution. We hope this book helps you enhance procurement in your company by giving you a detailed look into how SAP SRM works.

You should also now have a fairly good understanding of implementation, integration, and updates. This section is largely based on our own experiences and contains valuable information not found in other SAP resources. This is where you should have received the answers to your commonly encountered problems, issues, and needs.

To make this book a comprehensive and real-world guide, we delved deep into some specific industry solutions. These included procurement in the public sector and generally highlighted SAP PPS.

Then, we proceeded on to selected configuration issues, which was intended to be a guide for key setup and integration issues related to SAP SRM.

The appendices contain valuable extras, which should greatly help you in your projects. Here you can get an SAP SRM functionality matrix, job scheduling, a quiz to determine your SAP SRM knowledge, and more. We encourage you to read the appendices and use them as you need to.

I hope that you find this book useful and valuable for your needs. I have learned a lot while writing it and hope extensive knowledge and experience were passed on to you.

Appendices

A   SRM Functionality Matrix

The SAP SRM application has evolved at a rapid pace over the last six years, with each release of the application providing enhanced functionality. Each implementation team is faced with the task of gathering varied organizational requirements and then performing a gap analysis against the SAP SRM release being implemented. The SAP SRM scenario implementation type (Classic, Extended Classic, Standalone) has a considerable impact on this gap analysis. SAP continually aims to offer comparable functionality across the different implementation scenarios, but the inherent nature of each scenario results in restrictions.

SAP has developed an SAP SRM functionality matrix that provides a comparative analysis for the different implementation scenarios, the functional processes and the application releases. This document will be especially useful for organizations that want to compare — at a detail functionality level — which capabilities in SAP SRM are supported in the Classic, Extended Classic, or Standalone scenarios. Organizations can review the matrix for each of the SAP SRM core processes: strategic sourcing, operational procurement, and supplier enablement. Let's look at an example.

If your organization wants to implement the Request for External Staff functionality available within the operational procurement process, know whether this functionality is supported within the Classic, Extended Classic, or Standalone scenario. The SAP SRM functionality matrix illustrates that this functionality is only available in the Standalone scenario. As you can see, this information becomes valuable because it enables you to correctly blueprint and select your implementation scenario.

You can access and download the SAP SRM matrix document from *www.sap-press.com.*

B   Jobs that Require Scheduling

As part of a production SAP SRM system, you need to schedule and execute several jobs on a regular basis. This appendix discusses these jobs and the parameters that are required for each job.

Table B.1 provides an example of the frequency for the jobs you must schedule in the SAP SRM system. Organizations can change these frequencies, based on their requirements.

B.1   Jobs Required in SAP SRM

JOB NAME	DESCRIPTION	STEPS (PROGRAMS)	FREQ
CLEAN_ REQREQ_UP	This job executes report (SE38) CLEAN_REQREQ_UP to ensure that subsequent objects of shopping cart (SC) items and IDocs, which can be generated from confirmations and invoices, were updated successfully in the backend system. If the subsequent objects are created successfully, the report sets the status of the SC to 6 and deletes temporary data that is not needed anymore from the SAP EB system. (This is why it is called a CLEANER job.) Note: The entries in table BBP_ DOCUMENT_TAB represent the worklist for report CLEAN_ REQREQ_UP. This is why the runtime of the report increases with time. When the check is successful, the corresponding SC entries are deleted from table BBP_DOCUMENT_TAB.	CLEAN_REQREQ_UP	Every 15 minutes

Table B.1   Jobs Required for Scheduling in SAP SRM

JOB NAME	DESCRIPTION	STEPS (PROGRAMS)	FREQ
SPOOLER JOB	Similar to CLEAN_REQREQ_UP. You need to select either SPOOLER JOB or CLEAN_REQREQ_UP — Although SPOOLER JOB is not scheduled in SM37, it is still scheduled to execute in the system. You configure the job in the IMG: EBP • TECHNICAL BASIC SETTINGS • SET CONTROL PARAMETERS. The spooler transfers shopping cart data to the backend system. The preferred method is scheduling CLEAN_REQREQ_UP.		
APPROVALS — SEND EMAIL TO EXTERNAL MAIL SYSTEMS	This job enables offline approval functionality in SAP SRM and transfer of work items in an SAP SRM user's Inbox to their preferred email client (e.g., Microsoft Outlook, IBM Lotus Notes, Novell GroupWise, etc.) There are two steps in this job: The initial step moves the approval work-item from the SAP Inbox to SAP Connect (Transaction code: SCOT). The second step moves the same work item from SAP Connect to the organization's mail server, which then sends the email to the user's preferred email client.	Step 1: RSCONN01 Variant: SAP&CONNECTALL Step 2: RSWUWFMLEC Variant: EMAIL_VARIANT Attributes: Type of Mail: HTML Approval Buttons: NO Operation: FULL TEXT Email Address: EMAIL ADDRESS@COMPANY.com	Every 15 minutes

Table B.1 Jobs Required for Scheduling in SAP SRM (Cont.)

JOB NAME	DESCRIPTION	STEPS (PROGRAMS)	FREQ
GET STATUS OF SRM DOCUMENTS	This job retrieves status information back from the backend system. Once a Req. or a PO is generated in EBP, the spooler transfers it over to the backend. This job then gets the status of the created object and provides the appropriate input to the Check Status Transaction of the end user's shopping cart. If Check Status is not being updated in the shopping cart and the subsequent PO, Goods Receipt or Invoice has been created, and then check whether this job is running.	BBP_GET_STATUS_2 Variant might be required post production	Every 15 minutes
ORGANIZATION MODEL CLEAN-UP & PROFORMANCE IMPROVEMENT	This job cleans up the buffers of the organizational structure, which helps with the performance of the system. Additionally, it schedules inheritance of attributes within the organizational structure to allow for quicker access.	RHBAUPAT (for release <3.0) HRBCI_ATTRIBUTES_BUFFER_UPDATE (for releases >= 3.0) Variant might be required post production	Every night
RSPPF PROCESS	This report provides the mechanism to output local purchase orders for automatic message output.	RSPPFPROCESS	Every 30 minutes
EVALUATED RECEIPT SETTLEMENT EXECUTION	When ERS is being used, you need to schedule this report. This allows the ERS procedure execution in SAP SRM. Relevant for organizations using the local scenario. This executes the settlement. Assumption: Confirmation exists	BBPERS	1 – 2 times/day

Table B.1 Jobs Required for Scheduling in SAP SRM (Cont.)

JOB NAME	DESCRIPTION	STEPS (PROGRAMS)	FREQ
WORKFLOW: RUNTIME PROGRAMS	There are a number of jobs that are required to run so that workflow in the SAP SRM environment can be successfully executed. Typically, these jobs can be automatically scheduled using the Automatic Workflow Customizing in Transaction code SWU3. A background job is scheduled for the following: ▶ Missed deadlines ▶ Work items with errors ▶ Condition evaluation ▶ Event queue ▶ Clearing tasks	The following jobs need to be running in a production environment: ▶ SWWDHEX ▶ SWWERRE ▶ SWWCOND ▶ SWWCLEAR	Every 15 minutes
INVOICE: STATUS SYNCHRONIZATION	This report synchronizes the status of invoices in the SAP SRM system with the status in the corresponding SAP ERP backend system. Once invoices are "Paid" in the backend, the SRM status is synchronized to show "Paid."	BBP_IV_UPDATE_PAYMENT_STATUS	2 – 4 times/day
CHECK GOODS RECEIPTS FOR XML INVOICES	All invoices that come in via XML with a status of "Waiting for Preceding Document" to check if the preceding documents (such as Confirmations) have been posted and periodic attempts are made to post the relevant invoice.	BBP_IV_AUTO_COMPLETE	2 times/day

Table B.1   Jobs Required for Scheduling in SAP SRM (Cont.)

JOB NAME	DESCRIPTION	STEPS (PROGRAMS)	FREQ
CONTRACT EXPIRY CHECK	Organizations that use the Contract application in SAP SRM can schedule this report to check on the status of the contract. The report provides selection parameters to identify contracts that might be nearing expiry or where the quantity or release value is nearing completion. Organizations using the SAP NetWeaver Business Warehouse (BW) application can use the Alerts functionality in SAP SRM to trigger contract expiry reports in SAP NetWeaver BW.	BBP_CONTRACT_CHECK	Once/day
WORKFLOW: OFFLINE APPROVAL	Organizations using the Offline approvals functionality within SAP EB can schedule this report to enable receipt of status of approvals from external mail systems.	RBBP_NOTIFICA-TION_OFFAPP	Every 30 minutes

Table B.1 Jobs Required for Scheduling in SAP SRM (Cont.)

B.2 Jobs Required in SAP ERP

Table B.2 provides an example of the frequency for the job you have to schedule in the SAP ERP backend system. This job is only required if you have integrated the organizational structure in SAP SRM with the organizational model in the SAP ERP HCM application. Organizations can change this based on their requirements.

JOB NAME	DESCRIPTION	STEPS (PROGRAMS)	USER	FREQ
HR CHANGE POINTERS	Assumption: HR Org. Integration is active. When Org/Position changes are executed in SAP ERP HCM, then those changes/deletions need to be distributed to the SAP SRM system. SAP ERP HCM distributes the changes/deletions to SAP SRM and other systems via the IDoc interface. This job executes a report that creates IDocs from the change pointers in the SAP ERP HCM system. It then sends them to the receiving system (SAP SRM) and updates the organizational structure in SAP SRM.	STEP: RBDMIDOC Variant: HR_SRM_ORG Attributes: Message Type: HRMD_ABA		Once/day

Table B.2 Jobs Required for Scheduling in SAP ERP

In a production SAP SRM system that is linked to an SAP ERP backend, the BBP_GET_STATUS_2 report needs to be scheduled as described in Table B.1. For performance reasons, this report should be scheduled using a variant.

The BBP_GET_STATUS_2 report receives status information about documents that are pertinent to a backend system, for example, purchase requisition, PO, reservation, goods receipt, and invoice. The following parameters are available for setting up the variant:

- Shopping carts (interval)
- Logical system (if multiple backend systems are being used)
- Shopping carts in the last number of days (restrict variant based on range)
- Shopping cart status indicator (Deleted, Completed, etc.)

C   Using Different Browsers with SAP SRM

Every organization has policies regarding their support of applications used within the company, including Internet browsers. Probably the most used and supported browser is Microsoft Internet Explorer. However, other browsers such as Mozilla Firefox and Apple Safari are also used at many companies. It is important for an organization to know whether and to what extent the browser used in its company is supported by SAP for the SAP SRM application.

The main components within SAP SRM (Enterprise Buyer, Bidding Engine, Supplier Self-Services, and Catalog Content Management) are all accessed via a Web browser. End users can access the components directly via a URL representing the ITS (for SAP EB and Bidding Engine applications) or BSP (CCM and SUS applications) technologies.

Alternatively, they can access these components seamlessly via the SAP NetWeaver Portal system. No matter how these applications are accessed, a web browser is used (except when using the Microsoft Windows GUI for configuration). The following browsers are supported for use with SAP SRM 7.0:

▶ Microsoft Internet Explorer 6.0, 7.0, 8.0
▶ Mozilla Firefox 1.0 and Mozilla 1.7

> **Note**
> Detailed information on the browser support is available in the Service Marketplace under the PAM alias.

Additionally, organizations that are using SAP SRM 4.0 on computers running MAC OS should use Mozilla Firefox as their browser.

D   Using Business Add-Ins with SAP SRM

From SAP 4.6A, and for all SAP SRM releases, SAP provided a new enhancement technique in the form of Business Add-Ins (BAdIs). Business Add-Ins (BAdIs) are object-oriented enhancement options. Enhancements represent customer requirements that have not been developed in the standard SAP software. A BAdI is a standard exit within SAP programs whereby organizations can change SAP programs without carrying out any system modifications.

A common saying in SAP SRM projects is that BAdIs are your best friend and that you need to get to know them. This is because there is hardly any SAP SRM project where organizations have not utilized BAdIs to achieve their unique business requirements. A number of projects begin with the charter of no development and then realize that the only way to achieve some of their business requirements is by using BAdIs. Let's take a simple example: the *Shop* for transaction BBPSC01 contains different options for end users to create shopping carts.

Users can create shopping carts to order temporary labor, request for external staff, and others. If you do not plan to utilize the Services procurement functionality in SAP SRM implementation, then you might not want to give users the access to this these options. In our example, the only way to remove these from the Shop for transaction is either by using a BAdI or making HTML modifications. SAP provides a growing number of BAdIs with each SRM release.

With the help of BAdIs, organizations can implement business specific logic to gain flexibility without creating Customer modifications, because BAdIs are completely supported by SAP. According to SAP, Release upgrades do not affect enhancement calls from within the standard software nor do they affect the validity of call interfaces. Also, BAdIs are not required to be registered in the SAP Software Change Registration (SSCR).

D.1   Implementing a BAdI

To implement a BAdI in SAP SRM, development experts can navigate to the implementation through the IMG: (SUPPLIER RELATIONSHIP MANAGEMENT • SRM SERVER • BUSINESS ADD-INS) or use Transaction SE19 or SE18. To implement a BAdI, the first steps are to give an implementation name adhering to the customer naming standards and to define the required attributes. There are basically two types of attributes in a BAdI implementation, which are:

▶ Multiple Use
▶ Filter Dependent

These are described below.

D.1.1 Multiple Use

Multiple use for BAdI definitions means that there can be several active BAdI implementations in a single environment. When there is a call, they are all called up though, in an unpredictable sequence. If you have multiple-use BAdI definitions, the sequence must not play any role. Although SAP provides the functionality around multiple use BAdIs attributes, most BAdIs available in SAP SRM are filter dependent and not available for multiple-use.

D.1.2 Filter Dependent

Filters allow SAP to provide one technical object that can be used across multiple business documents. As a default, each BAdI definition method automatically has an importing parameter FLT_VAL assigned.

Let's take an example. The BAdI: BBP_VERSION_CONTROL has an attribute-type filter dependent checked. This means that this BAdI will be triggered for specific object types that are defined in the standard system configuration. Therefore, this same BAdI can be triggered for different documents, such as PO (BUS2201), contracts, and others. Figure D.1 illustrates the filter dependency for the PO business object.

Usually, a BAdI will have at least one method where a custom code can be written. Within this method, there will be parameters. These parameters can be importing, exporting, returning, or changing parameters. We can see the list of the available parameters during runtime by clicking the Signature button within the Implementation or by simply double clicking any of the Interface names in the BAdI definition.

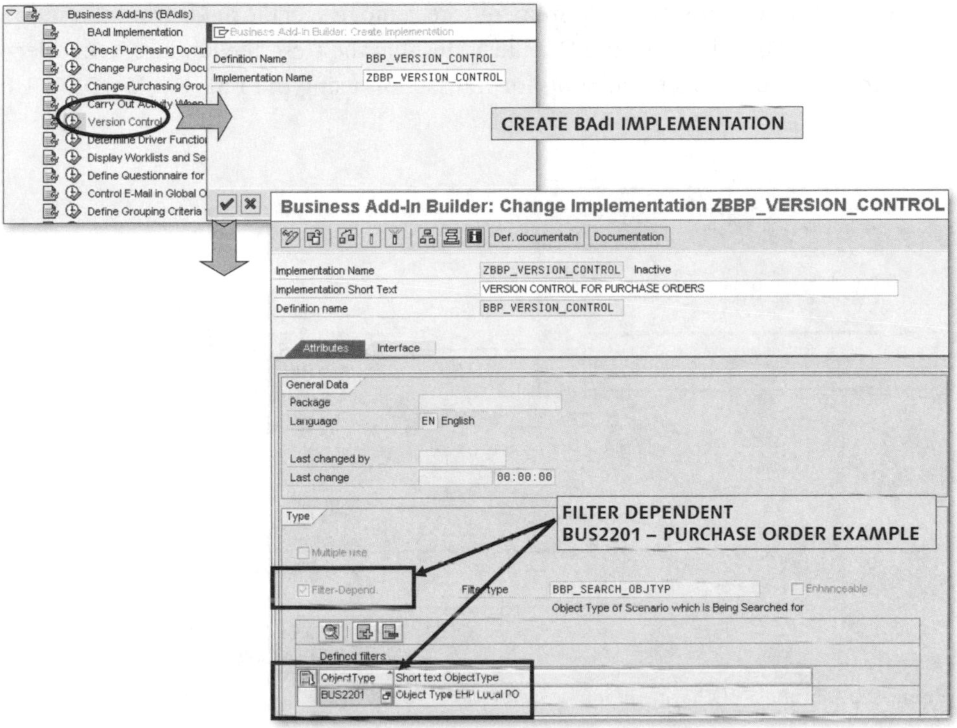

Figure D.1 Example of BAdI Definition and Filter Selection

D.2 Examples of BAdIs in SAP SRM

Each SRM implementation will experience a requirement of using BAdIs, based on their business requirements. This section provides a few examples where BAdIs can be implemented in SAP SRM.

D.2.1 BAdI: Change Display in Shopping Cart (BBP_SC_MODIFY_UI)

The Shop for transaction BBPSC01 in SAP SRM was designed with professional purchasers in mind. Many organizations enable this transaction for casual end users as well. However, most organizations want to remove specific access in this transaction from the casual users. This BAdI allows removing fields such as: Catalog Search, Catalogs, Limit Cart, Describe Requirement, Temporary labor, Product, Temp Labor Req, and Default Scr.

In this example, our business requirement is to remove specific fields from the shopping cart BBPSC01 screen. Figure D.2 illustrates that the Describe Requirement selection can be removed from the Shop for transaction using the BBP_SC_MODIFY_UI BAdI.

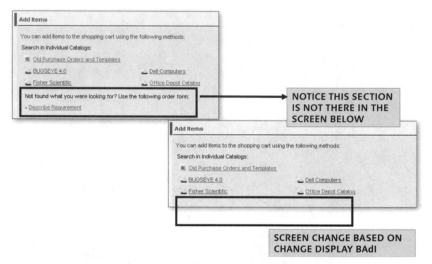

Figure D.2 Example of Change Shopping Cart Display BAdI

Here is a sample code that organizations can use to remove specific fields in the Shop for transaction. In our sample code, the Limit Cart, Temporary Labor, Product, and Catalog selections are cleared from user access. Let's take a look at the code now:

```
Definition: BBP_SC_MODIFY_UI
Method:SC_MODIFY_SCREEN
method IF_EX_BBP_SC_MODIFY_UI~SC_MODIFY_SCREEN.
   clear is_scr_itmchoice-LIMIT.
   clear is_scr_itmchoice-TEMP_LAB.
   clear is_scr_itmchoice-PRODUCT.
   clear is_scr_itmchoice-CATALOGS.
endmethod.
```

D.2.2 BAdI: Define Target Objects (BBP_TARGET_OBJECTS)

In SAP SRM, when implementing the Classic scenario, an organization has the choice to create a target document in the SAP ERP back-end. A purchase requisition, PO, or a reservation can be created in the backend once the shopping cart is approved in SAP SRM. In this example, our business requirement is to ensure that all shopping cart line items are converted into a PO.

Here is a sample code that organizations can use to force the target object in the backend system to be a PO. In this code, the backend object is being set as 3, which indicates PO creation; this can be set to *1* or *2* to create a purchase requisition or reservation based on your business requirements. Here is the code:

```
method IF_EX_BBP_TARGET_OBJECTS~DETERMINE_TARGET_OBJECTS.
 DATA: itM_data_OO TYPE bbp_bapipogn_eci,
 l_index TYPE sy-tabix.
* SET THE OBJECT TO BE GENERATED AS 3 FOR PO CREATION
 LOOP AT item_data INTO itm_data_OO.
 l_index = sy-tabix.
 itm_data_OO-obj_to_gen = '3'.
 MODIFY item_data FROM itm_data_OO INDEX l_index.
 ENDLOOP.
endmethod.
```

D.2.3 BAdI: Change Purchasing Document Data (BBP_DOC_CHANGE_BAdI)

The change purchasing document data BAdI is probably the single most utilized BAdI in SAP SRM implementations and can be utilized creatively to meet many unique business requirements. This BAdI allows organizations to change the data in the business document being created. For example, change data in the shopping cart or PO transactions. This example illustrates how organizations can utilize this BAdI to convert a preferred vendor in the shopping cart to a *fixed* vendor.

When creating a shopping cart, a user can select a preferred source of supply in the details of the shopping cart. If the business requirement empowers the end user to make the decision on the vendor selection and no further purchasing intervention is required, this preferred vendor would need to be converted into a fixed vendor in the system. This BAdI can be utilized for influencing this change in the shopping cart document data.

Here is a sample code that organizations can use to convert a preferred vendor in the shopping cart to a fixed vendor:

```
Method: BBP_SC_CHANGE  (FILTER BUS2121)

DATA: ls_partner TYPE bbp_pds_partner,
 l_index type sy-tabix.
CONSTANTS:
   c_prt_19 TYPE bbp_pds_partner-partner_fct VALUE '00000019',
   c_prt_39 TYPE bbp_pds_partner-partner_fct VALUE '00000039'.
```

```
* MOVE PARTNER DATA TO WORK AREA
 LOOP AT it_partner INTO ls_partner.
 l_index = sy-tabix.
* CHECK IF THE PARTNER FUNCTION IS PREFERRED VENDOR
 IF ls_partner-partner_fct EQ c_prt_39.
* IF TRUE CHANGE IT TO FIXED VENDOR
 ls_partner-partner_fct = c_prt_19.
 ENDIF.
* APPEND THE CHANGING PARAMETER TABLE
 APPEND ls_partner TO et_partner.
 ENDLOOP.
```

D.2.4 BAdI: Check Purchasing Document (BBP_DOC_CHECK_BAdI)

The check BAdI is another BAdI that is utilized heavily on SAP SRM projects. This BAdI allows the organization to ensure that the purchasing documents (shopping cart, PO, etc.) in SAP SRM are checked for validation using business rules specific to your organization. This example checks the shopping cart document to ensure that users are not using the Service radio button on the shopping cart line item.

In the shopping cart, users can choose the Service or Product radio button. Many organizations do not want to use the service option when creating shopping carts. The check BAdI can be utilized to ensure that if the user selects the service radio button during the creation of the shopping cart line item, the system should issue an error message. The example in figure D.3 illustrates the error message that a user receives if the Services product type radio button is selected in the shopping cart.

Here is a sample code that organizations can use to check the shopping cart if the Service radio button has been selected:

```
Method: BBP_DOC_CHECK
 DATA:
 wa_item TYPE bbp_pds_sc_item_d,
 wa_messages TYPE bbp_smessages_BAdI.
 LOOP AT lt_item INTO wa_item WHERE del_ind NE 'X'.
 IF wa_item-product_type EQ '02'.
 CLEAR wa_messages.
 wa_messages-msgty = 'E'.
 wa_messages-msgv1 = 'Product type service not allowed'
 APPEND wa_messages TO et_messages.
 ENDIF.
ENDLOOP.
```

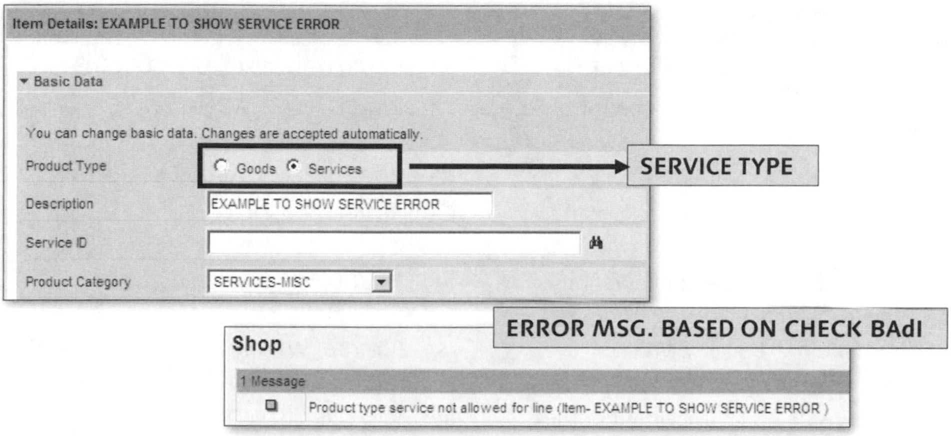

Figure D.3 Example of Document Check BAdI

D.3   List of BAdIs in SAP SRM

The purpose of this section is to provide users with a list of all the BAdIs that are available in SAP SRM as of release SAP SRM 7.0.

The list of BAdIs in Table D.1 is organized in a table format and when applicable are grouped together by function.

> **Note**
>
> This list has been compiled from the SAP SRM system, Search help, and the SAP SRM 7.0 Migration documents available on the SAP Service Marketplace.

Business Add-Ins (BAdIs)	Definition Name
Customer Enhancement of Document Search Functionality	/SAPSRM/BD_DOCUMENT_SEARCH
Handle Update of Customer Table Extension for BP Supplier	/SAPSRM/BD_DP_TE_BP_SAVE
SRM@FPM Extensibility: Subview Definition on OIF	/SAPSRM/BD_FPM_IDR_OIF_EXT
Action handling for customers	/SAPSRM/BD_MVC_ACTION
Control of IDR	/SAPSRM/BD_MVC_IDR
SRM MVC Architecture: Metadata Extensibility (Customer)	/SAPSRM/BD_MVC_METADATA
SRM MVC Architecture: WD Data Extensibility (Customer)	/SAPSRM/BD_MVC_WD_DATA

Table D.1   New BAdIs in SAP SRM 7.0.

Business Add-Ins (BAdIs)	Definition Name
Handle Field Extensions on PDO Layer	/SAPSRM/BD_PDO_FIELD_EXTENSN
Customer extension for SC monitor object adoptions	/SAPSRM/BD_PDO_MONITOR_SC
Customer Table Extension	/SAPSRM/BD_PDO_TABLE_EXT_CHNG
Enhancement Spot For Digital Signature BAdI	/SAPSRM/BD_SIG_DOC_ES
SRM Workflow Engine Configuration: BAdIs for Agent Deter	/SAPSRM/BD_WF_AGENTS
SRM Workflow: Dynamic Process Level Configuration	/SAPSRM/BD_WF_PROCESS
Internal BAdIs for Enhancement of the Context Navigation	/SAPSRM/BDI_CH_WD_CNP /SAPSRM/BDI_CLL_ACTION_EXT
Enhancement to filer out data before passing it into clipboard	/SAPSRM/BDI_CLL_COPY_CLIPBOARD
Internal BAdIs for extending the POWL Feeder	/SAPSRM/BDI_CLL_POWL_FEEDER
Enhancement of Document Search Functionality	/SAPSRM/BDI_DOCUMENT_SEARCH
Handle Update of Table Extension for BP Supplier	/SAPSRM/BDI_DP_TE_BP_SAVE
FPM Extensibility for IDR and OIF	/SAPSRM/BDI_FPM_IDR_OIF_EXT
Changes to Handling of Item Process Types in SRM	/SAPSRM/BDI_ITEM_PROCESS_TYPE
Internal Action Definitions for FPM	/SAPSRM/BDI_MVC_ACTION
IDR control	/SAPSRM/BDI_MVC_IDR
SRM MVC Architecture: Metadata Extensibility	/SAPSRM/BDI_MVC_METADATA
SRM MVC Architecture: WD Data Extensibility	/SAPSRM/BDI_MVC_WD_DATA /SAPSRM/BDI_PDO_ACTION_EXT /SAPSRM/BDI_PDO_FIELD_EXTENSN
Filtering of Items retrieved from PDO Layer	/SAPSRM/BDI_PDO_ITEM_FILTER
BAdI for Contract Mass Changes	/SAPSRM/CTR_MASS_CHANGE
ES for SOA Mapping	/SAPSRM/ES_SOA_MAPPING /SAPSRM/BD_CLL_MONITOR_SC /SAPSRM/BD_CLL_POWL_FEEDER

Table D.1 New BAdIs in SAP SRM 7.0. (Cont.)

D.3.1 Obsolete BAdIs for Organizations Implementing SAP SRM 7.0

▶ Change Display in Shopping Cart (ITS Technology)

▶ Deactivate Cross-Catalog Search (ITS Technology)

▶ Display of Input Helps, and Favorites (ITS Technology)

▶ Restrict the Display in Input Helps (ITS Technology)

▶ Internal Temporary Storage of Favorites for Input/Search Helps

▶ Final Saving of Favorites for Input Helps and Search Helps

▶ Determine Screen Variants (ITS Technology)

▶ Field Control in Purchasing Document (ITS Technology)

▶ Print Preview in Version Comparison

The majority of the BAdIs are available within the SAP EB application. However, certain BAdIs are also applicable for SUS, and are seen in Table D.2.

Business Add-Ins (BAdIs)	Definition Name	SAP SRM Application	Release
Check Purchasing Document	BBP_DOC_CHECK_BAdI	EBP	
Change Purchasing Document Data	BBP_DOC_CHANGE_BAdI	EBP & SUS	
Change Purchasing Group Assignment	BBP_PGRP_ASSIGN_BAdI		changed in 5.0
Carry Out Activity When Saving	BBP_DOC_SAVE_BAdI	EBP & SUS	
Version Control	BBP_VERSION_CONTROL	EBP & SUS	
Determine Driver Function Modules	BBP_DRIVER_DETERMINE		changed in 5.0
Display Worklist and Search Results Lists	BBP_WF_LIST		
Define Questionnaire for Vendor Evaluation in SRM	BBP_VE_QSTN_DET_BAdI		
Control E-Mail in Global Outline Agreement	BBP_CTR_MAIL_BAdI		
Define Grouping Criteria for Local Purchase Orders	BBP_GROUP_LOC_PO		
Define External Print Formatting for Office Documents	BBP_DOC_PRINTPROC		

Table D.2 Generic BAdIs in SAP SRM

Business Add-Ins (BAdIs)	Definition Name	SAP SRM Application	Release
Archive SRM Documents	BBP_ARCHIVING_BAdI	EBP & SUS	4.0
Upload/Download SRM Documents	BBP_PD_DOWNLOAD		4.0
Further Authorization Check for SRM Documents	BBP_AUTHORITY_CHECK	EBP & SUS	4.0
Activation of Vendor Monitor	BBP_BAdI_SUPP_MONI		4.0
Create Skills Profile	BBP_SKILLS		
Transfer Additional Characteristics to SAP CCM	BBP_CCM_CHAR_MAIN		
Filter for Scheduling Agreement Releases	BBP_SUS_FILTER_SCHAR		
Download Documents	BBP_SUS_DOWNLD_FILES	SUS	
Customer Text for Registration Screen	ROS_CUST_WEL_TXT	Supplier Registration	
Definition of Required Fields for Customers	ROS_REQ_CUF	Supplier Registration	
Default Quantity for Items in the Confirmation	BBP_SUS_QUAN_PROPOSE	SUS	
Field Checks for Customer-Defined Required Fields	ROS_BUPA_DATA_CHECK	Supplier Registration	

Table D.2 Generic BAdIs in SAP SRM (Cont.)

Table D.3 lists BAdIs for the Extended Classic scenario.

Business Add-Ins	Definition Note
Activate Extended Classic Scenario	BBP_EXTLOCALPO_BAdI
Transfer Purchase Order Data to Logistics Backend	BBP_ECS_PO_OUT_BAdI

Table D.3 BAdIs for Controlling the Extended Classic Scenario

Now, take a look at BAdIs for master data in Table D.4.

SAP SRM Application	Definition Name	Release
Customer Field Replication in Vendor Master Data	BBP_GET_VMDATA_CF	
Extension for Tax Number Mapping	BBP_SUS_BP_TAXNUMMAP	SUS
Extension for Duplication Check	BBP_SUS_BP_DUPLCHECK	SUS

Table D.4 BAdIs for Master Data

Table D.5 looks at BAdIs for shopping carts and requirements.

SAP SRM Application	Definition Name	Release
Shopping Cart: Determine Responsible Purchasing Group(s)	BBP_PGRP_FIND	
Determine Backend System / Company Code	BBP_DETERMINE_ LOGSYS	
Determine Target Object in BE System	BBP_TARGET_OBJECTS	Changed in 5.0 (new BAdI added)
Monitor Shopping Cart: Selection and List Display	BBP_MON_SC	
Change Display in Shopping Cart	BBP_SC_MODIFY_UI	4.0

Table D.5 BAdIs for Shopping Carts and Requirement Items

Table D.6 lists them for external web services.

SAP SRM Application	Definition Name
Transfer Shopping Cart from Catalog	BBP_CATALOG_TRANSFER
Transfer Additional Parameters	BBP_CAT_CALL_ENRICH
Deactivate Cross-Catalog Search	BBP_WS_AGENT_SFARCH

Table D.6 BAdIs for External Web Services (Catalogs, Vendor Lists, etc.)

Table D.7 lists BAdIs for follow-on document generation for the backend system, which is new in SAP SRM 5.0.

SAP SRM Application	Definition Name	Release
Determine Number Ranges and Grouping in Backend Documents	BBP_SC_TRANSFER_BE	Changed in 5.0 (new BAdI added)
Purchase Requisition in Backend System	BBP_CREATE_REQ_BACK	Changed in 5.0 (new BAdI added)
Purchase Order in Backend System	BBP_CREATE_PO_BACK	Changed in 5.0 (new BAdI added)
Grouping of Reservations	BBP_RESERVATION_GRP	Changed in 5.0 (new BAdI added)
Reservation in Backend System	BBP_CREATE_RES_BACK	Changed in 5.0 (new BAdI added)
Create Contract in Backend System	BBP_CTR_BE_CREATE	

Table D.7 BAdIs for Follow-on Document Generation in the Backend System

Learn about old and new definition names in Table D.8.

Business Add-Ins (BAdIs)	Old Definition Name	New Definition Name
Grouping of shopping cart items for follow-on documents	BBP_SC_TRANSFER_BE	BBP_BS_GROUP_BE
Purchase Requisition in Backend System	BBP_CREATE_REQ_BACK	BBP_CREATE_BE_RQ_NEW
Purchase Order in Backend System	BBP_CREATE_PO_BACK	BBP_CREATE_BE_PO_NEW
Grouping of Reservations	BBP_RESERVATION_GRP	BBP_BS_GROUP_BE
Reservation in Backend System	BBP_CREATE_RES_BACK	BBP_CREATE_BE_RS_NEW

Table D.8 New BAdIs in SAP SRM 5.0 for Follow-on Document Generation in the Backend System

Get a list of BAdIs relevant for sourcing in Table D.9.

Business Add-Ins (BAdIs)	Definition Name
Define Execution of Sourcing	BBP_SRC_DETERMINE
Define Sourcing via Vendor List	BBP_AVL_DETERMINE
Change Bid Invitation Data Before Transfer to Bidding Application	BBP_CREAT_RFQ_IN_DPE
Find and Check Sources of Supply	BBP_SOS_BAdI

Table D.9 BAdIs Relevant to Sourcing in SAP SRM

Table D.10 is your source for BAdIs that are needed for bid invitations.

Business Add-Ins (BAdIs)	Definition Name	Release
Dynamic Attributes in the Bid Invitation	BBP_DETERMINE_DYNATR	
Determine Bid Invitation Transaction Type	BBP_BID_DET_PROCTYPE	4.0
Control for Collaboration Folders	BBP_CFOLDER_BAdI	4.0

Table D.10 BAdIs Relevant for Bid Invitations

If you are interested in account assignment, you will find Table D.11 useful.

Business Add-Ins (BAdIs)	Definition Name
Change Account Assignment Category when Creating Backend Documents	BBP_ACCCAT_MAP_EXP
Change Account Assignment Category when Importing Backend Documents	BBP_ACCCAT_MAP_IMP
Determine SAP General Ledger Acct	BBP_DETERMINE_ACCT
Deactivate Automatic Budget Check	BBP_BUDGET_CHECK

Table D.11 Account Assignment Relevant BAdIs

Those interested in tax calculation will find Table D.12 interesting.

Business Add-Ins (BAdIs)	Definition Name
Determine Tax Code	BBP_DET_TAXCODE_BAdI
Change Tax Data	BBP_TAX_MAP_BAdI
Calculate Tax for Freight Costs	BBP_FREIGHT_BAdI

Table D.12 BAdIs Relevant for Tax Calculation

Gain important information about Controlling Pricing Configurator (IPC) in Table D.13.

Business Add-Ins (BAdIs)	Definition Name	Action
Switch On Simplified Pricing (Classic Scenario)	BBP_PRICEDATA_READ	
Switch off Buffer Refreshing IPC		REMOVED

Table D.13 BAdIs for Controlling Pricing Configurator

Confirmation and invoice verification BAdIs are found in Table D.13.

Business Add-Ins (BAdIs)	Definition Name
Define Target System for Sending of Confirmation	BBP_XML_CONF_LOGSYS
Send Confirmation via XML	BBP_XML_CONF_SEND
Control Default Values for Time Recording	BBP_TREX_BAdI
Control Entry Options for Unplanned Items	BBP_UNPLAN_ITEM_BAdI

Table D.14 BAdIs for Confirmation and Invoice Verification

Component Planning BAdIs are found in Table D.15.

Business Add-Ins (BAdIs)	Definition Name
Define Default Values for Component Planning	BBP_PM_DEFAULT_VAL
Check and Complete Component Data	BBP_PM_COMP_CHK

Table D.15 BAdIs for Component Planning

Direct material and plan-driven BAdIs are given in Table D.16.

Business Add-Ins (BAdIs)	Definition Name	Action
Control Direct Material Procurement	BBP_DP_PROD_CHK_BAdI	
Send XML Document to Planning System	BBP_XML_DET_SYSTEM	
Check Items for APO Relevance		REMOVED

Table D.16 BAdIs for Direct Material and Plan-Driven Procurement

SAP SRM workflow related BAdIs are found in Table D.17.

Business Add-Ins (BAdIs)	Definition Name	Release
Authorization to Change During Approval	BBP_WFL_SECUR_BAdI	
Determine Approver (Administrator)	BBP_WFL_ADMIN_APPROV	
Determination of Approver for n-Step Dynamic Approval Workflow	BBP_WFL_APPROV_BAdI	
Determine Shopping Cart Value for Purchasing Budget Workflow	BBP_SC_VALUE_GET	
Control Workflow for Stochastic Document Check	BBP_STOCH_CUST_BAdI	
Allow Changes to Approvers	BBP_CHNG_AGNT_ALLOW	4.0
Select Users when Creating/Changing Approvers	BBP_CHNG_AGNT_GET	4.0

Table D.17 BAdIs relevant for Workflow in SAP SRM

If you want to use BAdIs to create customer fields, you will find Table D.18 of use.

Business Add-Ins (BAdIs)	Definition Name	Release
Customer Field Control	BBP_CUF_BAdI	4.0
Customer Fields with Standard Table Control	BBP_CUF_BAdI_2	4.0

Table D.18 BAdIs for Creating Customer Fields

If you use BAdIs for SAP XML interfacing, Table D.19 will be of use to you.

Business Add-Ins (BAdIs)	Definition Name	Release
Change SAP XML Inbound Mapping	BBP_SAPXML1_IN_BAdIEBP & SUS	4.0
Change SAP XML Outbound Mapping	BBP_SAPXML1_OUT_BAdIEBP & SUS	4.0

Table D.19 BAdIs for Use with SAP XML Interfaces

For controlling document output you can use Table D.20.

Business Add-Ins (BAdIs)	Definition Name	Release
Output Shopping Cart with Customer Form	BBP_CHANGE_SF_SC	4.0
Output Contract with Customer Form	BBP_CHANGE_SF_CTR	4.0
Print Preview for Comparison of Purchase Order Versions	BBP_CHANGE_SF_POVERS	4.0
Change Smart Form for E-Mails Relating to Bids	BBP_CHANGE_SF_BID	

Table D.20 BAdIs for Controlling Document Output

To enhance user interface configuration you can use Table D.21.

Business Add-Ins (BAdIs)	Definition Name
Determine Screen Variants	BBP_SCREENVARIANT
Field Control in Purchasing Document	BBP_UI_CONTROL_BAdI
Display of Input Helps, Search Helps, and Favorites	BBP_F4_READ_ON_ENTRY
Restrict the Display in Input Helps and Search Helps	BBP_F4_READ_ON_EXIT
Internal Temporary Storage of Favorites for Input Helps and Search Helps	BBP_F4_MEM_UPDATE
Final Saving of Favorites for Input Helps and Search Helps	BBP_F4_SAVE_DB

Table D.21 BAdIs to Enhance the User Interface Configuration

E   Customer Fields in SAP SRM

Every SAP project brings forth unique business needs and requirements; this is one of the reasons for a common saying, "Every SAP project is different." The same is the case with SAP SRM projects. Organizations implementing SAP SRM often find the need to define customer-specific fields to capture information driven by their business needs. SAP uses the terms Customer-Specific fields or User-Defined fields to describe fields that are not delivered in the standard out-of-the-box solution, but organizations can create to meet their business requirements.

Organizations can use Customer-Specific fields in the SAP SRM system to enhance the standard SAP structures and store additional information that may be unique to their business and can display, change, and search for these customer fields.

User-defined fields provide the flexibility to enhance SAP SRM screens without MODIFICATION (or CORE MOD), because these fields are supported by SAP during application of notes, support packs, and implementation of upgrades.

E.1   Customer-Specific Fields in SAP SRM Document Types

In SAP SRM, User-Defined fields can be created at the Header and Item level for the different document types. As of SRM Release 4.0, User-Defined fields are no longer specified in the CI includes but in the INCL_EEW_* structure. These are shown in Table E.1.

Document Type	Structure
Shopping Cart**	INCL_EEW_PD_HEADER_CSF_SC
	INCL_EEW_PD_ITEM_CSF_SC
Purchase Order	INCL_EEW_PD_HEADER_CSF_PO
	INCL_EEW_PD_ITEM_CSF_PO
Confirmation	INCL_EEW_PD_HEADER_CSF_CONF
	INCL_EEW_PD_ITEM_CSF_CONF
Invoice	INCL_EEW_PD_HEADER_CSF_INV
	INCL_EEW_PD_ITEM_CSF_INV

Table E.1   Structures for SRM Document Types

Document Type	Structure
Contracts	INCL_EEW_PD_HEADER_CSF_CTR
	INCL_EEW_PD_ITEM_CSF_CTR
Quotations	INCL_EEW_PD_HEADER_CSF_QUOT
	INCL_EEW_PD_ITEM_CSF_QUOT
Bid Invitations	INCL_EEW_PD_HEADER_CSF_BID
	INCL_EEW_PD_ITEM_CSF_BID

Table E.1 Structures for SRM Document Types (Cont.)

Additionally, Customer-Specific fields can also be created in the account assignment section within the shopping cart, PO, and invoice document types.

As of SAP SRM 5.0, Customer-Specific fields in the shopping cart can also be created that appear directly underneath the item overview. This allows for additional flexibility when users are creating shopping carts and need to navigate to the detail of the item level (illustrated in Figure E.1).

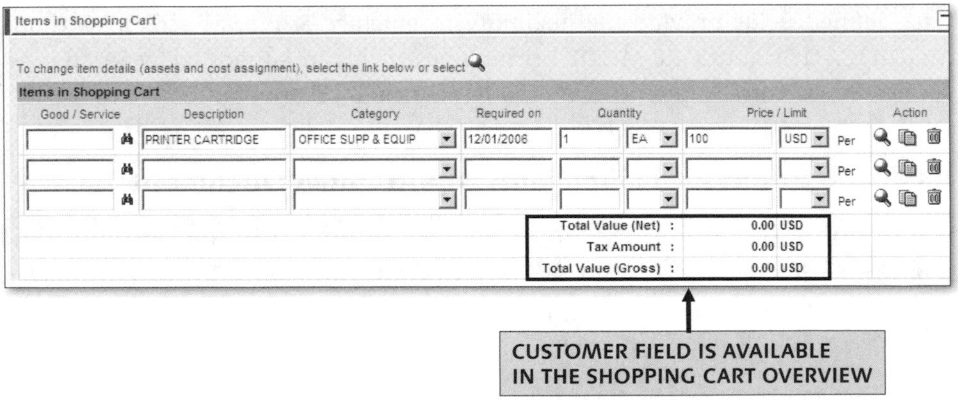

Figure E.1 Customer-Specific Fields in Shopping Cart Overview

E.1.1 Procedure for Creating a User-Defined Field

The following steps can be used as a guide for creating Customer-Specific fields in SAP SRM:

1. Identify the structure(s) to be utilized; based on the document type that needs to be changed. For example, if a new user-defined field needs to be created in the shopping cart, the structure INCL_EEW_PD_ITEM_CSF needs to be used (we use the *ITEM_CSF* instead of "HEADER_CSF*, because the header fields cannot be displayed; the shopping cart is not displayed in a Header and Item level.)

2. In Transaction SE11, append the structure identified in Step 1 with one or more User-Defined fields. Append the structure(s) using the SAP proposed structure "ZAINCL*" (e.g., for shopping cart use ZAINCL_EEW_PD_ITEM_CSF).

3. Define these document-specific fields in the append structures at the Header (INCL_EEW_PD_HEADER_CSF) and Item level (INCL_EEW_PD_ITEM_CSF) for the document type where the user-defined field needs to be created, as illustrated in Figure E.2.

4. Repeat Steps 1 through 3 above for each document type where this User-Defined field needs to be available (for example, in the PO and contract).

5. Activate all the appended structures.

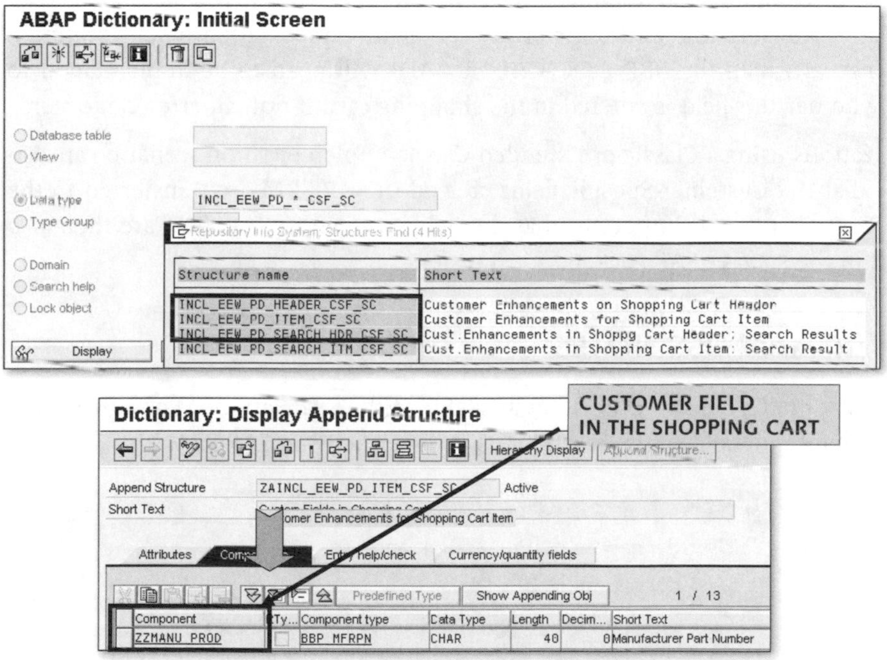

Figure E.2 Customer-Specific Field in Shopping Cart Document Type: View 2

Once the customer field is created, it is available in the document type, in our example, the shopping cart document. The customer fields created in SAP SRM are available in the Default Settings for Items section, as well as in the Item Details: ITEM section of the shopping cart.

A standard report BBP_CUF01 can be utilized to check the consistency and completeness of the User-Defined fields. It is important to understand that contents of a

User-Defined field can be transferred from a document to another only if the field is defined with exactly the same name in following document types.

The procedure for creating customer fields, defined in Section E.1.1, allows the creation of the Customer-Specific fields to store data in the SAP SRM system. These fields are then available for additional "checks" or processing in the various SRM BAdIs; in which case, the individual BAdI implementation is required. Development experts can further enhance the User-Defined fields by using the BAdI BBP_CUF_BADI_2 to control the changeability and the display of the fields. Additionally, other BAdIs can be utilized to further influence these Z fields. Let's take an example:

Assume that a new Customer-Specific field is created in the shopping cart (BUS2121) document, to capture the Manufacturer Part Number. Once this field is created, if you want to ensure that end users always enter this information when creating a shopping cart, then the BBP_DOC_CHECK_BADI will need to be implemented to check whether this field is entered in the shopping cart, if not, an error can occur.

Organizations using a Classic or Extended Classic implementation scenario can also ensure that the Customer-Specific fields created in SAP SRM are transferred to the SAP ERP backend. It is important that the fields created in SAP SRM are then also created in the specific SAP backend for transfer.

E.2   Related OSS NOTES

Table E.2 contains a list of OSS Notes available at the SAP Service Marketplace that provide helpful details on the creation of customer fields in SAP SRM.

Note	Description
458591	User-defined fields: Preparation and use
672960	User-defined fields 2
980074	Contents of old customer fields copied to new items
809630	Customer field in bid invitation and bid — How does it work?
762984	SRM40-SUS: Implementation of customer enhancement fields

Table E.2   Relevant OSS Notes

Note
A new SAP BAdI repository has been introduced on the SDN by SAP with the collaboration of the SAP community. Review it at *www.SDN.sap.com/IRJ/WIKI* and select the Supplier Relationship Management WIKI. The BAdI repository contains useful examples of BAdI code as implemented by other organizations.

F   Business Objects in SAP SRM

In SAP SRM, there are many business documents such as shopping carts, POs, contracts, bid invitations, and others. These documents are described as business objects (BOR Object) in the system. The following tables provide a list of the business objects that exist in SAP SRM and SAP ERP system. Table F.1 contains the business objects that exist in the SAP Enterprise Buyer (EB) functionality of SAP SRM.

Business Objects	Short Description
BUS2121	Shopping Cart
BUS2201	Purchase Order
BUS2209	PO Response
BUS2203	Confirmation
BUS2206	Vendor / Supplier List
BUS2205	Incoming Invoice
BUS2210	Invoice Default
BUS2000113	Purchase Contract
BUS2200	Bid Invitation
BUS2202	Vendor Bid
BUS2008	Auction

Table F.1   Business Objects in Enterprise Buyer

Table F.2 contains the business objects that exist in the supplier self-services (SUS) functionality of SAP SRM.

Business Objects	Short Description
BUS2230	Purchase Order in SUS
BUS2232	PO Confirmation in SUS
BUS2233	Confirmation in SUS
BUS2203	Confirmation/GR
BUS2231	Shipping Notification in SUS (ASN)
BUS2234	Invoice in SUS

Table F.2   Business Objects in SUS

Table F.3 contains the business objects that exist in the SAP ERP system.

Business Objects	Short Description
BUS2093	Reservation in ERP
BUS2009	Requisition in ERP
BUS2012	Purchase Order in ERP
BUS2013	Scheduling Agreement in ERP
BUS2014	Contract in ERP

Table F.3 Business Objects in SAP ERP

G Authorization Objects

In Chapter 11, we discussed the role of security in SAP SRM. You learned about roles, profiles, authorization objects, and transactions. The authorization concept protects transactions, programs, and services in SAP SRM from unauthorized access. This appendix contains a listing of the authorization objects that are available in SAP SRM as of release 4.0. Organizations can use these objects to control the level of authorization available to users when creating business documents in SAP SRM, such as shopping carts, POs, and invoices.

For example, in the Shopping Cart application, you can select a cost center or SAP General Ledger account by using the Binoculars icon (the F4 search help) from the corresponding SAP ERP backend.

If you want to enable or restrict this option, your security team can do this via the authorizations in Transaction PFCG. This can be achieved by using the authorization object BBP_FUNCT (or M_BBP_SHLP for release SAP SRM 4.0). If the value BE_F4_HELP is activated, then the call for F4 help is enabled in ERP.

Tables G.1 and G.2 give information on authorization objects in SAP SRM 5.0 and SAP SRM. Table G.3 provides information on the new authorization objects that have been created in SAP SRM 7.0.

Authorization Object	Description
S_BBP_PID	Authorization check for PID tree maintenance
M_BBP_ASS	Authorization for Create Attachment Master
M_BBP_ADM	Authorization for administration of application layer BBP
BBP_BUDGET	Authorization for budget display
M_BBP_CTR	Authorization for contracts
M_BBP_SHLP	Authorization for search helps
M_BBP_VE	Authorization for vendor evaluation in Enterprise Buyer
BBP_PD_AUC	Auction
BBP_PD_BID	Bid Invitation
BBP_PD_CNF	Confirmation
BBP_PD_CTR	Contracts

Table G.1 Authorization Objects in BBP Component Class in SAP SRM

Authorization Object	Description
BBP_PD_PCO	Purchase order response
BBP_PD_PO	Purchase orders
BBP_PD_QUO	Quotations
BBP_PD_SC	Shopping carts
M_BBP_BID	Bid Invitation in Enterprise Buyer
M_BBP_I_EX	External invoice entry in Enterprise Buyer
M_BBP_Q_EX	External bid creation in Enterprise Buyer
M_BBP_SES	External PO confirmation in Enterprise Buyer
M_BBP_I_IN	Internal invoice entry in Enterprise Buyer
M_BBP_CONF	Internal PO confirmation in Enterprise Buyer
M_BBP_Q_IN	Internal bid processing in Enterprise Buyer
BBP_BUYER	Maintenance (create or change) of buying company in EBP systems
M_BBP_PC	Procurement card master data
M_BBP_PO	Purchase order in Enterprise Buyer
M_BBP_AUC	SRM Live Auction
BBP_PD_VL	SRM: Edit vendor list
BBP_FUNCT	SRM: General access authorizations in EBP
BBP_PD_INV	SRM: Process Invoices
BBP_VEND	SRM: Vendor activities in EBP
BBP_SUS_PD	SUS: Document access in SUS (replaced in SAP SRM 5.0)
M_BBP_IM_1	Web goods receipt against purchase order: Plant

Table G.1 Authorization Objects in BBP Component Class in SAP SRM (Cont.)

Authorization Object	Description
BBP_CTR_2	Contracts (used in addition to the BBP_PD_CTR object)
BBP_SUS_AC	User authorization per SUS actions
BBP_SUS_P2	SUS documents (replaces BBP_SUS_PD authorization object)

Table G.2 Authorization Objects in SAP SRM 5.0

In SAP SRM 7.0, the following authorization objects have been newly created.

Authorization Object	Description
BBP_ADVS	SRM Advanced Search. This object is used to define which Business Objects are available in the Advanced Search
BBP_BID_EV	SRM Bid Evaluation Auth Object
BBP_ROLE	This object is used to identify the role of a particular user in SRM. (e.g., Employee, Manager, etc.)

Table G.3 New Authorization Objects in SAP SRM 7.0

H Quiz for Testing your SAP SRM Knowledge

We created this quiz for *www.searchsap.com*, in mid-2006. It should be beneficial for both beginners and experts, and the answers will help you understand many of the concepts discussed in this book. Additionally, this quiz will be helpful for consultants planning to take the SAP SRM certification exam, because you can expect similar questions and format on that exam.

H.1 Questions

Mark the correct response for the following questions and get the correct answers in Section H.2. Explanations for the answers appear in Section H.3.

1. **True or False: The terms Supplier Relationship Management (SRM) and Enterprise Buyer (EB) are the same, and can be used interchangeably.**
   a) True
   b) False

2. **Which of the following is not a standard scenario available for SRM?**
   a) Self-Service Procurement
   b) Plan-Driven Procurement
   c) Service Procurement
   d) Extended Classic Scenario
   e) Catalog Content Management
   f) Spend Analysis
   g) Strategic Sourcing

3. **The following technical component(s) is/are mandatory for the self-service scenario in SAP SRM 5.0:**
   a) SAP SRM Server 5.5
   b) SAP Catalog Content Management 2.0 (CCM)
   c) SAP NetWeaver Process Integration (SAP NetWeaver PI) Content for SAP SRM Server 5.5
   d) Live Auction Cockpit (LACWPS) 5.0

4. **Which of the following reports update the status of the follow-on documents within the shopping cart history?**

   a) BBP_GET_STATUS_2

   b) CLEAN_REQREQ_UP

   c) RSWUWFMLEC

   d) BBP_BW_SC2

5. **What is the function of the RSWUWFMLEC report in SAP EB?**

   a) To transfer POs from SAP EB to the backend system in a Standalone scenario.

   b) To allow printing of the shopping cart.

   c) To send notifications for work items via email to email recipients.

   d) To provide approval preview in the shopping cart.

6. **The following statements are true for the Extended Classic Implementation scenario:**

   a) The leading document is created in SAP SRM and a copy of the document is transferred to the backend SAP system.

   b) The follow-on documents of confirmation and invoice can only be entered in the SAP backend system.

   c) The PO can be changed in SAP ERP.

   d) The SAP NetWeaver Portal is not compatible with the Extended Classic Implementation scenario of SAP SRM.

7. **Which of the following statements are correct about the organization structure in SAP EB?**

   a) SAP SRM users can be created simply by using Transaction SU01.

   b) An organization structure is required. The self-service scenario cannot be implemented without the organization structure.

   c) The inheritance administration of attributes from PPOMA can be configured in table T77OMATTR.

   d) The report BBP_CHECK_CONSISTENCY checks the consistency of the organization plan.

8. **What statement(s) is correct regarding Plan-Driven Procurement in SAP SRM?**

   a) It is one of the business scenarios in SAP SRM.

   b) It only supports the sourcing or procurement of requirements generated in APO.

c) The requirements created in the backend system can be transferred to SAP EB where a shopping cart is created, and can then utilize the workflow start conditions rules to get approval(s).

d) The report BBP_EXTREQ_TRANSFER is utilized in the SAP backend to transfer the relevant requisitions to SAP EB.

9. **Which of the following is true concerning the workflows in SAP SRM?**

a) There is only one workflow template provided by SAP for the shopping cart workflow. All others need to be customized based on the project.

b) The approval preview allows the end user to visualize all required approvals in a graphical and tabular format.

c) As an alternative to the workflows supplied in the standard system, you can use the SLAPPROVER workflow to ensure more flexible assignment of users. This is a one-step approval workflow.

d) Ad-hoc approval functionality dynamically inserts approvers or reviewers within the approval chain for a document.

10. **What elementary step(s) is/are associated with workflow customizing in SAP SRM?**

a) The workflows have to first be activated in customizing.

b) The organization buffer of the organizational plan has to be refreshed first, using Transaction SWU_OBUF.

c) The IMG activity, "Maintain Standard Settings for SAP Business Workflow," can be configured by any user with access to this transaction.

d) Workflow start conditions need to be configured by business objects (e.g., BUS2121 for the shopping cart).

11. **What does the transaction BBPGETVD do?**

a) It transfers the materials from the backend SAP ERP system into SAP EB.

b) It transfers the terms of payment of the vendors from the backend into SAP EB.

c) It replicates the vendors from the backend system into the vendor organization (PPOMA_BBP).

d) All vendor master records are transferred from the backend and the business partner numbers are entered for these vendors in SAP EB.

12. **Which statement(s) concerning master data in SAP SRM is/are correct?**

a) Material Master Data is transferred from the SAP backend to SAP EB using middleware.

b) Product Categories correspond to material groups in the SAP backend.

c) Business partner master records correspond to the vendor master records in the SAP backend.

d) The vendors are downloaded into SAP SRM from the SAP backend via the middleware.

13. **What statements pertaining to the OCI interface are correct?**

a) OCI allows organizations to connect their SAP EB systems with online catalogs like Office Depot, Dell, and Grainger and transfer their catalog data into the SAP EB shopping carts.

b) OCI describes the data exchange between the SAP EB and external catalog applications.

c) The OCI is the Open Content Interface that ensures that the correct content is transferred to SAP EB from the catalog.

d) If products are contained in the catalog and are already maintained in the product master, SAP EB does not require any inbound parameters for transfer of the product data, because this data is already known in SAP EB.

e) The OCI interface contains inbound and outbound parameters.

14. **Which of the following are correct as of release SAP SRM 4.0?**

a) Customer-Specific fields can be created for the shopping cart, PO, and contract documents in SAP SRM.

b) The Procurement Card functionality in SAP EB can be implemented in the Classic and Extended Classic scenarios.

c) ITS can now be utilized integrated with the Web Application Server 6.40. This can decrease the total cost of ownership (TCO).

d) Archiving documents is not supported in SAP SRM.

15. **What statements pertaining to the account assignment in SAP SRM are correct?**

a) A real-time validation occurs in the SAP backend system.

b) A SAP General Ledger account has to be assigned to the product category for the validation of the accounts.

c) A local validation in SAP EB independent of a backend system is also possible.

d) The only account assignment categories available in SAP SRM are Cost Center (CC) and Asset (AS).

H.2   Answers

You can check your responses and see how many you got correct by going through Table H.1.

Question	Correct Answer
1	B
2	D
3	A, B
4	A
5	C
6	A
7	B, C, D
8	A, D
9	B, C, D
10	A, D
11	C
12	A, B, C
13	A, B, E
14	A, C
15	A, C

Table H.1   Correct Responses

H.3   Explanations for the Answers

This section is designed to give some insight into the correct answers and the thought processes involved in arriving at the correct response:

1. **True or False: The terms Supplier Relationship Management (SRM) and Enterprise Buyer (EB) are the same, and can be used interchangeably.**

    Answer: B

    SAP SRM and SAP EB are often used interchangeably, but they are not the same. Enterprise Buyer (EB) is a functionality within the SAP SRM application.

    SAP launched its e-Procurement solution in 1999 with B2B Procurement 1.0. later branded as Enterprise Buyer Professional (EBP). It started off as just a catalog-based Employee Self-Service tool and evolved into a robust e-Procurement solution. In 2003, SAP launched SRM, Supplier Relationship Management, which not only provided an e-Procurement solution but also added a supplier collaboration engine. Since then, SAP SRM has become a best of breed multi-purpose solution. Today, SAP SRM focuses on the core supply processes of procurement, sourcing, contract management, and supplier enablement.

2. **Which of the following is not a standard scenario available for SAP SRM?**

Answer: D

The Extended Classic Scenario is an Implementation Scenario for SAP EB. It is not a Business Scenario.

In the Extended Classic Scenario, the PO is created locally within SAP EB. If the data in the shopping cart is insufficient to generate a complete PO, the data is supplemented manually within SAP EB before being transferred to the backend system. The purchase order in SAP EB is the leading PO. Goods receipts (confirmations) and invoices can be entered in SAP EB or in the backend.

3. **The following technical component(s) is/are mandatory for the self-service scenario in SAP SRM 5.0:**

Answer: A, B

The self-service scenario does not require SAP NetWeaver PI or the Live Auction Cockpit as mandatory technical functionalities. SAP NetWeaver PI is only required if XML-based communication/integration is required (e.g., CCM material master replication from SAP ERP to SAP EB to SAP CCM). The Live Auction Cockpit is also not a mandatory component for the Self-Service Scenario.

According to the SAP SRM 5.0 functionality matrix published by SAP, the CCM component is a required install. However, organizations that choose not to utilize the CCM solution would have the option of not configuring CCM.

4. **Which of the following reports update the status of the follow-on documents within the shopping cart history?**

Answer: A

The BBP_GET_STATUS_2 job is scheduled to retrieve the status from the backend system. Once a Req. or a PO is generated in SAP EB, the spooler transfers it over to the backend. This job then gets the status of the created object and provides the appropriate input to the Check Status transaction of the end user's shopping cart.

The CLEAN_REQREQ_UP job ensures that the subsequent objects of shopping cart items and the IDocs, which can be generated from confirmations and invoices, are updated successfully in the backend system. If the subsequent objects are created successfully, the report sets the status of the shopping cart to ‚6' and deletes temporary data in the SAP EB system; it is not needed there anymore (this is the reason why it is called a "cleaner" job).

5. **What is the function of the RSWUWFMLEC report in SAP EB?**

   Answer: C

   This job is scheduled to enable offline approval functionality in SAP SRM and to allow the work items in the SAP SRM user's inbox to be transferred to their preferred email client (e.g., Microsoft Outlook, IBM Lotus Notes, Novell Group-Wise, etc.). Emails are only sent to those users for which the user attributes (FORWARD_WI) "Flag: Forward work item," are maintained in PPOMA_BBP. This is useful for users who do not use the integrated inbox of the SAP EB system, so that another mail client can process work items in their usual mail client.

   There are two steps in this job:

   1. The initial step moves the approval work item from the SAP inbox to SAP connect (TCode: SCOT). This step is executed by report: RSCONN01.

   2. The second step moves the same work item from SAP connect to the organization's mail server, which then sends the email to the user's preferred email client. This step is executed by report: RSWUWFMLEC.

6. **The following statements are true for the Extended Classic Implementation scenario:**

   Answer: A

   In the current SAP SRM 5.0 release, SAP provides three implementation scenarios for use: Classic, Extended Classic, and Standalone. In the Extended Classic scenario, the entire procurement process takes place locally in SAP EB and a copy of the data is replicated to the backend system. In essence, this scenario is an extension of the Classic scenario.

   The PO in the backend SAP system is a read-only copy that enables goods receipt, service entry, and invoice verification in the backend system. The backend PO cannot be changed. If you wish to make any changes to the PO, you must do so in SAP EB. Once you save these changes, they are transferred to the backend PO.

7. **Which of the following statements are correct about the organization structure in SAP EB?**

   Answer: B, C, and D

   Users in SAP SRM cannot simply be created using Transaction SU01. For valid system access, a user has to belong to an organization unit, a position, have a business partner ID, a central person, and a SU01-User ID.

   An organization structure and a set of user attributes are required for working with a SAP EB professional. Each user attribute represents a value that is stored under a particular name within the organizational structure. Depending on a user's role, a different set of attributes is required.

The report BBP_CHECK_CONSISTENCY (that can also be called via transaction BBP_ATTR_CHECK), checks the consistency of the organizational plan. It also checks whether the attributes for companies, purchasing organizations, purchasing groups, and users are defined correctly for the individual applications.

8. **What statement(s) is correct regarding Plan-Driven Procurement in SAP SRM?**

Answer: A, D

The Plan-Driven Procurement Scenario supports the sourcing and procurement of requirements from external planning systems within SAP EB. The requirements coming from an SAP backend system could result from an MRP run, or a PM or PS document or could be created manually. In addition, requirements from APO can be transferred into SAP EB. Once the requirements are transferred, if the data is complete and unique, PO(s) can be created automatically in SAP EB. If data is missing, the professional purchaser has to complete the missing information in sourcing or via process POs.

If customizing is set up for sourcing, the requirements appear in the sourcing transaction; technically, an interim shopping cart (BUS2121 object) is created, but this is not relevant for any approval(s).

Requirements from an SAP backend are replicated via RFC into the SAP EB. The report BBP_EXTREQ_TRANSFER can either be executed manually or scheduled in the background to transfer these requirements into SAP EB.

9. **Which of the following is true concerning the workflows in SAP SRM?**

Answer: B, C, and D

SAP provides multiple workflow templates for the shopping cart. One of the workflows is Single Step Approval Over limit, where the Requisitioners are assigned spending limits and approvers are assigned approval limits. Spending limit approvers are assigned via the attribute in the org structure SLAP-PROVER instead of depending on the hierarchy of orgs, positions, and users. Based on the shopping cart value, the approver with the ultimate approval value is determined.

In the SAP SRM shopping cart, approval preview provides a user with an approval flow simulation. The user can be aware of the approval chain, and if required, add approvers in addition to the ones determined by the system.

The process of adding additional approvers on the fly is Ad-Hoc approval functionality. In the approval preview, employees can specify a different approver for a shopping cart or other document at runtime. This might be necessary, if, for example, a manager is temporarily absent and has not specified a substitute for shopping cart approval.

10. **What elementary step(s) is/are associated with workflow customizing in SRM?**

Answer: A, D

Prior to using any of the scenarios in SAP SRM, the workflow environment needs to be configured. Even if no approvals are to be triggered in your business process, SAP SRM needs to be configured for triggering the "no-approval" workflows.

We can configure the standard workflow environment in the IMG • SRM • CROSS-APPLICATIONS • SAP BUSINESS WORKFLOW. Standard tasks and workflows can be activated for use.

A user who belongs to the super user group should perform the automatic workflow customizing activity. If you belong to the super user group, and the WF-BATCH user does not exist, it is created and automatically gets the maximum authorization of the current user (SY-UNAME). The system user must have the authorization SAP_ALL if the workflow system is to function without problems.

In the start conditions in customizing, you define which workflow is started under what conditions. The conditions always apply for the entire shopping cart, confirmation, or invoice. For example, you decide that shopping carts must be approved if the total value exceeds $1,000.

11. **What does the Transaction BBPGETVD do?**

Answer: C

Transaction BBPGETVD exists to download vendor information as business partner information from the backend system into the SAP EB. Take the following into account: whether the SAP EB is to assign numbers from the internal number range for business partners for the vendors to be copied or whether the vendor numbers are to be copied from the backend system.

However, it cannot be scheduled to automatically synchronize vendor master data between SAP SRM and SAP ERP. Instead, in customizing for vendor synchronization, you define between which SAP or SAP ERP backend systems and the SAP EB you wish to automatically synchronize the vendor master data. This setting is necessary to start a job-based execution of the synchronization, so that the vendor master data that is newly created or changed in the backend is updated regularly in the SAP EB System (SRM IMG: SRM SERVER • TECHNICAL BASIC SETTINGS • SETTINGS FOR VENDOR SYNCHRONIZATION).

12. **Which statement(s) concerning master data in SAP SRM is/are correct?**

Answer: A, B, C

Master data in SAP SRM can be downloaded from the SAP backend. This data includes product master records, business partner master records, and product categories, products (material), service masters, and product categories (material groups) are downloaded via the middleware. The middleware is a set of programs that exist partly in the SAP EB and partly in the SAP backend plug-in.

SAP EB uses the SAP business partner concept. An internal or external business partner is created in SAP EB for every person, organization, or group of people who could be involved in a business transaction. The vendor is an external business partner. Conversely, plant is an internal business partner. A shopping cart requester, a plant, an organization, a creditor, vendor, a bidder, or a marketplace are all business partners within SAP SRM.

Vendors are not downloaded via the middleware — instead using a transaction BBPGETVD or via the synchronization report.

13. **What statements pertaining to the OCI interface are correct?**

Answer: A, B, E

The Open Catalog Interface (OCI) describes the data exchange between the SAP EB and external catalog applications. OCI enables the transmission of selected goods and services from an external catalog to the SAP EB. The external catalog is located either within the intranet or somewhere on the Internet. SAP's Open Catalog Interface uses standard Internet protocols.

Punch-Out or Round-Trip allows suppliers to maintain branded content on their own websites and extend their e-commerce capabilities to buyers. By simply connecting to the supplier's website, buyers can select and configure products from the supplier's custom catalog. The supplier can provide buyer-specific items and pricing.

After products are selected, the Round-Trip service automatically brings the required item details back into the buying application. At this point, the order is routed through the normal requisition and approval processes and eventually converted into a PO that is sent back to the supplier for order fulfillment. The initial connection, authentication, and final return of the order information are all facilitated with the SAP Open Catalog Interface (OCI).

14. **Which of the following are correct as of release SAP SRM 4.0?**

    Answer: A, C

    Customer fields can be used in shopping carts, POs, confirmations, invoices, and contracts at the Header and Item level, and for account assignment. Customer fields can be displayed in the standard interface or on a custom screen. A BAdI is available for customer-defined subscreens.

    In SAP EB, you can specify procurement card as the payment method when purchasing items. However, this functionality is only supported in the Standalone or Local implementation scenarios. The Classic and Extended Classic scenarios do not support this functionality. Some organizations have handled this limitation via development.

    As of SAP NetWeaver ,04, ITS is available integrated with the SAP NetWeaver functionality, SAP Web Application Server 6.40, as an Internet Communication Framework (ICF) service. The integrated ITS runs on one machine, reducing the number of servers and decreases the total cost of ownership (TCO).

    Archiving is a process to remove bulk or outdated data from your database that is no longer needed in your system. Many documents including the shopping cart, PO, confirmation, and contracts can be archived in SAP SRM. In SAP SRM 4.0, the restoration of archived data is not yet possible.

15. **What statements pertaining to the account assignment in SAP SRM are correct?**

    Answer: A, C

    In the SAP EB, account assignment validation can be done in the following environments:

    ▶ In the SAP EB (local validation of FI data)
    ▶ In the backend system (real-time validation of FI data)
    ▶ You can choose not to validate at all.

    In the configuration, you can enter the SAP General Ledger account to be used based on product category and account assignment category.

    The account assignment categories used in the SAP EB system are Asset (AS) — the local counterpart of the backend account assignment category A. Cost Center (CC) — the local counterpart of the backend account assignment category K. FI — the local counterpart of the backend account assignment category K. NET — the local counterpart of the backend account assignment category N. Order (OR) — the local counterpart of the backend account assignment category F. SO — the local counterpart of the backend account assignment category C. And WBS — the local counterpart of the backend account assignment category P.

I   System Refresh Procedures

On many SAP SRM projects, a need arises to copy one system landscape to another. For example, the project testing strategy might require multiple testing cycles and for each cycle a separate client landscape is required. In this example, the project might want to have a Golden Client in the QA environment, let's say as 400, where all configuration and master data is created. Now for testing purposes, the project team needs four additional clients: 410, 420, 430, 440, each for a separate cycle of testing.

SAP SRM contains a number of different components and is often connected to one or more SAP backend systems. Therefore, the client copy or system landscape copy requires a number of steps that need to be followed by the BASIS and Functional teams. There are obvious tasks that are required of the BASIS team; however, in an SAP SRM environment a number of steps might be required of the Functional teams as well. Therefore, the project team needs to develop a task list and sequence of steps outlined that are owned by the BASIS and functional teams. Often, the BASIS teams are unaware of all the steps required.

Until recently, a comprehensive guide did not exist for project teams to follow to complete this task. However, SAP has recently published an OSS Note that is fairly comprehensive and will serve useful for project teams during this task. Project teams need to review this note and list all the activities that are relevant for their project scope. Assign responsibilities between the BASIS and Functional ownership. The sequence of steps is important to follow. For example, the functional team cannot make changes to the Organization Structure until the BASIS team has made the RFC and Logical system changes.

> **Note**
>
> Review OSS Note: 995771 — System Landscape Copy for SAP SRM 4.0 and 5.0

J Organization Structure Attributes

The Organization Structure is considered the heart of SAP SRM because it controls a number of different user and organizational attributes in SAP SRM. Table J.1 contains a list of the attributes available in SAP SRM. These attributes are maintained in the organization maintenance transaction PPOMA_BBP in SRM.

Attribute	Example Value	Description	Mandatory
ACS	BACKEND	▶ Key for the SAP ERP Financials Financial Accounting and SAP ERP Financials Financial Controlling backend. ▶ Required for Invoices without PO reference and ▶ Local Invoices. ▶ Define the backend system in the Customizing Path in the IMG ▶ SAP EB edition N Basic ▶ Settings N Define Backend Systems	X
ADDR_BILLT		Default bill-to party address in PO	
ADDR_SHIPT		Delivery address in PO. Specify at least one delivery address and set it as the default address.	
AN1		Account assignment (Asset) object permitted. Specifies the asset in the backend system.	
AN2		▶ Account assignment (Asset sub-number) ▶ Object permitted. Specifies the asset subnumber in the backend system	

Table J.1 Attributes in SAP SRM Organizational Structure

Attribute	Example Value	Description	Mandatory
ANK		<ul><li>Account assignment (Asset class) object permitted</li><li>Specifies the asset class in the</li><li>backend system</li></ul>	
ANR		<ul><li>Account assignment (Order) object permitted</li><li>Specifies the order in the back-end system</li></ul>	
APO		<ul><li>Account assignment (Sales Order Item) object permitted</li><li>Specifies the sales order item in the backend system</li></ul>	
APPRV_LIM		<ul><li>Approval limit for manager roles. Currency should be specified</li><li>Note that this attribute must be maintained in the Extended Attributes tab</li></ul>	
BSA	LOCAL\EC BACKEND\EC	<ul><li>Document type in backend/ local system</li><li>The document type you define here, has to be defined in the backend system, too.</li></ul>	X
BUK	LOCAL\1234 BACKEND\1234	Company code in backend and/ or local system if you are using backend and/or standalone.	X
BWA	BACKEND\201	Movement type in backend system. This is only required if reservations are created in the backend system.	X
CAT	CATALOG ID	<ul><li>Name of the catalog an organi-zation/user is allowed to use</li><li>This attribute must have been defined during customizing.</li></ul>	

Table J.1 Attributes in SAP SRM Organizational Structure (Cont.)

Attribute	Example Value	Description	Mandatory
CNT	LOCAL\1234 BACKEND\1234	▸ Account assignment (cost center) object permitted. Specifies the cost center in the backend system. ▸ If you are using only numerical cost centers in the backend system, you need to maintain leading zeros: <SYS>\0000001234 instead of <SYS>\1234	
COMPANY		▸ Company. Identifies a part of a company that functions as a separate legal entity ▸ Set by Type tab flag Company	
CUR	EUR	Key for the local currency	X
DP_PROC_TY		Transaction type: Direct material ▸ Specifies the transaction type used when POs for direct materials are created via BAPI, shopping cart, or bid invitation/bid ▸ This attribute MUST be maintained for the responsible purchasing group (see also TEND_TYPE) ▸ The specified transaction type must correspond to the document type used in the backend system for direct material POs with external number assignment ▸ Path in the Implementation Guide (IMG): ENTERPRISE BUYER PROFESSIONAL EDITION • APPLICATION-SPECIFIC BASIC SETTINGS • DEFINE TRANSACTION TYPES	

Table J.1 Attributes in SAP SRM Organizational Structure (Cont.)

Attribute	Example Value	Description	Mandatory
ITS_DEST	http://\<server\> /scripts/wgate/	Needed for the administrator application monitors and for tendering	X
IS_COMPANY		▶ Flag that identifies the org. unit as an independent legal entity ▶ Define an organizational unit near the top of the org. plan as a company by setting this flag ▶ If other org. units at a lower level in the plan represent subsidiaries, the flag should be set for these, too. ▶ Set by Type tab, flag Company	
IS_PGR		▶ Flag that identifies an org. unit as a purchasing group ▶ Set by Type tab	
IS_POR		▶ Flag that identifies an org. unit as a purchasing organization ▶ Set by Type tab	
KNT	CC	▶ Account assignments (account assignment category) permitted ▶ Has to be previously defined in Customizing: Enterprise Buyer professional edition Account Assignment ▶ Define Account Assignment Categories	X
LAG		Storage location	
PRCAT		▶ Product category that an organizational unit or user is allowed to order. As opposed to the WGR attribute, PRCAT is displayed in readable form ▶ Note that this attribute must be maintained in the Extended Attributes tab	

Table J.1 Attributes in SAP SRM Organizational Structure (Cont.)

Attribute	Example Value	Description	Mandatory
PRI	XXXX	Key for the printer that an organizational unit or user is going to use by default. Has to be defined previously.	
PRO		▶ Account assignment (WBS) object permitted ▶ WBS element (individual structural element in a work breakdown structure representing the hierarchical organization of an SAP ERP project) in the backend system	
PURCH_GRP		▶ Number of the organizational unit that is indicated as the local purchasing group in the organizational plan ▶ Set by Type tab, Purchasing Group	
PURCH_GRPX		▶ Number of the organizational unit that is indicated as the SAP ERP purchasing group in the organizational plan ▶ Set by Type tab, SAP ERP purchasing group	
PURCH_ORG		▶ Number of the organizational unit that is indicated as the local purchasing organization in the organizational plan ▶ Set by Type tab, Purchasing Organization	
PURCH_ORGX		▶ Number of the organizational unit that is indicated as the SAP ERP purchasing organization in the organizational plan ▶ Set by Type tab, R/3 purchasing organization	
REQUESTER	O 50000001	▶ Ship-to party for which a user or organizational unit will be allowed to order	

Table J.1 Attributes in SAP SRM Organizational Structure (Cont.)

Attribute	Example Value	Description	Mandatory
RESP_PGRP	O 50000001	▶ Only define for organizational units that are purchasing departments ▶ Organizational unit(s) or users for which this purchasing group is responsible ▶ This is a mandatory attribute for organizational units for which the attributes PURCH_GRP or PURCH_GRPX are defined ▶ See Responsible_POrg_PGrp	X
RESP_PRCAT		▶ Product category for which this department is responsible, in readable form (not GUID). Only define for organizational units that are purchasing departments. ▶ This attribute works in conjunction with the PRCAT attribute. It also must be maintained in the Extended Attributes tab.	
RESP_WGR	123	▶ Only define for organizational units that are purchasing departments: (optional)Product ▶ category for which this department is responsible. ▶ Maintain GUID — select product category via F4 search help. If system does not automatically convert product category into GUID, proceed as follows: <SM30> Table: T77OMATTR, choose	

Table J.1 Attributes in SAP SRM Organizational Structure (Cont.)

Attribute	Example Value	Description	Mandatory
		▶ Maintain, flag BBP, double-click on Attribute/Scenarios, go down to Attribute RESP_WGR, and change the matchcode from BBP_ATTR_F4 to BBP_ATTR_F4_PROD_CAT ▶ See Responsible_Porg_PGrp	
ROLE	SAP_BBP_STAL_EMPLOYEE	▶ All role(s) that can be adopted by a person belonging to this organizational unit ▶ Not relevant for vendors or bidders ▶ Use only the SAP_BBP_STAL_xxx composite roles, or customer amended versions. See Roles.	
SF_FOOTER		SAP Smart Forms: Footer line	
SF_GRAPHIC		Company logo. Used by Smart Forms when POs or contracts are printed.	X
SF_HEADER		SAP Smart Forms: Header line	
SLAPPROVER		Specifies the approver used in workflows based on a spending limit. If an employee with a spending limit of $500 orders a shopping cart with a total value of $600, the employee's spending limit has been exceeded and the spending limit approval workflow is started. The workflow determines the manager to approve the shopping cart on the basis of the value for the attribute SLAPPROVER.	

Table J.1 Attributes in SAP SRM Organizational Structure (Cont.)

Attribute	Example Value	Description	Mandatory
SPEND_LIM		▶ Spend limit for user. If this exceeded the spending limit, approval workflow is triggered. ▶ Currency should be specified. ▶ This attribute must be maintained in the Extended Attributes tab.	X
SYS	BACKEND	MM Backend system used (if backend system is used)	X
TEND_TYPE		Bid invitation transaction type ▶ Specifies the transaction type for bid invitations created automatically in the PLM (collaborative engineering) scenario ▶ Define this attribute or the purchasing group responsible for the organizational unit of the entry channel ▶ Path in the Implementation Guide (IMG): ENTERPRISE BUYER PROFESSIONAL EDITION • APPLICATION-SPECIFIC BASIC SETTINGS • DEFINE TRANSACTION TYPES	
TOG		Tolerance Group Using this attribute you define a user group for which tolerance checks are used when quantity or value tolerances for deliveries or invoices are exceeded	
VENDOR_ACS	BACKEND	Vendor Root: Accounting system for the vendor Specifies the backend system where the accounting for the vendor is checked	X
VENDOR_SYS	BACKEND and/or LOCAL	Vendor Root System in which POs can be created for this vendor	X

Table J.1 Attributes in SAP SRM Organizational Structure (Cont.)

Attribute	Example Value	Description	Mandatory
WGR (GUID32)	123	Product category that an organizational unit (or user) is allowed to order. Define a default value. For example, if a user mainly purchases office materials, it would make sense to specify office materials as the default value. Maintain GUID — select product category via F4 search help. If system does not automatically convert product cat into GUID proceed as follows: <SM30> Table: T77OMATTR, choose Maintain, flag BBP, double-click on Attribute/ Scenarios, go down to Attribute RESP_WGR and change the matchcode from BBP_ATTR_F4 to: -BBP_ATTR_F4_PROD_CAT -See also Create_Product_ Hierarchies to -enable searching to return GUID results	X
WRK	BACKEND\1234	Plant (in the backend system)	

Table J.1 Attributes in SAP SRM Organizational Structure (Cont.)

K Useful Transactions and Function Modules

In this appendix, we have provided some of the most utilized transactions and function modules in the SAP SRM system. You will find these to be extremely helpful during your SAP SRM project implementation and assist in troubleshooting issues.

This appendix is divided into multiple sections so it is easier for you to find transactions (TCode), function modules (FM), Programs, or Tables based on the application area within SAP SRM. Transaction codes can be executed directly in the SRM GUI. The Function Modules are executed using Transaction SE37 and then entering the individual function module. Programs are executed using Transaction SE38 and then entering the individual program name. Tables are found using Transaction SE16 and then entering the individual table name.

Let's begin with reviewing the different transactions, function modules, and tables that assist with the Shopping Cart (SC) application (Table K.1). Then we will continue with the different application areas further below. Tables K.1 through K.6 cover the transaction or function modules and their codes.

Transaction or Function Module	Description	Type
BBPSC01	Shopping Cart — Extended Form	TCode
BBPSC02	Shopping Cart — Wizard	TCode
BBPSC03	Shopping Cart — Limited Functions Form	TCode
BBPSC04	Check Status	TCode
BBPSC05	Public Template — Create	TCode
BBPSC06	Public Template — Change	TCode
BBPCF01	Vendor Confirmation	TCode
BBPCF02	Employee Confirmation	TCode
BBPCF03	Central Confirmation	TCode
BBPIV01	Vendor Invoice Entry	TCode
BBPIV02	Employee Invoice Entry	TCode
BBPIV03	Central Invoice Entry	TCode

Table K.1 Shopping Cart Application

Transaction or Function Module	Description	Type
BBPSOCO01	Carry out Sourcing	TCode
BBP_POC	Process Purchase Orders	TCode
BBP_CTR_MAIN	Process Contracts	TCode
BBPWLRA01	Redistribute Workload	TCode
BBPALVMAINT	Process Vendor Lists	TCode
BBPADM_COCKPIT	Application Monitors	TCode
BBP_QUOT	Process Bid	TCode
BBP_BW_SC2	Shopping Cart status Report in SAP SRM	TCode
BBP_PD	SRM Document Report — SC, PO, etc.	TCode
BBP_MON_SC	Monitor Shopping Cart — This is accessed using the Web application Monitor Shopping Cart. Typically in the SAP SRM Administrator role.	TCode
BBP_PD_DOC_CHECK	Makes all checks for the document — SC, PO, etc	FM
BBP_PD_SC_GETDETAIL	Shopping cart details	FM
CRMD_ORDERADM_H	Shopping cart header details	Table
CRMD_ORDERADM_I	Shopping cart Item details	Table
BBP_DOCUMENT_TAB	Table with documents in relationship with POs and confirmations not yet cleared in SAP SRM	Table

Table K.1 Shopping Cart Application (Cont.)

Transaction or Function Module	Description	Type
PPOCA_BBP	Create Organizational Structure	TCode
PPOMA_BBP	Maintain Organizational Structure	TCode
PPOSA_BBP	Display Organizational Structure	TCode
PPOMV_BBP	Create Vendor Organization	TCode
BBP_BP_OM_INTEGRATE	Synchronize / Verify Org Structure. Also used when integrating the SAP ERP HCM Organizational Structure	TCode
RHOMATTRIBUTES_ANALYZE	Analysis of attribute inheritance	Program
RHOMATTRIBUTES_CONSISTENCY	Consistency check for attributes	Program

Table K.2 Organizational Structure Application

Transaction or Function Module	Description	Type
RHOMATTRIBUTES_REPLACE	Mass change of attributes in organizational structure	Program
BBP_ATTR_CHECK	Check organizational model checks for consistency (e.g., to check if user's attributes are complete for creating shopping carts or POs)	FM
BBP_USER_GET_ATTRIBUTES	Get a list of all the attributes assigned to a user	FM
BBP_READ_ATTRIBUTES	Get a list of all attributes for a organizational object	FM
HRP1000	Organizational Structure objects	Table
HRP1001	Organizational Structure objects with relationships	Table
PFAL	Distributing the organizational structure from HR into SRM. This is a SAP ERP transaction.	TCode
PP01	Maintain Information for SAP ERP HCM Objects such as employee, position, organizational unit in SAP ERP	TCode
PA30	Employee master maintenance in SAP ERP	TCode

Table K.3 Table K.2 Organizational Structure Application (Cont.)

Transaction or Function Module	Description	Type
SWU3	Maintain standard workflow settings and configuration	TCode
SWB_PROCUREMENT	Workflow condition editor	TCode
SWI1	Workflow log	TCode
SWI5	Ability for administrator to review the list of work items that are awaiting approval in a user's inbox.	TCode
SOST	Log for all work items being sent to the external email address. This transaction is used for all external communication examples: Email, Fax, XML etc.	TCode
OOCU_RESP	Maintain Responsibility rules	TCode
SWUD	Workflow diagnosis for troubleshooting	TCode

Table K.4 Workflow Application

Transaction or Function Module	Description	Type
BBPGETVD	Download Vendors from SAP ERP into SAP SRM	TCode
BBPUPDVD	Update Vendors from SAP ERP into SAP SRM	TCode
BBP_UPDATE_PORG	Adjust the purchasing organization in SAP SRM when using Extended Classic scenario	TCode
BBPADDRINTC	Maintain addresses for the organization (Company)	TCode
BBPMAININT	Maintain external Vendor/Bidder	TCode
BBP_LOCMAP	Business Partner records for plants	Table
BBP_PD_SOS_FIND	Find all valid sources of supply	FM
BBP_VENDOR_READ_DETAIL	Get detail about a vendor	FM
COMM_HIERARCHY	Product Categories (or Material groups replicated from SAP ERP)	TCode
COMMPR01	Maintain Products (or Materials replicated from SAP ERP)	TCode
SMQ1	Outbound queue monitor when downloading master data from SAP ERP	TCode
SMQ2	Inbound queue monitor when downloading master data from SAP ERP	TCode

Table K.5 Master Data & Business Partner Application

Transaction or Function Module	Description	Type
BBPUM01	User Maintenance transaction from SAP SRM 5.0	TCode
BBPUSERMAINT	User Maintenance	TCode
BBPUM02	Settings for user data and attributes. New transaction in SAP SRM 5.0	TCode
BBPAT05	Settings for user data and attributes	TCode
USERS_GEN	Manage user and Employee data	TCode
BBP_USER_GET_DETAIL	Get details for a user	FM
SU01D	User master display	TCode
BBP_CHECK_USERS	Check users	TCode

Table K.6 Manage Users Application

Transaction or Function Module	Description	Type
SM12	Unlock user application sessions	TCode
ST22	View short dumps in the system	TCode
SXI_MONITOR	Monitor the SAP NetWeaver Process Integration (SAP NetWeaver PI) log for documents in SAP SRM	TCode
WE02	Monitor IDocs (e.g., confirmations)	TCode
SM21	Check logs for system issues	TCode
SLG1	Log for documents (e.g., download of vendor master)	TCode
WE20	Define partner profiles for EDI and ALE transfer	TCode
BD64	Create distribution model (e.g., for distributing Confirmations to SAP ERP)	TCode
WE19 / BD84	Repost IDocs in error	TCode
RZ20	Application monitor errors captured in the system	TCode
SE10	Transport management	TCode
RBDMIDOC	Creating IDocs for change pointers. Used when transferring HR data from SAP ERP into SAP SRM	Program
BBP_CLEANER	Starts synchronization with backend system	TCode
BBP_PROCDOC_CHECK	Makes all checks for the document	FM
BBP_PD_GETHISTORY	Get a history of all the documents	FM
BBP_PD_PO_TRANSFER_EXEC	Transfer PO data to backend after error in Extended Classic scenario	FM
BBP_REQREQ_TRANSFER	Transfer the shopping cart to the backend after error	FM
BBP_PD_PO_DOC_FLOW	Document flow between shopping cart, PO, confirmation, etc.	FM

Table K.7 General Administration

L   The Author

Sachin Sethi is an author, speaker, and agent of change for SAP SRM. He is the founder and Managing Partner of TSE (The SRM Experts), which provides business consulting and systems integration services focused around the SAP SRM solution. Find out more at *www.thesrmexperts.com*.

He has extensive experience globally as an advisor and subject matter expert to many leading companies. A certified SAP SRM expert, Sethi's track record includes serving clients at Deloitte Consulting, Ernst & Young, MarchFirst, IBM, and SEAL Consulting.

His services are frequently sought by industry leaders in the health care, consumer products, automotive, retail, manufacturing and higher education sectors. He has helped build business cases for SAP SRM, launch SAP SRM ramp-up and upgrades, and analyze many e-procurement solutions. His experience with SAP SRM and SAP EB products dates back to their inception — the initial B2B release.

As an industry leader, he has addressed audiences at the Logistics and Supply Chain conference, annual SAP Sapphire and America's SAP Users' Group (ASUG) conferences, e-business seminars, universities, and local ASUG chapters.

A resident SAP SRM solution expert at *www.searchsap.com*, he advises organizations globally and spends a considerable amount of time on customer engagements in the role of a strategic advisor, project lead, and solution architect.

Sethi has a dual degree in Computer Engineering and Business Administration and holds an Executive MBA degree.

He can be reached at *sachin.sethi@thesrmexperts.com*.

Index

S

T

Testing, 598
Texts, 86
Tial Download, 458
Tolerance, 176, 391
Total cost of ownership, 501
Tracking, 102
Traditional procurement process, 56
Transaction, 414
  MDMGX, 261
  MECCM, 263
  R3AC1, 458
Transaction integration, 344
Transfer to the catalog, 185
Two-step approval, 379

U

Under- or overdelivery tolerance, 105
United Nations Standard Products and
Services Code, 251, 465
Units of Measures, 261
Universal Worklist, 562, 572, 573, 576
Update contract, 188
Upgrade, 497, 503
  Assessment, 515, 519, 525
  Decision methodology, 503
  Functional, 504
  How to, 499
  Master Guide, 511
  Strategy, 502
  Technical, 504
Upload Content, 194, 604
US Defense Logistics Agency, 614
User access, 421
User authentication, 567
User creation process, 421
User interface, 60, 253, 509, 562
User management, 419, 423
User settings, 60
Utilization, 185

V

Valuation factors, 162
Value analysis, 546

Value-based cost distribution, 346
VA Support Package Manager, 566
Vendor landscape, 37
Vendor lists, 88, 145, 463, 464, 465
Vendor Master Record, 476
Vendor product number, 105, 177
Vendor Root, 473
Vendors, 470
Vendor-supplied content, 259
Vendor Synchronization, 477
Vendor text, 86
Vendor Transfer, 474
Version, 103
Version management, 184

W

Web-based e-training, 519
WebDynpro, 562, 570
Web templates, 532, 537
Weighting and ranking, 161
Wireless connectivity, 496
Withdraw, 159
Workflow, 96, 185, 366, 367, 370, 517
  Customizing, 384
  Event-driven, 368
  Restriction, 632
  Standard SAP delivered, 375
  Template, 370
Worklist, 97, 145
Work Order, 261
Worksets, 570

X

XML, 268, 390
  invoice, 125

Z

Z tables, 408
  Custom, 408